THE OXFORD HAN

TALENT
MANAGEMENT

David G. Collings is Professor of Human Resource Management (HRM) at Dublin City University Business School where he leads the HR Directors' Roundtable and is Director of the Leadership and Talent Institute. He previously held academic appointments at the University of Sheffield and National University of Ireland Galway and visiting appointments at Cornell university King's College London and Strathclyde University. His research and consulting interests focus on talent management and global mobility. He has been named as one of the most influential thinkers in the field of HR by HR Magazine on live occasions. He has published numerous papers in leading international outlets and seven books. He sits on a number of editorial boards including *Academy of Management Review* and *Journal of Management*. He is Consulting Editor at *Journal of World Business* and former Editor of *Human Resource Management Journal, Journal of World Business* and the *Irish Journal of Management*.

Kamel Mellahi is a Professor of Strategic Management at Warwick Business School where he teaches and researches in the areas of international business and strategic management. His research interests straddle international strategies of emerging markets multinationals, nonmarket strategy, and global talent management. He has published eight books and over 80 scholarly articles in top tier journals such as *Journal of International Business Studies, Journal of Management, Journal of Management Studies* and *Strategic Management Journal*. He serves as a Senior Editor for the *Journal of World Business* and Consulting Editor for the *British Journal of Management*. He is a previous (co)-Editor-in Chief of the *International Journal of Management Reviews*.

Wayne F. Cascio holds the Robert H. Reynolds Distinguished Chair in Global Leadership at the University of Colorado Denver. He has published 28 books, and more than 185 articles and book chapters. A former president of the Society for Industrial and Organizational Psychology, Chair of the Society for Human Resource Management Foundation, and member of the Academy of Management's Board of Governors, he is an elected fellow of the National Academy of Human Resources, the Academy of Management, the Society for Industrial and Organizational Psychology, and the Australian HR Institute. He received SHRM's Losey Award for Human Resources Research in 2010, and SIOP's Distinguished Scientific Contributions award in 2013.

THE OXFORD HANDBOOK OF

TALENT

MANAGEMENT

Edited by

DAVID G. COLLINGS,

KAMEL MELLAHI,

and

WAYNE F. CASCIO

OXFORD

UNIVERSITY PRESS

OXFORD
UNIVERSITY PRESS

Great Clarendon Street, Oxford, OX2 6DP,
United Kingdom

Oxford University Press is a department of the University of Oxford.
It furthers the University's objective of excellence in research, scholarship,
and education by publishing worldwide. Oxford is a registered trade mark of
Oxford University Press in the UK and in certain other countries

First published 2017
First published in paperback 2019

Published in the United States of America by Oxford University Press
198 Madison Avenue, New York, NY 10016, United States of America

British Library Cataloguing in Publication Data
Data available

Library of Congress Cataloging in Publication Data
Data available

ISBN 978-0-19-875827-3 (Hbk.)
ISBN 978-0-19-885035-9 (Pbk.)

Contents

SECTION 3 TALENT, TEAMS, AND NETWORKS

SECTION 4 MANAGING TALENT FLOWS

SECTION 5 TALENT MANAGEMENT IN CONTEXT

LIST OF FIGURES

LIST OF TABLES

LIST OF CONTRIBUTORS

Darren T. Baker is a researcher interested in applying psychosocial principles to the study of gender relations, class, and leadership. He draws on psychoanalytical theory for epistemological, methodological, and ontological inspiration. His research focuses on finance and accounting as well as low-skilled service-sector occupations, and includes: first, gender and diversity in organizations; second, leadership and ethics, including capacities to care and responsibility at work; and third, social mobility and precarity in organizations and wider society. Darren holds an MA from the University of Oxford, where he conducted research on masculinities, and studied for his PhD at the School of Business and Management, King's College London, where his research was funded by the ESRC and ACCA. Darren has taught at Queen Mary University and King's College London, and is currently a Visiting Fellow at Cranfield University, School Management.

Matthew Bidwell is an associate professor in Wharton's Management Department. His research examines new patterns in work and employment, focusing in particular on the causes and effects of more short-term, market-oriented employment relationships. He has conducted research on how firms balance internal mobility and hiring in staffing jobs and what the effects of those different strategies are. He has also studied the careers and management of highly skilled contractors. Before working at Wharton, he was an assistant professor at INSEAD. He received his PhD from the MIT Sloan School. He currently serves as a senior editor at *Organization Science*.

Ingmar Björkman is a professor of International Business and dean of Aalto University School of Business in Finland. His research interests focus on people issues in international organizations. His latest book is *Global Challenge: International Human Resource Management* (2017, Chicago Business Press), co-authored with Vladimir Pucik, Paul Evans, and Shad Morris.

Rocio Bonet is an associate professor of Human Resource Management at IE Business School. Her research interests lie at the intersection of labor economics and human resource management. One stream of her research focuses on the determinants of career advancement. She has explored how innovative work organizational practices that empower employees have affected promotions within organizations. Her ongoing research in the area of careers explores how prestigious affiliations are valued in the context of growing interorganizational mobility. Another stream of her research looks at the effects of new employment practices on firm-level outcomes. Her most recent research in this area focuses on how the use of contingent workers affects firm performance and employee retention in organizations. Her work has been published in several international outlets. She received a PhD in Management from the Wharton School, University of Pennsylvania.

Walter C. Borman received his PhD in Industrial/Organizational Psychology from the University of California (Berkeley). He was CEO and then chief scientist of Personnel Decisions Research Institutes until his retirement last year, and is a professor of Industrial-Organizational Psychology at the University of South Florida. He is a Fellow of the Society for Industrial and Organizational Psychology. Borman has written more than 350 books, book chapters, journal articles, and conference papers. He has served on the editor boards of several journals in the I/O field, including the *Journal of Applied Psychology, Personnel Psychology*, and the *International Journal of Selection and Assessment*. He was editor of *Human Performance, 2006–2014*. Finally, he was the recipient of the Society for Industrial and Organizational Psychology's Distinguished Scientific Contributions Award for 2003; the M. Scott Myers Award for Applied Research in the Workplace for 2000, 2002, 2004, and 2010; and the American Psychological Foundation's Gold Medal Award for Life Achievement in the Application of Psychology in 2011.

Paul Boselie, PhD, MSc, is a professor and research director in the Utrecht School of Governance at Utrecht University, The Netherlands. His research traverses human resource management, institutionalism, strategic management, and industrial relations. He currently focuses on public-value creation, employer engagement, health care management, professional performance, and talent management. Paul's teaching involves bachelor, master, PhD, and executive education. He is a member of the Editorial Board of the *Journal of Management Studies* and *Human Resource Management Journal*, and he is an associate editor of the *International Journal of Human Resource Management*. His 2010 and 2014 textbook, *Strategic HRM—A Balanced Approach*, is popular in bachelor and master programs.

John W. Boudreau, PhD, is a professor and research director at the University of Southern California's Marshall School of Business and Centre for Effective Organizations. His more than 200 publications include such books as *Lead the Work*, with Ravin Jesuthasan and David Creelman (Wiley, 2015); *Retooling HR* (Harvard Business, 2010); *Beyond HR*, with Peter M. Ramstad (Harvard Business, 2007); and *Short Introduction to Strategic Human Resources* with Wayne Cascio (Cambridge University Press, 2012), as well as articles in the *Journal of Applied Psychology, Personnel Psychology, Management Science*, and the *Journal of Vocational Behavior*. He has received the Michael Losey Award from the Society for Human Resource Management (SHRM), the Academy of Management's Organizational Behavior New Concept and Human Resource Scholarly Contribution Awards, and the Chairman's Award from the International Association for Human Resources Information Management. He is a Fellow of the National Academy of Human Resources, the Society for Industrial and Organizational Psychology, and the American Psychological Association.

Margaret E. Brooks is an associate professor in the Management Department at Bowling Green State University. She earned her PhD in Industrial-Organizational Psychology in 2004, from Bowling Green State University. She is a member of the Academy of Management, the Society for Industrial and Organizational Psychology, and the Society for Judgment and Decision Making. Her research focuses on applying behavioral decision research to solve organizational problems. She is interested in how decision making affects the organizational staffing process—including recruitment, attraction to the organization, job choice, and employee selection. She also is interested in employee well-being issues related to meaningful work and women's employment. Her work has been published in top journals in the field, including the *Journal of Applied Psychology* and the *Journal of Management*.

Peter Cappelli is the George W. Taylor Professor of Management at The Wharton School and Director of Wharton's Center for Human Resources. He is also a research associate at the National Bureau of Economic Research in Cambridge, MA. He served as senior advisor to the Kingdom of Bahrain for Employment Policy from 2003 to 2005, and since 2007 has been a Distinguished Scholar of the Ministry of Manpower for Singapore. He has degrees in industrial relations from Cornell University and in labor economics from Oxford, where he was a Fulbright Scholar. He has been a guest scholar at the Brookings Institution, a German Marshall Fund Fellow, and a faculty member at MIT, the University of Illinois, and the University of California at Berkeley. He was a staff member on the US Secretary of Labor's Commission on Workforce Quality and Labor Market Efficiency from 1988 to 1990, co-director of the US Department of Education's National Center on the Educational Quality of the Workforce, and a member of the Executive Committee of the US Department of Education's National Center on Post-Secondary Improvement at Stanford University. He was recently named by *HR Magazine* as one of the top five most influential management thinkers and by NPR as one of the fifty influencers in the field of aging, and has been elected a fellow of the National Academy of Human Resources.

Wayne F. Cascio holds the Robert H. Reynolds Distinguished Chair in Global Leadership at the University of Colorado, Denver. He has published 28 books and more than 185 articles and book chapters. A former president of the Society for Industrial and Organizational Psychology, chair of the Society for Human Resource Management Foundation, and member of the Academy of Management's Board of Governors, he is an editor of the *Journal of International Business Studies* and a former senior editor of the *Journal of World Business*. He received the SHRM's Losey Award for Human Resources Research in 2010, SIOP's Distinguished Scientific Contributions award in 2013, and the Georges Petitpas Lifetime Achievement Award from the World Federation of People Management Associations in 2016.

David G. Collings is a professor of human resource management at Dublin City University Business School where he leads the HR Directors' Roundtable and is a joint director of the Leadership and Talent Institute. From 2014–2017 he has been named as one of the most influential thinkers in the field of human resources by *HR Magazine*. He has published numerous papers in leading international journals and seven books. He sits on a number of editorial boards, including the *Academy of Management Review, Journal of Management*, and *Journal of Management Studies*. He is a deputy editor at the *Journal of World Business* and a former editor of *Human Resource Management Journal*.

Fang Lee Cooke, PhD, University of Manchester, UK, is a distinguished professor of Human Resource Management (HRM) and Asia Studies at Monash Business School, Monash University. Her research interests are in the area of employment relations, gender studies, diversity management, strategic HRM, knowledge management and innovation, outsourcing, Chinese outward FDI and HRM, employment of Chinese migrants, and HRM in the care sector. Fang is the author of the following books: *HRM, Work and Employment in China; Competition, Strategy, and Management in China*; and *Human Resource Management in China: New Trends and Practices*. Fang has also published more than 140 journal articles and book chapters. She is an associate editor of *Human Resource Management, International Journal of Human Resource Management, Gender, Work, and Organization*, and *Asian Business and Management*; senior editor of *Asia Pacific Journal of Management*; and co-editor-in-chief of *Asia Pacific Journal of Human Resources*. Fang's recent research projects consider Chinese firms in Africa and their employment/HRM practices and labor relations; employee resilience, HRM practices, and engagement in the finance sector in the Asian region; and HRM in the care sector.

Ormonde R. Cragun is a PhD student of Organizational Behavior and Human Resources at the Darla Moore School of Business School at the University of South Carolina. He received his Masters of Organizational Behavior from Brigham Young University and Bachelor of Arts in Personnel and Human Resource Management from Utah State University. Before entering academia, Ormonde was the vice president of Organizational Effectiveness at Conservice. Before Conservice, he spent the majority of his career at Bell Helicopter Textron, where he served in various human resources and continuous improvement roles, including director of HR Strategy, senior HR business partner, director of Continuous Improvement, and Six Sigma Master Black Belt. Ormonde's research interests include executive succession, executive personality, compensation, human capital, and strategic human resources.

David V. Day is a professor of Psychology and Eggert Chair in Leadership at Claremont McKenna College (USA), where he also holds the position of academic director of the Kravis Leadership Institute. Previous academic appointments include the University of Western Australia, Singapore Management University, Penn State University, and Louisiana State University. His research focuses primarily on issues related to leader and leadership development in organizational contexts. Day is a Fellow of the American Psychological Association, the Association for Psychological Science, the Society for Industrial and Organizational Psychology, and the International Association of Applied Psychology.

Giverny De Boeck is a doctoral researcher at the Research Centre for Organisation Studies, KU Leuven, Belgium. Her interests include human development and meaningful work. Central to her research are questions concerning employee experiences of (not) realizing potential at work. She is also an affiliated researcher at Vlerick Business School, cooperating with Professor De Stobbeleir on employee-proactivity behavior.

Gina Dokko is an associate professor at the University of California, Davis. Her research focuses on the consequences of job mobility and careers for individuals and organizations, including effects on innovation, learning, performance, and social capital. Her research has been published in the *Strategic Management Journal, Research Policy, Organization Science, Organization Studies*, and the *Academy of Management Journal*. She sits on the editorial review boards of the *Strategic Management Journal* and *Organization Science*. Professor Dokko holds a PhD in Management from the Wharton School of the University of Pennsylvania, an MS of Industrial Administration from Carnegie Mellon GSIA, and a BS of Economics from the Wharton School. Before her doctoral studies, she held various positions in marketing and strategy at firms such as 3M and American Express.

Nicky Dries is a research professor at KU Leuven (Belgium). She has been a visiting scholar at University of Tilburg, Wirtschaftsuniversität, Vienna; Reykjavik University; IESE Barcelona; and BI Oslo, and a Fulbright scholar at Boston University. Nicky's primary research interests are employee talent, potential, and success. Nicky is an active member of the two largest cross-cultural projects within the field of career studies: 5C (Consortium for the Cross-Cultural Study of Contemporary Careers) and the Career Adaptability/Life Design Project.

Martin R. Edwards is a reader in HRM and Organisational Psychology at King's College London—School of Management and Business. Martin has a background in organizational psychology, HRM, and industrial relations. He holds degrees in Social Psychology (BSc, Kent) and Industrial Relations and Personnel Management (MSc, London School of Economics), and a PhD in Organizational Psychology (King's College London). Martin has published in internationally renowned HR journals (*Human Resource Management, Human Resource Management Journal, Human Relations, European Journal of Work and Organisational Psychology*, and *International Journal of Management Reviews*) and is the co-author/co-editor of two highly successful HR books (*Predictive HR Analytics: Mastering the HR Metric*, 2016; *Human Resource Management in Transition*, 2013). Martin has worked for a number of years as an HR consultant and provides HR analytic training to HR teams. Martin's academic interests include organizational identification, social and multiple identities in organizations, employee/employer branding, employee responses to M&A activities, and the application of advanced analytic techniques to HR data.

Mats Ehrnrooth, PhD, is an associate professor at Hanken School of Economics, Finland. His research focuses on HRM, leadership, and organizational behavior from international, indigenous, cross-cultural, and various methodological perspectives. He has published in several prestigious academic journals including the *Journal of Management Studies, Strategic Management Journal, Journal of International Business Studies, Journal of World Business, Organization Studies, Human Resource Management,* and *International Journal of Human Resource Management.*

Marion Festing is a professor of Human Resource Management and Intercultural Leadership at the Berlin campus of ESCP Europe. Furthermore, she is the Business School's Academic Director of the Talent Management Institute. In her research, she focuses on topics such as international HRM strategies and approaches, with special emphasis on emerging countries, female careers, global talent management, and global performance and reward management. Her most recent book is *International Human Resource Management: Managing People in a Multinational Context* (7th edn., Cengage, forthcoming), which she wrote as part of a tricontinental team, together with Peter J. Dowling (Australia) and Allen D. Engle (USA).

Alexis A. Fink, PhD, is currently general manager, Talent Intelligence Analytics at Intel. Her organization provides original organizational effectiveness research, HR analytics, talent marketplace analytics, HR systems and tools, and consulting on talent solutions and strategic workforce planning. Before Intel, Alexis spent seven years at Microsoft, where her roles included director of Talent Management Infrastructure. Her career has been characterized by an integrative approach to HR, including developing and implementing competency systems and integrated talent-management systems. Her background also includes work in large-scale organizational transformation. Alexis earned her PhD in Industrial/Organizational Psychology and is a Fellow of the Society for Industrial and Organizational Psychology (SIOP). In addition to practicing and leading in organizations, she continues to teach, is a frequent SIOP contributor, and is an occasional author and journal editor.

Monika Hamori is a professor of Human Resource Management at IE Business School in Madrid, Spain. Her research interests include managerial and executive career paths and career success. Her articles have been published in *Human Resource Management, Organization Science,* the *Academy of Management Annals,* the *Academy of Management Perspectives,* the *Harvard Business Review,* and the *MIT Sloan Management Review,* among others. She received her PhD from the Wharton School of the University of Pennsylvania.

Katharina Harsch is a research assistant and PhD student at the Chair of Human Resource Management and Intercultural Leadership and an affiliated researcher at the Talent Management Institute, situated at ESCP Europe's Berlin campus. Her main research focus centers on talent management from different angles, concentrating on various working environments.

John P. Hausknecht is an associate professor of Human Resource Studies at Cornell University. He earned his PhD in 2003 from Penn State University, with a major in Industrial/Organizational Psychology and minor in Management. Professor Hausknecht's research addresses employee turnover and related staffing issues, and has appeared in the *Academy of Management Journal, Journal of Applied Psychology*, and *Personnel Psychology*. He currently serves on the editorial boards of the *Academy of Management Journal* and the *Journal of Applied Psychology*, and is an associate editor at *Personnel Psychology*. He is a member of the Academy of Management, the American Psychological Association, the Society for Industrial and Organizational Psychology, and the Society for Human Resource Management.

Scott Highhouse is a professor and Ohio Eminent Scholar in the Department of Psychology, Bowling Green State University. Scott is the founding editor of the journal *Personnel Assessment and Decisions*. He has been named a Fellow of the American Psychological Association, the Association for Psychological Science, and the Society for Industrial-Organizational Psychology. Scott formerly worked in organizational development at Anheuser Busch Companies in St. Louis, Missouri. His primary areas of expertise are assessment/selection for employment, and human judgment/decision making. His work has been featured in the popular press, including the *Washington Post, Wall Street Journal, Fortune, The Guardian*, and *The Boston Globe*.

Winnie Jiang is a doctoral student of Organizations and Management at Yale University. Her current research focuses on understanding individuals' experiences as they move across organizational and/or occupational boundaries, as well as the individual- and organizational-level antecedents and consequences of their movement. She also studies how individuals, especially those from marginalized groups, negotiate challenges in their work life and construct meaning from their work and careers, the findings of which provide helpful implications to organizations. To answer these research questions, she employs both qualitative and quantitative methodologies in unique social contexts. Before entering the doctoral program, Winnie received a BA of Economics and Psychology from Agnes Scott College in Atlanta, Georgia.

Rebecca R. Kehoe is an assistant professor of Human Resource Management at Rutgers University. Rebecca conducts research examining the interplay of human capital, social capital, and organizational context in the facilitation of innovation and competitive advantage in organizations. Against this backdrop, she maintains two active streams of research. In one, she studies how the characteristics, behaviors, and deployment of star performers influence the opportunities and performance enjoyed by stars' colleagues and broader organizations. In another, she studies the roles of alternative HR systems, collaborative exchange, and internal and external knowledge stocks and flows in supporting superior unit and organizational performance. Rebecca's research has appeared in the *Strategic Management Journal, Journal of Management, ILR Review*, and *Research in Personnel and Human Resources Management*. She serves on the editorial boards of the *Journal of Management, Personnel Psychology*, and the *International Journal of Human Resource Management*.

Elisabeth K. Kelan is a professor of Leadership at Cranfield School of Management, where she also directs the Global Centre for Gender and Leadership. Before this appointment, she held positions at King's College London and London Business School. She completed her PhD at the London School of Economics and Political Science. She is author of two books, as well as various peer-reviewed journal articles. During 2014–2015, she was a British Academy Midcareer Fellow and she explored the role of men as middle managers for gender equality. Her research centers on diversity and inclusion in organizations, with a specific focus on gender and generations.

JR Keller is an assistant professor of Human Resource Studies in the ILR School at Cornell University. His research focuses on how firms combine internal and external hiring to meet their human capital needs, as well as the various ways individuals build careers within and across organizations. He has explored the factors that lead firms to hire externally versus promote from within, supply chain approaches to talent management, the use of nonstandard work arrangements, and talent management more generally. His work has appeared in the *Academy of Management Journal, Academy of Management Review, Industrial & Labor Relations Review, Annual Review of Organizational Psychology*, and *Organizational Behavior*. Before pursuing a PhD, Keller had two careers—the first as a financial analyst and the second as a career consultant. He earned his PhD in Management from the Wharton School of Business and holds a Masters in Adult Education from Indiana University and undergraduate degrees in Finance and Computer Applications from the University of Notre Dame.

Shaista E. Khilji is a professor of Human and Organizational Learning & International Affairs at the George Washington University (GW), and founding editor-in-chief of the *South Asian Journal of Business Studies*. Dr. Khilji's most recent work focuses on social inequalities within organizations and conceptualizing macro global talent management. She has published her work in many tier 1 academic journals and presented more than one hundred papers at international conferences. She has won many awards, including the Best Reviewer and Best Service Achievement Awards from the Academy of Management, the Best Paper Award from Academy of International Business, GW's Service Excellence Award in the Collaborative Group category for hosting the Clinton Global Initiative University at GW, and the VALOR Award for cross-disciplinary work. She has served as a consultant to many public and private sector organizations, including working on President Obama's initiative to develop transparent culture in the US government.

Sydney Kroska is an undergraduate student at the University of Iowa in the Tippie College of Business. She is currently studying Management and Psychology. Her research interests include star performance, organizational behavior, and psychological flexibility. She currently is the president of Tippie Senate and Computer Comfort, an organization designed to help seniors to successfully navigate an increasingly technologically driven world and is an active member of Alpha Kappa Psi Business Fraternity. She plans to attend graduate school in Organizational Behavior.

Kristiina Mäkelä, PhD, is a professor of International Business at Aalto University School of Business in Helsinki. Her research focuses on people-related issues in multinational corporations, including those concerning HRM practices, the HR function, knowledge, social capital, and interpersonal interaction. Her work has appeared in more than twenty-five international peer-reviewed journals and books, including the *Journal of International Business Studies, Journal of Management Studies, Human Resource Management, Journal of World Business, International Business Review, Journal of Managerial Psychology*, and *International Journal of Human Resource Management*, among others. Before entering academia, she worked for more than ten years at Procter & Gamble, the world-leading consumer-goods multinational.

M. Travis Maynard, PhD, is an associate professor within the Department of Management at Colorado State University. He has conducted extensive research in the area of organizational team effectiveness, with primary interests centering on the role that team context has on team interactions and outcomes. In particular, some of his research has focused on the impact that interacting through virtual means has on team processes and performance. Beyond his work on virtual teams, Maynard also has conducted several research projects examining teamwork within healthcare settings. As a result of this line of research, he and his colleagues have seen dramatic increases in the teamwork skills of the healthcare providers they have work with, which has translated into substantial improvements in patient outcomes. Maynard's experiences with teams within the healthcare industry has led him to become increasingly interested in team adaptation, resilience, and teamwork in extreme contexts, which has led to numerous current projects on these topics.

Kamel Mellahi is a professor of strategic management at Warwick Business School where he teaches and researches in the areas of international business and strategic management. His research interests straddle international strategies of emerging markets multinationals, corporate social responsibility, and talent management. He has published eight books and over eighty scholarly articles in top-tier journals, such as the *Journal of International Business Studies, Journal of Management, Journal of Management Studies*, and *Strategic Management Journal*. He serves as a senior editor for the *Journal of World Business* and Consulting and an editor for the *British Journal of Management*.

Maria Christina Meyers is an assistant professor at the Department of Human Resource Studies of Tilburg University, The Netherlands. Her research interests include positive psychology in the contexts of organizations, employee strengths and talents, employee well-being, talent management, and field experiments. Part of her research is conducted in close collaboration with Dutch organizations. Christina has published her research in international journals such as *Human Resource Management Review*, the *Journal of World Business, Human Resource Management*, the *Journal of Counseling Psychology*, and the *European Journal of Work and Organizational Psychology*.

Amirali Minbashian is an associate professor of Organisational Behaviour in the School of Management at UNSW Business School, UNSW Sydney. His research focuses on the effects of personality and individual differences, emotions, motivation and time-varying factors (such as experience and aging) on performance at work. He has published research on these topics in a range of applied psychology and management journals, including *Journal of Applied Psychology, Organizational Research Methods, Leadership Quarterly, Journal of Vocational Behavior, Journal of Occupational and Organizational Psychology*, and *Applied Psychology: An International Review*.

Shad Morris, PhD, Cornell University, is the Georgia White Fellow and associate professor of Management at the Marriott School, Brigham Young University. Professor Morris conducts research on building global innovation capabilities through talent. In particular, he explores empirical problems related to how companies can more effectively invest in employee competencies and social networks to create firm value. He has published in outlets such as the *Academy of Management Review, Journal of International Business Studies, Strategic Management Journal, Journal of Operations Management*, and *Harvard Business Review*. Before becoming an academic, he worked for the World Bank, Management Systems International, and Alcoa.

Anthony J. Nyberg is a Moore Research Fellow at the Darla Moore School of Business at the University of South Carolina. Nyberg's research focuses on strategic human capital resources, with emphases on performance, compensation, employee movement, and executive succession. His work has been published in the *Academy of Management Journal, Academy of Management Review, Journal of Applied Psychology*, and *Journal of Management*, among others. He is an associate editor for the *Academy of Management Journal*, and has served on numerous editorial boards. Anthony has received teaching and research awards including the *Early Career Achievement Award*, best dissertation, and best published manuscript from the Human Resources Division of the Academy of Management. He received his doctorate from the University of Wisconsin-Madison. Before that, he served for nine years as the managing partner for an international financial services firm based in Northern California.

Ernest H. O'Boyle earned his doctorate in 2010 from Virginia Commonwealth University. He is currently an associate professor of management and organizations in the Tippie College of Business at the University of Iowa. His research interests include star performance, counterproductive work behavior, research methods, and ethical issues surrounding publication practices. He has more than thirty peer-reviewed journal publications in such outlets as the *Academy of Management Journal, Journal of Applied Psychology, Journal of Management, Organizational Research Methods*, and *Personnel Psychology*. His work has been featured in the *Wall Street Journal, Inc. Magazine, Bloomberg Businessweek*, National Public Radio's Morning Edition, and the NYT bestselling book *Work Rules!* He is the recipient of the Academy of Management Early Career Awards for the Research Methods Division and Human Resources

Division. O'Boyle sits on the editorial boards of *Personnel Psychology* and *Journal of Applied Psychology*, and is an associate editor at *Journal of Management*.

Patricia M. G. O'Connor is Chief Learning Officer at YPO and a global talent-management executive with recognized expertise in leadership development, succession planning, and cultural alignment. From 2008 to 2016, she served as general manager, Leadership Development & Talent Management at Wesfarmers, Ltd, an Australian conglomerate with 225,000 employees. Her primary responsibility was the development and deployment of high-return talent practices focused on the organization's top 275 executives. Before this appointment, Patricia worked for the Center for Creative Leadership (CCL). She served thirteen years with the CCL, progressing through a number of management, consulting, and research roles, culminating as research director in their Singapore office. Patricia holds an MBA in Management & Organization Behavior from the City University of New York and a Bachelor of Science degree in Human Resources from the University of Illinois, Champaign-Urbana. She is a published author and has addressed corporate, academic, and student audiences through speaking engagements across the globe.

Patrick Gavan O'Shea is the director of Private Sector Talent Management at Human Resources Research Organization (HumRRO), and lives in Louisville, Kentucky. Before joining HumRRO in 2006, Gavan was a senior research scientist at American Institutes for Research (AIR) in Washington, DC. His work has involved leadership assessment using 360-degree feedback, rich-media simulations, and assessment centers; job analysis and competency modeling; and employee selection, promotion, and development for jobs within the energy, aviation, and US law enforcement and intelligence communities. Gavan is also a certified coach and an adjunct professor within Villanova University's Department of Human Resource Development. Earlier in his career, he worked at a market research firm and with Volunteers in Service to America (VISTA). He received his PhD in Industrial-Organizational Psychology from Virginia Tech and his MS in General-Experimental Psychology from Villanova University.

James Oldroyd, PhD, Northwestern University, is the Ford/Richard Cook Fellow and Associate Professor of Strategy at the Marriott School, Brigham Young University. He has taught at SKK-GSB in Seoul, South Korea, and The Ohio State University. His research explores the intersection of stars, networks, and knowledge flows. He has published in outlets such as the *Academy of Management Review*, *Organization Science*, and *Harvard Business Review*. He teaches courses on strategy, strategy implementation, international business, and negotiations to undergraduates, MBAs, and executives.

Robert E. Ployhart is the Bank of America Professor of Business Administration and Chair of the management department at the University of South Carolina's Darla Moore School of Business. His PhD is in Industrial and Organizational Psychology from Michigan State University (1999). His research focuses on human capital, staffing, personnel selection, recruitment, staffing-related legal issues, and applied statistical models such as structural equation modeling, multilevel modeling (HLM/RCM), and longitudinal modeling. His most recent research focuses on the intersection of psychology with organizational strategy. He has served as an associate editor for the *Journal of Applied Psychology* and *Organizational Behavior and Human Decision Processes*, and on the editorial boards of six scientific journals. He has received many scholarly awards, and is a Fellow of the American Psychological Association, the Association for Psychological Science, and the Society for Industrial and Organizational Psychology.

Kerrin E. Puente is a research scientist in the Personnel Selection and Development program at Human Resources Research Organization (HumRRO) located in Alexandria, Virginia. Her work involves job analysis and competency modeling; selection and promotion; and managing and analyzing data to support a number of human capital solutions for public sector, private sector, and non-profit organizations. She is experienced in developing a variety of behavior-based assessments, including rich-media simulations, situational judgment tests, structured interviews, and assessment center exercises. Before joining HumRRO in 2014, Kerrin was an organizational effectiveness consultant at the Home Depot (in Atlanta, Georgia), where she supported the design and execution of large-scale talent-management solutions in a fast-paced retail environment. She received her PhD in Industrial-Organizational Psychology from the University of Georgia.

Blythe L. Rosikiewicz is a doctoral candidate in Management at the LeBow College of Business, Drexel University. Her research interests include interpersonal competition in the workplace, status and power dynamics, and the dark side of leadership.

Diana Sanchez is currently pursuing her PhD in Industrial-Organizational Psychology from Colorado State University. She obtained her MS in Industrial-Organizational Psychology from the University of Baltimore in 2010 and has a BS in Psychology from Portland State University. Her research expertise focuses on technology innovation and implementation, specifically looking at how organizations can integrate technological solutions to help manage their human capital. Her research primarily includes virtual teams, training simulations, and online assessment. Her applied experience includes over four years of work as a human capital consultant in Industrial-Organizational Psychology and over seven years of experience working in human resource management. Sanchez has previously worked for organizations such as John Hopkins University and Personnel Decisions Research Institute.

Lynn Schäfer heads the Talent Management Institute at ESCP Europe, Berlin campus. Her research interests include human resource management and talent management. Former research projects have focused on talent management in Germany, for instance gender inclusion and diversity elements in talent-management practices in the German media industry, and talent management in medium-sized companies.

Donald J. "DJ" Schepker is an assistant professor of Strategic Management in the Darla Moore School of Business at the University of South Carolina and a faculty member in the Center for Executive Succession. His research has appeared in outlets such as the *Journal of Management, Corporate Reputation Review,* and *Managerial and Decision Economics* and focuses on corporate governance, executive succession and turnover, and top management-team and board-level decision making. He received his PhD from the University of Kansas and his BS from Babson College. Before entering academia, he worked for the advisory practice of PricewaterhouseCoopers, assisting clients in business process engineering, fraud identification, and dispute resolution.

Randall S. Schuler is Distinguished Professor of Strategic International Human Resource Management and Strategic Human Resource Management, past director of the Masters in HRM Program, and founder and past director of the Center for Global Strategic Human Resource Management in the Department of Human Resource Management. He is also on the faculty of Luzern University Business School as a Visiting Scholar. His interests include managing talent, innovation and human resource management, global human resource management, strategic human resource management, the human resource management function in organizations, and the interface of business strategy and human resource management. He has authored or edited more than fifty books. In addition, he has contributed more than seventy chapters to books and has published over 150 articles in professional journals and academic proceedings. He is a Fellow of the American Psychological Association, the British Academy of Management, the Society for Industrial and Organizational Psychology, and the Academy of Management. Currently he is co-editing a Global HRM series for Routledge, with P. Sparrow and S. E. Jackson. It is composed of more than twenty-five books and involves more than 400 authors from around the world.

Hugh Scullion is a professor in International Human Resource Management in Hull University Business School. He has published in leading journals including the *Academy of Management Journal, Journal of World Business, Human Resource Management Journal,* and *Human Resource Management Review.* He is a co-author of recent books on *Global Talent Management* (Routledge, 2010), *Strategic Talent Management: Contemporary Issues in International Context* (CUP, 2014), and *Global Staffing* (Routledge, 2008). His current research interests include global talent management, SMEs, and the emerging markets.

Robert F. Silzer is managing director of HR Assessment and Development Inc., and doctoral faculty in Industrial-Organizational Psychology at Baruch/Graduate Center, City University of New York. He received his PhD in Industrial/Organizational and Counseling Psychology from the University of Minnesota and has served as a corporate senior director and as president of a major Industrial/Organizational psychology consulting firm. He has consulted with 150 organizations and thousands of leaders and executives. Rob was awarded the 2015 Distinguished Professional Contributions Award from the Society of Industrial and Organizational Psychology and the 2016 International Award for Excellence in Consultation from the Society of Consulting Psychology, a division of the American Psychological Association. He is a Fellow of the American

Psychological Association, the Association for Psychological Science, the Society for Industrial and Organizational Psychology and the Society for Consulting Psychology (a division of the American Psychological Association). He has taught graduate psychology courses at New York University, City University of New York and City University of New York - Singapore. He has served on numerous journal editorial boards and as president and officer in several professional psychology associations. He is widely published, including books on *Strategy-Driven Talent Management, The 21st Century Executive*, and *Individual Psychological Assessment.* He enjoys global adventure travel and lives in Greenwich Village, Manhattan, New York City.

Adam Smale is a professor in the Department of Management and head of the Human Resource Management research group at the University of Vaasa in Finland. His research interests focus on talent management, HRM, careers, and knowledge transfer in multinational corporations. He has published a teaching case on global talent management and more than twenty scientific articles in journals such as the *Journal of International Business Studies, Human Resource Management, Journal of World Business, International Business Review*, and *International Journal of Human Resource Management.* He is the HR Ambassador for Finland in the Academy of Management HR Division and the Finnish representative in both CRANET and the Cross-Cultural Collaboration on Contemporary Careers (5C).

Michael C. Sturman is a professor of Management and the Kenneth and Marjorie Blanchard Professor of Human Resources at Cornell University's School of Hotel Administration. There, he teaches undergraduate, graduate, and executive education courses on Human Resource Management and Compensation. His current research focuses on the prediction of individual job performance over time and the influence of compensation systems. He has published research articles in journals such as the *Journal of Applied Psychology, Academy of Management Journal, Personnel Psychology*, and *Journal of Management*, as well as hospitality-focused and practitioner-oriented papers in *Compensation and Benefits Review, Cornell Hospitality Quarterly, International Journal of Hospitality Management, Lodging Magazine, Lodging HR*, and the *American Compensation Association Journal.* Michael holds a PhD, MS, and BS from Cornell University's School of Industrial and Labor Relations, and is a senior professional of Human Resources, as certified by the Society for Human Resource Management.

Jennie Sumelius is an associate professor in the Department of Management at the University of Vaasa. She received her PhD from the Hanken School of Economics in Helsinki, and has been a visiting scholar at Uppsala University and the University of Melbourne. Her research focuses on people management issues in multinational corporations, including talent management, the HR function, identification, and employee perceptions. Her work has been published in the *Journal of International Business Studies, Journal of Management Studies, Human Resource Management*, and *Journal of World Business*, among others.

Marian Thunnissen, PhD, has more than twenty years of experience as a researcher and consultant in the field of Human Resource Management (HRM). Since 2016, she has worked as a professor at Fontys University of Applied Sciences in Eindhoven, The Netherlands. Her main research concentrates on talent management, employability, and HRM, with a particular interest in talent-management issues in public sector organizations and (Dutch) higher education institutes. Her work has been published in the *International Journal of HRM, Human Resource Management Review*, and *Employee Relations*, among others. Thunnissen wants to make a positive contribution to knowledge transfer between scholars in the academic fields of HRM and talent management and practitioners. She is an associate editor of the *Dutch Journal of HRM*.

Daniel Tzabbar is an associate professor of Strategy, at LeBow College of Business, Drexel University. He received his PhD from Rotman School of Management, University of Toronto. His research focuses on creating and testing organizational and strategic theories related to the mechanisms that facilitate learning and technological change. His work highlights the micromechanisms associated with human capital as a key driver of these transformations. By integrating human capital theory with knowledge-based view and power theories, his research provides a theoretical and empirical meeting ground for economists, organizational theorists, and strategic human capital scholars. His work has been published in premier outlets such as the *Academy of Management Journal, Strategic Management Journal, Organization Science*, and *Journal of Management*, where he also serves as an editorial review board member.

Matti Vartiainen is a professor of Work and Organizational Psychology at the Department of Industrial Engineering and Management, Aalto University School of Science. He is a mentoring professor in the Virtual and Mobile Work Research Unit (http://www.vmwork.net/). With his research teams, he is studying organizational innovations, digital work, leadership, and well-being in new ways of working, mobile and multilocational distributed teams and organizations, reward systems, knowledge and competence building, and e-learning systems. He has edited and authored the following books, among others: *Mobile Virtual Work: A New Paradigm?* (2006, with J. H. Erik Andriessen and M. Vartiainen, eds., Springer); *Distributed and Mobile Work—Places, People and Technology* (2007, with Marko Kakonen, Satu Koivisto, Petri Mannonen, Mika P. Nieminen, Virpa Ruohomäki, and Anni Vartola, Otatieto); and *Reward Management—Facts and Trends in Europe* (2008, with C. Antoni, X. Baeten, N. Hakonen, and H. Thierry, H., eds., Pabst Science Publishers).

Patrick M. Wright is Thomas C. Vandiver Bicentennial Chair in the Darla Moore School of Business at the University of South Carolina and director of the Center for Executive Succession. He teaches and conducts research in the area of Strategic Human Resource Management. He has published more than sixty research articles in journals and more than twenty chapters in books and edited volumes, and has co-authored two textbooks and two books on HR practice. He is the editor-in-chief for the *Journal of*

Management. He currently serves as a member on the board of directors for the Society for Human Resource Management and the National Academy of Human Resources (NAHR) and is a former board member of HRPS, SHRM Foundation, and World at Work. He has been named by *HRM Magazine* as one of the twenty "Most Influential Thought Leaders in HR" and has won SHRM's Michael R. Losey Award for Human Resource Research.

SECTION 1

CONTEXT

CHAPTER 1

....

INTRODUCTION

....

DAVID G. COLLINGS, WAYNE F. CASCIO, AND KAMEL MELLAHI

1.1 INTRODUCTION

....

TALENT management has become a key focus for management scholars and practitioners alike. This is reflected in the fact that at the time of this writing,[1] a search of the term *talent management* returns some 1,350,000 and 16,500,000 hits on Google Scholar and Google, respectively. Considering that mainstream practitioner interest in the topic only emerged in the mid-to-late 1990s, and that academic research on the topic did not begin to appear to any significant degree until 2009 or later (Gallardo-Gallardo et al., 2015; McDonnell et al., 2017), these numbers reveal an extremely steep trajectory of interest. Notwithstanding this interest, talent management remains a rather diffuse area of research, and its conceptual and intellectual boundaries remain relatively fluid. A key motivation for the current handbook was to bring together some of the leading scholars in the field of talent management, and to highlight the diversity of research themes in the area. Our hope is that the volume will be an influential reference work that offers academic researchers, advanced postgraduate students, and reflective practitioners a state-of-the-art overview of the key themes, topics, and debates in talent management. The current chapter provides a summary of the development of academic work in talent management, highlights some important research themes in the area, and concludes with an overview of the contributions to the current volume.

Interest in talent management can be traced to a number of factors. Although Peter Cappelli and JR Keller (2014, 2017), among others, chart a long history of talent management dating back some fifty years, recent mainstream interest in the area is generally considered to have emerged from the high-profile work of a group of McKinsey consultants who described "The War for Talent" in the mid-1990s. In response to the challenges of an aging population and a tightening labor market for certain skills in the United

States, these consultants sought to understand what differentiated high-performing organizations from others. A key conclusion from their work was that high-performing organizations differentiated themselves based on a focus on talent from the top to the bottom of the organization. Their focus on talent management was legitimized by high-profile advocates such as Jack Welch at GE. While the premise of much of this work around loading the organization with star performers or A players has been called into question more recently, the area has continued to evolve. While the focus may have shifted, the emphasis on talent management has endured (see Cappelli and Keller, 2017; Collings, 2014a). Indeed, scholars continue to identify the need to build effective talent pipelines as one of the greatest challenges facing organizations globally (Al Ariss, Cascio, and Paauwe, 2014; Cascio and Boudreau, 2016; Stahl et al., 2012; Tarique and Schuler, 2010). In a recent study, for example, more than 70% of chief executive officers (CEOs) highlighted the lack of availability of skills and capabilities as a key threat to the growth prospects of their organizations (PwC, 2015). Disturbingly, talent practitioners widely acknowledge their lack of capability in delivering on the talent agenda, given the limitations of talent programs, as well as their own skill sets (BCG, 2013; Mercer, 2016). Thus, the area of talent management remains of interest to scholars and practitioners alike.

In this introduction, we summarize some of the key debates in talent management and offer an overview of the content of the handbook. We begin by considering how *talent management* is defined in the academic literature. Thereafter, we provide an overview of the key trends and debates in the talent-management literature over the past decade and a half. We also point to some seminal research central to our understanding of talent management that has been omitted from a number of recent reviews of the field, owing to broader theoretical framing. We conclude with an overview of the content of the handbook.

1.2 Defining *Talent Management*

A key focus of much of the earlier academic literature on talent management has been on establishing the conceptual and intellectual boundaries of the field. Indeed, based on a review of the academic literature in the area through 2012, Thunnissen, Boselie, and Fruytier (2013: 1749) concluded, "the majority of the academic literature is still conceptual, trying to respond to the question of what talent management is." In their seminal review of the area in 2006, Lewis and Heckman identified three key themes in the talent-management literature as (1) rebranding of human resources (HR); (2) the management of A players; and (3) a focus on talent pools. Three years later Collings and Mellahi (2009) identified a fourth stream of research that focused on critical roles. Sparrow, Scullion, and Tarique (2014) framed these streams as (1) a practices approach—focused on the presence of key HR practices; (2) a people approach—focused on the categorization of people (generally captured as A, B, and C players); (3) a strategic-pools approach—reframing succession around talent pools and talent supply chains; and (4) a position approach—focused on the identification of key positions. Indeed, the fact that there was not a uniform definition of talent management was widely identified as a key constraint on the early development of the area.

Building on this work, Collings and Mellahi's (2009: 304) definition of *talent management* has become the most widely adopted definition (Gallardo et al., 2015). They define *talent management* as:

> the systematic identification of key positions which differentially contribute to the organization's sustainable competitive advantage, the development of a talent pool of high-potential and high-performing incumbents to fill these roles, and the development of a differentiated human resource architecture to facilitate filling these positions with competent incumbents, and to ensure their continued commitment to the organization.

This definition has its roots in the resource-based view and it emphasizes key positions as the point of departure for any talent-management system. These key positions are defined by their centrality to organizational strategy, their rarity (generally 10–20% of positions in any organization), and the fact that increasing the quality (quality pivotal) or quantity (quantity pivotal) of people in these positions is likely to generate a disproportionate return to the organization (Becker and Huselid, 2006; Boudreau and Ramstad, 2007; Cascio and Boudreau, 2016; Collings and Mellahi, 2009). Having identified these key positions, the talent-pool strategy emphasizes identifying high-potential and high-performing employees to fill those critical roles. This approach is premised on recruiting ahead of the curve as opposed to demand-led recruitment (Sparrow, 2007). Mitigating, managing, and optimizing human capital risk is also central to any talent pool strategy (Cascio and Boudreau, 2011, 2012). Finally, this definition recognizes the value of differentiating HR practices based on the differential potential of pivotal roles to generate value. This is a shift compared with historical approaches to HR, where HR professionals focused on developing and implementing relatively standardized HR polices and processes that applied to all employees, regardless of their positions or levels in an organization.

A further key theme that can be identified in the literature on defining talent management relates to using data and analytics to inform talent decisions (Vaiman et al., 2012). Indeed, linking talent management and management decision making is not particularly new. For example, John Boudreau introduced the term *decision science* in the context of talent management and HR in the late 1990s (Boudreau and Ramstad, 2007). According to Boudreau and Ramstad (2007: 25), the goal of a talentship decision science is "to increase the success of the organization by improving decisions that depend on or impact talent resources." Central to this perspective was HR repositioning itself through shifting the emphasis from services delivery to supporting key decisions within the business, particularly in relation to talent.

Research in talent management has broadly assumed a unitarist and managerialist orientation (Thunnissen et al., 2013). As noted by Al Ariss et al. (2014: 174), "a performance-driven version of TM is very common in TM processes." However, it is important to note that a limitation of the work in the area has been a failure to demonstrate the actual impact of talent management on organizational performance (Cascio and Boudreau, 2016; Collings 2014b; McDonnell et al., 2017). It is likely that the influence of talent-management research will significantly increase once research sheds light on if and how talent management affects organizational performance (broadly defined), much as the seminal papers of Mark Huselid and others did for the field of strategic HR management. We believe, however, that a narrow focus on shareholder value is likely to limit the potential contribution of talent management. We therefore echo the calls from others for a multistakeholder approach to talent management and a multidimensional consideration of organizational effectiveness (Cascio and Boudreau, 2016; Collings, 2014b; Schuler and Jackson, 2014; Thunnissen et al., 2013).

A key critique of the above approaches to talent management is that despite the profound shift in workforce management over the past three decades, they implicitly focus on practices associated with lifetime careers in organizations (Cappelli, 1999; Cappelli and Keller, 2014). More recently, however, there has been reduced commitment by organizations to lifetime careers and a growing reliance on external labor markets in staffing senior organizational positions (Cappelli, 1999; Bonet and Hamori, 2017). Indeed, the very notion of employment has been challenged. For example, John Boudreau and colleagues have argued that the workplace is fundamentally changing and moving "beyond employment" (Boudreau et al., 2015; Cascio and Boudreau, 2016). This trend reflects a shifting emphasis from managing employees to optimizing how work is done. More broadly, research has also considered what factors are linked to an individual's decision to pursue contract as opposed to full-time employment. While the assumption may have been that this decision is premised largely on a lack of career opportunities within organizations, research confirms that individuals with significant experiences often choose to contract in search of, *inter alia*, more meaningful work and greater control over work schedules (Bidwell and Briscoe, 2009). This means that there is growing availability of highly skilled talent available in the external labor market and available through a freelance or contractor relationship. This mirrors trends toward increased levels of self-employment and contracting that offer opportunities and challenges alike for talent management. This is arguably the key emerging trend in the field of talent management currently. Having identified some of the ways in which talent management has been defined and operationalized in the literature, we now consider some of the major trends in talent-management research over the past decade and a half or so.

1.3 TALENT MANAGEMENT RESEARCH: TRENDS AND DEBATES

Over the past few years, a number of reviews of the academic literature on talent management have been published (see Cappelli and Keller, 2014; Cascio and Boudreau, 2016;

Gallardo-Gallardo et al., 2015; McDonnell et al., 2017; Thunnisen et al., 2013). These reviews point to a number of key trends. First, virtually all of the academic literature published in peer-reviewed outlets has been published since 2008, with one review identifying only six peer-reviewed articles published before 2008 (McDonnell et al., 2017). Second, while the intellectual roots are firmly established in North America, the literature base is highly diverse geographically (Al Aris et al., 2014; Gallardo-Gallardo et al., 2015; McDonnell et al., 2017). One review identified peer-reviewed research from some thirty-five countries, with the United States and the United Kingdom leading the way with a respective 19% and 18% of all papers. Ireland and the Netherlands accounted for 8% of articles each, and Australia followed closely with some 7% (Gallardo-Gallardo et al., 2015). A third key theme in these reviews is that the volume of empirical work is larger than previously assumed, accounting for some 60% of all papers published on talent management (McDonnell et al., 2017). This contrasts with earlier work that was largely conceptual and focused on "respond[ing] to the question of what talent management is" (Thunnissen et al., 2013: 1749). Empirical research is also dominated by Anglo-Saxon sites, accounting for a combined 14% of empirical papers (Gallardo-Gallardo et al., 2015). However, India represented the single largest site of empirical work, at 12% of all empirical papers, followed by China (6%), Belgium (6%), Australia (5%), and Spain (5%). Indeed, European data accounted for 50% of all empirical studies (Gallardo-Gallardo et al., 2015). However, the quality of the empirical studies in much of this work is open to question, with a large reliance on single-site cases and basic research designs. This partially explains the failure of talent-management research to get traction at the leading international peer-reviewed outlets to date. Indeed, greater use of more sophisticated research designs will be central to ensuring the sustainable development of the academic area of talent management.

An additional factor that explains the types of outlets that dominate the publication of talent-management research (*Journal of World Business, International Journal of Human Resource Management*, and *Human Resource Management Review*) (McDonnell et al., 2017) is the phenomenon-driven nature of much of the work (Dries, 2013). For example, in a recent editorial, the editor-in-chief of the *Journal of World Business*, a journal that has published a significant amount of talent-management work, explicitly calls for more phenomenon-based research in that journal (Doh, 2015). Such an approach "starts with the generation of facts, most typically from large-sample analysis [although the empirical work on talent management often begins with smaller samples], that can inform us what we need a theory for" (Hambrick, 2007: 1349). Indeed, a common point of departure for much research on talent management is a reference to practitioner reports that cite the priority placed on the talent agenda by CEOs, the challenge of attracting and retaining key talent, or the limited capacity of HR professionals to deliver on the talent agenda (see, for example, BCG, 2013; Mercer, 2016; PWC, 2015), highlighting the phenomenon-driven nature of talent-management research. Two additional characteristics define phenomenon-driven research: there is a lack of available theory to account fully for the phenomenon or the cause-and-effect relationships that underly it, and there is neither a single methodological approach nor a research design superior to others in exploring the different aspects of the phenomenon (von Krogh, Lamastra, and Harfliger, 2012, cited in Gallardo-Gallardo et al., 2015). Based on the papers cited in these review articles, this does appear to be a fair assessment of the area of talent management. However, a wider body of literature that explicitly deals with talent and talent-management issues is missing from these reviews because the authors do not use the term *talent management* in their titles or keywords, which typically are the search criteria of such reviews. In our next section, we identify three bodies of literature that have significant implications for talent management but are missed from these reviews. We classify them as the literature on star employees, the portability of performance, and internal and external labor markets. Other key areas are highly relevant to talent management, and one of the objectives of the current volume is to try to capture some of this literature.

1.3.1 A Missing Literature Base

The first body of work that is absent from recent reviews on talent management looks at star performers in organizations. Given the focus of talent management on differentiated performance, this literature has clear relevance for talent management. (For comprehensive reviews, see Call, Nyberg, and Thatcher, 2015; Kehoe, Lepak, and Bentley, 2016; and O'Boyle and Kroska, 2017.) This literature generally appears in micro-oriented research outlets and has clear implications for research and practice in talent management. One key finding from this research is that in modern knowledge-driven organizations, employee performance is not normally distributed, as implied in utility analysis and in many early approaches to talent management, such as forced distributions of performance (Aguinis and O'Boyle, 2014). Star performance is much more likely to follow a Gaussian or power-law distribution. This has significant implications for how one thinks about and empirically examines star performance in organizations. The literature on stars provides some insights on the antecedents of star performance. For Call, Nyberg, and Thatcher (2015), "stars" are defined by disproportionately high and sustained performance, visibility, and relevant social capital. Their work provides important insights into the making, managing, and mobility of star employees. The impact of social capital on star performance is also a key theme in the literature on star performers. For example, by virtue of their reputation for high performance, stars benefit from greater access to organizational resources, greater autonomy in pursuing higher-reward ventures, and the potential to capitalize on a richer and denser social network (Kehoe et al., 2016). Conversely, stars can also suffer from the profile that comes with their stardom. Specifically, high-profile stars are likely to be sought by their colleagues for input, which, in turn, can lead to information overload and reduced performance (Oldroyd and Morris, 2012; Morris and Oldroyd, 2017).

A second body of literature that is often missed in the context of reviews of talent management concerns the portability of performance of high performers. Indeed, a longstanding assumption in the talent literature is that the performance of talent is mobile (Minbaeva and Collings, 2012). In other words, the assumption is that a higher performer in one context will maintain his or her performance when changing to a new employer. This is often not the case, however. For example, Groysberg and colleagues (2008), in a study of the performance of Wall Street's top market analysts over almost a decade, found that nearly 50% of the time, the performance of those analysts declined when they changed employers. Their performance dropped by an average of 20%, and it often took up to five years for their performance to return to pre-move levels. Groysberg et al. (2008) concluded that as little as 30% of analyst performance is determined by the individual. The other 70% is determined by resources and qualities specific to the firm. Such resources include reputation, IT, leadership, training, and team chemistry.

The importance of context in performance is supported by a study of cardiac surgeons performing the same surgical procedures across multiple hospitals contemporaneously (Huckman and Pisano, 2006). This study identified significant performance differences among surgeons working across different hospitals. Surgeons performed better (measured in terms of risk-adjusted mortality) in the hospitals where they performed a higher number of procedures. The differential in performance is explained by a surgeon's familiarity with critical assets in the hospital, such as specific employees, team structures, and operating routines, and by the fact that surgeons with higher volumes of patients at a specific hospital may be able to bring their influence to bear in ensuring access to better resources. Research on the performance of former CEOs who take on CEO roles at new organizations also points to the challenges of maintaining their performance in the new setting (Hamori and Koyuncu, 2015). This literature has important implications for talent management, particularly given the breakdown in traditional lifetime careers in organizations, which means that organizations increasingly rely on external labor markets for key hires (Cappelli and Keller, 2014). This work also raises important questions about labor market intermediaries such as executive headhunters, their role in talent acquisition, and the implications for the performance of stars (Bonet and Hamori, 2017).

The preceding discussion raises important questions around internal and external labor markets and how they combine in operationalizing organizational talent strategies. As Bidwell (2017) notes, "If we take a broader perspective than the individual job, though, we can also think about talent management as managing a flow of workers across different jobs, within and across organizations, over time." A key question in this context is "make or buy" decisions in the context of talent management. For example, research suggests that organizations are more likely to promote internally to pivotal roles (that is, strategically important roles with greater performance differentials) (Bidwell and Keller, 2014). This is a significant finding, as a separate study shows that individuals who were promoted internally produced significantly better performance compared with workers hired externally into similar jobs in the first two years in the new role. Those promoted internally also displayed lower rates of voluntary and involuntary turnover, whereas external hires were promoted more quickly (Bidwell, 2011). This occurred despite the fact that the external hires were paid about 18% more than comparable individuals who were promoted, and they entered the organization with higher levels of experience and education (Bidwell, 2011). Matthew Bidwell explores this broader debate in detail in Chapter 15 in the current volume. However, a further important theme in this stream concerns the end of an individual's tenure with an organization and how it manages the transition out (see Hausknecht, 2017). Drawing on social capital theory, Somaya, Williamson, and Lorinkova (2008) show that movement of employees both to and from clients known as "cooperators" may enhance firm performance. In contrast, only inward mobility from competitors, as opposed to outward mobility to competitors, benefits the original firm. The key implication is that organizations should develop differentiated strategies for turnover based on each individual's value to that organization, as well as whether he or she is moving to a competitor or to a cooperator. These considerations are reflected in the greater emphasis on alumni networks among many organizations. These offer a means of maintaining contact with former employees in the context of potential business and the potential of the individual to return as a boomerang hire.

The above review is intended as an illustrative rather than an exhaustive review of the types of research that have clear relevance for talent management and that are often missed from reviews of work in talent management because they fail to use the discourse of talent management in the papers. To explain why these papers are generally not framed in the discourse of talent management, we point to several reasons. One, research in these top-tier outlets is driven by a theoretical rather than by a phenomenon-based agenda. This requires authors to frame their work in terms of traditional discourse and theories. Because there is yet no grand theory of talent management, scholars have to position their work in the context of these cognate theoretical frames. Two, the traditional skepticism in the academy toward concepts that emerge from practice, similar to the emergence of employee engagement, may also constrain authors in integrating the talent discourse in these outlets. Our hope is that as the area of talent management continues to develop, and as academic work continues to evolve, talent management may increasingly be perceived as legitimate in leading outlets.

We now turn to summarizing the chapters in the current volume.

1.4 CONTRIBUTIONS TO THE HANDBOOK

1.4.1 Section 1

Section 1 outlines the scope of talent management and places the area in historical context. After the volume is introduced in Chapter 1, Chapter 2 considers the historical context of talent management.

In Chapter 2, Peter Cappelli and JR Keller note that the term *talent management* has developed into the most important term in HR during the early twenty-first century. They review the historical context of talent management and identify key issues and debates likely to shape the field going forward. Their definition of *talent management*—the process through which organizations anticipate and meet their needs for talent in strategic jobs—reflects how both academics and practitioners have come to view the field. Then they provide an overview of the conceptual history and a historical tour of the practice of talent management—focusing primarily on developments in the United States, where much more has been written on the subject—from the early days of industrial production to today. They conclude by identifying areas of inquiry that hold the most promise for those interested in advancing the science and practice of talent management.

1.4.2 Section 2

Section 2 focuses on the nature of talent and performance, and it includes five chapters.

In Chapter 3, Ernest O'Boyle and Sydney Kroska examine what we know about star performers—elite performers who either produce exceedingly high quantities of output or output not easily substituted by good or even very good workers. Although star performers have always existed, the decline of the manufacturing sector and the rise of the knowledge economy may be leading to a substantial increase in their numbers. Stars are important to individuals, teams, organizations, and even entire industries. This chapter reviews the theoretical and empirical work surrounding stars, distilling what is known and unknown, what is fact and what is myth. It concludes by identifying a research agenda designed to move investigations in this area from descriptive to predictive, from inductive to deductive, and from empirically and theoretically separated from the mainstream literature to integrated fully within it.

Chapter 4, by Amirali Minbashian, considers the often neglected questions of within-person variability in performance. This stands in contrast to debate on between-person variation in performance, which arguably has received far greater attention in talent-management research. He begins by reviewing the literature on within-person variability and presents a model of individual performance that incorporates short-term and long-term within-person performance variability and individual differences. The benefits of the model as a framework for explaining individual performance are outlined, as are its implications for the conceptualization of talent and the development of talent-management systems. Specific talent-management practices with respect to employee assessment and employee motivation are also considered. This chapter thus brings to the surface a number of important questions for research on talent management that have heretofore often been neglected.

Chapter 5, by Robert Silzer and Walter Borman, focuses on the identification of the potential for leadership—that is, having the qualities (e.g., personal characteristics, motivation, skills, abilities, experiences, and behaviors) that are early predictors of future leadership effectiveness. The authors review and summarize efforts in research and in practice to identify useful predictors or indicators of such potential, including those found in genetic, childhood/adolescent, early adult, and midcareer research. Based on their findings, they present a unifying, integrated model of leadership potential, the Blueprint of Leadership Potential. It includes foundational dimensions (personality characteristics and cognitive capabilities), growth dimensions (learning skills and motivation skills), and career dimensions (leadership skills and functional/techni-cal capability). After identifying factors that can support, stall, or disrupt someone who has an early, high-potential profile for leadership, the authors conclude by proposing emerging research questions related to identifying leadership potential in individuals.

Chapter 6, by Gina Dokko and Winnie Jiang, examines the fascinating topic of the portability of expertise, resources, and performance as talented individuals cross organ-izational boundaries. Drawing from career-mobility research, the authors develop a framework that considers the human capital, social capital, and identity issues in tal-ent movement. They also identify the implications for organizations as talent enters and exits, considering these issues separately because the effects of mobility in and out are asymmetric. They conclude that the acquisition of talent does not necessarily lead to the successful utilization of that talent. Evidence indicates that changes in organizational factors, as well as changes in the extent to which the context itself supports an individu-al's performance, will affect that performance. Conversely, departure of talent does not mean an absolute loss to organizations—losing talent can potentially bring organiza-tions unexpected gains, such as new social resources. Understanding the kinds of issues that prevent the perfect portability of performance and that reveal opportunities for firms to counterbalance talent losses will generate theoretical and practical insights.

In Chapter 7, Rob Ployhart and Ormonde Cragun consider the question of how firms create, manage, and leverage complementarities among human capital resources. They argue that extant research has largely neglected to conceptualize or measure directly the human capital resource. In contrast, they argue the extant literature has tended to directly link talent-management practices to firm performance, and assume that the effect was due to enhancing human capital resources. They point to the importance of work design and grouping individuals in ways that create unique relationships between their knowl-edge, skills, abilities, and other characteristics, and of designing these relationships to be accessible by the firm (i.e., creating human capital resources) in the innovation process. Synergistic relationships between two or more human capital resources are therefore con-ceptualized as *human capital resource complementarities*. Thus, they consider how talent management practices relate to the formation, maintenance, and bundling of human cap-ital resource complementarities. They begin by summarizing the key features of resource complementarities observed within the broader strategy literature. Next, the chapter con-siders the nature of complementarities specifically for human capital resources, and the numerous types of complementarities that may exist. The chapter concludes by proposing a research agenda to understand how talent-management practices are related to human capital resource complementarities and competitive advantage.

1.4.3 Section 3

Section 3 focuses on talent, teams, and performance, and it consists of four chapters.

In Chapter 8, Rebecca Kehoe, Blythe Rosikiewicz, and Daniel Tzabbar examine the impact of stars' influence on teams. The chapter starts with a critical and integrative review of the accumulated literature on talent in the team context. The review of the literature reveals that star team members tend to modify teams' interpersonal dynamics and work processes, as well as team performance. Star team members are also affected by surrounding team environments. Interestingly, the evidence suggests that the impact of an association with a star presence is not always positive. The impact is contingent on the characteristics of both the team and the star. The chapter provides a discussion of a set of conditions under which a star's membership on a team is likely to be positive for the star, the team, and the organization.

In Chapter 9, Maria Christina Meyers, Giverny De Boeck, and Nicky Dries examine employees' reactions to being designated as "talent." They review the empirical literature on how and whether employees display favorable attitudes to being identified as organizational talent. As perhaps expected, the evidence is not quite clear: while some studies show employees tend to react positively to being designated as talent, a number of studies do not support this finding. Several studies reveal that being designated as talent creates higher expectations that employees feel they may not be able to meet. The chapter provides interesting insights into the effects of talent designation on those identified as talent, as well as those excluded from the talent pool. The chapter concludes with an agenda for further research, calling for more research on the link between talent designation and performance.

In Chapter 10, Travis Maynard, Matti Vartiainen, and Diana Sanchez argue that virtual working has become a key means of collaborating in the global enterprise. This calls for a greater understanding of the factors that underlie virtual team performance. They note that extant research has pointed to the importance of factors such as team composition, leadership, communication, conflict, shared cognition, and trust. The chapter reviews and integrates recent research on talent management and virtual teams, to provide a different and, the authors argue, a better understanding of the current state of knowledge on virtual teams. The chapter provides a succinct summary of the state of the art of the talent management and virtual team literature, together with directions for future research and theoretical development.

Chapter 11, by James Oldroyd and Shad Morris, argues that owing to their disproportionate value and visibility, stars are more likely to be sought out by their lower-performing peers and to develop an information advantage through abundant social capital. They show that this social capital has the potential to impact star performance positively by endowing stars with greater access to information, which allows them to complete their work more effectively and further enhance their status with the organization. However, they also argue that not all of the informational effects of stardom are beneficial. Thus, stars' abundant social capital may produce an unintended side effect of information overload. They explore a curvilinear theory of social capital on the information performance of star employees. In the chapter, they highlight the role of talent management in mitigating these information-overload effects for stars and ensuring that they continue to shine. The chapter concludes by outlining a number of interesting avenues of potential future study that link stars, social capital, and information overload.

1.4.4 Section 4

Section 4 builds our understanding of talent flows into, through, and out of organizations. It consists of nine chapters.

In Chapter 12, Martin Edwards considers the intersection between employer branding and talent management. In considering this intersection, he reflects upon the phenomenon of HR practice differentiation in the context of both employer branding and talent management. In particular, he considers some similarities between brand management programs that are likely to differentiate HR practices on the basis of perceived talent versus employer brand segmentation, that is, more likely to differentiate HR practices on the basis of employee needs and wants. He also reflects upon the potential implications for an organization's employer brand and perceived employment offering when organizations take an object-versus-subject-oriented approach to differentiating the workforce based on talent identification. The chapter again concludes with an outline of the key potential avenues for future research in this area.

Chapter 13, by Rocio Bonet and Monika Hamori, considers the important role of talent intermediaries in the recruitment of talent to organizations. They define *talent intermediaries* as entities that stand between the individual worker and the organization that needs work done. These include online intermediaries, such as job boards or social networking sites, and search and placement firms, such as executive search firms and temporary-help service firms. They argue that talent intermediaries play an increasingly important role in the contemporary employment landscape. Specifically, not only do they influence how and which individuals are matched to organizations, but they also affect how tasks are performed or conflicts are resolved once talent is hired by the organization. The authors review the already extensive literature on talent intermediaries, focusing on their role in the identification, assessment, and hiring of talent. The chapter shows the advantages that talent intermediaries present to the talent-acquisition process compared with hiring organizations, and the ways in which their intermediation changes traditional talent-acquisition processes that involved only two parties: the job seeker and the hiring organization. It concludes with a consideration of key research questions for the area.

In Chapter 14, Scott Highhouse and Margaret Brooks explore and challenge five common myths and misconceptions about assessment and selection of talent for upper-management positions. First, they challenge the common assumption that the more information the organization has about the candidate, the better. They argue that while extensive information may provide a sense of diligence and rigor, it may add more cognitive complexity and more potential for bias. Second, they challenge the assumption that the practice of executive assessment ought to be more science than art. Third, they question the commonly held misconceptions that tests are less effective for upper-management assessment, and provide research evidence to show how tests, such as personality tests, can be a strong predictor of success of talent working at the top echelon of the organization. Fourth, they challenge the assumption that assessors need to discuss candidates and reach a consensus. The chapter provides a critical analysis of the team-approach assessment method and highlights its limitations. It posits that it is not necessary for assessors to reach consensus on candidate qualities. Finally, the chapter puts forward several arguments as to why interviews make little difference in executive assessment.

In Chapter 15, Matthew Bidwell examines talent management through the lens of worker flows, emphasizing the interdependence between staffing decisions across jobs and over time. Given that internal talent flows and external staffing both can generate potential benefits, the chapter reviews existing theories on how people flow across jobs within and across organizations. It also considers how organizations balance those internal and external flows in staffing jobs. Although different theories have generally been used to analyze internal and external mobility, this review reveals that organizations are using increasingly market-like structures to manage internal moves, while researchers are uncovering increasing amounts of structure in flows of workers across organizations. The chapter concludes by noting that studies continue to highlight the substantial benefits that organizations receive from staffing jobs through internal rather than external mobility, despite increases over time in outside hiring. At the same time, it stresses the need for additional evidence about what decision makers actually focus on in managing talent flows.

Chapter 16, by David Collings, considers workforce differentiation: formalized approaches to the segmentation of the workforce based on employees' competence or the nature of roles they perform that reflect their differential potential to generate value. Historically, HR professionals focused on developing and implementing HR policies and processes that ensured employees behaved in standardized ways in performing their jobs. More recently, however, researchers have questioned such a standardized approach to HR. In its place, workforce differentiation has emerged as a central element of talent management practice. Earlier research on workforce differentiation focused on individual talent as the locus of differentiation, but that focus has now shifted to strategic or pivotal jobs. This chapter reviews the emergence of workforce differentiation in the academic literature and identifies two routines that govern its implementation: identification of pivotal roles and of incumbents with the potential to fill those roles as they become available. The chapter concludes by describing emerging trends and potential avenues for future study in this area.

In Chapter 17, Anthony Nyberg, Donald Schepker, Ormonde Cragun, and Patrick Wright consider succession management, which they argue has long been considered a key tool for ensuring talent replacement, as part of a broad talent management strategy. They argue that creating a strong talent-development plan is essential to strengthening and sustaining the most important organizational resource, its talent. Although there is an increasing understanding of the relationship between talent and organizational performance, they argue that we still know little about the process involved in replenishing and sustaining talent. In the chapter, they summarize what we know, what we do not know, and what we speculate regarding the succession-planning process. In so doing, the chapter provides direction for academics and practitioners in considering how to maximize talent management by extending prior research and embarking on stronger, more robust and systematic succession-planning processes. They use a brief literature review to identify the current knowledge concerning succession research. Finally, they present findings from recent surveys on the succession-planning process.

Chapter 18, by David Day and Patricia O'Connor, provides an overview of talent development in organizations. It outlines why talent development is important, considers decisions about whom to invest in, and identifies some best practices in the field. The authors begin by reviewing the literature on talent development in young people. They argue that this literature is relevant to the leadership development but widely overlooked in understanding talent-management processes in organizations. The chapter elaborates on how nature, in the form of emergenic traits, and nurture, with regard to epigenetic experiences, interact to shape development. They then apply this perspective in understanding focal issues on building organizational capability through talent. The chapter shows how state-of-the-art talent development focuses on developing collective capability through the creation of systems, processes, practices, and culture required to achieve strategic objectives in a sustainable manner. The authors argue that talented individuals are integral architects of these types of collective phenomena and responsible for executing, stewarding, and improving them. Further, they argue that a comprehensive approach to building organizational capability does not rely on any one—or just a few—extraordinarily talented people. It involves the development of a broad-based organizational capacity for leadership.

In Chapter 19, John Hausknecht considers the end of the talent-cycle-talent turnover. He argues that despite longstanding research interest in understanding the causes and consequences of employee turnover, much less is known about the turnover of top talent, such as high performers or "stars." Building on the argument in earlier chapters, he defines star employees as disproportionately productive, highly visible, and often maintaining strong social networks, all of which make them desirable to organizations. The chapter begins by reviewing theory and research related to the retention of talented employees, including stars, high performers, high potentials, critical roles, and core employees. A key conclusion is that high performers are more likely than average performers to leave organizations, but much less is known about the factors that drive stars to leave organizations. However, equally he argues that it may not be always desirable to retain talent at all costs, and he points to some emerging literature around managing the exit of employees from organizations to retain key social capital. The review is structured around five key questions: (1) How is talent defined and measured? (2) Are talented employees more likely to quit? (3) What frameworks help us understand star performers? (4) What are the drawbacks of attempting to retain top talent? (5) What additional research is needed?

In Chapter 20, Alexis Fink and Michael Sturman argue that HR metrics and talent analytics present a renewed opportunity to help drive effective HR practices. HR metrics are operational measures, addressing how efficient, effective, and impactful an organization's HR practices are. In contrast, talent analytics focus on decision points, guiding investment decisions. The chapter provides an overview of the historic roots and current practices around HR metrics and talent analytics. Through this, the authors explore the role, benefits, and risks of benchmarking and utility analyses as two common approaches to HR metrics. They discuss how current advances in research and practice make the use of HR metrics and talent analytics a business necessity, and they argue that forces such as increased global competition, increased data availability, increased general analytic sophistication, and increased availability of data storage and computing power hold great promise for the continued evolution of talent analytics within organizations.

1.4.5 Section 5

The final section of the handbook, Section 5, considers a number of different contexts that affect talent management. It consists of eight chapters.

Chapter 21, by Shaista Khijli and Randall Schuler, focuses on the macro context of talent management. The chapter examines the role and influence of macro-level institutions such as governments and non-government organizations in talent development and utilization at the national level. The chapter proposes a conceptual framework for macro-level talent management that links macro-level factors with macro talent management and processes and what the authors refer to as first-level outcomes, such as educational attainment, jobs, talent mobility, and diaspora utilization, and second-level outcomes, such as talent rankings or country attractiveness, productivity, innovation, economic development, and overall national competitiveness.

In Chapter 22, Paul Boselie and Marian Thunnissen explore the important but underresearched issue of talent management in the public sector. The chapter reviews the large body of literature on HR management in this sector and discusses the unique characteristics of the sector, before providing a definition of talent management in this sector, taking into account the sector's unique characteristics and context. The chapter highlights a number of interesting issues that emerge when examining talent management in the public sector, such as the tensions between equality and differentiation, inclusiveness versus exclusiveness, talent-management outcomes, and the tension between delivering public value versus organizational excellence. The chapter concludes by providing an interesting agenda for future research on talent management in the public sector.

In Chapter 23, Fang Lee Cooke provides a comprehensive review of the talent-management literature in emerging economies. The chapter identifies the key talent-management challenges firms face in those economies. These challenges include talent shortages, mismatch of demand and supply expectations, and knowledge transfer in the context of multinational enterprises. The review reveals that talent-management research in emerging economies focuses on a small number of countries, such as China and India, and large, multinational enterprises. Cooke argues that in addition to broadening the geographical focus of talent-management research in emerging economies, the area would benefit from a broader set of disciplinary bases, solid research designs and analyses, and more attention to talent management-performance outcomes.

In Chapter 24, Ingmar Björkman, Mats Ehrnrooth, Kristiina Mäkelä, Adam Smale, and Jennie Sumelius review the status of talent-management practices that multinational enterprises use to manage employees designated as talent. The chapter draws on a case study of KONE, a Finland-based elevator and escalator company, to illustrate talent-management practices in a multinational enterprise. By examining the content of talent-management practices, the authors identified the actors involved in enacting talent management and their roles within their organizations, as well as the performance impact of talent-management practices within multinational enterprises. The chapter suggests a number of valuable research avenues, and it highlights the importance of examining the link between talent management and performance in multinational enterprises. The authors suggest three levels of analysis: the multinational enterprises as a whole, the unit/subsidiary level, and the individual level. With regard to performance, they suggest that scholars should distinguish between what they call *proximal outcomes* of talent management, and *distant outcomes* of talent management such as multinational performance.

In Chapter 25, Marion Festing, Katharina Harsch, Lynn Schäfer, and Hugh Scullion consider talent management in the context of small- and medium-sized (SME) businesses. They argue that despite the obvious economic importance of SMEs, talent management in this context is under-researched. Pointing to the liability of small size and scarce resources as typical features of SMEs, they call for a particular definition and approach to talent management in this sector. They argue that the limited knowledge about talent management in SMEs leads to major challenges in attracting and retaining talent. In drawing on the wider literature on HR management in SMEs, they position talent-management issues in that wider context. The chapter then reviews the scant literature on talent management in SMEs and outlines how HRM and talent-management networks and cooperation in industry clusters represent a means for SMEs to join forces in order to compete with larger, multinational companies. Given the paucity of research in the area, the chapter concludes with a summary of key research themes that should be explored in further research.

Chapter 26, by Wayne Cascio and John Boudreau, addresses talent management of nonstandard employees, those who work outside the bounds of regular, full-time employment. The chapter begins by examining why and when organizations choose to use nonstandard workers, followed by a description of the stages and objectives of the talent lifecycle. The authors then map the talent-lifecycle stages and objectives against several categories of nonstandard work, and develop a distribution of research attention across that map. Results reveal large areas of very sparse research, as well as two significant clusters of research. One of these focuses on more traditional arrangements (contractors, temporary, and outsourced work), and the other on less traditional arrangements (freelance platforms and crowdsourcing). A closer examination reveals striking differences in the research questions, theoretical frameworks, and disciplinary foundations within each cluster. The chapter concludes by considering questions and opportunities for future research, in order to deepen our understanding of this budding phenomenon.

In Chapter 27, Darren Baker and Elisabeth Kelan integrate the areas of diversity management and talent management. They show that in an increasingly globalized economy, organizations have had to invest significant financial resources in managing the talents of their diverse workforces. Further, it is often presumed that both talent and diversity management are complementary and interrelated, as they appear to share a similar aim to nurture the skills, attributes, and career progression of the workforce. In contrast, the authors argue that the two practices have in fact been at odds with one another. Specifically, talent management has, they argue, largely been defined by an exclusionary paradigm focused on developing the skills and attributes of an elite segment of the workforce, and rationalized using neoliberal meritocratic ideologies. In explicating how this has been problematic for progress on equality, they argue that it has assumed, firstly, that all employees are endowed with equal opportunity and secondly, that diverse individuals can overcome obstacles to success; thirdly, it has neglected collective identities through the individualization of discrimination. The chapter concludes with a number of recommendations on how talent management could be reframed as a catalyst for progress on equality in organizations, including future areas for research on the intersection between equality, diversity, and talent management.

Chapter 28, by Patrick Gavan O'Shea and Kerrin E. Puente, asks the intriguing question: "How is technology changing talent management"? Technological advances have touched nearly every aspect of human life in recent decades, and talent management is no exception. Organized around the primary elements of the talent-management life cycle (identifying talent, acquiring talent, developing talent, and evaluating talent), each section of the chapter provides a summary of current research findings and practice trends, examples illustrating those trends, and questions to guide future research. Several themes cut across these sections, including (1) the potential for technology to help individuals to identify, grow, and manage their talents in a more proactive way; (2) the increasing use of engaging simulations for recruitment, selection, and developmental purposes; and (3) the need for systematic research to investigate the many fascinating questions raised by technology's dramatic impact throughout the talent-management field.

1.5 Conclusion

There is little doubt that we are at an exciting juncture in the development of the area of talent management. As a whole, the contributions to the current volume represent a state-of-the-art overview of the key research and themes that are relevant to talent management. In evaluating the current development of the research in their respective areas, our authors have also charted a challenging and exciting research agenda for the broad area of talent management. Our hope is that the volume will provide a state-of-the-art reference work for the current knowledge base of talent management, as well as a platform for future research in this dynamic and exciting area.

NOTE

1. May, 2017.

REFERENCES

Aguinis, H., and O'Boyle, E. H. 2014. Star performers in twenty-first-century organizations. *Personnel Psychology*, 67, pp.313–50.

Al Ariss, A., Cascio, W.F., and Paauwe, J. 2014. Talent management: current theories and future research directions. *Journal of World Business*, 49, pp.173–9.

BCG. 2013. *Creating people advantage 2013: lifting HR practices to the next level*. New York: BCG.

Becker, B. E., and Huselid, M. A. 2006. Strategic human resources management: where do we go from here? *Journal of Management*, 32, pp.898–925.

Bidwell, M. 2011. Paying more to get less: specific skills, matching, and the effects of external hiring versus internal promotion. *Administrative Science Quarterly*, 56, pp.369–407.

Bidwell, M. 2017. Managing talent flows through internal and external labor markets. In D. G. Collings, K. Mellahi, and W. F. Cascio, eds. *The Oxford handbook of talent management*, pp.283–300. Oxford: Oxford University Press.

Bidwell, M., and Briscoe, F. 2009. Who contracts? Determinants of the decision to work as independent contractor among information technology workers. *Academy of Management Journal*, 52, pp.1148–68.

Bidwell, M., and Keller, JR. 2014. Within or without? How firms combine internal and external labor markets to fill jobs. *Academy of Management Journal*, 57, pp.1035–55.

Bonet, R., and Hamori, M. 2017. Talent intermediaries in talent acquisition. In D. G. Collings, K. Mellahi, and W. F. Cascio, eds. *The Oxford handbook of talent management*, pp.251–69. Oxford: Oxford University Press.

Boudreau, J. W., Jesuthasan, R., and Creelman, D. 2015. *Lead the work: navigating a world beyond employment*. Hoboken, NJ: John Wiley & Sons.

Boudreau, J. W., and Ramstad, P. M. 2007. *Beyond HR: the new science of human capital*. Boston: Harvard Business Press.

Call, M. L., Nyberg, A. J., and Thatcher, S. 2015. Stargazing: an integrative conceptual review, theoretical reconciliation, and extension for star employee research. *Journal of Applied Psychology*, 100, p.623.

Cappelli, P., and Keller, JR. 2014. Talent management: conceptual approaches and practical challenges. *Annual Review of Organizational Psychology and Organizational Behavior*, 1, pp.305–31.

Cappelli, P., and Keller, JR. 2017. The historical context of talent management. In D.G. Collings, K. Mellahi, and W. F. Cascio, eds. *The Oxford handbook of talent management*, pp.23–41. Oxford: Oxford University Press.

Cascio, W. F., and Boudreau, J. W. 2011. *Investing in people: financial impact of human resource initiatives*, 2nd edn. New York: Financial Times Press.

Cascio, W. F., and Boudreau, J. W. 2012. *A short introduction to strategic human resource management*. Cambridge: Cambridge University Press.

Cascio, W. F., and Boudreau, J. W. 2016. The search for global competence: from international HR to talent management. *Journal of World Business*, 51, pp.103–14.

Cascio, W. F., and Boudreau, J. F. 2017. Talent management of non-traditional employees. In D.G. Collings, K. Mellahi, and W. F. Cascio, eds. *The Oxford handbook of talent management*, pp.494–520. Oxford: Oxford University Press.

Collings, D. G. 2014a. The contribution of talent management to organisation success. In J. Passmore, K. Kraiger, and N. Santos, eds. *The Wiley Blackwell handbook of the psychology of training, development and feedback*, pp.247–60. London: Wiley Blackwell.

Collings, D. G. 2014b. Towards mature talent management: beyond shareholder value. *Human Resource Development Quarterly*, 25, pp.301–19.

Collings, D. G., and Mellahi, K. 2009. Strategic talent management: a review and research agenda. *Human Resource Management Review*. 19, pp.304–14.

Doh, J. P., 2015. From the editor: why we need phenomenon-based research in international business. *Journal of World Business*, 50, pp.609–11.

Dokko, G., and Jiang, W. 2017. Managing talent across organizations: the portability of individual performance. In D. G. Collings, K. Mellahi, and W. F. Cascio, eds. *The Oxford handbook of talent management*, pp.115–33. Oxford: Oxford University Press.

Dries, N. 2013. The psychology of talent management: a review and research agenda. *Human Resource Management Review*, 23, pp.272–85.

Gallardo-Gallardo, E., Nijs, S., Dries, N., and Gallo, P. (2015). Towards an understanding of talent management as a phenomenon-driven field using bibliometric and content analysis. *Human Resource Management Review*, 25, pp.264–79.

Groysberg, B., Lee, L. E., and Nanda, A. 2008. Can they take it with them? The portability of star knowledge workers' performance. *Management Science*, 54, pp.1213–30.

Hambrick, D. C. 2007. The field of management's devotion to theory: too much of a good thing? *Academy of Management Journal*, 50, 1346–52.

Hamori, M., and Koyuncu, B. 2015. Experience matters? The impact of prior CEO experience on firm performance. *Human Resource Management*, 54, pp.23–44.

Hauslknecht, J. P. 2017. Talent turnover. In D. G. Collings, K. Mellahi, and W. F. Cascio, eds. *The Oxford handbook of talent management*, pp.361–74. Oxford: Oxford University Press.

Huckman, R. S., and Pisano, G. P. 2006. The firm specificity of individual performance: evidence from cardiac surgery. *Management Science*, 52, pp.473–88.

Kehoe, R. R., Lepak, D. P., and Bentley, F. S. 2016. Let's call a star a star: task performance, external status, and exceptional contributors in organizations. *Journal of Management*, DOI: 10.1177/0149206316628644.

McDonnell, A., Collings, D. G., Mellahi, K., and Schuler, R. S. 2017. Talent management: a systematic review and future prospects. *European Journal of International Management*, 11, pp.86–128.

Mercer. 2016. *Future-proofing HR: bridging the gap between employers and employees*. London: Mercer.

Minbaeva, D., and Collings, D. G. 2013. Seven myths of global talent management. *The International Journal of Human Resource Management*, 24, pp.1762–76.

Minbashian, A. 2017. Within-person variability in performance. In D. G. Collings, K. Mellahi, and W. F. Cascio, eds. *The Oxford handbook of talent management*, pp.66–86. Oxford: Oxford University Press.

Morris, S. S., and Oldroyd, J. B. 2017. The challenges of being a star: network overload. In D. G. Collings, K. Mellahi, and W. F. Cascio, eds. *The Oxford handbook of talent management*, pp.215–33. Oxford: Oxford University Press.

O'Boyle, E. H., and Kroska, S. 2017. Star employees. In D. G. Collings, K. Mellahi, and W. F. Cascio, eds. *The Oxford handbook of talent management*, pp.43–65. Oxford: Oxford University Press.

Oldroyd, J. B., and Morris, S. S. 2012. Catching falling stars: a human resource response to social capital's detrimental effect of information overload on star employees. *Academy of Management Review, 37*, pp.396–418.

PWC. 2015. *PWC CEO Pulse Survey 2015*. London: PWC.

Schuler, R., and E. Jackson, S. 2014. Human resource management and organizational effectiveness: yesterday and today. *Journal of Organizational Effectiveness: People and Performance, 1*, pp.35–55.

Somaya, D., Williamson, I. O., and Lorinkova, N. 2008. Gone but not lost: the different performance impacts of employee mobility between cooperators versus competitors. *Academy of Management Journal, 5*, pp.936–53.

Sparrow, P. S., Scullion, H., and Tarique, I., eds. 2014. *Strategic talent management: contemporary issues in international context*. Cambridge: Cambridge University Press.

Stahl, G, Bjorkman, I., Farndale, E., Morris, S., Paauwe, J., Stiles, P., and Trevor, J. 2012. Six principles of effective global talent management. *MIT Sloan Management Review, 53*, pp.25–42.

Tarique, I., and Schuler, R. S. 2010. Global talent management: literature review, integrative framework, and suggestions for further research. *Journal of World Business, 45*, pp.122–33.

Thunnissen, M., Boselie, P., and Fruytier, B. 2013. Talent management and the relevance of context: towards a pluralistic approach. *Human Resource Management Review, 23*, pp.326–36.

Vaiman, V., Scullion, H., and Collings, D. G. 2012. Talent management decision making. *Management Decision, 50*, pp.925–41.

Von Krogh, G., Lamastra, C. R., and Haefliger, S. 2009. Phenomenon-based research in management and organization science: towards a research strategy. Working Paper. Zurich: ETH.

CHAPTER 2

....

THE HISTORICAL CONTEXT OF TALENT MANAGEMENT

....

PETER CAPPELLI AND JR KELLER

2.1 INTRODUCTION

....

HISTORIANS ask questions about the past to understand both the present and the future. In much the same way, seeing where talent management has come from and the forces that have shaped it in the past is helpful in understanding the current state of practice, as well as where it may go in the future.

The term *talent management* was coined in the late 1990s by McKinsey & Company as part of a research project that eventually led to the publication of *The War for Talent*, a book that colorfully argued that a company's success in the marketplace was increasingly tied to the performance of its top managers (Chambers, Foulon, Handfield-Jones et al., 1998). It reinforced the belief that "talent," in the sense of superior job performance, is more about the dispositions of the individuals than about the way they are, echoing a more general tendency to attribute outcomes such as job performance to individual characteristics (i.e., the fundamental attribution error). The book also anticipated the surge in outside hiring which became the dominant issue in human resources management.

Talent management has since developed into the most important term in the field of human resources of the early twenty-first century. Virtually all leading human resource consulting firms have developed new practice areas or have rebranded existing ones to provide so-called talent management solutions, and talent management is regularly cited as one of the top areas of concern in surveys of not only human resource professionals but also executives. While the term *talent management* has only recently entered our lexicon, the practices associated with talent management—from workforce planning to hiring, assessing potential, internal development, and succession planning—have much longer histories, dating back to the rise of large corporations in the United States in the 1950s.

We trace the historical context of talent management to identify the key issues and debates likely to shape the field going forward. We begin by offering a definition of talent management that reflects how both academics and practitioners have come to view the field. In doing so, we provide an overview of the conceptual history of talent management and a historical tour of the practice of talent management—focusing primarily on developments in the United States, where much more has been written on the subject—from the early days of industrial production to today. We conclude by offering our thoughts on the areas of inquiry we believe hold the most promise for those interested in advancing the science and practice of talent management.

2.2 A Conceptual History of Talent Management

Nearly every academic article written on the topic of talent management begins with handwringing over the conceptual boundaries of the term. Lewis and Heckman (2006: 139) noted the "disturbing lack of clarity regarding the definition, scope and overall goals of talent management." Collings, Scullion, and Dowling (2009: 1264) concluded that "the concept of talent management is lacking in terms of definition and theoretical development and there is a comparative lack of empirical evidence on the topic." As Gallardo-Gallardo, Dries, and Gonzalez-Cruz (2013: 2) assert, "it appears that talent can mean whatever a business leader or writer wants it to mean, since everyone has his or her own idea of what the construct does and does not encompass."

Yet from our perspective, we see a growing consensus around the meaning of the term *talent management,* which we define as *the process through which organizations anticipate and meet their needs for talent in strategic jobs.* This particular definition is useful for several reasons. First, it addresses the common criticism that the use of the term *talent management* is often little more than a rebranding of a range of typical human resources activities (Lewis and Heckman, 2006). Second, it reflects the interests of practitioners, for whom the interest in talent management is (and has long been) focused strongly on a small number of roles, typically senior-management and executive positions. Third, it is sufficiently suited to the academic need to stimulate theory development by capturing what academic researchers have been doing under the heading of talent management in recent years. In fact, this definition is grounded in two long-running theoretical debates. The first centers on the distinction between inclusive and exclusive approaches to talent management, and the second on whether workforce-differentiation efforts should begin with individuals or jobs.

2.2.1 Does Talent Management Apply to All Workers?

Inclusive approaches suggest that talent management should apply to all workers in all jobs. Post-World War II models of employment have tended to conform to the scientific management approach of dividing the workforce between production work-ers and white-collar employees, with most all of the focus of talent management being on the latter. But it was nevertheless true that supervisors, the first tier in the manage-ment ranks, tended to be promoted from the ranks of production workers. It was com-mon in the post-war period, with its virtually complete reliance on promotion from within, to extend talent-management frameworks all the way down to entry-level jobs. New regulations requiring equal treatment of all employees in areas such as retirement policies and health benefits, which started in the 1960s, no doubt contributed to this inclusiveness.

A key criticism of inclusive approaches has been in failing to recognize that the contributions of all workers are not equal, and, more importantly, that the squeeze of resources after the economic stagnation of the 1970s made it very difficult to sustain an inclusive approach to talent management. Conceptually, the idea that talent manage-ment applied to all employees contributed to the notion that talent management was simply a part of human resources management.

In light of this criticism and with the scaling back of corporate investments, especially in employee development and internal advancement, the academic literature on talent management shifted over the past decade or so toward a more exclusive orientation. It was reflected first in the growing interest in workforce differentiation (Collings and Mellahi, 2009; Huselid and Becker, 2011; Lepak and Shaw, 2008). In contrast to inclusive approaches, exclusive approaches see a subset of employees or jobs as creating dispro-portionate value (Gallardo-Gallardo et al., 2013), and suggest that organizations should disproportionately invest scarce resources in those individuals or jobs from which they expect the greatest return.

2.2.2 Should Talent Management Focus on Jobs or Individuals?

The exclusive approach leads to a second debate around whether the locus of workforce differentiation should be the individual or the job. Should the focus be on identifying a subset of individuals who might be slotted into an array of roles, as had been the case with the post-war model, or by identifying a specific population of jobs that are in some way "strategic" and then focusing on filling those roles with talent?

The individual differentiation perspective has its roots in personnel psychology and is consistent with the resource-based view of the firm, which suggests "the value of human capital is inherently dependent upon its potential to contribute to the compet-itive advantage or core competence of the firm" (Lepak and Snell, 1999: 35). The most prominent conceptual model remains the architectural theory of HRM (Lepak and Snell, 1999), which marries insights from the resource-based view, transaction-cost eco-nomics, and human capital theory to show how differential investments in workers pos-sessing highly valuable and unique human capital can lead to a competitive advantage. Several scholars have expanded on this work, including promising efforts to show how mobility constraints provide important boundary conditions on the link between firm-specific skills and competitive advantage (Campbell, Coff, and Kryscynski, 2012).

There is evidence that top performers contribute disproportionately to firm performance. Indeed, an entire body of research around star performers, following the *War for Talent* idea, has gained tremendous traction in recent years (see Call, Nyberg, and Thatcher, 2015 for a review). A defining characteristic of a star is that he or she contributes a disproportional amount of output relative to his or her peers, such that the addition or departure of a star will have "extraordinary" consequences on overall organizational productivity (Aguinis and O'Boyle Jr., 2014: 322). Research on the productivity of knowledge workers has demonstrated that top performers are many times more valuable than average performers (see Felin and Hesterly, 2007: 211–12).

This evidence supports the many practitioners who advocate for an "ABC" notion of talent management, popularized by Jack Welch's vitality curve, where there are really good performers (the A players), really poor performers (the C players), and most stuck in an average category (the B players). Implicit in this notion is the idea that performance is dispositional, so that the goal is to hire A players and get rid of the C players (Axelrod, Handfield-Jones, and Michaels, 2002; Smart, 2005).

The entire field of management, however, is dedicated to the proposition that performance is not entirely dispositional, but also a product of context, especially of management practices. Studies of investment bankers (Groysberg, Lee, and Nanda, 2008) and doctors (Huckman and Pisano, 2006), where we think individual performance per se should be paramount, have highlighted the importance intra-firm networks play in enabling the performance of any single individual. Groysberg and colleagues (2008) found that star investment analysts were often unable to replicate their previous levels of performance owing to the loss of social capital—staff support in particular—associated with the move to a new firm. Huckman and Pisano (2006) found cardiac surgeons practicing in multiple hospitals had higher mortality rates compared with those who practiced in fewer hospitals with more consistent staff support. Another study that casts further doubt on a "more is better" approach to talent management found a curvilinear relationship between group performance and the percentage of star analysts in investment-bank research groups; having a few stars helped performance, but when the percentage of stars eclipsed 45%, performance began to decline (Groysberg, Polzer, and Elfenbein, 2011). More generally, the field of human resource management is based on the notion that management practices, and not just individual differences, drive performance.

At a minimum, the value of a superior individual performance is often moderated by the job occupied. Hunter, Schmidt, and Judiesch (1990) found significant differences in output when comparing top performers to poor performers across a variety of jobs, but the gap varied significantly depending on the complexity of the job. Even further back, Jacobs (1981) modeled the relationship between individual performance, jobs, and organizational performance, showing how exemplary individual performance adds a significant increment to an organization's total performance in some jobs but not others.

These arguments led to advocating for jobs as the more appropriate locus of differentiation. From this perspective, some jobs are more critical to organizational performance
than others, and firms should devote more resources to those jobs in which individual performance has the greatest potential to impact firm performance (Boudreau and
Ramstad, 2007; Delery and Shaw, 2001; Huselid, Beatty, and Becker, 2005). These jobs
have been variously referred to as "key positions" (Collings and Mellahi, 2009); "linchpin positions" (Conger and Fulmer, 2003); "'A' positions" (Huselid, Beatty, and Becker,
2005); and "pivotal roles" (Boudreau and Ramstad, 2007; Collings and Mellahi, 2009).
We prefer the term *strategic job* as it reflects the choice to focus effort on them.

Concentrating on the job as the locus of differentiation does not dismiss individual
differences, of course. It simply gives primacy to the job, as the relative value of individual differences depends on the nature of the job (Gallardo-Gallardo et al., 2013;
Humphrey, Morgeson, and Mannor, 2009). As described by Becker and Huselid (2006:
904), "the value of employee skills within a firm is not just a supply-side phenomenon. It
is a function of how those skills are used and where they are used."

Humphrey, Morgeson, and Mannor's (2009) role-composition model of team performance provides support for the idea that jobs should be the locus of differentiation.
They find that certain roles are more important to team performance than others are, the
implication being that staffing decisions should take into account the strategic importance of different roles *before* considering individual attributes. A job-differentiation
perspective is also consistent with the historical view of talent management, where the
key jobs were executive positions, where assessing which individuals had the potential
to succeed in those jobs was a central task, and where development to make them successful in those jobs was the most significant expenditure. It also reflects the perspective
of most practitioners, where the focus is on filling a small number of key roles, typically
senior-management and executive roles, as well as key technical positions (e.g., Charan,
2005; Fernández-Aráoz, 2005).

A key insight from the recent workforce-differentiation literature is that while executive jobs are almost by definition strategic, strategic jobs can potentially be located anywhere in the organization, depending on the strategic objectives and competencies of
the organization. For example, a marketing-and-sales-focused company may find that
its sales positions are the key strategic jobs. That strategic jobs exist outside of the executive suite has been trumpeted as one of the most insightful aspects of this approach, as
"there is greater potential for distinctively competing for and with talent in areas that are
less recognized" (Boudreau and Ramstad, 2007: 69), and because it makes for broader
and stronger conceptual links between HR and business strategy.

Huselid, Beatty, and Becker (2005) argue that in order for a job to be classified as "strategic," it must meet the dual criteria of having a direct strategic impact and high variability in the performance of incumbents, representing upside potential. Hence, strategic
jobs are those in which investments in selection, evaluation, and development have the
greatest potential to generate a significant return through increasing revenue or decreasing costs. Jacobs (1981) similarly argues that individual performance is most likely to
affect firm performance in jobs located in a part of the organization with a direct impact

on firm performance and in jobs where success is comparatively infrequent. Boudreau and Ramstad (2007) focus on identifying jobs where increases in worker quality or availability most affect organizational success. Thus, strategic jobs can include such diverse roles as cashier at Costco (Huselid, Beatty, and Becker, 2005), street sweeper at Disneyland (Boudreau and Ramstad, 2007), and record producer (Jacobs, 1981).

Given the apparent dominance of the job-differentiation perspective, we can more clearly define *talent management* as *the process through which organizations meet their needs for talent in strategic jobs*. We define *talent* as *those individuals who are currently or have the potential to contribute differentially to firm performance by occupying strategic jobs* and *strategic jobs* as those *jobs in which exemplary individual performance contributes to a firm's competitive advantage*. We now turn our attention to the practice of talent management.

2.3 A History of Talent Management in Practice

Talent management was not much of an issue when firms were simple. Prior to the growth of the major railroads in the late nineteenth century, the typical firm had a simple structure where the owners were the managers (Chandler, 1977). Even then there was often little to manage, as organizations typically outsourced much of the work, from sales and distribution at companies such as DuPont (Zunz, 1990) to actual production tasks, which were often outsourced to contractors who found their own workers and managed them how they saw fit (Clawson, 1980: 72–80). Filling strategic jobs was therefore not a problem, because those jobs were either occupied by the owners or outsourced.

2.3.1 Early Attempts at Talent Management

Talent management first became a serious concern when companies grew complicated enough to have real management jobs to fill, which happened just prior to World War I. Starting with the railroads, organizations began to expand to the point where the need for standardization and coordination became paramount, leading to the creation of what we would now call senior-management or executive jobs.

These newly created jobs certainly met the criteria to be considered the first strategic jobs, as the ability to effectively manage mass production, deliver goods and services of consistent quality, and coordinate rapid expansion was often seen as a key to competitive advantage at this time. But, as business historian Thomas Cochran noted, while many of the administrative problems of running large corporations had been solved by World War I, one important issue had not: "… how were men to be trained, selected, and inspired to undertake the task of coordinating and directing the enterprise as a whole?"

(Cochran, 1960: 70). There was no way to assess the capabilities of the managers and predict who could handle one of these jobs, nor was there an understanding of how to develop candidates who might have some but not all of the requirements for these jobs. That is, companies suddenly found they had strategic jobs to fill but no available internal talent pool from which to fill those jobs, nor any processes in place to develop people to fill those jobs in the future.

As a result, firms came to rely almost exclusively on acquiring talent externally. It was not uncommon for larger firms to accomplish this by acquiring smaller companies and their founders, who were then installed as senior managers in charge of the very business that was acquired. This was an excellent approach given that nothing in the science of prediction and selection beats observing actual performance in an equivalent job (Cascio and Aguinis, 2008). Poaching talent from competitors was another common practice. In fact, it was so pervasive that when the World War I Manpower Commission was established by the government to ensure that companies had the workers and skills needed to maintain wartime production, one of its specific goals was to reduce the ubiquitous pirating of senior managers by competitors. Employers did promote top performers to frontline supervisory positions, a practice that had some limited success because the supervisory job was not so different from the worker's job. But the leap from frontline supervisor to middle- and senior-level manager roles was a big one, where success in the former role did not predict success in the latter.

The major consequence of this external approach to filling strategic jobs was that corporations were effectively prisoners to the supply of talent available in the outside market, which was often scarce. Recognizing this, a number of large companies established formal personnel departments to execute workforce-planning practices throughout the 1920s (Jacoby, 1985). GE was a leader in this regard, experimenting with several approaches to developing an internal pool of candidates for its strategic jobs. Yet these efforts were short-lived, as the Great Depression eroded the need for managers (Melman, 1951), and with it the need for talent management. One might have expected these efforts to be revived in the run-up to World War II, given the increase in demand for managers spurred by increases in wartime production. Instead, talent-development efforts at the management level remained stagnant throughout World War II, as most of the candidates who would have been hired into entry-level positions were serving in the military.

The lack of hiring and managerial development from the Depression through World War II led to a serious shortage of talent across nearly all industries (Whitmore, 1952). Organizations responded just as they had at the beginning of the century—by raiding their competitors. A prominent retail executive noted that "to go to another store for assistant buyers, buyers, and other executives" was the approach "almost universally used" to meet their human capital needs (Carden, 1956). Yet external hiring proved insufficient in meeting the demand for talent, as pension plans with onerous vesting requirements, high marginal tax rates, and a lack of housing decreased the attractiveness of switching employers, even when competitors were able to offer higher salaries. In fact, the demand for senior managers and executives exceeded the supply by such a margin that it created a talent bottleneck severe enough to dwarf any talent shortage before or since (Cappelli, 2010).

The difficulty in finding qualified external candidates to fill strategic jobs led companies to the realization that they needed to develop talent internally. With precious little experience doing so themselves, they turned to the military for help. Recognizing the need for a huge expansion of its officer ranks in a short period of time leading up to World War II, the Navy began what was arguably the first truly systematic effort at large-scale succession planning. That effort was based on lessons from a few leading companies before the Great Depression. It was summarized in the publication of "Personnel Administration at the Executive Level" in 1948, which the Industrial Relations faculty at Princeton (1949) summarized as:

> A principally graphic report of the composite practices of 53 companies in regard to executive inventory control. In these companies, reserves of trained executives are built up through five basic steps: (1) organization analysis, (2) selection, (3) evaluation, (4) development, and (5) inventory control.

The Navy's effort became a blueprint used by many companies as the basis for building their own talent-development programs, and a common model of internal talent management soon emerged.

2.3.2 The Organizational Man Model of Talent Management

That model was designed to provide a steady supply of internal talent capable of filling strategic jobs, which still consisted almost entirely of managerial and executive jobs. In this model, the companies developed their own talent pools, with the goal of creating a sufficient supply of internal talent to fill senior (strategic) jobs well into the future.

Companies developed detailed recruitment strategies and made substantial investments in identifying individuals with the potential to become executives, including the use of psychological, vocational, and intelligence testing. Careers and career planning unfolded within all these large corporations, with internal advancement supported by early investments in training and regular movements within the firm to provide development opportunities. In 1943, the Conference Board could not find enough employers offering talent-development programs to study them, yet by 1955 they were present in 60% of companies with 10,000 or more employees. External hiring at the executive level became virtually nonexistent; one study found that by 1950, 80% of current executives had been developed from within (Newcomer, 1955), and another shortly after found that few contemporary executives in any company had begun their careers elsewhere (Steel, 1957).

These programs, in turn, served as the basis for the Organizational Man model of the 1950s, in which expectations of lifetime employment and steady advancement opportunities emerged (Whyte, 1955). The implicit promise of lifetime employment provided a sense of stability to workers, who granted firms substantial control over their careers within the organization. Indeed, decisions related to investments in employee development and advancement were largely handled by centralized personnel offices. Advancement occurred in narrowly defined jobs located along clearly defined job ladders, structural features emerging from the need to maintain the overall efficiency and social stability of the closed employment system (Althauser, 1989). Workers were shielded from external competition, mobility was governed by bureaucratic rules (1981), and because jobs above entry level were not freely available to outsiders, there were limited opportunities for external advancement. Retention was rarely a concern.

The lifetime-employment model was predicated on stability in the economy, which, in turn, allowed for accurate, long-term business planning, and those plans required long-term human capital plans (see Cappelli, 2011: 676). Workforce planning, sometimes referred to as manpower planning, first caught the attention of researchers in the 1960s, with the publication of *Manpower Planning for High Talent Personnel* (Vetter, 1967). This was followed shortly by the publication of *Manpower Planning and Programming* (Burack and Walker, 1972), an edited volume describing the state of the art in forecasting models, with articles written by executives at GE, Standard Oil, North American Rockwell, Inland Steel, and McKinsey, alongside those of leading academics. It was during this period that firms began to collect and analyze data on workforce projection and employee outcomes, with a handful of firms even experimenting with simulations (Walker, 2013). Perhaps the most sophisticated of the models to emerge from this period was a late-1960s model called MANPLAN, which attempted to model the movement of individuals within a career system by including individual behavior and psychological variables, supervisory practices, group norms, and labor market outcomes (Cappelli, 2008a). The models led to the development of elaborate succession plans for strategic jobs, often identifying potential talent several years (and job levels) in advance. The assumption was that the supply of talent for executive positions was entirely internal, with career advancement and development centrally managed by the firm.

From the 1950s through the 1970s, all of the tools and practices commonly associated with internal talent management now were already in place: Workforce plans to set direction, sophisticated recruitment and selection techniques for hiring entry-level candidates, assessments of potential (including assessment centers, ability and personality tests, etc.), developmental assignments like job rotations, shadowing, action learning with coaches, assessments of performance (e.g., 360-degree feedback and forced rankings), career ladders, and succession planning to fill the important jobs. Virtually every contemporary practice in talent management was developed and in use during this period.

Yet these efforts were also short-lived, as changes in the way business operated in the early 1980s rendered the Organization Man approach to talent development obsolete.

2.3.3 Talent Management under Uncertainty

US firms experienced a sharp decline in the need for senior managers following the 1981 recession, and the subsequent process of "reengineering" led to flatter organizations and wholesale managerial layoffs (Cappelli, 1999). Competition increased because of product-market deregulation and international competition (Useem, 1993). Consumer demands began to change more rapidly (Ghemawat, 1986). The rising influence of financial markets and the shareholder-value notion (Davis, 2009) pushed public companies to squeeze spending on labor and make more of those costs variable.

This environment was characterized by uncertainty in demand and, in turn, the demand for labor, and, with the rise of lateral hiring and retention concerns, uncertainty in the supply of talent (Cappelli, 2008a). Together they led to the dismantling of the structures and processes supporting the Organizational Man model described above. Flattening organizational hierarchies, combined with broader job definitions, led to the gradual disappearance of well-defined job ladders. Lateral hiring took the place of internal development in many companies. Personnel decisions were largely decentralized, with decisions on promotions, transfers, and new hires being delegated to individual managers, which eroded long-term plans for careers, as well as purposeful internal mobility. No longer willing or able to provide any assurance of continued employment, employers encouraged workers to take control of their careers.

Uncertainty in demand has arisen from difficulties in forecasting consumer demand, creating difficulties in forecasting human capital needs. As a result, workforce planning has all but disappeared, replaced by the notion of workforce readiness. For a handful of companies, primarily those in the engineering and technology sectors, workforce readiness involves making substantial investments to ensure there will be a sufficient pool of talent that will possess those skills likely to be needed in the future, either through investments in current employees or in potential future employees.[1] Most companies are far less proactive, however, preferring to place the responsibility on individuals who are expected to somehow anticipate the future needs of employers and develop their skills accordingly (SHRM, 2015). In the mid-1960s, a study of personnel departments found that 96% did thorough enough planning to maintain a dedicated manpower planning function (Allen, 1966), but by the mid-1990s, only 19% of companies responding to a Conference Board survey reported engaging in any sort of structured workforce planning. A majority of large organizations once used elaborate statistical regression models to forecast talent needs, but by 1984 as few as 9% of employers reported using such models (Cappelli, 2008a). The decline in overall workforce planning was accompanied by a similar decline in succession planning. A 2005 survey found that only 29% of employers had succession-planning programs (Fegley, 2006), and of those that did, only about a quarter appeared to do any such planning more than two levels below the CEO (Cohn, Khurana, and Reeves, 2005).

Uncertainty on the supply side has arisen not just from retention issues but also from difficulties in predicting skills and competencies needed in the future and in predicting turnover. If the competencies needed in the future change dramatically, a talent pool that looks robust now may look deficient in the future. Companies are particularly concerned about dysfunctional or regrettable turnover, in which employees they want to keep walk out the door, but turnover rates among such employees are notoriously hard to predict (Allen, Bryant, and Vardaman, 2010). Increased hiring of experienced candidates from competitors has created retention concerns, further complicating estimates of internal supply.

Firms are often now back in the World War I–era situation of having limited control over the availability of skills and competencies because they rely on the labor market for them (Cappelli, 2008b). External hiring has become a de facto talent management strategy for many firms, with just-in-time hiring emerging as a substitute for workforce and succession planning, internal development, and even assessment (Cappelli, 2010). With ports of entry no longer restricted to lower-level jobs, employers now hire into almost all kinds of jobs at all levels of the organization. Jacoby (2005) surveyed senior HR executives in 145 US firms in 2001 and found that none of them considered only internal candidates for managerial vacancies, and a mere 1% considered only internal candidates for nonsupervisory vacancies—figures that would have been viewed as misprints only a few decades earlier. Cappelli and Hamori (2005) examined the top ten executives of the largest companies with the most sophisticated internal labor markets, the *Fortune 100* companies, in 2001, and compared their careers to those of their peers in 1980, finding that executives now spend significantly less time with a single employer and are much more likely to build careers across firms. Royal and Althauser (2003) and Bidwell (2011) found extensive external hiring to be common in mid- and upper-level jobs. These findings are consistent with extensive work documenting the steady decline in job tenure (particularly in the United States) over the past thirty-plus years (Hollister, 2011). While large employers in the United States filled only about 10% of their vacancies from outside in the period from World War II to the 1980s, current estimates suggest that they now fill more than 60% of vacancies from outside (Crispin and Mehler, 2013).

Just as in the 1920s, however, an overreliance on external hiring to fill strategic jobs leaves employers at the mercy of the labor market, resulting in talent shortfalls and other costs whenever labor markets tighten. Moreover, recent research has shown that even when firms are able to attract external talent, the results often fall short of expectations. Information asymmetries result in external candidates being paid a significant premium compared with internal candidates at all levels of the organization, up to and including the CEO (Agrawal, Knoeber, and Tsoulouhas, 2006; Bidwell, 2011). Firms require stronger signals of observable ability from external candidates, but these signals often fail to translate into higher levels of performance, with external hires underperforming their internal counterparts while simultaneously being more likely to both quit their jobs and be terminated (Bidwell, 2011). External hires often have trouble overcoming institutional and cognitive rigidities developed at their prior employers (Dokko, Wilk, and Rothbard, 2009), and it takes time for even the most accomplished external hires to rebuild internal networks (Groysberg, 2010). Filling strategic jobs through external hiring may also be perceived by external stakeholders as a negative signal (Groysberg, Lee, and Nanda, 2008).

In response to the challenges associated with external hiring, popular management books on talent management often suggest that firms should recreate many of the historical practices at older companies like GE (e.g., Charan, Drotter, and Noel, 2011). However, such models require extensive upfront investments that can be difficult to recoup if human capital needs change and if employees unexpectedly leave, both common occurrences. A recent survey of high-potential (HiPo) programs illustrates this problem: while 75% of firms report that HiPo employees are more than 50% more valuable than an average employee, less than a third reported realizing a significant return on their HiPo investments (Martin and Schmidt, 2010). Moreover, this approach would seem to be largely inconsistent with the way employees have come to view careers. As Collings and Mellahi (2009: 308) note, "solely relying on internal development and sourcing, with a general disregard for the external sourcing of talent, is at odds with an increasing realization that careers are more regularly characterized by interfirm mobility in the current environment."

2.4 THE FUTURE OF TALENT MANAGEMENT

The state of talent management now appears to be at something of a crossroads. The challenges associated with managing human capital are at the top of the list of concerns for organizational leaders around the world. The Conference Board surveyed more than 600 global CEOs in 2015 and asked them to select the top challenges facing their companies in the coming year. From a list of twenty-two challenges including issues as diverse as slowing economic growth in emerging markets, income inequality, growing trade protectionism, increasing global competition, and political instability, the respondents identified developing "next gen" leaders and the failure to attract and retain top talent as their top two challenges (Mitchell, Ray, and van Ark, 2016). In fact, respondents to this survey have ranked issues related to human capital as their top global business challenge every year since 2013. Yet at the same time, good data that describe the actual practices of companies are extremely difficult to find, and so we are left with drawing inferences from sources of information that are indirect to learn what is really happening in talent management.

Although it is sometimes difficult to know what aspects of human capital are the biggest concerns, there is no evidence of any return to the earlier models based on lifetime employment and long-term investments to meet talent needs. The overwhelming sense one gets from the business press, from the reports of industry associations, and from company pronouncements, is that the focus of employer interest is on hiring. Another way to say that is that for what seems like the vast majority of companies, talent management has mainly become a concern about external hiring, with firms worrying about filling more senior jobs through lateral hiring while churning through external hires at lower levels. No doubt this is sensible in countries like Singapore, where the unemployment rate is and has for years been extraordinarily low, or India and China, where school leavers with more practical degrees are in short supply. Why hiring should be the dominant factor in the case of countries like the United States and the United Kingdom, where there have been surpluses of educated job seekers, is a harder question.

It is difficult to generate attention for traditional topics such as workforce planning or succession planning when, as in the United States, two-thirds of positions are filled by outside hiring: filling jobs when they become vacant from the outside labor market is an approach to talent management, but it is an approach that short-circuits most of the traditional subtopics within talent management.

In the United States, the United Kingdom, Singapore, and now many countries in Europe, employer interest in "talent management through hiring" has now been pushed into the sphere of public policy. When employers move to filling more of their openings through outside hiring of experienced candidates and fewer of them through internal development, they become much more dependent on that outside labor market. When they cannot find the experienced talent they want at the wages they were expecting to pay, they have talent-management problems. Employers that have moved away from sophisticated programs for developing talent from within the firm cannot easily shift back to that approach to securing talent. Further, employers that still grow talent from within find it difficult to keep their talent when so many of their competitors have moved to the model of "poaching" candidates from competitors.

The response in this situation has been to ask the government to help them solve the talent-management challenges that employers face. That response comes in two forms. The first, which is prominent in many developed countries, is to ask the government to open up immigration from other countries. Another way to think about this is to extend the poaching model to other countries. Not surprisingly, this model is the preferred solution for many business groups, and they have led the lobbying campaigns to increase immigration of permanent or, especially in the United States, temporary employment of foreign workers from lower-wage countries. In the United States, this move has been especially prominent in the information-technology sector, where new college graduates can often contribute immediately.

The second response is through the postsecondary education system, pressing government-supported colleges to increase the number of graduates in STEM (science, technology, engineering, and math) fields, which include the engineering and IT fields, where new graduates can most easily contribute without training (see Cappelli, 2015 for a review).

To the extent that these campaigns succeed in increasing the supply of candidates whom employers want to hire, they obviously undermine traditional models of talent management, at least for positions where it is possible for new hires to contribute quickly. To the extent that they succeed, they also move the focus of talent management further in the direction of hiring, as noted above. Indeed, the recent innovations in talent management have largely related to finding new candidates, the most prominent of which focus on mining Internet-based social-networking sites such as LinkedIn.

More generally, one of the important developments in talent management that will likely continue is the growing importance of vendors, many of whom focus on the practice of hiring. A generation ago, systems for hiring, onboarding new hires, training, identifying potential, creating career paths, and assessing performance were all created inside companies. There are now dozens of large vendors providing services to address each of those tasks, and discussions about talent-management practices among even large employers frequently devolve into exchanges about which vendors they are using for what practices. Vendors in the recruitment outsourcing industry now integrate many of the separate tasks of talent management, allowing client firms to outsource entire chunks of the talent-management value chain. The practices used vary considerably across vendors, which could provide a good opportunity for researchers to examine the effectiveness of different practices.

The middle-term future of talent management is likely to be dominated by three important challenges. The first is whether employers will reengage in the development of talent. The complaints that employees will simply leave if employers invest in them sound to most people like rationalization. The ability to make development cost-effective and to persuade employers that it is remains the biggest challenge. Meeting this challenge will require researchers and practitioners to ask and answer questions such as: What factors might lead corporate employers to rediscover the benefits of work-based learning? Where are the innovations in internal development most likely to come from? Will corporations adapt the models that consulting firms and professional firms have long used? And What types of development are most likely to help firms attract and retain key talent?

The second challenge is whether the internal mobility of talent will become more purposeful. Most employers have abandoned the idea that there are clear career paths in their organizations and, if they do anything at all, they have yielded to employee-driven bidding and posting systems as the mechanism for employee mobility. Whether the constraints around those systems will loosen so that we have something more like a real market for talent inside firms is one of the interesting practical questions facing talent management. Another is whether employers will try to manage that internal market in some purposeful way. It is interesting to note that while a number of conceptual models of mobility within contemporary organizations have been proposed (e.g., the career lattice: Benko and Anderson, 2010), there is a startling lack of evidence detailing contemporary internal careers. Future research might therefore explore questions such as: What do career paths look like within contemporary organizations? What are the factors that predict the path an individual is likely to take? How do different career paths shape outcomes such as pay and performance?

A final question is whether employers will integrate in any systematic way the growing use of outsourcing and nonemployee labor into their regular talent-management thinking. At the moment, the decision as to whether to engage nonemployees as contractors, through temporary workers or other leased employment relationships, seems driven mainly by budget considerations: It is easier to spend money on contractors than on hiring, in part because of the apparent fixed costs of the latter. How to make those choices more purposefully, as well as to how use the options together, remains an underexamined and a potentially vibrant area for future research (Boudreau, Jesuthasan, and Creelman, 2015; see also Chapter 26 in this volume).

Talent management in the middle of the 2010s looks quite different than it did a generation ago, and it is a fair bet that it will look different again ten years hence. The hope for those who take the mission of talent management seriously is that it will be more purposeful and evidence-based than it has evolved to be now.

NOTE

1. Examples of investments intended to increase the pool of future employees include Google for Education (https://www.google.com/edu/resources/programs/), STEM @ Cisco (http://csr.cisco.com/pages/stem-at-cisco), and Project Lead the Way (https://www.pltw.org/).

REFERENCES

Agrawal, A., Knoeber, C. R., and Tsoulouhas, T. 2006. Are outsiders handicapped in CEO successions? *Journal of Corporate Finance*, 12(3), pp.619–44.

Aguinis, H., and O'Boyle Jr., E. O. 2014. Star performers in twenty-first century organizations. *Personnel Psychology*, 67(2), pp.313–50.

Allen, D. G., Bryant, P. C., and Vardaman, J. M. 2010. Retaining talent: replacing misconceptions with evidence-based strategies. *Academy of Management Perspectives*, 24(2), pp.48–65.

Allen, J. R. 1966. *Personnel administration: changing scope and organization*. New York: National Industrial Conference Board, No. 203.

Althauser, R. P. 1989. Internal labor markets. *Annual Review of Sociology*, 15, pp.143–61.

Althauser, R. P., and Kalleberg, A. L. 1981. Firms, occupations and the structure of labor markets: a conceptual analysis. In I. Berg, ed., *Sociological perspectives on labor markets*, pp. 119–49. New York: Academic Press.

Axelrod, B., Handfield-Jones, H., and Michaels, E. 2002. A new game plan for C players. *Harvard Business Review*, 80(1), pp.80–8.

Becker, B. E., and Huselid, M. A. 2006. Strategic human resources management: where do we go from here? *Journal of Management*, 32(6), pp.898–925.

Benko, C., and Anderson, M. 2010. *The corporate lattice: achieving high performance in the changing world of work*. Boston: Harvard Business Review Press.

Bidwell, M. J. 2011. Paying more to get less: the effects of external hiring versus internal mobility. *Administrative Science Quarterly*, 56(3), pp.369–407.

Boudreau, J. W., Jesuthasan, R., and Creelman, D. 2015. *Lead the work: navigating a world beyond employment*. Hoboken, NJ: John Wiley and Sons.

Boudreau, J. W., and Ramstad, P. M. 2007. *Beyond HR: the new science of human capital*. Cambridge, MA: Harvard Business School Publishing Corporation.

Burack, E. H., and Walker, J. W., eds. 1972. *Manpower planning and programming*. New York: General Learning Press.

Call, M. L., Nyberg, A. J., and Thatcher, S. M. B. 2015. Stargazing: an integrative conceptual review, theoretical reconciliation, and extension for star employee research. *Journal of Applied Psychology*, 100(3), pp.623–40.

Campbell, B. A., Coff, R., and Kryscynski, D. 2012. Rethinking sustained competitive advantage from human capital. *Academy of Management Review*, 37(3), pp.376–95.

Cappelli, P. 1999. *The new deal at work: managing the market-driven workforce*. Boston: Harvard Business School Press.

Cappelli, P. 2008a. *Talent on demand: managing talent in an age of uncertainty*. Cambridge, MA: Harvard Business School Publishing.

Cappelli, P. 2008b. Talent management for the twenty-first century. *Harvard Business Review*, 86(3), pp.74–81.

Cappelli, P. 2010. The rise and decline of managerial development. *Industrial and Corporate Change*, 19(2), pp.509–48.

Cappelli, P. 2011. Succession planning. In S. Zedeck, ed., *APA handbook of industrial and organizational psychology*, pp.673–90. Washington, DC: American Psychological Association.

Cappelli, P. 2015. *Will college pay off? A guide to the most important financial decision you'll ever make*. New York: Public Affairs.

Cappelli, P., and Hamori, M. 2005. The new road to the top. *Harvard Business Review*, 83(1), pp.25–32, 115.

Carden, C. J. 1956. Executive training. *Journal of Retailing*, 22, pp.1–4.

Cascio, W. F., and Aguinis, H. 2008. Staffing twenty-first century organizations. *Academy of Management Annals*, 2(1), pp.133–65.

Chambers, E. G., Foulon, M., Handfield-Jones, H., Hankin, S. M. et al. 1998. The war for talent. *The McKinsey Quarterly*, 3, pp.44–57.

Chandler, A. D. J. 1977. *The visible hand: the managerial revolution in American business*. Cambridge, MA: Belknap Press.

Charan, R. 2005. Ending the CEO succession crisis. *Harvard Business Review*, 83(2), pp.72–81.

Charan, R., Drotter, S., and Noel, J. 2011. *The leadership pipeline: how to build the leadership powered company*, 2nd edn. San Francisco: Jossey-Bass.

Clawson, D. 1980. *Bureaucracy and the labor process: the transformation of U.S. industry 1860–1920*. New York: Monthly Review Press.

Cochran, T. C. 1960. *The American business system: a historical perspective*. Cambridge, MA: Harvard University Press.

Cohn, J. M., Khurana, R., and Reeves, L. 2005. Growing talent as if your business depended on it. *Harvard Business Review*, 83(10), pp.62–70.

Collings, D. G., and Mellahi, K. 2009. Strategic talent management: a review and research agenda. *Human Resource Management Review*, 19(4), pp.304–13.

Collings, D. G., Scullion, H., and Dowling, P. J. 2009. Global staffing: a review and thematic research agenda. *International Journal of Human Resource Management*, 20(6), pp.1253–72.

Conger, J. A., and Fulmer, R. M. 2003. Developing your leadership pipeline. *Harvard Business Review*, 81(12), pp.76–84.

Crispin, G., and Mehler, M. 2013. *Sources of hire 2013: perception is reality*. CareerXRoads. http://www.careerxroads.com/news/SourcesOfHire2013.pdf.

Davis, G. F. 2009. The rise and fall of finance and the end of the society of organizations. *Academy of Management Perspectives*, 23(3), pp.27–44.

Delery, J. E., and Shaw, J. D. 2001. The strategic management of people in work organizations: Review, synthesis, and extension. In G. R. Ferris, ed., *Research in personnel and human resources management*, 20th edn., pp.165–97. Bingley, UK: Emerald Group.

Dokko, G., Wilk, S. L., and Rothbard, N. P. 2009. Unpacking prior experience: how career history affects job performance. *Organization Science*, 20(1), pp.51–68.

Fegley, S. 2006. *2006 talent management*. Alexandria, VA: Society for Human Resource Management.

Felin, T., and Hesterly, W. S. 2007. The knowledge-based view, nested heterogeneity, and new value creation: philosophical considerations on the locus of knowledge. *Academy of Management Review*, 32(1), pp.195–218.

Fernández-Aráoz, C. 2005. Getting the right people at the top. *Sloan Management Review*, 46(4), pp.67–72.

Gallardo-Gallardo, E., Dries, N., and González-Cruz, T. F. 2013. What is the meaning of "talent" in the world of work? *Human Resource Management Review*, 23(4), pp.290–300.

Ghemawat, P. 1986. Sustainable advantage. *Harvard Business Review*, 64(5), pp.53–8.

Groysberg, B. 2010. *Chasing stars: the myth of talent and the portability of performance.* Princeton, NJ: Princeton University Press.

Groysberg, B., Lee, L.-E., and Nanda, A. 2008. Can they take it with them? The portability of star knowledge workers' performance. *Management Science*, 54(7), pp.1213–30.

Groysberg, B., Polzer, J. T., and Elfenbein, H. A. 2011. Too many cooks spoil the broth: how high-status individuals decrease group effectiveness. *Organization Science*, 22(3), pp.722–37.

Hollister, M. 2011. Employment stability in the U.S. labor market: rhetoric versus reality. *Annual Review of Sociology*, 37(1), pp.305–24.

Huckman, R. S., and Pisano, G. P. 2006. The firm specificity of individual performance: evidence from cardiac surgery. *Management Science*, 52(4), pp.473–88.

Humphrey, S. E., Morgeson, F. P., and Mannor, M. J. 2009. Developing a theory of the strategic core of teams: a role composition model of team performance. *Journal of Applied Psychology*, 94(1), pp.48–61.

Hunter, J. E., Schmidt, F. L., and Judiesch, M. K. 1990. Individual differences in output variability as a function of job complexity. *Journal of Applied Psychology*, 75(1), pp.28–42.

Huselid, M. A., Beatty, R. W., and Becker, B. E. 2005. "A Players" or "A Positions"? The strategic logic of workforce management. *Harvard Business Review*, 83(12), pp.110–17.

Huselid, M. A., and Becker, B. E. 2011. Bridging micro and macro domains: workforce differentiation and strategic human resource management. *Journal of Management*, 37(2), pp.395–403.

Jacobs, D. 1981. Toward a theory of mobility and behavior in organizations: an inquiry into the consequences of some relationships between individual performance and organizational success. *American Journal of Sociology*, 87(3), pp.684–707.

Jacoby, S. M. 1985. *Employing bureaucracy: managers, unions, and the transformation of work in American industry*. New York: Columbia University Press.

Jacoby, S. M. 2005. *The embedded corporation: corporate governance and employment relations in Japan and the United States*. Princeton, NJ: Princeton University Press.

Lepak, D. P., and Shaw, J. D. 2008. Strategic HRM in North America: looking to the future. *International Journal of Human Resource Management*, 19(8), pp.1486–99.

Lepak, D. P., and Snell, S. A. 1999. The human resource architecture: toward a theory of human capital allocation and development. *Academy of Management Review*, 24(1), pp.31–48.

Lewis, R. E., and Heckman, R. J. 2006. Talent management: a critical review. *Human Resource Management Review*, 16(2), pp.139–54.

Martin, J., and Schmidt, C. 2010. How to keep your top talent. *Harvard Business Review*, 88(5), pp.54–61.

Melman, S. 1951. The rise of administrative overhead in the manufacturing industries of the United States, 1890–1947. *Oxford Economic Papers*, 3(1), pp.62–112.

Mitchell, C., Ray, R. L., and Van Ark, B. 2016. *CEO Challenge 2016*. Washington, D.C.

Newcomer, M. 1955. *The big business executive: the factors that made him, 1900–1950.* New York: Columbia University Press.

Royal, C., and Althauser, R. P. 2003. The labor markets of knowledge workers: investment bankers' careers in the wake of corporate restructuring. *Work and Occupations*, 30(2), pp.214–33.

Selected references on the selection and development of executives. 1949. Industrial Relations Section, Princeton University.

SHRM. 2015. *Workforce readiness and skills shortages*. Alexandria, VA. https://www.shrm. org/hr-today/trends-and-forecasting/labor-market-and-economic-data/Documents/ Workforce%20Readiness%20and%20Skills%20Shortages.pdf. Accessed May 18, 2017.

Smart, B. D. 2005. *Topgrading: how leading companies win by hiring, coaching, and keeping the best people*, 2nd edn. New York: Penguin Group.

Steel. 1957. Management development: the care and feeding of the junior executive. *Steel*, *140*(Feb. 11), pp.93–100.

Useem, M. 1993. Management commitment and company policies on education and training. *Human Resource Management*, *32*(4), pp.411–34.

Vetter, E. W. 1967. *Manpower planning for high talent personnel*. Ann Arbor: Bureau of Industrial Relations, University of Michigan.

Walker, J. W. 2013. The origins of workforce planning. In D. L. Ward and R. Tripp, eds., *Positioned: strategic workforce planning that gets the right person in the right job*, Chapter 1, pp.3–8. New York: American Management Association.

Whitmore, E. 1952. The executive manpower shortage—and what can be done about it? *American Business*, *22*(8–9), p.9.

Whyte, W. H. 1955. *The organizational man*. New York: Simon and Schuster.

Zunz, O. 1990. *Making America corporate*. Chicago: University Of Chicago Press.

SECTION 2

TALENT AND PERFORMANCE

CHAPTER 3

....

STAR PERFORMERS

....

ERNEST H. O'BOYLE AND SYDNEY KROSKA

ALTHOUGH by no means a new area of study, increased focus in management research has been shown on elite performers or stars over the past several years. Like talent management, the upsurge in research is partly in response to popular-press books such as Malcolm Gladwell's *Outliers* and Nassim Taleb's *The Black Swan*. A number of recent claims in the academic literature have further fueled a combination of both excitement and wariness toward star performers and their impact on organizations. This chapter's purpose is to introduce the theoretical and empirical work surrounding stars, to distill what is known and unknown, what is fact and what is myth, and to outline the direction of current and future research. We organize the chapter into broad themes beginning with what exactly a star is, as well as the performance distribution that typifies star output. We will then discuss the internal attributes and environmental qualities amenable to star performance. Finally, we will offer an agenda for future research that builds upon current understanding of assessing stars, determining the extent to which star effects generalize to negative behaviors, and how the source of star performance affects how best to recruit, manage, and compensate stars.

3.1 WHAT IS A STAR?

Simply put, a star exhibits exceptionally high quality and/or an exceptionally large quantity of output relative to his or her peers. That is, stars either produce much more than average or even very good workers do or they produce output where the alternatives of their peers are a poor substitute (Rosen, 1981). Although stars do not emerge in every industry or across every job, their frequency is alleged to be increasing, owing in part to the decline of the manufacturing sector and the rise of the knowledge economy (Powell and Snellman, 2004). This is because knowledge-economy jobs tend to possess features (e.g., autonomy and multiplicity of production) that lend themselves to star emergence (Aguinis and O'Boyle, 2014). Where stars are found, their influence is immense (Andriani and McKelvey, 2007, 2009). For example, in high-complexity jobs, the top percentile of workers more than doubles the productivity of average workers (Hunter, Schmidt, and Judiesch, 1990). For inventors working in the tech sector, the difference between the most and least productive is a factor of ten (Narin and Breitzman, 1995), and the top 20% of salespeople generate 80% of total sales (Aoyama, Yoshikawa, Iyetomi, and Fujiwara, 2010).

Beyond individual achievements, star performers can generate productivity that influences higher levels of analysis. For example, star expertise in software-design teams contributes to team-level outcomes beyond the team's overall expertise level (Volmer and Sonnentag, 2011). This possibly indicates that stars provide multiplicative value as opposed to a simple additive model in contributing to team outcomes. For organizations, especially those with substantial technology and service functions, stars can be the difference between excellence and mediocrity, and even survival or failure (Aguinis and O'Boyle, 2014; Bedeian and Armenakis, 1998). Perhaps most striking are those stars who substantially influence industries and society at large. For example, if listing the most widely known, quintessential stars, Michael Jordan would likely be at the top of many people's lists. Jordan's success was so profound that he is often credited with single-handedly raising the profile of the National Basketball Association to that of one of the "Big Three" premier sports in the United States. The evidence goes beyond sportswriter hyperbole. Hausman and Leonard (1997) calculated that Jordan generated an additional $53 million dollars a year for his *opponents* and increased annual road attendance by 23,294 tickets. Consider a lesser known but equally important figure to the video game industry, Shigeru Miyamoto. Miyamoto was a software designer for a fledgling Japanese company in the 1970s named Nintendo. His development of Donkey Kong saved the firm from bankruptcy. His development of Mario Bros., Legend of Zelda, Metroid, Star Fox, and many other titles, as well as his instrumental role in developing the Wii system, collectively helped fuel a multitrillion-dollar home-platform industry. Worth noting is that by saving his organization and helping to create a new industry, Miyamoto indirectly contributed to the decline of the multibillion-dollar arcade industry (Suellentrop, 2013)—star effects are not universally benevolent or beneficial. Outside of the world of entertainment, it is difficult to imagine fast food without Ray Kroc, the personal computer without Steve Wozniak, or the Internet without Larry Page and Sergey Brin. The output of these individuals helped shape society as a whole.

Although stars can be easily identified post hoc, and defining *stars* as those able to create much more output or much better output seems straightforward, the definition of *output* varies widely. In Rosen's (1981) development of superstar theory, he defined output in terms of economic activity. As a labor economist, his view is that of the marketplace; thus, superstar markets are those where economic activity is concentrated within a small minority of individuals, groups, and organizations. Stars dominate output because: (a) their talent is marginally better than the alternatives available to the consumer, and (b) the alternatives are a poor substitute (Rosen, 1981). In superstar markets, consumers, be they shoppers, HR representatives, or managers, are not satisfied with the performance of less talented alternatives, even when those alternatives are considerably cheaper and only marginally worse (Franck and Nuesch, 2012; Frey, 1988). In this way, we can start to see how jobs that allow stars to thrive diverge from traditional work. On an assembly line, there is no incentive to recruit or retain the fastest worker available because the line moves at the speed of the slowest worker. That the fastest is marginally more talented than the second fastest does not generate star effects because the alternative is an adequate substitute. On the other hand, when faced with the choice between the best brain surgeon and the second-best brain surgeon, the desire for the best exceeds the marginal differences in KSAs between the two. This disparity between consumer preference and talent differential is the same regardless of whether the consumer is a patient seeking care or a medical practice seeking a new partner. This is a fundamental principle underlying superstar theory—the intrinsic value of being "the best" receives a premium in the marketplace that far exceeds a linear relation between talent and value.

Interestingly, although Rosen's initial view included talent as an integral part of superstar emergence, Adler (1985), another renowned labor economist, contends star status is not a function, at least not directly, of any internal attribute of the person (i.e., talent). Rather, star status is bestowed purely by market response. Put differently, market response *is* output and vice versa. Therefore, the pop singer Taylor Swift is not a star because of her octave range, song-writing ability, or physical appearance. She is a star because she sold 3.66 million records in 2014 (Caulfield, 2014). Other fields define stars more in terms of the potential for output. For example, developmental psychologists identify prodigies by their ability to perform at professional levels at an early age (Feldman, 1986; Ruthsatz, Ruthsatz, and Stephens, 2014). The assumption here is that with additional practice, these prodigies will surpass even very good professionals at some point in the future. Their current output is merely an indicator of what will emerge at a later date. Nevertheless, the interest is still on output rather than individual attributes.

Within management research, output tends to be operationalized as either the frequency of some objective outcome (e.g., National Football League touchdown passes thrown) or the frequency of some qualitative judgment (e.g., Academy Award nominations). For example, O'Boyle and Aguinis (2012) and Aguinis, O'Boyle, Gonzalez-Mulé, and Joo (2016) studied a large number of samples (198 and 229, respectively) from a variety of professions, including research, entertainment, politics, sports, sales, and manufacturing, among others, to determine the shape of the output distribution. Similarly, Beck, Beatty, and Sackett (2014) examined the output, as well as some of the behaviors believed to lead to star output, of professional bowlers, undergraduates, and call-center workers. Although the definition of output varied across these studies, they all shared the common operationalization of being an output of behaviors and/or market responses.

3.2 THE STAR DISTRIBUTION

Regardless of theoretical perspective or definition of output, what must be kept in mind is that stars do not exist in a vacuum; rather, their status is relative. As such, when speaking of star performers, we are really speaking of star performance distributions—what is this person's performance relative to that of his or her peers? Here is where we arrive at the crux of an ongoing debate with massive implications for talent management (Sparrow and Makram, 2015). This goes well beyond any statistical consideration and is at the heart of whether stars even exist or are simply some methodological artifact best ignored in rigorous academic research. The debate centers on the distribution of job performance and the fact that stars cannot exist within a Gaussian (i.e., normal or bell-shaped) distribution (shown in Figure 3.1). Either stars are real phenomena and the normal distribution does not apply to many jobs and industries, or stars do not exist and normality generalizes across the population of workers. Given that the preponderance of management and applied psychology theories, methods, and statistics directly or indirectly rely on a normality assumption (Aguinis and O'Boyle, 2014), it is quite understandable how any challenge to normality is disruptive. The normal distribution is deeply ingrained in our fields, and any contention that it does not apply to a significant and increasing portion of workers should not be undertaken lightly.

Management research relies heavily on the natural sciences for many of its underlying principles, including the presumed distribution of variables. Height, weight, physical strength, blood pressure, and adult life expectancy are all alleged to follow a normal distribution, with most people in the middle and progressively fewer individuals farther away from the mean. Thus, it is quite understandable to assume that the distribution of job performance would also be normally distributed, especially since some of these variables (e.g., strength, stamina, and intelligence) have clear relations to performance for a number of jobs and careers. Further supporting normality is that supervisor ratings, the most commonly used job performance assessment tool (Aguinis, 2013), tend to be normally distributed.

On the surface there appears to be ample support for the "norm of normality," but with regard to stars, two considerations are worth mentioning. First, *normality* should not be confused with *prevalent* or *natural*. Many things are normally distributed, but most are not. In practice, normality appears to be the exception rather than the rule (Limpert, Stahel, and Abbt, 2001), and this is not a particularly recent finding either in

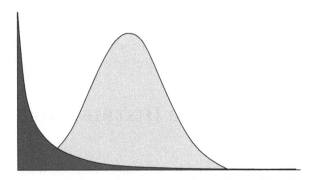

FIGURE 3.1 A Power Law (Black) Overlaying a Normal Distribution (Gray)

the natural sciences (Groth, 1914; Powers, 1936; Sinnot, 1937) or in the social sciences (Geary, 1947; Pearson, 1895). Even when limiting the scope to management and applied psychology research, normality is by no means certain. For example, in a *Psychological Bulletin* article, Micceri (1989) reviewed distributions of scores from 440 achievement and psychometric measures and found that everyone diverged from normality. Micceri concluded that normal curves were about as common as unicorns.

The second consideration regarding a Gaussian distribution of job performance is that, as previously stated, the compendium of evidence for its normality largely rests on supervisor ratings (Aguinis, 2013). Putting aside the amount of faith one can have in something where nearly half of its measurement is noise (LeBreton, Scherer, and James, 2014; Viswesvaran, Ones, and Schmidt, 1996), the bigger issue is that this may be an example of reverse causality. Researchers instruct supervisors to place employees onto normal distributions (e.g., Motowidlo and Borman, 1977; Schneier, 1977), and research-ers throw out any performance-evaluation items that fail to generate normal distribu-tions (e.g., Rotundo and Sackett, 2002). Then, with circular logic, these same data are used to verify that job performance is normally distributed.

Before moving on to what the distribution of stars resembles, we would be remiss not to address a commonly proposed solution to the debate, that stars are simply the right tail of a normal distribution. However, if this were true, then their performance would easily be replaced by a slight improvement in the second-best worker or the addition of a few average workers. This is counter to the definition of *stars*. The output of peers, even very good peers, must be unequivocally and substantially inferior to the output of the stars. Beyond the theoretical distinction, a truncated normal distribution does not follow the distribution of performance among those jobs believed dominated by stars. To illus-trate this difference, Figure 3.2 presents a truncated sample (n = 15,954) from a simulated normal distribution of 100,000 workers with only those values in excess of one standard deviation shown. As seen, it is definitely skewed, but compare it with the bottom panel of the academics from Study 1 (n = 490,185) of O'Boyle and Aguinis (2012), which is a star distribution). The truncated normal curve declines in frequency at a slower rate (i.e., it is fatter in the middle and less peaked on the left) than what is found in a star distri-bution. Notice also how the grade of a truncated normal curve slowly reduces in height from one frequency bar to the next. On the other hand, the distribution of star academ-ics exhibits an initial peak that is many times larger than the second frequency bar, and the third bar is less than half the height of the second, and so on—a much quicker initial decay rate, but a much longer tail overall. To illustrate this latter point, consider that if we convert the truncated distribution into standardized scores, only 3 of the 15,954 (0.019%) observations possess z-scores above 5.0. This is logical as even a truncated normal dis-tribution has a relatively short right tail. Compare this with the star distribution where 2,413 of the 490,185 (0.666%) possess z-scores above 5.0. These are small percentages and even with hundreds of thousands of observations, sampling error can still play a role, but the former percentage is more than thirty-five times smaller than the latter. Contrary to what has been presented in the past (e.g., Beck, Beatty, and Sackett, 2014), star distri-butions do not resemble truncated normal curves. Stars perform at five, ten, or twenty

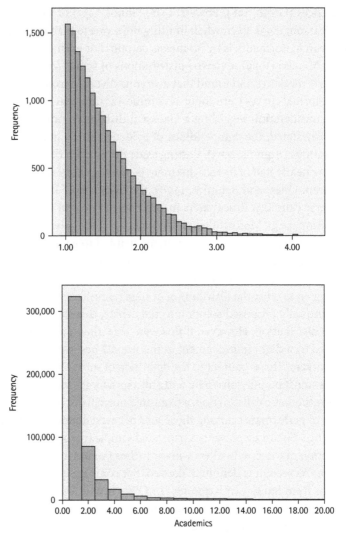

FIGURE 3.2 A Simulated Normal Distribution Truncated at +1 Standard Deviation and an Observed Star Distribution of Academics from O'Boyle and Aguinis (2012), Study 1

standard deviations above the mean, and their existence is highly improbable, bordering on impossible, under a normal distribution—truncated or otherwise.

So if performance is not normally distributed and it is not just the right tail of a normal curve, then what is it? Before relegating stars to this distribution or that, consider what we know about them. First, as expected in a non-normal distribution, the measures of central tendency in a star distribution are always drastically different from one another. The mode is the lowest possible value. The mean is considerably larger than the median, and thus the majority of workers in the distribution are below the arithmetic mean. Second, variances are difficult to interpret and highly unstable (Mandelbrot,

1960). The addition or deletion of one or two stars, even when sample sizes are large, can drastically affect both the mean and the variance. Third, star distributions exhibit a property known as scale invariance (Eliazar and Klafter, 2007). This means that the shape of the full star distribution shown in Figure 3.2 will be retained even if zoomed in on the top quartile, top decile, or even the top percentile—high-frequency peak to the left; long tail to the right. Many of the features of star distributions are consistent with a small group of non-normal distributions collectively known as heavy-tail distributions (Carmona, 2014).

At present, the heavy-tail distribution with the strongest (although by no means definitive) evidence is a power-law distribution. The term *power* is a reference to the exponential relation between one quantity (e.g., talent) and another quantity (e.g., performance and compensation) (see Clauset, Shalizi, and Newman, 2009 for an extensive review of its underlying equations). Power laws, as shown overlaying the normal distribution in Figure 3.1, exhibit the qualities of star distributions. The measures of central tendency are distanced from each other—the mean is much larger than the median, and the median is much larger than the mode. The addition or deletion of a small percentage of values at the right tail can drastically shift the mean. The variance is quasi-infinite, making traditional inferential statistics that rely on stable estimates of variance (e.g., ANOVA, OLS regression, and structural equation modeling) inappropriate and prone to both Type I and Type II errors (O'Boyle and Aguinis, 2012).

There are several noteworthy implications of power-law distributions to management research. First, overall production is largely attributable to a small minority of workers generating massive amounts of output. This is the opposite of a normal curve where overall production is largely attributable to a massive number of workers generating average output. Second, heavy-tail distributions allow individual output to affect firm-level outcomes without aggregation. This helps to address the paradox of human capital in the resource-based view that argues competitive advantage derives from resources that are valuable, rare, inimitable, and nonsubstitutable (VRIN). The paradox is how can average workers be rare, inimitable, and nonsubstitutable? Stars provide one solution to the paradox. Non-elite workers provide critical stability and support to organizational functioning, and in certain configurations, can become VRIN when aggregated (Coff and Kryscynski, 2011). Stars, on the other hand, provide the type of human capital that meets the VRIN definition without aggregation, and collectively the two forms of human capital meet the organizational goals of competitive advantage and longevity (Aguinis and O'Boyle, 2014). Third, heavy-tail distributions of output map better onto the heavy-tail distributions of reward allocation seen in a number of markets. For example, much has been made over the rapid increase in CEO compensation over the past few decades. Within large corporations in the United States, CEOs in 2003 earned six times as much as they collectively earned in 1980 (Edmans, Gabaix, and Landier, 2008). Within a normal curve, this rapid increase in compensation is nonsensical and unfair. However, this six-fold increase in compensation perfectly aligns with the six-fold increase in market capitalization these large firms experienced over the same period. The same can be found in the rapid increase in professional sports salaries, where increases in compensation correspond to increases in overall revenues in the sport (Leeds and Von Allmen, 2004).

In closing this section, we wish to note that just as there are valid criticisms against normal curves being the distributions most apt to describe job performance, there are also valid criticisms against power laws. First, it is unlikely there will ever be a single curve to explain performance in all jobs. Some jobs will be normally distributed; others will follow power laws; and others will follow something else entirely. (The comedian, Norm McDonald, proposed a Bernoulli distribution of job performance for professional cliff divers as taking on one of two values—either "grand champion" or "stuff on a rock".) Second, although O'Boyle and Aguinis (2012) concluded that 94% of the distributions conformed to a power law, they used a much looser definition of *power law* than a statistician would consider, and it is possible that what they concluded as overwhelming evidence for power laws was really overwhelming evidence for heavy-tail distributions. This was somewhat remedied in their tempered interpretation of the results in Aguinis, O'Boyle, Gonzalez-Mulé, and Joo (2016), but regardless, in a practical sense, the implications are largely the same—a small minority of workers dominates production and output. However, in a pure statistical sense, the evidence for power laws is far less certain.

3.3 WHAT, IF ANYTHING, MAKES STARS SPECIAL?

When discussing past events of epic importance, historians typically oscillate between great-person theory and the trends-and-forces perspective. The former suggests that certain individuals possess a particular set of traits and abilities that destine them for greatness regardless of environmental circumstances. Therefore, if Julius Caesar were born in nineteenth-century London, he would rise to a similar level of prominence as he did nearly two millennia prior, in late-republican Rome. The latter perspective holds that greatness is a function of environmental circumstances, and, to some extent, pure chance. So in all but the most extreme conditions, Adolf Hitler would have died in obscurity as a failed artist, but it just so happened that post-World War I Germany included the precise mix of trends and forces that allowed his rise to power. When discussing star performers, management scholars follow a similar course to historians, with some arguing that stars possess unique types or levels of human capital, while others argue that stars are simply placeholders within a hierarchy and their emergence is a function of a complex and sometimes random set of processes. Similar to nature–nurture debates (Simonton, 2014), the truth lies somewhere in between (for an example, see Kehoe, Lepak, and Bentley's (2016) excellent review and typology of stars), but as will be discussed, there are tremendous implications for research and practice, depending on whether stars emerge primarily because of external forces or, instead, rise on their own volition.

The predominant perspective in management and psychology research has been more aligned to great-person theory. Stars create and maintain their success with high levels of human capital. The dominance of this perspective is understandable, given the heritage of our fields. Whether applied or not, psychology is rooted in the person, and as such, differences in individual outputs are often presumed to be due to differences in individual inputs. Similarly, our economic heritage offers the efficient-market hypothesis, suggesting that visible star rewards (e.g., money and prestige) must be in response to and aligned with less visible, sometimes ambiguous, star productivity. Because some CEOs make twenty times as much as other CEOs do, they must be twenty times as valuable to their firms. However, there is increasing recognition of the role that forces outside the direct control of the individual play in allowing star distributions of productivity and performance. This is especially evident with regard to features of the work (e.g., autonomy and multiplicity of outputs) and the role of social networks. Below is a review of the extant evidence of the internal attributes and environmental features that allow for star emergence and star longevity.

3.3.1 Internal Attributes of Stars

As with any discussion of job performance and individual differences, the role of general mental ability (GMA) looms large. Ruthsatz, Ruthsatz, and Stephens (2014) reviewed the extant literature on child prodigies in music and art and concluded that their remarkable abilities were "highly dependent on a few features of their cognitive profiles, including elevated general IQs, exceptional working memories, and elevated attention to detail" (p. 60). Likewise, a longitudinal study of twelve children with exceptionally high IQs (scores in excess of 180) found that by the age of 22, nearly all had achieved star levels of productivity in their eventual professions (Hollingworth, 1942). Given the research (n = 1,326) linking childhood GMA to later job performance and career success (e.g., Bergman, Corovic, Ferrer-Wreder, and Modig, 2014), that stars tend to be smart is a rather obvious conclusion. What is less obvious, and merits more research, is whether there is a tipping point to stardom. For example, in a longitudinal study of twenty-six child geniuses (IQ scores in excess of 150), those that would eventually be classified as industry leaders in their respective fields (e.g., psychology, architecture, and law) all possessed IQ scores again in excess of 180, whereas the group of children with IQs between 150 and 179, although largely successful, failed to achieve star status (Feldman, 1984). If intelligence follows a normal distribution (as most agree it does), but performance output follows a heavy-tail distribution (as at least these authors believe), then there must come a point where small increases in intelligence yield massive differences in output.

With regard to GMA and star status, we see two areas ripe for exploration. First, if and where does the relation between GMA and job performance take on an exponential function (i.e., a tipping point)? Second, do the individual differences and contextual characteristics shown to interact with GMA to predict job performance (e.g., emotional intelligence; Cote and Miner, 2006) still hold at very high levels of GMA?

This is not simply an exercise in range restriction where we would expect attenuated interaction effects. Rather, it is entirely possible that weak or even nonexistent interactions observed at normal levels of GMA become quite strong when the population is limited to geniuses. For example, CEOs tend to be high in GMA (Wei and Rindermann, 2015). CEOs also tend to exhibit higher levels of narcissism and psychopathy compared with the general population (Babiak, Neumann, and Hare, 2010; Resick, Whitman, Weingarden, and Hiller, 2009). Do these maladaptive personality traits typified by grandiosity and callousness provide a competitive advantage when coupled with a high IQ that would not be observed among those with lower GMA?

Beyond GMA, there are a number of traits where either its magnitude or presence is proposed to be unique to stars. Ready, Conger, and Hill (2010) posited that high-potential stars possess such X-factors as a drive to excel, catalytic learning capability (i.e., the ability to scan for new ideas; the cognitive functioning to integrate new ideas into existing information and then translate ideas into action), enterprising spirit, and dynamic sensors. X-factors are by definition admittedly difficult to quantify, but collectively, these X-factors appear to fit within the classic motivation x ability = performance framework (Anderson and Butzin, 1974). For example, "catalytic learning capability" has strong similarities to fluid intelligence in that both deal with the speed of acquisition of new material, and "drive to excel" certainly aligns with achievement motivation. Also, within the realm of star athletes, a number of studies have found genetic factors related to elite performance (e.g., Alvarez et al., 2000; Montgomery et al., 1998; Yang et al., 2003). The extant evidence cannot rule out genetic factors in star emergence in fields other than athletics, but the generalizability of this evidence to less physically demanding jobs is questionable.

An admittedly "fuzzy" construct that has garnered attention in recent years is *grit*. Grit is continuing to pursue goals with passion over an extended period, even in the face of adversity (Duckworth, Kirby, Tsukayama, Berstein et al., 2011). In their conceptual review of the star literature, Call, Nyberg, and Thatcher (2015) identified grit as a key motivating factor to star emergence. The empirical support for grit is rather limited, but Duckworth, Kirby, Tsukayama, Berstein et al. (2011) examined 190 finalists in the Scripps National Spelling Bee and found a significant positive relation between grit and overall spelling performance.

Another interesting line of research suggests that at least in the entrepreneurial context, experience and education may be detrimental to star emergence. Several works in the mid-twentieth century found that the greater the experience, the lower the creative problem solving (Luchins, 1942; Wertheimer, 1945). And, when problem solving becomes mechanized, either owing to training or to individual experience, generating alternative solutions becomes more difficult (Gick and Lockhart, 1995). Entrepreneurs need to capitalize on new information, but those with greater education and experience may succumb to a Semmelweis reflex, where new information that runs counter to the established paradigm is rejected (McLaughlin, 2001). There are two notable caveats to this "less is more" effect when it comes to education and experience for entrepreneurs, and those in the fields where discovery is a premium (e.g., researchers). First, this does not appear to hold in established fields or content areas. For example, Nobel Laureates in most of the established sciences do their prize-winning work well after their 30s (Jones and Weinberg, 2011). Naiveté appears to benefit emerging realms most, where discovery is fast-paced and highly innovative, such as in quantum mechanics (Jones and Weinberg, 2011). The second caveat is the sociological perspective of the "marginal man" (Ben-David and Collins, 1966). It is not education or experience that stifles creativity and entrepreneurial success; rather, it is overspecialization (Baumol, Schilling, and Wolff, 2009). When education is interdisciplinary and experiences are diverse, these marginal entrepreneurs are successful because they are able to apply different assumptions and skills to problems and are willing to take larger risks (Baumol, Schilling, and Wolff, 2009; Gieryn and Hirsh, 1983). In sum, many knowledge-economy jobs require a certain degree of baseline knowledge and even considerable specialization and experience, but the likelihood of star emergence increases considerably when this specialization is coupled with wider exposure to ideas, methods, and fields of study.

One final individual difference of note is the role of practice. The widely discussed "10,000-hour rule" originally proposed in the works of Anders Ericsson and colleagues as the theory of deliberate practice (Ericsson and Charness, 1994; Ericsson, Krampe, and Tesch-Römer, 1993), and popularized in Malcolm Gladwell's *Outliers*, suggests that elite performance is largely, if not entirely, a function of deliberate practice. This idea of a tipping point of practice is found in a number of other works (e.g., Simonton, 1999; Simon and Chase, 1973), and it is difficult to argue that practice certainly has no effect on performance. However, a recent meta-analysis of 111 independent samples from a variety of domains found that deliberate practice played a role in every domain, but the accumulated evidence offered far from definitive support for its dominance (Macnamara, Hambrick, and Oswald, 2014). Attributable variance to deliberate practice ranged greatly, but in the domain most relevant to job performance—professional aptitude/success—practice contributed less than 1%. Practice may help, but it certainly does not make perfect.

3.3.2 Environmental Factors Affecting Stars

Again, innate talent, be it GMA, genetic factors, education, experience, or even deliberate practice, surely plays some role in star emergence. However, there is a growing body of literature to suggest that environmental features outside the control of stars can play just as important a role. These environmental features can serve to enhance star emergence and star performance (conductors) or serve to minimize and impede stars (insulators) (Aguinis, O'Boyle, Gonzalez-Mulé, and Joo, 2016). Collectively, these insulators and conductors can be viewed from the perspective of cumulative advantage. Cumulative advantage can help to explain why even in very efficient markets a widening gap can emerge between those with resources and those without. Sometimes referred to as the Matthew Effect (Merton, 1968) or 80-20 Rule, cumulative advantage posits that small initial advantages in wealth, skills, talent, or just plain luck will build over time to yield large differences in output and rewards.

Before discussing the external factors that facilitate or impede star emergence, we pause to note that our focus is squarely upon production stars (i.e., stars by virtue of their performance) as opposed to alternative star typologies, such as social capital stars or visibility stars, whose star status is bestowed upon them based on who they know and who knows them (Call, Nyberg, and Thatcher, 2015). Although there is certainly some overlap with performance stars, social capital stars and visibility stars likely have very different antecedents and outcomes.

For production stars, there are a number of conductors, but we will focus on two particularly strong conductors: multiplicity of production and monopolistic productivity. Multiplicity of production is the extent to which creating additional productivity requires less effort, resources, etc. than previous productivity (Aguinis, O'Boyle, Gonzalez-Mulé, and Joo, 2016). For example, Adler (1985) posited that superstardom in at least music and the arts is due almost entirely to initial and accumulating popularity (similar to Call, Nyberg, and Thatcher's (2015) definition of visibility stars). That is, part of enjoying a new band is being able to enjoy the band with others—"consumers prefer to consume what others also consume" (Adler, 2006: 4). In doing so, consumer interest feeds itself and begins to grow exponentially in a pattern consistent with multiplicity of production. In a more general sense, a star worker is able to capitalize on his or her past popularity to generate more productivity in the future with less individual effort. This may come in the form of greater access to organizational resources, more autonomy to pursue high-reward ventures, and capitalizing on a denser and more connected social network (Kehoe, Lepak, and Bentley, 2016). For example, publications are a form of output highly valued among academics. Regardless of initial skill level, the effort it takes a researcher to generate the first top-tier publication far exceeds the effort it takes later in their careers. Not only do the initial publications require more effort in learning the literature, developing one's voice, and acquiring the analytic skills necessary to test hypotheses, there is the added challenge of not yet having a reputation as a competent scholar. Editors faced with mixed reviews or ambiguous findings may give an established scholar the opportunity to revise, while the new scholar may be rejected outright (Macdonald and Kam, 2007). Either as a function of increased KSAs, greater access to resources, or increased reputation, later work requires fewer inputs, *ceteris paribus*.

The second conductor is monopolistic production. This is most likely to occur when rewards are rank-ordered as they are in tournament-style reward systems (Gerhart and Rynes, 2003). These winner-take-all systems allow stars to dominate output by diminishing the output of others. Returning to the example of a management professor, a star researcher will receive reduced teaching and service loads, higher salary, greater access to research assistants and doctoral students, etc. However, classes still need to be taught and committees still need to meet. The extra responsibilities and reduced access to resources lumped onto non-stars have the potential to box out and create cumulative disadvantage (Hannon, 2003). It may not be a conscious action of the star researcher, but the result is the same. Non-stars do the jobs that the stars do not and typically, this entails work that does not offer substantial extrinsic rewards.

Star production through monopolistic production can also have a deliberate component. Stars may use their position power to engage in informal means to signal to non-stars not to compete for top prizes (Connelly, Certo, Ireland, and Reutzel, 2011; Connelly, Tihanyi, Crook, and Gangloff, 2014). Beyond the individual level, the social and professional networks of stars may also lend themselves to monopolistic production, as stars' networks may "close ranks" as a means to dominate production (e.g., elite researchers turned editors may favor the work of other established stars over rising stars). Thus, unlike multiplicity of production that encourages star emergence, monopolistic production impedes star emergence, but may play an important role in star maintenance. Those that reach the top tend to stay at the top.

Whether the conductor of star productivity is primarily through multiplicity of production or primarily through monopolistic production has sweeping implications for an organization. Consider compensation. If stars are maintaining their status in large part by siphoning off the production of non-stars (i.e., monopolistic production), then resources are being misallocated. Star production should be symbiotic, not parasitic. Consider also selection and retention. If new potential stars recognize that the old, established stars dominate production through monopolistic practices, then the new stars will seek out better opportunities—potentially with a competitor. In essence, organizations will lose their future in order to preserve their past.

Regarding insulators, certain organizational practices affect stars and non-stars alike. These include anything that either hampers production (e.g., organizational constraints) or demotivates/disincentivizes (e.g., salary caps and nepotism), but there are certain insulators that are unique to stars. The one that we will focus on is the productivity ceiling. For most workers, productivity is capped by their own KSAs. As such, many organizations do not fully consider the absolute productivity ceiling (the amount of production capable by someone with ideal KSAs), but the absolute productivity ceiling can substantially affect stars. Aguinis and O'Boyle (2014) provided the example of a brokerage firm where the time it takes to close a sale is one hour, of which 30 minutes is completing paperwork. In an 8-hour day, the productivity ceiling is eight deals. For non-stars who may only close one or two deals a day, the paperwork is a minor constraint to their performance because their KSAs limit their production more so than the absolute ceiling. However, for a star broker closing deals at a fast rate, the one-deal-an-hour limit is considerably more detrimental. If this broker were to receive an administrative assistant to do the half-hour of paperwork, then this would double the broker's productivity ceiling.

The issue of a productivity ceiling extends beyond increasing the star's production maximum. It also is critical to retaining the star. Traditionally, when it comes to concerns about production, organizations have looked at the floor and not at the ceiling. Returning to the assembly-line example, the slowest worker sets the pace, so all efforts should be directed at increasing their productivity. At the department or branch level, the focus is usually on identifying "bottlenecks" in the organization and increasing their efficiency. Although ensuring minimum standards and clearing bottlenecks are still important in modern organizations, the new economy demands that organizations also look at the ceiling, because this may well be their source of competitive advantage. What can an organization offer to an incumbent star or recruited star that will allow him or her to maximize his or her productivity while decreasing their portability? In terms of VRIN, hiring an administrative assistant to fill out paperwork does increase productivity, but probably does not create competitive advantage because this benefit is easily imitated by a rival. On the other hand, a multinational corporation may offer the ability to transfer readily to locations that competitors cannot offer. Likewise, a diversified organization may be able to offer a spouse or dependent a career within their area of expertise.

Like many aspects of research into star performers, the antecedents of their emergence and retention are still in their infancy. However, the extant research does point to a number of promising areas. Still, before new theory can be built upon star performers, or they can be integrated into existing theory, there are some persistent and critical issues in the star literature. Next, we will offer a tentative research agenda for further understanding star performers.

3.4 A RESEARCH AGENDA INTO STAR PERFORMERS

Predicting the future course of any research stream is fraught with challenges. In the case of star performers, prognosticating is even more difficult, and the irony of trying to predict a stable course of research about a group that inherently brings instability to a system is not lost on us. That said, there are a few particular questions that are in dire need of addressing, and without resolution of these fundamental issues, star research is incapable of moving from descriptive to predictive, from inductive to deductive, or from empirically and theoretically separated from the mainstream literature to fully integrated within it.

3.4.1 The Criterion Problem

Whether at the individual, team, or firm level, operationalizing performance is one of the most debated topics in management research (Austin and Villanova, 1992; Venkatraman and Ramanujam, 1986). Thus, this issue is not unique to stars, but for a group that is explicitly defined by their performance, not being able to reach consensus on what exactly *is* performance significantly impedes progress. The criterion problem will require a multifront effort, but the greatest area of need at the moment is resolution about whether stars exist when performance is operationalized as multifaceted. Given the nascence of the debate in management concerning the nature of star performance, we are forced to rely on relatively few sources. Therefore, we will lean heavily on O'Boyle and Aguinis (2012) and Beck, Beatty, and Sackett (2014), but we remind the reader that there are more than these two positions, and in the coming years middle ground is likely to be struck, or perhaps the solution lies elsewhere entirely.

O'Boyle and Aguinis (2012) tested the distribution of productivity with single indicators of performance and found heavy-tail distributions more than 90% of the time. This led to their conclusion that in many contexts the distribution of performance is better modeled as a power-law rather than a Gaussian distribution. Therefore, one conductor of heavy-tail distributions is a single or a small number of job performance facets. This creates problems in two areas. First, Beck, Beatty, and Sackett (2014) argued that for most jobs, performance is multifaceted, and when performance is aggregated across these facets, the skewed individual facets will become normally distributed. So perhaps the heavy-tail distributions found in O'Boyle and Aguinis (2012) and elsewhere either represent small, nongeneralizable populations or reflect a deficiency bias where key facets of performance are omitted.

The second problem is that when a more holistic indicator of performance is used, unless it is disaggregated into its component parts, the measure can be quite coarse and possibly contaminated. For example, O'Boyle and Aguinis (2012) used Academy Awards nominations as one metric of performance for entertainers. Be it acting, directing, scoring, or editing, Academy Awards are given out for the holistic performance of the individual. That is, hitting one's mark, memorizing lines, emoting, etc. are all reflected in the Best Actor Award. This has some face validity, as Academy Award winners include well-known, highly successful stars such as Denzel Washington, Katherine Hepburn, and John Ford. At the same time, the measure is quite coarse, and as a result, many stars are likely underrepresented (e.g., Harrison Ford was nominated once, but never won) and perhaps some whose performance was misclassified as star quality (e.g., Three 6 Mafia's Academy Award for the song *It's Hard Out Here for a Pimp*).

However, the empirical and simulation evidence for normality when performance is multifaceted can be viewed as equally problematic and thus equally in need of future inquiry. Above we discussed the circular logic of instructing supervisors to place their employees into a normal distribution and then using supervisor ratings as evidence of normality. Given that supervisor ratings make up the preponderance of the normality evidence, this leaves much of the evidence for normality with simulations and Monte Carlo studies. For example, Beck, Beatty, and Sackett (2014) ran a series of simulations where they varied the number of facets (5, 20, and 35) of performance and the correlation (.00, .40, and .80) between facets (results shown in the nine panels in Figure 6 on p. 547). Their findings were quite interesting. Conditions where there were 20 to 35 unrelated facets were less skewed than conditions with fewer facets or when job facets correlated with one another. This is a critical finding, as Bandalos and Gagne stated that "even the most elegantly designed [simulation] may not be informative if the conditions included are not relevant to the type of data one typically encounters in practice" (2012: 96). Thus, the question for future research is which conditions are most relevant to "typical" job performance.

Are most jobs a large collection of unrelated facets or do most jobs consist of a few highly related core criteria? For example, a management professor's job performance largely consists of teaching management, researching management, mentoring management students, presenting at management conferences, and serving on academic committees in management departments. There is a distinct possibility that these facets are correlated with one another. On the other hand, there are jobs, even some touted as following a star distribution, where the facets that make up performance are quite distinct. For example, a professional baseball player's job can be divided into hitting, throwing, running, and catching. Not only are these facets likely to be differently correlated with one another, but there are some instances where they may be negatively related (e.g., pitchers in the modern era are notoriously bad hitters). As a final point, something not directly addressed in either Aguinis and O'Boyle (2012) or Beck, Beatty, and Sackett (2014) is the issue of facet weight. Are all job facets equally important to the overarching job performance construct? If not, which are more integral to performance? To what extent do the weights support or refute star existence? Again, future research is needed to supplement the descriptive evidence finding star distributions and the simulation evidence finding normality.

3.4.2 Do Star Effects Generalize to Negative Behaviors?

Are there "dark stars" within organizations that dominate counterproductive work behavior (CWB)? Put differently, does the distribution of positive star performance have a corresponding negative reflection? CWB is alleged to be a serious and frequent problem in organizations (Detert, Trevino, Burris, and Andiappan, 2007). To date, CWB is believed to be normally distributed, but the high frequency of CWB engagement, coupled with a normal distribution, means that most individuals engage in moderate amounts of CWB, with only a small percentage engaging in little CWB and a small percentage engaging in much CWB. This does not necessarily mean that most workers engage in a moderate amount of each particular CWB, such as sexual harassment, theft, sabotage, and physical violence against coworkers. Rather, normality advocates state that if one takes each worker's average engagement across all these behaviors, it will form a normal distribution. To illustrate, for an average worker, his or her high incidence of sexual harassment could be offset by very little engagement in embezzlement, such that he or she will score at the median CWB.

However, there are some indicators that dark stars may exist and can be highly detrimental. O'Boyle and Aguinis (2012) found star effects in narrow operationalizations of CWB in sports (e.g., flagrant fouls, red cards, and ejections). Using more broad operationalizations and more typical samples of workers, meta-analytic evidence also supports a highly skewed distribution of CWB, with the majority of individuals engaged in virtually no CWB, while a small minority dominates CWB engagement (Greco, O'Boyle, and Walter, 2015). Interestingly, there also appears to be a nonresponse bias in the study of CWB with those engaged in the most CWB, being the least likely to complete a CWB survey (Greco et al., 2015). This suggests that these dark stars are virtually a complete unknown. If dark stars act to the detriment of organizations at the same magnitude as positive stars contribute to organizations, then as an applied science, dark stars require far greater attention.

There is also a need to investigate the degree of overlap between star performers and dark stars. Lord Acton once quipped, "Great men are almost always bad men," and star productivity in one arena may be offset by deficits in other arenas. To what extent does positive behavior in terms of task performance justify negative behavior in a different realm of behavior (Fox, Spector, Goh, Bruursema et al., 2012)? How much leeway do organizations give their stars, and what effect does their differential treatment have on non-stars?

3.4.3 What Are the Best Ways to Recruit, Manage, and Compensate Stars?

The so-called war for talent posits that stars form the part of human capital that provides competitive advantage (Michaels, Handfield, and Axelrod, 2001). If true, then HR systems should always target elite acquisitions. The productivity attributed to the star certainly justifies such a targeted approach to recruitment, but such a ham-handed selection approach will likely do more harm than good. Stars are not cheap, and the costs of a selection error will be many orders of magnitude greater than the costs of selection errors for non-stars. Rather than simply trying to recruit all the available talent in the marketplace, research is needed into how HR systems evaluate stars in their assessment of strategic relevance, organizational fit, the job duties themselves, and alternative sources of their productivity.

There is also the issue of what determines the variance in star portability (Groysberg, Sant, and Abrahams, 2008). That is, when stars move from one organization to another, do they still perform at peak levels? Although this topic will be reviewed in far more depth in a later chapter by Dokko and Jiang, we will briefly review some of the extant literature in these areas. The evidence for star portability is mixed, but at present, the answer appears to be "sometimes." Groysberg et al. (2008) found that the larger the system that the star is embedded within, the lower their portability. So a wide receiver in professional football is deeply embedded within the offensive scheme, while a punter is somewhat autonomous. Thus, star wide receivers are less likely to maintain star production than star punters are. In a previous study, Groysberg and Lee (2009) found that one of the determining factors of whether stars are able to retain their productivity is when they are able to engage in the same behaviors as their previous position (referred to as exploitation). For example, star salespeople can retain their star production when they move to another organization as long as they are selling a similar product in a similar way. Groysberg and Lee also found that stars who moved with their colleagues from the previous organization also better maintained their elite performance. This not only reinforces that stars are specialized, but also suggests that the star himself or herself may simply be the tip of the iceberg, and stars' output is attributable as much to their network and support structure as it is to any internal attributes. Determining the source of star power is of the utmost importance; only rewarding the star may misalign incentives and demotivate the true source(s) of star power.

Stars shine brightly, and high performers in critical positions will garner the attention of competitors (Call, Nyberg, and Thatcher, 2015). Retaining stars will require organizations to reexamine their compensation policies and potentially make radical changes. For example, how acceptable to an organization is extensive variance in pay for the same position? An issue well known in professional sports, but largely unheard of in the private sector, is that stars create the possibility, even the inevitability, that certain employees will earn more than their supervisors do.

With regard to star compensation, the zeitgeist is to pay stars as much as possible—especially within prototypical star industries such as software development and technology. For example, Bill Gates allegedly said, "A great lathe operator commands several times the wage of an average lathe operator, but a great writer of software code is worth 10,000 times the price of an average software writer" (Veksler, 2010). This sentiment, common in Silicon Valley, encourages very high degrees of pay dispersion. For example, Google's Senior Vice President of People Operation (i.e., Head of HR), Laszlo Bock, reflecting on Google's compensation policy, stated: "two people doing the same work can have a hundred times difference in their impact, and in their rewards ... there have been situations where one person received a stock award of $10,000, and another working in the same area received $1,000,000" (Bock, 2015: 241). Unequal pay is only acceptable if it is equitable. Far greater research is needed into the group and environmental determinants of star performers.

Beyond monetary compensation, if it is determined that star effects are a result of networks of individuals, then this will also require substantial changes to a common retention tool for elite performers, known as idiosyncratic work arrangements or I-Deals (Rousseau, 2005). These are customized arrangements whereby stars receive special treatment and benefits. These range from relatively minor considerations (e.g., reduced hours) to complicated and expensive luxuries, such as taking an all-expenses-paid year off work to do underwater photography with one's partner (Rousseau, 2001). If stars are simply the beneficiaries of network effects, then not only is this a tremendous waste of resources, it can also have deleterious effects on the workers within the star network in terms of psychological contract breach and justice perceptions.

3.5 CONCLUSION

Research into star performers is a burgeoning area in management and applied psychology. Understanding their existence, their influence, and their antecedents will continue to be a hotly debated topic in the coming years. This chapter offered a brief overview of what constitutes a star, how stars fit into the existing research paradigm, and the factors that contribute to or impede star emergence. We concluded with a research agenda that we believe will help guide scholarly research.

REFERENCES

Adler, M. 1985. Stardom and talent. *American Economic Review*, 75, pp.208–12.

Adler, M. 2006. Stardom and talent. *Handbook of the Economics of Art and Culture*, 1, pp.895–906.

Aguinis, H. 2013. *Performance management*, 3rd edn. Upper Saddle River, NJ: Pearson/Prentice Hall.

Aguinis, H., and O'Boyle, E. H. 2014. Star performers in twenty-first-century organizations. *Personnel Psychology*, 67, pp.313–50.

Aguinis, H., O'Boyle, E., Gonzalez-Mulé, E., and Joo, H. 2016. Cumulative advantage: conductors and insulators of heavy-tailed productivity distributions and productivity stars. *Personnel Psychology*, 69(1), pp.3–66.

Alvarez, R., Terrados, N., Ortolano, R., Iglesias-Cubero, G. et al. 2000. Genetic variation in the renin-angiotensin system and athletic performance. *European Journal of Applied Physiology*, 82(1–2), pp.117–20.

Anderson, N. H., and Butzin, C. A. 1974. Performance = motivation × ability: an integration-theoretical analysis. *Journal of Personality and Social Psychology*, 30(5), p.598.

Andriani, P., and McKelvey, B. 2007. Beyond Gaussian averages: redirecting international business and management research toward extreme events and power laws. *Journal of International Business Studies*, 38, pp.1212–30.

Andriani, P., and McKelvey, B. 2009. Extremes and scale-free dynamics in organization science. *Organization Science*, 20, pp.1053–71.

Aoyama, H., Yoshikawa, H., Iyetomi, H., and Fujiwara, Y. 2010. Productivity dispersion: facts, theory, and implications. *Journal of Economic Interaction and Coordination*, 5, pp.27–54.

Austin, J. T., and Villanova, P. 1992. The criterion problem: 1917–1992. *Journal of Applied Psychology*, 77(6), p.836.

Babiak, P., Neumann, C. S., and Hare, R. D. 2010. Corporate psychopathy: talking the walk. *Behavioral Sciences & the Law*, 28(2), pp.174–93.

Bandalos, D. L., and Gagne, P. 2012. Simulation methods in structural equation modeling. In R. H. Hoyle, ed., *Handbook of structural equation modeling*, pp.92–110. New York: Guilford Publications.

Baumol, W. J., Schilling, M. A., and Wolff, E. N. 2009. The superstar inventors and entrepreneurs: how were they educated? *Journal of Economics & Management Strategy*, 18(3), pp.711–28.

Beck, J. W., Beatty, A. S., and Sackett, P. R. 2014. On the distribution of job performance: the role of measurement characteristics in observed departures from normality. *Personnel Psychology*, 67(3), pp.531–66.

Bedeian, A. G., and Armenakis, A. A. 1998. The cesspool syndrome: how dreck floats to the top of declining organizations. *Academy of Management Executive*, 12(1), pp.58–63.

Ben-David, J., and Collins, R. 1966. Social factors in the origins of a new science: the case of psychology. *American Sociological Review*, 31, pp.451–65.

Bergman, L. R., Corovic, J., Ferrer-Wreder, L., and Modig, K. 2014. High IQ in early adolescence and career success in adulthood: findings from a Swedish longitudinal study. *Research in Human Development*, 11(3), pp.165–85.

Bock, L. 2015. *Work rules!* New York: Grand Central Publishing.

Call, M. L., Nyberg, A. J., and Thatcher, S. 2015. Stargazing: an integrative conceptual review, theoretical reconciliation, and extension for star employee research. *Journal of Applied Psychology*, 100(3), p.623.

Carmona, R. 2014. Heavy tail distributions. In *Statistical Analysis of Financial Data in R*, (pp. 69–120). New York: Springer.

Caulfield, K. 2014. http://www.billboard.com/articles/columns/chart-beat/6422411/taylor-swift-1989-beats-frozen-top-selling-album-2014. Accessed Dec. 1, 2015.

Clauset, A., Shalizi, C. R., and Newman, M. E. 2009. Power-law distributions in empirical data. *SIAM Review*, 51(4), pp.661–703.

Coff, R., and Kryscynski, D. 2011. Invited editorial: drilling for micro-foundations of human capital–based competitive advantages. *Journal of Management*, 37(5), pp.1429–43.

Connelly, B. L., Certo, S. T., Ireland, R. D., and Reutzel, C. R. 2011. Signaling theory: a review and assessment. *Journal of Management*, 37, pp.39–67.

Connelly, B. L, Tihanyi, L., Crook, T. R., and Gangloff, K. A. 2014. Tournament theory: thirty years of contests and competitions. *Journal of Management*, 40, pp.16–47.

Cote, S., and Miners, C. T. 2006. Emotional intelligence, cognitive intelligence, and job performance. *Administrative Science Quarterly*, 51(1), pp.1–28.

Detert, J. R., Trevino, L. K., Burris, E. R., and Andiappan, M. 2007. Managerial modes of influence and counterproductivity in organizations: a longitudinal business-unit-level investigation. *Journal of Applied Psychology*, 92, pp.993–1005.

Duckworth, A. L., Kirby, T. A., Tsukayama, E., Berstein, H., and Ericsson, K. A. 2011. Deliberate practice spells success: why grittier competitors triumph at the national spelling bee. *Social Psychological and Personality Science*, 2(2), pp.174–81.

Edmans, A., Gabaix, X., and Landier, A. 2007. *A calibratable model of optimal CEO incentives in market equilibrium* (No. w13372). National Bureau of Economic Research.

Eliazar, I., and Klafter, J. 2007. Scale-invariance of random populations: from Paretian to Poissonian fractality. *Physica A: Statistical Mechanics and its Applications*, 383(2), pp.171–89.

Ericsson, K. A., and Charness, N. 1994. Expert performance: its structure and acquisition. *American Psychologist*, 49(8), p.725.

Ericsson, K. A., Krampe, R. T., and Tesch-Römer, C. 1993. The role of deliberate practice in the acquisition of expert performance. *Psychological Review*, 100(3), p.363.

Feldman, D. H. 1984. A follow-up of subjects scoring above 180 IQ in Terman's "Genetic Studies of Genius." *Exceptional Children*, 50(6), pp.518–23.

Feldman, D. H. 1986. *Nature's gambit: child prodigies and the development of human potential.* New York: Basic Books.

Fox, S., Spector, P. E., Goh, A., Bruursema, K., and Kessler, S. R. 2012. The deviant citizen: measuring potential positive relations between counterproductive work behaviour and organizational citizenship behaviour. *Journal of Occupational and Organizational Psychology*, 85(1), pp.199–220.

Franck, E., and Nüesch, S. 2012. Talent and/or popularity: what does it take to be a superstar? *Economic Inquiry*, 50(1), pp.202–16.

Frey, B. S. 1998. Superstar museums: an economic analysis. *Journal of Cultural Economics*, 22, pp.113–25.

Geary, R. C. 1947. Testing for normality. *Biometrika*, 34, pp.209–42.

Gerhart, B., and Rynes, S. 2003. *Compensation: theory, evidence, and strategic implications.* Thousand Oaks, CA: Sage Publications.

Gick, M. L., and Lockhart, R. S. 1995. Cognitive and affective components of insight. In R. J. Sternberg and J. E. Davidson, eds., *The Nature of Insight*, pp.197–228. Cambridge, MA: The MIT Press.

Gieryn, T. F., and Hirsh, R. F. 1983. Marginality and innovation in science. *Social Studies of Science*, 13, pp.87–106.

Greco, L. M., O'Boyle, E. H., and Walter, S. L. 2015. Absence of malice: a meta-analysis of non-response bias in counterproductive work behavior research. *Journal of Applied Psychology*, 100(1), p.75.

Groth, B. H. A. 1914. The golden mean in the inheritance of size. *Science*, 39, pp.581–4

Groysberg, B., and Lee, L. E. 2009. Hiring stars and their colleagues: exploration and exploitation in professional service firms. *Organization Science*, 20(4), pp.740–758.

Groysberg, B., Lee, L. E., and Nanda, A. 2008. Can they take it with them? The portability of star knowledge workers' performance. *Management Science*, 54(7), pp.1213–30.

Hausman, J. A., and Leonard, G. K. 1997. Superstars in the National Basketball Association: economic value and policy. *Journal of Labor Economics*, 15(4), pp.586–624.

Hannon, L. 2003. Poverty, delinquency, and educational attainment: cumulative disadvantage or disadvantage saturation? *Sociological Inquiry*, 73(4), pp.575–94.

Hollingworth, L. 1942. Children above 180 IQ. *The Teachers College Record*, 44(1), p.56.

Hunter, J. E., Schmidt, F. L., and Judiesch, M. K. 1990. Individual differences in output variability as a function of job complexity. *Journal of Applied Psychology*, 75(1), p.28.

Jones, B. F., and Weinberg, B. A. 2011. Age dynamics in scientific creativity. *Proceedings of the National Academy of Sciences*, 108(47), pp.18910–14.

Kehoe, R. R., Lepak, D. P., and Bentley, F. S. 2016. Let's call a star a star: task performance, external status, and exceptional contributors in organizations. *Journal of Management*, DOI: 10.1177/0149206316628644.

LeBreton, J. M., Scherer, K. T., and James, L. R. 2014. Corrections for criterion reliability in validity generalization: a false prophet in a land of suspended judgment. *Industrial and Organizational Psychology*, 7(4), pp.478–500.

Leeds, M., and Von Allmen, P. 2004. *The economics of sports.* New York.

Limpert, E., Stahel, W. A., and Abbt, M. 2001. Log-normal distributions across the sciences: keys and clues. *BioScience*, 51(5), pp.341–52.

Luchins, A. S. 1942. Mechanization in problem solving: the effect of Einstellung. *Psychological Monographs*, 54(6, Whole No. 248), pp.1–95.

Macdonald, S., and Kam, J. 2007. Ring a ring o'roses: quality journals and gamesmanship in management studies. *Journal of Management Studies*, 44(4), pp.640–55.

Macnamara, B. N., Hambrick, D. Z., and Oswald, F. L. (2014). Deliberate practice and performance in music, games, sports, education, and professions: a meta-analysis. *Psychological Science*, 25(8), pp.1608–18.

Mandelbrot, B. 1960. The Pareto-Levy law and the distribution of income. *International Economic Review*, 1(2), pp.79–106.

McLaughlin, N. 2001. Optimal marginality: innovation and orthodoxy in Fromm's revision of psychoanalysis. *The Sociological Quarterly*, 42(2), pp.271–88.

Merton, R. K. 1968. The Matthew effect in science. *Science*, 159(3810), pp.56–63.

Micceri, T. 1989. The unicorn, the normal curve, and other improbable creatures. *Psychological Bulletin*, 105(1), p.156.

Michaels, E., Handfield-Jones, H., and Axelrod, B. 2001. *The war for talent*. Cambridge, MA: Harvard Business Press.

Montgomery, H. E., Marshall, R., Hemingway, H., Myerson, S. et al. 1998. Human gene for physical performance. *Nature*, *393*(6682), pp.221–2.

Motowidlo, S. J., and Borman, W. C. 1977. Behaviorally anchored scales for measuring morale in military units. *Journal of Applied Psychology*, *62*, pp.177–83.

Narin, F., and Breitzman, A. 1995. Inventive productivity. *Research Policy*, *24*(4), pp.507–19.

O'Boyle, E. H., and Aguinis, H. 2012. The best and the rest: revisiting the norm of normality of individual performance. *Personnel Psychology*, *65*, pp.79–119.

Pearson, K. 1895. Contributions to the mathematical theory of evolution. II. Skew variation in homogeneous material. *Philosophical Transactions of the Royal Society of London*, A, *186*, pp.343–414.

Powell, W. W., and Snellman, K. 2004. The knowledge economy. *Annual Review of Sociology*, *30*, pp.199–220.

Powers, L. 1936. The nature of the interaction of genes affecting four quantitative characters in a cross between hordeum deficiens and hordeum vulgar. *Genetics*, *21*(5), p.624.

Ready, A. D., Conger, A. J., and Hill, A. L. 2010. Are you a high potential. *Harvard Business Review*, *88*(6), pp.78–84.

Resick, C. J., Whitman, D. S., Weingarden, S. M., and Hiller, N. J. 2009. The bright-side and the dark-side of CEO personality: examining core self-evaluations, narcissism, transformational leadership, and strategic influence. *Journal of Applied Psychology*, *94*(6), p.1365.

Rosen, S. 1981. The economics of superstars. *The American Economic Review*, *71*(5), pp.845–58.

Rotundo, M., and Sackett, P. R. 2002. The relative importance of task, citizenship, and counter-productive performance to global ratings of job performance: a policy-capturing approach. *Journal of Applied Psychology*, *87*(1), p.66.

Rousseau, D. M. 2001. The idiosyncratic deal flexibility versus fairness? *Organizational Dynamics*, *29*, pp.260–73.

Rousseau, D. M. 2005. *I-deals, idiosyncratic deals employees bargain for themselves*. New York: ME Sharpe.

Ruthsatz, J., Ruthsatz, K., and Stephens, K. R. 2014. Putting practice into perspective: child prodigies as evidence of innate talent. *Intelligence*, *45*, pp.60–5.

Schneier, C. E. 1977. Multiple rater groups and performance appraisal. *Public Personnel Management*, *6*, pp.13–20.

Simon, H. A., and Chase, W. G. 1973. Perception in chess. *Cognitive Psychology*, *4*(1), pp.55–81.

Simonton, D. K. 1999. *Origins of genius: Darwinian perspectives on creativity*. Oxford: Oxford University Press.

Simonton, D. K. 2014. Creative performance, expertise acquisition, individual differences, and developmental antecedents: an integrative research agenda. *Intelligence*, *45*, pp.66–73.

Sinnott, E. W. 1937. The relation of gene to character in quantitative inheritance. *Proceedings of the National Academy of Sciences of the United States of America*, *23*(4), p.224.

Sparrow, P. R., and Makram, H. 2015. What is the value of talent management? Building value-driven processes within a talent management architecture. *Human Resource Management Review*, *25*(3), pp.249–63.

Suellentrop, C. 2013. Divining what's next for video games. *The New York Times*. March 11. http://www.nytimes.com/2013/03/12/arts/video-games/shigeru-miyamoto-of-nintendo-on-wii-u-sales-and-game-violence.html Accessed Feb. 25, 2017.

Veksler, D. (2010). Some lesser-known truths about programming. https://www.facebook.com/notes/david-veksler/some-lesser-known-truths-about-programming/421427432044 Accessed Feb. 25, 2017.

Venkatraman, N., and Ramanujam, V. 1986. Measurement of business performance in strategy research: a comparison of approaches. *Academy of Management Review*, 11(4), pp.801–14.

Viswesvaran, C., Ones, D. S., and Schmidt, F. L. 1996. Comparative analysis of the reliability of job performance ratings. *Journal of Applied Psychology*, 81(5), p.557.

Volmer, J., and Sonnentag, S. 2011. The role of star performers in software design teams. *Journal of Managerial Psychology*, 26(3), pp.219–34.

Wai, J., and Rindermann, H. 2015. The path and performance of a company leader: a historical examination of the education and cognitive ability of Fortune 500 CEOs. *Intelligence*, 53, pp.102–7.

Wertheimer, M. [1945] 1959. *Productive thinking*. Chicago: University of Chicago Press.

Yang, N., MacArthur, D. G., Gulbin, J. P., Hahn, A. G., et al. 2003. ACTN3 genotype is associated with human elite athletic performance. *American Journal of Human Genetics*, 73(3), pp.627–31.

CHAPTER 4

···

WITHIN-PERSON VARIABILITY IN PERFORMANCE

···

AMIRALI MINBASHIAN

4.1 INTRODUCTION

···

INDIVIDUAL performance at work is a key mediating variable in the effect of strategic talent-management systems on organizational outcomes (Collings and Mellahi, 2009). Consequently, understanding the nature of performance variability and the factors that drive it is highly relevant for the development of talent-management systems that are maximally effective. In describing the nature of individual performance, an analogy can be drawn between the concepts of performance and body weight. Although differences between people in body weight can be easily observed, any given individual's weight may also fluctuate vastly across time. Like body weight, an individual's performance at work fluctuates up and down around a set point (i.e., a typical or "true" performance level) both within a day and across days and weeks. Furthermore, over long periods, an individual's set point itself may vary in response to one's experiences and developmental changes. Such *within-person variability in performance* (WPVP) has long been inferred from evidence of changes in the rank-order of performers across time, changes in the predictive validities of selection devices across time, and changes in mean performance across individuals over time (see Sturman, 2007). However, until recently, job performance researchers have primarily focused on *between-person variability* and its antecedents (see Fisher, 2008). This is perhaps unfortunate, as simply identifying the between-person factors that underlie performance differences provides limited information about how to maximize one's performance; much like the fact that individual differences in genetics and physical structure only provide a partial understanding of a person's weight at a given point in time.

Fortunately, over the past two decades, researchers have increasingly examined WPVP. The present chapter provides an overview of the literature on WPVP and the implications of its findings for talent management. In the first two sections of this chapter, I provide a definition of WPVP and summarize the evidence base for the existence of this type of variability. Following this, I discuss the main determinants of WPVP that are identified in theories of this construct, and outline a model that integrates these determinants. In the final section, I discuss some of the implications of WPVP and the model for the conceptualization of talent and the implementation of talent-management practices. It should be noted that the aim is not to provide a comprehensive review of the literature on WPVP. Several recent reviews have already done this (Dalal, Bhave, and Fiset, 2014; Sonnentag and Frese, 2012; Sturman, 2007), and I refer the interested reader to these articles. Rather, the present chapter aims to draw attention to some of the main issues and findings from this literature that are relevant for talent management.

4.2 WHAT IS WPVP?

WPVP refers to the idea that how well an individual performs at work (on a given dimension of performance) will vary across different situations and periods. Performance is conceptualized broadly to include a range of organizationally valued work behaviors— such as task performance (Borman and Motowidlo, 1997), organizational citizenship behavior (Organ, 1997), proactive behavior (Crant, 2000), and (a lack of) counterproductive work behavior (Sackett, 2002)—as well as the more general concept of overall job performance (see Murphy, 1989). Such behaviors can be assessed directly (e.g., using supervisor ratings or observations of the extent of sales calls made by a salesperson) or through their effects on valued outcomes (e.g., dollar sales generated by a salesperson). For the most part, the literature on WPVP has examined task performance, and, consequently, this chapter focuses largely on this outcome; however, relevant findings for the other forms of performance behavior are also included.

The definition of WPVP provided above differs from earlier conceptualizations of *dynamic performance*, which only indirectly captured within-person variability by focusing on how correlations between performance measures vary over time (see Sturman, 2007). Furthermore, though similar, my definition differs slightly from a recent definition provided by Dalal, Bhave, and Fiset (2014), who "define within-person performance variability simply as the change in an employee's performance level over time" (p. 1400). The definition presented in this chapter distinguishes explicitly between varying situations and the passage of time as two sources of within-person variability, and this forms the basis of a model of individual performance that is subsequently presented in the chapter.

4.3 EVIDENCE FOR WPVP

To assess the extent to which performance varies within-person in a given domain, researchers use research designs in which performance is assessed across multiple persons on multiple occasions, and they compute the proportion of total variance in performance (across and within persons) that is due to within-person (i.e., occasion to occasion) variability (see Fisher and To, 2012). The specific value that is obtained is likely to be influenced by various factors, such as the diversity of people included in the sample, the length of time and diversity of situations over which performance is assessed, and the specific performance measure that is used. Nevertheless, research conducted to date supports the view that within-person variability is a substantive component of overall variability. Dalal, Bhave, and Fiset (2014) summarized the findings from thirty-six such studies and found that on average 64% of the variability in job performance and 62% of the variability in task performance occurred within-person. Lower though still substantive values were found for other performance constructs, such as organizational citizenship behavior (43%), counterproductive work behavior (49%), and proactive behavior (39%). Moreover, the substantiveness of within-person variability seems to generalize across time frames, jobs, and objective versus subjective measures (Minbashian and Luppino, 2014). For example, Fisher and Noble (2004) asked 121 individuals across fifteen occupations to self-report their performance five times each day for two weeks. They found that 78% of total performance variability occurred within-person. In contrast, Stewart and Nandkeolyar (2006) focused on variability in the weekly sales (in root square transformed dollars) generated by sales representatives over 26 weeks, and they also found that within-person variability comprised the majority (73%) of total variability.

To illustrate further the effect of WPVP, the estimates reported by Stewart and Nandkeolyar (2006) can be used to make several inferences about performance within their sample. Figure 4.1 plots square root transformed sales per-week estimates for the average sales representative and the high-performing sales representative (where *high performing* is defined as one *between-person* standard deviation above the mean, or roughly among the top 15% of sales representatives). The estimates are based on the random-effects ANOVA results reported by Stewart and Nandkeolyar. Retransforming

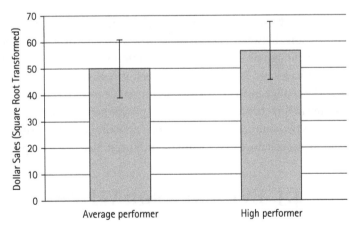

FIGURE 4.1 Square Root Transformed Sales Estimates for the Average Performer and High Performer in Stewart and Nandkeolyar's (2006) Study.
Error bars represent within-person variability.

these values back to raw dollar values, the average sales representative typically generated approximately $2515 per week, whereas the high performer typically generated $3214 per week. However, on a "good week" (defined as a week in which performance is one *within-person* standard deviation above the mean) the average and high performers generated $3719 and $4560, respectively. These results suggest that under the right conditions, the average performer can far exceed their own typical performance and even that of the high performer. Moreover, the results suggest that identifying the determining conditions of WPVP enables an organization to manage its talent in such a way as to increase greatly their performance. In a subsequent section, the concept of WPVP will be linked back to arguments around performance variability in the talent-management literature. However, next I discuss the determinants of WPVP.

4.4 Determinants of WPVP

A range of theories are relevant to explaining WPVP, and these can be grouped based on the time frame under question, the nature of the variability in performance, or the specific variables that are the antecedent causes of variability (see Dalal, Bhave, and Fiset, 2014). Below I discuss two groups of theories, namely, those that explain short-term fluctuations in performance and those that explain long-term performance trends.

4.4.1 Short-Term Variability in Performance

The first group of theories seeks to explain short-term situationally induced WPVP. A key explanatory mechanism underlying such theories is that performance varies over the short term owing to *resource-allocation processes*, where resources refer to *motivational* variables such as attention, effort, and time spent on a task (Kanfer, 1990). Performance on a given task is expected to increase when motivational resources are allocated to it and decrease when resources are withdrawn and allocated off task (Beal, Weiss, Barros, and MacDermid, 2005). The resource-allocation process is initially triggered by exposure to a particular situation (e.g., an event, task, or performance episode; see Dalal, Bhave, and Fiset, 2014) which activates various cognitive and affective processes that ultimately influence resource allocation (see Mischel and Shoda, 1995). Although the triggering situation can be conceptualized in terms of its nominal characteristics (e.g., the people present and the type of activity involved), it is the underlying psychological features of the situation (e.g., the perceived importance or difficulty of the task) that have been argued to be the key triggers of the cognitive and affective processes that influence resource allocation (e.g., Minbashian, Wood, and Beckmann, 2010).

The *cognitive processes* that underlie resource allocation were identified in earlier models of motivation. For example, motivation is likely to be higher when an individual perceives a strong link between effort and performance on a task and when high performance is perceived as leading to valued outcomes (Vroom, 1964). Goal setting also increases motivation, especially when the goals set are specific, difficult, and accompanied by feedback (Locke, Shaw, Saari, and Latham, 1981). *Self-efficacy*, which refers to beliefs in one's capability to attain a specific goal, is thought to enhance performance via its effects on motivation (Bandura, 1977; although see recent arguments and empirical evidence for null or even negative effects, e.g., Sitzmann and Yeo, 2013; Vancouver and Kendall, 2006). Kanfer and Ackerman (1989; Kanfer, 1987, 1990) integrated the concepts from these earlier models in a resource-based model of task motivation. Specifically, expectancies of the level of effort required to achieve different performance levels and judgments of the utility associated with different levels of task performance and effort expenditure determine the initial level of resources allocated to a task. Further resource-allocation processes may occur during task engagement as individuals distribute their attention and effort across on-task and off-task activities. This is achieved through self-regulation, in which individuals monitor and evaluate their performance in relation to their goals, which in turn influences their self-reactions, their self-efficacy beliefs, and the extent to which they allocate resources toward the task. This self-regulatory process will typically enhance performance by sustaining on-task attention when needed; however, it may also impair performance when it draws on attentional resources that are required by the task (Kanfer and Ackerman, 1989).

More recently, it has been discovered that the *capacity to engage in self-regulation* may itself vary from task to task, as it relies on a limited energy resource that is diminished by repeated use (Baumeister, Vohs, and Tice, 2007; Muraven and Baumeister, 2000). This limited resource is depleted by acts of self-regulation that occur over a broad range of activities such as difficult interpersonal interactions, physically demanding tasks, and situations that call for the resistance of impulses or the control of one's thoughts (Baumeister, Vohs, and Tice, 2007). Consequently, the level of regulatory resources available for a given performance episode will vary depending on the activities completed before that episode, and this will further contribute to WPVP. Rest and replenishment has been shown to play a role in the recovery of depleted self-regulatory resources and, therefore, can be used as a strategy for restoring performance. For example, engaging in recovery experiences such as psychological detachment, relaxation, and mastery experiences during the weekend has been shown to predict positively the state of being recovered at the beginning of the week, which in turn positively predicts task performance, organizational citizenship behavior, and personal initiative during that week (Binnewies, Sonnentag, and Mojza, 2010). Similarly, day-to-day fluctuations in task performance, organizational citizenship behavior, and personal initiative are positively predicted by the state of being recovered each morning (Binnewies, Sonnentag, and Mojza, 2009), and within-day fluctuations in performance are predicted by break activities during the day (Trougakos, Beal, Green, and Weiss, 2008).

The role of *affective processes* in WPVP was highlighted by Weiss and Cropanzano (1996) as part of affective events theory. Drawing on previous research in the literature on affect, Weiss and Cropanzano argue that emotional experiences at work fluctuate within a person as a function of reactions to work events. Specifically, events can trigger positive and/or negative affective responses based on appraisals of the relevance (with respect to opportunities and threats) and importance of the event to one's well-being, and other more elaborate appraisals. Affective states in turn may influence performance, although the direction of the effect will depend on the congruence of the thoughts and behaviors elicited by the experienced mood or emotion with the requirements of the task. For example, positive affect is likely to be useful for tasks that require the recall of positive material or heuristic information processing, whereas negative affect is likely to be useful for tasks that require the recall of negative material or systematic information processing (see Weiss and Cropanzano, 1996). In support of affect-congruent effects on performance, within-person experience sampling studies have found that positive emotions increase organizational citizenship behavior, whereas negative emotions increase counterproductive work behavior (e.g., Dalal, Lam, Weiss, Welch et al., 2009; Ilies, Scott, and Judge, 2006; Rodell and Judge, 2009; Yang and Diefendorff, 2009).

Beal, Weiss, Barros, and MacDermid (2005) proposed a model that integrates affective influences on within-person performance variability with the resource-allocation perspective proposed by Kanfer and Ackerman (1989; Kanfer, 1987, 1990). Although Beal, Weiss, Barros, and MacDermid (2005) acknowledge the influence of affect on performance, via its congruency with task requirements, they argue that affect primarily influences task performance via its effect on the regulation of attention. This effect may be positive, as occurs when affect that is generated by the performance task itself creates attentional pull toward the task. However, Beal, Weiss, Barros, and MacDermid (2005) argue that the effect will more often be detrimental, as affect that is incidental to the task creates attentional demands that takes people off task and depletes their capacity to self-regulate. The latter view is only partially supported by empirical findings. While some evidence exists for a negative within-person relationship between negative affect and task performance (e.g., Chi, Chang, and Huang, 2015; Fisher and Noble, 2004; Rothbard and Wilk, 2011), the within-person effect of positive affect on task performance is generally positive (e.g., Chi, Chang, and Huang, 2015; Fisher and Noble, 2004; Rothbard and Wilk, 2011; Totterdell, 1999).

Finally, several studies have focused on how short-term variability in situational factors—especially *task characteristics*—can influence performance as main effects and/or through their moderating effects on motivational processes. For example, Stewart and Nandkeolyar (2006) found that weekly variations in situational opportunity (specifically sales referrals) accounted for over 60% of WPVP among salespeople. Stewart and Nandkeolyar (2007) found a negative effect of constraints created by other people (teammates and opponents) on WPVP of professional footballers. Minbashian and Luppino (2014) examined within-person effects of task complexity on the performance of professional tennis players; they found that, in addition to its negative main effect on performance, tasks that are overly simple or overly complex constrain the effect of motivational resources on performance. Other researchers working within the theoretical framework of the Job Demands-Resources (JD-R) model (Demerouti, Bakker, Nachreiner, and Schaufeli, 2001) have recast this model in within-person terms, and have found that daily and weekly fluctuations in job resources (e.g., autonomy, feedback, coaching, and learning opportunities) are positively associated with WPVP (e.g., Bakker and Bal, 2010). Taken together, these findings demonstrate the main and moderating effects of short-term fluctuations in environmental opportunities and constraints on WPVP.

4.4.2 Long-Term Variability

A second type of within-person variability is in the form of long-term performance trends in studies that typically examine job performance over several months or years. Research indicates that performance typically increases at a decreasing rate over such periods, where the specific rate of change is likely to vary across individuals (e.g., Hofmann, Jacobs, and Gerras, 1992; Thoresen, Bradley, Bliese, and Thoresen, 2004). Furthermore, when assessed over long periods, performance has been observed to eventually decline (e.g., Minbashian, Earl, and Bright, 2013; Minbashian and Luppino, 2014). Although such effects are often proxied by temporal variables such as job experience, tenure, and aging, the true underlying causal factors are likely to result from changes in the knowledge, skills, abilities, and other attributes of individuals that covary with time (see Sturman, 2003), as well as from changes in the nature of the tasks and jobs that are performed.

The changing-subjects model and changing-tasks model (see Alvares and Hulin, 1972) have traditionally been the dominant models for explaining long-term performance variability. The changing-subjects model explains long-term performance variability as resulting from changes within individuals in the levels of the attributes that facilitate performance. That is, increasing practice and experience on a task or job leads to acquisition of the knowledge, skills, and abilities required to perform the job, and this in turn leads to changes in performance (see Sturman, 2007). Attitudinal variables may also change over time, either increasing or decreasing as a function of repeated exposure to and experiences with the work environment (Schleicher, Hansen, and Fox, 2010). For example, Boswell, Boudreau, and Tichy (2005) observed that job satisfaction initially increases after starting a new job ("the honeymoon effect") but then declines over time ("the hangover effect"). Consequently, to the extent that work attitudes such as job satisfaction and organizational commitment influence motivation and performance at work (see Katzell and Thompson, 1990), long-term changes in performance may come about as a result of changes in work attitudes.

In contrast, the changing-tasks model explains long-term performance variability as resulting from changes over time in the contributions of different attributes to performance. In this view, the levels of the attributes possessed by an individual need not change, although the effect of different attributes on performance change with experience (where some attributes may become less important, and others more so). Early explanations for this phenomenon focused on changes in task structure that occur as a result of skill acquisition (see Alvares and Hulin, 1972). For example, Ackerman (1988) has proposed a model in which skill acquisition on tasks with consistent information processing demands moves across three phases, characterized by increasing automaticity of information processing. As an individual moves across the phases, the initial demands on cognitive ability decline and are replaced by increasing demands on perceptual speed and psychomotor abilities.

Beyond changes in task structure, broader changes in tasks, responsibilities, and expectations can occur over time; for example, when a new technology is introduced, when a job is redesigned, or when a promotion results in new duties that the employee is required to fulfill (Murphy, 1989). Although such changes in job and organizational characteristics can ultimately lead to improved performance (e.g., when job redesign leads to greater autonomy or when new technology improves opportunities to perform), they may initially place demands on knowledge and skills that the individual does not possess. Murphy has proposed a stage-based model of performance that explains how such changes in aspects of the job interact with an individual's attributes to influence performance. Murphy distinguishes between two distinct stages of job performance: a *transitional stage* that follows change, in which the individual is performing novel tasks or under new conditions; and a *maintenance stage* in which no change has taken place and the major tasks are familiar to the individual. During transitional stages (e.g., when starting a new job) performance is low, but it increases rapidly as new knowledge and skills are acquired through experience. The rate of this acquisition is determined by cognitive ability. During maintenance stages performance increases less rapidly as tasks are already well learned, although further experience (e.g., in the form of deliberate practice; see Ericsson, Krampe, and Tresch-Römer, 1993) can continue to lead to improvements over many years, assuming adequate levels of motivation.

4.4.3 The Role of Individual Differences

The main effects of relatively fixed individual difference variables such as intelligence and personality on *between-person* variability in performance are well established. For example, general mental ability is widely considered as the best individual difference predictor of performance across jobs (see Schmidt and Hunter, 1998). Of the Big Five personality factors, conscientiousness has been shown to be the strongest predictor of performance across jobs, whereas other factors such as neuroticism, extroversion, openness to experience, and agreeableness predict performance in certain jobs and on certain criteria (Barrick, Mount, and Judge, 2001). However, additionally, such individual difference attributes may also play a role in WPVP through their moderating effects on within-person effects.

First, individual difference variables can have a top-down effect on the situational effects and resource-allocation processes that underlie short-term WPVP. This is particularly true in the case of personality, which has previously been conceptualized in terms of how strongly individuals respond to situational triggers (e.g., Tett and Burnett, 2003). For example, the within-person effect of aversive situational events at work on negative affect has been shown to be stronger for highly neurotic individuals compared to individuals low on neuroticism (e.g., Rodell and Judge, 2009; Yang and Diefendorff, 2009). In contrast, conscientiousness has been linked to self-regulatory processes involved in WPVP. For example, a high level of conscientiousness weakens the negative within-person effect of negative affect on-task performance (Chi, Chang, and Huang, 2015) and the positive within-person effect of negative affect on counterproductive workplace behavior (Yang and Diefendorff, 2009).

Second, individual difference variables predict between-person differences in long-term performance growth and decline. For example, according to Murphy's (1989) model, cognitive ability should predict the rate of increase in performance in the transition stages of a job. In support, Deadrick, Bennett, and Russell (1997) found that higher cognitive ability was associated with a stronger linear increase in performance among sewing machine operators in their first 24 weeks on the job. With respect to personality, conscientiousness has been proposed to predict performance growth, although tests of this hypothesis have provided mixed findings (Thoresen, Bradley, Bliese, and Thoresen, 2004). Openness to experience has been shown to predict performance changes in transitional job stages; the performance of highly open individuals plateaus at a slower rate compared with their low-openness colleagues (Thoresen, Bradley, Bliese, and Thoresen, 2004; Minbashian, Earl, and Bright, 2013).

Finally, although individual differences such as intelligence and personality are usually conceptualized as invariant aspects of individuals, longitudinal studies provide evidence for change over the lifespan and such change may at least partly account for long-term changes in performance. For example, although experiential and educational knowledge tends to increase across one's working life, fluid intelligence is known to peak in young adulthood and decline thereafter (see Kanfer and Ackerman, 2004). In contrast, desirable personality characteristics such as conscientiousness and emotional stability increase across one's working life (Roberts, Walton, and Viechtbauer, 2006), which may partially compensate for the loss in fluid intelligence.

4.4.4 Integrative Summary: A Three-Level Model of Individual Performance

As outlined by Minbashian and Luppino (2014), the three sources of performance variability discussed above (short-term WPVP, long-term WPVP, and individual differences) can be integrated within a single multilevel model. At any given point in time, each individual has a typical (or "true") level of performance that is determined by their relevant knowledge, skills, abilities, and other attributes, in the context of the opportunities and constraints inherent in the broader environment (e.g., job and organizational characteristics). In the short term (level 1 of the model), variability in performance around this true level can occur as a result of the variations in the situational cues individuals are exposed to, which trigger cognitive, affective, and self-regulatory processes that influence resource allocation. The specific effects on performance will also depend on situational opportunities and constraints, which may either directly influence performance or else moderate the effect of resource-allocation processes on performance. Over longer periods of time (level 2 of the model), the true level of the individual's performance and/or the sensitivity of their performance to situational cues may also change. This can occur, for example, as a result of the acquisition of new knowledge or skills that comes with increasing experience, changes in work attitudes, or changes in job characteristics. Finally, aspects of individuals that show little or no variability across time (level 3 of the model)—such as intelligence and personality (see Silzer and Church, 2009)—can affect between-person differences in true performance at a given point in time, between-person differences in the sensitivity of performance to situational cues, and between-person differences in the growth in true performance over time.[1]

4.5 Implications of WPVP for Talent Management

As part of their review of the strategic talent-management literature, Collings and Mellahi (2009) highlight the critical mediating role of individual performance in the relationship between strategic talent management and organizational outcomes. Thus, understanding the factors that drive individual performance is important for both the definition of what it means to be talented and the development of talent-management practices that are likely to be effective. To that effect, Collings and Mellahi presented the AMO model as a framework for explaining individual performance. The model describes performance as a function of the employee's ability (or capacity to perform), motivation (or willingness to perform), and opportunity to perform (see Blumberg and Pringle, 1982). This framework has heuristic value in identifying the broad classes of variables that influence individual performance, although the specific mechanisms and processes through which variables influence performance are left unspecified, thereby leaving unanswered questions about when and how performance is maximized. In this regard, the findings from the literature on WPVP and the three-level model presented in this chapter complement the AMO framework in at least three ways.

First, the three-level model explicitly distinguishes between the stable versus dynamic aspects of performance. This is important because, as will be discussed below, the extent of performance variability at each level is relevant for identifying the type of management practices that are likely to bring about an improvement in the performance of an organization's talent (cf. Meyers, Van Woerkom, and Dries, 2013). Second, the literature on WPVP identifies specific variables within the broad classes of ability, motivation, and opportunity that are relevant in facilitating performance at each of the three levels of the model. Table 4.1 provides a summary of how variables at each level map on to the three classes of the AMO framework. The table is provided for illustrative purposes; it does not exhaustively list all the relevant variables at each level and in each class. Relatedly, the talent-management literature uses a range of variables to assess talent, and these could be mapped on to the cells in Table 4.1. For example, Silzer and Church's (2009) foundational and career dimensions map onto levels 3 and 2 of the three-level model respectively; and the "meta-competencies" learning agility (Dries, Vantilborgh, and Pepermans, 2012) and emotional intelligence (Dries and Pepermans, 2007) fit at level 3.

Third, the three-level model provides a framework for considering various processes through which variables at each level influence performance, including how ability, motivation and opportunity variables dynamically interact both within and between levels. This is particularly important, as the AMO framework (as originally stated; see Blumberg and Pringle, 1982) assumes interactive relationships among ability, motivation, and opportunity. Furthermore, this assumption has important implications for how talent-management practices should be implemented, yet the veracity of the assumption may vary based on the level at which each variable is conceptualized. In this regard, the findings from the WPVP literature described above provide some insight into interactive effects that occur among variables at the same level and at different levels. For example, studies that have examined ability x motivation interactions among variables at level 3 (e.g., Mount, Barrick, and Strauss, 1999; Sackett, Gruys, and Ellingson, 1998) have failed to support an interaction effect; however, studies that have examined the interaction between level-3 ability and level-1 motivation variables have found significant interactions (e.g., Kanfer and Ackerman, 1989; Yeo and Neal, 2004), albeit in a different form to that originally predicted by the AMO framework.

The rest of this chapter will discuss the implications of the findings from the WPVP literature and the three-level model for the conceptualization of talent and specific talent-management practices.

Table 4.1 Ability, Motivation, and Opportunity Variables at Each Level of the Three-Level Model of Individual Performance

Form of Variability	Ability/Capacity	Motivation/Willingness	Opportunities and Constraints
Level 1: short-term WPVP	Self-regulatory capacity	Cognitive processes Affective reactions	Situational and task characteristics
Level 2: long-term WPVP	Job-relevant knowledge and skills	Work attitudes	Job characteristics Organizational characteristics
Level 3: individual differences	Intelligence	Personality	

WPVP = Within-person variability in performance.

4.5.1 The Conceptualization of Talent

Disagreement about the definition of *talent* has been the cause of much conceptual ambiguity in the talent-management field (Lewis and Heckman, 2006; Meyers, Van Woerkom, and Dries, 2013). In this regard, Dries (2013) has identified five sources of tension in the literature based on differing perspectives on talent. Below I outline each source of tension and discuss the position of a WPVP approach with respect to each.

The *object versus subject* tension distinguishes between talent as people (the subject perspective) and talent as characteristics of people (the object perspective). The object perspective conceptualizes talent in terms of an individual's attributes; that is, talent comprises unique abilities, in conjunction with knowledge and skills that are acquired through practice, and commitment, all of which facilitate the achievement of superior performance in a given context (Gallardo-Gallardo, Dries, and Gonzalez-Cruz, 2013). In the subject perspective, the term *talent* refers to people (rather than to their characteristics) as the source of what needs to be managed. Within this perspective, the term may be used broadly to apply to all employees within the organization, or may be applied more narrowly to those individuals who are high performers or who have high potential relative to others (Gallardo-Gallardo, Dries, and Gonzalez-Cruz, 2013). The distinction between object versus subject perspectives is important because of its implications for what talent management should manage (Dries, 2013). In this regard, the three-level model of performance is clearly based on an object perspective: Talent can be conceptualized in terms of the abilities, knowledge, and skills, and other personal attributes that define levels 2 and 3 of the three-level model, and that interact with the opportunities and constraints in the environment to influence performance. Talent management, in turn, is primarily concerned with selecting for and developing these characteristics, and, importantly, managing the situational and environmental factors that trigger resource-allocation processes or act as opportunities or constraints to performance.

The *inclusive versus exclusive* tension pertains to whether talent-management efforts should apply to all employees or a subset of employees. An inclusive approach assumes that all individuals have their talents and it seeks to maximize each individual's contribution. As noted by others (e.g., Thunnissen, Boselie, and Fruytier, 2013), an inclusive approach does not distinguish talent management from the more general discipline of human resource management. Furthermore, focusing on all employees in all positions fails to recognize that different positions may differentially contribute to the firm's strategic objectives; consequently, given a limited pool of resources, organizations need to identify and invest their resources in those positions that are likely to deliver the greatest strategic value (Collings and Mellahi, 2009). Beyond the identification of such key positions, a second consideration relates to the extent to which organizations differentiate between individuals within such strategic roles (see Collings, 2017; Collings and Mellahi, 2009). The three-level model suggests that a relevant factor in justifying an exclusive approach among employees in a given strategic position is the extent to which between-person (i.e., level 3) performance variability constitutes a substantive component of overall performance variability. When between-person variability is trivially small, individuals differ minimally in the value they generate for the organization, and, consequently, differentiating between employees is unwarranted. In contrast, Figure 4.1 demonstrates that even when between-person variability is moderate (27% in this case), the typical difference in value creation (in terms of dollar sales) between average and high performers is substantial.

The *innate versus acquired* tension refers to whether talent is best conceptualized as part of an individual's innate nature, or whether it is something that can be learned. As discussed by Meyers, Van Woerkom, and Dries (2013), the distinction describes a continuum upon which definitions of talent can range from the innate extreme (e.g., talent as the genetically determined aspects of intelligence) to the acquired extreme (e.g., talent as purely a function of deliberate practice). One's position on the continuum determines whether talent management should place more focus on the identification and selection of talent (at the innate end) versus the development of talent (Dries, 2013). The three-level model contains constructs that are largely governed by genetic factors (e.g., intelligence and personality; see Bouchard, 2004), as well as constructs that are acquired through experience (e.g., job-specific knowledge and skills). Consequently, the model is best positioned away from either of the extremes of the innate versus acquired continuum, although the specific contribution of innate versus acquired factors to performance is also likely to depend on the job. Moreover, to the extent that stable individual differences (at level 3) and learning experiences (at level 2) have a synergistic multiplicative effect on performance (e.g., see Yeo and Neal, 2004), it becomes particularly important to simultaneously combine both selection and developmental activities.

The *input versus output* tension distinguishes between talent as motivation and talent as ability. The input perspective sees talent as more about motivational factors such as effort and ambition, whereas the output perspective conceptualizes talent as an ability, as assessed via achievements, results, and hard performance data (Dries, 2013). The three-level model represents both ability and motivation at each of the three levels, although the relative effect of each is likely to vary across jobs and job stages (Murphy, 1989). Moreover, the two factors have been shown to interact in complex ways (e.g., Kanfer and Ackerman, 1989). Consequently, focusing predominantly on one factor in conceptualizing talent can result in a misleading assessment of an individual's potential performance.

Finally, the tension between the *transferable versus context-dependent* perspectives refers to whether talent can be transferred across environments or whether it is conditional on its environment (Dokko and Jang, 2017; Dries, 2013). In the context of an object approach to talent, this tension can be reinterpreted as the extent to which the individual attributes that comprise talent generalize across environments. In the three-level model, this tension is addressed by the possibility that individual attributes at levels 2 and 3 of the model have interactive effects with contextual factors (e.g., job and organizational characteristics). To the extent that interactive effects are absent, the effects of the attributes on performance can be said to generalize across contexts. However, evidence suggests that even innate attributes have contextually dependent effects. For example, context-dependence is widely evident in relation to personality factors, including the conscientiousness factor (see Tett and Burnett, 2003). Similarly, the effects of general mental ability are known to vary considerably across settings and time (see Murphy, 1989).

4.5.2 Specific Talent-Management Practices

In addition to their broad implications, the literature on WPVP and the three-level model highlights several specific practices for how organizations can better identify and manage their talent. Here I will discuss issues related to employee assessment and employee motivation.

4.5.2.1 *Employee Assessment*

A relevant approach to talent management comes from the personnel selection and performance appraisal traditions in the industrial-organizational psychology literature, which strongly emphasize employee assessment and individual differences (Dries, 2013; see also Highhouse and Brooks, 2017). In this approach, performance appraisal is used to assess an individual's performance aggregated over a given period. Such performance measures are then used as "criteria" in studies in which predictors, such as cognitive ability and personality measures, are validated for personnel selection purposes by demonstrating their correlation with the criteria (e.g., Schmidt and Hunter, 1998). Employee assessment is also one of the most prevalent approaches in the talent-management literature (Gallardo-Gallardo, Nijs, Dries, and Gallo, 2015). In this context, talent is conceptualized as comprising various intellectual and nonintellectual attributes that are assessed using measures of abilities and personal dispositions (Nijs, Gallardo-Gallardo, Dries, and Sels, 2014). The validity of such measures is demonstrated by their accuracy in predicting excellence in performance, where the latter criterion is typically operationalized using some aggregated measure of performance (see Nijs, Gallardo-Gallardo, Dries, and Sels, 2014).

The findings on WPVP contribute to the employee assessment approach in two ways. First, the three-level model of WPVP identifies two additional criteria beyond aggregated performance outcomes, namely, individual differences in performance trends over time and individual differences in performance fluctuations across situations. A performance trend captures the rate at which an individual's performance changes over time and, therefore, may indicate an individual's likely *future* performance. For example, an individual may initially perform at a lower level than their equally inexperienced colleagues, but display a faster rate of increase in their performance within a given time period, such that they ultimately perform at a higher level than their colleagues. Consequently, performance trends tap into an individual's propensity to learn from experience and, therefore, can be conceived as indicators of *potential* that can be used as a relevant criteria for the validation of specific tools that assess high-potential talent (see Church and Rotolo, 2013). Individual differences in performance fluctuations also carry useful information about the individual, although the specific interpretation of this information will depend upon the situational cues across which performance varies. For example, Minbashian, Wood, and Beckmann (2010) examined individual differences in the extent to which conscientious behavior varies as a function of task demand. They interpreted such differences as providing information about an individual's *adaptability*, a construct that is a core component in models of potential (see Silzer and Church, 2009).

Second, the use of performance trends and performance fluctuations as criteria provides new perspective on the usefulness of established predictors in identifying talent. For example, the personality variable *openness to experience* is one of the least useful of the Big Five for talent identification based on its negligible correlation with job performance in meta-analyses (see Barrick, Mount, and Judge, 2001). However, its validity in predicting how quickly individuals plateau over time (Minbashian, Earl, and Bright, 2013; Thoresen, Bradley, Bliese, and Thoresen, 2004) suggests that it may be useful for identifying individuals who are likely to perform well over the long term. In contrast, conscientiousness, which is considered the strongest Big Five predictor of performance (Barrick, Mount, and Judge, 2001), has been shown to correlate negatively with the extent to which conscious behavior fluctuates as a function of task demand (Minbashian, Wood, and Beckmann, 2010), thus indicating a potential negative implication of this personality factor in relation to being adaptable.

4.5.2.2 *Motivating Employees*

The critical role of motivation in talent management has previously been highlighted (e.g., Collings and Mellahi, 2009). The findings on WPVP suggest that motivation is largely a level-1 phenomenon; that is, a substantive part of the effect of motivation on performance is due to variability in resource-allocation processes that are reflected in short-term WPVP. Consequently, management practices are required that manage motivation at this level. In this regard, it is important to note that many procedures traditionally used to motivate employees—such as long-term goal setting that takes place in annual performance reviews, financial incentives that are linked to yearly performance, and job enrichment efforts (see Robbins, Judge, Millett, and Boyle, 2011)—do not directly address the issue of short-term WPVP. Such factors are constant across tasks and performance episodes and, therefore, do not explain why an individual performs well on some tasks but not so well on others. Rather, these latter deficits need to be addressed by considering motivational processes that occur at the level of the task.

The findings reported in this chapter provide several suggestions as to how this might be accomplished. First, individuals allocate less of their motivational resources to a task when the link between performance on the task and attractive rewards is not clear, or when they do not perceive a strong link between effort expenditure and performance on the task. Consequently, factors that increase the strength of these perceived links—such as task-related financial and social incentives, specific goal assignments, and performance feedback (see Kanfer, 1987)—can be used to increase motivation at the task level. Such task-level motivators are likely to be particularly effective on moderately complex tasks that have yet to be automatized (Minbashian and Luppino, 2014). However, given the limited nature of the self-regulatory resources available to individuals (Muraven and Baumeister, 2000), task-level motivators should not be used indiscriminately, but rather should be used as a tool for ensuring that individuals are maximally motivated when performing those tasks that are most important in contributing to the organization's strategic objectives.

Second, organizations can put in place initiatives that increase the amount of self-regulatory resources available to the individual, which in turn allows the individual to stay focused on a task for longer and to perform at a high level more consistently (see Dalal, Bhave, and Fiset, 2014). As described above, research on WPVP has provided evidence for the importance of rest and recovery experiences in restoring regulatory resources (Binnewies, Sonnentag, and Mojza, 2009, 2010; Trougakos, Beal, Green, and Weiss, 2008). Dalal, Bhave, and Fiset (2014) outline several suggestions for organizational interventions that would facilitate such recovery experiences. Beyond these, evidence exists that regulatory resources can be increased over the long term with practice on relatively simple self-control tasks (see Muraven and Baumeister, 2000). Consequently, organizations could develop training programs based on this evidence.

Finally, findings highlight the important role of affect in motivational processes that influence a range of performance outcomes. Positive affect tends to increase task performance and organizational citizenship behavior, whereas negative affect decreases task performance and increases counterproductive behavior (Chi, Chang, and Huang, 2015; Rodell and Judge, 2009). However, in some cases, moderate amounts of negative affect can facilitate performance, too, especially when elicited by the performance task itself (e.g., Beckmann, Beckmann, Minbashian, and Birney, 2013). Managerial practices that can be used to manage affect include personnel selection based on attributes that predict susceptibility to various emotions (a level-3 intervention), training programs that equip individuals with emotion management skills (a level-2 intervention), and the minimization of daily hassles at work (a level-1 intervention).

4.6 Conclusions and Future Directions

As part of her review of the psychology of talent management, Dries (2013) has called for further empirical work that, among other things, investigates the "shortitudinal" and "longitudinal" processes that underlie fluctuations and growth in performance. The chapter contributes to this aim by summarizing relevant research from the literature on WPVP and presenting a framework from the literature that can be used to organize such findings. Although this research was not originally framed in the language and concepts of talent management, it aligns well with current models of individual performance advocated in the talent-management literature (e.g., Collings and Mellahi, 2009), and, further, it explicitly distinguishes between the dynamic and stable factors that interact to determine performance. In terms of its conceptualization of talent, the framework adopts an object-oriented exclusive approach to talent that recognizes the potential importance of both innate and acquired attributes, motivational and ability-based factors, and the context-dependence of talent.

Future work is required to integrate the framework with talent-management research. An initial direction could be to map constructs from the tools currently used for talent assessment (e.g., Silzer and Church, 2009) onto the relevant cells in Table 4.1, and to evaluate their predictive validity in relation to the dynamic criteria outlined in the chapter. Second, although the framework identifies key factors that generate variability in performance at each level, the relative importance of the factors and the way they interact may differ from job to job, as may the relative proportions of variability at each level. As this has implications for the types of talent-management practices that are likely to be effective for any given job, another avenue for research will be to compare findings for strategic versus non-strategic jobs. Ultimately, the value of the framework for talent management should be judged by its ability to suggest effective strategies for managing talent. Consequently, studies are required that evaluate whether talent-management systems that are aligned with the nature of relationships captured by the framework lead to improved individual and organizational performance.

NOTE

1. The proposed framework also allows for examining between-person differences in the rate at which the sensitivity of performance to situational cues changes over time (see Minbashian and Luppino, 2014), although this more complex form of change is not considered here.

REFERENCES

Ackerman, P. L. 1988. Determinants of individual differences during skill acquisition: cognitive abilities and information processing. *Journal of Experimental Psychology: General, 117,* pp.288–318.

Alvares, K. M., and Hulin, C. L. 1972. Two explanations of temporal changes in ability-skill relationships: a literature review and theoretical analysis. *Human Factors: The Journal of the Human Factors and Ergonomics Society, 14*(4), pp.295–308.

Bakker, A. B., and Bal, P. M. 2010. Weekly work engagement and performance: a study among starting teachers. *Journal of Occupational and Organizational Psychology, 83,* pp.189–206.

Bandura, A. 1977. Self-efficacy: toward a unifying theory of behavioral change. *Psychological Review, 84,* pp.191–215.

Barrick, M. R., Mount, M. K., and Judge, T. A. 2001. Personality and performance at the beginning of the new millennium: what do we know and where do we go next? *International Journal of Selection and Assessment, 9,* pp.9–30.

Baumeister, R. F., Vohs, K. D., and Tice, D. M. 2007. The strength model of self-control. *Current Directions in Psychological Science, 16,* pp.351–5.

Beal, D. J., Weiss, H. M., Barros, E., and MacDermid, S. M. 2005. An episodic process model of affective influences on performance. *Journal of Applied Psychology*, 90, pp.1054–68.

Beckmann, N., Beckmann, J. F., Minbashian, A., and Birney, D. P. 2013. In the heat of the moment: on the effect of state neuroticism on task performance. *Personality and Individual Differences*, 54, pp.447–52.

Binnewies, C., Sonnentag, S., and Mojza, E. J. 2009. Daily performance at work: feeling recovered in the morning as a predictor of day-level job performance. *Journal of Organizational Behavior*, 30, pp.67–93.

Binnewies, C., Sonnentag, S., and Mojza, E. J. 2010. Recovery during the weekend and fluctuations in weekly job performance: a week-level study examining intra-individual relationships. *Journal of Occupational and Organizational Psychology*, 83, pp.419–41.

Blumberg, M., and Pringle, C. D. 1982. The missing opportunity in organizational research: some implications for a theory of work performance. *Academy of Management Review*, 7, pp.560–9.

Borman, W. C., and Motowidlo, S. J. 1997. Task performance and contextual performance: the meaning for personnel selection research. *Human Performance*, 10, pp.99–109.

Boswell, W. R., Boudreau, J. W., and Tichy, J. 2005. The relationship between employee job change and job satisfaction: the honeymoon-hangover effect. *Journal of Applied Psychology*, 90, p.882.

Bouchard, T. J. 2004. Genetic influence on human psychological traits: a survey. *Current Directions in Psychological Science*, 13, pp.148–51.

Chi, N. W., Chang, H. T., and Huang, H. L. 2015. Can personality traits and daily positive mood buffer the harmful effects of daily negative mood on task performance and service sabotage? A self-control perspective. *Organizational Behavior and Human Decision Processes*, 131, pp.1–15.

Church, A. H., and Rotolo, C. T. 2013. How are top companies assessing their high-potentials and senior executives? A talent management benchmark study. *Consulting Psychology Journal: Practice and Research*, 65, pp.199–223.

Collings, D. G. 2017. Workforce differentiation. In D. G. Collings, K. Mellahi, and W. F. Cascio, eds., *Oxford handbook of talent management*. Oxford: Oxford University Press.

Collings, D. G., and Mellahi, K. 2009. Strategic talent management: a review and research agenda. *Human Resource Management Review*, 19, pp.304–13.

Crant, J. M. 2000. Proactive behavior in organizations. *Journal of Management*, 26, pp.435–62.

Dalal, R. S., Bhave, D. P., and Fiset, J. 2014. Within-person variability in job performance: a theoretical review and research agenda. *Journal of Management*, 40, 1396–436.

Dalal, R. S., Lam, H., Weiss, H. M., Welch, E. R. et al. 2009. A within-person approach to work behavior and performance: concurrent and lagged citizenship-counterproductivity associations, and dynamic relationships with affect and overall job performance. *Academy of Management Journal*, 52(5), pp.1051–66.

Deadrick, D. L., Bennett, N., and Russell, C. J. 1997. Using hierarchical linear modeling to examine dynamic performance criteria over time. *Journal of Management*, 23, pp.745–57.

Demerouti, E., Bakker, A. B., Nachreiner, F., and Schaufeli, W. B. 2001. The job demands-resources model of burnout. *Journal of Applied Psychology*, 86, pp.499–512.

Dokko, G., and Jang, W. 2017. The portability of performance. In D. G. Collings, K. Mellahi, and W. F. Cascio, eds., *Oxford handbook of talent management*. Oxford: Oxford University Press.

Dries, N. 2013. The psychology of talent management: a review and research agenda. *Human Resource Management Review*, 23, pp.272–85.

Dries, N., and Pepermans, R. 2007. Using emotional intelligence to identify high potential: a meta-competency perspective. *Leadership and Organization Development Journal*, *28*, pp.749–70.

Dries, N., Vantilborgh, T., and Pepermans, R. 2012. The role of learning agility and career variety in the identification and development of high potential employees. *Personnel Review*, *41*, pp.340–58.

Ericsson, K. A., Krampe, R. T., and Tesch-Römer, C. 1993. The role of deliberate practice in the acquisition of expert performance. *Psychological Review*, *100*, pp.363–406.

Fisher, C. D. 2008. What if we took within-person performance variation seriously? *Industrial and Organizational Psychology*, *1*(2), pp.185–9.

Fisher, C. D., and Noble, C. S. 2004. A within-person examination of correlates of performance and emotions while working. *Human Performance*, *17*, pp.145–68.

Fisher, C. D., and To, M. L. 2012. Using experience sampling methodology in organizational behavior. *Journal of Organizational Behavior*, *33*, pp.865–77.

Gallardo-Gallardo, E., Dries, N., and González-Cruz, T. F. 2013. What is the meaning of "talent" in the world of work? *Human Resource Management Review*, *23*, pp.290–300.

Gallardo-Gallardo, E., Nijs, S., Dries, N., and Gallo, P. 2015. Towards an understanding of talent management as a phenomenon-driven field using bibliometric and content analysis. *Human Resource Management Review*, *25*, pp.264–79.

Highhouse, S. and Brooks, M. 2017. Talent selection. In D. G. Collings, K. Mellahi, and W. F. Cascio, eds., *Oxford handbook of talent management*. Oxford: Oxford University Press.

Hofmann, D. A., Jacobs, R., and Gerras, S. J. 1992. Mapping individual performance over time. *Journal of Applied Psychology*, *77*, pp.185–95.

Ilies, R., Scott, B. A., and Judge, T. A. 2006. The interactive effects of personal traits and experienced states on intraindividual patterns of citizenship behavior. *Academy of Management Journal*, *49*(3), pp.561–75.

Kanfer, R. 1987. Task-specific motivation: an integrative approach to issues of measurement, mechanisms, processes, and determinants. *Journal of Social and Clinical Psychology*, *5*, pp.237–64.

Kanfer, R. 1990. Motivation theory and industrial and organizational psychology. In M. D. Dunnette and L. M. Hough, eds., *Handbook of Industrial and Organizational Psychology*, 2nd edn., pp.75–170. Palo Alto, CA: Consulting Psychologists Press.

Kanfer, R., and Ackerman, P. L. 1989. Motivation and cognitive abilities: an integrative/aptitude-treatment interaction approach to skill acquisition. *Journal of Applied Psychology*, *74*, pp.657–90.

Kanfer, R., and Ackerman, P. L. 2004. Aging, adult development, and work motivation. *Academy of Management Review*, *29*, pp.440–58.

Katzell, R. A., and Thompson, D. E. 1990. An integrative model of work attitudes, motivation, and performance. *Human Performance*, *3*, pp.63–85.

Lewis, R. E., and Heckman, R. J. 2006. Talent management: a critical review. *Human Resource Management Review*, *16*, pp.139–54.

Locke, E. A., Shaw, K. N., Saari, L. M., and Latham, G. P. 1981. Goal setting and task performance: 1969–1980. *Psychological Bulletin*, *90*, p.125.

Meyers, M. C., Van Woerkom, M., and Dries, N. (2013). Talent—innate or acquired? Theoretical considerations and their implications for talent management. *Human Resource Management Review*, *23*, pp.305–21.

Minbashian, A., Earl, J., and Bright, J. E. H. 2013. Openness to experience as a predictor of job performance trajectories. *Applied Psychology: An International Review*, *62*, pp.1–12.

Minbashian, A., and Luppino, D. 2014. Short-term and long-term within-person variability in performance: an integrative model. *Journal of Applied Psychology*, 99, pp.898–914.

Minbashian, A., Wood, R. E., and Beckmann, N. 2010. Task-contingent conscientiousness as a unit of personality at work. *Journal of Applied Psychology*, 95, pp.793–806.

Mischel, W., and Shoda, Y. 1995. A cognitive-affective system theory of personality: reconceptualizing situations, dispositions, dynamics, and invariance in personality structure. *Psychological Review*, 102, pp.246–68.

Mount, M. K., Barrick, M. R., and Strauss, J. P. 1999. The joint relationship of conscientiousness and ability with performance: test of the interaction hypothesis. *Journal of Management*, 25, pp.707–21.

Muraven, M., and Baumeister, R. F. 2000. Self-regulation and depletion of limited resources: does self-control resemble a muscle? *Psychological Bulletin*, 126(2), p.247.

Murphy, K. R. 1989. Is the relationship between cognitive ability and job performance stable over time? *Human Performance*, 2, pp.183–200.

Nijs, S., Gallardo-Gallardo, E., Dries, N., and Sels, L. 2014. A multidisciplinary review into the definition, operationalization, and measurement of talent. *Journal of World Business*, 49, pp.180–91.

Organ, D. W. 1997. Organizational citizenship behavior: it's construct clean-up time. *Human Performance*, 10, pp.85–97.

Robbins, S., Judge, T. A., Millett, B., and Boyle, M. 2011. *Organisational behaviour*, 6th edn. Frenchs Forest, NSW, Australia: Pearson.

Roberts, B. W., Walton, K. E., and Viechtbauer, W. 2006. Patterns of mean-level change in personality traits across the life course: a meta-analysis of longitudinal studies. *Psychological Bulletin*, 132, pp.1–25.

Rodell, J. B., and Judge, T. A. 2009. Can "good" stressors spark "bad" behaviors? The mediating role of emotions in links of challenge and hindrance stressors with citizenship and counterproductive behaviors. *Journal of Applied Psychology*, 94, pp.1438–51.

Rothbard, N. P., and Wilk, S. L. 2011. Waking up on the right or wrong side of the bed: start-of-workday mood, work events, employee affect, and performance. *Academy of Management Journal*, 54, pp.959–80.

Sackett, P. R. 2002. The structure of counterproductive work behaviors: dimensionality and relationships with facets of job performance. *International Journal of Selection and Assessment*, 10, pp.5–11.

Sackett, P. R., Gruys, M. L., and Ellingson, J. E. 1998. Ability–personality interactions when predicting job performance. *Journal of Applied Psychology*, 83, pp.545–56.

Schleicher, D. J., Hansen, D., and Fox, K. E. 2010. Job attitudes and work values. In S. Zedeck, ed., *APA handbook of industrial and organizational psychology*, Vol. 3, pp.137–90. Washington, DC: APA.

Schmidt, F. L., and Hunter, J. E. 1998. The validity and utility of selection methods in personnel psychology: practical and theoretical implications of 85 years of research findings. *Psychological Bulletin*, 124, pp.262–74.

Silzer, R., and Church, A. H. 2009. The pearls and perils of identifying potential. *Industrial and Organizational Psychology*, 2, pp.377–412.

Sitzmann, T., and Yeo, G. 2013. A meta-analytic investigation of the within-person self-efficacy domain: is self-efficacy a product of past performance or a driver of future performance? *Personnel Psychology*, 66, pp.531–68.

Sonnentag, S., and Frese, M. 2012. Dynamic performance. In S. W. J. Kozlowski, ed., *Handbook of industrial and organizational psychology*, pp.548–75. New York: Oxford University Press.

Stewart, G. L., and Nandkeolyar, A. K. 2006. Adaptation and intraindividual variation in sales outcomes: exploring the interactive effects of personality and environmental opportunity. *Personnel Psychology*, 59, pp.307–32.

Stewart, G. L., and Nandkeolyar, A. K. 2007. Exploring how constrains created by other people influence intraindividual variation in objective performance measures. *Journal of Applied Psychology*, 92, pp.1149–58.

Sturman, M. C. 2003. Searching for the inverted U-shaped relationship between time and performance: meta-analyses of the experience/performance, tenure/performance, and age/performance relationships. *Journal of Management*, 29, pp.609–40.

Sturman, M. C. 2007. The past, present, and future of dynamic performance research. *Research in Personnel and Human Resources Management*, 26, pp.49–110.

Tett, R. P., and Burnett, D. D. 2003. A personality trait-based interactionist model of job performance. *Journal of Applied Psychology*, 88, pp.500–17.

Thoresen, C. J., Bradley, J. C., Bliese, P. D., and Thoresen, J. D. 2004. The big five personality traits and individual job performance growth trajectories in maintenance and transitional job stages. *Journal of Applied Psychology*, 89, pp.835–53.

Thunnissen, M., Boselie, P., and Fruytier, B. 2013. A review of talent management: infancy or adolescence? *The International Journal of Human Resource Management*, 24(9), pp.1744–61.

Totterdell, P. 1999. Mood scores: mood and performance in professional cricketers. *British Journal of Psychology*, 90, pp.317–32.

Trougakos, J. P., Beal, D. J., Green, S. G., and Weiss, H. M. 2008. Making the break count: an episodic examination of recovery activities, emotional experiences, and positive affective displays. *Academy of Management Journal*, 51(1), pp.131–46.

Vancouver, J. B., and Kendall, L. N. 2006. When self-efficacy negatively relates to motivation and performance in a learning context. *Journal of Applied Psychology*, 91, pp.1146–53.

Vroom, V. 1964. *Work and motivation*. New York: Jon Wiley and Sons.

Weiss, H. M., and Cropanzano, R. 1996. Affective events theory. *Research in Organizational Behavior*, 18, pp.1–74.

Yang, J., and Diefendorff, J. M. 2009. The relations of daily counterproductive workplace behavior with emotions, situational antecedents, and personality moderators: a diary study in Hong Kong. *Personnel Psychology*, 62, pp.259–95.

Yeo, G. B., and Neal, A. 2004. A multilevel analysis of effort, practice, and performance: effects; of ability, conscientiousness, and goal orientation. *Journal of Applied Psychology*, 89, pp.231–47.

CHAPTER 5

....

THE POTENTIAL
FOR LEADERSHIP

....

ROBERT F. SILZER AND WALTER C. BORMAN

5.1 INTRODUCTION

....

IN contemporary work organizations, the concept of *potential* is often used to focus on employees who have *high potential* for future roles in an organization. Current efforts to introduce strategically driven talent-management processes (Silzer and Dowell, 2010a, 2010b) into organizations have put a premium on identifying and developing employees who have the potential to make significant contributions to the organization in the future, mostly in leadership roles. There has been keen interest by business executives, human resource professionals, and organizational psychologists in building systems, processes, predictors, and tools that will help organizations achieve this goal.

Although typically there is interest in building the talent pool across an entire organization, special attention has been devoted to identifying talent with leadership potential (Church and Silzer, 2014; Silzer and Church, 2009a, 2009b, 2010, 2016). This chapter focuses on efforts in research and practice to identify useful predictors or indicators of *leadership potential* in individuals. Over the past twenty years, there has been a significant increase in the attention given to studying leadership in organizations, and in particular, to identifying effective future leaders. This chapter will concentrate on the research and practice focused on the long-term prediction of future leadership talent; we will not try to summarize the huge body of research literature related to current leadership effectiveness, including necessary competencies for success, processes to enhance future performance, and related issues (Hollenbeck, McCall, and Silzer, 2006; Zaccaro, 2007; and similar reviews). Instead, we explore the construct of *leadership potential* and review what we know about determining the leadership potential of individuals.

5.2 IMPORTANCE TO ORGANIZATIONS

"Having the right talent in the right roles at the right time" is a common talent objective in business organizations. The "war for talent" (Michaels, Handfield-Jones, and Axelrod, 2001) has promoted the importance of identifying and managing high-potential talent. The ability to define and identify that elusive variable known as *potential* in an individual or group of individuals is considered a critical competitive advantage in the marketplace (Silzer and Church, 2009a, 2010, 2016; Silzer and Dowell, 2010a, 2010b). The ability to identify accurately and consistently high potentials is arguably "one of the holy grails of Industrial-Organizational Psychology" (Church and Waclawski, 2010).

5.3 DEFINING *POTENTIAL*

The term *talent* may refer to a person's value or *natural abilities* (Michaels, Handfield-Jones, and Axelrod, 2001). However, we could distinguish individuals who have natural abilities in an area (who some might call *gifted*) from those who have *learned* their skills and knowledge. Of course, individuals are typically a mix of both natural abilities and learned skills. Ideally, their natural abilities should expand and blossom through what they learn.

Over the years, the nature of organizational talent has changed, and the management of talent has become more sophisticated. Silzer and Dowell define *talent management* as "an integrated set of processes, programs, and cultural norms in an organization designed and implemented to attract, develop, deploy, and retain talent to achieve strategic objectives and meet future business needs" (2010b: 18).

Silzer and Dowell (2010b) note that the term *talent* in organizations can refer to or be applied to three different constructs: (i) an individual's knowledge, skills, and abilities (i.e., *talents*), what the person has done, and what the person is capable of doing or contributing to the organization in the future; (ii) a specific person (e.g., she is *a talent* or she is *talented*), usually implying she has specific knowledge, skills, and abilities in some area); or (iii) a group (e.g., *the level of talent in the marketing function*) in an organization.

Currently, significant corporate resources (i.e., attention, time, and money) are being devoted to helping people improve performance in their current roles and developing them for the next positions in their career paths. However, this effort has been extended from development for *current and next positions* to development for *long-term future* performance. For our purposes, we define *leadership potential* as having the qualities (e.g., personal characteristics, motivation, skills, abilities, experiences, and behaviors) that are early predictors of future leadership effectiveness (Silzer and Church, 2009a).

Also, organizations typically differ in their definitions of potential or high potential (Karaevli and Hall, 2003; Silzer and Church, 2010). A recent corporate survey of twenty major corporations identified several different common definitions of *high potential*

(Silzer and Church, 2010): (i) *by role*, the potential to effectively move into top/senior management roles (35% of companies); (ii) *by level*, the potential to move into and effectively perform at two positions/levels above current role (25% of companies); (iii) *by breadth*, the capability to take on broader job scope and leadership roles, and to develop long-term leadership potential (25% of companies); (iv) *by record*, a consistent track record of exceptional performance (10% of companies); (v) *by strategic position*, key positions that may be at the core of an organization's success (perhaps a subset of *by level* definitions but targeting specific positions); and (vi) *by strategic area*, functions, business units, or geographical areas that are central to the organization's strategic objectives.

5.4 POTENTIAL IN ORGANIZATIONS

Organizations often use the term generically—*he has potential* or *she is a high-potential individual*. In these cases, *potential* is not specifically defined, and all *potential* is put in one general category. This suggests that *potential* can be identified and measured independent of the context and might be immutable across situations, much like general intelligence. Perhaps people who hold these views may actually mean general intelligence or personality characteristics when they use the term *potential* so generically.

The identification of potential is not usually matching an individual to specific, near-term, known positions and responsibilities, but rather predicting how likely an individual, with additional growth and development, can be successful in future, often unspecified, roles. In order to leverage organizational resources most effectively, there is growing interest in identifying individuals who have the greatest potential to be effective in higher-level, senior organizational roles. Today organizations are creating sophisticated systems and programs for identifying, assessing, and developing such high-potential talent (e.g., Church, 2006; Church and Silzer, 2013; Parasher and McDaniel, 2008; Silzer, 2006; Silzer and Church, 2009a, 2009b, 2010, 2016; Silzer, Hollenbeck, and Fulkerson, 2002; Wells, 2009).

The number of organizations that report having a high-potential identification program has been increasing. For example: (i) 42% of the twenty-one major corporations surveyed in 1994 (Silzer, Slider, and Knight, 1994); (ii) 31% of seventy-one small, medium, and large Canadian companies surveyed in 2004 (Slan and Hausdorf, 2004); (iii) 55% of one hundred companies surveyed in 2003 by Hewitt Associates (Wells, 2003); (iv) 100% of the companies in the 2003 Hewitt survey that were in the top quartile out of one hundred companies for total shareholder return (Wells, 2003); and (v) 100% of twenty major corporations surveyed in 2008 (Silzer and Church, 2010).

Some organizations have multiple categories of potential in their organizations, often labeled as talent pools (Dowell, 2010), and they distinguish the talent groups by addressing the question, *potential for what*? This view argues that although there may be some common characteristics or abilities that predict potential in general, for several different talent pools, there are also more unique abilities and characteristics that differentially predict potential for each talent pool and career path (such as technology leaders versus human resource leaders). This suggests that the question *potential for what?* may clarify and underlie the specific definition of potential.

At this point, we might ask the question: Can talent and potential be learned or developed? This is an interesting question, as many leaders, managers, and HR professionals view the concept of *potential* as an inherent individual capability (e.g., either one has or does not have potential), and some have asserted that potential factors are very difficult to develop (Rogers and Smith, 2007).

We disagree with this conclusion. The construct of *potential* implies that individuals can become something more than what they currently are. It implies further growth and development to reach some desired end state of behavior, skills, and abilities.

From this discussion, it is clear that there are different ways that organizations address the question of *potential for what?* Nonetheless, we now move forward to review and comment on four related categories of literature on the prediction of leadership potential. The categories are classified primarily by when the predictor measurement occurs. They are genetic, childhood/adolescence, early adult and early career, and midcareer studies.

5.5 Prediction of Potential

5.5.1 Genetic Studies

In recent years there has been significant interest in exploring genetic factors related to leadership potential (Arvey, Wang, Song, and Li, 2014). Based on existing population samples, these studies use genetically related participants, often of identical and fraternal twins, extensive life biographies, and additionally administered inventories and instruments that measure personality variables, cognitive skills, and leadership behavior. The initial studies utilized the twins' database for the Minnesota Twins Studies (Arvey and Bouchard, 1994; Bouchard, 1997; Lykken, Bouchard, McGue, and Tellegen, 1990; McGue and Bouchard, 1998). In Arvey and Bouchard (1994), the aim of the research was to predict later leadership role occupancy, transformational and transactional leadership ratings, and emergent leadership.

The sample of genetic studies relating to leadership potential that we reviewed indicates the following preliminary conclusions. Results suggest: (i) 30%–32% of variance could be attributed to genetic factors when leadership-role occupancy was the criterion; (ii) 37%–44% of variance was related to genetic factors in predicting emergent leadership; (iii) 43%–57% of variance was explained when the criteria were transformational leadership self-ratings; (iv) 33% of the variance in family factors related to leadership-role occupancy could be attributed to genetic factors; and (v) 31% of the variance in work-experience factors related to the leadership-role occupancy criterion was attributed to genetic factors (Arvey et al., 2006; Arvey, Zhang, Avolio, and Krueger, 2007;

Chaturvedi et al., 2012; Johnson, Vernon, Harris, and Jang, 2004; Li Arvey, Zhang, and Song, 2012).

It should be noted that studies using more objective criteria, such as past leadership roles, found 30%–33% of the variance explained by genetic factors. The studies using a more subjective criterion—leadership self-ratings—tend to be higher, in the range of 43%–47% variance accounted for. Li, Arvey, Zhang, and Song (2012) suggest that transformational leadership appears more heritable than leadership-role occupancy (Arvey et al., 2006; Arvey, Zhang, Avolio, and Krueger, 2007; Johnson, Vernon, Harris, and Jang, 2004; Johnson et al., 1998), although the apparent difference in the two heritability estimates was not significant. It suggests that occupancy of supervisory positions seems to be more determined by environmental factors than are transformational leadership behaviors. Some researchers hypothesize that people may need to be perceived as leader-like first, before being promoted into leadership positions by organizations (Lord, DeVader, and Alliger, 1986; Lord, Foti, and DeVader, 1984). Also, the genetic influence on leadership-role occupancy may hinge more on contextual factors, such as the support of the immediate manager (Zhang, Ilies, and Arvey, 2009).

One other interesting finding is that 49% of the variance in the Leadership Potential scale ratings on the California Psychological Inventory can be attributed to genetic factors (Bouchard, McGue, Hur, and Horn, 1998). Although there are other studies that examine the heritability of personality variables (Bouchard, 1997; Johnson, Vernon, Harris, and Jang, 2004), this scale is unusual in that it was designed to capture multiple personality variables related to leadership potential.

Genetic studies often have the challenges of small sample sizes and low statistical power. They tend to rely on existing population data sets (such as twin registries) and self-reported after-the-fact criterion ratings. It has also been noted that heritability estimates of IQ and personality can vary at different points in the life span (McGue, Pickens, and Svikis, 1992), although there is not yet a consensus on whether the heritability increases or decreases with age (Chaturvedi et al., 2012).

In general, there seems to be support for the *Diathesis Stress Model*, that behavior is best explained by biological factors (nature) and life experiences (nurture) (Gottesman, 1991). Arvey, Wang, Song, and Li (2014) outline a "Pathways from Genes to Leadership" model and suggest that genetic differences lead to differences in chemical (hormones and blood sugar), physiological (height/weight and gender/race), and psychological (perception, attention, and values) factors. These, in turn, lead to differences in cognitive functioning, personality, interests/values, and physical capacities, which then lead to leadership behaviors.

It should be noted that individuals can also shape the environment around them. They can evoke responses from others that shape the environment, which can give them special leadership opportunities (Avolio, 1999). Also, individuals can actively select or create environments that are consistent with their genetic propensities, called niche picking (Plomin, 1994). The fact that a significant part of the correlation between leadership and work experience is due to shared genetic/environment influences supports these possibilities.

5.5.2 Childhood and Adolescent Studies

Because of the widespread focus on leadership potential, there has been growing interest in exploring childhood and adolescence indicators that may be precursors of later leadership behavior. In particular, experts in childhood and adolescent psychology have devoted some attention to identifying early life predictors of later leadership behaviors. This raises the question: How early in life can we identify individuals who may have the potential for leadership?

Most of these studies require older participants to provide retrospective reports on their early family life. Those data are then often correlated with self-report ratings on leadership questionnaires. They might be considered longitudinal studies in the sense that the predictor data are information from earlier periods in a person's life. But there is the risk of less than fully objective data when people's memories of long past events are relied upon for predictor data.

The significant childhood and adolescent predictors against various leadership criteria focus on: (i) early family context (accounted for 4%–14% of criterion variance); (ii) parenting style (significant path coefficients of .22–.73; in one study the path was mediated by adolescent positive self-concept); (iii) childhood secure emotional attachment (accounted for 9%–19% criterion variance); (iv) childhood cognitive abilities (accounted for 5% of criterion variance in one study but in several other studies there was no significant relationship to the criterion); (v) childhood/adolescent motivation to learn (childhood motivation accounted for 7% of variance in motivation to lead [indirectly through adolescent motivation], while adolescent motivation directly accounted for 12% of motivation to lead variance); and (vi) adolescent personality (extraversion accounted for 3%–12% of the criterion variance, agreeableness 9%, conscientiousness 9%, neuroticism (negative correlation) 7%, and self-concept 12%–16%) (see Popper and Mayseless, 2007; Oliver et al., 2011; Avolio, Rotundo, and Walumba, 2009; Avolio and Gibbons, 1988; Popper and Amit, 2009; Popper, Mayseless, and Castelnovo, 2000; Murphy and Johnson, 2011; Guerin et al., 2011; Gottfried et al., 2011; Reichard et al., 2011; Gottfried and Gottfried, 2011; Dhuey and Lipscomb, 2008; Mumford et al., 1993; Daly, Egan, and O'Reilly, 2015; Fullerton Longitudinal Study, 1988).

The first three predictor factors may be primarily influenced by an interaction between the child's personal characteristics and the environmental context. The last three may be more influenced by the child's/adolescent's individual characteristics, as each individual learns to express his or her personality and influence the surrounding environment. The interaction of personal characteristics and developmental contexts has been identified as a key component in the development of leaders over time (Avolio, Rotundo, and Walumbwa, 2009; Popper, 2002; Popper and Amit, 2009; Popper and Mayseless, 2007). Early childhood context factors can also have a critical impact on early leader development, leadership self-identity (Johnson et al., 2012), and self-regulatory capabilities.

As mentioned, these childhood and adolescent studies usually require retrospective designs that rely on remembering past events and understanding the past from a current perspective, and may be open to forgetting, altering, or reconstructing the past (Avolio and Gibbons, 1988; Oliver et al., 2011). This introduces a number of research-method issues (Guerin et al., 2011). In most cases the "longitudinal" studies in this area rely on multiple surveys administered closely together in current time (Yukl, 2006), with one survey focusing on remembering past events (predictors), while the second survey measures current criterion behavior. There are a few true longitudinal studies, such as the Fullerton Longitudinal Study (1988), or the forty-year study by Daly, Egan, and O'Reilly (2015) that actually collected the predictor data in the past when the subjects were ages 10 and 11.

Nonetheless, we believe it is important to continue to study the prediction of leadership potential, focusing on the relatively early part of the life path. If we can achieve reasonably accurate forecasts of individuals' leadership potential at this life stage, it may be possible to understand better later links between potential measured in early career and subsequent leadership performance. Of course, we must be careful not to apply directly the relationships between childhood/adolescent predictors and later performance in ways that would in any way place children on narrow tracks toward management or non-management careers. Thus, the emphasis should be, as mentioned, on using these results to understand better the later early career predictors of leadership potential on leadership effectiveness.

5.5.3 Early Adult and Early Career Studies

Many studies on early career and early adult leadership potential use college students or military cadets. This is because college students are readily available to academic researchers as participant samples, and the U.S. government has been willing to fund numerous leadership studies involving cadets at the military academies. Few of these studies were done in business organizations. So the limitations of these samples and the college and military academy environments need to be considered when reviewing these results.

Numerous personality variables were found to correlate positively with various leadership criteria. The most frequent significant correlations were with dominance (for 2%–14% of the criterion variance) and extraversion (1%–19% of the variance across different criteria) (Foti and Hauenstein, 2007; Gough, 1990; Judge, Bono, Ilies, and Gerhardt, 2002; Lord, DeVader, and Alliger, 1986; Mumford et al., 1993; Nyquist and Spence, 1986; Smith and Foti, 1998; Bono and Judge, 2004; Hirschfeld, Jordan, Thomas, and Feild, 2008; Judge, Bono, Ilies, and Gerhardt, 2002; Riggio, Riggio, Salinas, and Cole, 2003).

Significant correlations with various later leadership criteria (see Reiter-Palmon, 2003; Gough, 1990; Hirschfield, Jordon, Thomas, and Field, 2008; Judge, Bono, Ilies, and Gerhardt, 2002; Harms, Spain, and Hannah, 2011; Johnsen et al., 2009; Popper et al., 2004; Judge, Bono, Ilies, and Gerhardt, 2002; Kenny and Zaccaro, 1983) were also found with:

- Cognitive flexibility (added significantly to the criterion variance accounted for in a regression equation)
- Capacity for status (accounted for 4% of variance)
- Conscientiousness (3%–13% of the variance)
- Diligence (1%–5% of the variance)

- Dispositional resiliency (15%–24% of the variance)
- Empathy (6% of the variance)
- Independence (8% of the variance)
- Internal locus of control (2%–9% of the variance)
- Openness to experience (4%–8% of the variance)
- Optimism (individuals who emerged as leaders had significantly greater optimism than others)
- Skills in perceiving the needs of others (estimated to account for 49%–82% of variance in leadership criteria that can be attributed to ability to perceive the needs and goals of others and adjust accordingly)
- Secure attachment style (individuals who emerged as leaders had higher levels of secure attachment style compared with others)
- Sociability (4%–21% of the variance; social skills were particularly predictive of adolescent leader emergence).

In addition, other characteristics emerged as early adult predictors of later leadership, including self-efficacy (7% of criterion variance, and individuals who emerge as leaders have higher levels of self-efficacy than others), self-acceptance (7% of the criterion variance), and self-esteem (2%–13% of the variance) (see Atwater et al., 1999; Avolio et al., 1996; Avolio, Rotundo, and Walumbwa, 2009; Foti and Hauenstein, 2007; Li, Arvey, and Song, 2011; Gough, 1990; Smith and Foti, 1998; Judge, Bono, Ilies, and Gerhardt, 2002; Popper et al., 2004; Riggio, Riggio, Salinas, and Cole, 2003). These variables do make some rational sense since they are often cited as key components of effective leadership. In addition, the more an individual gains leader self-efficacy and self-confidence in his or her own ability to lead a group, the more he or she is likely to engage in leadership experiences, which, in turn, serve to increase his or her leadership skills (Hannah, Avolio, Luthans, and Harms, 2008).

Self-monitoring was also a useful predictor. Self-monitoring is the ability to "read" social situations and to alter one's own behavior to fit in and act appropriately in them (Snyder, 1974, 1987). In one study, Foti and Hauenstein (2007) found high self-monitoring was associated with both leadership emergence and leader effectiveness. Other studies also support this variable as a useful predictor (accounts for 4%–20% of criterion variance) (see Dobbins, Long, Dedrick, and Clemons, 1990; Ellis, 1988; Ellis, Adamson, Deszca, and Cawsey, 1988; Kenny and Zaccaro, 1983; Riggio, Riggio, Salinas, and Cole, 2003; Zaccaro, Foti, and Kenny, 1991).

In addition, other personality variables have been found to correlate with later leadership criteria. They include *achievement orientation* (accounted for 8%–12% of variance in leadership criteria); *adjustment* (4%–6% of variance); *anxiety level* (2% of criterion variance); *dependability* (9% of variance); *diligence* (1%–5% of variance for military cadets); *imaginative* (4%–8% of variance for military cadets, all negative correlations); *masculinity–femininity* (12% of variance); *neuroticism* (2%–7% of variance with consistently negative correlations); *skeptical* (2%–4% of variance for military cadets with all negative correlations); and *social potency* (20%–22% of variance) (see Avolio, Rotundo, and Walumbwa, 2009; Harms, Spain, and Hannah, 2011; Judge, Bono, Ilies, and Gerhardt, 2002; Lord, DeVader, and Alliger, 1986; Popper et al., 2004).

Further, several studies have developed multiple regression equations and personality profiles against later leadership criteria. Some of the results were: (i) regression of dominance, intelligence, and self-efficacy (accounted for 45% of the variance in perceptions of leadership in others); (ii) pattern of high intelligence, high dominance, high self-efficacy, and high self-monitoring (accounted for 7%–30% of criterion variance); (iii) personality profile of extraversion, conscientiousness, and emotional stability (accounted for 4% of criterion variance); (iv) regression of extraversion, openness to experience, conscientiousness, neuroticism (negative weight), (accounted for 28% of criterion variance); (v) regression of academic ability and social skills (accounted for 4% of the criterion variance); (vi) regression of academic ability, social skills, behavioral flexibility, and cognitive flexibility (accounted for 9% of the criterion variance); and (vii) combination of self-monitoring and extraversion (accounted for 59% of variance in peer perceptions of leader emergence) (see Avolio, Rotundo, and Walumbwa, 2009; Foti and Hauenstein, 2007; Gough, 1990; Hirschfield, Jordon, Thomas, and Field, 2008; Judge, Bono, Ilies, and Gerhardt 2002; Reiter-Palmon, 2003; Smith and Foti, 1998; and Zaccaro, Foti, and Kenny, 1991).

Regarding personality as a predictor of leadership, we are aware of the criticisms of the early "great man" theory of leadership effectiveness. The observation was that the mixed results for these personality-leadership performance relationships suggested that "situations" should also be taken into account, with these correlations depending to some extent on the leadership environment (e.g., position power and leader-member relations). This was Fiedler's (1967) rationale for the mixed findings with the personality-leader effectiveness correlations.

Cognitive variables with significant correlations to leadership criteria included: (i) *general mental ability* (accounted for 2%–27% of the variance, except in one study when the predictor was *perceived intelligence* and the variance accounted for was 42%); (ii) *complex problem solving* (accounted for 17% of criterion variance); (iii) *divergent thinking* (accounted for 18% of criterion variance); (iv) *inductive and deductive reasoning* (added significant incremental variance accounted for in a regression equation); and (v) *creativity* (added significant incremental variance) (see Atwater et al., 1999; Foti and Hauenstein, 2007; Hogan, Raskin, and Fazzini, 1990; Judge, Colbert, and Ilies, 2004; Lord DeVader and Alliger, 1986; Mumford et al., 1993; Reiter-Palmon, 2003; Smith and Foti, 1998; Zaccaro et al., 2015).

Most important in this area is the emphasis on personality and cognitive factors as early career predictors. These are foundational variables that are stable, consistent, and more likely to predict across different leadership situations and across time. Also because most of these studies involved college-age participants, there were limited opportunities in early adulthood to observe, measure, and demonstrate early leadership behaviors as predictors.

There is an ongoing discussion of how much situations impact leadership behavior. Zaccaro, Foti, and Kenny (1991) and Kenny and Zaccaro (1983) found that emergent leadership is fairly stable across situations, and, therefore, they concluded that emergent leadership variance is more likely related to personal characteristics. Of course, early studies argued that leader emergence was strongly influenced by the situational context (Barnlund, 1962; Bell and French, 1950; Borgatta, Couch, and Bales, 1954; Carter and Nixon, 1949; Gibb, 1947). More recently there are emerging views that contextual factors can have a critical impact on leadership effectiveness (Silzer, 2016a, 2016c). So the leadership situation and context probably has an influence (e.g., Fiedler, 1967), although the degree of this influence is not clear.

5.5.4 Midcareer Studies from Practice

Business organizations have long had an interest in selecting effective leaders. After the AT & T Management Progress Study (Bray, Campbell, and Grant, 1974), there was a significant corporate interest in leadership. Dunnette (1971) reviewed available studies and identified common leader characteristics that correlated with later managerial success, including cognitive skills, interpersonal skills, organizing/planning skills, energy, motivation, emotional stability, and resistance to stress. Others (Bass, 1990) also concluded that traits such as intelligence, dominance, extroversion, and achievement motivation fairly consistently related to leadership effectiveness. And a recent meta-analysis (Hoffmann, Woehr, Maldagen-Youngjohn, and Lyons, 2011) found a number of individual differences correlated significantly with leader effectiveness, including achievement motivation, energy, dominance, honesty/integrity, self-confidence, creativity, charisma, interpersonal skills, oral and written communication skills, management skills, problem-solving skills, and decision making.

There has been a noticeable increase in the past several decades in efforts by organizations and consulting firms to specify the key components and predictors of later leadership effectiveness. Business organizations want to identify those individuals who are most likely to develop into highly effective leaders, and consulting firms want to market their own predictors and models of leadership potential to their business clients.

The predictor models of leadership potential that have emerged and are reviewed below were developed by external consulting firms, sometimes as part of a new product or service offering (Hay, 2008), and sometimes as a research outcome (Church, 2006; Silzer and Church, 2009a; Spreitzer, McCall, and Mahoney, 1997). In addition, some corporate organizations have developed their own internal models of potential in order to have a structured and standardized process in place for internal high-potential talent identification and development programs.

Silzer and Church (2009a) reviewed nine models from consultants and consulting firms (Barnett, 2008; Corporate Leadership Council, 2005; Hay, 2008; Hewitt, 2008;

Hogan, 2009b; McCall, 1998; Peterson and Erdahl, 2007; Rogers and Smith, 2007; Rowe, 2007), and two corporate surveys that asked organizations to indicate the predictors they use to identify high-potential talent (Silzer and Church, 2010; Slan and Hausdorf, 2004).

After analyzing the eleven models, Silzer and Church (2009a) identified common components in them. Those components are listed in Table 5.1.

Table 5.1 Common Components across Current Models and Surveys of High Potential Indicators (adapted from Silzer and Church 2009a)

Cognitive abilities

- Conceptual or strategic thinking, breadth of thinking
- Intellect, cognitive ability
- Dealing with complexity/ambiguity

Personality variables, Interpersonal skills

- Interpersonal skills, sociability
- Dominance
- Maturity, stability, resilience

Learning variables

- Adaptability, flexibility
- Learning orientation, interest in learning
- Openness to feedback

Motivation variables

- Drive, energy, engagement, tenacity
- Drive for advancement, ambition, career drive
- Results orientation, risk taking

Leadership skills

- Leadership capabilities, managing and empowering people
- Developing others
- Influencing, inspiring, challenging the status quo, change management

Performance record

- Performance track record
- Leadership experiences

Other variables

- Technical/functional skills and knowledge, business knowledge
- Cultural fit, values, behavioral norms
- Qualifiers, screening variables (mobility, individual-difference variables)

5.6 COGNITIVE ABILITIES

Cognitive abilities were included in all eleven models. The abilities include cognitive agility, conceptual thinking, navigating ambiguity, cognitive complexity, breadth of perspective, intellect, judgment, strategic reasoning, tactical problem solving, insightfulness, decision making, strategic thinking, and managing ambiguity.

Summarizing, the variables in this category, based on Silzer and Church's clustering, are: (i) *conceptual or strategic thinking and breadth of thinking*; (ii) *intellect and cognitive ability*; and (iii) *dealing with complexity/ambiguity*.

Although most of these more specific variables are likely to co-vary, some seem more distinct. For example, there has been growing interest in including *strategic thinking skills and ability to deal with ambiguity/complexity* (Dragoni, Oh, VanKatwyk, and Tesluk, 2011) as an important indicator of leadership potential. Jaques has advocated that conceptual thinking skills can be evaluated relatively early in life and are predictive of long-term success of leaders in organizations (Jaques and Clement, 1991). In addition, conceptual thinking skills and cognitive capabilities are relatively stable and unchanging throughout life.

Basic intellect and cognitive skills are likely to be useful indicators, particularly at midcareer levels, where there may be more variance than at senior-leader levels. That suggests that cognitive factors may be best used as an early differentiator when the variance is the greatest.

5.7 PERSONALITY VARIABLES AND INTERPERSONAL SKILLS

Personality variables and interpersonal skills were included in seven of the models from practice. The personality variables in the models include *dominance, sociability, stability, interpersonal skills, emotional intelligence, being authentic, optimism, understanding others, personal maturity, respect for people*, and *collaboration*.

Silzer and Church clustered these variables into three themes: (i) interpersonal skills, sociability; (ii) dominance; and (iii) maturity, stability, and resilience.

There has been a growing interest in differentiating individuals based on their social skills, balanced with interpersonal assertiveness and dominance. The third theme of maturity, stability, and resilience focuses on emotional self-control and management, particularly in stressful situations. Dominance and emotional stability variables have often been identified as indicators of potential, but the optimal level on these variables may depend to a degree on the context and company culture. As a specific example, some companies encourage and reinforce highly dominant leaders, whereas other organizations place a premium on maturity and emotional self-control. For example, in

2005 PepsiCo launched a study to predict high potentials and found that ambition and sociability were both predictive of high-potential identification (Church, 2006; Church and Desrosiers, 2006).

5.8 LEARNING VARIABLES

Learning variables were identified in eight of the models, and they included *learning orientation, versatility, openness to feedback, learning agility, adaptability, eagerness to learn, flexibility, seeks opportunities to learn, adapts to cultural differences, seeks feedback, learns from mistakes, is open to criticism*, and *learning ability*. The key clusters are: (i) adaptability and flexibility, (ii) learning orientation and interest in learning, and (iii) openness to feedback.

Silzer and Church (2010) found that 65% of the companies in their corporate survey include learning skills as an indicator of high-potential talent. They use a range of variables such as *learning ability, learning motivation*, and *learning agility*. Recently there has been a surge in interest in learning skills as important predictors, partially owing to the attention given to *learning from experience* as an important development approach (Lombardo and Eichinger, 2000; McCall, Lombardo, and Morrison, 1988; McCauley and McCall, 2014).

Adaptability and flexibility have long been considered useful predictors (Pulakos, Arad, Donovan, and Plamondon, 2000). They often include a consideration of both a person's mental flexibility (e.g., ability to understand and integrate new information quickly) and their behavioral flexibility (e.g., ability to modify one's own behavior and try out new behaviors and directions).

Learning orientation and an interest in learning can differentiate how successful managers' acquisition of knowledge may lead to higher-quality solutions to problems. Having the right context and external stimulation may influence an individual's learning orientation, just as a limited and unstimulating environment may decrease that orientation.

Openness to feedback is relatively new to the discussion of potential, although it has been found to influence performance in past studies (e.g., Kluger and DeNisi, 1996). It seems intuitively to be a precursor to continuous learning. The extensive use of multirater-feedback surveys has made this a more salient and core leadership skill (Bracken, Timmreck, and Church, 2001).

Learning agility is a newer and less well-researched construct. Recent reviews (DeRue, Ashford, and Myers, 2012; Silzer, 2015, 2016b, 2016d) have argued that more evidence is needed before its usefulness is determined. Silzer has suggested the construct might be better labeled *learning from experience*.

Learning variables are what we might call "meta skills" (Derry and Murphy, 1986; Ford et al., 1998). That is, they are intervening variables for personal growth and development and may indicate the "developability" of an individual and the developmental readiness of the individual (Avolio and Hannah, 2008).

5.9 Motivation Variables

Almost all the models and surveys reviewed (ten out of eleven) include a motivation variable. The models included a range of such variables, including *aspiration, engagement, propensity to lead, results orientation, initiative, taking responsibility, energy, drive for advancement, need for power/control, drive for change, upward motivation, results orientation, tenacity, courage to take risks, career drive,* and *commitment to the organization.*

The key categories identified by Silzer and Church are: (i) *drive, energy, engagement, and tenacity;* (ii) *need for advancement, ambition, career drive, and motivation to lead;* and (iii) *results orientation and risk taking.*

A high level of motivation and commitment seems a logical differentiator for assessing potential. Because of the demand put on leaders in organizations, it follows that the motivation variables of *drive, energy, engagement,* and *tenacity* are differentiators of high-potential talent. Similarly, results orientation and drive for results are almost universally expected of leaders. The emphasis on leadership risk taking and how it is defined will vary by organization. An additional variable that might be considered is *motivation to lead* (Chan and Drasgow, 2001).

More recent is the emerging importance of advancement drive, personal ambition, and career drive as important considerations. Leaders are now expected to take responsibility for their own careers. In the Silzer and Church survey (2010), 90% of the companies now consider managers' career drive in determining whether they are identified as a high potential.

5.10 Leadership Skills

It may seem circular thinking to include leadership skills as an indicator of later leadership effectiveness. However, foundational leadership skills such as influencing peers and encouraging, supporting, and collaborating with others are behavioral skills that can be found in early career individuals that seem to predict later leadership emergence and even end-state leadership effectiveness.

Eight of the eleven models and survey results included leadership skills as a useful predictor. The specific leadership variables cited included: *brings out best in people, manages people, challenges status quo, influences others, develops others, teamwork, inspires others, manages change efforts,* and *leadership capabilities.* The main categories identified by Silzer and Church were: (i) *leadership capabilities, managing, and empowering people;* (ii) *developing others;* and (iii) *influencing, inspiring, challenging the status quo, and embracing change management.*

In the Silzer and Church survey (2010), 100% of the companies included leadership competencies as indicators of high-potential talent. Two leadership behavioral themes—*developing others and influencing others*—are emerging as more critical as organizations focus on talent management, talent development, and change management as important leader responsibilities (Silzer and Dowell, 2010b). To perhaps state the obvious, leadership behaviors as predictors are most relevant to individuals interested in pursuing leadership careers, but perhaps less relevant for others, such as individuals interested in becoming leading-edge researchers, chief software design engineers, or those in similar individual contributor roles.

All leadership behaviors used as early predictors, (such as early career transformational and transactional leadership behaviors, see Judge and Piccolo, 2004) however, should assess behaviors that distinguish people at early career stages, and not evaluate those individuals against behavioral standards for seasoned, experienced, senior leaders.

5.11 PERFORMANCE RECORD

Silzer and Church (2010) note that 100% of the companies in their survey considered an individual's performance record when identifying high-potential talent. That is, organization members typically need to demonstrate that they have successfully performed in a range of responsibilities in diverse roles. This often leads to confusion in an organization about the difference between performance and potential. Many professionals in human resources organizations work hard at helping leaders understand the difference between current/past performance and potential for success in future roles.

Interestingly, there is evidence from Project A, the large-scale selection and classification study in the US Army (Campbell and Knapp, 2001), that a one-item measure of supervisory potential by peer and supervisor raters in the first tour of duty correlated higher with overall performance as a later supervisor during second tour than did a peer/supervisor rating of overall performance (first tour against the same criterion in the second tour). In short, even lay, non-Industrial/Organizational psychologist assessment practitioners seem to understand the difference between present job performance and potential for later supervisory performance (at Time 1 for predicting Time 2 actual supervisory performance). Also, these raters leverage this understanding into more valid predictions of subsequent supervisory performance.

There are two types of variables in this category, *performance track records* and *leadership experiences or career history*. Of course, there are risks in using a person's past performance record as a predictor of how well the person might handle higher-level, more complex, and broader responsibilities. However, it is still widely used as a screening variable for identifying high-potential talent. Although the argument that "past performance is the best predictor of future performance" (Wernimont and Campbell, 1968) is widely understood, what is often forgotten is the second part of that conclusion "in similar circumstances." In many situations senior-leadership roles *are not similar circumstances* to early career roles, and, therefore, predicting from one to the other is problematic.

Early career leadership experiences may be a more viable predictor. But that also assumes acceptable levels of performance and some learning and developmental growth across those experiences. Overall, having a consistent and solid performance record may be a necessary but not sufficient qualification. However, there may be individuals with strong potential to be successful at senior-leadership levels in an organization but poorly suited for lower-level, more tactical, and narrower responsibilities.

5.12 OTHER VARIABLES

Other variables are often found in related models and are usually specialized predictors and qualifiers. Common variables that are mentioned include: (i) technical/functional skills and knowledge, that may be career track-specific; (ii) cultural fit, values, and behavioral norms (with respect to, for example, country, company, or department); and (iii) qualifiers or screening variables, such as geographical mobility and individual-difference variables (e.g., gender or age).

Cultural fit or organizational fit is an emerging issue as organizations focus on identifying and selecting individuals who fit the company's values and norms (Ostroff and Judge, 2007). Of course, this can be problematic. By screening out people who do not closely fit the company's specific behavioral norms and thinking, the organization may also be screening out new ideas, innovative approaches, and individuals who tend to challenge the status quo. Screening for fit may limit diverse thinking and diversity inclusion, and there is some professional agreement that these qualities may be needed in many business organizations, in order to survive.

Some companies also list other qualifiers that may support or prevent a person from being identified as a high potential. Silzer and Church (2010) found that 80% of the companies listed *mobility* as an important consideration. There is now active discussion in many companies on whether someone needs to be willing to move to new geographical locations for new assignments in order to be considered high potential. Organizations may need to be more flexible on requiring mobility, as younger generations demonstrate more resistance to making frequent major moves (Church, Rotolo, Ginther, and Levine, 2015; Church and Waclawski, 2010; Zemke, Raines, and Filipczak, 2000). In addition, as some authors have noted (Nalbantian and Guzzo, 2009), there are significant costs associated with an overemphasis on mobility, and organizations need to articulate a clear business strategy before using mobility as a formal screening requirement.

5.13 ADDITIONAL OBSERVATIONS
ON LEADERSHIP POTENTIAL

As we have seen, there are many possible variables that might be related to identifying leadership potential in individuals. An effort was made by Silzer and Church (2009a; Church and Silzer, 2014) to organize these variables into a coherent framework.

5.13.1 A New Structure of Leadership Potential

In reviewing the themes presented in Table 5.1, Silzer and Church (2009a) developed an integrated framework for organizing predictors of high-potential talent. Some components of potential are relatively stable and difficult to change across a person's career, whereas other components are more easily developed. These types of components have often been discussed as selection variables or developmental variables. But there are other components that impact an individual's later emergence as a leader and act as intervening variables that can facilitate or inhibit a person's learning and development. See Figure 5.1 for the integrated framework—the Blueprint of Leadership Potential (Church and Silzer, 2014; Silzer and Church, 2009a, 2009b).

Silzer and Church (2009a) identified three types of *dimensions of potential*: foundational, growth, and career.

5.13.1.1 *Foundational Dimensions*

Foundational dimensions are consistent over time and difficult to change; in adulthood, they are relatively stable across situations, experiences, and time. They are unlikely to develop or change much without considerable intervention and support from others.

Typical examples are cognitive abilities and many personality variables, including interpersonal skills. There is some evidence that personality is moderately stable, beginning in early adulthood, and increasingly stable and consistent into older age (Roberts,

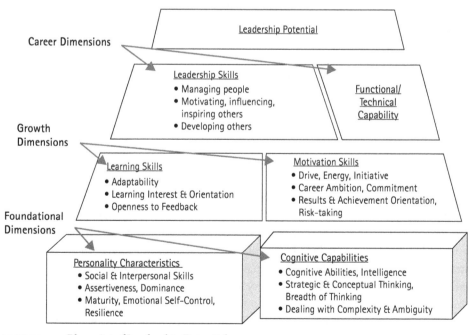

FIGURE 5.1 Blueprint of Leadership Potential

Adapted from Silzer and Church (2009a).

Wood, and Caspi, 2008), although certain life experiences and developmental efforts may result in modest changes (e.g., Boyce, Wood, Daly, and Sedikides, 2015; Edmonds, Jackson, Fayard, and Roberts, 2008; Roberts, Wood, and Caspi, 2008). These factors are included and evaluated in most individual management and executive assessments as stable, enduring characteristics.

5.13.1.2 *Growth Dimensions*

Growth dimensions can facilitate or hinder a person's growth and development. They are intervening variables to learning and can be useful indicators of whether a person will further develop and learn additional skills. They can be somewhat consistent and stable across situations, but might be more manifest and strengthen when a person has strong personal interests in an area, has an opportunity to learn more in those areas of interest, and has a supportive, encouraging environment. Individuals who are self-aware often can proactively engage and leverage these characteristics to learn important new behaviors, approaches, and strategies for greater leadership effectiveness. Typical examples are motivation, adaptability, and learning orientation.

5.13.1.3 *Career Dimensions*

These dimensions of potential are typically early indicators of the later end-state skills needed in a management career. For example, early career supervisory skills are likely to be an indicator of potential for higher leadership roles, as project management skills might be an indicator of potential for more senior managerial roles. The specific behavioral dimensions of potential may depend on the individual career path being considered and on the answer to the question *potential for what*? Often these dimensions can be learned and developed, providing the person has some of the growth characteristics that can be leveraged, and is in a work environment that provides the right experiences and the support to develop these skills.

5.13.2 The Complexity of Leadership

Predicting leadership effectiveness is difficult. Early life experiences reported in published research and reviewed in this chapter are primarily "leading indicators" that give early signs of who may excel. However, there are many contextual factors that can impact, disrupt, or support those early indications. The road to leadership effectiveness can have many hurdles, potholes, and disruptions along the way. Lagging indicators of leadership effectiveness include leadership skills and behaviors the individual demonstrates in early and midcareer leadership positions. By this time in a person's career, the individual often has had numerous opportunities to learn and demonstrate the leadership skills, abilities, and behavior that are associated with leadership effectiveness. But other contextual factors, such as a change in the CEO, a change in the economy or market, a merger or business sell-off, or a non-collaborative set of peers can impact leadership performance.

So a first step is to identify those individuals who seem to have the best profile of early indicators of later leadership success. This allows organizations to work with the best talent available who might be developed and leveraged. This is considered a wise investment of organizational resources in talent and careful risk management of those resources.

There are four groups of factors that can support, stall, or disrupt someone who has an early, high-potential profile for leadership.

The person him/herself. It is not uncommon for gifted or talented people to build and extend their talent but to not fully realize their potential. Someone who shows great promise in high school can fade in college for lack of motivation or skills to step up to the higher expectations. An interpersonally effective person living in a small rural town may become less self-confident and assured when moving to a large metropolitan city. People change, and not always in a positive direction. But there are some individual-difference predictors, such as learning orientation, openness to experience, and flexibility that can help the person adapt and learn in new situations.

Development opportunities. Early indicators of potential usually reflect where an individual is at a particular point in their life and career. These indicators are usually (or should be) normed against a peer group, so high-potential individuals usually stand out when compared with their cohorts. We know how important the right development opportunities can be in encouraging, supporting, and advancing the person in those areas (McCauley and McCall, 2014). However, a lack of development opportunities or learning the wrong lessons can take a person off the track for leadership effectiveness. Some examples of development opportunities include effective learning events in school; effective teachers; access to books, computers, and libraries; being assigned to or finding a skilled mentor; pursuing training; development in an organization, etc. The lack of these opportunities can discourage or sideline a person with a high-potential profile.

Contextual factors in life. Many of these factors, such as early family environment, family socioeconomic status, and parental support level, can influence developmental outcomes. But some of these factors are the result of personal choices, such as whether a person attends college and if so, where, and who the individual chooses as friends and advisors. The neighborhood the person lives in, early peers, parental attitudes, spouse, and family size are all factors that can support or discourage leveraging an early potential profile.

Contextual factors in an organization. Once a person begins working in an organization, numerous contextual factors can support or diminish a person's potential. Some examples are impact of good or bad immediate managers, the organizational culture, the talent level of peers and direct reports, and the financial resources in the organization (Silzer, 2016a, 2016c, 2016d). Individuals with high-potential indicators are more likely to leverage available resources and support and to take the initiative to find and use them. However, some individuals may not see those opportunities when they come along, or do not fully abstract the advantages and learnings from them. Of course, often the availability of these factors is out of a person's control. Nonetheless, they can still significantly impact whether individuals can fully realize their earlier potential.

Leadership effectiveness is the result of an interaction of the individual (skills, abilities, and behavior), the situation (job requirements and expectations), and the context (immediate manager, CEO, peers, organizational culture, etc.). However, there are many contextual factors that can significantly impact leadership effectiveness as well. All three factors—the individual, the situation, and the context—can interact in many different ways and can impact the predictability of a leader's end-state effectiveness.

These studies and conclusions add significantly to our knowledge about leadership potential. They lead to additional, emerging research questions related to identifying leadership potential in individuals, such as:

1. How do the indicators of leadership potential evolve over time and in an individual's life?
2. What factors influence whether these indicators emerge and grow, or decline and regress over time?
3. How do these indicators interact, and when do they act in concert with each other and when do they conflict with each other?
4. What situational, cultural, and organizational factors impact leadership potential at each life stage?
5. To what degree can intentional development efforts grow or hinder the leadership-potential indicators?

5.14 Conclusion

Identifying talent that has potential for leadership has become a major strategic goal for many business organizations and human resource departments. A great deal of time and resources are being focused on identifying and developing the talent that is needed to achieve future business strategies. The organizational resource of "talent" has gained significant importance, almost equal to financial resources, as a critical requirement for business success.

Talent with leadership potential is in great demand and it has become a competitive strategic advantage for many companies. Most large organizations now have formal talent strategies (Silzer and Dowell, 2010a, 2010b) that help them identify and compete successfully for the strategic talent that is needed for that organization. Leader development is a future planning effort that places the right potential talent in development opportunities having the greatest likelihood of creating and supporting successful organizational leaders for the future. Part of the challenge is to find talented individuals early in their careers so that the organization can shape and grow them to fit future organizational needs.

We have summarized the current state of predictors of leadership potential. We reviewed genetic, childhood/adolescence, early adulthood/early career, and midcareer predictors, and identified key indicators from each life stage. A useful midcareer model, the Blueprint for Leadership Potential (Church and Silzer, 2014; Silzer and Church,

2009a), has emerged, which captures the key predictors that organizations can look for in their current employees. This model can serve as the foundation for efforts to identify leadership potential in business and related organizations.

The research and organizational efforts reported here reflect major advances in the study of leadership potential. Future advancement in this field is likely to be based on bringing together two related, but somewhat unconnected, efforts. What is needed is an integration of the research efforts published in peer-reviewed journals with the results and findings from organizational efforts in practice that are often presented at professional conferences but often go unpublished.

The identification of leadership potential to meet business needs has a promising future. Both researchers and organizational professionals see it as a critical area to pursue. We need to continue to improve our understanding of the construct and how best to identify it in individuals. We hope that this chapter will stimulate both researchers and practitioners to consider how they think about high-potential talent, and that it will generate new research and organizational processes that advance and integrate our understanding of this construct.

REFERENCES

Arvey, R., Zhang, Z., Avolio, B. J., and Krueger, R. F. 2007. Developmental and genetic determinants of leadership role occupancy among women. *Journal of Applied Psychology*, 92(3), pp.693–706.

Arvey, R. D., and Bouchard, T. J., Jr. 1994. Genetics, twins, and organizational behavior. In L. L. Cummings and B. M. Staw, eds., *Research in organizational behavior*, Vol. 16, pp.47–82. Greenwich, CT: JAI Press Inc.

Arvey, R. D., Rotundo, M., Johnson, W., Zhang, Z. et al. 2006. The determinants of leadership role occupancy: genetic and personality factors. *The Leadership Quarterly*, 17, pp.1–20.

Arvey, R. D., Wang, N., Song, Z., and Li, W-D. 2014. The biology of leadership. In D. Day, ed. *The Oxford handbook of leadership and organizations*, pp.75–91. Oxford: Oxford University Press.

Arvey, R. D., Zhang, Z., Krueger, R. F., and Avolio, B. J. 2007. Developmental and genetic determinants of leadership role occupancy among women. *Journal of Applied Psychology*, 92, pp.693–706.

Atwater, L. E., Dionne, S. D., Avolio, B. J., Camobreco, J. F. et al. 1999. A longitudinal study of the leadership development process: individual differences predicting leadership effectiveness. *Human Relations*, 52, pp.1543–62.

Avolio, B. J. 1999. *Full leadership development: building the vital forces in organizations*. Thousand Oaks, CA: Sage.

Avolio, B. J., Dionne, S., Atwater, L., Lau, A. et al. 1996. *Antecedent predictors of a "full range" of leadership and management styles*. Technical Report 1040. US Army Research Institute.

Avolio, B. J., and Gibbons, T. C. 1988. Developing transformational leaders: a life span approach. In J. A. Conger and R. N. Kanungo, eds., *Charismatic leadership: the elusive factor in organizational effectiveness*, pp.276–308. San Francisco: Jossey-Bass.

Avolio, B. J., and Hannah, S. T. 2008. Developmental readiness: accelerating leader development. *Consulting Psychology Journal: Practice and Research*, 60, pp.331–47.

Avolio, B. J., Rotundo, M., and Walumbwa, F. O., 2009. Early life experiences as determinants of leadership role occupancy: the importance of parental influence and rule breaking behavior. *The Leadership Quarterly*, 20, pp.329–42.

Barnett, R. 2008. *Identifying high-potential talent*. Minneapolis, MN: MDA Leadership Consulting, Inc.

Barnlund, D. C. 1962. Consistency of emergent leadership in groups with changing tasks and members. *Speech Monographs*, 29, pp.45–52.

Bass, B. M. 1990. *Bass & Stogdill's handbook of leadership: theory, research and managerial applications*, 3rd edn. New York: Free Press.

Bell, G. B., and French, R. L. 1950. Consistency of individual leadership position in small groups of varying membership. *Journal of Abnormal and Social Psychology*, 45, pp.764–7.

Bono, J. E., and Judge, T. A. 2004. Personality and transformational and transactional leadership: a meta-analysis. *The Journal of Applied Psychology*, 89, pp.901–10.

Borgatta, E. F., Couch, A. S., and Bales, R. F. 1954. Some findings relevant to the great man theory of leadership. *American Sociological Review*, 19, pp.755–9.

Bouchard, T. J., Jr. 1997. The genetics of personality. In K. Blum and E. P. Noble, eds., *Handbook of psychiatric genetics*, pp.273–96. Boca Raton: CRC Press.

Bouchard, T. J., McGue, M., Hur, Y. M., and Horn, J. M. 1998. A genetic and environmental analysis of the California Psychological Inventory using adult twins reared apart and together. *European Journal of Personality*, 12, pp.307–20.

Boyce, C. J., Wood, A. M., Daly, M., and Sedikides, C. 2015. Personality change following unemployment. *Journal of Applied Psychology*, 100(4), pp.991–1011.

Bracken, D. W., Timmreck, C. W., and Church, A. H., eds., 2001. *The handbook of multisource feedback: the comprehensive resource for designing and implementing MSF processes*. San Francisco: Jossey-Bass.

Bray, D. W., Campbell, R. J., and Grant, D. L. 1974. *Formative years in business: a long term AT&T study of managerial lives*. New York: John Wiley.

Campbell, J. P., and Knapp, D. J. 2001. *Exploring the limits in personnel selection and classification*. Mahwah, NJ: Lawrence Erlbaum.

Carter, L., and Nixon, M. 1949. Ability, perceptual, personality, and interest factors associated with different criteria of leadership. *Journal of Psychology*, 27, pp.377–88.

Chan, K. Y., and Drasgow, F. 2001. Toward a theory of individual differences and leadership: understanding the motivation to lead. *Journal of Applied Psychology*, 86(3), pp.481–98

Chaturvedi, S., Zyphur, M. J., Arvey, R. D., Avolio, B. J. et al. 2012. The heritability of emergent leadership-age and gender as moderating factors. *Leadership Quarterly*, 23, pp.219–32.

Church, A. H. 2006. Bring on the high potentials: talent assessment at PepsiCo. In *Talent management: will the high potentials stand up? Allan Church* (Chair). Symposium at the Annual Conference of the Society of Industrial/Organizational Psychology (SIOP), Dallas, Texas.

Church, A. H., and Desrosiers, E. I. 2006. *Bring on the high potentials—talent assessment at PepsiCo*. Presentation at the Annual Meeting of the Society for Industrial and Organizational Psychological (SIOP), Dallas, Texas.

Church, A. H., Rotolo, C. T., Ginther, N. M., and Levine, R. 2015. How are top companies designing and managing their high-potential programs? A follow-up talent management benchmark study. *Consulting Psychology Journal: Practice and Research*, 67(1), pp.17–47.

Church, A. H., and Silzer, R. F. 2014. Going behind the corporate curtain with a blue print for leadership potential: an integrated framework for identifying high-potential talent. *People and Strategy Journal*, 36(4), pp.51–8.

Church, A. H., and Waclawski, J. 2010. Take the Pepsi Challenge: talent development at PepsiCo. In R. F. Silzer and B. E. Dowell, eds., *Strategy driven talent management: a leadership imperative*, pp.617–40. San Francisco: Jossey Bass.

Corporate Leadership Council. 2005. *Realizing the full potential of rising talent (volume I): a quantitative analysis of the identification and development of high potential employees.* Washington, DC: Corporate Executive Board.

Daly, M., Egan, M., and O'Reilly, F. 2015. Childhood general cognitive ability predicts leadership role occupancy across life: evidence from 17,000 cohort study participants. *Leadership Quarterly*, 26, pp.323–41.

Derry, S. J., and Murphy, D. A. 1986. Designing systems that train learning ability: from theory to practice. *Review of Educational Research*, 56, pp.1–39.

DeRue, D. S., Ashford, S. J., and Myers, C. G. 2012. Learning agility: in search of conceptual clarity and theoretical grounding. *Industrial and Organizational Psychology*, 5(3), pp.258–79.

Dhuey, E., and Lipscomb, S. 2008. What makes a leader? Relative age and high school leadership. *Economics of Education Review*, 27, pp.173–83.

Dobbins, G. H., Long, W. S., Dedrick, E. J., and Clemons, T. C. 1990. The role of self-monitoring and gender on leader emergence: a laboratory study and field study. *Journal of Management*, 16, pp.609–18.

Dowell, B. E. 2010. Managing leadership talent pools. In R. F. Silzer and B. E. Dowell, eds., *Strategy driven talent management: a leadership imperative*, pp.399–438. San Francisco: Jossey Bass.

Dragoni, L., Oh, I-S., VanKatwyk, P., and Tesluk, P. E. 2011. Developing executive leaders: the relative contribution of cognitive ability, personality and the accumulation of work experiences in predicting strategic thinking competency. *Personnel Psychology*, 64, pp.829–64.

Dunnette, M. D. The assessment of managerial talent. In P. McReynolds (Ed.), *Advances in psychological assessment* (vol. 2). Palo Alto, CA: Science and Behavior Books. Pgs 79–108.

Edmonds, G. W., Jackson, J. J., Fayard, J. V., and Roberts, B. W. 2008. Is character fate or is there hope to change my personality yet? *Social and Personality Psychology Compass*, 2(1), pp.399–413.

Ellis, R. J. 1988. Self-monitoring and leadership emergence in groups. *Personality and Social Psychology Bulletin*, 14, pp.681–93.

Ellis, R. J., Adamson, R. S., Deszca, G., and Cawsay, T. F. 1988. Self-monitoring and leader emergence. *Small Group Behavior*, 19, pp.312–24.

Fiedler, F. E. 1967. *A theory of leadership effectiveness.* New York: McGraw Hill.

Ford, J. K., Smith, E. M., Weissbein, D. A., Gully, S. M. et al. 1998. Relationships of goal orientation, metacognitive activity, and practice strategies with learning outcomes and transfer. *Journal of Applied Psychology*, 83, pp.218–33.

Foti, R. J., and Hauenstein, N. M. A. (2007). Pattern and variable approaches in leadership emergence and effectiveness. *Journal of Applied Psychology*, 92, pp.347–55.

Fullerton Longitudinal Study (FLS). 1988. *Inventory of family functioning (child report).* Unpublished manuscript, Department of Psychology, California State University, Fullerton, Fullerton, CA.

Gibb, C. A. 1947. The principles and traits of leadership. *Journal of Abnormal and Social Psychology*, 4, pp.267–84.

Gottfried, A., and Gottfried, A. 2011. Paths from gifted motivation to leadership. In S. R. Murphy and R. J. Reichard. eds., *Early development and leadership: building the next generation of leaders.* pp. 71–91. New York: Psychology Press/Routledge.

Gottfried, A. E., Gottfried, A. W., Reichard, R. J., Guerin, D. W., Oliver, P. H., and Riggio, R. E. 2011. Motivational roots of leadership: a longitudinal study from childhood through adulthood. *The Leadership Quarterly*, 22(3), pp.510–19.

Gottesman, I. I. 1991. *Schizophrenia genesis: the origins of madness*. New York: Freeman, Gould, LC.

Gough, H. G. 1990. Testing for leadership with the California psychological inventory. In K. E. Clark and M. B. Clark, eds. *Measures of Leadership*, pp.355–79. West Orange, NJ: Leadership Library of America.

Guerin, D. W., Oliver P. M., Gottfried A. W., Gottfried, A. E. et al. 2011. Childhood and adolescent antecedents of social skills and leadership potential in adulthood: temperamental approach/withdrawal and extraversion. *Leadership Quarterly*, 22, pp.482–94.

Hannah, S. T., Avolio, B. J., Luthans, F., and Harms, P. D. 2008. Leadership efficacy: review and future directions. *Leadership Quarterly*, 19, pp.669–92.

Harms, P. D., Spain, S. M., and Hannah, S. T. 2011. Leader development and the dark side of personality. *Leadership Quarterly*, 22, pp.495–509.

Hay Group. 2008. *Growth factor index: technical manual*. Retrieved from www.haygroup.com.

Hewitt Associates. 2003. *Managing high potentials*. Lincolnshire, IL: Hewitt Associates.

Hewitt Associates. 2008. *Getting to high potential: how organizations define and calibrate their critical talent*. Lincolnshire, IL: Hewitt Associates.

Hirschfeld, R. R., Jordan, M. H., Thomas, C. H., and Feild, H. S. 2008. Observed leadership potential of personnel in a team setting: big five traits and proximal factors as predictors. *International Journal of Selection and Assessment*, 16(4), pp.385–402.

Hoffmann, B. J., Woehr, D. J., Maldagen-Youngjohn, R., and Lyons, B. D. 2011. Great man or great myth? A quantitative review of the relationship between individual differences and leader effectiveness. *Journal of Occupational and Organizational Psychology*, 84, pp.347–81.

Hogan, R. 2009a. Hogan Assessment Systems Inc. *The Hogan development survey: overview guide*. Tulsa, OK: Hogan Assessment Systems.

Hogan, R. 2009b. Hogan Assessment Systems. *Sample High Potential, Candidate assessment report*. Tulsa, OK: Hogan Assessment Systems.

Hogan, R., Raskin. R., and Fazzini, D. 1990. The dark side of charisma. In K. E. Clark and M. B. Clark, eds., *Measures of leadership*, pp.343–54. West Orange, NJ: Leadership Library of America.

Hollenbeck, G., McCall, M., and Silzer, R. 2006. Leadership competency models. *Leadership Quarterly*, 17, pp.398–413.

Jaques E., and Clement, S. D. 1991. *Executive leadership*. Arlington, VA: Cason Hall.

Johnsen, B. H., Eid, J., Pallesen, S., Bartone, P. et al. 2009. Predicting transformational leadership in naval cadets: effects of personality hardiness and training. *Journal of Applied Social Psychology*, 39(9), pp.2213–35.

Johnson, R. E., Venus, M., Lanaj, K., Mao, C. et al. 2012. Leader identity as an antecedent of the frequency and consistency of transformational, consideration, and abusive leadership behaviors. *Journal of Applied Psychology*, 97(6), pp.1262–72.

Johnson, A. M., Vernon, P. A., McCarthy, J. M., Molson, M. et al. 1998. Nature vs. nurture: are leaders born or made? A behavior genetic investigation of leadership style. *Twin Research and Human Genetics*, 1(4), pp.216–23.

Johnson, A. M., Vernon, P. A., Harris, J. A., and Jang, K. L., 2004. A behavior genetic investigation of the relationship between leadership and personality. *Twin Research and Human Genetics*, 7(1), pp.27–32.

Judge, T. A., Bono, J. E., Ilies, R., and Gerhardt, M. W. 2002. Personality and leadership: a qualitative and quantitative review. *Journal of Applied Psychology*, 87, pp.765–80.

Judge, T., Colbert, A., and Ilies, R. 2004. Intelligence and leadership: a quantitative review and
test of theoretical propositions. *Journal of Applied Psychology*, 89, pp.542–52.

Judge, T. A., and Piccolo, R. F. 2004. Transformational and transactional leadership: a meta-
analytic test of their relative validity. *Journal of Applied Psychology*, 89(5), pp.755–68.

Karaevli, A., and Hall, D. T. 2003. Growing leaders for turbulent times: is succession planning
up to the challenge? *Organizational Dynamics*, 32(1), pp.62–79.

Kenny, D. A., and Zaccaro, S. J. 1983. An estimate of variance due to traits in leadership. *Journal
of Applied Psychology*, 68, pp.678–85.

Kluger, A. N., and DeNisi, A. 1996. The effects of feedback interventions on performance: a historical review. *Psychological Bulletin*, 119, pp.254–84.

Li, W-D, Arvey, R. D., and Song, Z. 2011. The influence of general mental ability, self-esteem,
and family socioeconomic status on leadership role occupancy and leader advancement: the
moderating role of gender. *Leadership Quarterly*, 22, pp.520–34.

Li, W. D., Arvey, R. D., Zhang, Z., and Song, Z. 2012. Do leadership role occupancy and transformational leadership share the same genetic and environmental influences? *Leadership
Quarterly*, 23, pp.233–43.

Lombardo, M. M., and Eichinger, R. W. 2000. High potentials as high learners. *Human Resource
Management*, 39(4), pp.321–29.

Lord, R. G., DeVader, C. L., and Alliger, G. M. 1986. A meta-analysis of the relation between
personality traits and leadership perceptions: an application of validity generalization procedures. *Journal of Applied Psychology*, 71, pp.402–10.

Lord, R. G., Foti, R. J., and DeVader, C. L. 1984. A test of leadership categorization theory: internal structure, information processing, and leadership perceptions. *Organizational Behavior
and Human Performance*, 34, pp.343–78.

Lykken, D. T., Bouchard, T. J., McGue, M., and Tellegen, A. 1990. The Minnesota twin family registry: some initial findings. *Acta Geneticae Medicae et Gemellologiae: Twin Research*,
39(1), pp.35–70.

McCall, M. W., Jr. 1998. *High flyers: developing the next generation of leaders*. Boston: Harvard
Business School Press.

McCauley, C. D., and McCall, M. W., Jr. 2014. Using experience to develop leadership talent.
San Francisco: Wiley.

McCall, M. W., Lombardo, M. M., and Morrison, A. M. 1988. *The lessons of experience: how
successful executives develop on the job*. New York: The Free Press.

McGue, M., and Bouchard Jr., T. J. 1998. Genetic and environmental influences on human
behavioral differences. *Annual Review of Neuroscience*, 21(1), pp.1–24.

McGue, M., Pickens, R. W., and Svikis, D. S. 1992. Sex and age effects on the inheritance of alco-
hol problems: a twin study. *Journal of Abnormal Psychology*, 101, pp.3–17.

Michaels, E., Handfield-Jones, H., and Axelrod, B. 2001. *The war for talent*. Boston: Harvard
Business School Press.

Mumford, M. D., O'Connor, J, Clifton T. C., Connelly, M. S. et al. 1993. Background data constructs as predictors of leadership behavior. *Human Performance*, 6(2), pp.151–95.

Murphy, S. W., and Johnson, S. K. 2011. The benefits of a long-lens approach to leader development: understanding the seeds of leadership. *The Leadership Quarterly*, 22, pp.459–70.

Nalbantian, H. R., and Guzzo, R. A. 2009. Making mobility matter. *Harvard Business Review*,
March, pp.3–11.

Nyquist, L. V., and Spence. J. T. 1986. Effects of dispositional dominance and sex role expecta-tions on leadership behaviors. *Journal of Personality and Social Psychology, 50*, pp.87–93.

Oliver, P. H., Gottfried, A., Guerin, D. W., Gottfried, A. E. et al. 2011. The adolescent family environmental antecedents to transformational leadership potential: a longitudinal media-tional analysis. *Leadership Quarterly, 22*, pp.535–44.

Ostroff, C. and Judge, T. A. 2007. *Perspectives on organizational fit.* New York: Lawrence Erlbaum.

Parasher, P., and McDaniel, S. L. 2008. *Executive talent management: creating and implement-ing practices that drive business results.* Workshop presented at the Annual conference of the Society of Industrial-Organizational Psychology, San Francisco, April 9.

Peterson, D. B., and Erdahl, P. 2007. *Early identification and development of senior leadership talent: the secret insider's guide.* Workshop presented at the Annual conference of the Society of Industrial-Organizational Psychology, New York, April.

Plomin, R. 1994. *Genetics and experience: the interplay between nature and nurture.* Thousand Oaks, CA: Sage.

Popper, M. 2002. Narcissism and attachment patterns of personalized and socialized charis-matic leaders. *Journal of Social and Personal Relationships, 19*, pp.797–809.

Popper, M., and Amit, K. 2009. Attachment and leader's development via experiences. *The Leadership Quarterly, 20*, pp.749–63.

Popper, M., Amit, K., Gal, R., Mishkal-Sinai, M. et al. 2004. The capacity to lead: major psycho-logical differences between leaders and non-leaders. *Military Psychology, 16*, pp.245–63.

Popper, M., and Mayseless, O. 2007. The building blocks of leader development: a psychological conceptual framework. *Leadership & Organizational Development Journal, 28*, pp.664–84.

Popper, M., Mayseless, O., and Castelnovo, O. (2000). Transformational leadership and attach-ment. *Leadership Quarterly, 11*, pp.267–89.

Pulakos, E. D., Arad, S., Donovan, M. A., and Plamondon, K. E. 2000. Adaptability in the work-place: development of a taxonomy of adaptive performance. *Journal of Applied Psychology, 85*(4), pp.612–24.

Reichard, R. J., Riggio, R. E., Guerin, D. W., Oliver, P. H., Gottfried, A. W., and Gottfried, A. E. 2011. A longitudinal analysis of relationships between adolescent personality and intelligence with adult leader emergence and transformational leadership. *The Leadership Quarterly, 22*(3), pp.471–48.

Reiter-Palmon, R. 2003. Predicting leadership activities: the role of flexibility. *Individual Differences Research, 1*, pp.124–36.

Riggio, R. E., Riggio, H. R., Salinas, C., and Cole, E. J. 2003. The role of social and emotional communication skills in leader emergence and effectiveness. *Group Dynamics: Theory, Research, and Practice, 7*, pp.83–103.

Roberts, B. W., Wood, D., and Caspi, A. 2008. The development of personality traits in adult-hood. In O. P. John, R. W. Robins, and L. A. Pervin, eds., *Handbook of personality: theory and research*, 3rd edn., pp.375–98. New York: Guilford Press.

Rogers, R. W., and Smith, A. B. 2007. *Finding future perfect senior leaders: spotting executive potential.* Bridgeville, PA: Development Dimensions International.

Rowe, K. 2007. How to identify leadership potential. *UK Guide to Skills and Learning,* pp.234–36.

Silzer, R. F. 2015. *Learning agility or learning from experience: define & measure, predict & develop.* In SIOP symposium, V. Harvey (Chair), Can learning agility be learned? At the Annual Conference of the Society for Industrial and Organizational Psychology, Philadelphia, PA.

Silzer, R. F. 2016a. *Leadership: new directions and paradigms for identifying & developing leaders*. Distinguished Professional Contributions Award address at the Annual Conference of the Society for Industrial and Organizational Psychology, Anaheim, CA.

Silzer, R. 2016b. *Learning agility or learning from experience*. In R. Silzer (Chair), Learning agility: fads, challenges and new directions. A symposium at the Midwinter Conference of the Society for Consulting Psychology, Orlando, FL.

Silzer, R. F. 2016c. *Leadership potential: predicting future leaders*. In R. F. Silzer (Chair), Identifying high potential: from bad HR to good behavioral science. A symposium at the Annual Conference of the Society for Industrial and Organizational Psychology, Anaheim, CA.

Silzer, R. 2016d. *Leadership potential: predicting future leaders*. In A. H. Church (chair). Leadership potential—leading edge thinking and applications in organizations. A symposium at the Midwinter Conference of the Society for Consulting Psychology, Orlando, FL.

Silzer, R., and Church, A. H. 2009a. The pearls and perils of identifying potential. *Industrial and Organizational Psychology: Perspectives on Science and Practice*, 2(4), pp.377–412.

Silzer, R. F., and Church, A. H. 2009b. The potential for potential. *Industrial and Organizational Psychology: Perspectives on Science and Practice*, 2(4), pp.446–52.

Silzer, R. F., and Church, A. H. 2010. Identifying and assessing high-potential talent: current organizational practices. In R. F. Silzer and B. E. Dowell, eds., *Strategy driven talent management: a leadership imperative*, pp.213–80. San Francisco: Jossey Bass.

Silzer, R., and Church, A. H. 2016. Strategic talent management. In S. Rogelberg, ed., *SAGE encyclopedia of industrial and organizational psychology*, 2nd edn., Thousand Oaks: Sage.

Silzer, R. F., and Dowell, B. E., eds. 2010a. *Strategy driven talent management: a leadership imperative*. San Francisco: Jossey Bass.

Silzer, R. F., and Dowell, B. E. 2010b. Strategic talent management matters. In R. F. Silzer and B. E. Dowell, eds., *Strategy driven talent management: a leadership imperative*, pp.3–70. San Francisco: Jossey Bass.

Silzer, R. F. 2006. Making a difference in talent management. In A. Church (chair), *Talent management: will the high potentials stand up?* A symposium at the Annual Conference of the Society of Industrial/Organizational Psychology, Houston, Texas.

Silzer, R., Hollenbeck, G., and Fulkerson, J. 2002. *Innovative practices for building 21st century executives*. A workshop at the annual conference of the Society of Industrial and Organizational Psychology, Dallas, Texas.

Silzer, R. F., Slider, R. L., and Knight, M. 1994. *Human resource development: a benchmark study of corporate practices*. St. Louis, MO, and Atlanta, GA: Anheuser-Busch Corporation and Bell South Corporation.

Slan, R., and Hausdorf, P. 2004. *Leadership succession: high potential identification and development*. Toronto: University of Guelph and MICA Management Resources.

Smith, J. A., and Foti, R. J. 1998. A pattern approach to the study of leader emergence. *The Leadership Quarterly*, 9, pp.147–60.

Snyder, M. 1974. Self-monitoring of expressive behavior. *Journal of Personality and Social Psychology*, 30, pp.526–37.

Snyder, M. 1987. *Public appearances/private realities: the psychology of self-monitoring*. New York: W. H. Freeman.

Spreitzer, G. M., McCall, M. W., and Mahoney, J. D. 1997. Early identification of international executive potential. *Journal of Applied Psychology*, 82(1), pp.6–29.

Wells, L. 2009. *Implementing talent management in complex organizations—challenges and approaches.* In Lyse Wells (Chair) Talent management. A symposium at the Annual Conference of the Society of Industrial and Organizational Psychology, New Orleans, Louisiana, 2009.

Wells, S. J. 2003. Who's next: creating a formal program for developing new leaders can pay huge dividends, but many firms aren't reaping those rewards. *HR Magazine, 48*(11), pp.44–64.

Wernimont, P. F., and Campbell, J. P. 1968. Signs, samples and criteria. *Journal of Applied Psychology, 52,* pp.372–76.

Yukl, G. A. 2006. *Leadership in organizations,* 6th edn. Upper Saddle River, NJ: Pearson Prentice-Hall.

Zaccaro, S. J. 2007. Trait-based perspectives of leadership. *American Psychologist, 62,* pp.6–16.

Zaccaro, S. J., Connelly, S., Repchick, K. M., Daza, A. I. et al. 2015. The influence of higher order cognitive capacities on leader organizational continuance and retention: the mediating role of developmental experiences. *Leadership Quarterly, 26,* pp.342–58.

Zaccaro, S. J., Foti, R. J., and Kenny, D. A. 1991. Self-monitoring and trait-based variance in leadership: an investigation of leader flexibility across multiple group situations. *Journal of Applied Psychology, 76,* pp.308–15.

Zemke, R., Raines, C., and Filipczak, B. 2000. *Generations at work: managing the clash of veterans, boomers, xers, and nexters in your workplace.* New York: American Management Association.

Zhang, Z., Ilies, R., and Arvey, R. D. 2009. Beyond genetic explanations for leadership: the moderating role of the social environment. *Organizational Behavior and Human Decision Processes, 110*(2), pp.118–28.

CHAPTER 6

MANAGING TALENT ACROSS ORGANIZATIONS

The Portability of Individual Performance

GINA DOKKO AND WINNIE JIANG

THE management of talent in organizations has largely been about the attraction and retention of valued employees (Lewis and Heckman, 2006). Organizations believe that hiring the most talented people will yield competitive advantage, and so go to great lengths to recruit them. Organizations also fear losing talented individuals, especially to competitors, so sometimes go to extraordinary measures to retain them. At the same time, talent is increasingly mobile. The psychological, social, and economic ties that have held individuals to employers have eroded as employment security, job ladders, and pensions have given way to boundaryless careers (Arthur and Rousseau, 1996) and market-driven employment practices (Cappelli, 1999; Cascio and Boudreau, Ch. 28, this volume).

Given the relatively free movement of individuals in contemporary labor markets, and the emphasis on talented individuals as a key element of strategic human resources practices, it is important to understand what individuals bring with them as they enter organizations. This question is more important than ever, since individuals now enter organizations at all hierarchical levels and in all sorts of jobs. In fact, only about a third of hires are internal, and many firms have backed away from succession planning in favor of external recruiting (Cappelli, 2015). Instead of a traditional internal labor market model where ports of entry into organizations are primarily at lower levels (Doeringer and Piore, 1971), talented individuals enter organizations in many positions, bringing with them widely varied levels and types of experience and knowledge.

Experienced talent is hired with the expectation that experience will convert to performance, but performance is not perfectly portable across organization boundaries. Research suggests that there are social and cognitive barriers that prevent easy transfer of skills and knowledge to new contexts (Dokko and Rosenkopf, 2009; Groysberg, Lee, and Nanda, 2008; Huckman and Pisano, 2006). Moreover, hiring for different types of experience might have different outcomes. Recruiting star performers and placing them in the same type of job in a new organization might bring relevant knowledge and skill or social connections (Somaya, Williamson, and Lorinkova, 2008), but recruiting more broadly might have positive effects on innovation (Song, Almeida, and Wu, 2003).

Just as individuals join organizations at all levels, they correspondingly leave organizations at all levels. Losing individuals who have deep firm-specific experience, or those who have been in strategic positions or made strategic contributions to a firm, could have significant consequences, which could vary according to where they go: for example, to competitors, to customers, or to start new ventures (Campbell, Ganco, Franco, and Agarwal, 2012b; Somaya, Williamson, and Lorinkova, 2008). Further, questions about what individuals take with them when they leave need to be considered independently from questions about what they bring when they join an organization, since the effects of hiring and losing employees are asymmetric (Dokko and Rosenkopf, 2010). Organizations do not necessarily lose the skills, knowledge, and social connections of departing employees, if they are able to appropriate their knowledge or relationships (Corredoira and Rosenkopf, 2010; Dokko and Rosenkopf, 2010).

Questions about the portability of performance are particularly important as they relate to talent. We take a broad view of talent, including individuals who are high performing or high potential (Stahl et al., 2012) and professionals (Mawdsley and Somaya, 2016), that is, those with high levels of human capital from superior education or experience. Since these individuals are valued for their superior skills and knowledge, and often are hired at a premium price (Groysberg, Nanda, and Nohria, 2004), it is critical to consider if their superior skills and knowledge will generate superior performance in a new organizational context. Given the high cost associated with recruiting and retaining talent, having a refined understanding of the portability of performance, along with ideas to address barriers to portability, is critical to enabling talent to contribute fully to organizational performance.

In this chapter, we discuss the portability of performance as talented individuals cross organizational boundaries, as well as the implications for an organization's talent-management strategy and practices. When organizations think about "poaching" talent, are they going to get what they want? What do organizations really lose when talent exits? To explore these questions, we will review the literature on job mobility and the portability of performance by developing a framework that considers human capital, social capital, and identity issues that arise when mobile talent crosses organizational boundaries. We consider organizational entry and exit separately because the effects of mobility in and out are asymmetric (Dokko and Rosenkopf, 2010). We will then turn to implications for organizations. Mobile talent is part of the reality of the modern workforce, and organizations whose talent-management practices can accommodate the careers of valuable workers are better positioned to take full advantage of their human resources.

6.1 Performance in Context: The Imperfect Portability of Individual Performance

When firms hire for experience, the underlying assumption is that the performance in a prior job can be easily replicated in a new organization. However, this simplifying assumption masks the complexity of work in context. The literature on the consequences of job mobility has grown rapidly in the past ten years, and evidence is mounting that individual performance is not perfectly portable. Individuals do not function in a vacuum. Rather, individual performance is a function of not only individual but also organizational factors, such as the team to which the person belongs, organizational routines, or other complementary assets, which are left behind as a person moves to a new organizational context.

To the extent that the context supports an individual's performance, a change in context will impinge on his or her performance. Job performance in context helps to explain why external hires to an investment bank performed worse than internal hires in comparable jobs, even though they appeared more qualified in terms of education and experience, and were paid more (Bidwell, 2011). Even star performers may suffer a performance decline when they change employers. Analyses of star security analysts' performance after they moved to a different firm revealed that they experienced a drop in rated performance that persisted for up to five years (Groysberg, Lee, and Nanda, 2008).

In order to understand the portability of performance, it is necessary to understand what individuals carry across organizational boundaries that enables or constrains their performance. Individuals' performance is generated by their human and social capital (Waldman and Spangler, 1989), so we start by examining the portability of these assets. In addition, changing employers involves changes to one's self-concept and social identity, as well as cognition (Ibarra and Barbulescu, 2010). Identity, mental models, and assumptions are increasingly recognized as playing a role in the transfer of performance across organizational boundaries, so we also discuss the findings and implications about these factors in work-role transitions. We consider the issues that arise for individuals at organizational entry and exit.

6.2 Human Capital

When considering what mobile talent brings into or takes away from an organization, often the first category that comes to mind is the individual's human capital, in other words, the knowledge, skills, and abilities embodied in a person. Since Becker (1962) proposed the concept of human capital, the literature has recognized the distinction between general and specific human capital. General human capital refers to knowledge, skills, and capabilities that are valuable to all firms, whereas specific human capital consists of those that are valuable only to a particular firm, occupation, or industry (Ang, Slaughter, and Ng, 2002; Harris and Helfat, 1997; Pennings, Lee, and Van Witteloostuijn, 1998). For example, an engineer's knowledge about physical laws, a computer scientist's programming skills, and a consultant's ability to identify and solve problems are all considered general human capital because they are likely to remain useful, regardless of organizational context.

Specific human capital, on the other hand, is only useful in a particular context or for a particular use. Most research has focused on firm-specific human capital, such as knowledge of the firm's unique product and market position, technology, and organizational structure, as well as the common language, identification, and culture shared among employees (Becker, 1975). More recent work has considered degrees of firm specificity or has extended the idea of specificity to occupations and industries (Campbell, Coff, and Kryscynski, 2012a; Mayer, Somaya, and Williamson 2012). Occupation- and industry-specific human capital comprises, for example, knowledge of particular professional practices and industry rules (Castanias and Helfat, 2001). Occupational experience is a key component of selection into organizations (Wilk and Cappelli, 2003). Organizations also pay a premium for talent coming from the same industry because industry-specific knowledge is useful to other industry participants (Ang, Slaughter, and Ng, 2002). When talented individuals move within occupations or industries, the occupation- and industry-specific human capital accumulated in their previous firms should be portable in a useful way, as occupational skills and industry knowledge should be applicable to other jobs in the same occupation or within the industry.

6.2.1 Human Capital at Organizational Entry

Organizations want to absorb the full value of incoming talent through successful acquisition of talented individuals' human capital, which is reflected in their prior performance. Leaders have a particularly strong effect. For instance, Pfeffer and Davis-Blake (1986), in their analysis of twenty-two teams in the National Basketball Association, found that a successor coach's prior experience and performance affect the team's subsequent performance. Incoming C-suite executives use what they know and direct new product entry into areas where they have prior experience (Boeker, 1997). Research on entrepreneurial ventures founded by ex-employees (i.e., "spin-outs") has also found that their parent firms' capabilities positively influence the spin-outs' survival and capabilities (Agarwal, Echambadi, Franco, and Sarkar, 2004), suggesting that the knowledge and skills employees acquired from parent firms can facilitate the formation and development of their new ventures.

Organizations expect that incoming talent will demonstrate comparable performance and impact with a new employer, which is one reason that talent is pursued so keenly. However, these expectations are not perfectly realizable. There is a growing body of evidence that there are barriers to the easy transfer of human capital across settings.

Even highly specialized professionals, whose skills seem like they should transcend organizational boundaries, have different performance levels in different organizations. For example, cardiac surgeons' success rates vary across the different hospitals where they perform surgeries, that is, patients operated on in the hospital where the surgeon performs a higher volume of procedures are more likely to survive (Huckman and Pisano, 2006). This finding suggests that individual performance depends in part on complementary assets like equipment, facilities, and other team members that enable performance (Campbell, Ganco, Franco, and Agarwal, 2012b), even for highly professionalized roles like that of cardiac surgeon. Indeed, the star financial analysts mentioned earlier whose performance fell as they changed employers experienced less of a performance decline if they moved collectively with their colleagues, a phenomenon commonly called "a lift out" (Groysberg, Lee, and Nanda, 2008; Groysberg and Lee, 2009). Therefore, a lack of complementary assets in a new setting can act as a barrier, preventing the full use of human capital.

In addition to these barriers to transfer, individuals can carry things they should have left behind. Mental models, cognitive and behavioral habits, and assumptions that enabled efficient performance in the previous firm can interfere with the effective application of human capital in a new context. Task-relevant knowledge and skills are not the only things employees acquire through their experience with past firms. Individuals also internalize an organization's norms, values, and cognitive conventions (Dokko and Rosenkopf, 2009). Internalized culture and cognitive habits can improve performance within an organization because they facilitate communication and mutual understanding with colleagues (Edwards and Cable, 2009), but because of their taken-for-granted nature, they can interfere with performance. For example, moving from an organization that values efficiency and cost saving to one that values premium customer service can result in aiming for the wrong performance target (Dokko and Rosenkopf, 2009). Once an individual moves to a different organization, his or her cognitions formed in the prior firm can become "baggage" that hinders performance in the new context, at least in the short term. Again, these effects can be especially consequential for mobile talent. Those who have held higher-ranked positions or demonstrated remarkable performance in their prior firms are generally more involved in the creation, enactment, and enforcement of the firms' routines (Hall and Schneider, 1972). Therefore, talented employees may actually be more likely to introduce unsuitable practices that may hurt the new organization (Phillips, 2002).

6.2.2 Human Capital at Organizational Exit

Even if exiting talent cannot fully perform for a new employer, the prior employer still loses human capital. However, the damage to the losing organization depends on the extent to which the knowledge and skill held by the mobile talent is replicated elsewhere in the organization. To some extent, each individual holds a unique set of firm-specific knowledge, so replacing a departing person always entails some friction, though the cost to an organization is lower when other individuals in the organization have the same skills (Hausknecht and Holwerda, 2013). Smaller firms, where fewer people perform a greater number of unique functions, could be particularly at risk for the loss of human capital. The loss of higher-level people and those occupying mission-critical jobs (i.e., jobs that are vital to the functioning of an organization), especially, can have larger impacts on organizations simply because there are fewer of them, and they are more likely to hold unique knowledge. Further, though losing executives is associated with firm failure, losing those with internally facing (i.e., administration, finance, and operations) jobs has a larger effect (Bermiss and Murmann, 2015).

Complicating the loss of human capital, the extent of loss depends on where talent goes. Mobile talent often has a variety of alternatives, and some destinations are more consequential than others are. Campbell, Ganco, Franco, and Agarwal (2012b) show that higher-paid individuals in the legal services industry are less likely to move, but when they do, they are more likely to start their own new firms. Notable in this study is that the new firms (i.e., law firms) compete with the existing firm, which suffers a drop in performance. The transfer of human capital from a firm to a startup via the mobility of individuals could even lead to the failure of the firm, especially when higher-level talent leaves (Phillips, 2002), or when groups of people leave together (Wezel, Cattani, and Pennings, 2006). Therefore, despite barriers to compete or efficient transfer of human capital to new organizations, the loss of human capital can still be harmful or even fatal to the source organization.

6.3 Social Capital

In addition to human capital, mobile talent can transport social capital across organizational boundaries. Although multiple definitions of *social capital* have been proposed (see Adler and Kwon, 2002), this concept is generally understood as the resources available to individuals as a result of their positions in the social structure or the quantity and quality of their social relations (Adler and Kwon, 2002; Leana and Pil, 2006). Social capital has been examined in such disciplines as sociology, economics, political science, and organization studies. Research has noted the important role it plays in affecting both individual-level outcomes, such as finding a job, pay and promotions, job performance, and innovativeness (Belliveau, O'Reilly, and Wade, 1996; Burt, 2004; Castilla, 2005; Granovetter, 1995/1974; Seibert, Kraimer, and Liden, 2001), and organizational-level outcomes, such as interfirm knowledge transfer, firm performance, and even firm survival (Gulati, 1998; Inkpen and Tsang, 2005; Pennings, Lee, and Van Witteloostuijn, 1998; Shane and Stuart, 2002).

For mobile talent, the social capital they carry across organizational boundaries depends on the relationships they can sustain. Relationships with clients, suppliers, alliance partners, or professional associations can all be valuable inputs to performance that might or might not be portable. Relationships enable performance in obvious ways by providing revenue or access to scarce supplies, but they also function in less obvious ways. The structure and content of relationships can provide information about the environment that can enable choices and actions that facilitate performance, as well as information about opportunities for new ways to create value (Burt, 1997; Podolny and Baron, 1997). A social network position that bridges otherwise disconnected parties can benefit the holder of this position by providing access to diverse sets of information that can be recombined into innovative ideas (Burt, 2004). Such a position can also enable control over the flow of information between the disconnected parties that can be parlayed into opportunities to profit from an intermediary role (Burt, 1992). Social capital's role in the portability of performance is complex in that mobility entails a change in position, and changes to relationships.

6.3.1 Social Capital at Organizational Entry

When organizations hire talent, they may also be thinking about the social capital brought into the firm. This is most clearly the case when sales representatives or service providers are hired for their client relationships. Individuals matter to firm-level relationships; for example, firms change auditors if their needs change, but they are less likely to change if there is a stable individual-level relationship between client and auditor (Seabright, Levinthal, and Fichman, 1992). If mobile individuals can keep their client relationships and the revenue associated with those relationships, then their performance can be maintained. There is some evidence that this might be the case. When account services executives leave an advertising agency, their clients are likely to switch agencies (Broschak, 2004). Patent law firms that hire from competitors get more business from the clients of those competitors, as does hiring from the clients themselves (Somaya, Williamson, and Lorinkova, 2008). Similarly, relationships with vendors and suppliers might also be portable, and of value to individual and organizational performance (Carnahan and Somaya, 2013). Excellent supplier relationships can lead to efficiencies and cost savings, and could be a valuable resource. In addition to market ties to customers and suppliers, firms may also think of using influence that individuals have to accomplish important firm outcomes. For example, in technical standards setting, firms hire individuals for their social capital, which leads to influence over which technology standards are adopted (Dokko and Rosenkopf, 2010). Therefore, individual-level social capital from interorganizational relationships can be portable, but the benefit to the organization depends on both the individual's ability to bring the relationships and the firm's ability to appropriate the social capital for its own uses.

6.3.2 Social Capital at Organizational Exit

Individuals can carry their own social capital when they leave a firm. Even if people are no longer working together, they may still talk, especially if they are in the same occupation or industry. Keeping relationships with co-workers can create new ties between organizations that can be appropriated for the organization's purposes. For example, Corredoira and Rosenkopf (2010) find that losing semiconductor engineers can open channels of learning with the hiring firms. However, the effect of talent losses for firms depends heavily on the connection between individual and firm social capital, as well as on where the talent goes (Carnahan and Somaya, 2015). Even though interfirm relationships are executed at the individual level, organizations that actively manage relationships can be protected even when their individual relationship managers move on (Bermiss and Murmann, 2015). The engineers in technical standards setting mentioned earlier carried their individual social capital to their new employer, increasing the new employer's social capital, but their old employers did not suffer a decrease in social capital (Dokko and Rosenkopf, 2010).

Finally, the talent's destination matters. Moving to competitors is harmful to the source firm, while moving to customers can result in more business from those customers, as the relationship between the firms becomes closer (Somaya, Williamson, and Lorinkova, 2008). And, even when talent moves to a competitor, competitive behavior at the individual level is attenuated when the individual encounters a former co-worker (Grohsjean, Kober, and Zucchini, 2016). Therefore, exiting individuals can retain their individual ties and even carry them to a new employer, but the effect on the losing firms is not always a loss. Firms that maintain their relationships at the firm level are insulated against the loss of individual social capital. They can even come out ahead, if they would benefit from learning from the new employer, or if the mobile talent moves to a customer or supplier.

6.4 IDENTITY AND COGNITION

Work is a central part of most people's identity. *Identity* (i.e., self-concept; Ibarra, 1999) and *social identity* (i.e., psychological attachment to a social group such as a work team, organization, or occupation; Ashforth and Mael, 1989; Tajfel and Turner, 1986) are shaped by individuals' experiences and affiliations, and they determine how individuals see themselves in relation to the world around them. Individuals' identities include aspects of self-definition, beliefs and values, and behaviors (Ashforth, Harrison, and Corley, 2008). Work is also situated in an organizational and institutional context and it shapes the way individuals think about their work and the assumptions and values they bring to work. Individuals build mental models about the way work should be done and about what constitutes good performance (Dokko, Wilk, and Rothbard, 2009; Kraatz and Moore, 2002). Since these identities and cognitions are set by or in relation to context, changing contexts through job moves can lead to mismatches with new employers that prevent the easy transfer of performance.

Unlike human and social capital, identity and cognition are not typically what organizations consider when they hire talent. However, as individuals move across firm boundaries, they carry aspects of identity and assumptions that enable or impede performance.

Identities are complex, in that multiple independent identities can be held at the same time (Ashforth and Johnson, 2001). Individuals can identify with multiple targets at once, such as organizations and occupations (Ashforth, Anand, and O'Leary-Kelly, 2013; Elsbach, 1999). An engineer, for example, can identify with both an employer and the occupation of engineering (Dokko, Nigam, and Rosenkopf, 2012). Occupations that are highly professionalized can be particularly strong targets of identification as the training and socialization for professions is both intensive and standardized (Ibarra, 1999; Pratt, Rockmann, and Kaufmann, 2006). Having multiple identifications can cause conflict, such as when the demands of an employing organization conflict with professional norms and values.

Second, both identity and cognition are sticky, such that even after a career change, identification with old employers or occupations can persist in conscious ways (e.g., joining a firm's alumni organization) or less conscious ways as peoples' identities shape values or attention processes (Dokko, Wilk, and Rothbard, 2009). Saying "we" when referring to a former employer is a common occurrence. This stickiness can be particularly consequential when talent moves. For example, CEOs and other organizational leaders bring mental models that can change the strategic direction of an entire organization (Boeker, 1997; Kraatz and Moore, 2002). Identity and cognition can also be consequential to individual performance, as they affect whom individuals pay attention to, and what aspects of performance they prioritize. Recognizing the role of identity and cognition in work transitions can enable smoother entry and more productive exit for talent.

6.4.1 Identity and Cognition at Organizational Entry

Identity and cognition carried by mobile talent can affect the portability of their performance. To the extent that existing identities, mental models, and assumptions are congruent with the demands of the new context, performance transfer can be easier. For professionals like medical doctors, engineers, or attorneys, identifying strongly with the profession may facilitate the portability of performance. Because professionals are relatively autonomous and they have control over their work and the standards by which their work is judged (Abbott, 1991), their professional identities might enable them to be effective across contexts, though they may still suffer transfer losses owing to imperfectly portable human or social capital (Huckman and Pisano, 2006). Occupations with less autonomy and less control over work may be more subject to losses owing to differences in organizational context, such that persistent identification with old employers or mental models that come from prior work lead individuals to limit their attention in the wrong way or to make incorrect assumptions about what kinds of behaviors and outcomes are valued.

When talented individuals join organizations, identity and cognition carried from past affiliations can shape their perspectives and influence their actions. Career backgrounds condition attention to social referents for learning or assessing legitimacy of actions. For example, Gaba and Dokko (2016) found that corporate venture capital managers in IT firms paid attention to and learned from the actions of venture capital firms if they were formerly venture capitalists, while internal hires followed IT industry peers. This direction of attention may or may not be desirable for the individual or the organization, depending on the strategic needs of the organization. Individuals also carry models of how firms should operate from their prior employers that can influence their decisions on how to structure their organizations, including functional structure (Beckman and Burton, 2008) and opportunity structure (Phillips, 2005). As talent is more likely to have influence or control over these major decisions, the way that attention and influence is carried through identity and cognition can have substantial impact on the employer and on the individual's performance.

Work-role transitions are usually accompanied by identity transitions (Van Maanen and Schein, 1979). Even though identity can be flexible and adaptive (Elsbach, 1999), identity construction or reconstruction requires psychological work (Creed, Dejordy, and Lok, 2010; Ibarra, 1999; Ibarra and Barbulescu, 2010). Adjustment to a new role entails learning not only the skills that enable productive work but also the mindset, values, and norms associated with the role. However, because identity and cognitions contain taken-for-granted beliefs, values, and assumptions, it is not always immediately obvious that such psychological work needs to happen, especially when occupation or industry stay constant. Moving from one software engineering job to another may seem like an easy transition, but may actually require psychological work to adjust rapidly to a new employment context (Ashforth, Harrison, and Corley, 2008; Ibarra, 1999).

6.4.2 Identity and Cognition at Organizational Exit

Exiting talent can continue to identify with his or her previous employers, which can also aid and facilitate the maintenance of social capital, as discussed in a previous section. Persistent identification can also be the source of a general propensity to favor the products or services of a previous employer. For example, former McKinsey & Company consultants often use their positions in management to contract for consulting services from McKinsey, even from divisions where they have no personal connections. On the other hand, moving to a competitor can increase the motivation to compete. Grohsjean, Kober, and Zucchini (2016) show that hockey players who change teams compete harder against their former teams, in an effort to de-identify with their former team. Joining a competing firm provides an incentive to do the psychological work necessary to change work identity, because it sets up a direct conflict between the old employer and new employer as identity targets.

Identity issues can also arise at organizational exit if the separation is acrimonious. Highly talented individuals, like anyone else, can have irreconcilable differences with employers or co-workers that lead to exit. To the extent that the feelings of the exiting talent or the character of his or her relationships within a firm are unfriendly or even hostile, exiting talent can disidentify with the firm. Organizational disidentification, that is, a negatively valenced separation between a person and an organization, can lead to negative behaviors, such as supporting an opposing organization or publicly criticizing the organization (Elsbach and Bhattacharya, 2001).

6.5 IMPLICATIONS FOR MANAGING MOBILE TALENT

The emphasis on acquiring talent has overshadowed the difficulties in actually using the talent for performance. By one estimate, half of all senior outside hires fail within their first eighteen months (Bauer, 2010). Given that organizations pay a substantial premium for outside talent (Bidwell, 2011), understanding what they bring to the workplace is a necessary step toward enabling them to do their best work. Ideally, organizations would like the acquired talent to demonstrate comparable or better performance in the new organizational context, through a smooth and perfect transmission of the individuals' human capital, their social capital, and the facilitative facets of their identity. However, as research in career mobility suggests, hiring talent does not necessarily lead to successful utilization of the talent's capital, and it does not guarantee that the talented individual would be able to successfully transfer his or her performance. On the other hand, losing talent does not have to be an absolute loss. The popular idiom applies: there is a silver lining. Losing talent can potentially bring to organizations unexpected gains, such as new social resources. Understanding the portability of performance through the lens of the human capital, social capital, and identity carried by individuals suggests actions that organizations can take to improve their talent-management practices. Table 6.1 summarizes the framework and implications we propose.

6.5.1 Implications for Organizational Entry: Talent Acquisition Does Not Mean Talent Utilization

The findings from mobility and portability research provide organizations with several practical implications. First and foremost, organizations' socialization practices, or "onboarding," are an opportunity to address the barriers to importing performance. Currently, most organizations focus intensively on attracting and acquiring talent, and assume that these high-performing and well-paid individuals will "hit the ground running." Leaving talented hires to figure out on their own how to use their skills and other resources to benefit their new employer may take time, and that could be avoided with better onboarding practices. Getting talent in is only the first step. Even highly experienced, skilled, and capable individuals can benefit from appropriate socialization into a new organization.

Table 6.1 Portability of Performance at Organizational Entry and Exit

	Human Capital	Social Capital	Identity and Cognition
Entry issues	Firm-specific knowledge and skills do not transfer • Complementary assets • Team capital Professional skills and knowledge will transfer more easily	Interfirm relationships might not transfer because they are at the firm level rather than the individual level • Client ties • Vendor ties • Alliances	Complex identity/identity conflict (professional vs. firm) Persistence of attachment to old employers Persistent mental models, and taken-for-granted assumptions
Exit issues	Loss of non-redundant knowledge and skill Competitive implications involving organizational knowledge and routines	Exiting individuals can create new interfirm ties Moves to customers can increase business Moves to competitors can decrease business	Desire to shed old identity because of unfavorable exit conditions • Exit owing to misfit • Disidentification
Implications	Consider context similarity Design customized socialization Processes • Address the need to unlearn • Consider hiring and socializing groups (lift-outs) • Specialized socialization for professionals—emphasis on adapting to organizational Context	Consider likelihood of client mobility in selection and salary process Socialization processes should include within-firm network building opportunities	Socialization that supports identity work Take advantage of professional identity for organizational improvement Offboarding processes that enable continued favorable identification Consider rehire opportunities Build and manage alumni communities

Specifically, to facilitate the transfer of useful human capital, organizations may consider designing customized socialization processes for incoming talent with different backgrounds. Especially for professionals, more specialized socialization processes that emphasize adapting to the new organizational context may be offered. These customized processes should acknowledge and address the need to help new hires unlearn the mental models and assumptions they have developed in previous organizations. In addition, organizations may consider hiring a group of employees who have worked well together and socializing them together into the new organizational context. Moreover, socialization should be treated as a continuous process instead of a set of separate activities and events (Adkins, 1995). Socialization processes could be used to help new hires develop valuable social capital and a new organizational identity, by including opportunities for within-firm relationship building and creating a supportive environment for new hires to form new organizational identities (Petrieglieri and Petrieglieri, 2010).

Organizations could also consider paying more attention to the similarity in context between the individuals' future and prior working environments in the process of identifying and acquiring potential talent, given that context plays an essential role in sustaining and supporting individuals' performance. If an organization is similar to the incoming talent's prior firm in several dimensions—for example, if they are geographically co-located or match in terms of organizational structure and culture—the incoming talent might find it easier to apply knowledge and skills and leverage his or her resources for the new employer. Recognizing the effect of context similarity on performance transmission will also help organizations avoid falling into the trap of overpaying for incoming talent's prior performance by properly accounting for onboarding costs or other transition costs to "get up to speed." On the other hand, organizations may also consider how they can take advantage of talent's professional or occupational identity for organizational improvement. Strong identification with a profession can imply a high standard of practice or state-of-the-art techniques and knowledge that can enhance organizational performance.

6.5.2 Implications for Organizational Exit: The Silver Lining in Losing People

To minimize the losses of potential talent departure, organizations should understand clearly what kinds of resources the talent is carrying and may consider ensuring that redundant skills, knowledge, and social connections are held elsewhere in the organization. Organizations spend significant time and resources in trying to retain talented employees, but human assets can walk out the door at any time (Coff, 1997). Talented workers are especially mobile, and organizations are often unprepared to handle the aftermath of talent departure. Talent departure, especially departure of individuals in key leadership positions, is least destructive if there is a ready successor in the organization who possesses similar knowledge and skills and occupies a similar social network position as the departing individual.

However, insulating against loss is not the only thing that organizations can do when talent exits. Organizations may be able to gain some benefit to counter losses by maintaining relationships with the departing talent. Some organizations have recognized the benefits of keeping prior employees connected by supporting or even creating firm alumni organizations. However, explicitly and thoughtfully maintaining relationships with talented ex-employees can partially offset the impact of losing them. For example, sustained contact with firm alumni can provide access to the ex-employee's expanded resources, especially social connections with their new firms. Since individuals can carry social connections as they change employers, they can continue to contribute to their old employer by opening an interfirm conduit that can lead to learning or cooperative relationships like alliances (Corredoira and Rosenkopf, 2010; Rosenkopf, Metiu, and George, 2001). Furthermore, organizations can design "offboarding" processes that encourage departing talent to hold a continued favorable identification with the firm. Current offboarding processes focus on gathering information about why employees quit or to ease the administrative transition. For departing talent, organizations may be better off taking a proactive and forward-looking approach that cultivates an ongoing relationship. They could even discuss the possibility of being rehired. Boomerang employees—those who leave but later return to an organization—have been found to represent a valuable staffing resource because of their previously established familiarity with the organization (Shipp, Furst-Holloway, Harris, and Rosen, 2014).

6.6 FUTURE DIRECTIONS FOR UNDERSTANDING THE PORTABILITY OF PERFORMANCE

As the relations between employees and employers change and workforce participants seek more diverse challenges and opportunities, individuals' careers have moved from the traditional, linear path to a multidirectional, boundaryless model (Arthur and Rousseau, 1996). Empirically, shorter employment relationships have been observed during the past thirty years (Bidwell, 2013), indicating an increasing level of individual mobility in the work force. The movement of individual employees across organizational contexts has been receiving growing attention from researchers and practitioners, with special attention to those who are labeled as talented.

Despite advances in knowledge about the portability of individual performance, there remain a number of interesting directions for future research. Still to be considered, for example, are interactions between human capital, social capital, and identity and cognition. Do human capital and identity interact for mobile talent such that identity constrains the use of skills and knowledge? If mobile talent identifies strongly with a prior employer, will it enable or constrain the formation of interfirm connections between old and new employers? Similarly, does identification with the prior employer have an amplifying or suppressing effect on the exercise of the mover's human capital?

There may be contingencies that shape the portability of performance. We have touched on some of these factors, such as professionalization or complementary assets, but other individual-level factors may affect how portable performance is. Adaptability, innovativeness, and conscientiousness are a few possible personal characteristics that might make some movers more likely to transfer their human capital, social capital, and identity to new situations. New generations with different values and priorities may also experience job mobility in a psychologically distinct way (Twenge, 2006), leading to differences in how their performance transfers. In addition to individual-level factors, macro-level factors (e.g., from organization, industry, or institutions) could also affect the portability of individual performance. We discussed earlier how moving within professionalized occupations or stable industries might facilitate transfer of performance. Likewise, moving between industries with similar structures or growth patterns or firms with similar strategies or organizational structures might allow for easier transfer than would moving between structures that are very different.

Future research can examine these factors and others to understand better the increasingly important effects of mobility on performance of firms and individuals. As individuals move more freely across organizational boundaries, the question of whether they could sustain their performance and bring about desired outcomes after the move becomes more important, especially since many organizations now spend a significant amount of time, effort, and resources in attracting the people they deem as talented (Cappelli, 2008). Our objective in this chapter was to develop a framework that provides a structured way of thinking about the portability of individual performance, and the implications for firms. Considering how human capital, social capital, and identity and cognition relate to mobile individuals' performance enables more precise understanding of the issues that both prevent the perfect portability of performance and reveal opportunities for firms to counterbalance talent losses.

REFERENCES

Abbott, A. D. 1991. The order of professionalization: an empirical analysis. *Work & Occupations*, *18*(4), pp.355–84.

Adkins, C. L. 1995. Previous work experience and organizational socialization—a longitudinal examination. *Academy of Management Journal*, *38*(3), pp.839–62.

Agarwal, R., Echambadi, R., Franco, A. M., and Sarkar, M. B. 2004. Knowledge transfer through inheritance: spin-out generation, development, and survival. *Academy of Management Journal*, *47*(4), pp.501–22.

Ang, S., Slaughter, S., and Ng, K. Y. 2002. Human capital and institutional determinants of information technology compensation: modeling multilevel and cross-level interactions. *Management Science*, *48*(11), pp.1427–45.

Arthur, M. B., and Rousseau, D. M. 1996. *The boundaryless career: a new employment principle for a new organizational era.* New York: Oxford University Press, p.394.

Ashforth, B. E., Harrison, S. H., and Corley, K. G. 2008. Identification in organizations: An examination of four fundamental questions. *Journal of Management*, *34*(3), pp.325–74.

Ashforth, B. E., Joshi, M., Anand, V., and O'Leary-Kelly, A. M. 2013. Extending the expanded model of organizational identification to occupations. *Journal of Applied Social Psychology*, *43*(12), pp.2426–48.

Ashforth, B. E., and Johnson, S. A. 2001. Which hat to wear? The relative salience of multiple identities in organizational contexts. In M. A. Hogg and D. J. Terry, eds., *Social identity processes in organizational contexts*, pp.31–48. Philadelphia: Psychology Press.

Ashforth, B. E., and Mael, F. A. 1989. Social identity theory and the organization. *Academy of Management Review*, *14*(1), pp.20–39.

Bauer, T. 2010. *Onboarding new employees: maximizing success.* Effective practice guidelines series. Alexandria, VA: SHRM Foundation.

Becker, G. S. 1962. Investment in human capital: a theoretical analysis. *Journal of Political Economy*, 70(5), pp.9–49.

Becker, G. S. [1964] 1975. *Human capital: a theoretical and empirical analysis, with special reference to education*, 2nd edn. New York: NBER.

Beckman, C. M., and Burton, M. D. 2008. Founding the future: path dependence in the evolution of top management teams from founding to IPO. *Organization Science*, 19(1), pp.3–24.

Belliveau, M. A., O'Reilly, C. A., and Wade, J. B. 1996. Social capital at the top: effects of social similarity and status on CEO compensation. *Academy of Management Journal*, 39(6), pp.1568–93.

Bermiss, Y. S., and Murmann, J. P. 2015. Who matters more? The impact of functional background and top executive mobility on firm survival. *Strategic Management Journal*, 36(11), pp.1697–716.

Bidwell, M. 2011. Paying more to get less: the effects of external hiring versus internal mobility. *Administrative Science Quarterly*, 56(3), pp.369–407.

Bidwell, M. J. 2013. What happened to long-term employment? The role of worker power and environmental turbulence in explaining declines in worker tenure. *Organization Science*, 24(4), pp.1061–82.

Boeker, W. 1997. Executive migration and strategic change: the effect of top manager movement on product-market entry. *Administrative Science Quarterly*, 42, pp.213–36.

Broschak, J. P. 2004. Managers' mobility and market interface: the effect of managers' career mobility on the dissolution of market ties. *Administrative Science Quarterly*, 49(4), pp.608–40.

Burt, R. S. 1992. *Structural holes: the social structure of competition*. Cambridge, MA: Harvard University Press, p.313.

Burt, R. S. 1997. The contingent value of social capital. *Administrative Science Quarterly*, 42(1), pp.339–65.

Burt, R. S. 2004. Structural holes and good ideas. *American Journal of Sociology*, 110(2), pp.349–99.

Campbell, B. A., Coff, R., and Kryscynski, D. 2012a. Rethinking sustained competitive advantage from human capital. *Academy of Management Review*, 37(3), pp.376–95.

Campbell, B. A., Ganco, M., Franco, A. M., and Agarwal, R. 2012b. Who leaves, where to, and why worry? Employee mobility, entrepreneurship and effects on source firm performance. *Strategic Management Journal*, 33(1), pp.65–87.

Cappelli, P. 1999. *The new deal at work: managing the market-driven workforce*. Boston: Harvard Business School Press, p.306.

Cappelli, P. 2015. Why we love to hate HR … and what HR can do about it. *Harvard Business Review*, 93(7–8), pp.54–61.

Carnahan, S., and Somaya, D. 2013. Alumni effects and relational advantage: the impact on outsourcing when a buyer hires employees from a supplier's competitors. *Academy of Management Journal*, 56(6), pp.1578–600.

Carnahan, S., and Somaya, D. 2015. The other talent war: competing through alumni. *MIT Sloan Management Review*, 56(3), p.14.

Cascio, W. F., and Boudreau, J. W. 2017. Talent management of nonstandard employees. In W. F. Cascio, D. Collings, and K. Mellahi, eds., *Oxford handbook of talent management*, pp.494–520. Oxford: Oxford University Press.

Castanias, R. P., and Helfat, C. E. 2001. The managerial rents model: theory and empirical analysis. *Journal of Management*, 27(6), pp.661–78.

Castilla, E. J. 2005. Social networks and employee performance in a call center. *American Journal of Sociology*, 110(5), pp.1243–83.

Coff, R. W. 1997. Human assets and management dilemmas: coping with hazards on the road to resource-based theory. *Academy of Management Review*, 22(2), pp.374–402.

Corredoira, R. A., and Rosenkopf, L. 2010. Should auld acquaintance be forgot? The reverse transfer of knowledge through mobility ties. *Strategic Management Journal*, 31(2), pp.159–81.

Creed, W. E. D., Dejordy, R., and Lok, J. 2010. Being the change: resolving institutional contradiction through identity work. *Academy of Management Journal*, 53(6), pp.1336–64.

Doeringer, P. B., and Piore, M. J. 1971. *Internal labor markets and manpower analysis*. Lexington, MA: Heath, p.214.

Dokko, G., Nigam, A., and Rosenkopf, L. 2012. Keeping steady as she goes: a negotiated order perspective on technological evolution. *Organization Studies*, 33(5-6), pp.681–703.

Dokko, G., and Rosenkopf, L. 2010. Social capital for hire? Mobility of technical professionals and firm influence in wireless standards committees. *Organization Science*, 21(3), pp.677–95.

Dokko, G., Wilk, S. L., and Rothbard, N. P. 2009. Unpacking prior experience: how career history affects job performance. *Organization Science*, 20(1), pp.51–68.

Edwards, J. R., and Cable, D. M. 2009. The value of value congruence. *Journal of Applied Psychology*, 94(3), p.654.

Elsbach, K. D. 1999. An expanded model of organizational identification. In L. L. Cummings and B. M. Staw, eds., *Research in organizational behavior*, pp.163–200. Greenwich, CT: JAI Press, Inc.

Elsbach, K. D., and Bhattacharya, C. B. 2001. Defining who you are by what you're not: organizational disidentification and the National Rifle Association. *Organization Science*, 12(4), pp.393–413.

Gaba, V., and Dokko, G. 2016. Learning to let go: social influence, learning, and the abandonment of corporate venture capital practices. *Strategic Management Journal*, 37, pp.1558–77.

Granovetter, M. [1974] 1995. *Getting a job: a study of contacts and careers*, 2nd edn. Chicago and London: University of Chicago Press, p.251

Grohsjean, T., Kober, P., and Zucchini, L. 2016. Coming back to Edmonton: competing with former employers and colleagues. *Academy of Management Journal*, 59(2), pp.394–413.

Groysberg, B., and Lee, L. E. 2009. Hiring stars and their colleagues: exploration and exploitation in professional service firms. *Organization Science*, 20(4), pp.740–58.

Groysberg, B., Lee, L. E., and Nanda, A. 2008. Can they take it with them? The portability of star knowledge workers' performance. *Management Science*, 54(7), pp.1213–30.

Groysberg, B., Nanda, A., and Nohria, N. 2004. The risky business of hiring stars. *Harvard Business Review*, 82(5), pp.92–101.

Gulati, R. 1998. Alliances and networks. *Strategic Management Journal*, 19(4), pp.293–317.

Hall, D. T., and Schneider, B. 1972. Correlates of organizational identification as a function of career pattern and organizational type. *Administrative Science Quarterly*, 17(3), pp.340–50.

Harris, D., and Helfat, C. 1997. Specificity of CEO human capital and compensation. *Strategic Management Journal*, 18(11), pp.895–920.

Hausknecht, J. P., and Holwerda, J. A. 2013. When does employee turnover matter? Dynamic member configurations, productive capacity, and collective performance. *Organization Science*, 24(1), pp.210–25.

Huckman, R. S., and Pisano, G. P. 2006. The firm specificity of individual performance: evidence from cardiac surgery. *Management Science*, 52(4), pp.473–88.

Ibarra, H. 1999. Provisional selves: experimenting with image and identity in professional adaptation. *Administrative Science Quarterly*, 44(4), pp.764–91.

Ibarra, H., and Barbulescu, R. 2010. Identity as narrative: prevalence, effectiveness, and consequences of narrative identity work in macro work role transitions. *Academy of Management Review*, 35(1), pp.135–54.

Inkpen, A. C., and Tsang, E. W. 2005. Social capital, networks, and knowledge transfer. *Academy of Management Review*, 30(1), pp.146–65.

Kraatz, M. S., and Moore, J. H. 2002. Executive migration and institutional change. *Academy of Management Journal*, 45(1), pp.120–43.

Lewis, R. E., and Heckman, R. J. 2006. Talent management: a critical review. *Human Resource Management Review*, 16(2), pp.139–54.

Mawdsley, J. K., and Somaya, D. 2016. Employee mobility and organizational outcomes: an integrative conceptual framework and research agenda. *Journal of Management*, 42(1), pp.85–113.

Mayer, K. J., Somaya, D., and Williamson, I. O. 2012. Firm-specific, industry-specific, and occupational human capital and the sourcing of knowledge work. *Organization Science*, 23(5), pp.1311–29.

Pennings, J. M., Lee, K., and Van Witteloostuijn, A. 1998. Human capital, social capital, and firm dissolution. *Academy of Management Journal*, 41(4), pp.425–40.

Petriglieri, G., and Petriglieri, J. L. 2010. Identity workspaces: the case of business schools. *Academy of Management Learning & Education*, 9(1), pp.44–60.

Pfeffer, J., and Davis-Blake, A. 1986. Administrative succession and organizational performance: how administrator experience mediates the succession effect. *Academy of Management Journal*, 29(1), pp.72–83.

Phillips, D. J. 2002. A genealogical approach to organizational life chances: the parent-progeny transfer among Silicon Valley law firms, 1946–1996. *Administrative Science Quarterly*, 47(3), pp.474–506.

Phillips, D. J. 2005. Organizational genealogies and the persistence of gender inequality: the case of Silicon Valley law firms. *Administrative Science Quarterly*, 50(3), pp.440–72.

Podolny, J. M., and Baron, J. N. 1997. Resources and relationships: social networks and mobility in the workplace. *American Sociological Review*, 62(5), pp.673–93.

Pratt, M. G., Rockmann, K. W., and Kaufmann, J. B. 2006. Constructing professional identity: the role of work and identity learning cycles in the customization of identity among medical residents. *Academy of Management Journal*, 49(2), pp.235–62.

Rosenkopf, L., Metiu, A., and George, V. P. 2001. From the bottom up? Technical committee activity and alliance formation. *Administrative Science Quarterly*, 46(4), pp.748–72.

Seabright, M. A., Levinthal, D. A., and Fichman, M. 1992. Role of individual attachments in the dissolution of interorganizational relationships. *Academy of Management Journal*, 35(1), pp.122–60.

Seibert, S. E., Kraimer, M. L., and Liden, R. C. 2001. A social capital theory of career success. *Academy of Management Journal*, 44(2), pp.219–37.

Shane, S., and Stuart, T. 2002. Organizational endowments and the performance of university start-ups. *Management Science*, 48(1), pp.154–70.

Shipp, A. J., Furst-Holloway, S., Harris, T. B., and Rosen, B. 2014. Gone today but here tomorrow: extending the unfolding model of turnover to consider boomerang employees. *Personnel Psychology*, 67(2), pp.421–62.

Somaya, D., Williamson, I. O., and Lorinkova, N. 2008. Gone but not lost: the different performance impacts of employee mobility between cooperators versus competitors. *Academy of Management Journal*, 51(5), pp.936–53.

Song, J., Almeida, P., and Wu, G. 2003. Learning–by–hiring: when is mobility more likely to facilitate interfirm knowledge transfer? *Management Science*, 49(4), pp.351–65.

Stahl, G., Björkman, I., Farndale, E., Morris, S. S. et al. 2012. Six principles of effective global talent management. *Sloan Management Review*, 53(2), pp.25–42.

Tajfel, H., and Turner, J. C. 1986. The social identity theory of intergroup behavior. In S. Worchel and W. G. Austin, eds., *Psychology of intergroup relations*, 2nd edn., pp. 7–24. Chicago: Nelson-Hall.

Twenge, J. M. 2006. *Generation me: why today's young Americans are more confident, assertive, entitled—and more miserable than ever before*. New York: Free Press, pp.vii, 292.

Van Maanen, J., and Schein, E. H. 1979. Toward a theory of organizational socialization. In L. L. Cummings and B. M. Staw, eds., *Research in organizational behavior*, pp.206–64. Greenwich, CT: JAI Press, Inc.

Waldman, D. A., and Spangler, W. D. 1989. Putting together the pieces: a closer look at the determinants of job performance. *Human Performance*, 2(1), pp.29–59.

Wezel, F. C., Cattani, G., and Pennings, J. M. 2006. Competitive implications of interfirm mobility. *Organization Science*, 17(6), pp.691–709.

Wilk, S. L., and Cappelli, P. 2003. Understanding the determinants of employer use of selection methods. *Personnel Psychology*, 56(1), pp.103–24.

CHAPTER 7

....

HUMAN CAPITAL RESOURCE COMPLEMENTARITIES

....

ROBERT E. PLOYHART AND ORMONDE R. CRAGUN

7.1 INTRODUCTION

....

THIS chapter poses a question that to date has received little scholarly attention: how do firms create, manage, and leverage complementarities among human capital resources? On the surface, the answer to this question seems obvious: firms use integrated talent-management practices to acquire, develop, and bundle human capital resources (Lepak, Liao, Chung, and Harden, 2006; Ployhart and Hale, 2014; Sirmon, Hitt, and Ireland, 2007). For our purposes we define *talent management* as the process through which firms anticipate and meet their needs for people in strategic jobs (adapted from Cappelli and Keller, 2014). The expectation is that different talent-management practices (e.g., recruitment, training, and compensation) enhance the ability, motivation, and opportunity of employees (Lepak, Liao, Chung, and Harden, 2006), and as a result, firms perform better (Collings and Mellahi, 2009; Lewis and Heckman, 2006). However, note that most research in this area does not directly conceptualize or measure the human capital resources (Wright and McMahan, 2011). It is far more common to link talent-management practices directly to firm performance, and assume that the effect was due to enhancing human capital resources (Becker and Huselid, 2006). Thus, when most human resource (HR) research talks about complementarities, it is essentially focusing on complementarities that may exist among the talent-management practices rather than the resources that are influenced by those practices.

Research is explicitly considering human capital resources. Indeed, research on human capital has exploded in recent years (see Nyberg, Moliterno, Hale, and Lepak, 2014; Wright, Coff, and Moliterno, 2014). The contemporary research is shifting the focus directly onto human capital, seeking to understand its structure, function, and properties (Ployhart and Moliterno, 2011; Raffiee and Coff, 2015). Early research on human capital was heavily grounded within the economic tradition and operationalized within human capital theory (Becker, 1964; Schultz, 1959). This has changed and resource-based theory (RBT) has become the dominant framework for conceptualizing human capital—that is, human capital resources (Ployhart and Hale, 2014).

Interestingly, one fundamental question spanning HR and strategy is whether there are one or multiple human capital resources. The extant literature has largely been silent on this issue. Most articles either conceptualize a single human capital resource or consider two distinct types (specific and generic) (Ployhart and Hale, 2014). Ployhart and Hale (2014) argued that there are multiple human capital resources because all such resources are based on combinations of individual knowledge, skill, ability, and other characteristics (KSAOs). Consequently, multiple types of human capital resources may exist, and these resources may be interrelated in different ways that form *resource complementarities*, defined for our purposes simply as *synergistic relationships between two or more human capital resources*.

Following in this scholarly tradition, we consider how talent-management practices may relate to the formation, maintenance, and bundling of human capital resource complementarities. We start by briefly summarizing the key features of resource complementarities observed within the broader strategy literature. We then consider the nature of complementarities specifically for human capital resources, and consider numerous types of complementarities that may exist. We conclude by proposing new connections between talent management and human capital resource complementarities—a topic that we believe has been neglected for far too long.

7.2 RESOURCE COMPLEMENTARITIES: INSIGHTS FROM STRATEGIC MANAGEMENT

In this section, we summarize the key features of resource complementarities observed within the broader strategy literature. We review the definition of complementarities, the resources that have been studied as complementarities, and the role of factor markets.

7.2.1 Definition of *Strategic Complementarities*

Strategy scholars use similar definitions for *complementarities*, also called *complementary assets*, which originate from two primary sources (Ennen and Richter, 2010; Teece, 2007). First, from an economics perspective, Milgrom and Roberts (1995: 181) state that "activities … are complements if doing (more of) any one of them increases the returns to doing (more of) the others." Second, as a precursor to dynamic capabilities (Teece, Pisano, and Shuen, 1997), Teece (1986: 288) describes *complementary assets* in relation to successful innovation when he states: "the successful commercialization of an innovation requires that the know-how in question be utilized in conjunction with other capabilities or assets." Subsequent scholars have developed definitions very closely aligned with these earlier definitions. For example, Crocker and Eckardt (2014: 5) state that the term *complementarities* refers to "situations in which the performance of one resource increases in the presence of another." Adegbesan (2009: 463) states, "a firm displays complementarity to a resource when their combination leads to the creation of a surplus over and above the sum of the amounts of value they could create independently." And Clougherty and Moliterno (2010) describe complementarities as synergistic resource combinations. The underlying theme is that the combination creates a synergy that is distinct from, yet more valuable than, the inputs.

7.2.2 Strategic Complementary Resources Studied

Strategy scholars study a wide variety of complementary resources at various levels. The firm itself can be a resource in a strategic alliance (Rothaermel, 2001) or the stakeholder in a value chain (Garcia-Castro and Francoeur, 2016). Technology and patents are also examples of firm-level resources (Rothaermel and Boeker, 2008). Complementary resources at lower levels of the firm can span a diverse spectrum including manufacturing equipment (Kapoor and Furr, 2015), "marketing capabilities, regulatory knowledge, client lists, and so on" (Stieglitz and Heine, 2007: 2). Finally, people such as star scientists can be part of a resource complementarity (Hess and Rothaermel, 2011).

7.2.3 The Role of Factor Markets

Complementarities may contribute to superior performance when the constituent resources can be acquired at a lower price than their true value (Denrell, Fang, and Winter, 2003). While the assumption is that factor markets are efficient and resources are correctly valued in relation to their existing uses (Barney, 1986), a firm is able to take advantage of the factor market through idiosyncratic information and subjective knowledge of its own resources. Information is idiosyncratic because complementarities are causally ambiguous and difficult to impute without firm-specific knowledge (Denrell, Fang, and Winter, 2003). For these reasons, the value of complementarities is also largely a subjective evaluation and known only within the firm (Schmidt and Keil, 2013).

Therefore, the factor market prices for the resource are set according to the resource's known value, not the subjective value of the resource tied to a specific firm. However, because the firm knows what current resource bundles have a complementary effect, and the resource bundle's costs versus benefits, the firm can identify valuable resources and acquire them at a relatively advantageous price. Thus, by adding complementary resources that add superior performance, while paying the same factor market prices as other firms, the firm may be able to get a disproportionately higher value from the resource. Therefore, it is the combination of resources purchased and not any one resource that allows for arbitrage.

To increase competitive positions in factor markets, firms need to identify new complimentary resource bundles. Denrell, Fang, and Winter (2003) suggest that opportunities for economic gain come from incrementally trying new things to take advantage of imperfect information and the existence of complementarities, and this is accomplished through effort, luck, alertness, and flexibility. The best way to innovate incrementally is to create new resource combinations by adding new resources to existing working combinations. Rather than looking outward at other firms where there is causal ambiguity for innovative solutions, the firm should look inward because it has insight into both its own operations and where it understands the complementarities. Innovation happens as something new is added to an already existing set of complementarities. Likely, many trials will fail, which encourages incrementalism through small, low-risk changes. Firms must purposefully choose to deviate from practice in order to innovate. Therefore, the factor market for the new opportunity is only valuable to the firm that sees the new opportunity and has the necessary unique set of complementarities.

7.3 THE NATURE OF HUMAN CAPITAL RESOURCE COMPLEMENTARITIES

In this section, we consider the nature of human capital resource complementarities—their structure and antecedents. First, however, it is necessary to understand the nature of human capital resources.

7.3.1 Human Capital Resources

Human capital resources are "… individual or unit-level capacities based on individual knowledge, skills, abilities, and other characteristics (KSAOs) that are accessible for unit-relevant purposes" (Ployhart and Hale, 2014: 371). It is important to recognize that human capital resources always originate within the KSAOs of individuals. KSAOs reflect the broad range of individual difference characteristics such as intelligence, cognitive ability, specific abilities (e.g., math), knowledge (e.g., accounting), skills (e.g., persuasion), and traits (e.g., personality). The common feature among KSAOs is that they are relatively stable across time and contexts. The stability of KSAOs is also the feature that excludes more state-like characteristics, such as attitudes, emotions, and moods, from comprising human capital resources.

Human capital resources may exist individually (e.g., a star manager; a CEO) or within a collective (e.g., a top-management team; the aggregate of a firm's KSAOs). Collective human capital resources emerge from the KSAOs of individuals (Ployhart and Moliterno, 2011). This emergence process is strongly shaped by the nature of the task environment. Task environments that are more complex require greater coordination and interaction and, hence, increase the likelihood that the collective human capital resource will not be isomorphic with the individual-level KSAO elements. However, even relatively simple task environments that only require pooling individual KSAOs can create a collective human capital resource that is different from the lower-level origins. For example, social loafing contributes to the collective resource being "less" than the sum of the individuals' potential, whereas ideas generated by diverse groups are more creative than are ideas generated by individuals (Karau and Williams, 1993; Sutton and Hargadon, 1996). Thus, the transformation from individual to collective human capital resource occurs in the nature of interactions among workers and it is why understanding these interactions is so important for organizational behavior (Kozlowski and Klein, 2000) and strategy (Barney and Felin, 2013).

Finally, human capital resources are capacities for action, not the behavior or consequences that follow from that action. This means that human capital resources are not job performance, firm performance, member interactions, or any similar outcomes. The distinction between the action and the capacity for action is important for a number of reasons, but can be most simply appreciated by noting that human capital resources are only valuable to the extent they relate to relevant business outcomes. Stated differently, a human capital resource may be valuable for certain outcomes but not others. If a firm chooses to enter a new market, it is unlikely to have the human capital resources to be effective for the new strategy and will thus need to rely on a talent-strategy and talent-management system to acquire or develop the necessary resources.

7.3.2 The Structure of Human Capital Resource Complementarities

Observing that human capital resources originate in individual KSAOs leads to the undeniable conclusion that multiple types of human capital resources exist (Ployhart and Hale, 2014). This in turn implies that these human capital resources may combine in different ways. The nearly infinite ways in which human capital resources combine adds a great deal of complexity to the understanding of human capital resources. Yet, this complexity is also the reason why the study of human capital resource complementarities has remained elusive—even though such complementarities exist naturally and are strong determinants of firm performance and competitive advantage.

Prior research on human capital resource complementarities has occurred primarily with a strong strategy and economic-based focus. For example, Campbell, Coff, and Kryscynski (2012) suggest that human capital resource complementarities are heterogeneous across firms, which affects human capital mobility constraints. Similarly, Crocker and Eckardt (2014) conducted a multilevel study and found that the relationship between individual human capital and individual performance is impacted by complementary functional and managerial unit-level human capital resources. However, some research has used the logic of complementarities to study HR practices. Laursen and Foss (2003) found evidence that links complementary HR management practices (i.e., interdisciplinary work groups, quality circles, employee suggestion systems, planned job rotations, delegation of responsibility, functional integration, performance-related pay, internal training, and external training) to innovation. Foss et al. (2014) further found evidence that individual-level rewards, when complimented with company-level HR management practices, positively affect knowledge sharing.

Other studies take slightly different approaches. One study conducted by MacDuffie (1995) found evidence that when the HR practices of team-based work systems, contingent compensation, and extensive training were bundled and then complemented with a flexible production system and low inventory buffers, it had a positive effect on performance. Economists have recognized that complementarities exist between technology and physical assets with an individual's KSAOs (Goldin and Katz, 1998), and that growth is shifting from physical asset accumulation to human capital accumulation (Galor and Malov, 2004). Finally, directly related to factor market costs, there is some evidence to suggest that some human capital resource complementarities can increase factor market costs. Datta and Iskandar-Datta (2014) find that strategic CFOs with generalist MBA backgrounds earn higher salaries than do strategic CFOs with accounting non-generalist master's degrees. Thus, a growing body of literature seeks to understand complementarities that are directly related to human capital.

Prior research has clearly examined human capital resource complementarities from a variety of disciplinary perspectives. Despite such variety, we propose that human capital resource complementarities may be defined concisely as the *synergistic relationships between two or more human capital resources*. This is an admittedly simple definition but it is not a simplistic definition one it captures the complexity of complementarities remarkably well. There are no claims that the complementarities exist with any specific type of human capital resource, or at any specific level. However, the definition does assume that the complementarities produce positive outcomes (and even this assumption is testable). Thus, the power of the definition lies in its ability to concisely capture the essence of a complementarity—a synergistic relationship between two or more resources.

Ployhart and Hale (2014) presented a broad framework for conceptualizing human capital resource complementarities. There are three broad types. First, within-level complementarities occur when two different types of human capital resources combine interactively or causally. An interactive relationship is typical of a synergy where the whole is more than the sum of the parts, such as when a highly motivated and capable workforce outperforms a workforce that is lower on motivation, capability, or both. A causal relationship reflects a situation where one resource contributes to the nature of the other resource, such as when higher amounts of human capital contribute to greater learning and absorptive capacity (Cohen and Levinthal, 1990).

Second, cross-level complementarities occur through a process of resource emergence. In this situation, lower-level resources are transformed through a task environment to produce a new, higher-level resource (Ployhart and Moliterno, 2011). These higher-level resources may be formed based on a consensus process, whereby the collective resource reflects (but is not identical to) the lower-level resources. An example of this type might occur when team human capital resources are averaged or summed across teams to create a firm-level human capital resource. On the other hand, these higher-level resources may be formed based on a process of compilation (Mathieu, Tannenbaum, Donsbach, and Alliger, 2014). In this case, each lower-level resource adds something new yet valuable to the collective, such as when different divisions have different human capital resources that are combined in such a way that the firm's human capital resources become a configural portfolio of interrelated component resources, as opposed to a simple average or aggregate.

Finally, hybrid complementarities exist when human capital resources are related within and across levels. Hybrid complementarities may exist in innumerable types of combinations. For example, a collective human capital intelligence resource based on composition (similarity) may lead to the formation of a collective human capital resource reflecting the diverse knowledge of many strategy managers (a compilation resource).

The human capital resource complementarities types presented in Ployhart and Hale (2014) are merely illustrative, but they operationalize the key point: that multiple human capital resources exist and these resources are, in different ways, interrelated. We now consider the consequences of such complementarities.

7.3.3 The Function of Human Capital Resource Complementarities

As noted above, resource complementarities generally do not have efficient factor markets, and hence, the value of a given resource within the complementarity may be undervalued (Denrell, Fang, and Winter, 2003). This enables complementarities to generate *competitive advantage*, defined roughly as generating above-normal returns from a resource, relative to what competitors are able to generate (Peteraf and Barney, 2003).

We can unpack this argument further by considering the characteristics of resources that may contribute to competitive advantage (Barney, 1991; Dierickx and Cool, 1989; Wernerfelt, 1984). *Valuable* resources are those that contribute to the design or implementation of a strategy that differentiate the firm and capture more value than competitors do (Barney, 1991). *Rare* resources are those that are not evenly distributed in a competitive environment, and hence, acquiring or accessing a rare and valuable resource enables one to have an advantage over competitors. However, to maintain any such advantage, the resource must also be *difficult or costly to imitate*. When resources are based on interactions among people (*social complexity*), require time for development (*path dependence*), and are developed in ways that are hard to understand (*causally ambiguous*), it is hard for competitors to duplicate the resource. Competitive advantage is further enhanced when the resource cannot be substituted with a different type of resource (nonsubstitutability).

The four characteristics of resources that underlie competitive advantage are the reasons why human capital resources are so important. Compared with many other types of resources, human capital resources are more likely to be valuable, rare, difficult, or costly to imitate, and difficult to substitute (Coff, 1997; Coff and Kryscynski, 2011). Yet human capital resource complementarities are even more difficult and costly to imitate than a stand-alone human capital resource (Dierickx and Cool, 1989). Indeed, because they reflect a web of relationships among resources, complementarities are more causally ambiguous, socially complex, and path dependent. And because there are no factor markets for complementarities and their value is subjectively determined, it is possible for a firm to generate a competitive advantage by bundling resources even when the component resources are generic and acquired from efficient factor markets (Denrell, Fang, and Winter, 2003; Ployhart and Hale, 2014).

7.3.4 A Wider Web of Resource Complementarities

Resource complementarities are not limited to human capital resources. As is well established in the strategy literature, complementarities may be based on combinations of tangible and intangible resources. Similarly, nothing in RBT requires that resource complementarities be based purely on human capital resources. Indeed, other psychological resources, such as collective attitudes, engagement, satisfaction, and motivation, may comprise strategically valuable resources (Ployhart, 2015; Ployhart and Hale, 2014). Because these other resources are not human capital resources, but have individual psychological origins, we refer to these as *psychological resources*.

Psychological resources may combine and relate to human capital resources via complementarities described in section 7.3.2. However, the precise structure and nature of these human capital and psychological resource complementarities are currently unknown. For example, do human capital resources contribute to the formation of collective attitudes? Do attitudes contribute to human capital resources, or are they interactive? Does engagement contribute to learning and knowledge, or vice versa? It is one thing to suggest human capital and psychological resources are interrelated, but it is quite another to specify how and why.

Essentially, no research in the entire field of management speaks to these interrelationships at the collective level. For example, the meta-analysis by Jiang, Lepak, Hu, and Baer (2012) included human capital and motivation, but causal relationships between these two constructs were not modeled. The closest research is found in the groups and teams literature, where it is widely recognized that team KSAO composition (what we are calling human capital resources) is an input to team processes (what we are calling psychological resources), which then contributes to performance and subsequent changes (Ilgen et al., 2005; Kozlowski and Ilgen, 2006; Mathieu et al., 2008). Although this research is highly related, the difference between a small-group setting and a firm are significant (Kenny et al., 2002; Sirmon, Hitt, Ireland, and Gilbert, 2011). Likewise, the research on collective attitudes or engagement is relevant but it neglects consideration of human capital resources (Ployhart, 2015).

Thus, as a scholarly discipline, we know almost nothing about how human capital resources and psychological resources combine (Ployhart, 2015)—even though they are inseparable in the real world. Research must begin to theorize and empirically test how these different types of resources interrelate. It seems highly unlikely, but not impossible, to envision individual-level research or small-group research generalizing to the firm level. Yet even if it does generalize, this micro research usually neglects consideration of factor markets and competitive environments. This research must not be conducted simply to understand the structure and function of resources; it should also investigate how to manage these resources within the context of talent management.

7.4 The Implications of Resource Complementarities for Talent Management

In this final section, it is now possible to realize fully the implications of resource complementarities for talent management. We first start by analyzing the existing talent-management research, and we conclude by pointing to directions for future research.

7.4.1 Limitations of Talent-Management Research

Recognizing that human capital resource complementarities are synergistic relationships among two or more human capital resources makes it obvious that there is no programmatic research attention devoted toward understanding how talent management contributes to the creation, development, and rebundling of human capital resource complementarities.

First, when HR research has considered complementarities, it has tended to focus on HR practices rather than resources. Giving privilege to practices is natural given the domain and history of HR, and the movement from studying the effects of individual practices to studying bundles of practices is a natural evolution. However, the fact remains that studying HR practices is not the same as studying human capital resources. The distinction between practices and resources has been made theoretically (Collings and Mellahi, 2009; Lepak, Liao, Chung, and Harden, 2006; Wright and McMahan, 1992), but it remains neglected empirically. That is, few studies have considered whether different types of HR practices produce different types of human capital resources or even changes in resources. This research would need to vary the practices, have measures of different types of resources, and observe relationships between the two. For example, how does recruitment versus training contribute to collective skills? Likewise, one would expect selection based on cognitive ability to contribute to the emergence of an "ability" resource, but would such emergence happen faster using different ability assessments? The closest research we have on this topic are studies linking different HR practices to individual-level outcomes, linking variations in HR practice use to firm performance, or linking perceptions of practices to perceptions of resources (e.g., Huselid, 1995; Jiang, Lepak, Hu, and Baer, 2012; Wright and Nishi, 2007; Van Iddekinge et al., 2009).

Second, even when research studies purposefully seek to examine complementarities among HR practices, they are usually operationalized in terms of an average among a set of practices. For example, a study will usually measure a variety of practices, argue they are theoretically consistent, and then average the practices together. This approach implicitly assumes a universalistic perspective (the same constellation of practices is always useful), relative to a configural perspective (different relationships among the practices are required to be effective) (Delery and Doty, 1996). Averaging practices into a single composite negates the ability to identify relationships among the practices. For example, does a firm with more effective recruitment use different development and training practices than a firm with ineffective recruitment? Similarly, "make or buy" decisions imply different practices and will be more or less important for different strategies, and hence, the relationships between practices are likely to change as well. In general, there is rarely an explicit theorizing or modeling of a specific causal or interactive structure among the practices.

Third, regardless of how HR practices are operationalized, most of this research focuses on a single human capital resource. The comprehensive meta-analysis by Jiang, Lepak, Hu, and Baer (2012), for example, models one human capital resource. Even the meta-analysis by Crook et al. (2011), which was devoted specifically to human capital resources, considered an overall human capital resource and generic-specific human capital resources that reflect the distinction made in human capital theory (Becker, 1964). As long as research considers only one broad, all-inclusive human capital resource, there will be no way to study meaningfully resource complementarities.

Thus, research is not examining whether different practices contribute to different types of human capital resources, and so there is no research linking talent management to human capital resource complementarities. Talent management does not imply the management of a single human capital resource in isolation. Talent management actually manages a bundle of human capital resources and, thus, will strongly shape the nature of any resource complementarities. It is the portfolio of human capital resources that must be managed, and the purpose of talent management is the creation and coordination of these complementarities. We now turn to the question of how this might occur.

7.4.2 Implications of Talent-Management Research

Talent-management practices are the integrated set of activities that influence and shape human capital resources to achieve a number of diverse outcomes (Collings and

Mellahi, 2009). This broad view of talent management is highly consistent with the nature of human capital resource complementarities forwarded in this chapter. Talent management should shape the entire talent lifecycle, and human capital resource complementarities are one way to operationalize that life cycle. Hence, the notion of human capital resource complementarities is closely aligned with the purpose of talent management. In this section we propose several directions for how future research might be conducted to demonstrate how talent management contributes to human capital resource complementarities.

First, research should consider how human capital resources are created, so that we may come to understand how to build complementary resources. Talent management recognizes human capital resources develop over time and in different ways. Different types of human capital resources are created or acquired, they are developed or transformed, they are bundled with other resources, and they ultimately must be refreshed or divested. This is the reality of the HR function, and talent management is closely aligned to this reality. What is missing in the literature is full appreciation of the human capital resources that are shaped by talent-management practices. Therefore, it would be useful for researchers to give as much attention to the creation of human capital resources as they do to talent-management practices. For example, how do human capital resources evolve over time? There is growing research on human capital pipelines and flows (Nyberg and Ployhart, 2013; Bryme, Molloy, and Gilbert, 2014), but this research barely taps the surface. We need to know how long resources exist before they start to decay, and which talent-management practices are needed at which times to offset any decay.

Second, we need to understand how different talent-management practices influence the relationships between resources. For example, generic human capital resources contribute to the formation of specific human capital resources (Ployhart and Moliterno, 2011). Human capital resources such as ability and personality influence the formation of resources such as knowledge and skill, which are in turn the proximal determinants of performance (Ployhart and Moliterno, 2011). Given this causal sequence, what talent-management practices might be employed to strengthen this relationship? Do practices that support autonomous learning and development lead to a stronger relationship between these resources? Or do firms that set higher standards for selection obtain employees who are more capable, who benefit more from training? The major shift in focus is from treating human capital resources as the dependent variables (which is itself scarcely done), to focusing on the relationship between the resources.

Third, research must explore the causal structure within HR practices. If resources follow a causal or interactive sequence, then talent-management practices must themselves be causally structured or sequenced to optimize the effects on human capital resource complementarities. This is not the same argument as using high-performance work systems because the emphasis is on causal effects among the practices themselves—it is a configural approach to talent management. We feel this is a critically overlooked issue because most research is focused on an overall average set of practices, rather than identifying how they fit together. For example, the first author worked with a large company where the selection group and the training group were fighting over resources, even though they both were in HR. The problem occurred because both groups operated relatively independently and did not understand how the actions of one group affected the actions of the other group. Had we administered an HR practice survey within this firm, the results would have shown they were using effective selection and training practices and had good performance. What the results could not have identified is how much better the firm would have performed if the selection and training functions were better sequenced and internally consistent. Work by Foss et al. (2014) highlights ways in which functions can be sequenced and aligned.

Fourth, research needs to consider whether different types of human capital resource complementarities contribute differently to competitive advantage. This is not unlike the micro research trying to understand how different combinations of KSAOs contribute to job performance, such as which combinations of ability and personality most strongly relate to performance (e.g., Sackett, Gruys, and Ellingson, 1998). For example, do firms that have greater ability-related human capital resources and engagement outperform firms that do not? Do firms that have stronger relationships between generic and specific human capital resources truly generate a more sustainable competitive advantage? Can firms who hire those with greater cognitive ability generate a competitive advantage if they are unable to sufficiently engage and motivate that workforce? The findings from the individual level are unlikely to generalize directly to the firm level, particularly when one realizes that most micro research does not focus on competitive advantage.

Finally, it may be worth revisiting the question of whether HR practices can contribute to competitive advantage. On the one hand, practices can easily be copied, and so it would seem unlikely that HR practices can contribute to competitive advantage. On the other hand, the human capital resources that are generated by those practices are not easily copied. Further, firms are unlikely to apply the same practices even though they may be similar, and the manner in which the practices are embedded within a larger system of talent-management practices is almost surely going to be firm-specific. Considering that the broader set of practices contributes to human capital resource complementarities, it stands to reason that the talent-management practices may very well contribute to competitive advantage.

7.5 CONCLUSION

In conclusion, we believe that research on talent management benefits from consideration of human capital resource complementarities. Multiple types of human capital resources exist, and they are interrelated in a variety of ways that contribute to performance and possibly competitive advantage. Research needs to move past a "singular" view of human capital resources, to consider how multiple types of resources are created, developed, bundled, and leveraged within the context of talent management. Much of this new terrain is uncharted, and we suspect it will lead to many surprises in our journey toward understanding how talent management and human capital resources contribute to competitive advantage.

REFERENCES

Adegbesan, J. A. 2009. On the origins of competitive advantage: strategic factor markets and heterogeneous resource complementarity. *Academy of Management Review*, 34(3), pp.463–75.

Barney, J. 1991. Firm resources and sustained competitive advantage. *Journal of Management*, 17(1), pp.99–120.

Barney, J. A. Y., and Felin, T. 2013. What are microfoundations? *The Academy of Management Perspectives*, 27(2), pp.138–55.

Barney, J. B. 1986. Strategic factor markets: expectations, luck, and business strategy. *Management Science*, 32(10), pp.1231–41.

Becker, B. E., and Huselid, M. A. 2006. Strategic human resources management: where do we go from here? *Journal of Management*, 32(6), pp.898–925.

Becker, G. S. 1964. *Human capital: a theoretical and empirical analysis, with special reference to education*, 3rd edn (1975). New York: Columbia University Press.

Brymer, R. A., Molloy, J. C., and Gilbert, B. A. 2014. Human capital pipelines: competitive implications of repeated interorganizational hiring. *Journal of Management*, 40(2), pp.483–508.

Campbell, B. A., Coff, R., and Kryscynski, D. 2012. Rethinking sustained competitive advantage from human capital. *Academy of Management Review*, 37(3), pp.376–95.

Cappelli, P., and Keller, J. R. 2014. Talent management: conceptual approaches and practical challenges. *Annual Review of Organizational Psychology and Organizational Behavior*, 1(1), pp.305–31.

Clougherty, J. A., and Moliterno, T. P. 2010. Empirically eliciting complementarities in capabilities: integrating quasi-experimental and panel data methodologies. *Strategic Organization*, 8(2), pp.107–31.

Coff, R. W. 1997. Human assets and management dilemmas: coping with hazards on the road to resource-based theory. *Academy of Management Review*, 22(2), pp.374–402.

Coff, R. W., and Kryscynski, D. 2011. Invited editorial: drilling for micro-foundations of human capital-based competitive advantages. *Journal of Management*, 37(5), pp.1429–43.

Cohen, W. M., and Levinthal, D. A. 1990. Absorptive capacity: a new perspective on learning and innovation. *Administrative Science Quarterly*, 35(1), pp.128–52.

Collings, D. G., and Mellahi, K. 2009. Strategic talent management: a review and research agenda. *Human Resource Management Review*, 19(4), pp.304–13.

Crocker, A., and Eckardt, R. 2014. A multilevel investigation of individual-and unit-level human capital complementarities. *Journal of Management*, 40(2), pp.509–30.

Crook, T. R., Todd, S. Y., Combs, J. G., Woehr, D. J. et al. 2011. Does human capital matter? A meta-analysis of the relationship between human capital and firm performance. *Journal of Applied Psychology*, 96(3), pp.443–56.

Datta, S., and Iskandar-Datta, M. 2014. Upper-echelon executive human capital and compensation: generalist vs specialist skills. *Strategic Management Journal*, 35(12), pp.1853–66.

Delery, J. E., and Doty, D. H. 1996. Modes of theorizing in strategic human resource management: tests of universalistic, contingency, and configurational performance predictions. *Academy of Management Journal*, 39(4), pp.802–35.

Denrell, J., Fang, C., and Winter, S. G. 2003. The economics of strategic opportunity. *Strategic Management Journal*, 24(10), pp.977–90.

Dierickx, I., and Cool, K. 1989. Asset stock accumulation and sustainability of competitive advantage. *Management Science*, 35(12), pp.1504–11.

Ennen, E., and Richter, A. 2010. The whole is more than the sum of its parts—or is it? A review of the empirical literature on complementarities in organizations. *Journal of Management*, 36(1), pp.207–33.

Foss, N. J., Pedersen, T., Reinholt-Fosgaard, M., and Stea, D. 2015. Why complementary HRM practices impact performance: the case of rewards, job design, and work climate in a knowledge-sharing context. *Human Resource Management*, 54(6), pp.955–76.

Galor, O., and Moav, O. 2004. From physical to human capital accumulation: inequality and the process of development. *The Review of Economic Studies*, 71(4), pp.1001–26.

Garcia-Castro, R., and Francoeur, C. 2016. When more is not better: complementarities, costs and contingencies in stakeholder management. *Strategic Management Journal*, 37(2), pp.406–24.

Goldin, C., and Katz, L. F. 1996. The origins of technology-skill complementarity. NBER (No. w5657).

Hess, A. M., and Rothaermel, F. T. 2011. When are assets complementary? Star scientists, strategic alliances, and innovation in the pharmaceutical industry. *Strategic Management Journal*, 32(8), pp.895–909.

Huselid, M. A. 1995. The impact of human resource management practices on turnover, productivity, and corporate financial performance. *Academy of Management Journal*, 38(3), pp.635–72.

Ilgen, D. R., Hollenbeck, J. R., Johnson, M., and Jundt, D. 2005. Teams in organizations: from input-process-output models to IMOI model. *Annual Review of Psychology*, 56(1), pp.517–43.

Jiang, K., Lepak, D. P., Hu, J., and Baer, J. C. 2012. How does human resource management influence organizational outcomes? A meta-analytic investigation of mediating mechanisms. *Academy of Management Journal*, 55(6), pp.1264–94.

Kapoor, R., and Furr, N. R. 2015. Complementarities and competition: unpacking the drivers of entrants' technology choices in the solar photovoltaic industry. *Strategic Management Journal*, 36(3), pp.416–36.

Karau, S. J., and Williams, K. D. 1993. Social loafing: a meta-analytic review and theoretical integration. *Journal of Personality and Social Psychology*, 65(4), pp.681–706.

Kenny, D. A., Mannetti, L., Pierro, A., Livi, S. et al. 2002. The statistical analysis of data from small groups. *Journal of Personality and Social Psychology*, 83(1), pp.126–37.

Kozlowski, S. W., and Ilgen, D. R. 2006. Enhancing the effectiveness of work groups and teams. *Psychological Science in the Public Interest*, 7(3), pp.77–124.

Kozlowski, S. W. J., and Klein, K. J. 2000. A multilevel approach to theory and research in organizations. contextual, temporal, and emergent processes. In *Multilevel theory, research, and methods in organizations*, pp.1–45. San Francisco: Jossey-Bass.

Laursen, K., and Foss, N. J. 2003. New human resource management practices, complementarities and the impact on innovation performance. *Cambridge Journal of Economics*, 27(2), pp.243–63.

Lepak, D. P., Liao, H., Chung, Y., and Harden, E. E. (2006). A conceptual review of human resource management systems in strategic human resource management research. *Research in Personnel and Human Resources Management*, 25, pp.217–71.

Lewis, R. E., and Heckman, R. J. 2006. Talent management: a critical review. *Human Resource Management Review*, 16(2), pp.139–54.

MacDuffie, J. P. 1995. Human resource bundles and manufacturing performance: organizational logic and flexible production systems in the world auto industry. *Industrial and Labor Relations Review*, 48(2), pp.197–221.

Mathieu, J., Maynard, M. T., Rapp, T. L., and Gilson, L. 2008. Team effectiveness 1997–2007: a review of recent advancements and a glimpse into the future. *Journal of Management*, 34(3), pp.410–76.

Mathieu, J. E., Tannenbaum, S. I., Donsbach, J. S., and Alliger, G. M. 2014. A review and integration of team composition models: moving toward a dynamic and temporal framework. *Journal of Management*, 40(1), pp.130–60.

Milgrom, P., and Roberts, J. 1995. Complementarities and fit strategy, structure, and organizational change in manufacturing. *Journal of Accounting and Economics*, 19(2), pp.179–208.

Nyberg, A. J., and Ployhart, R. E. 2013. Context-emergent turnover (CET) theory: a theory of collective turnover. *Academy of Management Review*, 38(1), pp.109–31.

Nyberg, A. J., Moliterno, T. P., Hale, D., and Lepak, D. P. 2014. Resource-based perspectives on unit-level human capital: a review and integration. *Journal of Management*, 40(1), pp.316–46.

Peteraf, M. A., and Barney, J. B. 2003. Unraveling the resource-based tangle. *Managerial and Decision Economics*, 24(4), pp.309–23.

Ployhart, R. E. 2015. Strategic organizational behavior (STROBE): the missing voice in the strategic human capital conversation. *The Academy of Management Perspectives*, 29(3), pp.342–56.

Ployhart, R. E., and Hale, D., Jr. 2014. The fascinating psychological microfoundations of strategy and competitive advantage. *Annual Review of Organizational Psychology and Organizational Behavior*, 1(1), pp.145–72.

Ployhart, R. E., and Moliterno, T. P. 2011. Emergence of the human capital resource: a multilevel model. *Academy of Management Review*, 36(1), pp.127–50.

Ployhart, R. E., Nyberg, A. J., Reilly, G., and Maltarich, M. A. 2014. Human capital is dead; long live human capital resources! *Journal of Management*, 40(2), pp.371–98.

Ployhart, R. E., Van Iddekinge, C. H., and MacKenzie, W. I. 2011. Acquiring and developing human capital in service contexts: the interconnectedness of human capital resources. *Academy of Management Journal*, 54(2), pp.353–68.

Raffiee, J., and Coff, R. 2015. Micro-foundations of firm-specific human capital: when do employees perceive their skills to be firm-specific? *Academy of Management Journal*, 59(3) pp.766–90.

Rothaermel, F. T. 2001. Incumbent's advantage through exploiting complementary assets via interfirm cooperation. *Strategic Management Journal*, 22(6–7), pp.687–99.

Rothaermel, F. T., and Boeker, W. 2008. Old technology meets new technology: complementarities, similarities, and alliance formation. *Strategic Management Journal*, 29(1), pp.47–77.

Sackett, P. R., Gruys, M. L., and Ellingson, J. E. 1998. Ability–personality interactions when predicting job performance. *Journal of Applied Psychology*, 83(4), pp.545–56.

Schmidt, J., and Keil, T. 2013. What makes a resource valuable? Identifying the drivers of firm-idiosyncratic resource value. *Academy of Management Review*, 38(2), pp.206–28.

Schultz, T. W. 1959. Investment in man: an economist's view. *Social Service Review*, 33(2), pp.109–17.

Sirmon, D. G., Hitt, M. A., and Ireland, R. D. 2007. Managing firm resources in dynamic environments to create value: looking inside the black box. *Academy of Management Review*, 32(1), pp.273–92.

Sirmon, D. G., Hitt, M. A., Ireland, R. D., and Gilbert, B. A. 2011. Resource orchestration to create competitive advantage breadth, depth, and life cycle effects. *Journal of Management*, 37(5), pp.1390–412.

Stieglitz, N., and Heine, K. 2007. Innovations and the role of complementarities in a strategic theory of the firm. *Strategic Management Journal*, 28(1), pp.1–15.

Sutton, R. I., and Hargadon, A. 1996. Brainstorming groups in context: effectiveness in a product design firm. *Administrative Science Quarterly*, 41, pp.685–718.

Teece, D. J. 1986. Profiting from technological innovation: implications for integration, collaboration, licensing and public policy. *Research Policy*, 15(6), pp.285–305.

Teece, D. J. 2007. Explicating dynamic capabilities: the nature and microfoundations of (sustainable) enterprise performance. *Strategic Management Journal*, 28(13), pp.1319–50.

Teece, D. J., Pisano, G., and Shuen, A. 1997. Dynamic capabilities and strategic management. *Strategic Management Journal*, 18(7), pp.509–33.

Van Iddekinge, C. H., Ferris, G. R., Perrewé, P. L., Perryman, A. A. et al. 2009. Effects of selection and training on unit-level performance over time: a latent growth modeling approach. *Journal of Applied Psychology*, 94(4), pp.829–43.

Wernerfelt, B. 1984. A resource-based view of the firm. *Strategic Management Journal*, 5(2), pp.171–80.

Wright, P. M., Coff, R., and Moliterno, T. P. 2014. Strategic human capital crossing the great divide. *Journal of Management*, 40(2), pp.353–70.

Wright, P. M., and McMahan, G. C. 1992. Theoretical perspectives for strategic human resource management. *Journal of Management*, 18(2), pp.295–320.

Wright, P. M., and McMahan, G. C. 2011. Exploring human capital: putting 'human' back into strategic human resource management. *Human Resource Management Journal*, 21(2), pp.93–104.

Wright, P. M., and Nishii, L. H. 2007. Strategic HRM and organizational behavior: Integrating multiple levels of analysis. *CAHRS Working Paper Series*, pp.1–25.

SECTION 3

TALENT, TEAMS, AND NETWORKS

CHAPTER 8

....

TALENT AND TEAMS

....

REBECCA R. KEHOE, BLYTHE L. ROSIKIEWICZ,
AND DANIEL TZABBAR

8.1 INTRODUCTION

....

THE increasing utilization of teams in the coordination and completion of work in organizations suggests a need to examine and better understand how organizations' key talent influences—and is influenced by—the broader team context within which it is so often employed. It is important that we begin by clarifying our areas of focus with respect to the notions of *talent* and *teams*. Whereas the term *talent* has variously been used to refer to the portfolio of knowledge, skills, abilities, and other attributes that create value for firms (Michaels, Handfield-Jones, and Axelrod, 2001; Schiemann, 2014) and/or the individuals who possess these valuable qualities (e.g., Gardner, 2005), in our discussion of talent in the present chapter, we will explicitly focus on star performers, whose personification of exceptional talent is evidenced in their disproportionately high productivity and significant external visibility relative to their industry peers (Groysberg, Lee, and Nanda, 2008; Oldroyd and Morris, 2012). We employ this definition based on its widespread use in prior research, and relatedly, on the broad evidence supporting the creation of exceptional value by individuals included in this classification (e.g., Kehoe and Tzabbar, 2015; Rothaermel and Hess, 2007; Zucker, Darby, and Armstrong, 2002).

In defining *teams*, we adopt the broad conceptualization suggested by Kozlowski and Bell (2003: 334), who define *teams* as "two or more individuals who (a) exist to perform organizationally relevant tasks, (b) share one or more common goals, (c) interact socially, (d) exhibit task interdependencies (i.e., work flow, goals, and outcomes), (e) maintain and manage boundaries, and (f) are embedded in an organizational context that sets boundaries, constrains the team, and influences exchanges with other units in the broader entity." Employing this inclusive definition allows us to synthesize research examining issues related to stars' employment in a variety of interdependent work arrangements with their colleagues in organizations. This is significant, as research in this area to date has tended to focus more broadly on stars' effects on their organizations and/or colleagues but has not often examined stars in the context of teams.

The purpose of this chapter is twofold. First, we provide a critical and integrative review of extant research related to talent in the team context. Second, based on this review, we propose several directions for future research that promise to leverage patterns of findings from extant research in the process of addressing gaps and limitations in our knowledge on this topic. In the first section of the chapter, we consider stars' effects on their teams and colleagues. Specifically, we review research on stars' roles as team and organizational boundary spanners, in which stars may leverage their broad status and favorable network positions to enhance their teams' access to external resources. We then examine stars' interpersonal influences within teams, which can take the form of collaborating with teammates, shaping work norms, or providing sponsorship or other forms of mentoring to other team members. We also examine stars' potential negative effects on colleagues, which can include constraining the utilization of colleagues' knowledge, limiting colleagues' opportunities, and undermining team decision-making processes.

In the second section, we shift our attention to the effects of the team context on stars. Here, we focus on extant research that has examined how various characteristics of the team environment (e.g., the number of star team members, and the relative alignment with a team's tasks with the core competencies of the broader organization) influence the value associated with stars' contributions in a particular team context. We then review research examining how the presence of resources that are complementary or redundant to a star in a team shape the star's behavioral propensities and performance outcomes. Finally, in the discussion, we draw on patterns of findings in the extant research we reviewed to identify critical directions for future research on stars and teams. Broadly, these focus on how differences in interdependence and task requirements at the team level shape stars' experiences and contributions across team contexts, and how teams and their star members are best managed to optimize the total effects associated with a star's presence, with an emphasis on the idea that neither stars as individuals nor teams as structural and social contexts are necessarily fixed over time.

8.2 STARS' EFFECTS ON TEAMS AND COLLEAGUES

Beyond stars' exceptional direct contributions through their own individual task performance, stars' broad external status and deep tacit knowledge position them to exert significant influence on their teams' learning and performance outcomes. In the sections that follow, we explore stars' effects on their teams and colleagues that materialize through stars' roles as team and organizational boundary spanners and through stars' interpersonal influences within their teams.

8.2.1 Stars as Boundary Spanners and Teams' Access to External Resources

Stars' deep knowledge, exceptional performance, central network positions, and broad external status tend to position them as critical boundary spanners in their teams and larger organizations. In their boundary-spanning roles, stars are instrumental in ensuring their teams' abilities and opportunities to access key external resources that fuel a team's capacity for innovation, adaptation, and renewal (Rothaermel and Hess, 2007). Access to these resources may be granted as a function of external stakeholders' more favorable perceptions of and attraction to a team with a star member or may come in the form of knowledge flowing through the preferential communication channels established in the development of the star's personal professional network (Hess and Rothaermel, 2011; Rothaermel and Hess, 2007).

Organizational and/or team boundaries often obscure the internal dynamics characterizing a team's operations, making it difficult for outsiders to accurately evaluate the team's resources and capabilities or to predict the quality of the team's future output. Thus, stars' broad external status can be leveraged by teams in the attraction of various external stakeholders who may rely on the star's affiliation with a team as a signal of the quality of team resources and performance potential. Such signaling may take two forms. First, stakeholders may develop expectations about a team's forthcoming performance based on a star's direct involvement in the team's operations (i.e., *The team will demonstrate exceptional performance based on the star's personal guidance and extraordinary contributions to team processes and output*). Second, stakeholders may infer that the team's less visible resources are of outstanding quality based on the star's membership on the team (i.e., *A star, who likely enjoys numerous employment alternatives, would certainly only join a team offering access to high-quality, complementary resources*) (Groysberg, Polzer, and Elfenbein, 2011).

8.2.1.1 *Stars' Status Spillover*

Indeed, scholars and practitioners alike have observed such positive spillovers of stars' broad status in the attraction of a variety of external stakeholder groups—and their demonstrated willingness to invest resources—in several industry contexts. For example, highlighting the spillovers of stars' status in the attraction of customers, Ravid (1999) noted higher revenues earned by films employing star actors. Further, Lucifora and Simmons (2003) pointed to customers' willingness to pay more for sporting event tickets involving star athletes—with both effects stemming from signaling of quality associated with the products or services of teams with which a star is involved. Others have examined this status spillover effect in the context of investors and firm valuation. For example, Higgins, Stephan, and Thursby (2011) found that technology firms employing Nobel laureate scientists realized greater initial public offering (IPO) proceeds than firms without such highly acclaimed employees did, suggesting a star's membership may positively influence investors' assessments of a firm's resources and capabilities and expectations about the firm's future performance. Similarly, Fuller and Rothaermel (2012) found that in the context of faculty entrepreneurship, entrepreneurial teams involving star faculty members had greater success in reaching an IPO than did teams without star members. This effect was argued to occur based on the increased quality signals associated with a star's involvement in an entrepreneurial team, with support for this explanation reflected in the reduced importance of a star's involvement when entrepreneurial teams came from universities that are more prestigious. While these two studies focused on firm-level valuation and entrepreneurial success, they are relevant in that both studies focus on entrepreneurial team membership, and their findings provide additional support for the notion that a star's membership can confer prestige to a collective, as well as bolster outsiders' perceptions and expectations of the collectives' capabilities. Finally, Coff and Kryscynski (2011) note that stars may help their organizations and teams to attract other talented human resources more effectively and at a lower cost. This likely recruiting benefit may emerge both from the attraction of quality employees to the prospect of working alongside talented colleagues and from the broader spillover of a star's external status to the status of the star's organization or team—both of which serve to reduce uncertainty and improve satisfaction associated with entry and employment for potential new hires, who may as a result be willing to accept relatively lower pay in exchange for the employment opportunity (Cable and Turban, 2003).

8.2.1.2 *Stars as Boundary Spanners*

In addition to helping their teams to attract resources by conveying quality signals to external stakeholders, stars can more directly leverage their professional networks (and their central positions within these networks) to increase a team's access to and abilities to utilize timely and relevant knowledge. In particular, occupying boundary-spanning and gatekeeping roles in the industry connects stars to key industry players at the core of knowledge development in the star's field and thus provides stars preferential access to new knowledge shortly after its development (Hess and Rothaermel, 2011; Rothaermel and Hess, 2007). This timely knowledge access, combined with stars' deep expertise and established abilities to evaluate and integrate knowledge, positions stars to identify, obtain, and apply relevant knowledge on behalf of their teams and organizations earlier and more successfully than other team or organizational members can. Importantly, these benefits have been shown to occur among star employees spanning boundaries at the organizational level (Hess and Rothaermel, 2011), among star employees spanning networks within organizations (Grigoriou and Rothaermel, 2014), and among external star collaborators who are not employed by the focal organization but who provide similar knowledge access benefits to their collaborators who are employed with the organization (Liebeskind, Oliver, Zucker, and Brewer, 1996; Zucker, Darby, and Armstrong, 2002), suggesting that the combined advantages of stars' status, network positions, and deep expertise span both formal and informal, as well as internal and external, organizational boundaries.

In summary, significant empirical research has demonstrated that teams with star members—or collaborative connections with star performers—may be well positioned to benefit from stars' occupation of boundary-spanning roles. These benefits—which come in the form of improved revenues, customer attraction, investor interest, recruitment outcomes, and knowledge access—tend to emerge from positive reputational spillovers conveyed from the star to the broader team or organization and/or from the preferential access to exchange channels provided by the star's central positions in key external professional networks. Subsequently, beyond connecting a team to increased resources, stars often help teams to better utilize externally sourced resources based on stars' deep tacit expertise and understanding of how best to integrate and apply resources to achieve success.

8.2.2 Stars' Interpersonal Influences in Teams

Stars tend to be well positioned to convey positive knowledge-based spillovers within their teams as a function of both their exceptional access to knowledge and their abilities to influence others (Kehoe and Tzabbar, 2015; Meyers, De Boeck, and Dries, 2017). First, stars' deep expertise, cumulative records of success, and occupation of preferential positions in broad external and internal networks provide stars with disproportionate access to knowledge relative to other team members—suggesting the potential for significant knowledge-sharing benefits should stars invest in sharing their knowledge with others (Hess and Rothaermel, 2011; Nerkar and Paruchuri, 2005, 2010). Second, because professional communities tend to give rise to social hierarchies based on individuals' relative skills and expertise, stars are likely to command substantial influence (and openness of colleagues to stars' perspectives) in their teams, and thus experience greater ease in using their knowledge to shape team outcomes. Importantly, the extents to which such knowledge-based benefits are realized are likely to depend on the individual characteristics of the star and on the team context in which the star is employed (Kehoe and Tzabbar, 2015).

8.2.2.1 *Stars' Influence on Team Norms and Practices*

At a broad level, stars' expert power and central network positions enable them to influence the norms and practices enacted within their teams (Lacetera, Cockburn, and Henderson, 2004) and serve as role models to their colleagues (Huckman and Pisano, 2006). This influence can benefit team functioning based on stars' preferential access to new knowledge and best practices in the professional community, as well as significant experiential knowledge of the behaviors associated with consistent success. Indeed, stars' positive influences on work practices have been documented, for example, in the adoption of progressive medical technologies, where Burke, Fournier, and Prasad (2007) found that surgeons were more likely to adopt such technologies when working in the presence of star surgeons, who were the most apt adopters of these advanced technologies themselves. Through imitation of this nature, as well as through other forms of less formal influence, such as colleagues' modeling of a star's work behaviors (Lacetera, Cockburn, and Henderson, 2004), a star's presence can reduce the uncertainty and improve the reliability of performance in their teams.

8.2.2.2 *Stars' Influence on Knowledge Transfer*

At the individual level, stars may also convey significant knowledge spillovers through their dyadic collaborations with colleagues. These spillovers may occur at multiple stages in the collaborative exchange process. Early on, stars may utilize their own deep expertise and their favorable network positions to provide team members preferential access to novel knowledge (Grigoriou and Rothaermel, 2014; Oldroyd and Morris, 2012). Subsequently, stars may help their colleagues to better integrate and utilize knowledge in the context of the team's tasks (Tzabbar and Vestal, 2015). Ongoing collaboration enables these knowledge benefits to be realized on a more consistent basis (Kehoe and Tzabbar, 2015). In particular, the proximity and frequent interaction facilitated by formal collaborative exchange fosters the trust, common language, and communication channels required for the effective transfer of tacit knowledge. Over time, the shared mental models and collective mindset that develop among colleagues engaged in close collaborative exchange enable the seamless integration of knowledge, such that a star's expert knowledge is not only shared, but is combined for broader application with the knowledge of other team members. Indeed, research conducted both in R&D and professional service contexts has demonstrated that stars' collaboration with colleagues benefits both individual (Azoulay, Zivin, and Wang, 2010; Groysberg and Lee, 2008; Oettl, 2012) and collective productivity (Kehoe and Tzabbar, 2015).

8.2.2.3 *Stars' Influences on Colleagues' Careers*

In other cases, stars' interpersonal influences relate less directly to team task performance and more closely to their colleagues' personal career outcomes. In particular, stars often assume roles as mentors of less experienced or less accomplished colleagues, wherein stars may provide support, guidance, feedback, and direction regarding job and career decisions. Additionally, in the mentoring role, stars may also leverage their own favorable network positions to provide sponsorship to mentees, thereby increasing a mentee's visibility and social standing within the organization and/or in the broader professional community (Noe, 1988). Indeed, stars are well equipped to help colleagues in these ways, based on their disproportionate human capital and social capital relative to other team or organizational members (Furukawa and Goto, 2006; Oldroyd and Morris, 2012).

8.2.2.4 *Differences in the Influences of Stars*

It is important to note that stars vary in the nature and level of interpersonal influences that they exert in teams. Indeed, Oettl (2012) demonstrated that stars vary significantly in their propensities to help colleagues, and Kehoe and Tzabbar (2015) found significant differences in stars' formal collaboration with others. Furthermore, stars' interpersonal influences on colleagues are not always positive. For instance, stars have been shown to use their disproportionate influence to limit the utilization and integration of newcomers' knowledge in a firm's operations—presumably based on stars' interest in maintaining the centrality and value of their own unique knowledge to a firm's performance

(Tzabbar, 2009) and reinforcing the firm's strategic commitments along proven, star-led knowledge trajectories (Audia and Goncalo, 2007). This type of behavior can ultimately hinder teams' and organizations' opportunities to leverage new knowledge, as well as to adapt to environmental change. In addition to limiting opportunities for new knowledge integration, star scientists' desires to maintain their own uniqueness and value, combined with their abilities to wield significant influence within a team or organization, can also hamper the development of their colleagues. For example, Kehoe and Tzabbar (2015) found that star scientists who held narrower expertise (and thus fewer unique bases of knowledge) were more likely to limit the opportunities for innovative leadership afforded to their colleagues. Arguably, such stars may be driven to such behavior based on their perceptions of being at greater risk of redundancy given the emergence of another scientist with similar expertise who also possesses the experience and capabilities required to assume the role of innovative leader.

In summary, stars' expert power and favorable network positions enable them to wield significant influence over colleagues' work and career outcomes. These influences can occur at the collective level, with stars shaping the work norms and practices adopted by a team, or can take place through dyadic exchange, with stars improving colleagues' access to and utilization of knowledge in formal collaborative arrangements and/or providing career support and guidance as mentors. Importantly, stars are not all equal in their influences on colleagues, and some stars may exert negative interpersonal influences in their teams. Thus, we suggest it is critical to consider both stars' individual characteristics and attributes of the team social context in considering stars' likely interpersonal effects within their teams.

8.3 Teams' Contextual Effects on Stars

While a substantial body of research has examined stars' influences on their colleagues, teams, and organizations, much less attention has been devoted to how stars themselves are influenced by their surrounding environments. In this section, we discuss how stars' abilities to create value are shaped by the broader team and organizational contexts in which they are employed. Beginning from a macro perspective, we focus on how the inherent strategic value associated with the role of a star and his or her team in an organization influences a star's potential contributions to the firm's competitive advantage. Then, shifting to a more micro perspective, we examine the role of resources available in a star's task context in supporting or limiting the star's abilities to create value.

8.3.1 Stars' Positions in the Organizational Context

Aguinis and O'Boyle (2014) draw on Strategic Core Theory in highlighting the need to account for a star's (and the star's team's) position in the broader context of an organization's strategy and structure in predicting the star's contributions to value crea-tion. Specifically, Strategic Core Theory suggests that the relationship between individ-ual productivity and firm performance is moderated by the proximity of an individual's role to the firm's core competence (Delery and Shaw, 2001). That is, this perspective sug-gests that a star's capacity to create value in a particular team or organizational context depends not only on the star's individual productivity, but also on how central the star's contributions are to the source of competitive advantage pursued by the star's organi-zation. Importantly, this perspective reinforces the logic underlying Tzabbar's (2009) finding that stars often limit the integration of novel perspectives brought by newcom-ers, as any strategic shifts that such integration may instigate threaten to reposition the firm's core away from the star's domain of expertise and thus threaten the star's capacity to contribute to organizational value creation.

8.3.2 Complementary Resources in the Team Context

While a star's proximity to an organization's strategic core may enhance or limit the total value associated with a particular level of star productivity, several aspects of the team context in which a star is employed have been shown to influence more directly the level of productivity the star achieves in the first place.

Although stars are recognized for their exceptional *individual* performance, stars' achievements are generally supported by a wealth of resources that receive less attention. Resource complementarities are said to exist when the marginal return to one resource increases in the presence of the other (Hess and Rothaermel, 2011). The importance of complementary resources to stars' exceptional performance is highlighted quite clearly in Groysberg and Lee's (2009) study of mobile star security analysts, where the authors found that stars suffer an immediate performance decline following their movement to another firm. Importantly, performance declines for those stars who were hired into exploitation (i.e., as opposed to exploration); roles were shorter in duration, presumably because firms are more likely to have an established base of complementary resources required to support familiar exploitation tasks than novel exploration tasks. In addition, the authors found that those stars hired with a team of colleagues from their previous firm (as opposed to hired alone) experienced less drastic performance losses in their new roles, arguably because these stars had a team of familiar colleagues on whom they could efficiently draw for support in their new roles. Together, these findings suggest that supporting resources that complement the task requirements of a particular role, as well as resources that complement the expertise of a star himself, are critical in ena-bling a star's exceptional performance. Indeed, these findings are also consistent with broader research in the strategy and strategic human resource management literature that suggests that interdependencies exist among the intellectual, human, and social capital within organizations (Subramaniam and Youndt, 2005; Tzabbar, Aharonson, Amburgey, and Al-Laham, 2008) and with more focused research in the stars literature highlighting the importance of complementary human and organizational resources in supporting stars' success (Groysberg, Lee, and Nanda, 2008; Groysberg and Lee, 2008; Groysberg and Lee, 2010).

We can also view resource complementarities as central to stars' contributions to value creation at the collective team or organizational level. For instance, Hess and Rothaermel (2011) found that star scientists' positive effects on firms' innovation outcomes were stronger when a firm was also engaged in downstream alliances that provided access to commercialization channels for the firm's products. That is, these authors found that stars—as providers of the basic knowledge which serves as inputs in the innovation process—were complements to downstream alliances in pharmaceutical firms' supply chains, as the contributions associated with one of these resources (e.g., stars' inputs to the innovation process) were more valuable to a firm that also possessed the other resource (e.g., downstream alliances which enabled more effective and efficient product commercialization). Together with the findings of other studies reviewed here, these findings suggest that stars' individual productivity and broader contributions to organizational value creation may be supported and even enhanced by the presence of complementary resources.

8.3.3 Redundant Resources in the Team Context

Just as complementary resources can enhance the value creation associated with a star, resources that are redundant—or substitutive—to a star can limit the unique value associated with the star's contributions (Hess and Rothaermel, 2011). Research has identified such substitutive resources in a variety of forms, including organizational alliances (Hess and Rothaermel, 2011), non-star colleagues (Kehoe and Tzabbar, 2015), or other stars in a team (Groysberg, Polzer, and Elfenbein, 2011). Importantly, the presence of redundant resources can limit a star's value creation in both direct and indirect ways (Kehoe, Lepak, and Bentley, 2016).

Most directly, resources that act as substitutes for stars reduce a star's value creation by decreasing the unique incremental value associated with a star's contributions. For instance, Hess and Rothaermel (2011) found that stars' positive effects on firms' innovation outcomes were reduced when firms were also engaged in upstream alliances, with the rationale that upstream alliances, *like stars*, improve firms' innovation potential by providing access to basic scientific knowledge. As another example, Groysberg, Polzer, and Elfenbein (2011) suggest that as the number of stars on a team increases, the reputation benefits provided by the multiple stars become redundant, thereby reducing the incremental value associated with each additional star on the team.

The direct threats to a star's uniqueness posed by redundant resources may also trigger stars to engage in undesirable behaviors that result in less direct but equally detrimental consequences for value creation. For instance, Groysberg, Polzer, and Elfenbein (2011) suggested that when multiple stars are part of the same team, they may engage in status competitions with one another, which can disrupt team activities and undermine effective decision making. This logic was supported by the authors' finding that the decreases in team performance associated with the presence of additional stars were mitigated when star team members held diverse (and thus less redundant) areas of expertise. Kehoe and Tzabbar's (2015) finding that stars with narrower expertise (i.e., which was more prone to redundancy) were more likely to limit their colleagues' opportunities for innovative leadership provides further support for this reasoning.

In summary, stars' behaviors and contributions in organizations occur in the broader contexts of the teams and organizations in which stars are employed. These contexts influence stars' individual productivity, interactions with colleagues, and potential to contribute to value creation and competitive advantage of the organization. Thus, in hiring and placing stars, organizations would be well advised to position stars for maximum success by (a) recruiting stars whose knowledge and skills enable them to fill roles that are central to an organization's basis for competitive advantage; (b) focusing on star skill sets that are sufficiently unique yet related enough to existing team or organizational capabilities to provide beneficial knowledge spillovers to colleagues; and (c) surrounding stars with required support resources, especially talented colleagues, with whom the star is either already well acquainted or whom the star will have ample opportunities to get to know.

8.4 Discussion

We noted at the outset of this chapter that relatively little empirical research has specifically examined stars in the team context. Nonetheless, we have identified and reviewed a significant and growing body of research examining the mutual influences between stars and both their colleagues and broader organizations that bears definite relevance to stars in teams.

Importantly, on one hand, our review suggests this extant research offers a foundation to understand the bases on which stars may directly and indirectly influence teams, as well as many of the ways in which the team context is likely to shape stars' experiences and contributions. In particular, we know from prior research that, in addition to stars' exceptional individual productivity, stars may benefit the capabilities and performance of their colleagues, teams, and organizations by sharing their preferential access to external resources (including broad stakeholder support, key network connections, and cutting-edge knowledge) (Rothaermel and Hess, 2007; Zucker, Darby, and Armstrong, 2002), conveying knowledge spillovers through collaboration and informal helping behaviors (Kehoe and Tzabbar, 2015; Oettl, 2012), and positively influencing organizational norms to support more effective work behaviors (Lacetera, Cockburn, and Henderson, 2004). Alternatively, stars may limit the utilization of others' knowledge (Tzabbar, 2009), constrain colleagues' opportunities for development (Kehoe and Tzabbar, 2015; Tzabbar and Kehoe, 2014), and/or disrupt team processes in their efforts to maintain their unique value and status (Groysberg, Polzer, and Elfenbein, 2011). In addition, extant research has demonstrated that stars' abilities to make sustained exceptional contributions may be influenced by their positioning within a firm (Aguinis and O'Boyle, 2014), their ongoing access to quality colleagues and other complementary resources (Groysberg and Lee, 2008, 2009), and the presence of potential substitutes for stars' contributions in the team or broader organization (Groysberg, Polzer, and Elfenbein, 2011; Hess and Rothaermel, 2011).

8.4.1 Directions for Future Research: Establishing the Generalizability of Extant Findings

On the other hand, our review highlights several gaps in our understanding of how and when stars are most likely to exert influence, and be influenced, in teams, which point to important questions for future research. First, there is a significant question of the generalizability of extant research findings to different team, organizational, and industry contexts. As evidenced in our review, in the star literature to date, there is a significant overrepresentation of professional service and R&D firms. The resulting *under-representation* of many other work contexts in this research points to limitations in our knowledge of how different team and organizational task environments might shape the mutual influences between stars and their teams. For example, the work conducted in professional service and R&D settings relies heavily on the integration and application of tacit knowledge, and is conducive to—and in some cases requires—at least moderate interdependence among employees. Our review suggests that stars may exert significant positive influences in organizations by collaborating with and shaping the work norms of colleagues, and likewise points to the importance of high-quality colleagues who complement a star's expertise and contributions in supporting stars' superior performance across time and jobs. However, it is unclear how beneficial any of these influences are in teams whose tasks rely less on tacit knowledge developed through individuals' cumulative successful experiences and/or which allow less room for the integration of multiple interdependent members' ideas and expertise. Thus, there is a pressing need for future research to examine the bidirectional influences between stars and their colleagues in a broader array of contexts—both to assess the generalizability of extant research findings from professional service and R&D settings and to determine whether other organizational and team environments lend themselves to additional, previously unexplored influences between stars and teams.

8.4.2 Directions for Future Research: Achieving a More Nuanced Understanding of Stars' Distinct Influences

Second, and relatedly, while our review focuses on extant research that has defined *stars* as those individuals who both have demonstrated exceptional productivity and who enjoy disproportionate visibility relative to their industry peers, scholars have recently pointed to the likelihood that this conceptualization of stars may cause us to overlook individuals who create exceptional value in their teams and organizations but fail to conform to this characterization (Kehoe, Lepak, and Bentley, 2016; Tzabbar and Kehoe, 2014). For instance, as Kehoe, Lepak, and Bentley (2016) suggest in their expanded typology of stars, it is possible that individuals in some contexts create disproportionate value but demonstrate only one of these two criteria (i.e., exceptional task performance or broad external status) inherent in the traditional approach to identifying stars. That is, some individuals may solely (or primarily) benefit their teams and organizations through their exceptional task performance *or* through the resources and opportunities made available through their broad external status. As a result, such stars—if we accept these individuals into our definition—may be likely to exert influence, and be influenced, in their teams in distinct ways, pointing to a variety of important questions for future research. For example, future research would benefit from an exploration of (a) *the characteristics of team contexts in which value creation is more and less likely to benefit from stars with either one (but not both) of these exceptional qualities; (b) the extent to which stars with either one (but not both) of these exceptional qualities rely on complementary resources within their teams to maintain their exceptional contributions to value creation; and (c) how the interpersonal dynamics and patterns of status and influence within a team are differentially shaped by the presence of a star with either one (but not both) of these qualities.*

8.4.3 Directions for Future Research: Approaches to Managing Stars and Their Work Environments

Third, while a growing body of scholarship has begun to explore contingencies associated with the mutual influences between stars and their colleagues and organizations, there is a lack of empirical research exploring how stars and their surrounding contexts are best managed to maximize the benefits and minimize the costs associated with a star's presence in a team. While research of this nature could be approached from a variety of perspectives, we believe the findings from extant scholarship on stars point to two particularly promising directions for future research in this vein. With respect to stars' influences in teams, while we know that important differences exist in stars' individual capabilities, as well as in their abilities and propensities to provide resources and support to colleagues (Kehoe, Lepak, and Bentley, 2016; Kehoe and Tzabbar, 2015; Oettl, 2012), extant research sheds little light on (a) the extent to which various individual differences across stars are fixed versus malleable; (b) what, if any, approaches to managing stars and teams are effective in maximizing the positive spillovers that stars convey to their teams; and (c) the conditions under which stars' efforts to share knowledge, guidance, and other forms of support to improve their teammates' performance negatively affect stars' opportunities to maximize and/or sustain their own exceptional productivity. Thus, we suggest future research would benefit from an exploration of the relative malleability and manageability of relevant star attributes (e.g., propensity to collaborate and willingness to empower others), the extent to which tradeoffs are necessarily associated with different types of star contributions to a team (e.g., individual task performance; collaborative helping), whether the nature of stars' contributions and influences in teams tends to vary with their career stage, and how organizations can best shape the social and technological contexts that allow stars to excel, while shining light on—rather than casting shadows over—their teams.

With respect to teams' influences on stars, while extant research has demonstrated the general importance of resource-rich work contexts and quality colleagues in supporting stars' superior performance, prior work has also suggested that the presence of multiple stars in a team may lead to competition for status and influence which ultimately results in suboptimal team decision-making and performance outcomes. Given the relatively scant research examining the influences of these various contextual factors, combined with our limited knowledge concerning the consequences of stars' mobility between organizations in general (Groysberg, Lee, and Nanda, 2008), we suggest an important area for future research relates to how differences in the configurations of human capital, social structures, and other resources available in different teams or organizations affect stars' abilities to transfer their capabilities and exceptional performance across work contexts. For example, how might a star's mobility from a more hierarchical social structure to a more democratic structure influence the star's ability to maintain his or her disproportionate productivity and influence?

8.4.4 Directions for Future Research: Implications of Multiple Stars in the Work Context

Finally, we have noted that despite recent theoretical and empirical advancements in scholarship on stars, little is known about the dynamics associated with the presence of multiple stars on a team (for an exception, see Groysberg, Lee, and Nanda, 2008), and more specifically about the optimal approaches to managing the team context to maximize the benefits and mitigate the challenges associated with the presence of multiple star team members. From a resource orchestration perspective (Sirmon and Hitt, 2009), the presence of multiple stars on a team introduces a managerial and theoretical dilemma. Resource deployment decisions that focus on maximizing the utilization of stars' human capital are likely to increase the quality and reliability of a team's performance (Huckman and Pisano, 2006), but they are also likely to limit opportunities for the development of the team's non-stars' human capital and may foster an over-dependence on the team's star members (Tzabbar and Kehoe, 2014). However, investments more heavily focused on the utilization of non-star team members are likely to promote such team members' development but may leave stars' human capital underutilized, resulting in the erosion of the very human capital at the root of the team's potential competitive advantage (Sirmon, Hitt, Arregle, and Campbell, 2010). Thus, we suggest future research should explore the implications of not only having different numbers of stars present on a team, but also different approaches to resource orchestration that entail distinct patterns of bundling and leveraging a team's multiple stars among its other members.

8.5 Conclusion

Our review confirms that scholars' and practitioners' increasing interest in the dynamics and outcomes associated with stars' presence in teams—and more broadly in organizations—is quite justified. Indeed, beyond the exceptional productivity stars contribute to their teams on an individual basis, extant research suggests that star team members alter teams' interpersonal dynamics, work processes, and performance outcomes, and are themselves affected by their surrounding team environments. Importantly, evidence suggests that the consequences associated with a star's presence on a team are not always positive and are likely to vary based on relevant characteristics of both the team and star. Thus, while we have identified several potential avenues for future research in this area, we highlight that the underlying question across all of these lines of inquiry is: how and under what conditions is a star's membership on a team likely to produce the most positive outcomes for the star, the team, and the broader organization?

References

Audia, P. G., and Goncalo, J. A. 2007. Past success and creativity over time: a study of inventors in the hard disk drive industry. *Management Science*, 53(1), pp.1–15.

Aguinis, H., and O'Boyle, E. 2014. Star performers in twenty-first century organizations. *Personnel Psychology*, 67(2), pp.313–50.

Azoulay, P., Zivin, J. S. G., and Wang, J. 2010. Superstar extinction. *The Quarterly Journal of Economics*, 125, pp.549–89.

Burke, M. A., Fournier, G. M., and Prasad, K. 2007. The diffusion of a medical innovation: is success in the stars? *Southern Economic Journal*, 73, pp.588–603.

Cable, D. M., and Turban, D. B. 2003. The value of organizational reputation in the recruitment context: a brand-equity perspective. *Journal of Applied Social Psychology*, 33(11), pp.2244–66.

Campbell, B. A., Coff, R., and Kryscynski, D. 2012. Rethinking sustained competitive advantage from human capital. *Academy of Management Review* 37, pp.376–95.

Coff, R. W., and Kryscynski, D. 2011. Invited editorial: drilling for micro-foundations of human capital-based competitive advantages. *Journal of Management*, 37(5), pp.1429–43.

Delery, J. E., and Shaw, J. D. 2001. The strategic management of people in work organizations: review, syntheses, and extension. *Research in Personnel and Human Resources Management*, 20, pp.165–97.

Fuller, A. W., and Rothaermel, F. T. 2012. When stars shine: the effects of faculty founders on new technology ventures. *Strategic Entrepreneurship Journal*, 6, pp.220–35.

Furukawa, R., and Goto, A. 2006. Core scientists and innovation in Japanese electronics companies. *Scientometrics*, 68(2), pp.227–40.

Gardner, T. M. 2005. Interfirm competition for human resources: evidence from the software industry. *Academy of Management Journal*, 48(2), pp.237–56.

Grigoriou, K., and Rothaermel, F. T. 2014. Structural microfoundations of innovation the role of relational stars. *Journal of Management*, 40(2), pp.586–615.

Groysberg, B., and Lee, L. E. 2008. The effect of colleague quality on top performance: the case of security analysts. *Journal of Organizational Behavior*, 29(8), pp.1123–44.

Groysberg, B., and Lee, L. E. 2009. Hiring stars and their colleagues: exploration and exploitation in professional service firms. *Organization Science*, 20(4), pp.740–58.

Groysberg, B., and Lee, L. 2010. Star power: colleague quality and turnover. *Industrial and Corporate Change*, 19, pp.741–56.

Groysberg, B., Lee, L. E., and Nanda, A. 2008. Can they take it with them? The portability of star knowledge workers' performance. *Management Science*, 54(7), pp.1213–30.

Groysberg, B., Polzer, J. T., and Elfenbein, H. A. 2011. Too many cooks spoil the broth: how high-status individuals decrease group effectiveness. *Organization Science*, 22(3), pp.722–37.

Hess, A. M., and Rothaermel, F. T. 2011. When are assets complementary? Star scientists, strategic alliances, and innovation in the pharmaceutical industry. *Strategic Management Journal*, 32(8), pp.895–909.

Higgins, M. J., Stephan, P. E., and Thursby, J. G. 2011. Conveying quality and value in emerging industries: star scientists and the role of signals in biotechnology. *Research Policy*, 40, pp.605–17.

Huckman, R. S., and Pisano, G. P. 2006. The firm specificity of individual performance: evidence from cardiac surgery. *Management Science*, 52(4), pp.473–88.

Kehoe, R. R., Lepak, D. P., and Bentley, F. S. 2016. Let's call a star a star: task performance, external status, and exceptional contributors in organizations. *Journal of Management*, DOI: 10.1177/0149206316628644.

Kehoe, R. R., and Tzabbar, D. 2015. Lighting the way or stealing the shine? An examination of the duality in star scientists' effects on firm innovative performance. *Strategic Management Journal*, 36(5), pp.709–27.

Kozlowski, S. W. J., and Bell, B. S. 2003. Work groups and teams in organizations. *Handbook of Psychology*, 2(14), pp.333–75.

Lacetera, N., Cockburn, I. M., and Henderson, R. 2004. Do firms change capabilities by hiring new people? A study of the adoption of science-based drug discovery. In J. A. C. Baum and A. M. McGahan, eds., *Business strategy over the industry lifecycle (advances in strategic management)*, Vol. 21, pp.133–59. Bingley, UK: Emerald Group Publishing Limited.

Liebeskind, J. P., Oliver, A. L., Zucker, L., and Brewer, M. 1996. Social networks, learning, and flexibility: sourcing scientific knowledge in new biotechnology firms. *Organization Science*, 7(4), pp.428–43.

Lucifora, C., and Simmons, R. 2003. Superstar effects in sport evidence from Italian soccer. *Journal of Sports Economics*, 4(1), pp.35–55.

Meyers, M. C., De Boeck, G., and Dries, N. 2017. Talent or not: employee reaction to talent designations. In D. G. Collings, K. Mellahi, and W. C. Cascio, eds., *Oxford handbook of talent management*. Oxford: Oxford University Press.

Michaels, E., Handfield-Jones, H., and Axelrod, B. 2001. *The war for talent*. Boston: Harvard Business School Press.

Nerkar, A., and Paruchuri, S. 2005. Evolution of R&D capabilities: the role of knowledge networks within a firm. *Management Science*, 51(5), pp.771–85.

Noe, R. A. 1988. An investigation of the determinants of successful assigned mentoring relationships. *Personnel Psychology*, 41(3), pp.457–79.

Oettl, A. 2012. Reconceptualizing stars: scientist helpfulness and peer performance. *Management Science*, 58(6), pp.1122–40.

Oldroyd, J. B., and Morris, S. S. 2012. Catching falling stars: a human resource response to social capital's detrimental effect of information overload on star employees. *Academy of Management Review*, 37(3), pp.396–418.

Paruchuri, S. 2010. Intraorganizational networks, interorganizational networks, and the impact of central inventors: a longitudinal study of pharmaceutical firms. *Organization Science*, 21(1), pp.63–80.

Ravid, S. A. 1999. Information, blockbusters, and stars: a study of the film industry. *The Journal of Business*, 72(4), pp.463–92.

Rothaermel, F. T., and Hess, A. M. 2007. Building dynamic capabilities: innovation driven by individual-, firm-, and network-level effects. *Organization Science*, 18(6), pp.898–921.

Schiemann, W. A. 2014. From talent management to talent optimization. *Journal of World Business*, 49(2), pp.281–88.

Sirmon, D. G., and Hitt, M. A. 2009. Contingencies within dynamic managerial capabilities: Interdependent effects of resource investment and deployment on firm performance. *Strategic Management Journal*, 30, pp.1375–94.

Sirmon, D. G., Hitt, M. A., Arregle, J. L., and Campbell, J. T. 2010. The dynamic interplay of capability strengths and weaknesses: investigating the bases of temporary competitive advantage. *Strategic Management Journal*, 31(13), pp.1386–409.

Subramaniam, M., and Youndt, M. A. 2005. The influence of intellectual capital on the types of innovative capabilities. *Academy of Management Journal*, 48(3), pp.450–63.

Tzabbar, D. 2009. When does scientist recruitment affect technological repositioning? *Academy of Management Journal*, 52(5), pp.873–96.

Tzabbar, D., Aharonson, B. S., Amburgey, T. L., and Al-Laham, A. 2008. When is the whole bigger than the sum of its parts? Bundling knowledge stocks for innovative success. *Strategic Organization*, 6(4), pp.375–406.

Tzabbar, D. T., and Kehoe, R. R. 2014. Can opportunity emerge from disarray? An examination of exploration and exploitation following star scientist turnover. *Journal of Management*, 40(2), pp.449-82.

Tzabbar, D., and Vestal, A. 2015. Bridging the social chasm in geographically distributed R&D teams: the moderating effects of relational strength and status asymmetry on the novelty of team innovation. *Organization Science*, 26(3), pp.811–29.

Zucker, L. G., Darby, M. R., and Armstrong, J. S. 2002. Commercializing knowledge: university science, knowledge capture, and firm performance in biotechnology. *Management Science*, 48(1), pp.138–53.

CHAPTER 9

TALENT OR NOT

Employee Reactions to Talent Designations

MARIA CHRISTINA MEYERS, GIVERNY DE BOECK,
AND NICKY DRIES

9.1 Talent or Not: Employee Reactions to Talent Designations

FROM an employee perspective, being designated as talent by one's employer is commonly seen as a highly desirable, major career event. King defines *talent designation* as "the process by which organizations selectively identify employees for participation in the organization's talent programs [which vary by organization and by maturity of talent management practices]" (2016: 5). Being selected for these often very prestigious and exclusive programs is interpreted as a signal that the organization is recognizing an employee's (high) potential and is committed to develop and use this potential in the future. From an organizational perspective, talent designation is a critical component of talent management, which is commonly understood to be the key to gaining a sustainable competitive advantage (Becker, Huselid, and Beatty, 2009).

Talent management is defined as "activities and processes that involve the systematic identification of key positions which differentially contribute to the organization's sustainable competitive advantage, the development of a talent pool of high-potential and high-performing incumbents to fill these roles, and the development of a differentiated human resource architecture to facilitate filling these positions with competent incumbents and to ensure their continued commitment to the organization" (Collings and Mellahi, 2009: 305). The 1%–20% of employees who are identified as members of the talent pool (Dries, 2013)—the talent—typically stand out because of their highly valuable and unique knowledge, skills, and abilities (Lepak and Snell, 1999); superior performance records (Aguinis and O'Boyle, 2014); or promise and potential for the future (Silzer and Church, 2009). In line with literature on the resource-based view of the firm (Barney, 1991) and workforce differentiation (Lepak and Snell, 1999), talent management draws on the assumption that talented employees are more valuable than others are because they have the ability to make substantial contributions to organizational performance when placed in strategic roles within the organization (Boudreau and Ramstad, 2005; Collings and Mellahi, 2009). As a consequence, talent-management scholars advocate differentiated management of employees based on their talent-pool membership, implying that a major share of organizational resources is invested in activities to identify, attract, develop, motivate, and retain talent and only a minor share in all other employees. These disproportionate investments in talent are justified by the disproportionate returns that they are expected to deliver.

Conversely, all expectations about disproportionate performance gains through talent management hinge on the assumption that talent will react in a positive way to talent-management initiatives by, for instance, displaying more motivation and effort. Even though many scholars and practitioners take positive reactions among talent for granted, to date, not much is actually known about how talent reacts to having a special status within their organization (Dries and De Gieter, 2014). To close this knowledge gap, several scholars have been starting to conduct empirical studies in which they investigate reactions to talent-management practices among employees who either have or have not been identified as organizational talent (e.g., Björkman et al., 2013; Gelens, Dries, Hofmans, and Pepermans, 2015).

In this chapter, we first provide an overview of the empirical—both qualitative and quantitative—studies that explore the effects of talent designation on those identified as "talent" versus those not identified as "talent." The studies are broadly organized according to the investigated outcome variables, that is, a focus on positive attitudes of talented employees, psychological contracts, or potential costs of talent designation. Subsequently, we integrate the findings and discuss and explain them in the light of the most commonly adopted theoretical frameworks in the empirical studies, that is, social exchange theory (Blau, 1964), signaling theory (Spence, 1973), psychological contract theory (Rousseau, 1989), equity theory (Adams, 1965), talent-perception incongruence (Sonnenberg, van Zijderveld, and Brinks, 2014), and theories on identity struggles (Winnicott, 1960). Finally, we discuss debates and issues with regard to talent designation and point out avenues for future research.

9.2 RESEARCH FINDINGS

An overview of all studies that have explored employee reactions to talent identification can be found in Table 9.1. The studies can be roughly organized in three categories according to their research focus. First, a majority of studies focused on comparing one or several groups of talented employees to a control group of average (non-talented) employees. The differentiation between talent and non-talent was either based on organizational ratings (official talent status) or on the employees' own beliefs about whether or not they were seen as talent by the organization (perceived talent status). Second, some studies

Table 9.1 Overview of Empirical Studies Investigating Employee Reactions to Talent Identification

Author(s)	Type of study	Research context	Research focus/IV		Outcomes
Bethke-Langenegger (2012)	Quantitative	Swiss organization (financial service provider)	Official talent status (talent/ non-talent)	ns + -	Job satisfaction Turnover intention Work engagement
			Perceived talent status (talent/ non-talent)	ns ns ns	Job satisfaction Turnover intention Work engagement
Björkman et al. (2013)	Quantitative	Eleven Scandinavian MNE's	Perceived talent status (talent/non-talent/not knowing whether talent or not)	+ + + + ns (-)	Acceptance of increasing performance demands Commitment to building skills Support of strategic priorities Identification with the unit Identification with the MNE Turnover intentions *(only in comparison to non-talent)*
Dries and de Gieter (2014)	Qualitative	Nine organizations (six different industries), all identified as best practice organizations	Interviews with employees with an official talent status		Talent expected to be provided with customized career support and interesting training and development opportunities (whereas organizations expected the talent to manage their own careers). Talent reported to feel insecure and confused by ambiguous signals with regard to talent management
Dries and Pepermans (2007)	Quantitative	Three organizations (finance, insurance, and telecom sector)	Official talent status (talent/ non-talent)	ns	Career commitment

(continued)

Table 9.1 Continued

Author(s)	Type of study	Research context	Research focus/IV		Outcomes
Dries and Pepermans (2008)	Qualitative	Six MNE's (all interviewees employed in Belgium)	Interviews with employees with an official talent status		Talent mentioned to expect upward career moves on a regular basis They feared not meeting organizational expectations (source of stress) and resented being constantly monitored for failure
Dries, Forrier, De Vos, and Pepermans (2014)	Quantitative	Five Belgian for-profit organizations (different industries)	Official talent status (talent/ non-talent)	ns +	Perceived employee PC obligations (display high loyalty and performance) Perceived employer PC obligations (offer long-term job security and opportunities for development)
Dries, Hofmans, and Pepermans (2013)	Quantitative	Twelve internationally active, for-profit organizations (different industries)	Official talent status (high potentials/ key experts/ non-talent)	+ + (+) (+) (+) (+)	Job security Salary increase since entry Organizational support *(only for high potentials, not key experts)* Promotions since entry *(only for high potentials, not key experts)* Organizational commitment *(only for high potentials, not key experts)* Career satisfaction *(only for high potentials, not for key experts)*
Dubouloy (2004)	Qualitative	Diverse (interviewees followed an executive MBA program)	Interviews with employees with an official or perceived talent status		Talent might display "false selves" in response to the pressure to assimilate into an organization's culture and may have feelings of insecurity with regard to their job and career prospects

Author(s)	Type of study	Research context	Research focus/IV		Outcomes
Gelens, Dries, Hofmans, and Pepermans (2015)	Quantitative (two studies)	Two Belgian organizations (finance sector)	Official talent status (talent/ non-talent)	+ (+)	POS Affective organizational commitment *(only in Study 1, not in Study 2)*
Gelens, Hofmans, Dries, and Pepermans (2014)	Quantitative	Belgian organization (finance sector)	Official talent status (junior high-potential/ senior high-potential/ non-talent)	+ + (+)	Perceived distributive justice Job satisfaction Work effort *(only for senior high potentials)*
Khoreva and Vaiman (2015)	Quantitative	Eight MNEs	Talent status self-awareness (self-aware talent/ unaware talent)	ns ns	Willingness to participate in leadership development activities Actual participation in leadership development activities
Khoreva, Kostanek, and van Zalk (2015)	Quantitative	Eleven Nordic MNCs	Talent status self-awareness (self-aware talent/ unaware talent)	+ + +	Acceptance of increasing performance demands Commitment to building competencies Utilization of corporate socialization mechanisms
Smale et al. (2015)	Quantitative	Six Finnish MNCs	Talent status self-awareness (self-aware talent/ unaware talent)		For self-aware talent, there was a stronger relationship between psychological contract fulfillment and perceived talent obligations (moderation) For self-aware talent, there was a weaker relationship between performance appraisals and talent obligations (moderation)
Sonnenberg, van Zijderveld, and Brinks (2014)	Quantitative	Twenty-one European, internationally active, private- and public-sector organizations	Talent-perception incongruence	−	Psychological contract fulfillment

(continued)

Table 9.1 Continued

Author(s)	Type of study	Research context	Research focus/IV	Outcomes
Swailes and Blackburn (2016)	Mixed method	State-owned, specialist technology organization	Interviews with employees either identified as emerging talent, scientist, future senior leader, or non-talent	Talent perceived talent-management procedures as more fair, felt more supported by their organizations and supervisors, were more satisfied with development opportunities, and were more motivated to develop themselves More senior talent displayed a "sense of entitlement," i.e., they expected others to create opportunities for them
Tansley and Tietze (2013)	Qualitative	Global accountancy practice (headquartered in London)	Interviews with employees with an official talent status	Talent indicated that their status was associated with benefits (e.g., early promotions), but also with certain costs (stress; little private time) They reported a tension between the need to belong (having an "appropriate" identity) and the need to be unique
Thunnissen (2015)	Mixed method	Five Dutch public universities	Interviews with employees with an official talent status	Talent said to be more committed to their career than to their organization and expressed dissatisfaction with talent-management programs, their lack of transparency, the slow pace of career advancement, and a lack of job security

Notes. IV = independent variable; "+" = significant positive relationship; "-" = significant negative relationship; "ns" = not significant focused solely on employees who have officially been identified as talent by the organization, while differentiating between talent who are aware of their status and talent who are not (talent status self-awareness). Third, several (qualitative) studies focus on groups of talented employees only, who are mostly officially identified as talent and are aware of their talent status. Employee-reaction variables that are investigated in these studies encompass (positive) employee attitudes (toward their job, the talent-management program, their organization, and their career), effects on employees' psychological contracts (PCs), and potential costs or downsides of having a talent status.

9.3 Effects of Talent Designation on Employee Attitudes

9.3.1 Attitudes toward Work

Research findings about effects of talent identification on employees' attitudes toward their work or job have delivered mixed findings so far. Contrary to common expectations, Bethke-Langenegger (2012) found a negative relationship between an employee's official talent status and work engagement and no relation between an employee's perceived talent status and work engagement. Similarly, neither official nor perceived talent status was found to be related to job satisfaction. By contrast, Gelens, Hofmans, Dries, and Pepermans (2014) found that both official groups of talent that were included in their study (high potentials and key experts) scored higher on job satisfaction than average employees did.

9.3.2 Attitudes toward the Organization

Findings with regard to the attitudes of talent toward their organizations are ambiguous, as well, yet slightly more supportive of positive than negative employee reactions. Gelens, Dries, Hofmans, and Pepermans (2015) conducted two studies—one comparing high-potential to non-high-potential employees and the other comparing élite management trainees to non-trainees—which revealed that individuals with an official, organization-assigned talent status scored higher on perceived organizational support than non-talent. Moreover, both studies revealed that perceived organizational support mediated the relationship between having a talent status and affective organizational commitment. However, in the second study, no mean difference in commitment was found when comparing management trainees and non-trainees. Positive effects of being officially identified as talent on both perceived organizational support (POS) and organizational commitment were also found in Dries, Van Acker, and Verbruggen's (2012) study. The effects were, however, only significant for "high potentials" (defined as *employees with exceptional leadership potential*), not for key experts (defined as *employees with exceptional leadership skills*). In line with the results of these two quantitative studies, qualitative studies also yielded ambiguous results. In one study, interviewed talent reported feeling well supported by both their organization and supervisor (Swailes and Blackburn, 2016), but they mentioned being much less committed to their organization than to their career in another study (Thunnissen, 2015).

Adding to the list of inconclusive results, the only two studies that investigated turnover intentions as an outcome revealed contradictory findings. Björkman et al. (2013) reported that employees who perceived having talent status scored lower on turnover intention compared with employees who did not perceive having talent status (but not with employees who did not know whether they were seen as talent or not). By contrast, Bethke-Langenegger (2012), meanwhile, discovered that perceived talent status was unrelated to and official talent status was positively related to turnover intentions.

Little research has specifically focused on how talent perceives the talent-management program implemented by their organization. Qualitative research among public-sector employees has shown that talent are, at times, dissatisfied with their organizations' talent-management programs, especially when these programs lack transparency and do not lead to quick career advancement (Thunnissen, 2015). Concerning the perceived fairness of talent management, however, results of another qualitative study indicated that talent, especially senior-level talent, rated talent-management procedures as fairer than non-talent did (Swailes and Blackburn, 2016). In line with this, quantitative research demonstrated that being officially designated as talent is associated with higher ratings of perceived distributive justice, which, in turn, affects job satisfaction (Gelens, Hofmans, Dries, and Pepermans, 2014). Moreover, the authors found a positive effect on work effort of being identified as a senior high potential (no effect for junior high potentials). The authors specified that there was a conditional indirect effect of high-potential status on work effort via distributive justice as a mediator, moderated by procedural justice. That is, the effect of distributive justice on work effort was conditional on perceived procedural justice, implying that the effect was only significant for either very low or high levels of procedural justice (Gelens, Hofmans, Dries, and Pepermans, 2014). This means that having a fair (equity-based) distribution of resources is not sufficient to trigger more work effort but rather has to be complimented by a fair distribution process (procedural justice).

9.3.3   Attitudes toward the Career

As indicated earlier, in a qualitative study, talented employees in public-sector organizations reported being more committed to their career than to their employer (Boselie and Thunnissen, 2017; Thunnissen, 2015). By contrast, no effect of official talent status on career commitment was found in a quantitative study (Dries and Pepermans, 2007). Moreover, investigating career satisfaction as an outcome variable, Dries, Van Acker, and Verbruggen (2012) found that an official status as high potential, but not as key expert, was related to higher career satisfaction. Effects of being identified as high potential on career satisfaction were furthermore found to be mediated by POS, organizational commitment, and promotions since organizational entry (Dries, Van Acker, and Verbruggen, 2012).

9.4 Effects of Talent Designation on Psychological Contracts

When discussing effects on employees' PCs (Rousseau, 1989), a distinction can be made between perceptions of PC obligations of employees toward their employer, the perceived PC obligations of the employer toward employees, and the perceived fulfillment or breach of PCs.

9.4.1 Perceived PC Obligations of the Employee toward the Employer

On the one hand, several studies have found that being identified as a talent or being aware of one's talent status is linked to increased perceptions of "talent obligations" (the obligations of talented employees toward their employers). One study, for instance, found that employees who believed they had talent status were more likely to accept increased performance demands, to be committed to develop their competencies, to support their employer's strategic priorities, and to identify with their focal unit than were employees who believed they were not or did not know whether they were seen as talented (Björkman et al., 2013). The same positive effects on the acceptance of increasing performance demands and commitment to building competencies were found when comparing officially identified talent who were aware of their talent status with talent who were unaware (Khoreva, Kostanek, and van Zalk, 2015; Smale et al., 2015). In addition, talent indicated greater motivation to develop themselves (Swailes and Blackburn, 2016). On the other hand, empirical studies have also revealed that there were no effects of perceived talent status on identification with the MNE (Björkman et al., 2013), no effects of actual talent status on perceived talent obligations in terms of loyalty toward the organization and commitment to improving one's performance (Dries, Forrier, De Vos, and Pepermans, 2014), and no effect of talent status self-awareness on willingness to participate and actual participation in leadership development activities (Khoreva and Vaiman, 2015).

9.4.2 Perceived PC Obligations of the Employer toward the Employee

While results with regard to the perceived talent obligations toward their employer are ambiguous, results with regard to the perceived employer obligations toward talent unanimously point to increased expectations of talent. In a quantitative study, it was found that officially being designated as talent was related to higher perceived employer obligations in terms of offering job security and opportunities for development (Dries Forrier, De Vos, and Pepermans, 2014). Moreover, qualitative studies emphasized that talent expected to be provided with interesting development opportunities and customized career support (Dries and De Gieter, 2014), and to be promoted on a regular basis (Dries and Pepermans, 2008). Swailes and Blackburn (2016) even mention that higher-level talent in particular can display a "sense of entitlement," manifesting itself in a more demanding attitude with regard to inducements and opportunities that they feel the organization should offer them. Some hints that these heightened expectations of talent can be fulfilled are provided by results of Dries, Van Acker, and Verbruggen's (2012) study, indicating that official talent status is related to higher perceived job security, higher salary increases since organizational entry, and number of promotions since entry.

9.4.3 Psychological Contract Fulfillment

A large-scale study that focused explicitly on the consequences of a mismatch between employees' perceived talent status and organization-assigned talent status ("talent-perception incongruence") revealed that such a mismatch was negatively related to psychological contract fulfillment (Sonnenberg, van Zijderveld, and Brinks, 2014). This implies that an incorrect perception of one's talent status can create flawed expectations about one's employment relationship that are doomed to remain unfulfilled. Note that the variable talent-perception incongruence covers both employees who do not officially belong to the talent pool but think they do and employees who officially belong to the talent pool but think they do not (Sonnenberg, van Zijderveld, and Brinks, 2014).

Another study revealed that talent who are aware of their talent status are particularly sensitive to psychological contract fulfillment: Smale et al. (2015) found that the awareness of one's talent status moderated the positive relationship between psychological contract fulfillment and perceived obligations toward the organization in such a way that the effect was stronger for the "aware" talent. The status-aware managers seemed to have become more sensitive to, or more demanding with regard to, the fulfillment of their psychological contract, whereas managers who were not aware of their talent status were committed to their obligations toward their organization independent of the fulfillment of their PCs.

9.5 POTENTIAL COSTS OF TALENT DESIGNATION

While being designated as talent is supposed to bring about rewards and benefits for outstanding employees, results of qualitative studies indicated that these rewards often come at a certain price. Interviewees in Tansley and Tietze's (2013) study, for instance, reported that having a high-potential status helped them to make quick career progress, but also heightened their stress levels and cut back their private time. In Dries and Pepermans' (2008) study, the interviewed talent specified that, in particular, the fear of failing to meet the organization's expectations is a major source of stress. In line with this, the talent indicated resenting the feeling of being constantly monitored (in their eyes, for failure) by the organization. Along similar lines, Dubouloy (2004) found that many (beginning) managers felt a lot of pressure to conform to their employers' expectations, not only in terms of showing the desired behaviors but also in terms of having the "right" personality. Because of this pressure and feelings of insecurity, managers seemed prone to submit to their desire to please others and to develop a "false self," while losing sight of their true talent and desires. Similar struggles with regard to the identity or felt sense of self of high-potential managers were uncovered in the study by Tansley and Tietze (2013), revealing that talent felt the need to display an "appropriate identity" in order to progress within the organization. This requirement can generate tensions between, on the one hand, the need to assimilate into the organization's culture and, on the other, the need to be unique and to stand out, which, in turn, adds to the experienced level of stress.

Furthermore, talent reported feeling insecure (Dubouloy, 2004; Thunnissen, 2015) or even confused and frustrated (Dries and De Gieter, 2014), which seemed to be particularly the case in a context of strategic ambiguity, where high potentials are completely sure of neither their status within the organization nor the content of available talent-management programs (Dries and De Gieter, 2014). In particular, employees often experienced promotion procedures as unintelligible and "haphazard," and they demonstrated a strong desire for fair and transparent talent management (Thunnissen, 2015).

9.6 Theoretical Explanations

One of the key assumptions among both talent-management scholars and practitioners is that talent management and the related differential treatment of employees according to their talent status will cause mainly favorable reactions among the talented employees. In scientific literature, most hypotheses about these reactions are based on social exchange theory (Blau, 1964) and the central idea that individuals have a tendency to reciprocate favorable treatment by others. Applying social exchange theory to talent management, scholars propose that employees who are identified as talent gain certain benefits provided by the organization (e.g., training and promotion opportunities; Björkman et al., 2013; Dries, Forrier, De Vos, and Pepermans, 2014; Gelens, Dries, Hofmans, and Pepermans, 2015; Gelens, Hofmans, Dries, and Pepermans, 2014; Swailes and Blackburn, 2016). In return for these benefits, employees adopt more favorable attitudes toward the organization (e.g., enhanced loyalty and commitment) and invest more effort in their work tasks and personal development. Moreover, positive reciprocation by the employee is even expected when the designation as talent is not linked to immediate, visible benefits. Signaling theory (Spence, 1973) proposes that the mere act of designating someone as a talent can serve as a strong organizational "signal" indicating that an employee is valued by the organization, which can be sufficient to trigger a positive reciprocation process in anticipation of benefits that will be provided in the future (Dries, Forrier, De Vos, and Pepermans, 2014; Gelens, Dries, Hofmans, and Pepermans, 2015).

In many (albeit not all) studies comparing talent with non-talent, support for the ideas of social exchange and signaling theory was found. Results of several studies corroborated that talented employees score higher on desirable attitudes toward the organization such as affective organizational commitment, job satisfaction, and commitment to build their competencies and keep up with increasing performance demands (e.g., Björkman et al., 2013; Gelens, Dries, Hofmans, and Pepermans, 2015). Some evidence was found that being identified as high potential signals POS in the first place, which, in turn, contributes to affective commitment and career satisfaction (Dries, Van Acker, and Verbruggen, 2012; Gelens, Dries, Hofmans, and Pepermans, 2015). Moreover, the effect of talent designation on career satisfaction was found to be mediated by the number of promotions since organizational entry and organizational commitment (Dries, Van Acker, and Verbruggen, 2012). Based on studies that included employees from different talent pools, however, we know that these favorable effects on high potentials do not always hold across talent pools (Dries, Van Acker, and Verbruggen, 2012; Gelens, Hofmans, Dries, and Pepermans, 2014). Gelens and colleagues (2014) reasoned that rather than getting a "high-potential" label, the amount of organizational resources one receives, which differs per talent pool, might be decisive in eliciting favorable employee attitudes. Support for this assumption was delivered by studies that investigated the effects of the number of talent-management practices someone has access to on individual attitudes and behaviors (e.g., Buttiens, Hondeghem, and Wynen, 2014; Chami-Malaeb and Garavan, 2013; Marescaux, De Winne, and Sels, 2013). Some studies comparing talent and non-talent found no relationship between being a talent and positive attitudinal variables such as career satisfaction (e.g., Dries and Pepermans, 2007), or even unfavorable relationships such as higher turnover intentions and lower engagement among talented employees (Bethke-Langenegger, 2012).

Based on initial empirical evidence, two potential explanations for not finding the expected effects of talent designation can be derived. First, the effect of talent designation on employee reactions might be susceptible to moderating factors. In one of the few studies in which moderation was tested, Gelens, Hofmans, Dries, and Pepermans (2014) pointed out that perceptions of organizational justice might be an important boundary condition that affects how (non-)talent react to talent designation. The authors found that employees designated as talent score higher on perceived distributive justice, which, in turn, only leads to more work effort if the talent perceives high procedural justice as well (Gelens, Hofmans, Dries, and Pepermans, 2014). Based on equity theory (Adams, 1965), it can be argued that a distribution of resources (outputs) that reflects the delivered inputs (e.g., work effort and performance) is desirable (distributive justice). Next to that, the processes that are used to allocate the resources need to be fair and transparent as well (procedural justice). The notion that both talent and non-talent are sensitive to fair procedures was also supported by results of qualitative studies (Swailes and Blackburn, 2016; Thunnissen, 2015): Overall, non-talent voice more complaints about the unfairness of talent-management procedures than talent do—probably because they overestimate their own contributions, which creates expectations of high rewards that will not be fulfilled (cf. theoretical work by Gelens, Dries, Hofmans, and Pepermans, 2013). Nonetheless, talent, especially at the organizational entry level, also seem concerned about fairness of talent management and criticize, for instance, the lacking clarity and transparency of promotion procedures (Thunnissen, 2015).

A second explanation why some studies that compared talent and non-talent did not find the expected results might lie in the fact that many labeled talent are unaware of their talent status (e.g., Khoreva and Vaiman, 2015). This unawareness results from policies of secrecy with regard to talent management, which organizations often opt for to prevent potential negative reactions among the employees who are not considered talent (Dries and De Gieter, 2014; Silzer and Church, 2010). Overall, it has been found that a mismatch in one's perceived and actual talent status (talent-perception incongruence), which also includes employees who have no official talent status but think they do, will lead to unfavorable employee reactions (Sonnenberg, van Zijderveld, and Brinks, 2014). Conversely, studies that compared the reactions of talent who are aware of their talent status and talent who are unaware did not result in unambiguous evidence that being aware of one's status is related to reactions that are more positive. Khoreva and Vaiman (2015), for instance, did not find differences between self-aware and unaware talent with regard to their willingness to participate in leadership development activities, whereas Khoreva et al. (2015) found that self-aware talent reported a stronger commitment to developing themselves. A similar positive relationship (correlation) between self-aware talent and commitment to perform and to develop themselves was found by Smale et al. (2015). However, the authors also found hints that self-aware talent became more demanding and difficult to manage (Smale et al., 2015), which corresponds to findings from qualitative studies (e.g., Dries and De Gieter, 2014). In detail, findings by Smale et al. (2015) revealed that employees who are aware of their talent status have a heightened sensitivity for the fulfillment of their psychological contract compared to unaware employees. Furthermore, a non-significant relation between target setting and evaluative feedback and organizational obligations was found in status-aware employees, whereas it was significantly negative for employees unaware of their talent status, indicating a reduced sensitivity for performance appraisals in the first group.

To explain this more demanding attitude of talent, talent-management scholars draw on psychological contract theory (Rousseau, 1989) and reason that talent-management influences an employee's expectations with regard to their unique exchange relationship with the organization (Gelens, Hofmans, Dries, and Pepermans, 2014; Sonnenberg, van Zijderveld, and Brinks, 2014). When identified as talented, employees develop heightened expectations of the obligations of their employer toward them (they expect to receive more benefits), and, in turn, toward their employer (they expect that they have to deliver more)—which King (2016) describes as the "talent deal." Interestingly, results reveal that the two sorts of obligations are not always in balance, meaning that talent expects to receive, but not necessarily to deliver, more (Dries and De Gieter, 2014; Dries, Forrier, De Vos, and Pepermans, 2014). Taken together, findings point to a considerable risk of psychological contract breach among high-potential employees resulting from: (a) a sensitivity to psychological contract fulfillment (Smale et al., 2015); (b) the talent's feeling that they are "entitled" to special treatment (Swailes and Blackburn, 2016); and (c) a mismatch between what the high potentials expect to obtain and what the organization is expecting to provide (Dries and De Gieter, 2014).

While the latter findings highlight one potential risk of talent designation for talented employees, results of qualitative studies suggest that there are even more downfalls of being identified as talent. Employees who are designated as talent experience more stress owing to the felt requirement to live up to expectations and a resulting fear of failure (Dries and Pepermans, 2008; Tansley and Tietze, 2013). At times, they feel insecure and confused, because many organizations are not very transparent about the specific employees who have a talent status or about the requirements to keep or obtain such a status (Dries and De Gieter, 2014). Furthermore, interviews with high-potential employees revealed that they are prone to face identity struggles as a consequence of a perceived pressure to develop an identity that conforms to standards and ideals of the employing organization (Dubouloy, 2004; Tansley and Tietze, 2013). Referring to literature on psychoanalysis (Winnicott, 1960), Dubouloy (2004) explains that high-potential managers face a highly uncertain environment that does not allow for any clear predictions of future employment expectations, job security, or career opportunities. To regain a feeling of security in this insecure context, high-potential managers strive to conform to the supposed norms of the person or institution they depend upon (i.e., of higher-level managers or the organization) at the cost of behaving according to their own norms—that is, they will develop a "false self" (Dubouloy, 2004; Winnicott, 1960).

9.7 Key Issues and Debates Regarding Talent Designation

9.7.1 The Dark Side of Talent Designation: Negative Reactions in Talent

A first issue that is present in the literature on talent designation concerns its outcomes for talented employees. Following the social exchange logic, it is assumed that employees who are identified as talent will react positively to the talent designation in return for the advantages offered to them by the organization. Several studies find evidence for favorable attitudes and behaviors, showing that talent score higher on organizational commitment, work effort, and job and career satisfaction (Dries, Van Acker, and Verbruggen, 2012; Gelens, Dries, Hofmans, and Pepermans, 2015; Gelens, Hofmans, Dries, and Pepermans, 2014). These positive results, however, do not capture the complete picture. Talent designation also seems to trigger reactions in talented employees that are less favorable, ranging from feeling insecure and confused because of uncertain career prospects and ambiguous communication about the talent-management program (Dries and De Gieter, 2014); to suffering from stress, fear of failure, and an impaired work-life balance (Dries and Pepermans, 2008; Tansley and Tietze, 2013); to struggling to behave in accordance with both one's "true identity" and the "appropriate identity" desired by the organization (Dubouloy, 2004; Tansley and Tietze, 2013).

The available evidence revealed that talent designation can be a double-edged sword, meaning that researchers as well as organizations might need to refrain from seeing it as a solely positive experience for talent. To avoid an overly positive focus in research, talent-management scholars are required to look beyond social exchange theory (Blau, 1964) to underpin their reasoning about employee reactions to talent designation. In the light of the available research evidence, the job demands-resources model (Bakker and Demerouti, 2007) presents itself as a feasible theoretical framework for future research, as gaining talent status seems associated with both increased job resources (e.g., access to training) and job demands (e.g., job insecurity, workload, and role ambiguity). Using a framework that considers both costs and benefits of talent designation is essential to further our understanding of the potential negative consequences of talent identification for talented employees, which, in the worst case, might undermine the purpose of talent nominations in the first place.

9.7.2 Talent Designation: the Effect of Status or Associated Talent Investments

A second issue that needs to be addressed concerns the distinction between the effects of talent status per se (getting a "talent" label) and the effects of *benefits* related to having this status (e.g., getting access to talent-management practices). The impact that having a certain status in itself can have on individuals has been illustrated by research on self-fulfilling prophecies or Pygmalion effects (Merton, 1948; Rosenthal and Jacobson, 1968). Rosenthal and Jacobson (1968), for example, assigned students at random to two groups—one experimental group labeled "intellectual bloomers" and one control group—and found that the experimental group scored significantly higher on a subsequent IQ test than the control group did. This effect was attributed to altered expectations in the teacher that were likely to affect positively the students' self-confidence and self-efficacy. A similar reasoning could be applied to talent management, as selecting an employee for talent-pool membership is related to raised management expectations of employee capabilities, which likely motivates the selected employees to live up to the expectations (Swailes and Blackburn, 2016).

Next to this explanation related to self-fulfilling prophecies, a second explanation for finding the effects of talent status alone can be found in signaling theory (Spence, 1973) and in King's (2016) theoretical work. It is assumed that employees interpret gaining talent status as a token of organizational appreciation and a sign of long-term commitment to the employment relationship on side of the organization (Dries, Forrier, De Vos, and Pepermans, 2014; King, 2016). As such, talent designation in itself should trigger positive employee reactions in the short term. One issue to be aware of, however, is that talented employees also interpret gaining talent status as a promise that the organization will invest in the exchange relationship in the future (King, 2016). As a consequence, the long-term effects of talent designation depend upon the fulfillment of those perceived promises (i.e., the actual access to talent-management practices), which only becomes apparent over time. This reasoning has essential implications for research on talent designation as it points to the necessity to account for the passage of time after talent designation. While employees who have just been identified as talent are likely to display favorable reactions to talent management, talent who were identified several months or even years ago will have had the chance to assess whether the organization is living up to the perceived promises, and might thus display differential reactions to talent management based on the outcomes of that assessment (cf. psychological contract theory; Rousseau, 1989).

Untangling the effects of talent status per se from the effects of (not) receiving benefits associated with this status might help us to explain the conflicting outcomes of research on talent designation (see the description of research findings earlier). Researchers can explore this further by making a distinction between short- and long-term effects and by exploring how each of the different theoretical lenses used to understand employee reaction seem to be linked to different phases of the talent-designation process.

9.7.3   Limited Attention to the Effects of Talent Designation on Non-Talent

A fourth issue in current studies on the reactions of employees to talent designation is the fact that these often only focus on members of the talent pool. Hardly any attention is given to the impact that talent designation may have on employees not identified as talent (King, 2016). Nevertheless, reactions of non-talent employees to talent designation might well be very interesting to study. In a proposition paper, Malik and Singh (2014) argue that even though many organizations do not communicate openly about their talent programs (Dries and Pepermans, 2008), non-talent (B-players) can be expected to use various informational and contextual cues to draw inferences about talent nominations. Through social comparison, this information might provoke feelings of disadvantage in non-talent employees, given that nominations are often tied to differential access to organizational resources (Marescaux, De Winne, and Sels, 2013). In addition, theoretical work on self-fulfilling prophecies suggests that not being selected as talent typically lowers both the employee's and management's expectations of the employee's potential contributions, which can cause demotivation and even frustration (i.e., the Golem effect; Bethke-Langenegger, 2012; Swailes and Blackburn, 2016). As the group of non-talent employees represents the majority of the workforce, their potential negative reactions could diminish or even outbalance the gains that are achieved owing to positive reactions among talent (Marescaux, De Winne, and Sels, 2013).

Hence, assessing the benefits and costs of talent designation requires researchers to take into account its effects on non-talent employees as well. Not paying attention to the reactions of non-talent is problematic because these influence the total effect of talent designation in terms of organizational outcomes. Therefore, future research should further explore the reactions of non-talent employees to talent designation and analyze their impact.

9.7.4 The Phenomenon of Talent-Management Secrecy

A fifth and final issue concerns communication about talent designation. In general, organizations display a high level of secrecy regarding their talent-management program (Dries and Pepermans, 2008). For example, they do not communicate openly about whether they employ an inclusive or exclusive strategy, and rarely reveal who is included in the pool of talent (Sonnenberg, van Zijderveld, and Brinks, 2014). Deliberately creating information asymmetries, organizations prefer the strategy of "strategic ambiguity" as it allows them to maintain control and is believed to prevent negative reactions in both talent and non-talent employees (Dries and De Gieter, 2014). Research findings, however, contradict this assumption and show that talent-management secrecy can yield undesired reactions in employees. Not openly communicating about talent designation is likely to create talent-perception incongruence (a mismatch between one's actual and perceived talent status), which, as mentioned earlier, is negatively related to psychological contract fulfillment (Sonnenberg, van Zijderveld, and Brinks, 2014). Similarly, Dries and De Gieter (2014) reason that communicating ambiguously about talent designation increases the risk of psychological contract breach (Dries and De Gieter, 2014) because ambiguity potentially creates unrealistic expectations that are unlikely to be met by the organization. Consequently, communication about who is seen as talented, on the one hand, and what a talent status entails (in terms of mutual expectations), on the other, might be a key factor that determines employee reactions to talent management, and should thus be further explored in future research.

9.8 FUTURE RESEARCH AGENDA

9.8.1 Theoretical Advancement: Exploring Boundary Conditions

The findings reviewed in this chapter show that the effect of talent designation on employee behaviors and attitudes is not univocal. More specifically, talented employees do not always seem equally inclined to react to the organization's talent designations in a positive way (Dries, Van Acker, and Verbruggen, 2012; Gelens, Hofmans, Dries, and Pepermans 2014). This implies that the effect of talent designation on employee reactions might be susceptible to boundary conditions, which was supported in Gelens and colleagues' (2014) study identifying procedural justice as key moderator. However, much more needs to be learned about moderators in the relationship between talent designation and employee reactions. As their study suggests, future research should, for instance, pay attention to the potential impact of the degree of exclusiveness (i.e., the relative proportion of employees included into the talent pool), as well as of the transparency of the talent-management program, on justice perceptions. Both are important information sources for employees to assess whether the talent designation is fair or not.

An additional moderator that is worth investigating has been identified in the conceptual work of King (2016) highlighting the importance of the direct supervisor as a gatekeeper to organizational resources (e.g., rewards and developmental opportunities). In particular, King (2016) proposes that the positive relationship between an employees' (perception of) talent designation and perceived supervisor support will be moderated by perceived supervisor talent status, such that less supervisor support will be perceived when the supervisor of a "talent" is not identified as talent him- or herself. Although it is likely that direct supervisors influence employee reactions to talent designation, it is, however, not yet clear how their influence would manifest itself. Future research could benefit from the further exploration of this moderator by, for example, introducing established theoretical frameworks such as leader-member exchange (Graen and Uhl-Bien, 1995).

Future research could also investigate theoretical frameworks related to employees' perceptions of talent status. One framework that could be relevant is self-serving bias (i.e., the tendency to attribute positive outcomes to personal factors such as ability and negative outcomes to contextual factors such as the complexity of a task) (Campbell and Sedikides, 1999). Since self-serving attributions are especially strong in situations characterized by skill and chance (Myers, 1980), it is likely that this bias will be present in the context of talent designation, implying, for instance, that employees will believe that their talent status is the result of their own making. Research evidence revealing that most talent ascribe their career success to their own assertiveness instead of organizational initiatives (Dries and Pepermans, 2008; Thunnissen, 2015) indicates that such self-serving bias might be present among talent. This, again, increases the risk of psychological contract breach because overestimating one's own contributions while underestimating the organization's will create a perceived imbalance in the exchange relationship (Morrison and Robinson, 1997). This could explain why researchers find that the identification as high potential is unrelated to employee obligations such as attachment and performance, but is significantly related to perceived employer obligations (Dries, Forrier, De Vos, and Pepermans, 2014). Future research could thus enhance our understanding of employee reactions to talent designation by focusing on employees' perceptions of the reasons behind having received the talent label or getting access to talent-management practices as moderating factors. If employees think that the label reflects their own efforts, talent designation is less likely to trigger positive reciprocation (e.g., displaying enhanced loyalty and effort).

9.8.2 Methodological Advancements: Experimental, Longitudinal, and Multilevel Designs

We propose that future research on employee reactions to talent designation could greatly benefit from the use of more advanced and rigorous methodologies because the available studies are subject to four main limitations. The first limitation is that the majority of existing studies uses cross-sectional designs that do not allow drawing causal interferences (e.g., Dries, Forrier, De Vos, and Pepermans, 2014). Although the implicit assumption is made that talent designation precedes employee reactions, reverse causality—meaning that employees who show the attitudes or behaviors desired by organizations are more likely to be selected into the talent pool—cannot be excluded (Björkman et al., 2013; Khoreva and Vaiman, 2015). This limitation can be addressed by adopting experimental research designs. To guarantee ecological validity (Gelens, Hofmans, Dries, and Pepermans, 2014), preference is given to case control field experiments in which researchers randomly assign employees to two groups—one nominated as talent and one control—and in which variables of interests are measured before and after the random talent designation. This approach would allow researchers to determine whether the talent nomination has a causal influence on talent's attitudes or behaviors, non-talent's attitudes or behaviors, or both. Moreover, experimental designs can also be used to investigate whether employee reactions result from the talent label as such, or from the resources associated with the talent status. Finally, vignette studies, a specific type of experimental design in which respondents' evaluations are assessed after presenting hypothetical stories, would allow researchers to study the effects of talent designation on employees who are informed about their status with varying degrees of transparency versus ambiguity (Gelens, Dries, Hofmans, and Pepermans, 2013). This is a practical advantage, as organizations often prefer to keep their talent-management practices secret (Dries and Pepermans, 2008)—cf. the literature on pay dispersion and pay secrecy (Colella, Paetzold, Zardkoohi, and Wesson, 2007).

A second limitation related to the cross-sectional research design used in most studies is that the time lapse between the moment of talent identification and the measurements is ignored (Smale et al., 2015). This is problematic because employees experience talent nomination as a major career event that holds the promise of organizational opportunities (e.g., training) in the future (Dries, Forrier, De Vos, and Pepermans, 2014; King, 2016). Since the fulfillment of expectations over time is experienced as an essential element of talent designation, placing employees at risk of future disappointments (Swailes and Blackburn, 2016), timing must purposively be taken into account to develop a comprehensive understanding of employee reactions. This time centrality is also reflected in transitional perspectives that focus on how talent experiences the effects of talent designation and related practices throughout the different stages of the talent-management program over time (King, 2016; Tansley and Tietze, 2013).

Previous limitations can be addressed by researchers with a longitudinal approach starting from the moment that employees first acquire their talent status. Longitudinal studies that control for changes in employee reactions over time would, for example, be especially suited to gain insight into the role of talent identification as a "critical incident" that can trigger a cycle of career progress (Dries, Van Acker, and Verbruggen, 2012) and can change the perceived psychological contract (Dries and De Gieter, 2014). Furthermore, longitudinal studies would also allow researchers to check whether talented employees remain with the organization long enough to fill the identified key position and, in that role, realize the competitive advantage that was the reason for the talent nomination in the first place (Collings and Mellahi, 2009).

A third limitation refers to the absence of multilevel research studying employee reactions to talent designation. Modeling different levels of analysis (e.g., individual, team, and organizational), however, is promising for future research on employee reactions to talent designation for two reasons. First, existing studies often draw their samples from multiple, diverse organizations but find it difficult to control for and draw inferences about differences between these (e.g., different high-potential programs) (Dries and De Gieter, 2014). Second, by collecting data on the team or departmental level, researchers could account for the fact that line managers often implement and communicate talent-management policies other than those intended by top management (Wright and Nishii,

Table 9.2 Suggested Research Questions, Levels of Analysis, and Research Designs

Research question	Level of analysis	Research design
Does talent designation influence employee attitudes and behaviors or the other way round (causal effects)?	Individual	(Field) experimental study
What are the experienced costs (job demands) and benefits (job resources) associated with talent designation?	Individual	Longitudinal study
How does talent experience the effects of talent designation over time? What are the short- and long-term effects?	Individual	Longitudinal study
Can the effects of talent designation be attributed to having a talent status or to receiving benefits associated with this status?	Individual	Cross-sectional study
What are the effects of talent designation on employees that are <u>not</u> designated as talent?	Individual	Longitudinal study
How do boundary conditions at the individual (e.g., justice perceptions), team (e.g., supervisor support), and organizational level (e.g., size of the talent pool) influence the talent designation–employee-reaction relationship?	Individual/ Team/ Organizational	Longitudinal study Multilevel study
To which factors do employees attribute their designation as talent (e.g., internal vs. external; to own assertiveness versus to sponsoring by a supervisor)? How do these attributions influence the talent designation–employee-reaction relationship?	Individual	Cross-sectional study
How does the policy of talent-management secrecy (not clearly communicating who the designated talent is) affect employee reactions to talent-management?	Individual/team/ organizational	Multilevel study Vignette study
How do variables at the level of nations (e.g., culture) influence the talent designation–employee-reaction relationship?	Individual/team/ organizational/ national	Cross-sectional, cross-cultural study Multilevel study

2012). Accounting for the role of the supervisor is essential for future research as a "lack of research attention to the specific mechanisms between supervisors and employees managed in the talent pool also limits our understanding of the exchange relationship and response of employees to the 'talent deal'" (King, 2016).

A fourth and final limitation concerns the generalizability of the findings. To date, most research on employee reactions to talent designation has been conducted in European countries (Gallardo-Gallardo, Nijs, Dries, and Gallo, 2015). Exploring cultural differences between countries (e.g., power distance), however, might yield interesting insights regarding employee reactions to talent designation (Gelens, Hofmans, Dries, and Pepermans, 2014). Björkman et al. (2013), for example, note that employees sampled from Nordic countries, which are characterized by egalitarian values, might hold different attitudes regarding differentiation compared with employees in Anglo-American cultures who are more accepting of differentiation. Studying the relation between talent designation and employee reactions in different countries would allow researchers to cross-validate findings (Dries, Forrier, De Vos, and Pepermans, 2014; Khoreva, Kostanek, and van Zalk, 2015).

Table 9.2 provides an overview of the most relevant questions for future research that have been identified in this chapter.

9.9 Conclusion: Does Talent Designation Achieve Its Ultimate Goal?

From an organizational point of view, talent designation is an essential part of talent management, and talent management, in turn, is seen as a critical driver of organizational success. A few employees are designated as talent based on the idea that they will deliver disproportionate contributions to organizational performance when developed appropriately and placed in suitable strategic positions (Collings and Mellahi, 2009). Implicitly, organizations assume that granting talent status to employees and providing them with extra opportunities unequivocally results in positive reactions among the talent (cf. social exchange theory; Blau, 1964). In particular, it is often assumed that talented employees will be more motivated to develop themselves and more committed to their organization. If they were not to react in this positive way, it would be unlikely that talent-management initiatives would result in performance gains for the organization.

Although research does find that talented employees score higher on desirable outcomes such as the commitment to build their competencies and affective organizational commitment (Björkman et al., 2013; Gelens, Dries, Hofmans, and Pepermans, 2015), these positive reactions are not always guaranteed. Evidence also shows unfavorable reactions in talented employees, including lower scores on engagement and higher scores on turnover intentions (Bethke-Langenegger, 2012). The only universal reaction that talent designation seems to evoke in talented employees is an increase in perceived employer obligations (Dries, Forrier, De Vos, and Pepermans, 2014), that is, a more demanding attitude on the side of the talented employees. To the best of our knowledge, there is no available research on talent designation that includes (objective) performance outcomes on either the individual or the organizational level. Based on the available research evidence, we thus cannot draw any valid conclusions about whether talent designation reaches its ultimate goal: to improve organizational performance through the development, motivation, and retention of talent. We therefore argue that it is crucial to investigate further the effects of talent designation on performance—and the boundary conditions under which they do and do not hold. In the absence of these assumed effects, the high investment in talent would be neither justified nor worth the effort.

References

Adams, J. S. 1965. Inequity in social exchange. In L. Berkowitz, ed., *Advances in experimental social psychology*, Vol. 2, pp.267–300. New York: Academic Press Inc.

Aguinis, H., and O'Boyle, E. 2014. Star performers in twenty-first century organizations. *Personnel Psychology*, 67(2), pp.313–50.

Bakker, A. B., and Demerouti, E. 2007. The job demands-resources model: state of the art. *Journal of Managerial Psychology*, 22(3), pp.309–28.

Barney, J. B. 1991. Firm resources and sustained competitive advantage. *Journal of Management*, 17(1), pp.99–120.

Becker, B. E., Huselid, M. A., and Beatty, R. W. 2009. *The differentiated workforce: transforming talent into strategic impact*. Boston: Harvard Business Press.

Bethke-Langenegger, P. 2012. *The differentiated workforce—effects of categorisation in talent management on workforce level*. Zurich: University of Zurich.

Björkman, I., Ehrnrooth, M., Mäkelä, K., Smale, A. et al. 2013. Talent or not? Employee reactions to talent identification. *Human Resource Management*, 52(2), pp.195–214.

Blau, P. M. 1964. *Exchange and power in social life*. New York: Wiley.

Boselie, P., and Thunnissen, M. 2017. Talent management in the public sector. In D. G. Collings, K. Mellahi, and W. C. Cascio, eds., *Oxford handbook of talent management*. Oxford: Oxford University Press.

Boudreau, J. W., and Ramstad, P. M. 2005. Talentship, talent segmentation, and sustainability: a new HR decision science paradigm for a new strategy definition. *Human Resource Management*, 44(2), pp.129–36.

Buttiens, D., Hondeghem, A., and Wynen, J. 2014. *How does talent management influence job satisfaction in the public sector? Integrating the construct of Basic Needs Satisfaction*. Paper presented at the Annual Work Conference Netherlands Institute of Government, Delft, NL.

Campbell, W. K., and Sedikides, C. 1999. Self-threat magnifies the self-serving bias: a meta-analytic integration. *Review of General Psychology*, 3(1), pp.23–43.

Chami-Malaeb, R., and Garavan, T. 2013. Talent and leadership development practices as drivers of intention to stay in Lebanese organisations: the mediating role of affective commitment. *The International Journal of Human Resource Management*, 24(21), pp.4046–62.

Colella, A., Paetzold, R. L., Zardkoohi, A., and Wesson, M. J. 2007. Exposing pay secrecy. *Academy of Management Review*, 32(1), pp.55–71.

Collings, D. G., and Mellahi, K. 2009. Strategic talent management: a review and research agenda. *Human Resource Management Review*, *19*, pp.304–13.

Dries, N. 2013. The psychology of talent management: a review and research agenda. *Human Resource Management Review*, *23*(4), pp.272–85.

Dries, N., and De Gieter, S. 2014. Information asymmetry in high potential programs. *Personnel Review*, *43*(1), pp.136–62.

Dries, N., Forrier, A., De Vos, A., and Pepermans, R. 2014. Self-perceived employability, organization-rated potential, and the psychological contract. *Journal of Managerial Psychology*, *29*(5), pp.565–81.

Dries, N., and Pepermans, R. 2007. Using emotional intelligence to identify high potential: a metacompetency perspective. *Leadership and Organization Development Journal*, *28*(8), pp.749–70.

Dries, N., and Pepermans, R. 2008. "Real" high-potential careers: an empirical study into the perspectives of organisations and high potentials. *Personnel Review*, *37*(1), pp.85–108.

Dries, N., Van Acker, F., and Verbruggen, M. 2012. How "boundaryless" are the careers of high potentials, key experts and average performers? *Journal of Vocational Behavior*, *81*(2), pp.271–79.

Dubouloy, M. 2004. The transitional space and self-recovery: a psychoanalytical approach to high-potential managers' training. *Human Relations*, *57*(4), pp.467–96.

Gallardo-Gallardo, E., Nijs, S., Dries, N., and Gallo, P. 2015. Towards an understanding of talent management as a phenomenon-driven field using bibliometric and content analysis. *Human Resource Management Review*, *25*(3), pp.264–79.

Gelens, J., Dries, N., Hofmans, J., and Pepermans, R. 2013. The role of perceived organizational justice in shaping the outcomes of talent management: a research agenda. *Human Resource Management Review*, *23*(4), pp.341–53.

Gelens, J., Dries, N., Hofmans, J., and Pepermans, R. 2015. Affective commitment of employees designated as talent: signalling perceived organisational support. *European Journal of International Management*, *9*(1), pp.9–27.

Gelens, J., Hofmans, J., Dries, N., and Pepermans, R. 2014. Talent management and organisational justice: employee reactions to high potential identification. *Human Resource Management Journal*, *24*(2), pp.159–75.

Graen, G. B., and Uhl-Bien, M. 1995. Relationship-based approach to leadership: development of leader-member exchange (LMX) theory of leadership over 25 years: applying a multi-level multi-domain perspective. *The Leadership Quarterly*, *6*(2), pp.219–47.

Khoreva, V., Kostanek, E., and van Zalk, M. 2015. *Managing high-potential employees in MNCs: the mediating role of socialization mechanisms.* Paper presented at the Academy of Management Annual Meeting 2015, Vancouver, Canada.

Khoreva, V., and Vaiman, V. 2015. Intent vs. Action: talented employees and leadership development. *Personnel Review*, *44*(2), pp.200–16.

King, K. 2016. The talent deal and journey: understanding how employees respond to talent identification over time. *Employee Relations*, *38*(1), pp.94–111.

Lepak, D. P., and Snell, S. A. 1999. The human resource architecture: toward a theory of human capital allocation and development. *The Academy of Management Review*, *24*(1), pp.31–48.

Malik, A. R., and Singh, P. 2014. "High potential" programs: let's hear it for "B" players. *Human Resource Management Review*, *24*(4), pp.330–46.

Marescaux, E., De Winne, S., and Sels, L. 2013. HR practices and affective organisational commitment: (when) does HR differentiation pay off? *Human Resource Management Journal*, 23(4), pp.329–45.

Merton, R. K. 1948. The self-fulfilling prophecy. *The Antioch Review*, 8(2), pp.193–210.

Morrison, E. W., and Robinson, S. L. 1997. When employees feel betrayed: a model of how psychological contract violation develops. *Academy of Management Review*, 22(1), pp.226–56.

Myers, D. 1980. *The inflated self*. New York: Seabury.

Rosenthal, R., and Jacobson, L. 1968. Pygmalion in the classroom. *The Urban Review*, 3(1), pp.16–20.

Rousseau, D. M. 1989. Psychological and implied contracts in organizations. *Employee Responsibilities and Rights Journal*, 2(2), pp.121–39.

Silzer, R., and Church, A. H. 2009. The pearls and perils of identifying potential. *Industrial and Organizational Psychology: Perspectives on Science and Practice*, 2(4), pp.377–412.

Silzer, R., and Church, A. H. 2010. Identifying and assessing high-potential talent: current organizational practices. In R. Silzer and B. E. Dowell, eds., *Strategy-driven talent management: a leadership imperative*, pp.213–79. San Francisco: Jossey-Bass.

Smale, A., Ehrnrooth, M., Björkman, I., Mäkelä, K. et al. 2015. *Letting the chosen ones know: the psychological effects of talent status self-awareness*. Paper presented at the Academy of Management Annual Meeting 2015, Vancouver, Canada.

Sonnenberg, M., van Zijderveld, V., and Brinks, M. 2014. The role of talent-perception incongruence in effective talent management. *Journal of World Business*, 49(2), pp.272–80.

Spence, M. 1973. Job market signaling. *The Quarterly Journal of Economics*, 87(3), pp.355–74.

Swailes, S., and Blackburn, M. 2016. Employee reactions to talent pool membership. *Employee Relations: The International Journal*, 38(1), pp.112–28.

Tansley, C., and Tietze, S. 2013. Rites of passage through talent management progression stages: an identity work perspective. *The International Journal of Human Resource Management*, 24(9), pp.1799–815.

Thunnissen, M. 2015. *Talent management in academia: an exploratory study in Dutch universities using a multi-dimensional approach*. Utrecht, the Netherlands: University of Utrecht.

Winnicott, D. W. 1965. Ego distortion in terms of true and false self. In D. W. Winnicott, *The maturational processes and the facilitating environment*, pp.140–52. London: Hogarth.

Wright, P. M., and Nishii, L. H. 2013. Strategic HRM and organizational behaviour: integrating multiple levels of analysis. In J. Paauwe, D. E. Guest, and P. M. Wright, eds., *HRM and performance: achievements and challenges*. pp. 97–110. Chichester: Wiley.

CHAPTER 10

....

VIRTUAL TEAMS

*Utilizing Talent-Management Thinking to Assess
What We Currently Know about Making
Virtual Teams Successful*

....

M. TRAVIS MAYNARD, MATTI VARTIAINEN, AND DIANA SANCHEZ

10.1 INTRODUCTION

THE environment in which today's organizations are functioning is quite different from those faced by organizations previously (e.g., Bigley and Roberts, 2001). Given the complexities and challenges currently faced by organizations, they are continually seeking out ways in which to improve their performance. One area that research has examined in hopes of linking it to enhanced organizational performance is talent management. In fact, there is a substantial body of literature to suggest that talent management is an important aspect of organizational success as it enhances a company's ability to maintain a competitive advantage (Ashton and Morton, 2005; Collings and Mellahi, 2009; Tarique and Schuler, 2010). In the 1990s, the term *war for talent* became emblematic of a time when people were seen as a primary resource worth attracting and retaining (e.g., Michael, Handfield-Jones, and Axelrod, 2001; Tulgan, 2001). That said, the value of talent management is believed to have increased in the twenty-first century owing to the changing nature of work (e.g., Cappelli, 2008b; Dries, 2013).

During this period, the task of acquiring skilled employees to fill roles within an organization has become more difficult for companies who discovered that individual talent was not easily duplicated (e.g., Iles, 1997) or globally accessed (e.g., Stahl et al., 2012). Likewise, the relationship between employers and employees has altered as the power has shifted from the employer to the employee (e.g., Rousseau, 2001). In response, organizations have had to consider the tradeoff between two opposing risks with regard to human capital: *capacity risk* (i.e., the undersupply of skilled workers, which causes roles within an organization to go unfilled) and *productivity risk* (i.e., an oversupply of workers who become less knowledgeable and skilled as they age in an ever changing workplace) (e.g., Calo, 2008; Currie, Tempest and Starkey, 2006).

This major concern regarding a possible mismatch in supply and demand of employees demonstrates the clear importance of talent management for organizational success (Cappelli, 2008a; Collings and Mellahi, 2009). Although there is consensus among researchers on the importance of talent management, there is less agreement on the definition and framework of *talent management* (e.g., Huang and Tansley, 2012). This lack of consensus has had a negative impact on the progress of research regarding talent management (Collings and Mellahi, 2009; Dries, 2013). Likewise, given that largely, organizations are relying on team-based structures (e.g., Salas, Cooke, and Rosen, 2008), it is noteworthy that the talent-management and team-effectiveness literatures have seemed to develop in isolation from one another, with little cross-fertilization of ideas.

This disconnect is interesting given that, as evidenced by numerous literature reviews regarding the use of teams within organizations (e.g., Mathieu, Maynard, Rapp, and Gilson, 2008), this literature is also seeking ways in which to enhance team performance so that in turn, organizational performance can be improved. For instance, research within the team-effectiveness literature has considered topics such as team composition, leadership, communication, conflict, shared cognition, and trust (e.g., Cohen and Bailey, 1997; Gully, Incalcaterra, Joshi, and Beaubien, 2002), among others. Likewise, given technology improvements that have occurred over the past couple of decades, the teams used within organizations presently are quite different from the traditional teams that were previously used within organizations (e.g., Wageman, Gardner, and Mortensen, 2012). This trend has led to an increased prevalence of research attention devoted to the topic of virtual teams (e.g., Bell and Kozlowski, 2002; Kirkman et al., 2002). In fact, over the past couple of decades, there have been numerous reviews of the virtual team (VT) literature (e.g., Gilson et al., 2015; Martins, Gilson, and Maynard, 2004). However, while each of these reviews provides unique contributions in terms of encapsulating the research that has been conducted on VTs to date and identifying opportunities for future research, it is interesting to note that none of these reviews has specifically connected the VT literature to the talent-management literature. As such, we strive to address this gap within the chapter.

10.2 TALENT-MANAGEMENT FRAMEWORK

In a broad sense, talent management is understood as anticipating and planning an organization's human capital needs (Cappelli, 2008b). This includes making sure the right people with the right sets of skills are in the right positions at the time they are needed (e.g., Ashton and Morton, 2005; Tarique and Schuler, 2010). However, there is much confusion around several more specific aspects of talent management, such as how to conceptualize "talent" (Dries, 2013) and who to focus on (e.g., all employees, managers, "pivotal" positions) (Collings and Mellahi, 2009).

Within the chapter, we leverage the definition of *talent management* introduced by Collins and Mellahi as:

> activities and processes that involve the systematic identification of key positions which differentially contribute to the organization's sustainable competitive advantage, the development of a talent pool of high potential and high performing incumbents to fill these roles, and the development of a differentiated human resource architecture to facilitate filling these positions with competent incumbents and to ensure their continued commitment to the organization. (2009: 305)

This definition includes three parts: identify pivotal roles, develop individuals in the talent pool, and align human resource systems with the organization's strategic objectives. These parts serve as the framework used to guide our discussion of talent management within the context of VTs (see Table 10.1). The framework is similar to others that have been used by researchers in talent-management and global talent-management studies (e.g., Dries, 2013; Roberts, Kossek, and Ozeki, 1998; Tarique and Schuler, 2010).

10.2.1 Step 1—Identify Pivotal Roles

There is a growing agreement that focusing talent-management efforts on the entire workforce may be a waste of resources because such efforts may result in an over-investment in nonessential positions. In response, some suggest that organizations should focus on a subgroup of the organization (Collings and Mellahi, 2009). While there has been some debate regarding what group should be the focus of talent management (e.g., Dickson, Hartog, and Mitchelson, 2003; Jackson, Schuler, and Rivero, 1989; Scullion and Collings, 2006), more recently there has been growing agreement suggesting that the focus should be on *pivotal* roles within an organization. In fact, recent research supports this shift toward pivotal roles, making a clearer distinction between human resource practices that service all employees and talent-management practices that service those who occupy and have high potential for key roles in organizations (Collings and Mellahi, 2009).

Accordingly, the first step in the talent-management framework includes identifying key positions or pivotal roles within the organization (Boudreau and Ramstad, 2005, 2007; Huselid, Beatty, and Becker, 2005). These pivotal roles are defined as positions in an organization that "differentially contribute to the organization's sustainable competitive advantage" (Collings and Mellahi, 2009: 304). Rather than placing emphasis on the individual employees, this step involves emphasizing the opportunity in the role with an emphasis on jobs that have an above-average impact on the organization rather than a marginal impact (Boudreau and Ramstad, 2007; Collings and Mellahi, 2009). For instance, many talent-management researchers have emphasized the critical role that leaders play and thus have focused on how best to manage these pivotal positions.

Table 10.1 Virtual Team Talent–Management Framework

	Virtual Team Talent-Management Framework	
Identify Pivotal Roles	Develop a Talent Pool	Align Human Resource with the Organization
What We Know • **VT Leadership** a) Transformation/Transactional b) Leader Emergence c) Physical Location *What We Don't Know* • **Strategic Core Members in VT** a) Effect of Location • **Subgroups** a) Effect on Leader Emergence • **Type of Technology Used** a) Effect on Leader Emergence b) Effect on Strategic Core	**Step 1: Attract** *What We Know* • Team Composition a) Demographics Personality, Culture *What We Don't Know* • Team Collective Orientation • Political Skill • Team Member Adaptability • Generational Makeup of Members **Step 2: Develop** *What We Know* • Team Training *What We Don't Know* • Value of Team Training • Timing of Training • Format of Training **Step 3 : Retain** *What We Know* • Motivation & Commitment *What We Don't Know* • Rewards a) Impact of Cultures • OCB a) Effect of Subgroups and Virtuality	*What We Know* • **Culture** a) Effect of cultural on technologies used *What We Don't Know* • **Context** • **Bracketing** a) Organizational level constructs b) Individual–level constructs

10.2.2 Pivotal Roles—VT Research

10.2.2.1 *What We Know*

Overlaying the concept of pivotal roles from the talent-management literature to the VT literature is interesting given that, thus far, the VT leadership position is the primary pivotal role that has been examined. That said, this is one of the more well-developed constructs within the VT literature, and, therefore, leadership within VTs has been examined from varying perspectives. For example, research has considered the different effects that various leadership styles and behaviors have on team dynamics and ultimately performance. Specifically, researchers have given significant attention to the effects of transformation and transactional leadership within VTs (e.g., Huang, Kahai, and Jestice, 2010). Overall, such work would suggest that transformational leadership is more beneficial within teams that are virtual (e.g., Purvanova and Bono, 2009). Additionally, researchers have provided evidence that VT members were more satisfied with transformational rather than transactional leaders. In fact, leaders who were more focused on relationships rather than task-based factors were perceived as more intelligent, creative, and original. In contrast, transactional leaders were described as authoritative, having higher levels of self-esteem, and being more task-focused (e.g., Ruggieri, 2009; Strang, 2011).

Additionally, research has examined factors that can contribute to individuals emerging as leaders within VTs (e.g., Gluckler and Shrott, 2007). For instance, Sutanto, Tan, Battistini, and Phang (2011) use social network analysis to document that patterns of interactions predict whether an individual was perceived as a leader by others in the group. Specifically, highly effective emergent leaders were those individuals who performed more mediating activities and fewer directing activities, and avoided monitoring activities. Having leaders that emerge within a VT appears particularly salient, as Carte, Chidambaram, and Becker (2006) found that higher performing VTs have members who display significantly more leadership-focused behaviors and shared leadership than those in lower-performing teams did.

Beyond what the VT leader actually does and how they lead, interestingly, the location of leaders within VTs also seems relevant, as it appears beneficial to have a leader who is not co-located with the team members. Specifically, Henderson (2008) examined project managers and found that team members were more satisfied with their team and their leader if the leader was geographically distant from the team. Furthermore, team members perceived their leader as being better able to decode messages when the team and leader were geographically dispersed (Henderson, 2008).

10.2.2.2 *What We Don't Know*

As demonstrated by the previous section, the topic of leadership within VTs is quite popular. However, the talent-management literature has seen debate about who the pivotal employees are (e.g., Dickson, Hartog, and Mitchelson, 2003; Jackson, Schuler, and Rivero, 1989; Scullion and Collings, 2006). Accordingly, it is an unanswered question whether VT members beyond the leader may also play a pivotal role in shaping VT dynamics and performance. Relatedly, this raises the question of whether VT members are able to lead themselves (i.e., should a self-leadership strategy be utilized within VTs? See, e.g., Panagopoulous and Ogilvie, 2015). Within the broader organizational team literature, this conversation has already commenced, with Humphrey, Morgeson, and Mannor (2009) articulating that certain members within an organizational team may play a larger role (i.e., the team's strategic core). Accordingly, it will be interesting for future VT research to apply this line of thinking and dig a bit deeper regarding which members of a VT are part of the strategic core.

Likewise, as articulated above, it appears that geographic location may be important in determining whether a VT member is pivotal or not. For instance, there has been growing interest within the VT literature regarding the presence of subgroups (e.g., Polzer, Crisp, Jarvenpaa, and Kim, 2006). In fact, O'Leary and Mortensen (2010) found that geographic subgroups within VTs can prove detrimental to the level of identification within the team, result in less effective shared cognition, cause more conflict within the team, and impair coordination. However, there has not been an extensive amount of work on the presence of subgroups within VTs and certainly more can be learned regarding the impact of subgroups, not just on the overall performance of the team, but also on the individual members of the VTs. Specifically, we think that it could be promising for future empirical examinations of VTs to explore whether VT members who are part of a subgroup within a VT are more or less likely to emerge as a leader, to be a part of the team's strategic core, or to play another pivotal role within the VT.

Similarly, within the VT research stream, there has been a wealth of attention paid to the types of technology utilized. As such, future research could examine whether the type of technology utilized by VT members influences whether that individual becomes a leader within that team or otherwise becomes a central player within the VT. Based on the research conducted to date, there is limited evidence to suggest that using certain technology or adapting the technology that is used within the VT may be beneficial. Specifically, within their research, Suh, Shin, Ahuja, and Kim (2011) evidenced that personalized computer-mediated communication (CMC) (i.e., e-mail and instant messaging) helped expand VT network size, whereas communal CMC (i.e., audioconferences and videoconferences) improved intragroup-tie strength.

10.2.3 Step 2—Develop a Talent Pool

This second step includes creating a pool of high-potential, high-performing individuals to fill these pivotal roles (Collings and Mellahi, 2009), moving away from vacancy-driven action toward proactive recruitment of individuals. These preemptive actions involve three specific activities that are frequently seen in the talent-management research: namely, developing a talent pool includes attracting, developing, and retaining skilled employees (e.g., Collings and Mellahi, 2009; Dries, 2013; Tarique and Schuler, 2010). In the sections below, we will first describe each of these categories and then describe how the VT literature to date could be described using this framework, and how future VT research can also further develop work within each of these categories.

10.2.4 Attract: Recruitment and Selection of Applicants

Multiple components go into recruiting and selecting employees from a pool of applicants. Part of the process includes developing a positive organizational reputation that attracts applicants in the first place (e.g., Bhattacharya, Sen, and Korschun, 2008). However, it is not enough just to attract applicants; these need to be individuals who would be a good fit for the identified pivotal positions (Chapman et al., 2005). Then, the focus becomes selecting the individuals that fit within the organization (Seigel, 2008; Tarique and Schuler, 2010). As such, the goal is to select individuals that are talented but also capable with regard to the organization's strategic objectives (Collings and Mellahi, 2009).

10.2.5 Recruitment and Selection—VT Research

10.2.5.1 *What We Know*

As suggested above, to evaluate applicants, organizations need to learn about the individual characteristics of those within the applicant pool. The corollary within the VT literature is work, which has addressed VT composition. In fact, as was the case with the topic of leadership, there has been substantial research attention paid to the compositional makeup of VTs and how it affects performance. Research has examined the impact of VT compositional factors such as sex, race, age, status, and nationality (e.g., Mockaitis, Rose, and Zettinig, 2012; Sutanto, Tan, Battistini, and Phang, 2011). Likewise, researchers have explored technical expertise (e.g., Luse, McElroy, Townsend, and DeMarie, 2013; Martins and Shalley, 2011), competencies (e.g., Krumm, Kanthak, Hartmann, and Hertel, 2016), past performance (Algesheimer, Dholakia, and Gurău, 2011), ego strength, and attitudes (Leonard and Haines, 2007).

Additionally, as is the case within traditional organizational team research, individual member personality has been the focus of several VT research projects (e.g., Turel and Zhang, 2010). Luse and colleagues (2013) found that personality and, in particular, openness to experience, resulted in greater individual preference for VTs as compared with face-to-face (FtF) teams. However, when the comparison was working in a VT versus working alone, extroverts tended to trust VT environments more highly than introverts did. Likewise, given that many VTs are composed of members located across the globe, researchers have also considered the impact of cultural influences. For instance, Mockaitis and colleagues (2012) found that VT members who have a more collectivistic rather than individualistic orientation are more likely to have more favorable impressions of team processes, trust, task interdependence, information sharing, and task conflict. Similarly, Paul, Samarah, Seetharaman, and Mykytyn (2004) examined VT members' individual-versus-collectivist orientations.

Likewise, as alluded to above, organizations need to assess not only candidates' individual characteristics but also how that individual will fit within the organization. Along similar lines, within the VT literature, work has examined the cultural diversity of VT members, with Au and Marks (2012) finding that perceived differences between VT members in regard to national culture impaired the level of identification within the team.

10.2.5.2 *What We Don't Know*

While the topic of team composition has been a popular topic within the VT literature, unanswered questions remain regarding the roles of certain individual characteristics and how they may work within a VT to affect team dynamics and performance. Specifically, while the broader organizational team literature has started to appreciate the role that team membership's collective orientation plays in team performance (e.g., Driskell, Salas, and Hughes, 2010), only a few studies have examined collective orientation, or individuals' preference for group work, within the context of VTs (e.g., Stark and Bierly, 2009). Accordingly, future research in this area could seek to better understand the effect that such an orientation has within VTs. Linking to the idea that not all individuals within a team are equal, research could examine whether everyone within a VT needs a high level of collective orientation or whether only certain pivotal persons need to possess this orientation.

In addition to collective orientation, some additional compositional factors deserve more attention within the VT literature. Specifically, over the past decade, there has been increasing attention to the impact of political skill in organizations (e.g. Ferris et al., 2007) and within teams (e.g., Ahearn et al., 2004). That said, the level of political skill possessed by VT members has not received adequate consideration. This gap in the literature is noteworthy given that research suggests that conflict may be more likely within VTs (e.g., Furumo, 2009). Accordingly, it stands to reason that teams with higher levels of political skill should be able to overcome this tendency.

Likewise, given that Luse and colleagues (2013) found value in having VT members with higher levels of openness to experience, it is also likely that having members who possess adaptability should be beneficial. However, as noted by Gilson and colleagues (2015), the topic of adaptation and adaptability has not as of yet received significant research attention within the context of VTs. This fact is unfortunate, given that VTs may experience an increasing number of disruptions that give rise to the need for the team to adapt. In fact, VTs may encounter increasing team-member churn (e.g., Wageman, Gardner, and Mortensen, 2012) and cross-cultural membership (e.g., Zhang, Lowry, Zhou, and Fu, 2007), and a greater need to adapt their technology (e.g., Qureshi and Vogel, 2001). Accordingly, we would encourage future research on VTs to include the expanding body of literature on team adaptation (e.g., Baard, Rench, and Kozlowski, 2014; Maynard, Kennedy, and Sommer, 2015). Specifically, by using the framework introduced by Maynard and colleagues (2015), research could examine how adaptability shapes processes and performance within VTs.

Fortunately, research has begun to consider more complex compositional variables within VTs, such as multiple team membership and the amount of time members allocate to a focal team (e.g., Cummings and Haas, 2011; Maynard, Mathieu, Rapp, and Gilson, 2012). Building upon this trend, we feel that there is also potential to consider factors such as the generational makeup of VT members. Again, as noted by Gilson and colleagues (2015), there is much potential here, given that there is evidence to suggest that millennials may be more comfortable with technology and working in VTs may align with millennials' preferred work-life balance expectations (e.g., Carless and Wintle, 2007). As a result, it will be interesting for future examinations of VTs to include consideration of the generational makeup of the teams being studied. Likewise, researchers may want to examine the role and functionality of online labor platforms in recruiting talent into VTs.

10.2.5.3 *Development: Develop and Train Key Individuals*

Research on talent management has a long history of considering the activities necessary to enhance the development of key individuals (e.g., Dickson, Hartog, and Mitchelson, 2003). Major considerations in this area include identifying the individuals who will benefit most from developmental opportunities (Caligiuri, 2006), given that research suggests not all individuals benefit equally from the same types of development (Tarique and Schuler, 2010). Developing individuals is a core part of talent management because it cultivates the current knowledge and skills possessed by organizational members (Roberts, Kossek, and Ozeki, 1998; Tarique and Schuler, 2010). In particular, research recommends focusing developmental efforts on the broad context of the organization rather than focusing on a specific plan for an individual.

Likewise, research focused on this part of talent management has shown that organizations that make leadership development part of their culture and involve leaders in the process are those who excel most at talent-management activities (Novicevic and Harvey, 2004; Seigel, 2008; Tarique and Schuler, 2010). In part, this strategy is successful as it better aligns with the current dynamic workforce (e.g., Collings and Mellahi, 2009). However, while there is evidence documenting the positive ramifications of training and development initiatives within organizations, studies have shown that the most recently trained employees are those most likely to consider leaving an organization (e.g., Cappelli, 2008b). As a result, understanding the potential turnover and mobility of newly trained employees leads to the third hallmark activity of this step of talent management—retention, which will be discussed in the section below.

10.2.6 Development—VT Research

10.2.6.1 *What We Know*

While Martins and colleagues (2004) noted that at the time of their writing there were few studies that considered training with VTs, more recently Gilson and colleagues (2015) highlighted that there has been progress in this area over the past decade.

Research has started to explore the effects of training VT members on a variety of topics. One of the first studies focused on training in VTs was conducted by Warkentin and Beranek (1999), who provided support that VT communication training can result in higher levels of trust, commitment, and perceived frank expression between team members. Bierly, Stark, and Kessler (2009) suggested that the perceived level of training provided to VT members would be positively related to levels of trust and that this relationship would be dampened as team virtuality increased, but these hypothesized relationships were not supported. More recently, given that VT members often work across cultural boundaries, Holtbrugge, Schillo, Rogers, and Friedmann (2011) studied individuals working virtually in India and the value of providing intercultural behavioral training to such individuals.

10.2.6.2 *What We Don't Know*

First, there is a need to understand the real value of providing training to VT members. As such, it would be valuable to understand more fully the competencies and skills needed in VTs because this should likely serve as a starting point for developing the content of any required training. Likewise, understanding the return on investment that can accrue from such training offerings is salient from both a theoretical and a practical standpoint as it may demonstrate to organizations the need to offer such programs more fully. Documenting this relationship between VT training and resulting performance is especially important if the statistic presented by Rosen and colleagues (2006) that 60% of organizations do not provide any training to VT members still holds true. Likewise, as within the training and development literature, there is a need to understand precisely when such training of VT members should occur. Specifically, it remains an empirical question as to whether such training can be a one-time endeavor at the start of an employee's employment within an organization or whether it should be more continuous (e.g., Kirkman et al., 2002).

Additionally, research could consider both the optimal format of VT training and whether the format should be altered depending on the specific topic area of the training. For instance, is the format choice the same for more technical-oriented training sessions as compared with more interpersonal-oriented training sessions such as teamwork? Rosen and colleagues (2006) provided a prototype for a VT training program that includes both FtF and technology-based training components. However, based on our review of the literature, there has not been any empirical examination of such recommendations to ensure that these are the most desirable formats to ensure enhanced learning and changes in behavior. Furthermore, given that these recommendations were made several years ago and there have been numerous advancements in the breadth of training formats being offered, there is a need to reconsider the VT training best practices introduced by Rosen and colleagues (2006).

10.2.6.3 *Retention: Retain Employees*

The main actions to retain employees involve reducing turnover and increasing employee engagement. Several researchers have discussed ways in which to increase employee retention (e.g., Lee et al., 2004). For example, research has demonstrated that retention can be enhanced by variables such as the extent to which employees are satisfied (e.g., Harter, Schmidt, and Hayes, 2002), receive adequate supervisor support (e.g., Eisenberger et al., 2002), and believe that there are limited job alternatives (e.g., Mitchell et al., 2001). Likewise, Collings and Mellahi (2009) proposed that talent management can shape organizational performance through its impact on employee motivation (e.g., Meyer, Becker, and Vandenberghe, 2004), organizational commitment (e.g., D'Amato and Herzfeldt, 2008), and organizational citizenship behaviors (e.g., Koys, 2001). Similarly, related work has considered how talent management can assist with the retention of employees within a global context (Lazarova and Caligiuri, 2001; Lazarova and Cerdin, 2007). In addition to noting the importance of employee satisfaction (e.g., Vidal, Valle, and Ma Isabel, 2008), and organizational commitment (e.g., Tarique and Schuler, 2010), research on the retention of employees within global contexts has also acknowledged the salience of perceptions of justice (Siers, 2007). Accordingly, organizations that do a better job managing and retaining their employees are able to enhance these important mediating mechanisms and ultimately enhance overall organizational performance.

10.2.7 Retention—VT Research

10.2.7.1 *What We Know*

Interestingly, while the broader organizational team literature has examined the role of various team-based reward systems (e.g., Johnson et al., 2006; Kirkman and Shapiro, 2000), this topic has not been nearly as prevalent within the VT literature. In fact, even though Kirkman and colleagues (2002) acknowledged that the organization that they studied struggled with determining the appropriate mix of rewards for their VTs, based on our review of the literature, we have only noticed a single article addressing the topic of rewards within VTs, namely, Hertel, Konradt, and Orlikowski (2004), which demonstrated in its examination of thirty-one VTs that team-based rewards were positively related to team effectiveness.

While the topic of rewards has not received significant attention to date, researchers have given at least some consideration to other topics that are discussed within the retention category of talent management. In particular, topics such as motivation and commitment have been examined within the context of VTs. For instance, Johri (2012) focused on impressions within VTs and the role that they had in shaping VT members' motivation. Likewise, Staples and Webster (2008) examined knowledge sharing in teams and linked it to team performance, which included a measure of VT members' intention to remain. Additionally, while it has not received substantial research attention, Hakonen and Lipponen (2008) provide intriguing evidence that the link between procedural justice and team identification is stronger within VTs that have fewer FtF meetings.

10.2.7.2 *What We Don't Know*

Obviously, given the dearth of research attention given to the topic of rewards within the VT literature, there is a great opportunity to address this gap in the literature with future research projects. In particular, given that there is quite a bit of documentation regarding teams and how best to structure their reward systems, it could be quite productive for future research to examine whether such relationships hold within VTs and whether the extent of virtuality moderates such direct relationships. Consideration of rewards within VTs also has cultural ramifications, and, therefore, such research should use the literature on rewards that is most applicable given cultural preferences. As such, research may need to examine rewards not just at the team level of analysis but also at the individual level, to understand the effects that a VT's reward system is having on individual members.

Similarly, other retention-focused topics, such as organizational citizenship behavior (OCB), have been documented as important within organizational teams (e.g., Foote and Li-Ping Tang, 2008) but have not yet been examined extensively within the context of VTs. Therefore, we suggest that future research in this area seeks to understand more about the effects of OCB within VTs, given that such behaviors can enhance retention from both the person exhibiting such behaviors and the recipients of such behaviors. More importantly, perhaps, research could explore the factors that impede such behaviors within VTs. For instance, as mentioned before, within VTs, it is often likely that subgroups may emerge based on a myriad of factors. Accordingly, future research could explore whether OCB is more evident within geographically proximal subgroups as compared with across geographically dispersed subgroups. Likewise, research could explore whether the extent of team virtuality affects the presence of such behaviors within the team.

Finally, while there is some work within the telecommuting literature exploring employee satisfaction (e.g., Golden, 2007), this topic has not been sufficiently examined within the VT literature. Instead, whereas much of the VT literature has focused on team-level phenomenon exclusively, there is work that has looked at team-level satisfaction within VTs (e.g., Zornoza, Orengo, and Penarroja, 2009). Accordingly, as emphasized in the section below, we see great opportunity in examining some of the cross-level relationships that exist within VTs. For example, do team-level phenomenon shape individual-level constructs such as employee job satisfaction and ultimately employee retention within the organization?

10.2.8 Step 3—Align Human Resources with the Organization

The purpose of this final stage is to align the human resource system with the organizational strategies to fill and service pivotal roles in an effort to support organizational performance (e.g., Collings and Mellahi, 2009). Considering that globalization has had a large impact on the strategies that organizations must use to be successful, we are reminded that talent management needs to account for the dynamic nature of work that exists today (Cappelli, 2008b). As a result, consensus is growing that a flexible approach to talent management is most beneficial (Tarique and Schuler, 2010).

In part, this idea of flexibility regarding an organization's talent management is based on the thinking that the goal should be to align or find *fit* between the organization's culture, policy, objectives, and practices and the organization's talent-management system (e.g., Dries, 2013). This *contingency approach* applies practices that best fit the needs of the context (Collings and Mellahi, 2009). For example, researchers have identified that at the global level, the definition of *talent management* changes based on the context (Scullion and Collings, 2006; Tarique and Schuler, 2010). Likewise, research has shown that applying different human resource practices to different contexts can lead to positive outcomes at the employee and organizational levels (e.g., Lepak et al., 2007; Tsui, Pearce, Porter, and Tripoli, 1997).

10.2.9 Alignment—VT Research

10.2.9.1 *What We Know*

In terms of alignment, there is some work within the VT literature that has sought to ascertain how best to align the dynamics within a VT to the culture from which its members are drawn. Much of this work is built upon the prominent cultural dimensions introduced by Hofstede (2001). Specifically, Duranti and de Almeida (2012) found that the preferred technologies differ depending on culture, with some cultures (e.g., Brazil) preferring richer forms of CMC, while other cultures (e.g., the United States) were more accepting of weaker CMC tools.

10.2.9.2 *What We Don't Know*

Given the diversity of cultures that are often included within the membership of VTs, understanding how the team should align with these cultural preferences is important. However, cultural dimensions are not the only consideration in terms of how best to align the practices of a given VT. In particular, the importance of considering the role of context in our examinations of behavior within organizations is increasingly discussed (e.g., Johns, 2006). Context is of particular salience to teams, given that many definitions of *organizational teams* include that they "are embedded in an organizational context that sets boundaries, constrains the team, and influences exchanges with other units in the broader entity" (Kozlowski and Bell, 2003: 334). Within VTs, context may be even more pertinent to consider as the context often changes and VT members may work in different contexts, which can bring along a hard-to-anticipate level of dynamism to considerations of context within VTs. Accordingly, the role of context is key in shaping how the team functions and ultimately the performance levels it attains.

There have been many suggestions within the broader organizational team literature advocating for a greater appreciation of context. In particular, Hackman provides a compelling argument that research should include "constructs that exist one level lower, but also one level higher, than those that are the main subject of study" (2003: 906). Accordingly, given that VT research is primarily focused on team-level phenomena, Hackman's (2003) bracketing idea would suggest that such research should also consider individual- and organizational-level constructs.

However, such a sentiment has not been adequately adopted within the VT literature to date. Instead, typically, research on VTs has exclusively focused on team-level constructs (e.g., Maynard, Mathieu, Rapp, and Gilson, 2012). While such work can certainly help us understand what is happening within such teams, it may only provide part of the picture. In fact, as Hackman (2003) outlines, without considering higher- and lower-level constructs, a researcher may miss what is actually going on at the focal level of analysis. Thus, there are numerous opportunities for future research involving VTs to consider both individual- and organizational-level constructs.

For instance, in terms of individual-level considerations, as articulated by Gilson and colleagues (2015), the topic of team-member well-being has not been adequately examined within the VT literature. Obviously, such research could focus exclusively on the individual level of analysis. However, we would advocate that by using the *alignment* idea from the talent-management literature, research could examine individual well-being by considering whether there is a proper fit between that team member and the VT they are a part of. Specifically, could the communication processes within the team (team-level construct) have an impact on individual-level well-being? Likewise, examining possible cross-level relationships between various team emergent states (i.e. trust, cohesion, and potency) and well-being could prove fruitful. Furthermore, while we are using the construct of well-being as an example, we also see the need for examinations of how team-level constructs impact constructs such as intention to remain, employee satisfaction, and other individual-level variables.

Similarly, the limited amount of VT research that has considered higher-level constructs in order to see how they may be associated with the dynamics and performance of VTs is shocking. Again, there are precedents from the broader organizational team effectiveness literature that can be used as a template. Specifically, team research has recently started to consider how team-level constructs can have an impact on organizational-level outcomes (e.g., Barrick, Bradley, Kristof-Brown, and Colbert, 2007). Likewise, organizational team research has examined the effect that higher-level constructs such as organizational-level global integration (e.g., Zelmer-Bruhn and Gibson, 2006), multiteam system coordination (e.g., Marks et al., 2005), and organizational climate (e.g., Kirkman and Rosen, 1999) may have on team-level constructs and relationships. For instance, Mathieu and colleagues (2007) considered how the organization's climate, as well as whether there was coordination across teams within an organization (higher-level constructs), affected team processes and performance in their study of service and repair teams.

Given the robust findings from the traditional, organizational team literature, which have demonstrated the value of considering cross-level relationships, it is interesting that this approach has yet to take hold within the VT literature. Accordingly, given this substantial gap within studies examining VTs, there remain numerous opportunities within this literature to apply the bracketing approach suggested by Hackman (2003) and more fully understand how higher-level constructs may shape VT phenomena and, likewise, how VT constructs may have cross-level ramifications on individual-level constructs of interest.

10.3 FUTURE RESEARCH OPPORTUNITIES

As highlighted throughout this chapter, several areas within the VT literature have been examined extensively from a talent-management perspective. In particular, as detailed in Table 10.1, research within the "identify pivotal roles" category has considered the pivotal role that leadership plays in shaping VT performance. Additionally, research has sought to understand better how to develop a VT talent pool by examining the effect of various team composition factors in shaping VT effectiveness, as well as the role of team commitment and motivation within VTs. Likewise, over the past decade, there has been an increased presence of work examining training initiatives within VTs. Finally, in keeping with the "Align Human Resources with the Organization" line of thinking within the talent-management literature, research has examined the effect of cultural backgrounds of VT members and, in particular, how such cultural backgrounds can shape the types of technologies used within VTs.

So, as noted by Gilson and colleagues (2015), the VT literature has progressed quite a bit over the past decade. However, this is not to say that we know all there is to know about VTs. In fact, by utilizing the talent-management framework within the chapter, we have identified several areas that could be fruitful for VT researchers to examine more fully. Specifically, in order to understand better the pivotal roles that may be present within VTs, we would encourage researchers to use the strategic core thinking introduced by Humphrey and colleagues (2009). By doing so, researchers could explore the roles that different types of technologies used within VTs have in the creation of strategic core members, as well as the role that geographic and other forms of subgroups play in the delineation of strategic and non-strategic core VT members.

Additionally, there are several opportunities for researchers interested in understanding the *talent pools* present within VTs. Again, as demonstrated within Table 10.1, these opportunities can be categorized within the attract, develop, and retain categories. For instance, VT research could benefit from a more in-depth examination of the factors that are the most salient sources of member competencies within VTs. Namely, researchers may find it valuable to examine the role that factors such as members' collective orientation, political skill, and adaptability play in shaping VT performance. Likewise, we echo the sentiments of Gilson and colleagues (2015), who suggested that more research is needed to understand the impact that generational differences have within VTs. Additionally, while researchers have examined the role of various training programs on the development of VT members over the past decade, there remain unanswered questions in this area. Specifically, gaining a clearer understanding of the "true" value of such training interventions is a practical consideration that remains underexplored. Additionally, we suggest it is salient to examine the effect of various team-training formats, as well as whether it matters when such trainings occur within the team.

Furthermore, there remain numerous research opportunities centered on the effects of various reward structures within VTs. For example, do rewards used within a VT need to be altered depending on the cultural makeup of the VT members and does offering such personalized rewards create unintended consequences? Likewise, given the importance that OCB can have within VTs, research is needed examining the impact that virtuality has on such behaviors and whether VT subgroups enhance or impair the demonstrations of such behaviors. Finally, we contend that VT research could benefit from a greater appreciation of the role of context, and we strongly advocate for a greater adoption of Hackman's (2003) bracketing approach of considering the impact that both organizational- and individual-level constructs have in shaping team-level constructs within VTs.

10.4 CONCLUSION

In this chapter, we have attempted to provide an assessment of the current state of the VT literature, as well as some recommendations on how this literature stream could be improved going forward. Granted, such efforts have also been made by other authors recently (e.g., Gilson et al., 2015). However, in this chapter, we have taken a different perspective to this effort by applying a talent-management lens to our assessment and recommendations. We feel that by utilizing the talent-management framework that we outline here, we were able to provide a different picture of the VT literature and, more specifically, a different appreciation of what we know about VTs and where more can be learned in future research endeavors. Our hope is that through the recommendations made within the current chapter, the VT literature can continue to develop and address key ways in which the performance of such teams can be enhanced, given the central role that VTs play in today's organizations.

REFERENCES

Ahearn, K. K., Ferris, G. R., Hochwarter, W. A., Douglas, C. et al. 2004. Leader political skill and team performance. *Journal of Management, 30*(3), pp.309–27.

Algesheimer, R., Dholakia, U. M., and Gurău, C. 2011. Virtual team performance in a highly competitive environment. *Group & Organization Management, 36*(2), pp.161–90.

Ashton, C., and Morton, L. 2005. Managing talent for competitive advantage: taking a systemic approach to talent management. *Strategic HR Review, 4*(5), pp.28–31.

Au, Y., and Marks, A. 2012. Virtual teams are literally and metaphorically invisible: forging identity in culturally diverse virtual teams. *Employee Relations, 34*, pp.271–87.

Baard, S. K., Rench, T. A., and Kozlowski, S. W. J. 2014. Performance adaptation: a theoretical integration and review. *Journal of Management*, *40*, pp.48–99.

Barrick, M. B., Bradley, B. H., Kristof-Brown, A. L., and Colbert, A. E. 2007. The moderating role of top management team interdependence: implications for real teams and working groups. *Academy of Management Journal*, *50*, pp.544–57.

Bell, B. S., and Kozlowski, S. W. 2002. A typology of virtual teams implications for effective leadership. *Group & Organization Management*, *27*(1), pp.14–49.

Bhattacharya, C. B., Sen, S., and Korschun, D. 2008. Using corporate social responsibility to win the war for talent. *MIT Sloan Management Review*, *49*(2), pp.37–44.

Bierly, P. E., Stark, E. M., and Kessler, E. H. 2009. The moderating effects of virtuality on the antecedents and outcome of NPD team trust. *Journal of Product Innovation Management*, *26*, pp.551–65.

Bigley, G. A., and Roberts, K. H. 2001. The incident command system: high-reliability organizing for complex and volatile task environments. *Academy of Management Journal*, *44*(6), pp.1281–99.

Boudreau, J. W., and Ramstad, P. M. 2005. Talentship, talent segmentation, and sustainability: a new HR decision science paradigm for a new strategy definition. *Human Resource Management*, *42*, pp.129–36.

Boudreau, J. W., and Ramstad, P. M. 2007. *Beyond HR: the new science of human capital*. Boston: Harvard Business School Press.

Caligiuri, P. 2006. Developing global leaders. *Human Resource Management Review*, *16*, pp.219–28.

Calo, T. J. 2008. Talent management in the era of the aging workforce: the critical role of knowledge transfer. *Public Personnel Management*, *37*(4), pp.403–16.

Cappelli, P. 2008a. *Talent on demand*. Boston: Harvard Business School Press.

Cappelli, P. 2008b. Talent management for the twenty-first century. *Harvard Business Review*, *86*(3), pp.74–81.

Carless, S. A., and Wintle, J. 2007. Applicant attraction: the role of recruiter function, work-life balance policies and career salience. *International Journal of Selection and Assessment*, *15*, pp.394–404.

Carte, T., Chidambaram, L., and Becker, A. 2006. Emergent leadership in self-management virtual teams. *Group Decision and Negotiation*, *15*, pp.323–43.

Chapman, D., Uggerslev, K., Carroll, S., Piasentin, K. et al. 2005. Applicant attraction to organizations and job choice: a meta-analytic review of the correlates of recruiting outcomes. *Journal of Applied Psychology*, *90*, pp.928–44.

Cohen, S. G., and Bailey, D. E. 1997. What makes teams work: group effectiveness research from the shop floor to the executive suite. *Journal of Management*, *23*, pp.239–90.

Collings, D. G., and Mellahi, K. 2009. Strategic talent management: a review and research agenda. *Human Resource Management Review*, *19*(4), pp.304–13.

Cummings, J. N., and Haas, M. R. 2012. So many teams, so little time: time allocation matters in geographically dispersed teams. *Journal of Organizational Behavior*, *33*, pp.316–41.

Currie, G., Tempest, S., and Starkey, K. 2006. New careers for old? Organizational and individual responses to changing boundaries. *International Journal of Human Resource Management*, *17*, pp.755–74.

D'Amato, A., and Herzfeldt, R. 2008. Learning orientation, organizational commitment and talent retention across generations: a study of European managers. *Journal of Managerial Psychology*, *23*(8), pp.929–53.

Dickson, M., Hartog, D., and Mitchelson, J. 2003. Research on leadership in a cross-cultural context: making progress, and raising new questions. *The Leadership Quarterly*, 14, pp.729–68.

Dries, N. 2013. The psychology of talent management: a review and research agenda. *Human Resource Management Review*, 23(4), pp.272–85.

Driskell, J. E., Salas, E., and Hughes, S. 2010. Collective orientation and team performance: development of an individual differences measure. *Human Factors: The Journal of the Human Factors and Ergonomics Society*, 52, pp.316–28.

Duranti, C. M., and de Almeida, F. C. 2012. Is more technology better for communication in international virtual teams? *International Journal of e-Collaboration*, 8, pp.36–52.

Eisenberger, R., Stinglhamber, F., Vandenberghe, C., Sucharski, I. L. et al. 2002. Perceived supervisor support: contributions to perceived organizational support and employee retention. *Journal of Applied Psychology*, 87(3), pp.565–73.

Ferris, G. R., Treadway, D. C., Perrewé, P. L., Brouer, R. L. et al. 2007. Political skill in organizations. *Journal of Management*, 33(3), pp.290–320.

Foote, D. A., and Li-Ping Tang, T. 2008. Job satisfaction and organizational citizenship behavior (OCB): does team commitment make a difference in self-directed teams? *Management Decision*, 46(6), pp.933–47.

Furumo, K. 2009. The impact of conflict and conflict management style on deadbeats and deserters in virtual teams. *Journal of Computer Information Systems*, 49, pp.66–73.

Gilson, L. L., Maynard, M. T., Jones Young, N. C., Vartiainen, M. et al. 2015. Virtual teams research: 10 years, 10 themes, and 10 opportunities. *Journal of Management*, 41(5), pp.1313–37.

Gluckler, J., and Schrott, G. 2007. Leadership and performance in virtual teams: exploring brokerage in electronic communication. *International Journal of e-Collaboration*, 3, pp.31–52.

Golden, T. 2007. Co-workers who telework and the impact on those in the office: understanding the implications of virtual work for co-worker satisfaction and turnover intentions. *Human Relations*, 60(11), pp.1641–67.

Gully, S. M., Incalcaterra, K. A., Joshi, A., and Beaubien, J. M. 2002. A meta-analysis of team-efficacy, potency, and performance: interdependence and level of analysis as moderators of observed relationships. *Journal of Applied Psychology*, 87(5), pp.819–32.

Hackman, J. R. 2003. Learning more by crossing levels: evidence from airplanes, hospitals, and orchestras. *Journal of Organizational Behavior*, 24(8), pp.905–22.

Hakonen, M., and Lipponen, J. 2008. Procedural justice and identification with virtual teams: the moderating role of face-to-face meetings and geographical dispersion. *Social Justice Research*, 21(2), pp.164–78.

Harter, J. K., Schmidt, F. L., and Hayes, T. L. 2002. Business-unit-level relationship between employee satisfaction, employee engagement, and business outcomes: a meta-analysis. *Journal of Applied Psychology*, 87(2), pp.268–79.

Henderson, L. S. 2008. The impact of project managers' communication competencies: validation and extension of a research model for virtuality, satisfaction, and productivity on project teams. *Project Management Journal*, 39, pp.48–59.

Hertel, G., Konradt, U., and Orlikowski, B. 2004. Managing distance by interdependence: goal setting, task interdependence, and team-based rewards in virtual teams. *European Journal of Work and Organizational Psychology*, 13(1), pp.1–28.

Hofstede, G. 2001. *Culture's consequences: comparing values, behaviors, institutions and organizations across nations*. Thousand Oaks, CA: Sage.

Holtbrugge, D., Schillo, K., Rogers, H., and Friedmann, C. 2011. Managing and training for virtual teams in India. *Team Performance Management*, 17, pp.206–23.

Huang, J., and Tansley, C. 2012. Sneaking through the minefield of talent management: the notion of rhetorical obfuscation. *International Journal of Human Resource Management*, 23(17), pp.3673–91.

Huang, R., Kahai, S., and Jestice, R. 2010. The contingent effects of leadership on team collaboration in virtual teams. *Computers in Human Behavior*, 26, pp.1098–110.

Humphrey, S. E., Morgeson, F. P., and Mannor, M. J. 2009. Developing a theory of the strategic core of teams: a role composition model of team performance. *Journal of Applied Psychology*, 94(1), pp.48–61.

Huselid, M. A., Beatty, R. W., and Becker, B. E. 2005. "A players" or "A positions"? The strategic logic of workforce management. *Harvard Business Review*, 83(12), pp.110–17.

Iles, P. 1997. Sustainable high potential career development: a resource-based view. *Career Development International*, 2(7), pp.347–53.

Jackson, S. E., Schuler, R. S., and Rivero, J. C. 1989. Organizational characteristics as predictors of personnel practices. *Personnel Psychology*, 42, pp.727–86.

Johns, G. 2006. The essential impact of context on organizational behavior. *Academy of Management Review*, 31(2), pp.386–408.

Johnson, M. D., Hollenbeck, J. R., Humphrey, S. E., Ilgen, D. R. et al. 2006. Cutthroat cooperation: asymmetrical adaptation to changes in team reward structures. *Academy of Management Journal*, 49(1), pp.103–19.

Johri, A. 2012. From a distance: impression formation and impression accuracy among geographically distributed coworkers. *Computers in Human Behavior*, 28(6), pp.1997–2006.

Kirkman, B. L., and Rosen, B. 1999. Beyond self-management: antecedents and consequences of team empowerment. *Academy of Management Journal*, 42, pp.58–74.

Kirkman, B. L., Rosen, B., Gibson, C. B., Tesluk, P. E. et al. 2002. Five challenges to virtual team success: Lessons from Sabre, Inc. *The Academy of Management Executive*, 16(3), pp.67–79.

Kirkman, B. L., and Shapiro, D. L. 2000. Understanding why team members won't share an examination of factors related to employee receptivity to team-based rewards. *Small Group Research*, 31(2), pp.175–209.

Koys, D. J. 2001. The effects of employee satisfaction, organizational citizenship behavior, and turnover on organizational effectiveness: a unit-level, longitudinal study. *Personnel Psychology*, 54(1), pp.101–14.

Kozlowski, S. W. J., and Bell, B. S. 2003. Work groups and teams in organizations. In W. C. Borman, D. R. Ilgen, and R. J. Klimoski, eds., *Handbook of psychology: industrial and organizational psychology*, Vol. 12, pp.333–75. London: Wiley.

Krumm, S., Kanthak, J., Hartmann, K., and Hertel, G. 2016. What does it take to be a virtual team player? The knowledge, skills, abilities, and other characteristics required in virtual teams. *Human Performance*, 29, pp.123–42.

Lazarova, M., and Caligiuri, P. 2001. Retaining repatriates: the role of organization support practices. *Journal of World Business*, 36, pp.389–401.

Lazarova, M., and Cerdin, J. 2007. Revising repatriation concerns: organizational support versus career and contextual influences. *Journal of International Business Studies*, 38, pp.404–29.

Lepak, D. P., Taylor, M. S., Teklead, A., Marrone, J. A. et al. 2007. An examination of the use of high-involvement human resource systems for core and support employees. *Human Resource Management*, 46, pp.223–46.

Lee, T. W., Mitchell, T. R., Sablynski, C. J., Burton, J. P. et al. 2004. The effects of job embeddedness on organizational citizenship, job performance, volitional absences, and voluntary turnover. *Academy of Management Journal, 47*(5), pp.711–22.

Leonard, L. N., and Haines, R. 2007. Computer-mediated group influence on ethical behavior. *Computers in Human Behavior, 23*(5), pp.2302–20.

Luse, A., McElroy, J. C., Townsend, A. M., and DeMarie, S. 2013. Personality and cognitive style as predictors of preference for working in virtual teams. *Computers in Human Behavior, 29*, pp.1825–32.

Marks, M. A., DeChurch, L. A., Mathieu, J. E., Panzer, F. J. et al. 2005. Teamwork in multiteam systems. *Journal of Applied Psychology, 90*(5), pp.964–71.

Martins, L. L., Gilson, L. L., and Maynard, M. T. 2004. Virtual teams: what do we know and where do we go from here? *Journal of Management, 30*(6), pp.805–35.

Martins, L. L., and Shalley, C. E. 2011. Creativity in virtual work: effects of demographic differences. *Small Group Research, 42*, pp.536–61.

Mathieu, J., Maynard, M. T., Rapp, T., and Gilson, L. 2008. Team effectiveness 1997–2007: a review of recent advancements and a glimpse into the future. *Journal of Management, 34*(3), pp.410–76.

Mathieu, J. E., Maynard, M. T., Taylor, S. R., Gilson, L. L., and Ruddy, T. M. 2007. An examination of the effects of organizational district and team contexts on team processes and performance: a meso-mediational model. *Journal of Organizational Behavior, 28*(7), pp.891–910.

Maynard, M. T., Kennedy, D. M., and Sommer, S. A. 2015. Team adaptability: a synthesis and framework for how this literature needs to "adapt" going forward. *European Journal of Work & Organizational Psychology, 24*, pp.652–77.

Maynard, M. T., Mathieu, J. E., Rapp, T. L., and Gilson, L. L. 2012. Something(s) old and something(s) new: modeling drivers of global virtual team effectiveness. *Journal of Organizational Behavior, 33*, pp.342–65.

Meyer, J. P., Becker, T. E., and Vandenberghe, T. 2004. Employee commitment and motivation: a conceptual analysis and integrative model. *Journal of Applied Psychology, 39*, pp.991–1007.

Michaels, E., Handfield-Jones, H., and Axelrod, B. 2001. *The war for talent.* Boston: Harvard Business School Press.

Mitchell, T. R., Holtom, B. C., Lee, T. W., Sablynski, C. J. et al. 2001. Why people stay: using job embeddedness to predict voluntary turnover. *Academy of Management Journal, 44*(6), pp.1102–21.

Mockaitis, A. I., Rose, E. L., and Zettinig, P. 2012. The power of individual cultural values in global virtual teams. *International Journal of Cross Cultural Management, 12*, pp.193–210.

Novicevic, M., and Harvey, M. 2004. The political role of corporate human resource management in strategic global leadership development. *The Leadership Quarterly, 15*, pp.569–88.

O'Leary, M. B., and Mortensen, M. 2010. Go (con) figure: subgroups, imbalance, and isolates in geographically dispersed teams. *Organization Science, 21*(1), pp.115–31.

Panagopoulous, N. G., and Ogilvie, J. 2015. Can salespeople lead themselves? Thought self-leadership strategies and their influence on sales performance. *Industrial Marketing Management, 47*, pp.190–203.

Paul, S., Samarah, I. M., Seetharaman, P., and Mykytyn, Jr, P. P. 2004. An empirical investigation of collaborative conflict management style in group support system-based global virtual teams. *Journal of Management Information Systems, 21*(3), pp.185–222.

Polzer, J. T., Crisp, C. B., Jarvenpaa, S. L., and Kim, J. W. 2006. Extending the faultline model to geographically dispersed teams: how collocated subgroups can impair group functioning. *Academy of Management Journal*, 49(4), pp.679–92.

Purvanova, R. K., and Bono, J. E. 2009. Transformational leadership in context: face-to-face and virtual teams. *The Leadership Quarterly*, 20, pp.343–57.

Qureshi, S., and Vogel, D. 2001. Adaptiveness in virtual teams: organizational challenges and research directions. *Group Decision and Negotiation*, 10, pp.27–46.

Roberts, K., Kossek, E., and Ozeki, C. 1998. Managing the global workforce: challenges and strategies. *Academy of Management Executive*, 12, pp.93–106.

Rosen, B., Furst, S., and Blackburn, R. 2006. Training for virtual teams: an investigation of current practices and future needs. *Human Resource Management*, 45(2), pp.229–47.

Rousseau, D. M. 2001. Schema, promise and mutuality: the building blocks of the psychological contract. *Journal of Occupational and Organizational Psychology*, 74, pp.511–41.

Ruggieri, S. 2009. Leadership in virtual teams: a comparison of transformational and transactional leaders. *Social Behavior and Personality*, 37, pp.1017–22.

Salas, E., Cooke, N. J., and Rosen, M. A. 2008. On teams, teamwork, and team performance: discoveries and developments. *Human Factors: The Journal of the Human Factors and Ergonomics Society*, 50(3), pp.540–47.

Scullion, H., and Collings, D. 2006. *Global staffing*. London: Routledge.

Seigel, J. 2008. *Global talent management at Novartis*. Harvard Business School, Case #9-708-486.

Siers, B. 2007. Relationships among organizational justice perceptions, adjustment, and turnover of United States-based expatriates. *Applied Psychology, An International Perspective*, 56, pp.437–59.

Stahl, G. K., Björkman, I., Farndale, E., Morris, S. S. et al. 2012. Six principles of effective global talent management. *MIT Sloan Management Review*, 53, pp.25–32.

Staples, D. S., and Webster, J. 2008. Exploring the effects of trust, task interdependence and virtualness on knowledge sharing in teams. *Information Systems Journal*, 18(6), pp.617–40.

Stark, E. M., and Bierly, P. E., III. 2009. An analysis of predictors of team satisfaction in product development teams with differing levels of virtualness. *R&D Management*, 39, pp.461–72.

Strang, K. D. 2011. Leadership substitutes and personality impact on time and quality in virtual new product development projects. *Project Management Journal*, 42, pp.73–90.

Suh, A., Shin, K. S., Ahuja, M., and Kim, M. S. 2011. The influence of virtuality on social networks within and across work groups: a multilevel approach. *Journal of Management Information Systems*, 28, pp.351–86.

Sutanto, J., Tan, C. H., Battistini, B., and Phang, C. W. 2011. Emergent leadership in virtual collaboration settings: a social network analysis approach. *Long Range Planning*, 44(5), pp.421–39.

Tarique, I., and Schuler, R. S. 2010. Global talent management: literature review, integrative framework, and suggestions for further research. *Journal of World Business*, 45(2), pp.122–33.

Tsui, A. S., Pearce, J. L., Porter, L. W., and Tripoli, A. M. 1997. Alternative approaches to the employee organization relationship: does investment in employees payoff? *Academy of Management Journal*, 40, pp.1089–121.

Tulgan, B. 2001. Winning the talent wars. *Employment Relations Today*, 23(1–2), pp.37–51.

Turel, O., and Zhang, Y. 2010. Does virtual team composition matter? Trait and problem-solving configuration effects on team performance. *Behaviour and Information Technology*, 29(4), pp.363–75.

Vidal, S., Valle, R. S., and Ma Isabel, B. 2008. International workers' satisfaction with the repatriation process. *International Journal of Human Resource Management*, 19, pp.1683–702.

Wageman, R., Gardner, H., and Mortensen, M. 2012. The changing ecology of teams: new directions for teams research. *Journal of Organizational Behavior*, 33(3), pp.301–15.

Warkentin, M., and Beranek, P. M. 1999. Training to improve virtual team communication. *Information Systems Journal*, 9(4), pp.271–89.

Zellmer-Bruhn, M., and Gibson, C. 2006. Multinational organization context: implications for team learning and performance. *Academy of Management Journal*, 49(3), pp.501–18.

Zhang, D. S., Lowry, P. B., Zhou, L. N., and Fu, X. L. 2007. The impact of individualism—collectivism, social presence, and group diversity on group decision making under majority influence. *Journal of Management Information Systems*, 23, pp.53–80.

Zornoza, A., Orengo, V., and Peñarroja, V. 2009. Relational capital in virtual teams: the role played by trust. *Social Science Information*, 48(2), pp.257–81.

CHAPTER 11

STARS THAT SHIMMER AND STARS THAT SHINE

How Information Overload Creates Significant Challenges for Star Employees

SHAD MORRIS AND JAMES OLDROYD

11.1 INTRODUCTION

A company's overall value proposition is due, in part, to a small group of elite employees known as stars (Aguinis and O'Boyle, 2014; Lepak and Snell, 2002; O'Boyle, 2017; Ready, Conger, and Hill, 2010). Not only are stars much higher performing than their peers, but they are also much more visible within the firm (Oldroyd and Morris, 2012). Because of their disproportionate value and visibility, stars are often sought out by others for advice and expertise (Burkhardt and Brass, 1990).

High visibility and frequent interaction make it likely that the stars will develop abundant social capital. This capital benefits stars by endowing them with access to more information, which, in turn, allows them to complete their work more effectively and further enhance their status as stars in the organization (Coleman, 1990; Kang, Morris, and Snell, 2007).

Yet, while an abundance of social capital can positively impact stars' performance, not all the effects of robust social capital are likely to be positive (Leenders and Gabbay, 2013). The purpose of this chapter is to demonstrate how social capital can produce an unintended outcome that is likely to plague star employees. More specifically, because of stars' unique social capital, they are likely to be placed in greater jeopardy of suffering from performance-crippling information overload (Edmunds and Morris, 2000; Eppler and Mengis, 2004; O'Reilly, 1980).

The chapter begins by reviewing the link between social capital and star employees. We emphasize that owing to the affiliatory nature of network formation, stars are likely to have exponentially higher levels of social capital than their peers who are less visible and average performing. We then discuss how this abundance of social capital may uniquely contribute to information overload for star employees. Noting that information overload calls into question prior assumptions of preferred structural position, we explore the implications of a curvilinear theory of social capital on the information performance of star employees. We specifically highlight the talent-management implications of this information overload for developing and managing stars. Finally, we conclude by outlining several avenues of potential future research linking stars, social capital, and information overload.

11.2 STAR EMPLOYEES AND SOCIAL CAPITAL

Strategic human resource management scholars have emphasized that firm-specific human capital is a key source of competitive advantage for organizations because it consists of intangible resources that are valuable and rare (Huselid, 1995; Lepak and Snell, 1999). Examples of firm-specific human capital include knowledge about how to accomplish complex tasks in a particular firm, trust among a team of employees, a sense of commitment to a firm's success, and so forth (Barney and Hansen, 1994; Conner and Prahalad, 1996).

Prior studies have demonstrated that firm-specific skills play an important role in the performance of employees (e.g., Baks, 2003; Peteraf, 1993), with high performers providing critical resources to the organization such as effective customer interaction (Batt, 2002), customer loyalty (Greenwood, Hinings, and Brown, 1990), and unique knowledge assets (Groysberg, Lee, and Nanda, 2008). As certain employees exhibit more productivity and value, they become much more visible in their labor markets than their peers, receiving a disproportionate amount of attention from managers, peers, competitors, and even the media (Morris, Alvarez, Barney, and Molloy, 2016).[1] It is at this point, when performance and visibility are high, that employees become stars (Groysberg, Lee, and Nanda, 2008).

As stars' reputations develop, the likelihood that they will be sought out by both organizational and external constituents increases. For instance, Burkhardt and Brass (1990) found that technical experts were likely to be sought out by others within the organization and over time become central in the firm's network of experts. Similarly, Lazear (1986) noted that stars were likely to be highly sought after by external agents, causing these agents to engage in bidding wars for star talent. In other words, others are more likely to be aware of stars and seek to leverage their human capital, resulting in abundant social capital for stars (Groysberg and Lee, 2008).

11.2.1 Benefits of Social Capital for Star Employees

Top performers are able to develop and maintain networks of colleagues who contribute to their advancement as stars (Ibarra, 1995; Burt, 1987). Moreover, star employees' robust connections are advantageous because they endow the star with organizational influence and information (Adler and Kwon, 2002; Sandefur and Laumann, 1998).

Because stars are likely to be central in organizational networks, they have access to a multitude of contacts, increasing the amount of information they receive (Lechner, Frankenberger, and Floyd, 2010). Furthermore, once information is obtained, abundant social capital enables stars to leverage their structural position, acting in arbitrage roles that facilitate the flow of new and valuable information across structural boundaries or holes in the network space (Burt, 1997).

While the benefits of social capital are abundant, much of the research has examined the direct social capital-to-performance link, ignoring what goes on in the "black box," linking structure to performance or the actual information flow within the networks (Sparrowe, Liden, Wayne, and Kraimer, 2001). In consequence, structural benefits are frequently assumed to provide information access, the ability to control the temporal pace of information flow, and the ability to tap robust connections when needing access to additional information or other resources (Burt, 1997). Moreover, much of the research linking social capital to performance assumes a linear relationship between information flow and stars, such that the more information a star (or any other actor) receives, the better his or her performance will be (e.g. Burt, 1992, 1997). On the other hand, the theory of information overload, based on the cognitive limits of individuals, suggests that the information benefits of social capital may be limited by the flow of information and the information processing capacity of the individual.

11.3 INFORMATION SIDE EFFECTS OF SOCIAL CAPITAL

Recent work in physics (Barabasi and Crandall, 2003), information technology (Ebel, Mielsch, and Bornholdt, 2002), and biology (Jeong et al., 2000), among other fields, indicates that the formation of networks often follows an "affiliatory" pattern, meaning that rather than random associations between actors, they form their associations by choice based on preferences to what they are searching for or hoping to gain (Newman, 2002). Numerous studies demonstrate that affiliatory networks are more representative of social and work life because people tend to gravitate toward a certain few who are seen as key in being able to obtain their objectives (e.g., Newman and Park, 2003). For instance, in social networks, because of their high visibility and performance, star employees are likely to be more sought after for advice, influence, and association, causing the majority of employees in the organization, and beyond, to seek them out.

Because stars are likely to be connected to many times more individuals than others are, the distribution of social capital in organizations is likely to follow a power-law or Pareto distribution of ties. This means that rather than having just a few more ties compared with average non-star employees, stars are likely to have exponentially more ties

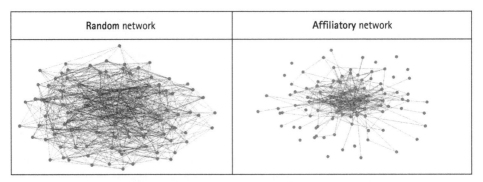

| Random network | Affiliatory network |

FIGURE 11.1 Simulated Star Connections

in the organization. As a result, a star's status is likely to be exponentially higher than a non-stars, but, more problematically, the information by-product of stardom is not a marginal increase but rather an exponential increase in information flow.

Understanding the difference between random and affiliatory networks is vital when investigating the cognitive burden of information flow to star employees. To illustrate this point, Oldroyd and Morris (2012) constructed a simulation with hundred-person networks, comparing the difference in network structures developed in a random versus affiliatory manner. In their simulation, whereas both networks consist of one hundred people and both have an equal average number of ties, the distribution of ties in the networks differs. As Figure 11.1 demonstrates, in the affiliatory networks, the majority of the relationships are formed with a few stars in the center of the network.

Oldroyd and Morris's simulation goes on to show that stars in affiliatory networks receive more than two-and-a-half times as many associations as those most central in random networks do, and stars are connected to nearly nine times as many ties as the average node in the network. Realizing that both incoming and outgoing information flows emerge from each tie implies that, in a conservative estimate, stars are likely to receive eighteen times the information load of other employees if information flows were constant among actors. In reality, because stars are likely to be sought out for advice, input, and affiliation, they are likely to receive the majority of the information flow in the organization and thus bear an even greater information load. Hence, Oldroyd and Morris (2012) found that stars have exponentially higher levels of social capital compared with their non-star peers, and these ties are likely to magnify their information load.

11.3.1 The Effects of Information Overload for the Star

Information processing theory enriches our understanding of the potential side effects of information overload on star employees. The theory of information overload asserts that individuals benefit from the recipient of information until they reach a point beyond which they are unable to process the incoming information (Tushman and Nadler, 1978;

O'Reily, 1980). Once information exceeds this point, additional information becomes a liability rather than a benefit to the recipient (Eppler and Mengis, 2004), and, in a state of overload, performance rapidly declines (Chewning and Harrell, 1990). If the amount of information a star receives exceeds the star's information-processing ability, then extra information may not only be rendered useless, but may actually become harmful and may denigrate his or her performance (Boone, Olffen, and Witteloostuijn, 2005; Carpenter and Fredrickson, 2001; Meier 1963; Rudolph and Repenning, 2002; Wadhwa and Kotha, 2006). This curvilinear relationship is compared with a linear relationship in Figure 11.2.

There are numerous examples of the detrimental effect of information overload. For instance, Meier's (1963) study of library workers found that overwhelmed individuals and organizations were required to halt information flow until they could catch up on processing tasks. Oskamp (1965) found that information improved decision-making ability up to a certain point, but past that point, more information did not improve decision outcomes. Herbert Simon wrote:

> In an information-rich world, the wealth of information means a dearth of something else: a scarcity of whatever it is that information consumes. What information consumes is rather obvious: it consumes the attention of its recipients. Hence, a wealth of information creates a poverty of attention and a need to allocate that attention efficiently among the overabundance of information sources that might consume it. (1957: 40–1)

In line with studies of network structure and load (e.g., Watts, Dodds, and Newman, 2002), even if the relative cognitive costs of processing information per message are very low for the star employee, and the star employee has expert information-processing capabilities, the cumulative exponential information burden imposed upon stars is likely to result in their overload.

Moreover, because others often seek advice, recognition, and friendship from stars, they are likely to experience frequent task interruptions hindering the star's ability to complete their own tasks. Grove, for example, describes the constant request

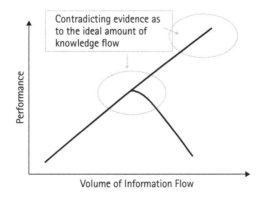

FIGURE 11.2 Contradicting Theories of Information Flow and Performance

for information and advice received by managers as "the plague of managerial work" (1983: 67). Similarly, Perlow (1999) showed that frequent coworker interruptions experienced by software engineers led to "a time famine," wherein engineers are plagued by the sense of having too many information requests to perform their jobs properly. Because stars have exponentially higher levels of social capital, these damning effects of interruptions are likely to be more frequent in their work (Oldroyd and Morris, 2012).

11.3.2 The Effects of Information Overload for the Organization

Because stars are the most valuable individuals in the organization, they are likely to have vital information. As a result, star employees are likely to receive many requests for advice and information, increasing the amount of information stars are required to process. And, while inflows (in-degree centrality) to stars may not be directly proportional to their outflow (out-degree centrality), they are likely to be highly correlated. As a result, the volume of sending information required by stars similarly adds exponentially to their information load.

Yet, as stars are likely to be overloaded with information, they are likely to become bottlenecks in the organization (Cross and Parker, 2004). In other words, by receiving too much information, not only does a star's individual performance deteriorate, but, because they are less able to share information with others, the organization's performance may also decline. This decline is not only in ignored requests for information. Further, as the number of information requests received increases, a star becomes more likely to turn to preexisting knowledge and associations, rather than use a careful "bottom-up" consideration of the details of what is being requested (Abelson, 1981). As stars attempt to grapple with over-abundant information, they are likely to attempt to simplify their information processing efforts. Fiske and Taylor (1991) found that employees use cognitive schemas to help process all this information so that it can be appropriately used and distributed. Schemas can be thought of as people's simplified theories about the way the world works. However, schemas can not only decrease one's ability to process information for their own use, but can also decrease one's ability to respond to information requests (Dutton and Jackson, 1987). As a result, scholars are careful to point out that the ability to process information when inflows are high may lead to information outflows that are poor in terms of quantity and quality (Lord and Maher, 1990).

11.4 Managing Stars' Social Capital

To this point, we have argued that stars are likely to be overloaded with information, and this state of overload likely has significant effects for both the individual star and the organization to which they belong. We now turn our attention to potential talent-management solutions that may help mitigate the problem of information over-load for stars.

While managing and developing the cognitive abilities to process and share increased information within the organization may be peripheral to the importance of manag-ing their human capital for competitive advantage, it is imperative for the human capi-tal's own future development, as well as that of the organization. As stated by Lorsch and Tierney (2002: 26), "employing stars is necessary but insufficient. They must also be aligned; that is, they must behave in ways that move the firm toward its goals" (see, also, Ployhardt and Cragun, 2017). Unfortunately, such behavior is usually an unnatural act. Because of this, organizations must consider not only the social capital of stars but also how to mitigate the potential negative effect of their information overload. This can pri-marily be achieved in one of two ways: by either decreasing the stars' information load or increasing their ability to process and share information.

11.4.1 Decreasing Stars' Information Load

The primary factor impacting information overload is the volume of information (including requests) an individual receives. For example, one way for the organization to reduce the volume of information is to focus on information-filtering mechanisms and information technologies (Bawden, 2001; Edmunds and Morris, 2000). Stars can increase their ability to reach more of the people in the network with valuable informa-tion if they have systems in place to help them sort out knowledge more efficiently and effectively. Grant (1996) argued that processing information for application requires organizational processes and information systems that enable an individual to use the information coming to them. Such information systems allow information from others to be codified and made simpler to understand, and captured in a storage system that allows for longevity of the information.

One example is seen in organizations where valuable information is captured in short "lessons learned" or templates that allow users to apply information coming to them from others in a more comprehensive and understandable format (Morris and Oldroyd, 2009). They are also able to apply this information more quickly, allowing them to deal with larger amounts of information flow. In addition, information systems can work to eliminate fluctuations in the flow of information. Oldroyd and Gulati (2009) found that individuals who experience more variation in the flow of information they receive are likely to have poorer performance. Thus, the standardization of information of both content and volume may reduce stars' cognitive burden.[2]

The standardization of how information is received and disseminated is also rel-evant to decreasing information overload (e.g., Snell, Youndt, and Wright, 1996). Specific processes and systems consist of set routines or guidelines in how informa-tion should be received and disseminated (Itami 1987; Walsh and Ungson 1991; Hall 1992; Subramaniam and Youndt 2005). Such systems provide a template to help over-come the complexities and ambiguities in trying to process information. For example, at P&G, web-based interfaces support the so-called communities of practice used to share knowledge—providing a platform for employees to process and share information more rapidly.

Through information systems and processes, knowledge becomes decontextualized and articulated in databases and other codified systems that allow employees to more easily understand how certain aspects of it might be helpful to them in their specific context. In this regard, processes and systems provide employees with an appropriate structural mechanism to receive information from others and to share it as well (Brockbank and Ulrich, 2002; Davenport and Prusak, 1998). An example can be drawn from Morris et al. (2009), where they found that the ability to codify knowledge and embed it into existing operations allows people in organizations to capture, roll out, maintain, promote, and distribute information with others in the organization.

Finally, it may be easier for stars to seek directly to limit the volume of information rather than make changes to their physical network structure or rely upon processes and information systems. Information filters can be implemented to reduce the burden of information flowing in the network. For instance, a few companies have imposed e-mail holidays, days where employees are encouraged not to send e-mail messages (Kessler, 2007). These actions, which are designed to reduce the volume of information flow within the organizations, will have the most profound effect on stars, who suffer most from the burden of information load.

11.4.2   Increasing Stars' Information-Processing and Sharing Capabilities

Another way to manage high levels of social capital consists of working with stars to enhance their information-processing capabilities (Haas, 2006; Tushman and Scanlan, 1981). Because information is often context-specific, stars with backgrounds that are more diverse are better able to quickly understand the subtle nuances of the information and share it with others (Tushman and Scanlan, 1981). Hansen and Haas (2001), Daft and Huber (1987), Kostova and Roth (2003), Sproull and Kiesler (1991), and Whittaker, Swanson, Kucan, and Sidner (1997) all argued that knowledge sharing provides almost no benefit when actors lack the ability to act on shared information and distinguish reusable from non-usable information.

Linguists have extensively examined the information-processing requirements of unique or novel information. Universally, they have found that information that does not fit into existing schema (Rumelhart, 1975), scripts (Schank and Abelson, 1977), frames (Minsky, 1975), or categories (Lakoff, 1987) requires additional effort and may even require the adaptation of existing or the creation of new linguistic frameworks. For example, Morris et al. (2009) found that when people lack shared vision or a shared framework of what is and is not important within the organization, much of the information is not transferred or processed. Furthermore, a more robust exposure also increases the transactive memory of the brokers, allowing them to know where in the corpus of information to look for specific information (Wegner, 1986).

Another way to increase information-processing and sharing capabilities consists of skill development around architectural knowledge (Kang et al., 2007). Henderson and Clark (1990) identified two separate forms of knowledge that are needed to process information: component and architectural. Component knowledge refers to knowledge of the parts or "components" of how or why something is done. Architectural knowledge is related to a shared understanding of the interconnection of all components, or how things fit together (Matusik and Hill, 1998). Star employees have often developed specialized skills that allow them to deliver value to the client. However, to utilize different sources of knowledge, as well as their own, they need to possess some degree of architectural knowledge. Such knowledge can be built by training stars on the various components and processes that go together to allow the firm to deliver value to a client. Assigning stars to be mentors and to provide on-the-job training can also enable them to build strong social and cognitive connections that allow them to better integrate information (Gittell, 2000; Mullen and Noe, 1999; Orlikowski, 2002). Similarly, team-building activities can also increase the cognitive processing skills of stars by helping them to understand better the problems and challenges facing colleagues (Wright and Snell, 1991). In addition, long-term partner contracts may not only increase stars' commitment to the organization but also encourage them to develop capabilities necessary to process and share information more effectively (Dyer and Nobeoka, 2000).

Kang et al. (2007) discussed the importance of flexible work structures for employees to more effectively process information. Flexible work structures provide greater autonomy to stars in being able to choose when, where, and how they will process information. For example, many organizations allow knowledge-based employees to do their work away from the office, whether at home, on the road, or elsewhere. Such flexibility is especially attractive to stars, as their ability to process and share information is not as much tied to the internal networks and structure of the firm. This flexibility provides a degree of autonomy that increases the decision-making latitude of the stars (Hambrick and Cannella, 1993; Huselid, 1995; Jelinik and Schoonhoven, 1995).

A commonly explored talent-management approach has been to give stars greater decision rights in the governance of the firm (Coff, 1997). While decision rights are seen to cause greater information processing regarding the activities of the business, for star employees, they provide greater status. Stars will use this status to push their desire to become more familiar with the general issues and problems faced by colleagues. As stars become more productive in processing and sharing information with others, organizations often provide greater decision-making power and ability to shape the direction of the company. They do this not only to keep them from leaving the organization, but also to encourage them to develop architectural knowledge and a shared vision.

Furthermore, to increase a star's ability to process information, organizations such as McKinsey and Company have transitioned some of their star employees to the position of "thought leader," where their incentives for information processing and sharing are aligned with their roles in the organization (Rasiel and Friga, 2002). This, of course, is not done for every star employee—usually only those more willing to shift the amount of time spent processing client information to spending more time processing colleague information. Within the World Bank Group, project leaders who have become stars have their processing burdens eased by requiring project teams and managers from other offices to pay for the star's time to provide information and expertise. In this way, the "costs" of processing more information are calculated into the organization and into the employee's work schedule, and, as a result, fewer burdens are placed on the stars.

Similarly, university professors who become research stars find themselves bombarded with information. To help ease the burden and ensure they maintain "stardom," universities will often offer reduced teaching loads, employ administrative assistants, and lower service requirements for these individuals. While these strategies may not directly reduce the information flowing to and from the star, they reduce the burden of performing other tasks, freeing their cognitive processing abilities to focus on their information load. In all these examples, the organization increases the time available for stars to process and pass information.

11.5 FUTURE DIRECTIONS

In sum, we have drawn upon social capital, information processing, and talent-management research to show how social capital can prove detrimental to star employees and how companies might more effectively help to manage the negative side effect of information load for star employees. Specifically, as information load continues to increase, it is increasingly important for organizations to understand how talent-management interventions might be implemented to reduce information overload of stars within an organization, and optimize information flow surrounding them.

Future avenues for research might examine what stars actually do to manage information overload and determine if this is something that only occurs within traditional boundaries of the firm. For example, more and more professionals are finding themselves loosely affiliated with organizations: acting as independent contractors outside the firm. While globalization and modularity contribute largely to this movement, employees may find additional motivation to engage in freelance work because it might help reduce a person's information load. For example, being outside the boundaries of a firm may provide increased independence and decreased need to respond to requests in a firm.

But not being tied to a firm may not necessarily reduce one's affiliatory ties. Because freelancers can more easily pick the projects or work they like, more pressure may exist for them to ensure their social networks are strong and dense. Scholars need to examine these types of network affiliations and determine how they affect star workers and the information load they bear.

Notes

1. Morris and colleagues (2016) argue that investments in firm-specific human capital signal to the external market that such employees are willing and able to make firm-specific investments in another firm. Hence, even though stars gain much of their value through firm-specific human capital investments, these investments are highly valued by the external market.

2. These strategies at the individual level mirror the efforts of firms. Typically, organizations engage in two strategies to cope with uncertainty and increased information needs. First, they implement structural mechanisms and information-processing capability to limit the information flow and thereby reduce uncertainty, and second, they develop buffers to reduce the effect of uncertainty (Daft and Lengel, 1986). A classic example of the first strategy is the redesign of business processes in organizations and the implementation of integrated information systems that improve information flow and reduce uncertainty within organizational subunits. A similar strategy is creating better information flow between organizations to address the uncertainties in the supply chain. An example of the second strategy is building inventory buffers to reduce the effect of uncertainty in demand or supply; another example is adding extra safety buffers in product design to address uncertainty in product working conditions.

References

Abelson, R. P. 1981. Psychological status of the script concept. *American Psychologist, 36*(7), p.715.

Adler, P. S., and Kwon, S. W. 2002. Social capital: prospects for a new concept. *Academy of Management Review, 27*(1), pp.17–40.

Aguinis, H., and O'Boyle, E. 2014. Star performers in twenty-first century organizations. *Personnel Psychology 67*(2), pp.313–50.

Baks, K. P. 2003. On the performance of mutual fund managers. Working Paper, Emory University, Atlanta.

Barabasi, A. L., and Crandall, R. E. 2003. Linked: the new science of networks. *American Journal of Physics 71*(4), pp.409–10.

Barney, J. B., and Wright, P. M. 1998. On becoming a strategic partner: the role of human resources in gaining competitive advantage. *Human Resource Management, 37*(1), p.31.

Batt, R. 2002. Managing customer services: human resource practices, quit rates, and sales growth. *Academy of Management Journal, 45*(3), pp.587–97.

Bawden, D. 2001. Information overload. *Library & Information Briefings, 92*, pp.1–15.

Boone, C. A. J. J., Van Olffen, W., and Van Witteloostuijn, A. 2005. Personality composition, leadership, information acquisition, and informed decision making in teams: a simulation game study of the locus-of-control. *Academy of Management Journal, 47*, pp.633–56.

Brockbank, W., and Ulrich, D. 2005. Higher knowledge for higher aspirations. *Human Resource Management, 44*(4), pp.489–504.

Burkhardt, M. E., and Brass, D. J. 1990. Changing patterns or patterns of change: the effects of a change in technology on social network structure and power. *Administrative Science Quarterly, 35*(1), pp.104–27.

Burt, R. S. 1987. Social contagion and innovation: cohesion versus structural equivalence. *American Journal of Sociology*, 92(6), pp.1287–335.

Burt, R. S. 1992. *Structural holes: the social structure of competition*. Cambridge, MA: Harvard University Press.

Burt, R. S. 1997. The contingent value of social capital. *Administrative Science Quarterly*, 42(2), pp.339–65.

Buskens, V., and Van de Rijt, A. 2008. Dynamics of networks if everyone strives for structural holes. *American Journal of Sociology*, 114(2), pp.371–407.

Carpenter, M. A., and Fredrickson, J. W. 2001. Top management teams, global strategic posture, and the moderating role of uncertainty. *Academy of Management Journal*, 44(3), pp.533–45.

Chewning, Jr., E. C., and Harrell, A. M. 1990. The effect of information load on decision makers' cue utilization levels and decision quality in a financial distress decision task. *Accounting, Organizations and Society*, 15, pp.527–42.

Coff, R. W. 1997. Human assets and management dilemmas: coping with hazards on the road to resource-based theory. *Academy of Management Review*, 22, pp.374–402.

Coleman, J. S. 1990. *Foundations of social theory*. Cambridge, MA; Harvard University Press.

Conner, K. R., and Prahalad, C. K. 1996. A resource-based theory of the firm: knowledge versus opportunism. *Organization Science*, 7(5), pp.477–501.

Cross, R., and Parker, A. 2004. *The hidden power of social networks: understanding how work really gets done in organizations*. Boston: Harvard Business School Press.

Daft, R. L., and Huber, G. P. 1987. How organizations learn: a communication framework. *Research in the Sociology of Organizations*, 5, pp.1–36.

Daft, R. L., and Lengel, R. H. 1986. Organizational information requirements, media richness and structural design. *Management Science*, 32(5), pp.554–71.

Davenport, T., and Prusak, L. 1998. *Working knowledge: how organizations manage what they know*. Boston: Harvard Business School Press.

Dutton, J. E., and Jackson, S. E. 1987. Categorizing strategic issues: links to organizational action. *Academy of Management Review*, 12(1), pp.76–90.

Dyer, J. H., and Noboeka, K. 2000. Creating and managing a high performance knowledge-sharing network: the Toyota case. *Strategic Management Journal*, 21, pp.345–68.

Ebel, H., Mielsch, L. I., and Bornholdt, S. 2002. Scale-free topology of email networks. *Physical Review E*, 66(3) p.035103.

Edmunds, A., and Morris, A. 2000. The problem of information overload in business organisations: a review of the literature. *International Journal of Information Management*, 20(1), pp.17–28.

Eppler, M. J., and Mengis, J. 2004. The concept of information overload: a review of literature from organization science, accounting, marketing, MIS, and related disciplines. *The Information Society*, 20(5), pp.325–44.

Fiske, S. T., and Taylor, S. E. 1991. *Social cognition*. Reading, MA: Addison-Wesley.

Gittell, J. H. 2000. Organizing work to support relational co-ordination. *International Journal of Human Resource Management*, 11, pp.517–39.

Grant, R. M. 1996. Toward a knowledge-based theory of the firm. *Strategic Management Journal*, 17, pp.109–22.

Greenwood, R., Hinings, C. R., and Brown, J. 1990. "P2-Form" strategic management: corporate practices in professional partnerships. *Academy of Management Journal*, 33(4), pp.722–55.

Grove, A. S. 1983. *High output management*. New York: Random House.

Groysberg, B., and Lee, L. E. 2008. The effect of colleague quality on top performance: the case of security analysts. *Journal of Organizational Behavior*, 29(8), pp.1123–44.

Groysberg, B., Lee, L. E., and Nanda, A. 2008. Can they take it with them? The portability of star knowledge workers' performance. *Management Science* 54(7), pp.1213–30.

Haas, M. R. 2006. Knowledge gathering, team capabilities, and project performance in challenging work environments. *Management Science*, 52(8), pp.1170–84.

Hall, S. 1992. How technique is changing science. *Science*, 257, pp.344–9.

Hambrick, D. C., and Cannella, A. A. 1993. Relative standing: a framework for understanding departures of acquired executives. *Academy of Management Journal*, 36, pp.733–62.

Hansen, M. T., and Haas, M. R. 2001. Competing for attention in knowledge markets: electronic document dissemination in a management consulting company. *Administrative Science Quarterly*, 46, pp.1–28.

Henderson, R. M., and Clark, K. B. 1990. Architectural innovation: the reconfiguration of existing product technologies and the failure of established firms. *Administrative Science Quarterly*, 35(1), pp.9–30.

Huselid, M. A. 1995. The impact of human resource management practices on turnover, productivity, and corporate financial performance. *Academy of Management Journal*, 38(3), pp.635–72.

Ibarra, H. 1995. Race, opportunity, and diversity of social circles in managerial networks. *Academy of Management Journal*, 38(3), pp.673–703.

Itami, H. 1987. *Mobilizing invisible assets*. Cambridge, MA: Harvard University Press.

Jelinek, M., and Schoonhoven, C. B. 1995. Organizational culture as a strategic advantage: insights from high-technology firms. In L. R. Gomez-Mejia and M. W. Lawless, eds., *Implementation management in high technology*. Greenwich, CT: JAI Press.

Jeong, H., Tombor, B., Albert, R., Oltvai, Z. N. et al. 2000. The large scale organization of metabolic networks. *Nature*, 47, pp.651–54.

Kang, S. C., Morris, S. S., and Snell, S. A. 2007. Relational archetypes, organizational learning, and value creation: extending the human resource architecture. *Academy of Management Review*, 32(1), pp.236–56.

Kessler, G. S. 2007. *Internet wisdom*. Bloomington, IN: Authorhouse.

Kostova, T., and Roth, K. 2003. Social capital in multinational corporations and a micro-macro model of its formation. *Academy of Management Review*, 28, pp.297–317.

Lakoff, G. 1987. *Fire, women, and dangerous things*. Chicago: University of Chicago Press.

Lazear, E. P. 1986. Raids and offer matching. *Research in Labor Economics*, 8, pp.141–65.

Lechner, C., Frankenberger, K., and Floyd, S. W. 2010. Task contingencies in the curvilinear relationships between intergroup networks and initiative performance. *Academy of Management Journal*, 53(4), pp.865–89.

Leenders, R. T. A., and Gabbay, S. M., eds. 2013. *Corporate social capital and liability*. Springer Science & Business Media.

Lepak, D. P., and Snell, S. A. 1999. The human resource architecture: toward a theory of human capital allocation and development. *Academy of Management Review*, 24(1), pp.31–48.

Lepak, D. P., and Snell, S. A. 2002. Examining the human resource architecture: the relationships among human capital, employment, and human resource configurations. *Journal of Management*, 28(4), pp.517–43.

Lord, R. G., and Maher, K. J. 1990. Alternative information-processing models and their implications for theory, research, and practice. *Academy of Management Review*, 15(1), pp.9–28.

Lorsch, J. W., and Tierney, T. J. 2002. *Aligning the stars: how to succeed when professionals drive results*. Boston: Harvard Business School Press.

Matusik, S., and Hill, C. 1998. The utilization of contingent work, knowledge creation, and competitive advantage. *Academy of Management Review*, 23, pp.680–97.

Meier, R. L. 1963. Communications overload: proposals from the study of a university library. *Administrative Science Quarterly*, 7(4), pp.521–44.

Minsky, M. A. 1975. *A framework for the representation of knowledge. The psychology of computer vision.* New York: McGraw-Hill.

Morris, S. S., Alvarez, S. A., Barney, J. B. and Molloy, J. C. 2017. Firm-specific human capital investments as a signal of general value: revisiting assumptions about human capital and how it is managed. *Strategic Management Journal*, 38(4), pp.912–19.

Morris, S., and Oldroyd, J. B. 2009. To boost knowledge transfer, tell me a story. *Harvard Business Review*, 87(5), p.23.

Morris, S. S., Wright, P. M., Trevor, J., Stiles, P., Stahl, G. K., Snell, S., Paauwe, J. and Farndale, E. 2009. Global challenges to replicating HR: the role of people, processes, and systems. *Human Resource Management*, 48(6), pp.973–95.

Mullen, E. J., and Noe, R. A. 1999. The mentoring information exchange: when do mentors seek information from their proteges? *Journal of Organizational Behavior*, 20, pp.233–42.

Newman, M. E. J. 2002. Assortative mixing in networks. *Physical Review Letters*, 89, p.208701.

Newman, M. E. J., and Park, J. 2003. Why social networks are different from other types of networks. *Physical Review Letters*, 68, p.036122.

O'Boyle, E., and Kroska, S. 2017. Star employees. In D. G. Collings, K. Mellahi, and W. F. Cascio, eds., *Oxford handbook of talent management.* Oxford: Oxford University Press.

Sparrow, P. R. and Makram, H. 2015. What is the value of talent management? Building value-driven processes within a talent management architecture. *Human Resource Management Review*, 25(3), pp.249–63.

O'Reilly, C. A. 1980. Individuals and information overload in organizations: is more necessarily better? *Academy of Management Journal*, 23(4), pp.684–96.

Oldroyd, J., and Gulati, R. 2010. Network centrality, information flow and cognitive overload: identifying the burdens of volume, variance, and non-unique information flows. Working Paper. Northwestern University.

Oldroyd, J. B., and Morris, S. S. 2012. Catching falling stars: a human resource response to social capital's detrimental effect of information overload on star employees. *Academy of Management Review*, 37(3), pp.396–418.

Orlikowski, W. J. 2002. Knowing in practice: enacting a collective capability in distributed organizing. *Organization Science*, 10, pp.249–73.

Oskamp, S. 1965. Overconfidence in case-study judgments. *Journal of Consulting Psychology*, 29(3), pp.261–65.

Perlow, L. A. 1999. The time famine: toward a sociology of work time. *Administrative Science Quarterly*, 44(1), pp.57–81.

Peteraf, M. A. 1993. The cornerstones of competitive advantage: a resource-based view. *Strategic Management Journal*, 14(3), pp.179–91.

Ployhardt, R. and Cragun, O. 2017. Collective human capital complementarities. In D. G. Collings, K. Mellahi, and W. F. Cascio, eds., *Oxford handbook of talent management.* Oxford: Oxford University Press.

Rasiel, E. M., and Friga, P. N. 2002. *The McKinsey mind: understanding and implementing the problem-solving tools and management techniques of the world's top strategic consulting firm.* New York: McGraw-Hill.

Ready, D. A., Conger, J. A. and Hill, L. A. 2010. Are you a high potential. *Harvard Business Review*, 88(6), pp.78–84.

Rudolph, J. W., and Repenning, N. P. 2002. Disaster dynamics: understanding the role of quantity in organizational collapse. *Administrative Science Quarterly*, 47(1), pp.1–30.

Rumelhart, D. E. 1975. Notes on a schema for stories. In D. G. Bobrow and A. Collins, eds., *Representation and understanding: studies in cognitive science*. pp. 211-236. New York: Academic Press.

Sandefur, R. L., and Laumann, E. O. 1998. A paradigm for social capital. *Rationality and Society*, 10(4), pp.481–501.

Schank, R. C., and Abelson, R. P. 1977. *Scripts, plans, goals, and understanding*. Hillsdale, NJ: Lawrence Erlbaum Associates.

Simon, H. 1957. *Models of man*. New York: John Wiley & Sons.

Snell, S. A., Youndt, M. A., and Wright, P. M. 1996. Establishing a framework for research in strategic human resource management: merging resource theory and organizational learning. *Human Resource Management*, 14, pp.61–90.

Sparrowe, R. T., Liden, R. C., Wayne, S. J., and Kraimer, M. L. 2001. Social networks and the performance of individuals and groups. *Academy of Management Journal*, 44(2), pp.316–25.

Sproull, L. and Kiesler, S. 1991.Computers, networks and work. *Scientific American*, 265(1991), pp.116–23.

Subramaniam, M., and Youndt, M. A. 2005. The influence of intellectual capital on the types of innovative capabilities. *Academy of Management Journal*, 48(3), pp.450–63.

Thompson, J. D. 1967. *Organizations in action: social science bases of administrative theory*. New York: McGraw-Hill.

Tushman, M. L., and Nadler, D. A. 1978. Information processing as an integrating concept in organizational design. *Academy of Management Review*, 3(3), pp.613–24.

Tushman, M. L., and Scanlan, T. J. 1981. Boundary spanning individuals: their role in information transfer and their antecedents. *Academy of Management Journal*, 24(2), pp.289–305.

Wadhwa, A., and Kotha, S. 2006. Knowledge creation through external venturing evidence from the telecommunication equipment manufacturing industry. *Academy of Management Journal*, 49(4), pp.819–35.

Walsh, J. P., and Ungson, G. R. 1991. Organizational memory. *Academy of Management Review*, 16(1), pp.57–91.

Watts, D. J., Dodds, P. S., and Newman, M. E. 2002. Identity and search in social networks. *Science*, 296(5571), pp.1302–5.

Wegner, D. M. 1986. Transactive memory: a contemporary analysis of the group mind. In B. Mullen and G. R. Goethals, eds., *Theories of group behavior*, pp.185–205. New York: Springer-Verlag.

Whittaker, S., Swanson, J., Kucan, J., and Sidner, C. 1997. Managing lightweight interactions in the desktop. *ACM Transactions on Computer-Human Interaction*, 4(2), pp.137–68.

Wright, P. M., and Snell, S. A. 1991. Toward an integrative view of strategic human resource management. *Human Resource Management Review*, 1, pp.203–25.

SECTION 4

MANAGING TALENT FLOWS

CHAPTER 12

EMPLOYER BRANDING AND TALENT MANAGEMENT

MARTIN R. EDWARDS

12.1 BACKGROUND AND CONTEXT

WITH a book that has a principal focus on talent management, it may not be obvious where a chapter focusing on employer branding sits; however, there are many elements of the employer-branding project that can add to debates around talent management. In the first instance, employer-branding authors (Dell and Ainspan, 2001; Martin, Beaumont, Doig, and Pate, 2005; Edwards, 2012) have argued that one of the reasons for the growth in employer branding as a field is the growing pressure to compete in the "war for talent." Arguably, having a strong, attractive employer brand should help organizations ensure they attract and retain talented people. In defining *employer branding*, some proponents of the project argue that attracting talent is a central aim. The United Kingdom's Chartered Institute of Personnel and Development, for example, argues that a successful employer brand will be one that appeals to "people who thrive and perform to their best in its culture" (2007: 3). Looking at employer branding from the perspective of talent management, a successful employment brand would be one that helps to attract and retain talented employees who perform to their full potential and thrive in the organization's culture. Of course, as discussed in other parts of this book, what *talent* and *talent management* mean may depend on one's definition; thus, exactly how it applies to employer branding will depend largely on one's frame of reference. Before discussing the links between talent management and employer branding, it is important to sketch out some of the central aspects of employer branding. Importantly, the area of employer-brand segmentation, which is a relatively recent addition to discussions linked to employer branding, will be explored. It has potential similarities or links with aspects of talent management.

12.2 EMPLOYER BRANDING

Although much has been written about employer branding over recent years, there is still no real agreed definition that helps us quickly identity what it involves as an human resource (HR) activity (Kudret, 2015). However, it can be seen as "an HR activity which involves the systematic management of how an organisation is perceived as an employer; specifically to potential new recruits as well as current employees" (Edwards, 2014: 71). Further, the management of an organization's employer brand is increasingly considered a core activity on which strategic HR functions need to be focusing their energies (Cascio and Graham, in press). Importantly, the exact nature of employer-branding programs across organizations will vary; however, they are likely to all share an aim of increasing the quality and number of applicants that seek employment in the firm, and such initiatives will also intend to help foster an increased degree of employee appreciation (and understanding) of the "unique employment experience" on offer by the organization. Of central importance to any employer-branding activity is the identification of the distinctive and unique features of the employment experience that employees enjoy through their employment; these unique selling-point features are then communicated to help retain current employees and attract potential new recruits (Edwards, 2005, 2014).

The potential breadth of the content of employment experiences that an organization's employer-branding project could identify might be considerable, and thus, definitions of what is encompassed within an employer brand will allude to this. If we consider one of the first definitions presented by Ambler and Barrow, who indicated that an employer brand will include "the package of financial, economic and psychological benefits provided by employment and identified with the employing company" (1996: 187), the potential breadth of the employment experience is clearly implied with this definition. This is also the case with Backhaus and Tikoo's (2004) definition. They argued that the employer brand "suggests differentiation of a firm's characteristics as an employer from those of its competitors, the employment brand highlights the unique aspects of the firm's employment offerings or environment" (Backhaus and Tikoo, 2004: 502).

In theorizing and researching aspects of an employer branding, authors have recently drawn on a range of established theoretical and conceptual frameworks to help clarify aspects of the employer brand. For example, Albert and Whetten's (1985) concept of "organisational identity" refers to current employees' perceptions of what they see as central, enduring, and distinctive characteristics of the organization (Edwards, 2010; Edwards and Edwards, 2013; Lievens and Slaughter, 2016) and organizational identification/commitment as potential desired consequences of a positive employer brand with an internal focus on current employees (Edwards and Edwards, 2013). Also, authors have drawn on the idea of "organizational image" (Lievens and Slaughter, 2016) to help frame the aspect of an employer brand that involves external perceptions of the organization's employment brand. Other authors (e.g., Ambler and Barrow, 1996; Cable and Turban,

2003) have drawn on ideas of employer "brand equity" when considering external perceptions of an organization's employer brand (and applicant knowledge of an employer); as with corporate and product brands, an effective employer brand would have "brand equity," defined by Aaker as "a set of brand assets and liabilities linked to a brand, its name, and symbol that add to or subtract from the value provided by a product or service to a firm and/or to that firm's customers" (1991: 15).

A strong product brand should result in customers' willingness for repeat investment in a product. Customers would also recommend it to others and be happy to pay a price premium for the product. The translation of these marketing ideas into employer brand is central to the idea of employer-brand equity. Lievens (2007) draws on marketing frameworks that are more oriented toward product brands and consumers (Aaker, 1991; Keller, 1993) in considering key elements of the brand's unique characteristics or the content of the employer brand. Lievens (2007) applies an established marketing framework of symbolic (psychological) and functional (instrumental) attributes associated with a brand to ideas of employer brand content. Instrumental attributes are associated with the employer and are tangible attributes considered to have value (e.g., training, benefits, or advancement opportunities); symbolic attributes are linked to inferences that people make about an employer that are less tangible, and their value is more symbolic in nature (Lievens, 2007; Highhouse, Thornbury, and Little, 2007).

Importantly, an effective employer brand (one with a high degree of employer-brand equity) should do two fundamental things. First, a strong and effective employer brand should ensure that potential and actual job applicants (as potential recruits) find the organization, its employer brand, and the potential unique employment experience, highly attractive. Associated with this, potential recruits should have a desire to work at the organization and concrete intentions to apply for a job at the organization. Second, a positive and strong employer brand should mean that existing employees will want to continue working at the organization; they should also be committed to the organization, have a higher degree of organizational identification, and be willing to put themselves out for the good of the organization (Edwards, 2005, 2010, 2012, 2014; Edwards and Edwards, 2013; Hanin, Stinglhamber, and Delobbe, 2013). Importantly, the brand equity of an organization that has a strong employer brand would be at its greatest if the people that it attracts and retains were highly talented individuals that could make a considerable difference to the success of the organization. Thus, being able to attract and keep "talented individuals" can be considered a key aim or aspired outcome of a successful employer-branding program.

12.3 EMPLOYER BRANDING AND "TALENT"

As mentioned, many of the earliest commentators and authors on the employer-branding project have been very clear that a strong and effective employer brand will help in the "war of talent." In an early paper focusing on employer branding, Dell and

Ainspan's (2001) Conference Board paper made numerous references to the importance of talent, as well as how a strong employer brand can help attract and retain talent. In one of the first works to address employer branding, Ambler and Barrow (1996) argued that one of the key aims of employer branding was to help attract the "best applicants" and employ the "best people." One can reasonably translate "best" applicants and people to the idea of "talented" applicants and people; thus, one of the key aims of employer branding is to attract and retain talented employees. However, the degree to which one can comfortably make this statement may depend on one's definition of *talent*. As other authors in this book will mention (see Cappelli and Keller, 2017; O'Boyle and Kroska, 2017), there are many different perspectives that one can take when attempting to understand what is meant by talent. A number of reviews of the talent literature have highlighted that talent can mean very different things to different people. In a review of the meaning of talent, Gallardo-Gallardo, Dries, and González-Cruz (2013) identified many possible ways to view talent in the world of work. One of the key distinctions that they drew from the literature is the idea that talent can be "object" oriented or "subject" oriented. Subject-oriented talent refers to particular people who can be identified or deemed as "talent," whereas object-oriented talent refers to particular characteristics that people can have (rather than the people themselves).

From an employer-branding perspective where we follow the rationale that employer branding aims to attract and retain the best people, whether the "best" label is referring to the individuals themselves or individuals with particular characteristics may initially seem like a moot point, as long as they are "the best." Interestingly, if we follow Ambler and Barrow's narrative that employer branding aims to help attract (and retain) the best people, we may be led to make particular inferences that employer branding as a project might be most interested in identifying and retaining particular individuals (i.e., "the best"). This idea may naturally lend itself to an "exclusive" rather than "inclusive" perspective on talent: a second key distinction that Gallardo-Gallardo, Dries, and González-Cruz (2013) draw from the literature on talent. They argue that talent literature (and practice) can take an exclusive approach, where particular individuals are singled out and identified as "talent" to be carefully managed, or it can take an inclusive approach. The latter approach assumes that all employees are deemed as talent and every employee has her or his own particular strengths. With regard to employer branding, especially from some of the early work on the field, one may assume that in trying to attract and retain the best people, a subject-oriented inclusive approach may be implied. However, there is no reason why employer brand itself couldn't incorporate an inclusive and object-oriented talent framework as part of its employment experience; and some authors may be implying this when they argue that a strong employer brand can help "leverage" the full potential of (presumably all) employees.

Ultimately, with *employer-branding* definitions such as that presented by the United Kingdom's Chartered Institute of Personnel and Development, where employer branding aims to attract and retain the "people who thrive and perform to their best in its culture," it seems that there is an implied assumption that some people within the organization will not thrive or perform to their best. Thus, the idea of "thriving or performing" to "their best" also has shades of "fulfilling their potential," another idea that has been associated with "talent" in the talent-management field. Thus, implicitly, employer branding can be assumed to have an aim of helping people perform to their potential. It can also be assumed that an organization with a strong employer brand will have the "best employees" working or performing to their "full potential."

12.4 Employer-Branding Segmentation and Differentiation of the Workforce Employment Experience

One of the key developments in the field that has direct relevance to theory and practice of talent management is the idea of employer-branding segmentation. Originating from the field of marketing, segmentation can be considered a fairly standard marketing activity, where experts take into account the fact that customers or consumers can be separated into subsets or groups of people with similar interests or needs (intrasegment similarity). The key assumption involved is that market researchers can differentiate subsets of consumers (intersegment differences can be identified), and, importantly, key messages (and potentially what is provided or sold to them) as a product should be tailored toward each segment according to their specific needs.

In recent years, theorists and practitioners in the area of employer branding have taken this idea on board; the introduction of segmentation into the employer-branding field is to some degree a natural development because of its marketing roots. A number of authors have suggested that an important employer-branding activity should involve a segmented employment experience and a segmented employer brand (Moroko and Uncles 2009; Tuzuner and Yuksel, 2009). An important question to ask here is: What does this involve in practice (or indeed in theory) in relation to an employment brand? In the very nature of organizations there will generally be subgroups of employees within the organization (vertically or horizontally across function specialisms) that will tend to have rather varied employment experiences. As explained above, although an employer-branding project is likely to involve the clarification and presentation of a unique employment experience that is offered by the organization, in reality, no organization will have a single employment experience shared by all. Even if an organization tries to identify the shared aspect of any employment experience on offer to employees, what is offered to different groups within the organization will inevitably be differentiated (see Collings, 2017; Meyers, De Boeck, and Dries, 2017). To some extent, identification of a unique shared employment experience in clarifying what an organization's employer brand is may tend to ignore or deemphasize these natural differences. Potentially, however, when trying to identify the unique shared employment experience on offer, this may be made easier if there is a universal set of HR practices/terms and conditions offered to all. Employer-brand segmentation potentially implies, however, deliberate differentiated HR practices offered to different segments.

The concept of having differentiated HR practices, terms, and conditions within organizations is not new, and a number of different theoretical models have been presented over the years that explicitly suggest or recommend this. For example, Atkinson's (1986) flexible firm model and the resource-based view of the firm-linked models (in particular, Lepak and Snell's [1999] Human Resource Architecture model) both propose that there should be differentiated levels of investments to different groups of employees and thus different employment experiences across organizations. An assumption underpinning the resource-based view of the firm revolves around the idea that different groups of workers receive varied levels of investment/HR practices, depending upon their relative strategic value. Similarly, Atkinson's flexible firm model revolves around the idea that different HR practices (and thus employment experiences) should be given to different categories of worker, specifically, elements of the core versus the periphery. However, distinct from RBV-based models, although employer-brand segmentation may allow for differentiated employment experiences being offered to different groups of workers, and thus there should be variation in HR practices, this variation is driven by the fact that different segments will desire and value different employment experiences.

The idea of providing differentiated HR practices to different groups (or segments) of workers is to some extent a natural process that often occurs with many forms of talent-management practices. In considering how employer-branding activities relate to the field of talent management it is important to clarify what one might mean by *talent management*, and a definition presented by Collings and Mellahi (2009) would be useful here. They define strategic talent management as "activities and processes that involve the systematic identification of key positions that differentially contribute to the organisations sustainable competitive advantage" (Collings and Mellahi, 2009: 304). Thus a "segment" is identified in organizations that conduct talent management, and the segment has been chosen as those who "contribute to the organization's sustainable competitive advantage" versus those who do not. Collings and Mellahi's definition then goes on to clarify that talent management can involve:

> [...] the development of a talent pool of high potential and high performing incumbents to fill these roles and the development of differentiated human resource architecture to facilitate filling these positions with competent incumbents, and to ensure their continued commitment to the organisation. (2009: 304)

Thus, organizations that conduct talent management in line with this definition will offer differentiated employment experiences to the talent versus the non-talent roles.

While it can be argued that one feature of presenting an organization's employer brand is to identify the shared employment experience and communicate this to potential recruits and current employees (which implies homogeneity rather than heterogeneity in employment experiences), the idea of differentiated employment experience probably represents a realistic picture of what happens in organizations.

According to Lawler (2011), the evidence is scant to support the idea that all employees within organizations tend to experience the same set of HR practices, implying that a differentiated employment experience is the norm in organizations. As Guest has suggested, "Many large organisations are likely to have a number of quite highly differentiated internal labour markets, each of which can have a distinctive set of HR policies and practices. In short, one size does not fit all" (2011: 8). Such a suggestion is supported by Lepak et al. (2007), who found consistent evidence of the existence of multiple, identifiable sets of HR practices being in place within organizations.

To a degree, differentiated employment experiences and HR provision are almost inevitable, and many organizations automatically segment the potential job market into different possible groups; the variation in imagery and messages being communicated to different groups and segments of potential employees is often marked. For example, as of 2016, the Apple.com job opportunities website is divided into three main functional groups: "retail," "corporate," and "students." These are clearly three fundamentally varied segments within the employer brand at Apple. The imagery of the potential incumbents in the *corporate* segment identified in the website features people in casual clothes and jeans; the *retail* employees all wear the same colored uniform (blue polo shirt); and the *student* segment are generally portrayed to be working flexibly from home. These differences reflect the norm within organizations that different roles tend to have different employment experiences, and, thus, different (differentiated) experiences are being offered to different segments. With organizations that carry out talent management as defined by Collings and Mellahi (2009), however, the different employment experience to be offered as part of the organization's employer brand will be based on talent segments. Segmenting on talent is of course only one possible way to segment the employment experience, but it could be a recognizable one nonetheless.

In one of the few articles written about segmentation and employer branding, Moroko and Uncles (2009) outline a number of possible groups that could form the basis of a segmentation of employee groups. These include groupings or segments across age categories (baby boomers versus generation X versus millennials/generation Y), groupings by seniority (e.g., managers versus graduates), or more traditional job-type-based segmentation, such as support services versus technical versus client-facing. It is commonly argued that organizations should consider segmenting the workforce specifically to take into account the different needs or wants of different generational groups (Lawler, 2011). It is clear from the number of authors who have recently argued for the consideration of segmentation in employer branding that there is a call for an increasingly sophisticated understanding of the target population. To carry out employer-brand segmentation, the designers of the brand will need to have a very sophisticated awareness of the possible heterogeneity in interests and values of the workforce or target population. If the main reason for segmenting the workforce from an employer-branding point of view is to attract and retain different groups of employees who have different interests and values, the employer brand/HR architects will need to think about the potential for considerable degrees of HR differentiation required to keep all groups happy, which could end up leading to a confused and overly complex employment-experience offering. Thus, an aspect of employer branding as an activity involves identifying and communicating a focused message about a unique shared employment experience associated with an organization. Segmentation introduces a fundamental tension. This tension involves the idea that employer-branding activities should ideally account for different wants and needs of different groups, but satisfying these different needs and wants would require the existence of multiple sub-brands within one organization. Where differentiated groups exist among the workforce the organization will need to choose between designing a differentiated HR architecture and providing varied terms and conditions, and HR systems, to different groups or not doing so. If an organization chooses differentiation, then the employment brand that it offers to potential and current employees will need to reflect the fact that the employment experience is not shared across the workforce. This would lead to difficulties in identifying and communicating (and potentially providing) a shared and unique employment experience. The alternative to offering and communicating a differentiated employment experience is that the organization presents a simplified brand message without actually highlighting real differences in employment experience across different groups within the workforce. Either way, employer-brand segmentation potentially challenges the idea central to employer branding that the shared unique employment experience can be identified, which helps to differentiate an organization from other employers and can be used to communicate to current and potential employees in order to attract and retain them.

Importantly, the examples of segments and differentiated HR provision that tend to be presented in association with employer-brand segmentation form a different narrative of differentiation than that associated with talent management. With employer-branding segmentation, the employment-experience differentiation tends to be driven by the desire to attract and retain people with varied interests, needs, and values; with talent management, the differentiation of HR provision and workforce segmentation tends to be driven by the desire to differentially invest in, reward, and develop people who will make the difference to the bottom line.

12.5 Segmentation on Talent

The discussion above relating to employer-brand segmentation refers to using "talent" as potential criteria for determining a segment of the workforce to target differential aspects of the organization's employer brand. However, the focus of the above discussion is the activity of employer-brand segmentation in itself. The implications of using talent as an employer-brand segment are explored further here. From an employer-branding perspective, a possible reason why an organization might want to segment their workforce on the basis of talent identification could simply involve the same rationale used for brand segmentation in general: that the workforce may be divided into groups where the groupings have a high degree of intracategory similarity in terms of needs, wants, and values (Moroko and Uncles, 2009; Tuzuner and Yuksel, 2009). Thus, identifying a talent versus non-talent group may imply that the two groups have different needs and wants that must be recognized. The organization can adjust or vary the employment experience offered to the talent versus non-talent group accordingly to ensure that the organization has an attractive employment offering to the different groups. Arguably, this would help ensure that the best people will want to apply for and stay in the jobs in the different segments (talent versus non-talent). Presumably, if one takes this argument further, differentiated terms and conditions (and employment conditions) may be offered to the two (or more) talent (or not) groupings. What such a segmentation may imply, however, is that the organization assumes there will be a group of the workforce that can be classed as non-talent, with identifiable needs and wants that are associated with people not being interested in fulfilling their potential or being considered talented. The logic of this does not seem to follow from an employer-branding point of view, and organizations are unlikely to segment actively their workforce with the assumption that some groups want to be considered talent and others do not. Thus, if an organization does actively segment their workforce on the basis of talent (as Collings and Mellahi [2009] suggest occurs in organizations that conduct talent-management practices), and adjusts its employment-brand offering accordingly (with differentiated employment experiences), then the main rationale for this is likely to be the the desire to invest selectively in different groups on the basis of their potential value or contribution to the firm. Thus, where an organization includes a talent segment, the reason for doing this is likely to be in accordance with standard arguments that have been presented associated with the resource-based view of the firm as a guiding theoretical model (which might be used to justify organizational variation in HR practices). The assumption here would be that talented employees would have more strategic "value" and potentially "greater human capital worth or value." These ideas seem to be quite commonplace in the HR field, and talent-management initiatives may now be the most obvious example of the application of the RBV of the firm and differentiated HR architecture. As mentioned, proponents of talent-management programs recommend that the workforce should be segmented into groups of talent versus other/non-talent (see Capelli, 2008) and greater developmental (and other) opportunities should be provided to the "talented" segment.

Although not labeled explicitly as talent versus other groups, other examples of segmentation based on talent/potential include the "Differentiated Workforce" model of Becker et al. (2009). Becker et al. suggest providing quite different opportunities to "C players" compared with "B" and "A" players. Ultimately, talent-management initiatives can be seen as formal, business-driven segmentations of an organization's employment brand. Such exclusionary and subject-based talent-management initiatives will inevitably create tensions in an organization's ability to present a unified shared employment experience as part of a coherent and distinctive employment brand. Such a differentiated approach implies many things from an employer-brand point of view. As mentioned, the organization's values, its symbolic characteristics, will help to form the shared employment experience within an organization. An organization that conducts differentiated talent-management practices that have a segmented employment brand will inherently imply particular values—values that provide favorable employment experience to different groups.

Aside from the challenges that talent-management initiatives will bring to an organization's identification of a unified coherent employment experience, the potential negative impact that differential employment-experience provision (of this sort) will have on workplace morale will need to be considered. A number of authors present the potential downsides of talent management. Pfeffer (2001), for example, argued that a focus on talent can lead to elitism and arrogance, and that "A, B, C" labeling can become a self-fulfilling prophecy (and thus not represent valid differentiation between employees).

12.5.1 Justice and Equity Concerns

Apart from the logistical challenge that the HR function will face in having to manage different sets of HR practices, different groups get different sets of terms and conditions, and potentially favoring particular groups may have other downsides. It could cause a fair degree of dissatisfaction among the workforce staff as certain segments make instrumental relative comparisons. Collings (2014) discusses some of these issues in a recent paper. He argues that exclusionary differentiating talent-management programs can lead to larger wage dispersion between the higher and lower earners (talent versus non-talent) in an attempt to motivate and retain key talent; however, in doing so, this can potentially have a negative impact on retention and cooperation within the organization in the long term (because of the inequities that occur with such wage dispersion). Related to this issue, Marescaux, De Winne, and Sels argue that "special care must be given towards the 'have nots,' who may develop negative perceptions of favourability and subsequently lower affective organisational commitment" (2013: 342). Such a point was also made by Martin in considering the implications of differential provision of terms and conditions to "non-talent" versus "talent" employee segments: "segmentation can lead to invidious comparisons and endemic employee relations problems because the 'losers' in the war for talent resent the success of 'winners'" (2009: 230).

The equity-based challenges of such an approach are obvious. Individuals make relative comparisons about how much other people receive in exchange for their efforts and weigh this up against their own inputs and outputs, as Adams' (1963) equity theory suggests. Thus, the existence of different terms and conditions across different groups may be expected to foster problems of morale across certain groups (see also Meyers, Dries, and De Boeck, 2017). It would be expected that employees will be aware of different employment experiences offered and provided to different groups and ask: Is this fair? This point has been addressed to some extent by Gelens, Dries, Hofmans, and Pepermans (2013), who point out that differentiating talent/high-potential status is likely to lead to differences in perceptions of distributive justice, which, importantly, can lead to negative outcomes. This was demonstrated empirically in a different paper, in which Gelens, Hofmans, Dries, and Pepermans (2014) showed that employees who were "non-high potentials" reported significantly lower levels of distributive justice than those identified as "high potentials." A considerable collection of theoretical work and empirical research exists indicating that that when organizations have variations in the distribution of resources or rewards across the workforce, the decision making that led to the variation must be just and fair. Employees' judgments of the fairness of both the procedures in place and how resources have been distributed when making decisions are extremely important in leading to positive or negative employee responses (Colquit et al., 2001). Thus, any organization that has differentiated employment experiences offered to talent versus non-talent populations runs the risk of having a negative rather than positive employer brand, which may undermine the aims of attracting potential employees and retaining existing workers.

Some talent-related research exists that recognizes individual differences in the extent to which employees (and potential employees) might respond negatively to an exclusionary, subject-based talent initiative. Gelens, Dries, Hofmans, and Pepermans (2013) suggest that equity sensitivity is likely to play a big role in moderating how employees may react to talent-based differentiation. From an employer-branding point of view, the implications of this research with regard to who might be attracted to an exclusionary subject-based talent-segmented employment experience would not be straightforward. It would depend upon the degree to which the individual applicants think they are likely to be treated favorably (as talent) and their degree of sensitivity to this. Presumably, individuals who are treated favorably as talent and who feel that they could or do contribute more than non-talent does may respond positively even if they have high degrees of equity sensitivity. Research by Marescaux, De Winne, and Sels indicates that "organisations may benefit from differentiating HR practices across employees when this leads to perceptions of positive favourability as this is associated with higher affective organisational commitment than perceived equality" (2013: 342). Of course, the potential "have nots" who are highly equity sensitive will not find such an organization an attractive place to work.

In research published by Blume, Rubin, and Baldwin (2013) that looked at potential employee responses toward a forced-distribution performance-management system that forced a particular distribution identifying a population of high, average, and low performers, it was clear that the majority of respondents did not find such a system particularly attractive, as compared with less forced and individualized appraisal systems. Presumably, in a similar vein, a talent system that rewards a population of haves and have nots is not likely to be attractive to all possible applicants or future employees who may have the potential to flourish. Interestingly, Blume, Rubin, and Baldwin (2013) found that the respondents who showed higher levels of cognitive ability were more likely to find an organization with a performance-management system that actively forced a workforce population partitioning as more attractive. Additionally, respondents who felt that a performance-management system that recognizes the relative contribution of employees and rewards accordingly (akin to talent-management initiatives) was fair were more likely to find the organization as attractive.

We can potentially draw a number of logical conclusions from some of the research mentioned here when considering talent management from an employer-branding perspective. Ultimately, if an exclusive subject-oriented talent-versus-non-talent segmentation becomes part of the offered employment experience at an organization and this becomes recognized as part of the distinctive employee value proposition of this organization's employment brand, then it is highly likely that the potential applicant pool will be fundamentally restricted. Such organizations may only attract those who believe that they are likely to be identified as talent and that they are special, and who expect preferential treatment from their unique input. Interestingly, exclusive subject-oriented talent-management initiatives that identify talent populations and treat them differently only identify a small subset of the population as talent. Paradoxically, although such an employment experience may be attractive to those who think such systems are fair, that they would thrive in such a system, and that the potential applicant pool will be made up of such people, most of these people will end up not receiving the reified talent status label.

The discussion of employer-brand segmentation on the basis of talent versus other here has assumed that the norm of such a talent-management initiative involves an exclusionary and subject-oriented approach, which identifies individuals and provides a differentiated employment experience. However, as recognized above, there are different ways to consider and define the treatment of talent in organizations (Gallardo-Gallardo, Dries, and González-Cruz, 2013). If an organization were to have more of an object-oriented and inclusive approach to the management of talent, where everyone is considered "talent" (with their own unique strengths) and their particular combination of abilities, characteristics, and skills are considered to reflect talent, then such an approach will imply a very different set of organizational values than those of the exclusive subject-based approach (which, as Collings [2014] argues implies a profit-maximizing value proposition). With such an approach, it is likely to be much easier for an organization to identify a shared employment experience that can help form the basis of a positive, unique employment experience that can help differentiate that organization from other potential employers. Furthermore, an inclusive and object-oriented talent-management program may also help ensure that the organization's employer brand involves a more sustainable relationship with employees (potentially answering some of the problems that Collings (2014) raises with particular forms of talent management). It is likely that a more inclusive object-oriented formulation and treatment of talent should lead to the organization having a more attractive employer brand that is likely to enable a much wider net to be cast in terms of the potential applicant pool.

12.6 Possible Avenues for Future Research

There are a number of potentially interesting research avenues that one could consider in order to explore further some of the possible employer-brand implications of having different forms of differentiated HR systems—differentiated on both employer-brand segmentation and talent-driven segmentation. It would be worth exploring whether having differentiated HR practices driven by brand segmentation (serving different needs and wants of employees) leads to fundamentally fragmented perceptions of the organization that might lead to perceptions of a confused unique value proposition on offer to potential (and current) employees. This could have serious implications for recruiters, who may not even be aware of the mixed messages that might be coming across in recruitment material and job adverts/job websites. However, potential applicants may become aware of an organization appearing to present different employment offerings to different groups. This could have negative implications in that it may lead to a perception that the organization might have a problem with fairness and equity in its offering. If potential applicants differ in how important they deem issues of justice, fairness, and equity, the organization could be excluding a potential applicant pool that they would rather attract (as in, people who are motivated by fairness and justice). In terms of the employer-brand implications of different types of talent-management systems (object- versus subject-oriented programs), it might also be a good idea to try to identify the types of applicant who may or may not find jobs operating within the different systems to be attractive (or not). With research indicating that only a minority of potential recruits are attracted to employment systems that actively identify a population of better-versus-worse performers (Blume, Rubin, and Baldwin, 2013), further studies need to be conducted (either by researchers or by HR within the organizations themselves) to identify the type of candidate that such systems exclude through self-selection (before application stage). This population (people who have not applied to an organization because of the differentiated employment offering) may actually be potential employees who could end up having a positive influence on the organization's culture; people who are particularly sensitive to inequity (Gelens, Dries, Hofmans, and Pepermans, 2013), who may be motivated (if hired) to ensure that the organization acts with fairness and equity.

12.7 CONCLUSION

Talent management and employer branding as topics are two areas that have the potential for overlapping interests. When an organization operates a formal strategic talent-management program, this will have profound implications for the employer brand linked to the firm. Organizations would do well to consider carefully the implications that any talent-driven differentiated HR system has for both the values-based message that any particular form of talent program sends to potential recruits, in particular with regard to the organization's fairness and equity credentials, and the effect that any differentiated HR practices may have on the organization's ability to identify and communicate a coherent (and, importantly, shared) employment experience that forms the core of its employer-brand offering. It is also important to recognize that a differentiated

HR system driven by an employer-brand segmentation strategy may have consequences for how the organization is seen from a fairness and equity point of view; it may also produce similar tensions for the organization in terms of its ability to identify and communicate a coherent (and, importantly, shared) employment experience expected to be at the core of its employer-brand offering.

REFERENCES

Adams, J. S. 1963. Towards an understanding of inequity. *The Journal of Abnormal and Social Psychology*, 67(5), p.422.

Aaker, D. A. 1991. *Managing brand equity*. New York: The Free Press.

Albert, S., and Whetten, D. A. 1985. Organizational identity. *Research in Organizational Behaviour*, 7, pp.263–95.

Ambler, T., and Barrow, S. 1996. The employer brand. *Journal of Brand Management*, 4(3), pp.185–206.

Apple. 2016. https://www.apple.com/jobs/us/.

Atkinson, J. 1984. Manpower strategies for flexible organisations. *Personnel Management*, 16(8), pp.28–31.

Backhaus, K., and Tikoo, S. 2004. Conceptualizing and researching employer branding. *Career Development International*, 9(5), pp.501–17.

Becker, B. E., Huselid, M. A., and Beatty, R. W. 2009. *The differentiated workforce: transforming talent into strategic impact*. Boston: Harvard Business Press.

Blume, B. D., Rubin, R. S., and Baldwin, T. T. 2013. Who is attracted to an organization using a forced distribution performance management system? *Human Resource Management Journal*, 23(4), 360–78.

Cable, D. M., and Turban., D. B. 2003. The value of organizational reputation in the recruitment context: a brand-equity perspective. *Journal of Applied Social Psychology*, 33(11), pp.2244–66.

Cappelli, P. 2008. Talent management for the twenty-first century. *Harvard Business Review*, 86(3), pp.74–81.

Cappelli, P., and Keller, J. R. 2017. The historical context of talent management. In D. G. Collings, K. Mellahi, and W. Cascio, eds., *Oxford handbook of talent management*, pp.23–42. Oxford: Oxford University Press.

Cascio, W. F., and Graham, B. Z. (In press). New strategic role for HR: leading the employer-branding process. *Organization Management Journal*.

Chartered Institute of Personnel and Development. 2007. *Employer branding: a no nonsense approach*. CIPD guide.

Collings, D. G., and Mellahi, K. 2009. Strategic talent management: a review and research agenda. *Human Resource Management Review*, 19(4), pp.304–13.

Collings, D. G. 2014. Toward mature talent management: beyond shareholder value. *Human Resource Development Quarterly*, 25(3), pp.301–19.

Collings, D. G. 2017. Workforce differentiation. In D. G. Collings, K. Mellahi, and W. Cascio, eds., *Oxford handbook of talent management*, pp.301-17. Oxford: Oxford University Press.

Colquitt, J. A., Conlon, D. E., Wesson, M. J., Porter, C. O. et al. 2001. Justice at the millennium: a meta-analytic review of 25 years of organizational justice research. *Journal of Applied Psychology*, 86(3), pp.425–45.

Dell, D., and Ainspan, N. 2001. *Engaging employees through your brand*, The Conference Board, Report, No. R-1288-01-RR, April. Washington, DC.

Edwards, M. R., and Edwards, T. 2013. Employee responses to changing aspects of the employer brand following a multinational acquisition: a longitudinal study. *Human Resource Management*, 52(1), pp.27–54.

Edwards, M. R. 2005. Employer and employee branding: HR or PR? In S. Bach, ed., *Managing human resources: personnel management in transition*, 4th edn., pp.266–86. Malden: Blackwell Publishing.

Edwards, M. R. 2010. An integrative review of employer branding and OB theory. *Personnel Review*, 39(1), pp.5–23.

Edwards, M. R. 2012. Employer branding: developments and challenges. In S. Bach and M. R. Edwards, eds., *Managing human resources: human resource management in transition*, 5th edn. New York: John Wiley and Sons.

Edwards, M. R. 2014. Employer branding. In D. E. Guest and D. Needle, eds., *Wiley encyclopedia of human resource management*, Vol. 5. London: Human Resource Management: International HRM, Wiley.

Gallardo-Gallardo, E., Dries, N., and González-Cruz, T. F. 2013. What is the meaning of "talent" in the world of work? *Human Resource Management Review*, 23(4), pp.290–300.

Gelens, J., Dries, N., Hofmans, J., and Pepermans, R. 2013. The role of perceived organizational justice in shaping the outcomes of talent management: a research agenda. *Human Resource Management Review*, 23(4), pp.341–53.

Gelens, J., Hofmans, J., Dries, N., and Pepermans, R. 2014. Talent management and organizational justice: employee reactions to high potential identification. *Human Resource Management Journal*, 24(2), pp.159–75.

Guest, D. E. 2011. Human resource management and performance: still searching for some answers. *Human Resource Management Journal*, 21(1), pp.3–13.

Hanin, D., Stinglhamber, F., and Delobbe, N. 2013. The impact of employer branding on employees: the role of employment offering in the prediction of their affective commitment. *Psychologica Belgica*, 53(4), pp.57–83.

Highhouse, S., Thornbury, E. E., and Little, I. S. 2007. Social-identity functions of attraction to organizations. *Organizational Behavior and Human Decision Processes*, 103(1), pp.134–46.

Keller, K. L. 1993. Conceptualizing, measuring, and managing customer-based brand equity. *The Journal of Marketing*, 57(1), pp.1–22.

Kudret, S. 2015. The Perceived Employer Brand (PEB): a three-component conceptualisation and an exploration of its relationship with organisational commitment. Unpublished PhD Thesis, King's College London.

Lawler, E. E. 2011. Creating a new employment deal: total rewards and the new workforce. *Organizational Dynamics*, 40(4), pp.302–9.

Lepak, D. P., and Snell, S. A. 1999. The human resource architecture: toward a theory of human capital allocation and development. *Academy of Management Review*, 24(1), pp.31–48.

Lepak, D. P., Taylor, M. S., Tekleab, A. G., Marrone, J. A. et al. 2007. An examination of the use of high-investment human resource systems for core and support employees. *Human Resource Management*, 46(2), pp.223–46.

Lievens, F. 2007. Employer branding in the Belgian Army: the importance of instrumental and symbolic beliefs for potential applicants, actual applicants, and military employees. *Human Resource Management*, 46(1), pp.51–69.

Lievens, F., and Slaughter, J. E. 2016. Employer image and employer branding: what we know and what we need to know. *Annual Review of Organizational Psychology and Organizational Behavior*, 3, pp.407–40.

Martin, G., Beaumont, P., Doig, R., and Pate, J. 2005. Branding: a new performance discourse for HR? *European Management Journal*, 23(1), pp.76–88.

Marescaux, E., De Winne, S., and Sels, L. 2013. HR practices and affective organizational commitment: (when) does HR differentiation pay off? *Human Resource Management Journal*, 23(4), pp.329–45.

Martin, G. 2009. Driving corporate reputations from the inside: a strategic role and strategic dilemmas for HR? *Asia Pacific Journal of Human Resources*, 47(2), pp.219–35.

Meyers, M. C., De Boeck, G., and Dries, N. 2017. Talent or not? Employee reactions to talent designations. In D. G. Collings, K. Mellahi, and W. F. Cascio, eds., *Oxford handbook of talent management*, pp.169–92. Oxford: Oxford University Press.

Moroko, L., and Uncles, M. D. 2009. Employer branding and market segmentation. *Journal of Brand Management*, 17(3), pp.181–96.

O'Boyle, E., and Kroska, S. 2017. Star performers. In D. G. Collings, K. Mellahi, and W. Cascio, eds., *Oxford handbook of talent management*, pp.43–65. Oxford: Oxford University Press.

Pfeffer, J. 2001. Fighting the war for talent is hazardous to your organization's health. *Organizational Dynamics*, 29(4), pp.248–59.

Tuzuner, V. L., and Yuksel, C. A. 2009. Segmenting potential employees according to firms' employer attractiveness dimensions in the Employer Branding Concept. *Journal of Academic Research in Economics*, 1, pp.47–62.

CHAPTER 13

TALENT INTERMEDIARIES IN TALENT ACQUISITION

ROCIO BONET AND MONIKA HAMORI

13.1 INTRODUCTION

THE employment relationship has witnessed dramatic changes in the past decades. In much of the developed world, organizations have moved away from a model of lifetime employment and the practices that accompanied the lifetime-employment model, namely, long-term workforce planning, succession planning, and predictable internal career development (see Cappelli and Keller, 2017). This implies that talent needs to be found outside the boundaries of the firm (Bidwell, 2017). At the same time, many workers are opting for short-term employment, which they may find more lucrative and less constraining compared with long-term contracts. Over half of all job openings in large US corporations are filled by outside hires today (CareerXroads, 2014), and this percentage is likely higher in small employers. In a survey of 500 UK business leaders, 55% said that they are more likely to recruit externally to address skill shortages than to provide learning and development to talent inside the organization (Skillsoft, 2015). These data represent a significant change compared with data from the 1960s or 1970s, when close to 90% of vacancies were filled by internal candidates (Cappelli, 2008).

The increase in outside hiring has fostered businesses that match candidates to open jobs. Organizations also increasingly use temporary-help firms and contractors that establish work relations that are not employment per se (Cascio and Boudreau, 2017). In Europe, where legislation enforces the job security of full-time employees, the use of agency temporary employees is greater than in any other region.

We refer to the above businesses as talent intermediaries, entities that stand between the individual worker and the organization that needs work done. Talent intermediaries mediate between these two parties to facilitate, inform, or regulate how workers are matched to firms, how work is accomplished, and how conflicts are resolved (Autor, 2009).

Figure 13.1 shows all of the important types of intermediaries that operate in the labor market, and definitions for each. With the exception of membership-based intermediaries (e.g., unions or professional associations) and public sector intermediaries (such as unemployment agencies), all of these intermediaries operate in the private sector.

However, not all of these labor market intermediaries would qualify as talent intermediaries. Collings and Mellahi define *strategic talent management* as:

> activities and processes that involve the systematic identification of key positions which differentially contribute to the organization's sustainable competitive advantage, the development of a talent pool of high potential and high performing incumbents to fill these roles, and the development of a differentiated human resource architecture to facilitate filling these positions with competent incumbents and to ensure their continued commitment to the organization. (2009: 304)

Based on this definition, we'll focus this chapter only on certain types of intermediaries in the labor market—online talent intermediaries, which include job boards and social networking websites, and place and search firms, which include executive search firms, contingency search firms, and temporary-help agencies—because these types of intermediaries focus on supplying key high-potential and high-performing individuals to organizations.

Talent intermediaries play an important role in today's economy. They are taking over human resource functions that were performed by employers in the past. Corporate recruitment and selection practices, for example, disappear when organizations use search firms to hire talent. Employers' focus on outside hiring demolishes internal labor markets and the training, development, and succession planning associated with them. In place of the traditional bilateral employer–employee relationship, intermediaries create triangular relationships that make work organization more complex. For example, employee relations change when temporary-help service firms become the legal employer of workers and the client organizations merely supervise the workers.

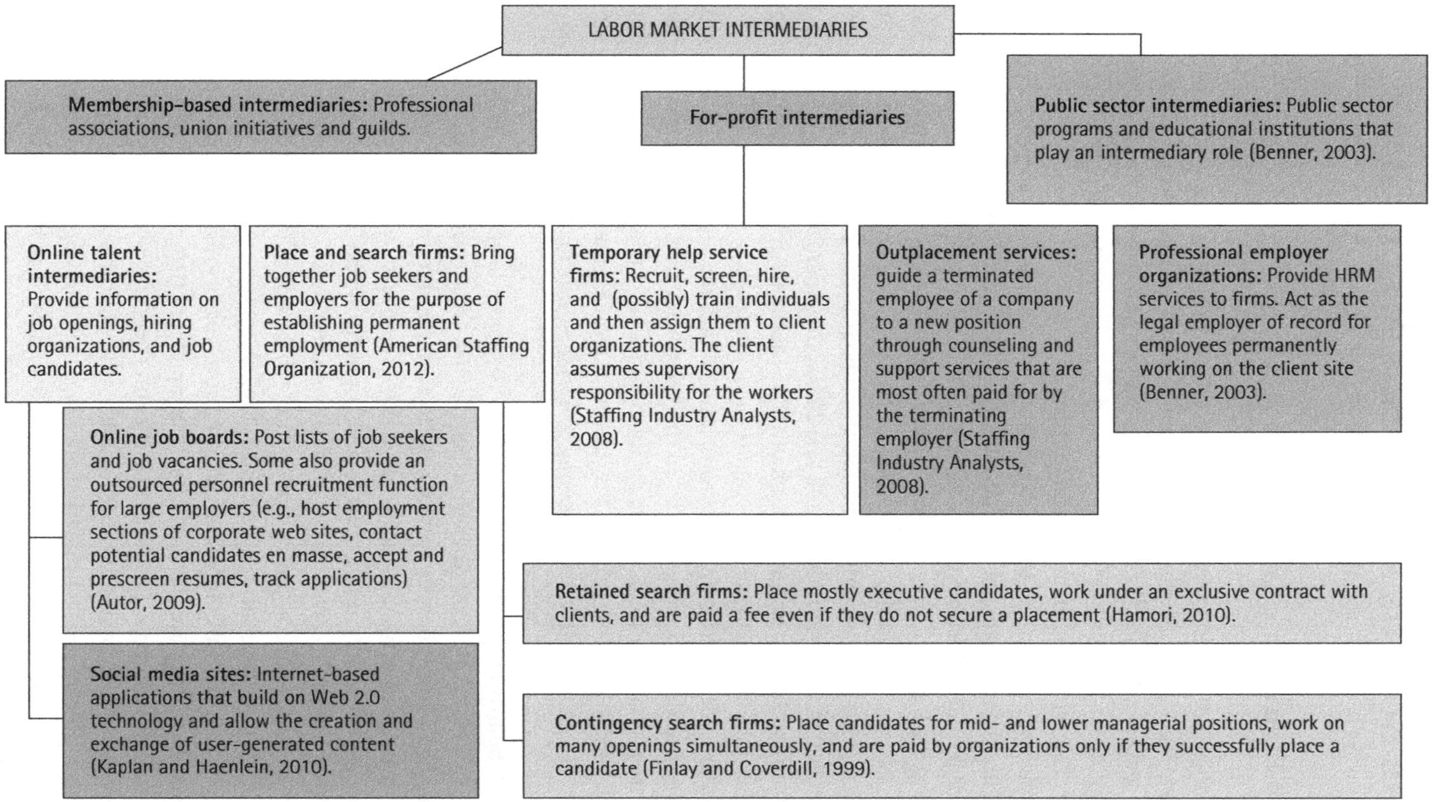

LABOR MARKET INTERMEDIARIES

Membership-based intermediaries: Professional associations, union initiatives and guilds.

Public sector intermediaries: Public sector programs and educational institutions that play an intermediary role (Benner, 2003).

For-profit intermediaries

Online talent intermediaries: Provide information on job openings, hiring organizations, and job candidates.

Place and search firms: Bring together job seekers and employers for the purpose of establishing permanent employment (American Staffing Organization, 2012).

Temporary help service firms: Recruit, screen, hire, and (possibly) train individuals and then assign them to client organizations. The client assumes supervisory responsibility for the workers (Staffing Industry Analysts, 2008).

Outplacement services: guide a terminated employee of a company to a new position through counseling and support services that are most often paid for by the terminating employer (Staffing Industry Analysts, 2008).

Professional employer organizations: Provide HRM services to firms. Act as the legal employer of record for employees permanently working on the client site (Benner, 2003).

Online job boards: Post lists of job seekers and job vacancies. Some also provide an outsourced personnel recruitment function for large employers (e.g., host employment sections of corporate web sites, contact potential candidates en masse, accept and prescreen resumes, track applications) (Autor, 2009).

Social media sites: Internet-based applications that build on Web 2.0 technology and allow the creation and exchange of user-generated content (Kaplan and Haenlein, 2010).

Retained search firms: Place mostly executive candidates, work under an exclusive contract with clients, and are paid a fee even if they do not secure a placement (Hamori, 2010).

Contingency search firms: Place candidates for mid- and lower managerial positions, work on many openings simultaneously, and are paid by organizations only if they successfully place a candidate (Finlay and Coverdill, 1999).

FIGURE 13.1 Labor Market Intermediaries

Adapted from Bonet, R., Cappelli, P., and Hamori, M. 2013. Labor market intermediaries and the new paradigm for human resources, *The Academy of Management Annals, 7*(1), p.339.

13.2 Online Talent Intermediaries: Job Boards and Social Media Sites

13.2.1 Job Boards

Online job boards match job seekers to job vacancies through the job advertisements that they post. They also give hiring organizations access to a large talent pool, by requiring the job seekers who use their services to register and provide demographic and career history data, which enables them to store detailed information on a large number of job seekers (Marchal, Mellet, and Rieucau, 2007).

In identifying suitable talent for a job opening, job boards have several advantages compared with hiring organizations that launch a talent search on their own. First of all, job boards provide information on a wider and more diverse pool of candidates than a single hiring organization may tap into (Parry and Wilson, 2008) because they have hundreds of job openings at the same time and typically cover more job functions and industries than hiring organizations do. Since job boards can present a huge amount of candidate-related information in just a few clicks, they increase hiring speed (Parry and Wilson, 2008). Owing to the large quantity of candidate-related information that they store, they may also facilitate the comparison of job seekers. A university job board, for example, provided hiring organizations information on the grades of individual students, as well as on the average grades in their database, enabling potential employers to compare a job seeker to the entire graduate population (Bagues and Sylos Labini, 2009). By allowing such a comparison, the job board reduced the risk of placing unsuitable job seekers into an open position owing to a lack of information on the applicants' characteristics.

How do job boards affect other aspects of the corporate talent-acquisition process? There is mixed evidence on whether they help hiring organizations secure talent. On the one hand, online job boards were found to facilitate the moves of the employed to another organization by making it easier for employers to identify passive (i.e., employed) candidates who may be open to other opportunities (Nakamura et al., 2008). Job boards also provide access to larger numbers of candidates. Nevertheless, job seekers typically apply for several job openings on a job board, which makes it harder to secure them for a particular job (Bagues and Sylos Labini, 2009).

Because job boards have information on more job candidates than individual employers may have, they are also more likely to facilitate a better candidate/job match. Freeman (2002), for example, proposes that the Internet can reach out to a much larger and diverse pool of candidates and break down "the old boys' networks." It can also demolish geographical barriers by posting openings in other geographical locations and helping individuals take jobs from lower-qualified applicants in local areas. Bagues and Sylos Labini (2009) document that the university job board that they looked at helped job seekers' moves across geographic areas, with most graduates ending up at employers that were located in regions other than the one where the individual graduated. They found that the monthly wages of graduates from universities that were associated with the job board increased by 3%, and job stability increased, too, again pointing to better job seeker/job match. They argued that the pool of job seekers and hiring organizations that intermediaries can tap into is larger, more diverse, and more geographically dispersed, which makes establishing the right match easier.

At the same time, job boards are found to create important biases in the corporate hiring process. Marchal, Mellet, and Rieucau (2007) show that job boards disadvantage applicants whose skill set spans several occupations or who have skills in emerging fields that are harder to find when searching with traditional search terms on the job board. They are also more likely to overlook credentials that could not be quantified or anticipated. Because job seekers are paired up by software with ads for which their work experience represents a match, they need both technical and semantic skills to navigate the job boards effectively and to be matched with the jobs of their choice. In sum, rather than simply connecting talent and job openings, job boards may screen candidates out in ways that do not serve the interests of the hiring organization (Marchal, Mellet, and Rieucau, 2007).

13.2.2 Social and Professional Networking (or Social Media) Websites

The users of social and professional networking sites create public profiles on the site and form relationships with other users. The largest professional social networking site, LinkedIn, started in 2003 and now has 400 million members in 200 countries. Much of the activity on LinkedIn is individuals looking for new jobs and corporations vetting candidates. In 2015, LinkedIn had 3 million active job openings at any one time. Of US employers, 94% say that they use LinkedIn to perform background checks on job applicants (DMR, 2015).

Research on social media sites is in its infancy. The available evidence suggests that social media sites may present a number of advantages in the talent-sourcing process: First of all, they have information on a broader segment of employees than a single employer may have. Second, they have more in-depth information that employers would have a hard time obtaining from other sources. In fact, the bulk of the existing research on social media sites addresses the use of that in-depth information, exploring whether social networking sites provide complete, cost-effective, and accurate candidate-related information (Brown and Vaughn, 2011; Slovensly and Ross, 2012) that observes legal and ethical norms (Brown and Vaughn, 2011; Clark and Roberts, 2010) in order for employers to reliably select candidates from among a pool of applicants. Social media sites enable their members to post as much information on themselves as they want to as well as to update it. This information is then sifted by hiring organizations on the basis of search criteria such as job function, geographic location, position, number of years of work experience, employer name, or university. Since most social media sites such as LinkedIn require users to display their real name, employers are able to see the comments or materials that they have posted or that others have posted about them (McGrath, 2012), which increases the reliability of the data. Social media sites also offer employers information on individuals who are happily employed in their jobs and not actively applying for jobs, enabling them to find high-performing "passive" candidates. In fact, professional networking sites help not only employing organizations but also other talent intermediaries, such as search firms and employment agencies, in identifying their pool of candidates.

13.2.2.1 *Search Firms*

The search firms that operate in the talent marketplace are of two types. Retained search firms are paid a standard fee irrespective of whether a candidate is hired by the client organization. Contingency search firms are paid only if a proposed candidate is hired. Search firms differ from online talent intermediaries in the functions that they perform. They not only aggregate and package the information on candidates, but also take an active role in the selection process: they act as the very first filter on the candidate pool by presenting only certain candidates to the client and have a huge impact on which candidate gets access to which job (King, Burke, and Pemberton, 2005). They also take an active part in matching job candidates to hiring organizations by mediating between clients and candidates and guaranteeing the quality of their placement, especially in the case of retained executive search firms.

Search firms bring many advantages to the corporate talent-acquisition process: they may facilitate higher-quality matches between individuals and hiring organizations than hiring organizations would achieve on their own, because they have access to a larger and more diverse pool of candidates as a result of the candidate-related information that they amassed in previous searches.

The pool of talent that search firms have access to is different from the pool that client organizations may tap into. Both retained and contingency search firms tend to reach out to employed individuals who are satisfied and productive in their positions, are not seeking jobs, and may therefore remain hidden from hiring organizations (Cappelli and Hamori, 2014; Finlay and Coverdill, 1999). While hiring organizations may wait for resumes to come in after a job advertisement is posted, contingency search firms are shown to be full-time talent seekers (Finlay and Coverdill, 1999), spending a lot of time identifying and tracking talent—even passive candidates, whom they consider to be easily moveable if an attractive offer presents itself.

In principle, search firms should also enjoy an advantage compared with hiring organizations in having more accurate information on each candidate, because they have greater experience and expertise in collecting and checking candidate-related information (Bidwell and Fernandez-Mateo, 2010; King, Burke, and Pemberton, 2005). The issue of whether search firms indeed have more accurate information on job candidates, however, is a debated one. On the one hand, search firms were found to obtain more accurate information on each candidate than hiring organizations did if they had a longer-term relationship with the candidate (i.e., they had previously placed or were trying to place the candidate) and therefore had "private" information on him or her (King, Burke, and Pemberton, 2005; Bidwell and Fernandez-Mateo, 2010).

Conceptual work by Biglaiser (1993) proposes that search firms may be better in assessing candidates than hiring organizations are, because they have more expertise in this area. Furthermore, they have to protect their own reputation in order to be able to run their business, which forces them to put effort into detecting candidate characteristics accurately. Accurate assessment is especially important for retained search firms that guarantee the quality of their placements and take on the responsibility to replace a candidate at no additional cost to the client company if performance problems arise in the first year (Cepin, 2012).

Other researchers, however, question the superior skill set of search firms in candidate assessment. Clark (1992) finds that executive search firms did not use more valid selection tools (i.e., tools that were able to forecast candidates' future on-the-job performance more accurately) than client organizations did. Of executive search firms, 88% used reference checks, one of the least valid selection tools, and many search firms resorted to two other tools of low validity: unstructured interviews (i.e., interviews with a random set of questions) and graphology (i.e., detecting applicant personality traits from analyzing their handwriting; Clark, 1992). Executive search firms used these tools despite their low validity because they argued that their role lay not in assessing candidates but rather in mediating between the candidate and the client, in an effort to ease the moves of executives between jobs.

Similar to Clark (1992), Khurana's (2002) ethnographic study shows that the assessment undertaken by executive search consultants does not improve search efficiency. Search consultants often base their decision on CEO qualities such as "chemistry," "articulation," or "stature." It is questionable whether these attributes relate at all to on-the-job performance. Search consultants also heavily rely on the visible characteristics of the candidates such as their previous position and previous employer. They focus on executives who work at peer organizations, especially well-performing and reputable ones, while they often ignore less visible candidate characteristics such as job performance. Khurana (2002) concludes that the real advantage of search firms over corporate clients lies not in the type of information that they may have, but in their ability to mediate between candidates and the client organization.

Finally, Bidwell (2011) finds that professionals who are hired from the outside through an executive search firm or an employment agency perform worse than those who are promoted from the inside or come from the outside through employee referrals and unsolicited hires. Bidwell (2011) argues that it is unlikely that the hires that came through a search firm misrepresented their knowledge and skills during the search process. Since they were already employed, they had little motivation to do so. Rather, the hiring organization may have placed too much trust in the search firms that it contracted and underestimated the challenges that the hires may face in the new environment (see also Bidwell, 2017).

Besides talent identification and selection, search firms also play an important intermediary role. They are often called in to mediate in situations in which the firm needs to find a replacement for an incumbent who is still in place, a task that may be politically difficult for internal human resource executives to handle (Shulman and Chiang, 2007). In other cases, client organizations may want to hire talent from direct competitors, which may also be too risky for corporate recruiters to do (Brooks, 2007).

What kind of impact do the identification, assessment, and mediation activities of search firms have on the talent composition and talent processes of hiring organizations? Search firms may increase the rate of voluntary turnover by presenting job opportunities to individuals who are not searching for jobs (Cappelli and Hamori, 2014; Finlay and Coverdill, 1999; Khurana, 2002). Retained executive search firms believe that attracting "hard to move" individuals to client companies is one of their most important roles.

Search firms are also effective in finding jobs for the individuals whom they represent. In the film industry, core agencies increased the chances of scriptwriters whom they represented getting jobs (Bielby and Bielby, 1999). The agency's influence was so important that the impact of the scriptwriters' past successes on the probability of finding the next assignment diminished when the moves were mediated by a search firm.

The efficiency of search firms in placing candidates, however, also introduces biases to the hiring process and distorts organizational talent pools. Search firms were found to be more likely to place white males in open positions than females or racial minorities, because they were also disproportionately more likely to collect information on white male professionals. The candidates in the databases of the executive search firms that belonged to a professional association were 89% male, 88% white, and 71% from middle-income, white-collar socioeconomic backgrounds (Dreher, Lee, and Clerkin, 2011). Among the film scriptwriters studied by Bielby and Bielby (1999), females, racial minorities, and older scriptwriters were less likely to secure the representation of an agency. Fernandez-Mateo and King (2011) found that a large staffing firm was less likely to present women for high-paid projects. Researchers, however, could only guess at why gender-, race-, and age-based discrimination takes place in the search process: it is possible that search firms will have less information about female and minority managers and executives (Dreher, Lee, and Clerkin, 2011); or, while skills are a prerequisite for jobs, it is the "chemistry" or the fit between the applicant and the organization that is important in making a match, and it is less risky to present a candidate who is socially similar to the hiring managers in the client organization (Coverdill and Finlay, 1998; Dreher, Lee, and Clerkin, 2011).

Search firms also introduce biases that reflect their own preferences: to ensure the high quality of the individuals whom they place, they follow a "conservative" approach in identifying talent. They overwhelmingly choose executives whose organizations are featured in prominent business rankings such as those by *Fortune* magazine or *Business Week*. The actual performance of executives from "high-status" organizations matters less for the selection (Khurana, 2002). Quantitative analyses of a large multinational executive search firm's database by Hamori (2010) confirm Khurana's findings: executive search firms were more likely to store information on executives from large, well-performing, reputable companies in their databases. Of the executives, 34% worked for organizations that were among *Fortune* magazine's "America's Most Admired" or "Global Most Admired." Of the employers, 36% were on either the Fortune 500 or the Forbes 500 list. In a similar vein, search firms were shown to favor candidates with high-status credentials such as graduate degrees from elite schools, international work experience, and a lack of career interruptions (Clerkin, 2005). Additional biases resulted from search firms' lack of target-job-specific knowledge, which led to applying excessively universal selection criteria to the assignment and screened out worthy candidates (Ammons and Glass, 1988).

A final driver of the biases in the talent-identification process is the candidate's history with the matchmaker. The probability that the employment agency would consider an individual for a job opening decreased with the number of times that the individual had been considered, but not chosen, for previous placements, and increased if the individual had actually been placed before (King, Burke, and Pemberton, 2005). Individuals' history with the agency was more important in listing them for a job opening than were the candidate's work experiences or skills.

What is the impact of search firms on salaries? There is ample evidence showing that search firms manage to obtain higher pay for the individuals whom they place into a job than the individuals would have negotiated on their own: Scriptwriters represented by core agencies in the film industry had higher earnings than did writers represented by noncore agencies or writers without representation (Bielby and Bielby, 1999). Candidates who used contingency and retained search firms received higher initial offers than those using any other method of referral did, and negotiated higher increases to that initial offer than candidates who used any other method of referral except for referral by a friend (Seidel, Polzer, and Stewart, 2000). The initial disadvantage in salary offers for minority and female candidates diminished when these candidates were referred by search firms. Seidel, Polzer, and Stewart (2000) concluded that "headhunters" were trusted, and their recommendations were treated similarly to employees' referrals. Finally, Bidwell (2011) also found that "intermediated" hires had a higher salary and a higher total compensation than did hires from other recruitment sources, including unsolicited applications, employee referrals, rehired former employees, or temporary workers. Whether higher salaries result in higher labor costs will depend on other factors such as whether talent that is brought through a search firm tends to exhibit less turnover or whether it tends to be a better fit with the firm, and therefore ends up performing better. The scarce existing evidence on this seems to suggest that those brought through the search agency did worse than employees brought through other means such as referrals (Bidwell, 2011).

The quality of candidates' ties to the search firm played an important role in setting salary levels. The length and the intensity of the relationship between the search firm and the candidate predicted pay level better than did traditional human capital factors such as years of work experience, the candidate's skill set, or tenure at past employer. Clerkin (2005) found that the total number of contacts that executives had with executive search firms was positively related to their pay level, frequency of promotions, and subjective career success. Dreher and colleagues (2011) showed that executives who had regular contacts with search firms fared much better in pay when changing employers. "Core" search firms (i.e., the ones that assumed a central and high-status role in the labor markets that they served) were able to secure even higher pay levels because of the important signaling and candidate certification functions that they provided to their candidates (Bielby and Bielby, 1999).

13.2.2.2 *Temporary-Help Service Firms*

Temporary-help service firms (THS) directly hire workers, become their legal employer of record, and supply their workers to a client organization with which they have established a contractual relationship (Cappelli and Keller, 2013). THS play an important role in sourcing talent for organizations. While traditionally THS were mostly used by companies to achieve numerical flexibility by delivering warm bodies on time and at a low cost (Peck and Theodore, 1998), which would hardly qualify as talent, later years have seen an increase in the role of THS in providing highly specialized workers who may be needed only for a specific project or period of time, such as interim managers or workers with very specialized technical skills (Matusik and Hill, 1998). According to the Ciett 2015 economic report, providing short-term access to key strategic skills was rated as one of the most important benefits of using THS workers. Not only may THS play a key role in providing specific hard-to-find skills, but they also allow organizations to pay higher market wages at the margin to get additional workers without necessarily disrupting the pay of core employees. Hospitals, for example, offered higher wages to new agency nurses than to permanent ones in a tight labor market in order to avoid having to raise the wages of their regular workforce (Houseman, Kalleberg, and Erickcek, 2003). THS thus serve as a vehicle to circumvent the rigidities imposed by the internal structure of the firm and may be particularly relevant for companies that have difficulties in attracting hard-to-get talent at their current pay levels.

All THS engage in hiring workers and placing them in the client organizations. In addition, THS may also undertake other talent-management responsibilities, such as the induction, training, and performance monitoring of workers, although there is substantial variation with respect to the amount and type of the other talent-management responsibilities undertaken.

What about the quality of the matches THS form and the benefits and costs associated with the talent they bring in? THS may help by reducing uncertainty about the unobserved ability, skills, and values of the worker, which in turn determines the quality of the job-person fit. In addition, THS may improve the quality of the matches by shaping the skills, attitudes, and behaviors of their temporary workers, a function previously carried out within organizations.

There are several reasons to expect that the quality of the matches will improve when workers are hired through THS. First, THS allow firms to screen workers before hiring them for their permanent ranks. Cappelli and Keller (2013) find that about 2% of the workforce in a typical US establishment is hired from the ranks of that establishment's agency-based temporary workforce. For establishments that use temporary agencies, 4.5% of their employees are hired from that "temp" pool. Matches between the individual and the employer should be better through a THS because both the individual and the employer have experience with each other before agreeing to the match (Kvasnicka, 2009).

THS may also improve the quality of their matches because they usually prescreen workers, both for general skills and for the specific requirements of client firms or work assignments. The screening functions of THS firms are especially important for highly skilled individuals: those who had previously worked at a THS firm were more likely to obtain permanent employment and less likely to move to new jobs compared with workers who had been hired directly by a client firm. In addition, THS may learn from their workers as they place them in different jobs. Fernandez-Mateo (2007) found that workers who have been affiliated with the THS firm for longer periods of time receive higher pay rates, suggesting better matches between the THS firm and the workers.

While THS may help improve the quality of the matches, the issue of developing THS workers after their placement is problematic. The temporary aspect of THS work is likely to diminish the incentives of both firms to invest in workers. Client organizations may have little incentive to train THS employees beyond the skills needed to perform the current job, as they will not have the chance to capitalize on their investment (Nollen, 1996). Empirical studies have provided indirect support for this argument. For example, Davis-Blake and Uzzi (1993) found that companies were less likely to use temporaries in jobs that required high degrees of firm-specific training. Although they looked at directly hired temporaries, we may expect the same pattern for THS workers. In fact, Cappelli and Keller (2013) found that establishments that trained workers less were more likely to use THS workers.

THS firms themselves, however, have been found to provide their temporary workers with general training, usually in end-user computer skills or similar (see, e.g., Krueger, 1993; Autor, 2001). Interestingly, THS workers typically are offered the opportunity to receive such training upfront on their own time (Krueger, 1993; Autor, 2001; Benner, Leete, and Pastor, 2007). Autor (2001) argues that this training (tightly coupled with worker skills testing) is a screening device to identify good workers, but higher-skilled temporary workers can also be billed at a higher rate, which works in the agency's favour. Obviously, this statement implies that THS may have access to deep knowledge about what skills are necessary in the client company, an assumption that is sometimes questionable (Benner, Leete, and Pastor, 2007).

As in the general notion of human resource strategy, the employment arrangements for THS employees may ultimately depend on the objectives of the client organizations. When THS are used to acquire highly specialized skills that are hard to find in the market, THS may have an incentive to do a better job in developing the skills of the workers. Peck and Theodore (1998) found that those THS whose main task was to offer qualitative in addition to numerical flexibility and who acted more as a strategic partner in deals that required workers that are more specialized tended to provide their workers with higher levels of training. Similarly, Lautsch (2002) found that THS workers enjoyed better training in contexts where firms used agency workers to provide flexibility and where technology was not easily adjustable because the client needed to integrate temporary workers with core employees.

Another way THS may affect the quality of the match is by shaping the attitudes and behaviors of their workers. THS may help to shape workers' affective commitments toward the agency and the client organization in which they are placed by providing support to their workers (Liden, Wayne, Kraimer, and Sparrowe, 2003; Connelly, Gallagher, and Gilley, 2007). As in the traditional employment relationship, social-exchange processes have been found to be an important determinant of commitment across the THS agency and the client organization. When workers perceive high organizational support from the agency through factors such as career support, communication, quality of the facilities and interpersonal supportiveness, they reciprocate by increasing their commitment and loyalty toward the agency (Liden, Wayne, Kraimer, and Sparrowe, 2003; Connelly, Gallagher, and Gilley, 2007; Luo, Mann, and Holden, 2010; Van Breugel, Van Olffen, and Olie, 2005). Importantly, the support from the client organization also leads to higher commitment toward the client (Coyle-Shapiro, Morrow, and Kessler, 2006; Liden, Wayne, Kraimer, and Sparrowe, 2003; Connelly, Gallagher, and Gilley, 2007).

In addition, fair treatment and perceived organizational support (i.e., employees' global beliefs concerning the extent to which the organization values their contributions and cares about their well-being) from the client company and from the intermediary have been shown to lead to higher organizational citizenship behavior (Connelly, Gallagher, and Webster, 2011; Liden, Wayne, Kraimer, and Sparrowe, 2003) and to reduce counterproductive behaviors (Connelly, Gallagher, and Webster, 2011) at each organization. There is also some evidence that perceptions formed in one organizational context may spill over and affect attitudes and behaviors in the other context. For example, Connelly and colleagues (2011) found that when the client company treated agency employees fairly, employees showed behaviors toward the agency that were more positive. Similarly, employees' perceptions of fair treatment by the temporary agency related positively to organizational citizenship behaviors at the client organization and reduced counterproductive behaviors. George and colleagues (2010) found that opportunities for development in the client organization produced spillover effects on positive behaviors at the agency. However, they also found evidence for negative spillover effects. In particular, when one organization clearly expressed demands about the performance of a particular role, workers exerted higher extra-role behaviors toward that organization (i.e., they were willing to go beyond the explicit terms in their job contracts, even if the immediate returns for the employee were uncertain)—and that increase came at the cost of extra-role behaviors at the other organization. This implies that client companies should pay attention to the type of THS practices when hiring talent from them as they probably will affect how these workers end up performing.

Another interesting question that arises is whether the talent brought by THS companies is more or less expensive than that brought through other sources. From a labor-cost perspective, does it make sense to use THS to bring talent to the organization?

One of the main reasons why firms may use THS workers is because they allow them to bring workers at higher pay rates that would be impossible to give if they were direct employees without disrupting the internal equity of the firm. Similarly, client firms may find an advantage when using temporary workers, as they are not required by regulation to pay them the same benefits they pay their permanent employees. In addition, if workers are only needed on a temporary basis, neither the client organization nor the agency may have incentives to nurture its relationships with employees; thus providing generous benefits will be less important for this type of worker. The issue of whether using THS workers ends up reducing labor costs is remarkably underexplored. In some cases, even if the company may want to hire the employees directly, they may not have that option because employees may prefer to be employed through a THS agency to enjoy greater pay and less commitment (see also Cascio and Boudreau, 2017). As a recent article in the *Financial Times* states, "in roles such as engineering and IT, the same companies that are hiring contractors also have open permanent roles. They are looking for permanent workers but they cannot find them" (Cadman, 2015).

Importantly, also, THS may affect the retention of the talent directly employed by their clients. Research has found that when companies blend THS workers and standard employees, they introduce job competition, threatening the security and mobility opportunities of standard employees (Davis-Blake, Broschak, and George, 2003; Broschak and Davis-Blake, 2006; Way, Lepak, Fay, and Thacker, 2010). In addition, THS workers are likely to make the jobs of their standard employees more demanding because they typically have less firm-specific knowledge, receive little training and orientation from the client company, and require more help and time from regular employees, which are rarely compensated (Broschak and Davis-Blake, 2006). As a result, directly employed workers have been found to show lower loyalty toward the organization and higher intentions to leave when THS are hired (George, 2003; Davis-Blake, Broschak, and George, 2003). Other evidence shows, however, that the use of temporary workers reduces the voluntary turnover of permanent workers across all skill levels in the organization (Bonet, Elvira, and Visintin, 2015), which suggests that THS may serve as a complement and not a substitute for permanent workers (e.g., as helping hands) and that companies may still be able to retain talent in key positions when using talented THS workers. Interestingly, also, THS may help in developing permanent employees by positively affecting the learning curve of incumbent employees through new ideas and a fresh look at organizational routines and processes (Matusik and Hill, 1998; Wiersma, 2007).

13.3 CONCLUSIONS AND FUTURE RESEARCH DIRECTIONS

Talent intermediaries are changing many aspects of contemporary workplaces, including how employees are managed in them. In the past, organizations needed to have recruiting and selection operations to be able to hire workers. Now they can go to search firms or to staffing agencies that provide a ready-made workforce. They no longer need a performance-evaluation process to manage the performance of the individuals who work for them, nor do they need processes to determine pay levels. These practices may be turned over to THS firms. Employers no longer need to do any workforce or career planning. Rather, they may address talent-management needs on a "just-in-time" basis, by relying on talent intermediaries. The entire talent-management process may now be pushed onto a marketplace of vendors.

Although many organizations may still follow the standard corporate talent-management practices that are based on internalizing the tasks of workforce management, it is no longer possible to ignore the large proportion of employers that do not, or to think of talent intermediaries as exceptions to standard practices. While academic researchers have started to address the role that intermediaries play in transforming the labor market, and consequently the employment outcomes for individuals and organizations, there are still many unanswered questions that deserve future attention. We examine them below.

13.3.1 Understanding the Effect of Intermediaries on Organizational Outcomes

Most studies about the effectiveness of different human resource practices have focused on a regular, full-time workforce that is entirely managed by the organization that employs them. But how do the conclusions of academic research about the effectiveness of alternative human resources management practices change when we add talent intermediaries to the picture? To what extent are intermediaries more effective than organizations are in managing human capital?

Talent intermediaries allow organizations to implement a just-in-time or a "talent-on-demand" (Cappelli, 2008) model of talent acquisition. However, this model may not be equally suitable for all organizations. Organizations that require more firm-specific skills or that have a strong corporate culture are less likely to benefit from using intermediaries to acquire workers for strategic positions, instead of developing their own talent. Existing research needs to focus on understanding the potential contingencies that influence the value of talent intermediaries for the organization. Factors such as the culture of the organization, the specificity of the skills required in a job at a given company, or the density of employees' social networks within the firm could all diminish the benefits of using intermediaries to source talent.

At the same time, by favoring interorganizational mobility talent intermediaries may facilitate the transmission of human and social capital across organizations, either fostering or hindering organizational performance. Existing research has investigated the performance consequences of interorganizational employee mobility and has found that the performance consequences of interorganizational employee mobility depend, among other things, on whether employees move to competitors or cooperators (Somaya, Williamson, and Lorinkova, 2008), on whether employees are moving to closely located versus remotely located companies (Corredoira and Rosenkopf, 2010), or on the type of employee that is moving outside the organization (Campbell, Ganco, Franco, and Agarwal, 2012; Dokko and Rosenkopf, 2010). Since a crucial role of talent intermediaries is to facilitate these types of moves, we may expect these intermediaries to have a pronounced effect on organizational performance. Future research could integrate the findings of the studies on interorganizational employee mobility to analyze how talent intermediaries may be shaping organizational performance.

In addition, the use of talent intermediaries may lead to a blended workforce managed with different employment practices, which has important performance consequences. For example, if the workers employed by the intermediary (e.g., temporary workers or contractors) see that their equivalent permanent workers in the organization receive very different treatment from them, they may be less willing to collaborate or share knowledge with them. Similarly, permanent workers may resent the presence of intermediary workers who are paid much higher salaries than they are, even when this comes at the cost of lower security for the temporary workers. As a result, knowledge integration in the organization is less likely to happen in the presence of both types of workers. Companies that rely strongly on coordination among workers may see a greater reduction the benefits of using intermediary workers than those in which work can be done more independently.

13.3.2 Talent Intermediaries and Careers

Talent intermediaries have an important effect on how careers unfold. They play a gatekeeper role, introducing their own biases to the selection process. Their reputation and networks may constrain the types of jobs and opportunities candidates get. Some intermediaries have been found to make information more transparent and harder to misrepresent by workers (see, e.g., Leung, 2014). Future research needs to investigate how intermediaries shape careers and how the characteristics of intermediaries, such as their size or reputation or the length and the quality of their ties with the individuals that they represent, substitute or complement traditional predictors of career success such as individuals' previous records of work experience, educational background, or demographic attributes.

In summary, we believe that talent intermediaries are very important to the practice of management. Their presence alters many of the assumptions that underlie a great deal of knowledge about managing employees. Yet our academic understanding of them is currently quite limited compared with their prevalence in the labor market.

264 ROCIO BONET AND MONIKA HAMORI

REFERENCES

Ammons, D. N., and Glass, J. J. 1988. Headhunters in local government: use of executive search firms in managerial selection. *Public Administration Review*, 48(3), pp.687–93.

Autor, D. 2001. Why do temporary help firms provide free general skills training? *Quarterly Journal of Economics*, 116, pp.1409–48.

Autor, D. H. 2009. Studies of labor market intermediation: introduction. In D. Autor, ed., *Studies of labor market intermediation*, pp.1–26. Chicago: University of Chicago Press.

Bagues, M., and Sylos Labini, M. 2009. Do on-line talent intermediaries matter? The impact of AlmaLaurea on the university-to-work transition. In D. Autor, ed., *Studies of labor market intermediation*, pp.127–54. Chicago: University of Chicago Press.

Benner, C., Leete, L., and Pastor, M. 2007. *Staircases or treadmills? Talent intermediaries and economic opportunity in a changing economy*. New York: Russell Sage Foundation.

Bidwell, M. J. 2011. Paying more to get less: the effects of external hiring versus internal mobility. *Administrative Science Quarterly*, 56(3), pp.369–407.

Bidwell, M. 2017. Managing talent flows through internal and external labor markets. In D. G. Collings, K. Mellahi, and W. F. Cascio, eds., *Oxford handbook of talent management*. Oxford: Oxford University Press.

Bidwell, M., and Fernandez-Mateo, I. 2010. Relationship duration and returns to brokerage in the staffing sector. *Organization Science*, 21(6), pp.1141–58.

Bielby, W. T., and Bielby, D. D. 1999. Organizational mediation of project-based labor markets: talent agencies and the careers of screenwriters. *American Sociological Review*, 64, pp.54–85.

Biglaiser, G. 1993. Middlemen as experts. *RAND Journal of Economics*, 24(2), pp.212–23.

Bonet, R., Elvira, M., and Visintin, S. 2015. The consequences of temporary hiring on individual voluntary turnover: a longitudinal examination. Working Paper. IESE Business School and IE Business School, Madrid, Spain.

Brooks, S. 2007. Getting a hand hiring top talent. *Restaurant Business*, 106(10), pp.22–6.

Broschak, J. P., and Davis-Blake, A. 2006. Mixing standard work and nonstandard deals: the consequences of heterogeneity in employment arrangements. *Academy of Management Journal*, 49(2), pp.371–93.

Brown, V. R., and Vaughn, E. D. 2011. The writing on the (Facebook) wall: the use of social networking sites in hiring decisions. *Journal of Business Psychology*, 26(2), pp.219–25.

Cadman, E. 2015. Employers tap 'gig' economy in search of freelancers. *Financial Times*, September 6, 2015.

Campbell, B. A., Ganco, M., Franco, A. M., and Agarwal, R. 2012. Who leaves, where to, and why worry? Employee mobility, entrepreneurship and effects on source firm performance. *Strategic Management Journal*, 33(1), pp.65–87.

Cappelli, P. 2008. *Talent on demand*. Boston: Harvard Business School Press.

Cappelli, P., and Hamori, M. 2014. Understanding executive search. *Organization Science*, 25(5), pp.1511–29.

Cappelli, P., and Keller, JR. 2013. A study of the extent and potential causes of alternative employment arrangements. *Industrial and Labor Relations Review*, 66(4), pp.874–901.

Cappelli, P., and Keller, JR. 2017. The historical context of talent management. In D.G. Collings, K. Mellahi, and W.F. Cascio, eds., *Oxford handbook of talent management*. Oxford: Oxford University Press.

CareerXroads. 2014. Sources of hire study. Retrieved from http://www.careerxroads.com/news/2014_SourceOfHire.pdf.

Cascio, W. F., and Boudreau, J. 2017. Talent management on non-traditional employees. In D. G. Collings, K. Mellahi, and W. F. Cascio, eds., *Oxford handbook of talent management*. Oxford: Oxford University Press.

Cepin, G. C. 2012. Choose wisely when hiring a search firm to recruit for key positions. *CPA Practice Management Forum*, 8(10), 8–11.

Ciett. 2015. About the industry—overview. Retrieved from http://www.wecglobal.org/fileadmin/templates/ciett/docs/Leaflet_Ciett.pdf.

Clark, L. A., and Roberts, S. J. 2010. Employers' use of social networking sites: a socially irresponsible practice. *Journal of Business Ethics*, 95(4), pp.507–25.

Clark, T. 1992. Management selection by executive recruitment consultancies: a survey and explanation of selection methods. *Journal of Managerial Psychology*, 7(6), pp.3–10.

Clerkin, T. 2005. *An exploratory study of the antecedents and consequences of relationships with executive search firms: implications for a model of career attainment*. Unpublished doctoral dissertation, Indiana University.

Collings, D. G., and Mellahi, K. 2009. Strategic talent management: a review and research agenda. *Human Resource Management Review*, 19(4), 304–13.

Connelly, C. E., Gallagher, D. G., and Gilley, K. M. 2007. Organizational and client commitment among contracted employees: a replication and extension with temporary workers. *Journal of Vocational Behavior*, 70(2), pp.326–35.

Connelly, C. E., Gallagher, D. G., and Webster, J. 2011. Predicting temporary agency workers' behaviors. Justice, volition, and spillover. *Career Development International*, 16(2), pp.178–94.

Corredoira, R. A., and Rosenkopf, L. 2010. Should auld acquaintance be forgot? The reverse transfer of knowledge through mobility ties. *Strategic Management Journal*, 31(2), pp.159–81.

Coverdill, J. E., and Finlay, W. 1998. Fit and skill in employee selection: insights from a study of headhunters. *Qualitative Sociology*, 21(2), pp.105–27.

Coyle-Shapiro, J. A., Morrow, P. C., and Kessler, I. 2006. Serving two organizations: exploring the employment relationship of contracted employees. *Human Resource Management*, 45(4), pp.561–83.

Davis-Blake, A., Broschak, J. P., and George, E. 2003. Happy together? How using nonstandard workers affects exit, voice, and loyalty among standard employees. *Academy of Management Journal*, 46(4), pp.475–85.

Davis-Blake, A., and Uzzi, B. 1993. Determinants of employment externalization: a study of temporary workers and independent contractors. *Administrative Science Quarterly*, 38(2), pp.195–223.

DMR (Digital Marketing Ramblings). 2015. LinkedIn Company Page and Group Statistics. Retrieved from http://expandedramblings.com/index.php/linkedin-business-page-and-group-statistics/.

Dokko, G., and Rosenkopf, L. 2010. Social capital for hire? Mobility of technical professionals and firm influence in wireless standards committees. *Organization Science*, 21(3), pp.677–95.

Dreher, G. F., Lee, J., and Clerkin, T. A. 2011. Mobility and cash compensation: the moderating effects of gender, race, and executive search firms. *Journal of Management*, 37(3), pp.651–81.

Fernandez-Mateo, I. 2007. Who pays the price of brokerage? Transferring constraint through price setting in the staffing sector. *American Sociological Review*, 72(2), pp.291–317.

Fernandez-Mateo, I., and King, Z. 2011. Anticipatory sorting and gender segregation in temporary employment. *Management Science*, 57(6), pp.989–1008.

Finlay, W., and Coverdill, J. E. 1999. The search game: organizational conflicts and the use of headhunters. *Sociological Quarterly*, 40(1), pp.11–30.

Freeman, R. B. 2002. The labour market in the new information economy. *Oxford Review of Economic Policy*, 18(3), pp.288–305.

George, E. 2003. External solutions and internal problems: the effects of employment externalization on internal workers' attitudes. *Organization Science*, 14(4), pp.386–402.

George, E., Levenson, A., Finegold, D., and Chattopadhyay, P. 2010. Extra-role behaviors among temporary workers: how firms create relational wealth in the United States of America. *International Journal of Human Resource Management*, 21(4), pp.530–50.

Hamori, M. 2010. Who gets headhunted—and who gets ahead? The impact of search firms on executive careers. *Academy of Management Perspectives*, 24(4), pp.46–59.

Houseman, S. N., Kalleberg, A. L., and Erickcek, G. A. 2003. The role of temporary agency employment in tight labor markets. *Industrial & Labor Relations Review*, 57(1), pp.105–27.

Khurana, R. 2002. *Searching for a corporate savior: the irrational quest for charismatic CEOs*. Princeton, NJ: Princeton University Press.

King, Z., Burke, S., and Pemberton, J. 2005. The "bounded" career: an empirical study of human capital, career mobility, and employment outcomes in a mediated labor market. *Human Relations*, 58(8), pp.981–1007.

Kvasnicka, M. 2009. Does temporary help work provide a stepping stone to regular employment? In D. Autor, ed., *Studies of labor market intermediation*, pp.335–72. Chicago: University of Chicago Press.

Krueger, A. B. 1993. How computers have changed the wage structure: evidence from microdata, 1984–1989. *Quarterly Journal of Economics*, 108(1), pp.33–60.

Lautsch, B. A. 2002. Uncovering and explaining variance in the features and outcomes of contingent work. *Industrial & Labor Relations Review*, 56(1), pp.23–43.

Leung, M. D. 2014. Dilettante or renaissance person? How the order of job experiences affects hiring in an external labor market. *American Sociological Review*, 79(1), pp.136–58.

Liden, R. C., Wayne, S. J., Kraimer, M. L., and Sparrowe, R. T. 2003. The dual commitments of contingent workers: an examination of contingents' commitment to the agency and the organization. *Journal of Organizational Behavior*, 24(5), pp.609–25.

Luo, T., Mann, A., and Holden, R. 2010. The expanding role of temporary help services from 1990 to 2008. *Monthly Labor Review*, August, pp.3–16.

Marchal, E., Mellet, K., and Rieucau, G. 2007. Job board toolkits: Internet matchmaking and changes in job advertisements. *Human Relations*, 60(7), pp.1091–113.

Matusik, S. F., and Hill, C. W. 1998. The utilization of contingent work, knowledge creation, and competitive advantage. *Academy of Management Review*, 23(4), pp.680–97.

McGrath, L. C. 2012. Social media and employment: is there a limit? *Interdisciplinary Journal of Contemporary Research in Business*, 4(1), pp.17–24.

Nakamura, A. O., Shaw, K. L., Freeman, R. B., Nakamura, E. et al. 2009. Jobs online. In D. Autor, ed., *Studies of labor market intermediation*, pp.27–65. Chicago: University of Chicago Press.

Nollen, S. D. 1996. Negative aspects of temporary employment. *Journal of Labor Research*, 17(4), pp.567–82.

Parry, E., and Wilson, H. 2009. Factors influencing the adoption of online recruitment. *Personnel Review*, 38(6), pp.655–73.

Peck, J., and Theodore, N. 1998. The business of contingent work: growth and restructuring in Chicago's temporary employment industry. *Work Employment & Society*, 12(4), pp.655–74.

Seidel, M. L., Polzer, J. T., and Stewart, K. J. 2000. Friends in high places: the effects of social networks on discrimination in salary negotiations. *Administrative Science Quarterly*, 45(1), pp.1–24.

Shulman, B., and Chiang, G. 2007. When to use an executive search firm and how to get the most out of the relationship. *Employment Relations Today*, 34(1), pp.13–19.

Skillsoft (2015). Skill builders versus skill buyers. Research report. Retrieved from http://www.skillsoft.com/assets/offers/SK0156_Research_Report.pdf.

Slovensly, R., and Ross, W. H. 2011. Should human resource managers use social media to screen job applicants? Managerial and legal issues in the USA. *Info*, 14(1), pp.55–69.

Somaya, D., Williamson, I. O., and Lorinkova, N. 2008. Gone but not lost: the different performance impacts of employee mobility between cooperators versus competitors. *Academy of Management Journal*, 51(5), pp.936–53.

Van Breugel, G., Van Olffen, W., and Olie, R. 2005. Temporary liaisons: the commitment of "temps" towards their agencies. *Journal of Management Studies*, 42(3), pp.539–66.

Way, S. A., Lepak, D. P., Fay, C. H., and Thacker, J. W. 2010. Contingent workers' impact on standard employee withdrawal behaviors: does what you use them for matter? *Human Resource Management*, 49(1), pp.109–38.

Wiersma, E. 2007. Conditions that shape the learning curve: factors that increase the ability and opportunity to learn. *Management Science*, 53(12), pp.1903–15.

CHAPTER 14

....

STRAIGHT TALK
ABOUT SELECTING FOR
UPPER MANAGEMENT

....

SCOTT HIGHHOUSE AND MARGARET E. BROOKS

14.1 STRAIGHT TALK ABOUT SELECTING FOR UPPER MANAGEMENT

....

THE most critical positions in an organization are often filled using the least systematic and scientific approaches. For instance, one of the authors worked briefly for a Fortune 50 firm that selected vice presidents using a headhunter, of dubious qualification, to identify a handful of finalists. These finalists were then interviewed by members of the executive team who arrived at a consensus about who to hire—often deferring to the team member with the greatest authority. Other large corporations employ consultants to do full-day assessments of candidates, using in-depth psychological interviews, role-play simulations, and a battery of psychological tests (Ryan and Sackett, 1987). The consultants provide reports, based on their "holistic" integration of the information, and provide graphical profiles of the candidates' strengths and weaknesses. Unfortunately, many of the consultants' practices are based on personal philosophy, and are contrary to the existing evidence on best practices (Kuncel and Highhouse, 2011).

Identifying future stars involves limiting, as much as possible, error in prediction—recognizing, however, that identifying the best person for the position is a probabilistic dilemma. Mistakes *will* be made. Professional sport teams use state-of-the-art methods to identify which players to draft. Yet, they occasionally draft duds. This, in itself, does not invalidate the procedures used to evaluate prospects; rather, it illustrates that even the best methods of prediction will result in error. Uncertainty is not simply owing to the limits of technology in assessment—it is inherent in nature (Salsburg, 2001). The question one must ask, therefore, is how many more mistakes would be made if poorer assessment practices were used?

This chapter is about identifying the best procedures for assessing candidates for upper-management positions, and selecting those candidates with the most potential to be successful. Many of the recommendations in this chapter are counter-intuitive, and are often met with resistance from employers and consultants. They are, however, based on a century of science in applied psychology and decision making.

Many other chapters in this volume deal with the identification and development of future stars within the organization. Our focus is on assessment and selection at the time of hire. Although there are many benefits to grooming people for upper management, there are limitations as well. Promoting from within by definition requires limiting the pool of applicants to those who already work for the organization. We agree with Ones and Dilchert that we need:

> . . . wider and stronger executive search practices that do not limit candidate pools based on prior achievement but instead take into account the large variability of personal characteristics and individual differences that exist among executives. (2009:169)

Moreover, arguments about fit with the organization's culture can often be excuses to limit diversity within the applicant pool (Dipboye, 1997) and ignore the advantages of external candidates with different experiences and viewpoints.

In the sections that follow, we present five myths about upper-management selection. We believe that widespread belief in these myths results in less than optimal decision making when selecting for upper management.

14.2 SOME GENERAL MYTHS ABOUT MANAGEMENT ASSESSMENT

Candidates for upper management are complex humans. And, so the argument goes, their assessment requires complex methods for combining information to make a holistic decision. Myths 1 and 2 concern separate but related issues in upper-management selection: (1) how much information is considered and (2) how that information is combined to form a judgment.

14.2.1 Myth 1: The More You Know about a Candidate, the Better

When it comes to information about candidates, executive assessment has typically taken a "more is better" approach. The assumption inherent in this approach is that more information yields better prediction. Executive assessors holistically integrate impressions from psychological tests, structured and unstructured interviews, work and family history, mannerisms and behavior, fit with an organization's culture, fit with job requirements, and so forth. Such extensive information provides a sense of diligence and rigor, yet is highly susceptible to common biases. For an illustration of how nuance and detail can easily derail judgments, consider this simple example of the conjunction fallacy (see Plous, 1993):

Which scenario has a higher probability of occurring?

Scenario A:

An all-out nuclear war between Russia and the United States

Scenario B:

An all-out nuclear war between Russia and the United States in which neither country intends to use nuclear weapons, but is triggered by the actions of a third party such as Libya, Pakistan, or Israel

Given that Scenario B (i.e., one possible way that Russia and the United States could go to war) is a subset of Scenario A (i.e., all possible ways that Russia and the United States could go to war), it is impossible for Scenario B to be more likely to occur. Yet, people asked to indicate which is more likely overwhelmingly find Scenario B more likely.

The allure of detail is also evident in the holistic school of thought's assumption that assessors can identify idiosyncrasies that standardized procedures ignore. The problem with this argument is that people over-rely on idiosyncratic cues, not distinguishing the useful from the irrelevant. Assessors find too many "broken leg" cues (Camerer and Johnson, 1997). Thus, "more" information may add more cognitive complexity (distinguishing trivial from important information) and more potential for bias, but it does not seem to add more predictive power. Decades ago, Huse (1962) found that the validities of assessor ratings based on complete data were no higher than validities based on standardized tests alone. Things have not changed (Highhouse and Kostek, 2013).

14.2.2 Myth 2: Executive Assessment Is an Art, not a Science

There is an art to interpreting vast assessment information, using expertise and intuition gathered through experience to create a holistic picture of the candidate. Research on holistic versus actuarial judgment (Dawes, 1993), however, suggests that the sterile, scientific approach of mechanically combining a few predictors is more effective. Simple (i.e., additive) combinations of objective predictors overwhelmingly outperform predictions of judges who have access to the scores on these predictors (Kuncel, Klieger, Connelly, and Ones, 2013). Although much of the research on holistic judgment in executive assessment is dated, it points toward the same conclusion: simple mechanical combinations of ratings and scores outperform judgments of experts (see Highhouse and Kostek, 2013). Meyer (1956), for example, compared the validity of holistic ratings of executive assessors versus scores on a simple test of general mental ability (GMA). Four out of five of the validity coefficients for the judgments of assessors who had access to the GMA test scores were below the validity of the GMA test alone. A meta-analysis by Morris, Daisley, Wheeler, and Boyer (2015) showed that the validity of individual assessments (.30) was substantially lower than the typical validity of a GMA test or a structured interview used alone. This is especially disturbing given that assessors have access to scores on these predictors when they make their holistic predictions. Moreover, there is no evidence to support the idea that assessors can take into account constellations of traits. This is despite oft-made arguments, such as that of Silzer and Jeanneret (1998: 467), that "Assessors need to understand the interaction of beliefs, values, and behavior in order to understand the individual in a more holistic way." Assessors are unable to process cognitively the unique configurations of data that are possible with even a small number of cues—just as astrologers are unable to conduct "whole chart" interpretations of the stars (Ruscio, 2003).

Related to the above issue is the idea that different qualities are needed in different types of organizations. This argument is based on the idea that trait by context interactions exist and must be acknowledged to properly assess upper managers for distinct roles. For instance, contingency theories of leadership posit that different leaders are needed for different organizational contexts. Most of these theories posit non-monotonic (i.e., crossed) interactions as shown on the left side of Figure 14.1. The idea here is that people-oriented leaders are only effective in highly structured task environments—task-oriented leaders are needed in unstructured task environments. A more common interaction, however, is shown on the right side of Figure 14.1. This monotonic (i.e., non-crossed) interaction suggests that people-oriented leaders always perform better than task-oriented ones do, but that people-oriented leaders are especially effective in structured environments. Although non-monotonic interactions are intuitively appealing, there is very little evidence for them in the leadership literature (Day and Antonakis, 2012). According to Hastie and Dawes, "It is easy to hypothesize

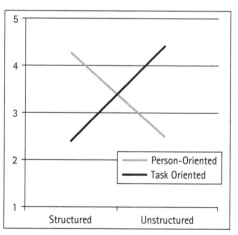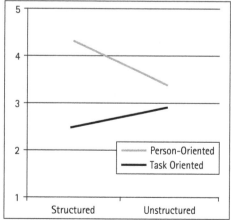

FIGURE 14.1 Non-Monotonic versus Monotonic Interactions of Leadership Style and Task Structure

crossed interactions but extraordinarily difficult to find them, especially in the areas of psychology and social interactions" (2001: 61).

Because interactions among predictors are also seldom found (see Sackett, Gruys, and Ellingson, 1998; Robertson, Brummel, and Foster, 2016), and are almost always non-crossed interactions (Guay et al., 2013; Perry, Hunter, Witt, and Harris, 2010; Wang, Wu, and Mobley, 2013; Witt, Burke, Barrick, and Mount, 2002), there is no advantage to deviating from simple formulas that add up the predictors. Thus, even if assessors could integrate configurations of traits in their heads, it would be unlikely to lead to a prediction advantage.

14.2.3 Myth 3: Tests Don't Work for Upper Management

It is commonly believed that tests have little value for upper-management assessment, because there is little variability in intelligence and personality for those who have risen to higher levels of the organization. Stagner (1957) contended about executive assessment:

> Simple, straightforward tests of intelligence and other objective measures seem not to have too much value, largely because an individual is not considered for such a position until he has already demonstrated a high level of aptitude in lower level activities. (1957: 241)

This view is so widely held that it has reached the level of stylized fact (e.g., Hollenbeck, 2009; Sessa, Kaiser, Taylor, and Campbell, 1998).

Are upper-management candidates so smart as to render cognitive ability measures impotent? Are they so ambitious and emotionally stable that personality tests are unable to discriminate among them? The evidence suggests otherwise. Ones and Dilchert (2009) examined normative data on multiple cognitive ability and personality instruments to see if the variability of scores at the executive level was severely restricted. The authors found very little reduction in variability for cognitive ability and only moderate range restriction on personality traits for executives.

Despite the lay notion that "book smarts" do not explain executive success, one of the most basic findings in the assessment literature is that the validity of cognitive ability increases as the complexity of the job increases (Schmidt and Hunter, 1998). Unless one believes that upper-management jobs lack complexity, it is difficult to deny that cognitive ability is an important component of success. Moreover, contrary to the notion that an executive needs "just enough" cognitive ability, research clearly shows that job performance is linearly related with scores on cognitive ability tests, regardless of the job level (Coward and Sackett, 1990). These findings should not be surprising, given that research on the profoundly gifted (Lubinski, 2009) shows that outstanding achievements, such as doctoral degrees, scholarly publications, and patents, are more frequent for those with higher scores *within* the top 1% of the ability distribution. As noted by

Kuncel and Hezlett, "Remarkably, those around the 99.13th percentile published less research and obtained fewer patents than those at the 99.88th percentile, even when controlling for type of institution and degrees earned" (2010: 342).

The fact that personality tests are not highly correlated with cognitive ability tests makes them particularly useful for predicting incremental variance in performance (Schmidt and Hunter, 1998). Bentz (1967) examined the characteristics of successful Sears executives and found that traits related to achievement and status were related to a number of success outcomes. Ones and Dilchert's (2009) review suggested that top executives score extremely high on emotional stability, energy, and dominance, and that they score higher than midlevel managers do on openness to experience, conscientiousness, extraversion, agreeableness, and emotional stability. Although Ones and Dilchert (2009) did observe less variability in personality among executives than among middle managers, research suggests that personality can be a potent predictor of success, even at the highest levels of the organization (see Hogan and Kaiser, 2005; Judge, Klinger, Simon, and Yang, 2008).

14.2.4 Myth 4: Assessors Need to Discuss Candidates

The assessment center is widely considered the Rolls Royce of management selection (Lievens, 2002). Head-to-head comparison on the basis of samples, jobs, and criteria suggests that the method is indeed unparalleled (Shewach, Sackett, and Keiser, 2015). The assessment center typically includes a number of individual and group managerial simulations, during which the candidates are observed by assessors and rated on a number of dimensions (e.g., communication, problem solving, and tolerance for stress).

The team approach to assessment is one of the hallmarks of the assessment-center method (Finkle, 1976; Highhouse and Nolan, 2012). This approach had its origins in the Office of Secret Services (OSS) assessment program led by Henry Murray. Murray's medical background often involved the use of "grand rounds," where the medical problems and treatment of a patient are presented to a team of doctors, residents, and medical students. During World War II, Murray applied this team approach to the OSS for the assessment of future spies (Highhouse, 2002). Douglas Bray borrowed the approach for the assessment of AT&T managers in their Management Progress Study (Bray, Campbell, and Grant, 1974).

Thornton and Byham (1982) described the typical process used in operational assessment centers: (a) assessors individually observe and rate exercises; (b) they derive consensus dimension ratings via group discussions; and (c) they integrate the dimension ratings to form a final overall assessment. In the typical group discussion, assessors are asked to report their preliminary dimension ratings. These are recorded on a flipchart for discussion to arrive at a consensus on the final dimension ratings. In the final stage, the team arrives at an overall assessment rating (OAR). The entire group discussion process can take several days to complete, and no mechanical or statistical formulas are used. Howard reported that "Many assessors report a potent sense of satisfaction from putting the evidence together and creating a holistic view of the assessee" (1997: 36).

Despite the central role given to the OAR in making selection decisions, research has not supported the use of this costly and time-consuming practice. Early research by Wollowick and McNamara (1969), for example, found that the OAR correlated .37 with the criterion, whereas a statistical combination of test scores, dimensions, and exercises provided a multiple correlation of .62. A meta-analysis by Arthur, Day, McNelly, and Edens (2003) showed that validities of preconsensus assessor ratings of organizing and planning (.37), problem solving (.39), and influencing (.38) were *by themselves* higher than the validity of the OAR (.36). Perhaps most compelling was a study of assessment-center validity for a large sample of top-level managers (*n* = 1923) by Dilchert and Ones (2009). The authors examined the incremental validity of the OAR over-and-above measures of GMA and conscientiousness, comparing it with the incremental validity of the average of dimension scores and an optimally weighted combination of dimension scores. The results are as follows:

Increment over GMA and conscientiousness			
	OAR	Average of dimension scores	Optimally weighted scores
Midlevel managers (N = 3062)	.00	.11	.13
Top-level managers (N = 1923)	.00	.10	.12

As you can see, the OAR offered no increment in prediction, after controlling for GMA and conscientiousness. When the ratings were mechanically combined, however, the increment in prediction was substantial.

14.2.5 Myth 5: The Interview Is Pivotal

In his popular book *Blink*, author Malcolm Gladwell (2007) presents many examples in which people successfully used "thin slicing" to make predictions about future outcomes. For instance, Gladwell recounts how a well-known marital expert can predict whether a couple will divorce within 15 minutes of meeting them. *Thin slicing* refers to the ability to make quick decisions with minimal amounts of information (Ambady and Rosenthal, 1992). Social psychologists suggest that thin slicing enables interviewers to make accurate predictions about job success, accounting for as much as 15% of the variance (Ambady, Bernieri, and Richeson, 2000). This is in stark contrast to the literature on the unstructured interview showing that, under optimal circumstances, they predict at best 4% of the variance in job performance (Huffcutt and Arthur, 1994). Eisenkraft (2013) noted, however, that the paradigm used in the social psychology literature involves aggregating thin-slice judgments over a large sample of judges; this process corrects for unreliability in individual judgments. The *individual* predictions in thin-slicing studies account for only 3% of the variance in the criterion. According to Eisenkraft, "Individual-level intuitive judgments are too encumbered by idiosyncratic biases and random noise to consistently produce valid predictions of job performance" (2013: 279). Gut feelings are useful for making aesthetic judgments—not for making predictions (Dijkstra, Pligt, and Kleef, 2013). And, despite people's strong intuition otherwise, the data suggest that there is little difference in interviewer accuracy across interviewers—it is not true that some interviewers are better than other interviewers (Pulakos, Schmitt, Whitney, and Smith, 1996).

No organization would ever hire an executive without conducting an in-person interview. And we are not foolish enough to recommend doing so. The most popular way to overcome the limitations of the unstructured interview is to structure it. Structuring the interview involves providing the same set of job-relevant questions to all applicants, who are evaluated using a pre-determined scoring guide. Note the similarity between a structured interview and an inventory or test. In fact, one might argue that the structured interview is little more than an orally administered test. Research suggests that structured interviews invariably outperform unstructured ones, and that they provide incremental validity over and above tests of cognitive ability and conscientiousness (see Cortina and Luchman, 2013). We suspect, however, that they are seldom used for hiring upper-level managers.

There are reasons for maintaining an unstructured interview for hiring upper management (although none have to do with validity). For instance, Dipboye (1997) noted that structured interviews turn off interviewees, who perceive the standardization as restricting their ability to have a high-quality interaction with the interviewer. Executive interviewers may also be turned off by structured interview procedures that inherently constrain their autonomy (Klehe, 2004; Nolan and Highhouse, 2014), as well as deny their perceived ability to "size up" people (Lodato, Highhouse, and Brooks, 2011).

We believe that, given likely resistance to structuring the interview for upper-management hires, the best solution for incorporating an unstructured interview is to first use data-driven screening based on proven assessment methods to narrow the pool to a small number of (e.g., two or three) qualified applicants. At this stage of a typical hiring process, finalists are roughly equally likely to succeed, given what is possible to know at the time of hire (i.e., they are Pareto efficient). We are not saying that any two or three candidates who survive screening are equally likely to be successful. We are saying, however, that, given what is possible to predict at the time of hire, the finalists have roughly equal probability of success.[1] These finalists are then interviewed in any way the employer deems appropriate. As Kuncel put it, "Decision makers can exercise their preference for unstructured interviews, firm handshakes, and holistic impressions without gross deviation from top-down decision making" (2008: 343). Such a process preserves the benefits of data-based assessment, while allowing: (a) the employer to feel a sense of control and (b) those who are wary of data-based decision making to see that a person, not data, made the final decision.

14.3 Determinism versus Error
as Inevitable

As we noted earlier in this chapter, reducing error in prediction is a probabilistic dilemma (Einhorn, 1986; Salsburg, 2001). One of the most difficult challenges for people charged with selecting upper management is accepting mistakes as inevitable. Even though there are specific examples of testing programs showing remarkable success at the executive level (Bentz, 1990; Sparks, 1990), these case studies showed that selling such programs to top management is extremely challenging. Even though these programs showed impressive validity estimates, they highlight the fact that considerable variance in executive performance is left unexplained. If one believes that perfect prediction is possible, then explained variance estimates can seem quite unimpressive. Figure 14.2 shows the difference between a deterministic viewpoint and an error-as-inevitable viewpoint on selection. The deterministic viewpoint is the belief that *person-job fit + accurate assessment = certain success* (see Highhouse, 2008). People holding this view have a reference point at the right side of Figure 14.2. For them, typical variance explained represents a considerable loss from explaining all of the variance. If, however, one views error as inevitable, their baseline is random selection (i.e., zero variance explained by flipping a coin). For them, reducing even a relatively small amount of error represents a considerable gain in utility.

Even selection experts seem to believe that we are on the cusp of validity breakthroughs, using such cutting-edge methods as neuroimaging and computational modeling. We believe that this shows that even highly educated and experienced scholars often fall prey to the deterministic view of performance prediction. There are many other contextual and chance factors that influence whether or not a candidate will live up to predictions (LeBreton, Scherer, and James, 2014). Why we continue to believe otherwise remains a mystery.

We believe that more research effort needs to be focused on understanding how to better communicate the utility of existing decision aids, rather than on pursuing the holy grail of perfect prediction. Johns (1993) noted that managers see personnel practices as matters of administrative style, rather than as technological innovations. Thus, whereas managers may have no trouble accepting analytics as applied to product customization, applying them to upper-management selection may be much harder to accept. This is likely why these methods remain popular.

FIGURE 14.2 Different Reference Points for Determinism versus Error-as-Inevitable

14.4 FINAL THOUGHTS

We have suggested that five pervasive myths limit our work in the area of executive assessment—and that understanding our unavoidable imperfection and the limitations inherent in prediction are necessary to dispel these myths and continue to move forward. We believe that less research needs to be aimed at validity breakthroughs, and more needs to be aimed at communication breakthroughs. Research needs to better understand how potential users can be convinced that standardized procedures are superior to unstandardized ones.

Many potential users of selection technology lack the necessary knowledge about statistics and probability to fully grasp the impact of data-based assessment practices. Big data exacerbates this problem by creating algorithms that are even more complex. One possible solution to this problem is to incorporate visual aids for presenting data to make it more user-friendly. Other possibilities include developing better methods of contextualizing effect size information so that consumers can gauge how the observed effect relates to others commonly found in the literature, or how it relates with effects of current methods in use. We envision a new research program aimed as examining how to debunk assessment myths—only then can we realize a deliberate, science-based approach to upper-management selection.

In this chapter, we argue for less—less information, less artistry, less interpretation, less discussion, and less intuition. The idea that "less is more" when it comes to assessing complicated human beings, and predicting their future job performance, is quite counter-intuitive, but it is one of the major discoveries of applied psychology.

NOTE

1. This of course assumes that there is a sufficient effort to recruit a diverse and talented applicant pool.

REFERENCES

Ambady, N., Bernieri, F. J., and Richeson, J. A. 2000. Toward a histology of social behavior: judgmental accuracy from thin slices of the behavioral stream. *Advances in Experimental Social Psychology*, 32, pp.201–71.

Ambady, N., and Rosenthal, R. 1992. Thin slices of expressive behavior as predictors of interpersonal consequences: a meta-analysis. *Psychological Bulletin*, 111(2), pp.256–74.

Arthur, W., Day, E. A., McNelly, T. L., and Edens, P. S. 2003. A meta-analysis of the criterion-related validity of assessment center dimensions. *Personnel Psychology*, 56(1), pp.125–53.

Bentz, V. J. 1967. The Sears experience in the investigation, description, and prediction of executive behavior. In F. R. Wickert and D. E. McFarland, eds., *Measuring executive effectiveness*. pp. 147–206.New York: Appleton-Century-Crofts.

Bentz, V. J. 1990. Contextual issues in predicting high-level leadership performance: contextual richness as a criterion consideration in personality research with executives. In K. E. Clark and M. B. Clark, eds., *Measures of leadership*. pp. 131–143. West Orange, NJ: Leadership Library of America.

Bray, D. W., Campbell, R. J., and Grant, D. L. 1974. *Formative years in business: a long-term AT&T study of managerial lives*. New York: John Wiley & Sons.

Camerer, C. F., and Johnson, E. J. 1997. The process-performance paradox in expert judgment: how can experts know so much and predict so badly? In K. A. Ericsson and J. Smith, eds., *Toward a general theory of expertise: prospects and limits*, pp.195–217. Cambridge: Cambridge University Press.

Cortina, J. M., and Luchman, J. N. 2013. Personnel selection and employee performance. *Handbook of psychology*, 12, pp.143–83.

Coward, W. M., and Sackett, P. R. 1990. Linearity of ability-performance relationships: a reconfirmation. *Journal of Applied Psychology*, 75, pp.297–300.

Dawes, R. M. 1993. Prediction of the future versus an understanding of the past: a basic asymmetry. *American Journal of Psychology*, 106, pp.1–24.

Day, D. V., and Antonakis, J. 2012. *The nature of leadership*. Los Angeles: Sage.

Dijkstra, K. A., Pligt, J., and Kleef, G. A. 2013. Deliberation versus intuition: decomposing the role of expertise in judgment and decision making. *Journal of Behavioral Decision Making*, 26(3), pp.285–94.

Dilchert, S., and Ones, D. S. 2009. Assessment center dimensions: individual differences correlates and meta-analytic incremental validity. *International Journal of Selection and Assessment*, 17(3), pp.254–70.

Dipboye, R. L. 1997. Structured selection interviews: why do they work? Why are they underutilized? In N. Anderson and P. Herriot, eds., *International handbook of selection and assessment*, pp.455–73. John Wiley and Sons.

Einhorn, H. J. 1986. Accepting error to make less error. *Journal of Personality Assessment*, 50(3), pp.387–95.

Eisenkraft, N. 2013. Accurate by way of aggregation: should you trust your intuition-based first impressions? *Journal of Experimental Social Psychology*, 49(2), pp.277–79.

Finkle, R. B. 1976. Managerial assessment centers. In M. D. Dunnette, ed., *Handbook of industrial and organizational psychology*, pp.861–88. Chicago: Rand McNally.

Gladwell, M. 2007. *Blink: the power of thinking without thinking*. New York: Back Bay Books.

Guay, R. P., Oh, I. S., Choi, D., Mitchell, M. S. et al. 2013. The interactive effect of conscientiousness and agreeableness on job performance dimensions in South Korea. *International Journal of Selection and Assessment*, 21(2), pp.233–8.

Hastie, R., and Dawes, R. M., eds. 2010. *Rational choice in an uncertain world: the psychology of judgment and decision making*. Los Angeles: Sage.

Highhouse, S. 2002. Assessing the candidate as a whole: a historical and critical analysis of individual psychological assessment for personnel decision making. *Personnel Psychology*, 55, pp.363–96.

Highhouse, S. 2008. Stubborn reliance on intuition and subjectivity in employee selection. *Industrial and Organizational Psychology*, 1(3), pp.333–42.

Highhouse, S., and Kostek, J. A. 2013. Holistic assessment for selection and placement. In *APA handbook of testing and assessment in psychology*, pp. 565–578. Washington, DC: American Psychological Association.

Highhouse, S., and Nolan, K. P. 2012. One history of the assessment center. In D. J. R. Jackson, C. E. Lance, and B. J. Hoffman, eds., *The psychology of assessment centers*, pp.25–44. New York: Routledge.

Hogan, R., and Kaiser, R. B. 2005. What we know about leadership. *Review of General Psychology*, 9(2), p.169.

Hollenbeck, G. P. 2009. Executive selection—What's right … and what's wrong. *Industrial and Organizational Psychology*, 2(2), pp.130–43.

Howard, A. 1997. A reassessment of assessment centers: challenges for the 21st century. *Journal of Social Behavior and Personality*, 12, pp.13–52.

Huffcutt, A. I., and Arthur, W. 1994. Hunter and Hunter (1984) revisited: interview validity for entry-level jobs. *Journal of Applied Psychology*, 79(2), pp.184–90.

Huse, E. F. 1962. Assessments of higher-level personnel: IV. The validity of assessment techniques based on systematically varied information. *Personnel Psychology*, 15(2), pp.195–205.

Jeanneret, R., and Silzer, R. 1998. An overview of individual psychological assessment. In R. Jeanneret and R. Silzer, eds., *Individual psychological assessment: predicting behavior in organizational settings*, pp.3–26. San Francisco, CA: Wiley/Jossey-Bass.

Johns, G. 1993. Constraints on the adoption of psychology-based personnel practices: lessons from organizational innovation. *Personnel Psychology*, 46(3), pp.569–92.

Judge, T. A., Klinger, R., Simon, L. S., and Yang, I. W. F. 2008. The contributions of personality to organizational behavior and psychology: findings, criticisms, and future research directions. *Social and Personality Psychology Compass*, 2(5), pp.1982–2000.

Klehe, U. C. 2004. Choosing how to choose: institutional pressures affecting the adoption of personnel selection procedures. *International Journal of Selection and Assessment*, 12(4), pp.327–42.

Kuncel, N. R. 2008. Some new (and old) suggestions for improving personnel selection. *Industrial and Organizational Psychology*, 1(03), pp.343–46.

Kuncel, N. R., and Hezlett, S. A. 2010. Fact and fiction in cognitive ability testing for admissions and hiring decisions. *Current Directions in Psychological Science*, 19(6), pp.339–45.

Kuncel, N. R., and Highhouse, S. 2011. Complex predictions and assessor mystique. *Industrial and Organizational Psychology*, 4(3), pp.302–6.

Kuncel, N. R., Klieger, D. M., Connelly, B. S. et al. 2013. Mechanical versus clinical data combination in selection and admissions decisions: a meta-analysis. *Journal of Applied Psychology*, 98(6), p.1060.

LeBreton, J. M., Scherer, K. T., and James, L. R. 2014. Corrections for criterion reliability in validity generalization: a false prophet in a land of suspended judgment. *Industrial and Organizational Psychology*, 7(4), pp.478–500.

Lievens, F. 2002. An examination of the accuracy of slogans related to assessment centres. *Personnel Review*, 31(1), pp.86–102.

Lodato, M. A., Highhouse, S., and Brooks, M. E. 2011. Predicting professional preferences for intuition-based hiring. *Journal of Managerial Psychology*, 26(5), pp.352–65.

Lubinski, D. 2009. Exceptional cognitive ability: the phenotype. *Behavior Genetics*, 39(4), pp.350–58.

Meyer, H. 1956. An evaluation of a supervisory selection program. *Personnel Psychology*, 9, pp.499–513.

Morris, S. B., Daisley, R. L., Wheeler, M., and Boyer, P. 2015. A meta-analysis of the relationship between individual assessments and job performance. *Journal of Applied Psychology*, 100(1), p.5.

Nolan, K. P., and Highhouse, S. 2014. Need for autonomy and resistance to standardized employee selection practices. *Human Performance*, 27(4), pp.328–46.

Ones, D. S., and Dilchert, S. 2009. How special are executives? How special should executive selection be? Observations and recommendations. *Industrial and Organizational Psychology*, 2(2), pp.163–70.

Perry, S. J., Hunter, E. M., Witt, L. A., and Harris, K. J. 2010). P = f (conscientiousness × ability): examining the facets of conscientiousness. *Human Performance*, 23(4), pp.343–60.

Plous, S. 1993. *The psychology of judgment and decision making*. New York: McGraw-Hill, Inc.

Pulakos, E. D., Schmitt, N., Whitney, D., and Smith, M. 1996. Individual differences in interviewer ratings: the impact of standardization, consensus discussion, and sampling error on the validity of a structured interview. *Personnel Psychology*, 49(1), pp.85–102.

Robertson, L. N., Brummel, B., and Foster, J. April, 2016. Examining the replicability of trait-trait interactions in local validation studies. Presented at the *Annual Meeting of the Society for Industrial and Organizational Psychology*, Anaheim, CA.

Ruscio, J. 2003. Holistic judgment in clinical practice: utility or futility? *Scientific Review of Mental Health Practice*, 2, pp.38–48.

Ryan, A., and Sackett, P. R. 1987. A survey of individual assessment practices by I/O psychologists. *Personnel Psychology*, 40(3), pp.455–88.

Sackett, P. R., Gruys, M. L., and Ellingson, J. E. 1998. Ability–personality interactions when predicting job performance. *Journal of Applied Psychology*, 83(4), pp.545–56.

Salsburg, D. 2001. *The lady tasting tea: how statistics revolutionized science in the twentieth century*. New York: W. H. Freeman & Company.

Schmidt, F. L., and Hunter, J. E. 1998. The validity and utility of selection methods in personnel psychology: practical and theoretical implications of 85 years of research findings. *Psychological Bulletin*, 124(2), p.262.

Shewach, O. R., Sackett, P. R., and Keiser, H. N. (2015, April). Assessment centers vs. ability: a new perspective on criterion-related validity. Presented at the *30th Annual Conference for the Society for Industrial and Organizational Psychology*, Philadelphia, PA.

Sessa, V. I., Kaiser, R., Taylor, J. K., and Campbell, R. J. 1998. Executive selection. *Center for Creative Leadership*, Greensboro, NC.

Sparks, C. P. 1990. Testing for management potential. In K. E. Clark and M. B. Clark, eds., *Measures of leadership*. West Orange, NJ: Leadership Library of America.

Stagner, R. 1957. Some problems in contemporary industrial psychology. *Bulletin of the Menninger Clinic*, 21, pp.238–47.

Thornton, G. C., and Byham, W. C. 1982. *Assessment centers and managerial performance*. San Diego: Academic Press, Inc.

Wang, Y., Wu, C. H., and Mobley, W. H. 2013. The two facets of conscientiousness: interaction of achievement orientation and dependability in predicting managerial execution effectiveness. *Human Performance*, 26(4), pp.275–96.

Witt, L. A., Burke, L. A., Barrick, M. A., and Mount, M. K. 2002. The interactive effects of conscientiousness and agreeableness on job performance. *Journal of Applied Psychology*, 87(1), p.164.

Wollowick, H. B., and McNamara, W. J. 1969. Relationship of the components of an assessment center to management success. *Journal of Applied Psychology*, 53, pp.348–52.

··

CHAPTER 15

MANAGING TALENT FLOWS THROUGH INTERNAL AND EXTERNAL LABOR MARKETS

··

MATTHEW BIDWELL

PERHAPS the most basic challenge in talent management is ensuring that a company has the right people in the right places when it needs them. A wide variety of research has explored different aspects of attracting and selecting workers, highlighting the different ways in which firms can ensure a fit between a particular person and a particular job (e.g., Ryan and Tippins, 2004; Sackett and Lievens, 2008; Schmidt and Hunter, 1998). If we take a broader perspective than the individual job, though, we can also think about talent management as managing a flow of workers across different jobs, within and across organizations, over time. Thinking of talent management as a set of flows through jobs is descriptive because we generally don't expect workers to stay in most jobs for very long. Many will leave the firm within a few years, and many others will be promoted or moved into a different job. More importantly, thinking of talent management as a set of flows through jobs is useful because it focuses our attention on the interdependences that exist across jobs, reminding us that the way that we fill a job today depends in part on who gained the necessary skills and preparation through the job that they were in yesterday, and on who wants or needs to take the job because of the roles that they hope to take tomorrow.

Prior research on internal labor markets provided a useful, systems-level perspective on how human capital flowed within organizations during the 1970s and 1980s (DiPrete, 1987; Doeringer and Piore, 1971; Stewman and Konda, 1983). Firms' staffing systems underwent radical change during the 1990s, though, coming to rely more and more on external hiring to fill critical roles at all levels (Bidwell, 2013; Bidwell, Briscoe, Fernandez-Mateo, and Sterling, 2013; Cappelli, 1999). Understanding talent-management systems now, therefore, requires us to examine how firms are managing the flows of talent both into and within the organization. In this chapter, I outline some of the progress that we have made in understanding talent flows in internal and external labor markets, as well as some of the major gaps in that understanding.

I approach this topic using two complementary perspectives. First, I describe the different models that have traditionally been used to describe how people move through jobs in internal labor markets versus external labor markets. Although these models build on very different premises, I argue that many of the practical differences are becoming increasingly blurred, both as firms draw on market mechanisms to manage less structured talent flows within their firms, and as firms' increased reliance on external sources of talent encourages the development of greater structure within the external labor market. Second, I examine the factors that shape when firms should, and do, rely on internal versus external labor markets to fill jobs. Although recent decades have seen a clear trend toward the increased use of external hiring to fill jobs at all levels, I note that the existing evidence suggests that internal mobility still has real advantages.

15.1 Understanding Processes in Internal and External Labor Markets

Although both internal mobility and external hiring end up with the same result—a new worker in a job—very different conceptual models have been applied to understanding each of them. Internally, flows are expected to be constrained, with a limited number of lower-level jobs feeding higher-level jobs. Our theories therefore seek to describe the factors that will regulate that flow. Externally, a much greater number of moves are possible, giving rise to questions about which worker, of all of the various possibilities, is most likely to be directed toward a given job.

15.1.1 Mobility in Internal Labor Markets

The dominant models that describe mobility within organizations explain how individuals move up into higher-level jobs along well-structured job ladders. Seminal work by Doeringer and Piore (1971) and Osterman (1987) described a number of influences shaping these job ladders. Among the most important of those influences were both economic factors, such as the way that lower-level jobs build specific skills necessary for the higher-level job, and institutional factors, such as tradition, fairness perceptions, and unions' desire to limit managers' discretion. Although studies showed that internal careers did not always follow prescribed job ladders (DiPrete, 1987; Miner, 1987), nonetheless the metaphor of the job or career ladder proved useful in understanding internal mobility.

Perhaps the strongest advantage of modeling talent flows along job ladders is that it allows us to identify factors that affect how quickly workers move through jobs. A worker's ability to move from one job to the next job on that career ladder is likely to depend on the availability of job openings, or "vacancies," in that next job. Moreover, that worker's move upward into a vacancy can also create an opening in the job that he or she left, allowing advancement by somebody at a yet lower level. Sociological studies of labor flows in internal labor markets emphasized the way that these "vacancy chains" shaped workers' movements and created an interdependence between the movements of people all along the job ladder (White, 1970). These models also showed how the rate of flow between jobs depended on the "grade ratio" or relative numbers of jobs at different levels of the ladder, the rate of growth within the organization, levels of turnover, and managerial preferences for hiring versus promotions in filling jobs (Konda and Stewman, 1980; Stewman and Konda, 1983; Stewman, 1986).

Of course, even if jobs in career ladders are filled from lower levels, it still leaves open the question of which worker at the lower level will be promoted to fill the job. Hence, work on career ladders also gave rise to analysis of competition among workers to move to the next level through promotion "tournaments" (Lazear and Rosen, 1981; Rosenbaum, 1979). This research highlights how a worker's move into a higher-level job is not just a means by which the organization solves a staffing problem; it almost always also represents an increase in pay and status for the worker involved (Spilerman and Lunde, 1991). The prospect of promotion is therefore an important source of motivation for workers, which can, in turn, then shape how firms manage mobility along the career ladder, and even the relative pay attached to the jobs within it (Lazear and Rosen, 1981).

Although the idea of vacancy-driven mobility along defined job ladders has been the most influential perspective for understanding internal labor markets, there are many ways in which actual organizations have always varied from this ideal type. In practice, mobility frequently takes place across job ladders, as well as within them (DiPrete, 1987). Much mobility also takes place without the presence of a defined vacancy at a higher level (Rosenbaum, 1990), either because the organization is continually creating new kinds of positions (Miner, 1987) or because, as in academia, workers can be advanced to higher-level positions based on their own performance or seniority, regardless of whether or not a vacancy exists (Pinfield, 1995; Stewman and Yeh, 1991).

15.1.2 Mobility in External Labor Markets

Where mobility within internal labor markets has traditionally been viewed as structured moves along job ladders, labor flows in external labor markets have more often been characterized as a product of search processes. Canonical models within economics and sociology emphasize that workers will be better off in jobs that provide the best fit for their skills and their preferences (Heckman and Sedlacek, 1985; Logan, 1996; Roy, 1951). Often, however, workers may only learn which jobs will provide such a fit after having tried them (Halaby, 1988; Jovanovic, 1979). As a consequence, the basic nature of labor flows within the external labor market is often depicted as an unstructured search process in which workers move from job to job in search of one that fits them well. When such a fit is established, mobility will cease.

Modeling external mobility as a search process fosters an image of Brownian motion within the labor market—highly unstructured, random movement across different kinds of jobs and organizations. A number of factors, though, can serve to generate clearer patterns in this movement.

Most obviously, the acquisition and utilization of skills is likely to be a strong constraint on mobility. There is evidence that industry-specific skills play an important role in labor markets, as workers who move within industries tend to receive stronger pay gains than those moving across industries (Bidwell and Mollick, 2015; Neal, 1995; Sturman, Walsh, and Cheramie, 2008). This desire to leverage existing skills should make within-industry mobility more common than cross-industry mobility (although moving within the industry may conflict with workers' desire to use mobility to find a different kind of job that would be a better fit for them).

A second factor that can generate structure in external labor market flows is the way that social networks shape access to information about job opportunities. A large proportion of jobs within the United States and elsewhere are filled using referrals by employees, and social networks play a strong role in how individuals learn about opportunities (Boxman, Graaf, and Flap, 1991; Fernandez, Castilla, and Moore, 2000; Granovetter, 1973; Sterling, 2014; Yakubovich, 2005). As a consequence, people will be more likely to follow career paths blazed by those people that they know, creating established tracks across different organizations, as well as within them (Dobrev, 2005).

15.1.3 Toward Convergence

Although our understanding of internal and external labor markets has tended to draw on very different baseline models, the distinctions across these markets have often blurred, providing us with a much more nuanced account of talent flows.

For example, various work has started to show how internal models of career ladders and vacancy chains can inform how we think about external labor markets. Heather Haveman and Lisa Cohen (1994; see also Haveman, 1995) showed how vacancy-chain models also explain the rate of talent flows across organizations, as the jobs and opportunities created by the growth of new organizations induce turnover from more established firms. Similarly, there is also evidence that jobs across organizations can become linked within career ladders. Just as movements across jobs within organizations can be driven by the acquisition and utilization of skills, so movements across organizations should reflect similar dynamics, where some organizations are better at providing workers with skills, while others make more intensive use of those skills. Forrest Briscoe and I provided some evidence of such flows, showing how IT workers were more likely to begin their careers in large organizations that provide more training before moving on to smaller organizations that engage in less skill provision, as well as to more technologically intensive firms where skills were more valuable (Bidwell and Briscoe, 2010).

An even more intriguing possibility is that career ladders can start to link specific organizations, as hiring firms learn that certain organizations provide skills that fit well with their needs. Brymer, Molloy, and Gilbert (2014) argue that some firms rely on particular "talent pipelines" to fill their jobs, focusing their recruiting on a small number of sources. Interesting questions surround the competitive dynamics that such pipelines provoke. On the one hand, it is likely that such pipelines will often be seen as a threat to the "sending" firms, who find their workers being poached by another organization, and such behavior may even provoke retaliation over time (Gardner, 2005). On the other hand, we are beginning to understand how such talent flows can benefit those sending firms, either because they enable them to build and strengthen relationships with critical stakeholders (Somaya, Williamson, and Lorinkova, 2008), or because the prospects of attractive future employment options help those sending firms to attract applicants in the first place (Bidwell, Won, Barbulescu, and Mollick, 2015; Lehmberg, Rowe, White, and Phillips, 2009). It is worth noting that the papers that highlight the benefits of being a source for other organizations' talent have studied law firms, investment banks, and General Electric—all organizations that are characterized by rapid upward mobility in their internal talent flows. These organizations may often have a strong need for turnover at higher levels in order to create opportunities for rapid upward mobility at lower levels. Other kinds of organizations may be distinctly less excited to find themselves used as a training ground for others.

At the same time that models of internal talent flows are becoming useful in understanding hiring, so hiring models can help us to understand internal mobility. Many organizations have been seeking to de-layer, reduce bureaucracy, and move to more fluid organizational structures based around broader job descriptions. These changes are intended to increase organizational flexibility and make better use of modern team working and communication technologies. An unintended consequence, though, has been to dismantle many of the well-defined career ladders that previously guided talent flows through organizations. Centralized career management has also fallen out of fashion in many large organizations, as staffing decisions have been devolved to individual line managers rather than being the responsibility of human resource departments (Cappelli, 2008).

Absent the guiding hand of career ladders and staffing specialists, talent flows within organizations are increasingly coming to resemble the search processes found outside them. JR Keller (2013) documents how organizations move people from job to job using internal job-posting systems that closely resemble the external job-boards run by Monster.com or LinkedIn. Anecdotally, we also see workers resorting to networking strategies to find their next internal posting, just as they long have for external job searches.

What we know less about is whether these moves to decentralized management flows are positive for organizations and workers. Keller's study found that workers performed better when they entered a job following a formalized posting process compared to when they were selected through an informal process, and that formalized posting processes were associated with better pay. It is less clear, though, how these posting processes affect firms' ability to develop employees effectively. An advantage of the old job-ladder model was that workers could use one job to prepare for the next, and staffing decisions could be made with a longer-term goal of developing workers for senior roles. Where neither the worker nor the firm know what that next job is likely to be, and where staffing decisions are made on the basis of fit with the current role rather than the development of a rounded profile, we might expect the quality of talent development to suffer. Although this de-emphasis of development in shaping talent flows may be a rational response to increased external mobility, it may also lead to longer-term problems in staffing the most senior roles.

15.2 BALANCING INTERNAL AND EXTERNAL LABOR MARKETS

Perhaps the most important questions in understanding how firms combine internal and external labor markets are when firms should and do fill jobs from the inside versus the outside. A number of theoretical perspectives provide clear predictions about what firms should do. Our empirical understanding of what they do in practice is perhaps more rudimentary, but is gradually growing.

Probably the easiest way to understand firms' use of internal versus external labor markets is by comparing the expected benefits of internal staffing and of external staffing. In general, we would expect firms to make use of the staffing approach that provided the biggest benefit in their particular situation. Below, I review theories about the benefits of internal and external staffing, what evidence there is to support those benefits, and what we know about when those benefits drive staffing decisions. I begin by reviewing the benefits of internal staffing.

15.2.1 Benefits of Internal Staffing

Arguments for the benefits of internal staffing largely stem from related theories on transaction cost economics (Coase, 1937; Williamson, Wachter, and Harris, 1975) and internal labor markets (Doeringer and Piore, 1971). At the heart of both theories is the idea that employment allows for mutual learning between workers and employers. Workers learn about the firm and how to be effective there, while firms learn about the abilities of the workers. That learning is very valuable when it comes to moving workers into different jobs within the organization.

15.2.1.1 *Firm-Specific Skills*

The knowledge that workers acquire during employment at a particular firm is usually described as "firm-specific skills" (Becker, 1993). Because workers who have acquired those skills can be more productive within that organization, they are more valuable to the firm than would be potential hires. This asymmetry was used by Williamson, Wachter, and Harris (1975) and Doeringer and Piore (1971) to explain why internal labor markets look so different from external ones. Williamson and colleagues argue that specific institutions are necessary to protect mutual investments in workers' skills, while Doeringer and Piore argue that the need to spur training of new workers encourages firms to provide protections to existing employees. More generally, the presence of firm-specific skills, by definition, should favor internal mobility over external hiring. Workers who enter the job from inside the firm already have firm-specific skills; new hires do not, reducing their productivity.

Although firm-specific skills play a central role in multiple theories of employment and human resources (see also, e.g., Chadwick and Dabu, 2009; Coff, 1997; Lepak and Snell, 1999), we lack clear evidence on what those skills comprise or where they come from. Some studies have emphasized the role of tools and technology in shaping firm specificity. Drawing on their fieldwork in manufacturing plants, Doeringer and Piore (1971) emphasized familiarity with the specific and often idiosyncratic requirements of the machines and technologies that are used in a given workplace. In studying the information technology (IT) department of a large financial services organization (Bidwell, 2009, 2010), I found that deep familiarity with particular proprietary software applications was critical to a worker's ability to make valuable contributions to the organization. Other work has emphasized relationships and culture. For example, Groysberg (2010) argued that the network of relationships that investment analysts built within their firms were critical for their effectiveness, and that it took time to replicate that network when analysts moved employers. Dokko, Wilk, and Rothbard (2009) also found evidence that adapting to new cultures is challenging for workers, so that those coming from different organizations must learn how to be effective in a new setting. Finally, Lazear (2009) argued that firm specificity may simply stem from differences in the precise mix of skills demanded by each firm. If each job requires a slightly different mix of skills, then those insiders who have had time to learn the exact combination of skills demanded will be most effective in performing it.

Regardless of the source of firm-specific skills, research shows that it is consequential for staffing decisions. I found evidence in three separate organizations that workers who were hired into jobs have worse initial performance compared with those promoted into similar jobs, but that those differences disappeared over time (Bidwell, 2011), a pattern that is consistent with the presence of firm-specific skills. Groysberg, Lee, and Nanda's (2008) study of investment analysts also demonstrates how those firm-specific skills make performance less portable across organizations, as analysts' external rankings dipped when they moved to similar firms.

Such theory and evidence suggest that firms should be less likely to hire into jobs that require higher levels of firm-specific skills. The evidence for such a supposition is mixed, though. Early work on the presence of internal labor markets did find that organizations were more likely to have internal labor markets and structured job ladders when they offered more training (Baron, Davis-Blake, and Bielby, 1986; Pfeffer and Cohen, 1984). Bayo-Moriones and Ortin-Angel (2006) found that Spanish plants were more likely to fill jobs through promotion when they were undergoing higher levels of technological change and had a larger proportion of permanent contracts. Although these studies link these measures of training, change, and permanent contracts to firm-specific skills, they are open to multiple alternative interpretations.[1]

In a more direct attempt to assess the impact of firm-specific skills, I found little effect of these skills on staffing decisions. Specifically, although I found that external hires at an investment bank were rated as lower performers than promoted workers were for two to three years, a follow-up study did not find that the extent of performance differentials across jobs predicted when the bank would promote and when it would hire (Bidwell and Keller, 2014). A scenario study by De Stefano and co-authors (2015) also found that managers paid little attention to firm-specific skills when deciding whether to fill a job from outside or inside. Indeed, a variety of scholars appear to be reaching the similar conclusion that workers and managers may systematically underestimate the importance of firm-specific skills (Coff and Raffiee, 2015; Groysberg, 2010); instead, they may mistakenly assume that workers' talent drives performance regardless of context. If true, this conjecture suggests that firm-specific skills shape firms' use of internal talent flows much less than they should.

15.2.1.2 *Information Asymmetry*

A second difference between internal and external talent flows is driven by employers' learning about the abilities of workers. Williamson and colleagues (1975) and Doeringer and Piore (1971) noted how managers' ability to observe the performance of their employees gave them valuable information about how those workers could best be matched with jobs. These information asymmetries create obvious advantages to filling jobs using internal mobility rather than external hiring—advantages that then affect how firms use internal and external labor markets in a variety of ways.

We might, for example, expect information asymmetry in the labor market to create adverse selection problems, where workers only want to move jobs when their existing employer is not prepared to promote them or make efforts to retain them, and where employers are, as a result, very suspicious of external hires (Greenwald, 1986). Although theoretically sound and intuitively plausible, such arguments do not accord well with our impressions of today's labor market, where external hiring is very common at all levels. There is evidence, however, that information asymmetries affect whom firms choose to hire.

In particular, where firms are not able to screen external candidates on their actual performance, they will hold those external candidates to a higher standard on their observable credentials than they will internal candidates (Bidwell, 2011; Oyer, 2007). We would therefore expect that those people hired into jobs would have stronger credentials compared with those promoted from within. Consistent with this argument, Oyer (2007) found that external hires in academia have stronger publication records compared with tenured insiders, while the studies of Baker, Gibbs, and Holmstrom (1994) and my own work (Bidwell, 2011) found that workers hired into jobs had more education and more experience compared with those who were promoted into them. In a study of alumni careers, Ethan Mollick and I were able to add further detail to these effects, showing that workers moving across companies tended to move into jobs with similar levels of responsibility to the ones that they had just left (as measured by job title and number of subordinates), while workers moving jobs internally experienced substantial increases in responsibility (Bidwell and Mollick, 2015).

An important corollary of these differences in credentials is that external hires are paid more than those promoted internally, as their external options should be better. Harris and Helfat (1997) demonstrated evidence of such pay differentials among CEOs, while I showed that hires within an investment bank were paid 18% more than those promoted to equivalent jobs (despite having substantially weaker performance evaluations) (Bidwell, 2011). Our research on alumni careers also showed that executives' moves across firms were associated with substantial increases in pay, even though they involved little increase in responsibility (Bidwell and Mollick, 2015).

There is also evidence that information asymmetries shape when firms source talent using internal versus external labor markets. Bayo-Moriones and Ortin-Angel (2006) found that firms were more likely to fill jobs by promotion when they made stronger attempts to screen hires and assess workers' performance, presumably reflecting the greater importance of ability in determining performance. Looking at how an investment bank balanced hiring with internal promotion across all of its (above entry-level) jobs, Keller and I found that hiring was less likely into those jobs where workers tend to have more varied performance evaluations. We argued that when there are bigger differences between weak and strong performers, it is more important for the firm to staff jobs with workers whose performance they can accurately predict.

15.2.1.3 *Promotion Ladders*

A third advantage of internal promotion is the signal that it sends to other workers about their prospects for internal mobility. As I noted above, promotions serve as important rewards in many organizations, and research links perceived promotion opportunities to firms' abilities to retain their talent (Griffeth, Hom, and Gaertner, 2000). The value that workers place on promotion means that employers will want to foster the belief that good work will result in promotion. If those beliefs were shaped by observing how jobs tend to be filled inside the firm, then favoring internal mobility would help to motivate and retain workers at lower levels (Chan, 1996; Williamson, Wachter, and Harris, 1975).

This desire to protect promotion incentives has been invoked as an alternative explanation for why firms should choose to hire more qualified workers than the ones that they promote (Chan, 1996; Oyer, 2007), and Chan (2006) provides evidence of such effects, showing that external hires get promoted out of their jobs more rapidly than do workers who were initially promoted into the job.[2]

There is also some evidence that the desire to preserve promotion incentives affects the kinds of jobs that are more likely to be filled by promotion. In my work with Keller, I found that focal jobs were more likely to be filled by promotion when there was a greater supply of workers eligible to be promoted into that job, and that this supply seemed to pre-empt consideration of other factors (Bidwell and Keller, 2014). Bayo-Moriones and Ortin-Angel (2006) argued that promotion should also be more important in the absence of other incentives, where there was less supervision, and where teamwork was not needed. They found little evidence, though, that these characteristics of jobs made firms more likely to fill them by promotion. A study of law firm hiring by Kim et al. (2016) advanced a very different perspective, suggesting that the benefits of external hiring in professional services may be greater when the knowledge of the new hire can be leveraged over more lower-level employees. Their results indicated that higher leverage ratios were indeed associated with stronger benefits to outside hiring of partners.

15.2.2 Benefits of External Talent Flows

Although the past thirty years have seen a tremendous increase in the extent to which organizations rely on external talent flows to fill their positions, there are not the same kinds of integrated theories of external sourcing that we see for internal labor markets. Instead, arguments about the benefits of external hiring revolve around the use of new hires as vectors of change, and the ability of external hiring to overcome some of the challenges of internal labor markets, such as the costs of developing workers from inside, restrictions on the number of candidates available internally, and the difficulties of dealing with large swings in demand through internal labor markets.

15.2.2.1 *Mitigating the Costs of Internal Labor Markets*

Although the use of internal labor markets carries a number of benefits, as articulated above, it is also associated with a number of costs. Clearly, external hiring provides a means of reducing those costs.

One potential cost of internal labor markets is the effort needed to provide workers with the skills necessary to move up in the organization. At least since Becker (1962), scholars have been aware of the very real concern that training workers makes them more attractive to other employers, either raising attrition or enabling workers to bargain for higher wages. A key attraction of external hiring may well be the ability to transfer those costs to competitors.

It is likely that much of the most valuable development that takes place in internal labor markets is the result of on-the-job learning rather than formal training. Certainly, most accounts of development emphasize the importance of experiential learning, and providing workers the opportunity to experience challenging assignments. Nonetheless, while such on-the-job learning may not incur direct costs, it can require significant investments of managerial time, as well as the need to pay workers even when they are still struggling to master the details of their jobs. The greater those costs, the more attractive external hiring may be as a means of acquiring experienced talent.

A second major cost of internal labor markets is the restriction of choice that they entail. Because employers are only looking within the firm to fill jobs, they can only pick from among those who are currently employees. Such restriction is likely to be a problem in two situations. First, the greater the number of upper-level jobs to be filled, the less likely it is that the lower level will be able to supply them. Hence, growing organizations are more likely to outstrip their internal supply of talent. Second, when organizations are struggling, there is more likely to be a perception (rightly or wrongly) that lower-level employees lack the skills necessary to be effective at the higher level. Certainly, scenario studies by DeStefano, Netchaeva, and Camuffo (2015) found that poor organizational performance was the central determinant of participants' decisions to fill a job from outside rather than inside. Similarly, research on CEO succession finds that poor performance is associated with outside succession, unless internal constituents have sufficient influence to protect the internal candidate (Cannella, Jr. and Lubatkin, 1993; Zhang and Rajagopalan, 2004).

Of course, one way to ensure that there is sufficient internal supply to fill jobs is to focus on maintaining a strong pool of internal talent. As Cappelli (2008) points out, though, maintaining such a supply can be costly if it requires organizations to stockpile talent while they wait for vacancies to materialize. In addition to the direct costs of employing surplus talent, such stockpiling can accelerate turnover among workers who see their careers stagnate while waiting for an opening. Perhaps the most important cost of internal labor markets, therefore, comes from the challenges that they have in dealing with uncertainty. Ideally, the organization should be able to deliver effective candidates when needed; yet developing candidates for higher-level positions can take years, and organizations simply lack the ability to forecast far enough ahead how many positions will be needed, how quickly higher-level jobs will open up, and how many of their high potentials will leave before moving into those higher-level jobs. Without being able to make those forecasts, external hiring provides a critical buffer between rapidly fluctuating organizational demands and slowly adjusting internal supply.

15.2.2.2 *Learning from External Hiring*

Perhaps the most frequently cited benefit of external hiring is its capacity to provide organizations with new knowledge (March, 1991). Where firms lack important skills and knowledge, they can often acquire them by hiring the right people. A variety of research has therefore explored how firms learn through hiring.

Much of the literature on learning through hiring has been developed using information from patents. Because patents list their inventors and are publicly available, they allow scholars to track inventors across organizations (provided they continue to patent) and allow their innovative output to be measured (if their innovations result in patents). Patents have therefore provided a fount of information for scholars interested in understanding how knowledge is carried across firms by individuals. Among other things, studies have shown that the mobility of inventors leads to knowledge flows between organizations (Almeida and Kogut, 1999; Rosenkopf and Almeida, 2003) and that the learning is greater when the new firm is larger (Almeida, Dokko, and Rosenkopf, 2003). Research has also pointed to a number of factors that can inhibit knowledge flows across organizations, including firms' internal focus on developing their own technology. Perhaps as a consequence, an organization's ability to learn from hiring seems greatest when people are hired into areas away from the core knowledge domain of the new firm (Song, Almeida, and Wu, 2003). One important question is how much such learning by hiring comes simply through the incorporation of a new expert into the organization versus the ability of the new expert to teach his or her knowledge to others in the organization. Work on patenting citation patterns suggests that the diffusion of new knowledge to others in the organization may often be quite limited (Singh and Agrawal, 2011).

Beyond the context of patenting, studies have also shown that new hiring is related to the introduction of new products and decisions to enter new markets. For example, Boeker (1997) found that hiring senior managers was often a prelude to launching products that competed with the managers' former companies. Within the context of mutual funds, Rao and Drazin (2002) showed that younger and less connected firms were more likely to engage in external hiring, potentially reflecting their lack of other resources for innovating, and that recruiting helped to predict product innovation, particularly when the recruits come from higher-performing, larger, and older organizations. Other studies have linked external hiring to forms of organizational change that are more dramatic. For example, Kraatz and Moore (2002) found that liberal arts colleges were more likely to adopt professional programs following the hiring of a president from a college with professional programs or from a lower-status institution.

A second kind of resource that organizations can acquire through hiring is relationships, as new hires bring with them the contacts that they formed through their prior employment. Hence, for example, Somaya and colleagues (2008) found that hiring from other law firms allowed the hiring firm to poach some of their clients. Using data from technical standards committees, Dokko and Rosenkopf (2010) showed that firms were able to gain influence by hiring people who were rich in social capital.

15.3 CONCLUSION

Understanding talent management as a set of worker flows forces us to elevate our perspectives from that of the individual job, and instead examine the broader set of interdependencies in how jobs both within and across organizations are staffed. The review of the literature laid out above demonstrates that current theory and evidence are strong when it comes to understanding certain aspects of these flows. Within the organization, we have very good theories of the determinants of promotion and job mobility along structured career ladders. We also have strong theories about why such pathways should exist within organizations. Across organizations, we understand multiple aspects of how people find jobs. Theories of search and job matching predict when people will move jobs and what kinds of jobs people are more likely to move to. Extensive literature also documents the important role that social networks play in shaping mobility between organizations.

In addition to the established literature, there are a number of emerging areas where good progress has been made but where important questions remain. This category includes work on the factors that shape the flows of workers between specific organizations and that generate interdependencies in mobility across firms. Among other things, this literature is beginning to think about some of the benefits that firms receive when their workers move elsewhere; there is the possibility that further work in this area may help to advance a more nuanced view on when firms may gain from losing workers. Work on these cross-firm flows also suggests the value of a more systems-level perspective on labor markets, where the employment strategies of different firms are inextricably interlinked through the mobility of their workers. Our understanding of those linkages between firms is still in its infancy and needs further fleshing out.

Another important new area of study is the use of market-like systems to govern mobility within organizations. Although the early evidence suggests benefits from such market mechanisms, the decentralization of these internal labor markets also implies a less deliberate approach to developing workers. An important question in this developing line of research will be to understand how organizations are trading off finding the right match for a job today versus developing workers for tomorrow.

A third area of emerging research deals with the tradeoffs between internal staffing and external mobility. I think that we have made progress in understanding the basic tradeoffs between the two strategies for staffing jobs. What we are still missing, though, is a clearer understanding of the contingencies: on an empirical level, at least, we could do with a stronger understanding of which jobs firms will gain most from filling internally, and when hiring is a good idea.

What then are the questions about which we still know very little? Where I believe that we are still missing out is in understanding the sets of processes that organizations are employing to manage these flows. A great strength of internal labor market theory was that it described clear sets of rules that organizations used to decide whom to move into which job. Those rules have largely disappeared as organizations have sought greater flexibility, decision-making has been delegated to line managers, and unions have declined (Bidwell, 2013; Cappelli, 2008). I think that we need a stronger understanding of the processes that have replaced them.

Research in other domains has emphasized that decisions are often not made through analytical optimization, but rather reflect the outcomes of structured processes that end up favoring some considerations over others (Bower, 1970; Burgelman, 1983; March, 1994; Ocasio, 1997). We should therefore expect that a central determinant of how, and how effectively, talent flows through organizations is the specific processes used to define the structure of jobs, allocate headcount, trigger job search and promotion, and guide the consideration of candidates for each post. We have anecdotal accounts of some of these processes, such as GE's "Session C" talent reviews or Google's engineer-promotion processes. It is my impression, though, that a focus on how organizations manage the overall staffing process is not yet a major part of academic discourse around talent management.

As we continue to explore how talent flows within and across organizations, I therefore hope that we will start to attend to the organizational decision processes that structure those flows. We now have a good sense of what organizations should attend to in managing talent flows. If we can bolster those theories with more evidence on what decision-makers actually do focus on, we will be able to build a robust understanding of how talent flows within organizations and what firms can do to optimize outcomes from those talent flows.

Notes

1. For example, firms should be more likely to promote permanent workers than temporary workers (Barnett and Miner, 1992), and we might expect that firms that invest more in training would prefer structures that help them to retain workers, regardless of the specificity of the skills required for work.
2. Bidwell (2011) finds a similar effect but offers a different explanation.

References

Almeida, P., Dokko, G., and Rosenkopf, L. 2003. Startup size and the mechanisms of external learning: increasing opportunity and decreasing ability? *Research Policy*, 32(2), pp.301–15.

Almeida, P., and Kogut, B. 1999. Localization of knowledge and the mobility of engineers in regional networks. *Management Science*, 45(7), pp.905–17.

Baker, G., Gibbs, M., and Holmstrom, B. 1994. The internal economics of the firm: evidence from personnel data. *The Quarterly Journal of Economics*, 109(4), pp.881–919.

Barnett, W. P., and Miner, A. S. 1992. Standing on the shoulders of others: career interdependence in job mobility. *Administrative Science Quarterly*, 37(2), pp.262–81.

Baron, J. N., Davis-Blake, A., and Bielby, W. T. 1986. The structure of opportunity: how promotion ladders vary within and among organizations. *Administrative Science Quarterly*, 31(2), pp.248–73.

Bayo-Moriones, A., and Ortín-Ángel, P. 2006. Internal promotion versus external recruitment in industrial plants in Spain. *Industrial and Labor Relations Review*, 59(3), pp.451–70.

Becker, G. S. 1962. Investment in human-capital—a theoretical analysis. *Journal of Political Economy*, 70(5), pp.9–49.

Becker, G. S. 1993. *Human capital: a theoretical and empirical analysis with special reference to education*, 3rd edn. Chicago: University of Chicago Press.

Bidwell, M. J. 2009. Do peripheral workers do peripheral work? Comparing the use of highly skilled contractors and regular employees. *Industrial and Labour Relations Review*, 62(2), pp.200–25.

Bidwell, M. J. 2010. Problems deciding: how the make or buy decision leads to transaction misalignment. *Organization Science*, 21(2), pp.362–79.

Bidwell, M. J. 2011. Paying more to get less: specific skills, incomplete information and the effects of external hiring versus internal mobility. *Administrative Science Quarterly*, 56(3), pp.369–407.

Bidwell, M. J. 2013. What happened to long-term employment? The role of worker power and environmental turbulence in explaining declines in worker tenure. *Organization Science*, 24(4), pp.1061–82.

Bidwell, M., and Briscoe, F. 2010. The dynamics of interorganizational careers. *Organization Science*, 21(5), pp.1034–53.

Bidwell, M., Briscoe, F., Fernandez-Mateo, I., and Sterling, A. 2013. The employment relationship and inequality: how and why changes in employment practices are reshaping rewards in organizations. *The Academy of Management Annals*, 7(1), pp.61–121.

Bidwell, M., and Keller, JR. 2014. Within or without? How firms combine internal and external labor markets to fill jobs. *Academy of Management Journal*, 57(4), pp.1035–55.

Bidwell, M., and Mollick, E. 2015. Shifts and ladders: comparing the role of internal and external mobility in managerial careers. *Organization Science*, 26(6), pp.1629–45.

Bidwell, M., Won, S., Barbulescu, R., and Mollick, E. 2015. I used to work at Goldman Sachs! How firms benefit from organizational status in the market for human capital. *Strategic Management Journal*, 36(8), pp.1164–73.

Boeker, W. 1997. Executive migration and strategic change: the effect of top manager movement on product-market entry. *Administrative Science Quarterly*, 42(2), pp.213–36.

Bower, J. L. 1970. *Managing the resource allocation process: a study of corporate planning and investment*. Boston: Harvard University, Division of Research, Graduate School of Business Administration.

Boxman, E. A., De Graaf, P. M., and Flap, H. D. 1991. The impact of social and human capital on the income attainment of Dutch managers. *Social Networks*, 13(1), pp.51–73.

Brymer, R. A., Molloy, J. C., and Gilbert, B. A. 2014. Human capital pipelines: competitive implications of repeated interorganizational hiring. *Journal of Management*, 40(2), pp.483–508.

Burgelman, R. A. 1983. A process model of internal corporate venturing in the diversified major firm. *Administrative Science Quarterly*, 28(2), pp.223–44.

Cannella, A. A., and Lubatkin, M. 1993. Succession as a sociopolitical process: internal impediments to outsider selection. *Academy of Management Journal*, 36(4), pp.763–93.

Cappelli, P. 1999. *The new deal at work: managing the market-driven workforce*. Boston: Harvard Business School Press.

Cappelli, P. 2008. *Talent on demand: managing talent in an age of uncertainty*. Boston: Harvard Business Press.

Chadwick, C., and Dabu, A. 2009. Human resources, human resource management, and the competitive advantage of firms: toward a more comprehensive model of causal linkages. *Organization Science*, 20(1), pp.253–72.

Chan, W. 1996. External recruitment versus internal promotion. *Journal of Labor Economics*, 14(4), pp.555–70.

Chan, W. 2006. External recruitment and intrafirm mobility. *Economic Inquiry*, 44(1), pp.169–84.

Coase, R. H. 1937. The nature of the firm. *Economica*, 4(16), pp.386–405.

Coff, R. W. 1997. Human assets and management dilemmas: coping with hazards on the road to resource-based theory. *The Academy of Management Review*, 22(2), pp.374–402.

Coff, R. W., and Raffiee, J. 2015. Toward a theory of perceived firm-specific human capital. *Academy of Management Perspectives*, 29(3), pp.326–41.

DeStefano, F., Netchaeva, E., and Camuffo, A. 2017. Questioning the effect of firm-specific human capital on staffing decisions: an experimental approach. Conference Presentation, Strategic Management Society Special Conference, Milan, Italy.

DiPrete, T. A. 1987. Horizontal and vertical mobility in organizations. *Administrative Science Quarterly*, 32(3), pp.422–44.

Dobrev, S. D. 2005. Career mobility and job flocking. *Social Science Research*, 34(4), pp.800–20.

Doeringer, P. B., and Piore, M. J. 1971. *Internal labor markets and manpower analysis*. Lexington, MA: Heath.

Dokko, G., and Rosenkopf, L. 2010. Social capital for hire? Mobility of technical professionals and firm influence in wireless standards committees. *Organization Science*, 21(3), pp.677–95.

Dokko, G., Wilk, S. L., and Rothbard, N. P. 2009. Unpacking prior experience: how career history affects job performance. *Organization Science*, 20(1), pp.51–68.

Fernandez, R. M., Castilla, E. J., and Moore, P. 2000. Social capital at work: networks and employment at a phone center. *American Journal of Sociology*, 105(5), pp.1288–356.

Gardner, T. M. 2005. Interfirm competition for human resources: evidence from the software industry. *Academy of Management Journal*, 48(2), pp.237–56.

Granovetter, M. S. 1973. The strength of weak ties. *American Journal of Sociology*, 78(6), pp.1360–80.

Greenwald, B. C. 1986. Adverse selection in the labor market. *The Review of Economic Studies*, 53(3), pp.325–47.

Griffeth, R. W., Hom, P. W., and Gaertner, S. 2000. A meta-analysis of antecedents and correlates of employee turnover: update, moderator tests, and research implications for the next millennium. *Journal of Management*, 26(3), pp.463–88.

Groysberg, B. 2010. *Chasing stars: the myth of talent and the portability of performance*. Princeton, NJ: Princeton University Press.

Groysberg, B., Lee, L. E., and Nanda, A. 2008. Can they take it with them? The portability of star knowledge workers' performance. *Management Science*, 54(7), pp.1213–30.

Halaby, C. N. 1988. Action and information in the job mobility process: the search decision. *American Sociological Review*, 53(1), pp.9–25.

Harris, D., and Helfat, C. 1997. Specificity of CEO human capital and compensation. *Strategic Management Journal*, 18(11), pp.895–920.

Haveman, H. A. 1995. The demographic metabolism of organizations: industry dynamics, turnover, and tenure distributions. *Administrative Science Quarterly*, 40(4), pp.586–618.

Haveman, H. A., and Cohen, L. E. 1994. The ecological dynamics of careers: the impact of organizational founding, dissolution, and merger on job mobility. *American Journal of Sociology*, 100(1), pp.104–52.

Heckman, J. J., and Sedlacek, G. 1985. Heterogeneity, aggregation, and market wage functions: an empirical model of self-selection in the labor market. *Journal of political Economy*, 93(6), pp.1077–125.

Jovanovic, B. 1979. Job matching and the theory of turnover. *The Journal of Political Economy*, 87(5), pp.972–90.

Keller, J. H. Posting and slotting: how hiring processes shape quality of hire and compensation in internal labor markets. Working Paper, Cornell ILR School.

Kim, K. H., Kim, T. H., Kim, T. Y., and Byun, H. 2016. Lateral hiring and the performance of professional service firms: the moderating effects of leverage ratio. *The International Journal of Human Resource Management*, 27(3), pp.338–54.

Konda, S. L., and Stewman, S. 1980. An opportunity labor demand model and Markovian labor supply models: comparative tests in an organization. *American Sociological Review*, 45(2), pp.276–301.

Kraatz, M. S., and Moore, J. H. 2002. Executive migration and institutional change. *Academy of Management Journal*, 45(1), pp.120–43.

Lazear, E. P. 2009. Firm-specific human capital: a skill-weights approach. *Journal of Political Economy*, 117(5), pp.914–40.

Lazear, E. P., and Rosen, S. 1981. Rank-order tournaments as optimum labour contracts. *The Journal of Political Economy*, 89(5), pp.841–64.

Lehmberg, D., Rowe, W. G., White, R. E., and Phillips, J. R. 2009. The GE paradox: competitive advantage through fungible non-firm-specific investment. *Journal of Management*, 35(5), pp.1129–53.

Lepak, D. P., and Snell, S. A. 1999. The human resource architecture: toward a theory of human capital allocation and development. *Academy of Management Review*, 24(1), pp.31–48.

Logan, J. A. 1996. Opportunity and choice in socially structured labor markets. *American Journal of Sociology*, 102(1), pp.114–60.

March, J. G. 1991. Exploration and exploitation in organizational learning. *Organization Science*, 2(1), pp.71–87.

March, J. G. 1994. *A Primer on decision making: how decisions happen*. New York: Free Press.

Miner, A. S. 1987. Idiosyncratic jobs in formalized organizations. *Administrative Science Quarterly*, 32(3), pp.327–51.

Neal, D. 1995. Industry-specific human capital: evidence from displaced workers. *Journal of Labor Economics*, 13(4), pp.653–77.

Ocasio, W. 1997. Towards an attention-based view of the firm. *Strategic Management Journal*, 18(51), pp.187–206.

Osterman, P. 1987. Choice of employment systems in internal labor markets. *Industrial Relations*, 26(1), pp.46–67.

Oyer, P. 2007. Is there an insider advantage in getting tenure? *The American Economic Review*, 97(2), pp.501–5.

Pfeffer, J., and Cohen, Y. 1984. Determinants of internal labor markets in organizations. *Administrative Science Quarterly*, 29(4), pp.550–72.

Pinfield, L. T. 1995. *The operation of internal labor markets: staffing practices and vacancy chains*. Columbus, OH: Springer.

Rao, H., and Drazin, R. 2002. Overcoming resource constraints on product innovation by recruiting talent from rivals: a study of the mutual fund industry, 1986–94. *Academy of Management Journal*, 45(3), pp.491–507.

Rosenbaum, J. E. 1979. Tournament mobility: career patterns in a corporation. *Administrative Science Quarterly*, 24(2), pp.220–41.

Rosenbaum, J. E. 1990. Structural models of organizational careers: a critical review and new directions. In R. L. Breiger, ed., *Social mobility and social structure*, pp.272–307. Cambridge: Cambridge University Press.

Rosenkopf, L., and Almeida, P. 2003. Overcoming local search through alliances and mobility. *Management Science*, 49(6), pp.751–66.

Roy, A. D. 1951. Some thoughts on the distribution of earnings. *Oxford Economic Papers*, 3(2), pp.135–46.

Ryan, A. M., and Tippins, N. T. 2004. Attracting and selecting: what psychological research tells us. *Human Resource Management*, 43(4), pp.305–18.

Sackett, P. R., and Lievens, F. 2008. Personnel selection. *Annual Review of Psychology*, 59(1), pp.419–50.

Schmidt, F. L., and Hunter, J. E. 1998. The validity and utility of selection methods in personnel psychology: practical and theoretical implications of 85 years of research findings. *Psychological Bulletin*, 124(2), p.262.

Singh, J., and Agrawal, A. 2011. Recruiting for ideas: how firms exploit the prior inventions of new hires. *Management Science*, 57(1), pp.129–50.

Somaya, D., Williamson, I. O., and Lorinkova, N. 2008. Gone but not lost: the different performance impacts of employee mobility between cooperators versus competitors. *Academy of Management Journal*, 51(5), pp.936–53.

Song, J., Almeida, P., and Wu, G. 2003. Learning-by-hiring: when is mobility more likely to facilitate interfirm knowledge transfer? *Management Science*, 49(4), pp.351–65.

Spilerman, S., and Lunde, T. 1991. Features of educational attainment and job promotion prospects. *American Journal of Sociology*, 97(3), pp.689–720.

Sterling, A. D. 2014. Friendships and search behavior in labor markets. *Management Science*, 60(9), pp.2341–54.

Stewman, S. 1986. Demographic models of internal labor markets. *Administrative Science Quarterly*, 31(2), pp.212–47.

Stewman, S., and Konda, S. L. 1983. Careers and organizational labor markets: demographic models of organizational behavior. *American Journal of Sociology*, 88(4), pp.637–85.

Stewman, S., and Yeh, K. S. 1991. Structural pathways and switching mechanisms for individual careers. *Research in Social Stratification and Mobility*, 10, pp.133–68.

Sturman, M. C., Walsh, K., and Cheramie, R. A. 2008. The value of human capital specificity versus transferability. *Journal of Management* 34(2), pp.290–316.

White, H. C. 1970. *Chains of opportunity: system models of mobility in organizations*. Cambridge, MA: Harvard University Press.

Williamson, O. E., Wachter, M. L., and Harris, J. E. 1975. Understanding the employment relation: the analysis of idiosyncratic exchange. *The Bell Journal of Economics*, 66(1), pp.250–78.

Yakubovich, V. 2005. Weak ties, information, and influence: how workers find jobs in a local Russian labor market. *American Sociological Review*, 70(3), pp.408–21.

Zhang, Y., and Rajagopalan, N. 2004. When the known devil is better than an unknown god: an empirical study of the antecedents and consequences of relay CEO successions. *Academy of Management Journal*, 47(4), pp.483–500.

CHAPTER 16

....

WORKFORCE
DIFFERENTIATION

....

DAVID G. COLLINGS

16.1 INTRODUCTION

....

HISTORICALLY, a key focus of human resource (HR) professionals was developing and implementing HR policies and processes focused on ensuring employees behave in a similar way in performing their jobs. Thus, the focus was on standardization of HR policy and practice, and, relatedly, employees' experiences of working in an organization (Wayne, 2015). This was premised on a belief that standardizing employment conditions through wage structure and benefits policies promoted trust and cooperation in organizations (Lazear, 1981), and that inequitable compensation and inconsistent treatment of workers could diminish trust both among workers and between workers and their employer (Cowherd and Levine, 1992; Rousseau, 2005). Concerns around legal compliance and managers' ineptitude in, and lack of appetite for, delivering tough performance evaluations historically also contributed to the perpetuation of undifferentiated workforce strategies (Becker, Huselid, and Beatty, 2009). Academic research on HR practices was generally premised on a rather homogeneous view of the employment relationship and an assumption that the HR practices used across firms were relatively consistent (cf. Gerhart and Trevor, 1996; Huselid, 1995; Lepak and Snell, 1999).

It has been argued that the squeeze on resources after the economic stagnation of the 1970s precipitated a more exclusive approach to talent management and a greater degree of differentiation in HR practices, as it became more difficult to sustain an inclusive approach (see Cappelli and Keller, 2017). More broadly, it was increasingly recognized that investing equally in all employees resulted in unnecessarily high costs for organizations (Becker and Huselid, 2006). In the academic literature, since the mid-1990s, there has been an increasing recognition of the limitations of an overly simplistic perspective on the nature of investments in human capital, and the idea of a single "optimal HR architecture" for the management of all employees has been questioned (Lepak and Snell, 1999). This change in perspective was premised on an understanding that homogeneous best practices can actually destroy value for organizations, as differentiation should be at the heart of strategic decisions, including HR decisions (Bonabeau, 2004). Lepak and Snell (1999) were among the first to foreground the consideration of variation in investment for different types of human capital. Their framework explicated how HR configurations did not necessarily represent an entire organization, but rather, subgroupings within organizations. This work was significant in highlighting questions around uniqueness and value in driving decisions around the HR architecture and investments in human capital.

As interest in talent management has grown, so too has the focus on greater differentiation in HR systems. Indeed, Michaels, Handfield-Jones, and Axelrod (2001) devote an entire chapter in their highly influential book on "the war for talent" to differentiation. The locus of differentiation in much of this early literature is the employee level. As the literature matured, the locus of differentiation shifted to the job or role, and arguably it became more strategic (see Boudreau and Ramstad, 2007; Becker et al., 2009; Collings and Mellahi, 2009). I define the term *workforce differentiation* as formalized approaches to the segmentation of the workforce based on employees' competence or the nature of roles performed to reflect differential potential to generate value. Such workforce differentiation is generally accompanied by a differentiated HR system.

Workforce differentiation results in heterogeneity in aspects of the employment experience through, for example, differential investment in development, rewards, or career opportunity, within and between workgroups. While this offers significant potential to motivate, it also opens the risk of perceptions of inequity or injustice. Therein lies the key tension in the notion of workforce differentiation and the challenge for managing workforce differentiation effectively.

A key objective of the current chapter is to review the emergence of workforce differentiation in the academic literature and to chart key trends in this regard. The implications of a workforce-differentiation strategy for employees will also be considered. The chapter will conclude with a consideration of emerging trends and potential avenues for future study in the area.

16.2 WORKFORCE DIFFERENTIATION

Workforce differentiation has its roots in the strategy literature and reflects the notion that as with any strategic decisions, workforce decisions also require choices about where to invest in human capital. Broadly, workforce differentiation is premised on the notion that the organization can create value through differences in how it designs and manages its workforce strategy (Becker et al., 2009). In practice, workforce differentiation involves making disproportionately higher investments in employees who are expected to deliver greater return on investment or value for the organization (Gallardo-Gallardo et al., 2014; Huselid and Becker, 2011). Indeed, the presence of differentiation is recognized by Guest, who argued: "Many large organizations are likely to have a number of quite highly differentiated internal labor markets, each of which can have a distinctive set of HR policies and practices. In short, one size does not fit all" (2011: 8). Employees are often differentiated on the basis of current or past performance in the context of pre-defined competencies, often focused on leadership potential, at the organizational level (Nijs et al., 2014).

Earlier approaches to workforce differentiation very much focused on the individual as the nexus of differentiation. From an academic perspective, this work takes a bottom-up focus in theory development, emphasizing the idea that employees can contribute to the firm's strategic objectives simply because of their value and uniqueness (Becker and Huselid, 2006). This approach was closely aligned with the high-profile McKinsey work around the war for talent, and it was popularized by high-profile advocates such as Jack Welch at GE. It represents an exclusive approach to talent management, where a relatively small group of employees is recognized as generating the greatest value for the organization. On the surface, this philosophy classifies employees into two broad groups: a small group of stars or A players "with talent," and a much larger group of those considered average or below-average performers: B and C players "without talent" (Meyers and von Woerkom, 2014).

In this philosophy, talent is seen as relatively stable and reflected in intelligence and other individual differences (DeLong and Vijayaraghavan, 2003; Meyers and von Woerkom, 2014; Pfeffer, 2001) or graduating from a top school (Gladwell, 2002). This philosophy places a priority on recruitment and selection in terms of attracting top talent, given the relatively stable and innate view of talent underpinning it (Vaiman et al., 2012). While work that is more recent has introduced a far more nuanced understanding of the nature of star performance (see Kehoe, Lepak, and Bentley, 2016; Call et al., 2015; O'Boyle and Kroska, 2017), the focus was narrowly on task performance in much of this early work.

This approach also brings performance management to the fore in driving high performance and differentiation. Central to this approach was the view that managers were reluctant to judge employees, particularly when such judgments influence key issues like salary, promotion, and career development, making these decisions overly lenient on many occasions (Berger, Harbring, and Sliwka, 2013). As managers were considered reluctant to differentiate in performance reviews, forced-ranking systems were suggested as a means of compelling them to evaluate an individual's performance relative to his or her peers (Grote, 2005). One of its strongest advocates, Dick Grote, argued that forced distribution "both demands and guarantees differentiation" (2005: 7).

These systems were premised on the idea that in any population, employee performance should map to a normal distribution. Thus, the majority of employees would be rated as "B players"; 10% to 20% of employees should be ranked as "A players" or stars; and 5% to 10% of employees are designated as "C players." While A players are handsomely rewarded under this model, reflecting the idea of rewards being a means of attracting and retaining talent (Gerhart and Milkovich, 1990), C players got limited or no incentive rewards, and in many cases were managed out of the organization (Grote, 2005).

The broad objective of the system is to continually shift the performance curve to the right and to manage poor performers out of the organization (Collings and Mellahi, 2009). Indeed, the McKinsey consultants who promoted the notion of forced distribution argued that 96% of senior managers that they surveyed advocated a more aggressive approach in addressing low performers (Axelrod, Handfield-Jones, and Michaels, 2002). This is premised on an often unstated assumption in performance management that organizational performance is simply an aggregation of individual performance (Pfeffer, 2001). A key overarching assumption is that by improving individual performance, organizational performance would *de facto* improve. However, this assumption is open to question, and research suggests that the link to organizational-level performance outcomes is much more complex (Chattopadhayay and Ghosh, 2012; DeNisi and Smith, 2014; Lawler, 2002; Ployhardt and Moliterno, 2012). Indeed, theories such as the resource-based view would reinforce the notion that collective interactions, interconnections, and path dependence, as opposed to individual efforts and contributions, are at the core of competitive advantage (Bowman and Hird, 2014).

In considering employees' reactions to forced distributions and the wider drive to differentiate based on individual performance, Blume et al. (2009) found, based on a student sample, that respondents were most attracted to forced-distribution systems with less stringent treatment of low performers, high differentiation of rewards, frequent feedback, and large comparison groups. This reflects the preference for less harsh outcomes for poor performers, in that they were less likely to be dismissed, where frequent feedback was a hallmark of the system. Indeed, the literature on downsizing points to a negative link between reduction in employee numbers and firm performance more broadly (Cascio, 1998; Cascio, Young, and Morris, 1997; Guthrie and Datta, 2008). There is also a preference for high performers to be disproportionately rewarded. However, the broader literature on pay dispersion suggests that while high levels of pay dispersion between the highest and lowest earners in organizations have been shown to yield short-term benefits, the long-term repercussions in terms of performance are negative (Connelly et al., 2013). The preference for larger comparison groups reflects the expectation that in a larger population, the distribution of performance is more likely to reflect a normal distribution. In a later study, the same authors found that respondents who scored higher on a cognitive-ability test were more attracted to working in an organization using a forced-distribution system than were those who had lower scores. Those with higher levels of collectivism were also particularly sensitive to perceived lack of fairness in forced-distribution systems (Blume et al., 2013). Hence, there is some tentative evidence that points to certain situations or potential employees who may be positively disposed toward forced distribution as a means of workforce differentiation.

However, notwithstanding the popularity of forced-distribution systems as a means of workforce differentiation and in improving organizational performance, the evidence on their effectiveness is mixed. Some studies do show a performance benefit of forced distributions. For example, Berger, Harbring, and Sliwka (2013) found an 8% improvement in performance under forced-distribution systems. However, while research demonstrates some short-term benefits of forced distribution as low performers are managed out of the organization, the effects become smaller over time (Scullen, Bergey, and Aiman-Smith, 2005), as those who may have been higher performers in a traditional model become demotivated as they realize the difficulty of attaining the higher ratings received in the past (Berger, Harbring, and Sliwka, 2013). Further, raters find ratings in forced-distribution systems more difficult and less fair than under a traditional system (Schleicher, Bull, and Green, 2009). Indeed, Jeffrey Pfeffer (2001) argues that the winner-takes-all culture which is an outcome of such forced-distribution systems is detrimental to teamwork, and also to learning and sharing of best practice, as it creates destructive internal competition through its invariable emphasis on the individual (see also Pfeffer and Sutton, 2006). Research shows "that the nearly single-minded focus on individuals that is endemic to companies' strategies for fighting the talent war often backfires and reduces, rather than enhances individuals, teams and organizations" (Beechler and Woodward, 2009: 277).

This tension is key, given that modern organizations can be viewed as highly interdependent "network[s] of workers" (Mailath and Postlewaite, 1990) carrying out interconnected tasks. Indeed, the division of labor (Marengo and Dosi, 2005) and task interdependence in modern organizations have created strong interactions and functional dependencies between individuals (Mailath and Postlewaite, 1990). As a result, the effectiveness of high-performing individuals is significantly dependent on colleagues who perform complementary and interrelated tasks (Groysberg and Lee, 2008; Groysberg, 2010; Huckman and Pisano, 2006; Kehoe et al., 2017).

A more recent critique of the idea of forced distribution questions the very premise that individual performance is normally distributed (see also O'Boyle and Kroska, 2017). The forced-distribution model suggests that the majority of employees perform at an average level, while very few actually achieve levels of performance associated with being a star (Aguinis and Bradley, 2015; O'Boyle and Kroska, 2017). Research that is more recent presents a strong case that, in fact, performance does not follow a normal distribution, and rather is subject to a Pareto or power distribution (O'Boyle and Kroska, 2017). In simple terms, this research suggests that around 20% of employees generate about 80% of output. This means that there are potentially more stars than a normal distribution would suggest, owing to the longer "tail." This distribution also has significant implications for where the "mean" of performance really lies in the workplace. The presence of star performers shifts the average to the right of the distribution compared with a normal distribution. Hence, a far greater percentage of performers fall below the mean. This perspective highlights how, to date, PM has been operating under the assumptions of a normal distribution and has a number of implications for performance management. For example, forcing a normal distribution on performance scores might result in a number of high performers being designated as average. Obviously, this could have significant demotivating effects. However, equally it calls the very premise of forced-distribution models into question.

Another key critique of the focus on a players or star performers includes the question of the portability of performance (see Bidwell, 2011; O'Boyle and Kroska, 2017;

Dokko, Wilk, and Rothbard, 2009; Groysberg, 2010). Indeed, there is an increasing awareness that organizations pay a premium in recruiting talent from outside the firm, compared with developing it internally (Bidwell, 2011). However, more worryingly, this literature highlights that high performance in one context does not necessarily translate into high performance in another. Studies of investment bankers (Groysberg, 2010), cardiac surgeons (Huckman and Pisano, 2006), and CEOs (Groysberg, 2010; Hamori and Koyuncu, 2015) all point to the challenges of transferring high performance from one organizational context to another. The lack of transferability of performance is traced to differences between generic (or transferable) versus firm-specific (and hence non-transferable) human capital (Dokko and Jiang, 2017; Groysberg, 2010; Huckman and Pisano, 2006). Indeed, based on his empirical work, Groysberg argues that as little as 30% of individual performance is determined solely by the individual, and that the remaining 70% is determined by firm-specific factors. Other explanations focus on negative learning transfer. For example, Hamori and Koyuncu (2015) posit that past job experience harms performance in a new role; thus, the CEOs in their sample needed to "unlearn" much of their knowledge and skills to be able to work effectively in the changed context. Dokko, Wilk, and Rothbard (2009) also point to the potential for rigidities owing to norms, schemas, and scripts that are acquired in one role leading to inappropriate behavior in another role, which can at least partially offset the benefits of prior related experience. In other words, the cognitions that are central to performance in one firm can become "baggage" that hinders performance, at least in the short term, when an individual moves to another organization (Dokko and Jiang, 2017).

These and other critiques have shifted the debate to the job as the locus of differentiation and highlighted strategic or pivotal jobs as the key drivers of differentiation. This is in contrast to the extant situation in many organizations where over-investment in non-strategic roles is common (Boudreau and Ramstad, 2008; Becker et al., 2009). This represents a top-down focus in theorizing, based on the argument that "When employees are able to contribute to a firm's strategic objectives they have (strategic) value" and that "not all strategic processes will be highly dependent on human capital" (Becker and Huselid, 2006: 904). It also reflects broader trends in the strategic HR literature, where research has only recently begun to focus on the practices that impact human capital rather than the human capital itself (Wright and McMahon, 2011). It is premised on the idea that human capital is of little economic value unless it is deployed in a manner consistent with an organization's strategic intent (Becker and Huselid, 2006; Bowman and Hird, 2014; Boxall and Purcell, 2015), and that the organizational capabilities that harness this human capital are as central as the human capital itself (Linden and Teece, 2014). In line with the resource-based view, it puts the emphasis on collective interactions, interconnections, and path dependence, and not particularly on the individual (Bowan and Hird, 2014).

Dynamic capabilities are identified as the fulcrum of workforce differentiation. This is based on the argument that competitive advantage is predicated on the unique way in which a firm can execute one or more business processes in implementing its strategy. Such capabilities are built and not bought (Rumelt, 1984), and they reflect the unique history, assets, and capabilities that any firm possesses (Bowan and Hird, 2014). While some capabilities are stable (ordinary capabilities) and enable the production and sale of a relatively defined and stable portfolio of goods and services, in more fast-paced or evolving contexts, more dynamic capabilities are called for (Linden and Teece, 2014). In the context of a business environment that is constantly in flux, scholars increasingly recognize that static conceptualizations of human capital requirements are no longer effective (Cascio and Aguinis, 2008; Cappelli, 2008; Lepak et al., 2012). The potential impact of the future value of human capital beyond its present value is also brought to the fore (Lepak et al., 2012). Such dynamic capabilities are evident in the firm's capacity to integrate, build, and reconfigure internal and external resources in adapting and responding to the evolving business environment (Linden and Teece, 2014). The dynamic-capabilities perspective identifies routines as key in reconfiguring intangible assets, such as human and social capital, in ways that facilitate the renewability, augmentation, and creative responses to dynamic and unpredictable business conditions (Teece et al., 1997). Such organizational routines—repetitive, recognizable patterns of interdependent actions involving various actors through which work is accomplished in organizations—have been proposed as a key means of guiding organizational activity, creating stability, and boosting efficiencies in organizations (Feldman and Pentland, 2003; Gupta and Govindarajan, 2002).

I identify two key routines that emerge as key in the consideration of a workforce-differentiation strategy in the context of talent management.

The first routine is the identification of pivotal roles. Indeed, one of the most cited definitions of talent management (see Gallardo-Gallardo et al., 2015), that of Collings and Mellahi (2009), places key roles at the center of their framework. Their definition is premised on the idea that the point of departure for any talent-management system should be the systematic identification of the key positions that differentially contribute to an organization's sustainable competitive advantage. These key positions are differentiated by their centrality to the organization's strategic intent and the potential for variability in performance between an average and top performer in those roles, or by an increase in the number of people in those roles (Becker and Huselid, 2006; Boudreau and Ramstad, 2007; Cascio and Boudreau, 2016; Collings and Mellahi, 2009).

This is consistent with an increasing recognition that there should be a greater degree of differentiation of roles within organizations, with a greater focus on strategic over non-strategic jobs (Becker and Huselid, 2006), or between those organizational roles that promise only marginal impact vis-à-vis those that can provide above-average impact (Boudreau and Ramstad, 2007). The underlying objective is to invest resources disproportionately in positions where one expects the greatest potential returns (Huselid and Becker, 2011). This does not mean, as is sometimes implied in critiques of exclusive approaches to talent management, that other roles and individuals receive no investment. Rather, the organization should make informed decisions around the optimum level of talent required in other roles (Huselid and Becker, 2011) and the level of HR investment in the individuals in those roles. Indeed, key proponents of the exclusive approach to talent management argue that the baseline of investment in human resource practice in any organization should be high and recognize that appropriately designed and coherent HR practices have the potential to advance individual and organizational performance outcomes (Collings and Mellahi, 2013).

A second key routine is a talent-pool strategy (Collings, 2014). Although on the surface this approach has some resonance with the A-player approach advocated in earlier research, it is more aligned with a resource-based perspective owing to its focus on the development of an organizational routine to capture the value from high-performing human capital across the organization.

A key advantage of talent pools is that they advance organizational practice from demand-led recruitment to recruitment "ahead of the curve" (Sparrow, 2007). This is significant, as the path-dependent effect of human capital development has been recognized since Penrose's (1959) contribution. She demonstrated how managerial efforts to expand organizations were constrained owing to the time required to develop the managerial talent. Thus, there is a temporal element to the impact of human capital and performance, and those organizations that invest in the development of human capital "ahead of the curve" are likely to display higher performance levels. This is in line with developments in the theory of human capital, which reflect a shift from "static" or "stock" notions of human capital toward "flow" or "process" notions of human capital (Buron-Jones and Spender, 2011).

A talent-pool strategy places the emphasis on the proactive identification of incumbents with the potential to fill key positions as they become available. Cappelli (2008: 77), building on the supply-chain management perspective, advocates a talent-pool strategy as a means of managing the risks of mismatches between talent supply and demand (see also Cappelli and Keller, 2017).

Human capital accumulation is most valuable when retained in the context where it is developed (Hitt et al., 2001). *Ceteris paribus*, this points to the value of talent pools in terms of building an internal pipeline of human capital vis-à-vis the buying of human capital from the external labor market. Although the latter may be preferable in some circumstances, such as a change in strategic direction of the organization, or when key skills are required quickly and on short notice, in most circumstances internal development is preferable. An additional benefit of a talent-pool strategy is that the focus can be on the development of talent within the broader context of the organization, rather than with a particular succession role in mind (Collings and Mellahi, 2009). This means that rather than developing talent in narrow, specialized ways, employees can be developed more broadly, targeting competencies that would fit a range of roles (Cappelli, 2008) and reflecting the values of the organization. This has the benefit of focusing on firm-specific human capital, which is less transferable and may assist in the retention of pivotal talent.

16.3 THE IMPACTS OF WORKFORCE DIFFERENTIATION

By definition, *workforce differentiation* results in heterogeneity in aspects of the employment experience. A key tension that emerges in this regard is that while differentiation offers significant potential to motivate, it also opens the risk of perceptions of inequity or injustice. There is a limited but growing literature base that highlights some of the key trends in the impact of workforce differentiation on those designated as talent and those outside of the talent pool (for a complete review, see Meyers, De Boeck, and Dries, 2017).

It is important to state at the outset that there is little empirical research that shows a direct relationship between workforce differentiation, or strategic talent management more broadly, and organizational performance outcomes (Collings, 2014; Meyers, De Boeck, and Dries, 2017). In the first comprehensive review of the impact of talent designations, Meyers, De Boeck, and Dries (2017) conclude that while those employees who are designated as talent do generally score higher on desirable outcomes such the commitment to build their competencies and affective organizational commitment (Björkman et al., 2013; Gelens, Dries, Hofmans, and Pepermans, 2015), these positive reactions are not universal. Their review also points to some negative reactions to talent designations among those designated as talent, in terms of lower levels of engagement and higher turnover intentions (Bethke-Langenegger et al., 2011). They conclude that one certainty of the designation of talent is a more demanding attitude toward their employer from the perspective of the talented employees (Dries, Forrier, De Vos, and Pepermans, 2014).

The extant research on the impact of differentiated-talent systems has tended to focus on proxy measures of performance at the individual level, as opposed to organizational-level outcomes. A key example is affective commitment. Theoretically affective commitment has been proposed as a key bridge between talent management and organizational performance (Collings and Mellahi, 2009; Gelens, Dries, Hofmans, and Pepermans, 2015). In the context of workforce differentiation, research has found that employees who felt they received more favorable treatment in the workplace displayed higher levels of affective commitment (Marescaux et al., 2013). More specifically, the study by Björkman et al. (2013) found that those individuals who were explicitly identified as talent and aware of their talent status again displayed higher levels of affective commitment. Later studies (Gelens et al., 2015), drawing on signaling theory, proposed and empirically demonstrate that being designated as talent is perceived as a signal of organizational support, which in turn triggers affective commitment. Hence, the research suggests that knowing you are identified as talent has a stronger signaling effect than simply thinking you are talent (Gelens et al., 2015). Indeed, signaling theory (Biron, Farndale, and Paauwe, 2010; Spence, 1973) represents an important frame for understanding how key talent practices represent choices made by the organization as to what it expects from employees and rewards them for, and what employees can expect in return. Thus, talent decisions and practices provide strong signals as to what the organization values (Sonnenberg, Van Zijderveld, and Brinks, 2014). Indeed, Sonnenberg and colleagues' (2014) study confirms that an increased use of perceived talent-management practices is positively associated with psychological contract fulfillment.

Informed by insights from psychological contract theory, there is a strong case for making talent decisions explicit (see Festing and Shaffer, 2014; Sonnenberg, Van Zijderveld, and Brinks, 2014). This is consistent with more recent literature in the HR field emphasizes the importance of employee perceptions of HR practices in determining the impact of these practices. This is based on the assumption that in order for HR systems to have the desired effects on employees, it is important that employees understand the intention behind those practices, as the attributions they make about these practices are associated with commitment and satisfaction (Nishii, Lepak, and Schneider, 2008). Indeed, Sonnenberg and co-authors (2014) point to incongruence in talent perception, where the organization views an individual as a talent but the individual is unaware of that, or, *vice-versa*, as a key driver of psychological contract breach and violation. They further argue that there is greater scope for misinterpretation and perceptions of incongruence in organizations that claimed to pursue inclusive talent-management approaches. This was because those organizations were found to apply distinction-making terms such as *high performers*, but not to communicate this openly to employees, and more broadly that employees perceived the approaches as exclusive regardless of the posited inclusive strategy. In another practitioner study, Sonnenberg and Van Zijderveld (2011) suggest that most talent-management practices were not perceived by employees as intended by the organization. Similarly, Gelens and co-authors (2014) show that stars and non-stars may not perceive workforce-differentiation practices in the same way.

A key implication of this research is that workforce differentiation as a social exchange should not be regarded as an objective process, but rather as a subjective one informed by perceptions of distributive and procedural justice (Gelens, Hofmans, Dries, and Pepermans, 2014). In explaining how employees may evaluate the fairness or justice of talent identification in the context of workforce differentiation, Gelens et al. (2014) draw on Greenberg's (1990) earlier work to highlight the role of perceived distributive justice and perceived procedural justice. The former is focused on comparing one's talent designation to one's personal estimation of contributions. The latter is premised on evaluating the procedures used to differentiate among employees. Gelens and co-authors' (2014) study found that those individuals identified as high potentials had significantly higher perceptions of distributive justice. Perceptions of distributive justice also mediated the relationship between identification as a high potential and job satisfaction. Procedural justice emerged as a key mediator of the relationship between identification as a high potential and job satisfaction and work effort in this study. This study reinforces the point that procedures of talent identification and workforce differentiation must be perceived to be fair by those identified as talent and others.

Indeed, Rousseau (2005: 140–60) identifies four key levels that frame how employees may react to differentiation in the workplace (see also Marescaux et al., 2013). These are: (1) The organizational level, including values, climate, and social norms. For example, one might expect a very different reaction to workforce differentiation in a public-sector organization compared with a tech company. Similarly, the level of interdependence between co-workers may influence comparisons. (2) The interpersonal level, which is based on relationships with colleagues and supervisors in the workplace; for example, the level of trust in the organization or perceptions of supervisor support in the workplace are key interpersonal factors. Theoretically, insights from psychological contract, justice and the trust literatures can help explain this level. (3) The process level, which focuses on how the negotiation unfolded and was managed. There is clear resonance with procedural justice here. Additionally, it reinforces the debate around the nature of communicating workforce-differentiation decisions openly. (4) Finally, there is the level of differentiation or the perception content and distributive fairness. Again, this level resonates with distributive justice. We noted above, for example, how high levels of pay dispersion between the highest and lowest earners in organizations have been shown to yield short-term benefits. The long-term repercussions in terms of performance are negative (Connelly et al., 2013). Indeed, Marescaux and colleagues' (2013) empirical research confirms that differentiation of different HR practices led to different employee outcomes, with developmental practices argued to be the least suited to differentiation.

This research stream also points to the communication of talent decisions, the practices underlying these decisions, and the implications for one's development and career in the organization as a key weakness in many talent systems. As Rousseau notes in the context of ideals:

> If only the employer and employee who negotiated the deal know its exact terms, others will learn about them incompletely and inaccurately, often through rumor and innuendo ... co-workers are generally biased against perceiving these deals as fair if they are made behind closed doors, as this secretive process raises suspicions that there is something to hide. (2005: 148)

On balance, this research reinforces the importance of organizations being more explicit about talent designations that underpin workforce differentiation and ensuring the fairness of systems is communicated.

A final theme that emerges in the workforce-differentiation literature is the extent to which a designation as talent creates expectations among talent as to the organization's contribution to their development or career. In this regard, many organizations explicitly limit the size of their talent pools in order to minimize the inflated expectations of rapid promotion or significant investment in their development on entering the talent pool. On balance, the literature points to increased expectations among those designated as talent. Swailes and Blackburn (2016), based on their qualitative study, go as far as to argue that those designated as talent develop a "sense of entitlement" around the organization's investment in their development. Indeed, some research points to increased expectations of talent around the level of support provided. Theoretically, King (2016) introduces the idea of career-anchor events as key in understanding the downstream implications of talent identification. Drawing on social-exchange theory (SET) (Blau, 1964), she argues that critical exchanges, such as being identified as talent, can "suddenly and durably change the rules" (Ballinger and Rockmann, 2010: 373) of the employment relationship. Such critical exchanges can be considered anchoring events within a relationship by which subsequent social exchanges can be evaluated (Ballinger and Rockmann, 2010). For example, Dries, Forrier, De Vos, and Pepermans (2014) found that those designated as high potentials had greater expectations of their organizations in terms of job security and development opportunities. This finding was supported in two other studies by the same author, which found that those designated as talent expected more interesting development opportunities and customized career support (Dries and De Gieter, 2014), as well as more regular promotions (Dries and Pepermans, 2008). Additionally, research points to the potential for psychological contract breach and violation where expectations of talent are not met (Sonnenberg, Van Zijderveld, and Brinks, 2014). In this regard, the career-anchoring event of being designated as talent was a key reference point in considering investments (or lack thereof) made by the organization in one's development or career progression.

16.4 Conclusions and Implications for Further Study

There is little doubt that the emergence of talent management has brought a far greater emphasis on workforce differentiation in organizations. Indeed, it could be argued that differentiation is one of the most controversial aspects of talent management from an academic perspective (Pfeffer, 2001; Swailes, 2013). As has been illustrated above, one key evolution in the talent-management literature is the shift in emphasis in the differentiation debate from the individual level to the level of jobs. The theoretical logic for a focus on differentiation at the level of the job is compelling. In line with the resource-based view, this approach emphasizes collective interactions, interconnections, and path dependence in delivering on the organization's strategic intent (Bowman and Hird, 2014). It recognizes that human capital is of limited value unless it is deployed effectively, and it emphasizes the role of organizational capabilities (Linden and Teece, 2014). However, there is little evidence as of yet of the impact of workforce differentiation on organizational-level outcomes (Collings, 2014). As noted above, the first comprehensive review of the impact of talent designations (Meyers, De Boeck, and Dries, 2017) concludes that while those employees who are designated as talent do generally score higher on desirable outcomes, such as the commitment to build their competencies and affective organizational commitment (Björkman et al., 2013; Gelens, Dries, Hofmans, and Pepermans, 2015), these positive reactions are not universal. Further, there may also be negative implications such as lower levels of engagement and higher turnover intentions (Bethke-Langenegger, 2012). However, the vast bulk of this research is at the individual level.

Thus, one key conclusion of the current chapter is a call for further empirical work that considers the impact of workforce differentiation at the unit or organizational level. This calls for multilevel theorizing and empirical work around the impacts of workforce differentiation. Indeed, a recent review of empirical research in talent management suggested that there was a very limited tradition of multilevel work in the extant literature (Gallardo-Gallardo and Thunnissen, 2016). This is similar to the earlier evolution of research on strategic human resource management (SHRM), whereby the micro and macro traditions evolved over distinct trajectories (Wright and Boswell, 2002). However, it emerges as a key limitation of our understanding of the effectiveness of talent management and workforce differentiation. Similar to Wright and Boswell's conclusion on the potential of SHRM research a decade and a half ago, I argue that research that unfolds at the intersection of the micro and macro traditions in talent management and workforce differentiation will have the greatest potential to advance our understanding of their impact on sustainable organizational performance and effectiveness. This will also facilitate a greater understanding of the overall pros and cons of workforce differentiation and the tradeoffs that occur at different levels, such as at a unit or organizational level.

A second key avenue that merits greater research attention concerns the level of differentiation in talent-management systems. This could include questions around the percentage of the workforce that is designated as talent, and the differential level of investment in those who are members of the talent pool. As noted above, extant research on forced-distribution (Blume et al., 2005) has pointed to a preference for higher levels of differentiation in rewards. However, this should be interpreted with caution. While high levels of differentiation in rewards in organizations have been shown to deliver short-term benefits, the long-term repercussions in terms of performance are negative (Connelly et al., 2013). Marescaux and colleagues' (2013) empirical research also raised important questions of which practices are more suited to differentiation, with their research suggesting that developmental practices were less suited to differentiation. Clearly, a key boundary condition on these questions is likely to relate to national cultural differences. Cultural differences in reactions to workforce differentiation would also be a worthwhile area for future study. Theoretically, the broad areas of trust and justice represent key avenues through which the impact of talent differentiation on employees could be evaluated. Indeed, it is clear that stars and non-stars may not perceive workforce-differentiation practices in the same way (Gelens, Hofmans, Dries, and Pepermans, 2014), and a key focus for research should be ensuring that all organizational stakeholders perceive such practices equally.

A further key focus for future study relates to the impact of the shifting boundaries of talent and organizations and workforce differentiation. In their chapter in the current volume, Cascio and Boudreau trace the increasing reliance on non-standard employment contracts in tapping into talent markets. Hence, more and more, key contributors to organizational success may be engaged on atypical contracts, such as e-lancers, contractors, etc. An important avenue for further work is to consider the implications of a greater reliance on these atypical relationships for talent management. It may well be that some of the roles that these individuals occupy fit the definition of critical positions, which, in turn, will challenge our understanding of how to design a differentiated-workforce strategy that was developed largely based on the ideas of a more typical employment contract.

Given the recent focus on performance management in organizations globally, there is little doubt that the data that feed into evaluations of individual performance are likely to change significantly in many cases. In this regard, high-profile organizations such as Accenture, Deloitte, Microsoft, and Goldman Sachs have also indicated a shift away from numerical performance ratings in their performance-management systems. Notwithstanding the well-documented limitations of performance ratings, historically, these ratings fed into evaluations of performance in many differentiated-talent systems. A key question for research is how performance can best be evaluated in the absence of quantitative inputs from performance management systems.

Workforce differentiation is clearly a distinguishing feature of talent management, and it could be considered the most controversial aspect of exclusive talent-management systems. While research does provide some indicators of the potential of workforce differentiation, many questions remain, and workforce differentiation represents an important area for future study in talent management. Thus, workforce differentiation is one of the more exciting areas for future research on talent management.

References

Aguinis, H., and Bradley, K. J. 2015. The secret sauce for organizational success. *Organizational Dynamics*, 44, pp.161–8.

Axelrod, B., Handfield-Jones, H., and Michaels, E. 2002. A new game plan for C players. *Harvard Business Review*, 83, pp.80–8.

Ballinger, G. A., and Rockmann, K. W. 2010. Chutes versus ladders: anchoring events and a punctuated-equilibrium perspective on social exchange relationships. *Academy of Management Review*, 35(3), pp.373–91.

Becker, B. E., and Huselid, M. A. 2006. Strategic human resources management: where do we go from here? *Journal of Management*, 32(6), 898–925.

Becker, B. E., Huselid, M. A., and Beatty, R. W. 2009. *The differentiated workforce: transforming talent into strategic impact*. Cambridge, MA: Harvard Business Press.

Beechler, S., and Woodward, I. C. 2009. The global "war for talent". *Journal of International Management*, 15(3), pp.273–85.

Berger, J., Harbring, C., and Sliwka, D. 2013. Performance appraisals and the impact of forced distribution-an experimental investigation. *Management Science*, 59(1), pp.54–68.

Bethke-Langenegger, P., Mahler, P., and Staffelbach, B. 2011. Effectiveness of talent management strategies. *European Journal of International Management*, 5(5), pp.524–39.

Bidwell, M. 2011. Paying more to get less: the effects of external hiring versus internal mobility. *Administrative Science Quarterly*, 56(3), pp.369–407.

Biron, M., Farndale, E., and Paauwe, J. 2011. Performance management effectiveness: lessons from world-leading firms. *The International Journal of Human Resource Management*, 22(06), pp.1294–311.

Björkman, I., Ehrnrooth, M., Mäkelä, K., Smale, A., and Sumelius, J. 2013. Talent or not? Employee reactions to talent identification. *Human Resource Management*, 52, pp.195–214.

Blau, P. M. 1964. *Exchange and power in social life*. New York: Wiley.

Blume, B. D., Baldwin, T. T., and Rubin, R. S. 2009. Reactions to different types of forced distribution performance evaluation systems. *Journal of Business and Psychology*, 24(1), pp.77–91.

Blume, B. D., Rubin, R. S., and Baldwin, T. T. 2013. Who is attracted to an organisation using a forced distribution performance management system?. *Human Resource Management Journal*, 23(4), pp.360–78.

Bonabeau, E. 2004. The perils of the imitation age. *Harvard Business Review*, 82(6), pp.45–54.

Boudreau, J. W., and Ramstad, P. M. 2007. *Beyond HR: the new science of human capital.* Cambridge, MA: Harvard Business Press.

Bowman, C., and Hird, M. 2014. A resource based view of talent management. In P. Sparrow, H. Scullion, and I. Tarique, eds. *Strategic talent management: contemporary issues in international context.* Cambridge: Cambridge University Press.

Boxall, P. and Purcell, J. 2015. *Strategy and human resource management*, 4th edn. Baskingstoke: Palgrave MacMillan.

Burton-Jones, A., and Spender, J. C. 2011. *The Oxford handbook of human capital.* Oxford: Oxford University Press.

Cappelli, P. 2008. *Talent on demand: managing talent in an uncertain age.* Cambridge, MA: Harvard Business School Press.

Cappelli, P., and Keller, JR. 2017. The historical context of talent management. In D. G. Collings, K. Mellahi, and W.F. Cascio, eds. *Oxford handbook of talent management.* Oxford: Oxford University Press.

Cascio, W. F. 1998. Learning from outcomes: financial experiences of 300 firms that have downsized. In M. K. Gowing, J. D. Kraft, and J. C. Quick, eds., *The new organizational reality: downsizing, restructuring, and revitalization*, pp.55–70. Washington, DC: American Psychological Association.

Cascio, W. F., and Aguinis, H. 2008. Staffing twenty-first-century organizations. *The Academy of Management Annals*, 2(1), pp.133–65.

Cascio, W. F., and Boudreau, J. W. 2016. The search for global competence: from international HR to talent management. *Journal of World Business*, 51(1), pp.103–14.

Cascio, W. F., Young, C. E., and Morris, J. R. 1997. Financial consequences of employment-change decisions in major U.S. corporations. *Academy of Management Journal*, 40(5), pp.1175–89.

Call, M., Nyberg, A. J., and Thatcher, S. 2015. Stargazing: an integrative conceptual review, theoretical reconciliation, and extension for star employee research. *Journal of Applied Psychology*, 100(3), pp.623–40.

Chattopadhayay, R., and Ghosh, A. K. 2012. Performance appraisal based on a forced distribution system: its drawbacks and remedies. *International Journal of Productivity and Performance Management*, 61(8), pp.881–96.

Collings, D. G. 2014. The contribution of talent management to organisation success. In J. Passmore, K. Kraiger, and N. Santos, eds., *The Wiley Blackwell handbook of the psychology of training, development and feedback*, pp.247–60. London: Wiley Blackwell.

Collings, D. G., and Mellahi, K. 2013. Commentary on: "Talent—innate or acquired? Theoretical considerations and their implications for talent management." *Human Resource Management Review*, 23(4), pp.322–25.

Collings, D. G., and Mellahi, K. 2009. Strategic talent management: a review and research agenda. *Human Resource Management Review*, 19, pp.304–13.

Connelly, B. L., Haynes, K. T., Tihanyi, L., Gamache, D. L., and Devers, C. E. 2013. Minding the gap: antecedents and consequences of top management-to-worker pay dispersion. *Journal of Management*, DOI: 10.1177/0149206313503015.

Cowherd, D. M., and Levine, D. I. 1992. Product quality and pay equity between lower level employees and top management: an investigation of disruptive justice theory. *Administrative Science Quarterly*, 37, pp.302–20.

DeLong, T. J., and Vijayaraghavan, V. 2003. Let's hear it for B players. *Harvard Business Review*, 81, pp.96–102.

DeNisi, A., and Smith, C. E. 2014. Performance appraisal, performance management, and firm-level performance: a review, a proposed model, and new directions for future research. *The Academy of Management Annals*, 8(1), pp.127–79.

Dokko, G. and Jiang, W. 2017. Managing talent across organizations: the portability of individual performance. In D. G. Collings, K. Mellahi, and W. F. Cascio, eds., *Oxford handbook of talent management*. Oxford: Oxford University Press.

Dokko, G., Wilk, S. L., and Rothbard, N. P. 2009. Unpacking prior experience: how career history affects job performance. *Organization Science*, 20(1), pp.51–68.

Dries, N., and De Gieter, S. 2014. Information asymmetry in high potential programs. *Personnel Review*, 43(1), pp.136–62.

Dries, N., Forrier, A., De Vos, A., and Pepermans, R. 2014. Self-perceived employability, organization-rated potential, and the psychological contract. *Journal of Managerial Psychology*, 29(5), pp.565–81.

Dries, N., and Pepermans, R. 2008. "Real" high-potential careers: an empirical study into the perspectives of organizations and high potentials. *Personnel Review*, 37(1), pp.85–108.

Feldman, M. S., and Pentland, B. T. 2003. Reconceptualizing organizational routines as a source of flexibility and change. *Administrative Science Quarterly*, 48, pp.94–118.

Festing, M., and Schäfer, L. 2014. Generational challenges to talent management: a framework for talent retention based on the psychological-contract perspective. *Journal of World Business*, 49(2), pp.262–71.

Gallardo-Gallardo, E., Nijs, S., Dries, N., and Gallo, P. 2015. Towards an understanding of talent management as a phenomenon-driven field using bibliometric and content analysis. *Human Resource Management Review*, 25(3), pp.264–79.

Gallardo-Gallardo, E., and Thunnissen, M. 2016. Standing on the shoulders of giants? A critical review of empirical talent management research. *Employee Relations*, 38(1), p.31.

Gelens, J., Dries, N., Hofmans, J., and Pepermans, R. 2015. Affective commitment of employees designated as talent: signalling perceived organisational support. *European Journal of International Management*, 9(1), pp.9–27.

Gelens, J., Hofmans, J., Dries, N., and Pepermans, R. 2014. Talent management and organisational justice: employee reactions to high potential identification. *Human Resource Management Journal*, 24(2), pp.159–75.

Gerhart, B., and Milkovich, G. T. 1990. Organizational differences in managerial compensation and financial performance. *Academy of Management Journal*, 33, pp.663–91.

Gerhart, B., and Trevor, C. 1996. Employment variability under different managerial compensation systems. *Academy of Management Journal*, 39, pp.1692–712.

Gladwell, M. 2002. The talent myth. Are smart people overrated? *New Yorker* (July), p.22.

Greenberg, J. 1990. Organizational justice: yesterday, today, and tomorrow. *Journal of management*, 16(2), pp.399–432.

Grote, D. 2005. *Forced ranking: making performance management work*. Boston: Harvard Business School Press.

Groysberg, B. 2010. *Chasing stars: the myth of talent and the portability of performance.* Princeton: Princeton University Press.

Groysberg, B., and Lee, L. E. 2008. The effect of colleague quality on top performance: the case of security analysts. *Journal of Organizational Behavior, 29*(8), pp.1123–44.

Guest, D. E. 2011. Human resource management and performance: still searching for some answers. *Human Resource Management Journal, 21*(1), pp.3–13.

Gupta, A. K., and Govindarajan, V. 2002. Cultivating a global mindset. *The Academy of Management Executive, 16*(1), pp.116–26.

Guthrie, J. P., and Datta, D. K. 2008. Dumb and dumber: the impact of downsizing on firm performance as moderated by industry conditions. *Organization Science, 19*(1), pp.108–23.

Hamori, M., and Koyuncu, B. 2015. Experience matters? The impact of prior CEO experience on firm performance. *Human Resource Management, 54*(1), pp.23–44.

Huckman, R. S., and Pisano, G. P. 2006. The firm specificity of individual performance: evidence from cardiac surgery. *Management Science, 52*(4), pp.473–88.

Huselid, M. A. 1995. The impact of human resource management practices on turnover, productivity, and corporate financial performance. *Academy of Management Journal, 38*, pp.635–72.

Huselid, M. A., and Becker, B. E. 2011. Bridging micro and macro domains: workforce differentiation and strategic human resource management. *Journal of Management, 37*, pp.421–8.

Kehoe, R. R., Lepak, D. P., and Bentley, F. S. 2016. Let's call a star a star: task performance, external status, and exceptional contributors in organizations. *Journal of Management*, DOI: 10.1177/0149206316628644.

Kehoe, R. R., Rosikiewicz, B. L., and Tzabbar, D. 2017. Talent and teams. In D. G. Collings, K. Mellahi, and W. F. Cascio, eds., *Oxford handbook of talent management*, pp.153–68. Oxford: Oxford University Press.

King, K. A. 2016. The talent deal and journey: understanding the employee response to talent identification over time. *Employee Relations, 38*, pp.94–111.

Lawler, E. E. III. 2002. The folly of forced ranking. *Strategy & Business, 28*, pp.28–32.

Lazear, E. P. 1981. Agency, earnings profiles, productivity, and hours restrictions. *American Economic Review, 71*, pp.606–20.

Lepak, D. P., Jiang, K., Han, K., Castellano, W. G., and Hu, J. 2012. Strategic HRM moving forward: what can we learn from micro perspectives? *International Review of Industrial and Organizational Psychology, 27*, pp.231–58.

Lepak, D. P., and Snell, S. A. 1999. The human resource architecture: toward a theory of human capital allocation and development. *Academy of Management Review, 24*(1), pp.31–48.

Linden, G., and Teece, D. J. 2014. Managing expert talent. In P. Sparrow, H. Scullion, and I. Tarique, eds., *Strategic talent management: contemporary issues in international context*, pp. 87–116. Cambridge: Cambridge University Press.

Mailath, G. J., and Postlewaite, A. 1990. Asymmetric information bargaining problems with many agents. *The Review of Economic Studies, 57*(3), pp.351–67.

Marengo, L., and Dosi, G. 2005. Division of labor, organizational coordination and market mechanisms in collective problem-solving. *Journal of Economic Behavior & Organization, 58*(2), pp.303–26.

Meyers, M. C, De Boeck, G., and Dries, N. 2017. Talent or not: reactions to talent designations. In D. G. Collings, K. Mellahi, and W. F. Cascio, eds., *Oxford handbook of talent management*, pp.169–92. Oxford: Oxford University Press.

Meyers, M. C., and van Woerkom, M. 2014. The influence of underlying philosophies on talent management: theory, implications for practice, and research agenda. *Journal of World Business*, 49(2), pp.192–203.

Michaels, E., Handfield-Jones, H., and Axelrod, B. 2001. *The war for talent*. Cambridge, MA: Harvard Business Press.

Nijs, S., Gallardo-Gallardo, E., Dries, N., and Sels, L. 2014. A multidisciplinary review into the definition, operationalization, and measurement of talent. *Journal of World Business*, 49(2), pp.180–91.

Nishii, L. H., Lepak, D. P., and Schneider, B. 2008. Employee attributions of the "why" of HR practices: their effects on employee attitudes and behaviors, and customer satisfaction. *Personnel Psychology*, 61, pp.503–45.

O'Boyle, E., and Kroska, S. 2017. Star performers. In D.G. Collings, K. Mellahi, and W.F. Cascio, eds., *Oxford handbook of talent management*, pp.43–65. Oxford: Oxford University Press.

Penrose, E. T. 1959. *The theory of the growth of the firm*. New York: Sharpe.

Pfeffer, J. 2001. Fighting the war for talent is hazardous to your organization's health. *Organizational Dynamics*, 29(4), pp.248–59.

Pfeffer, J., and Sutton, R. I. 2006. Evidence-based management. *Harvard Business Review*, 84(1), pp.62–74.

Ployhart, R. E., and Moliterno, T. P. 2011. Emergence of the human capital resource: a multilevel model. *Academy of Management Review*, 36(1), pp.127–50.

Rousseau, D. M. 2005. *I-Deals: idiosyncratic deals employees bargain for themselves*. New York: M.E. Sharpe.

Rumelt, R. 1984. Toward a strategic theory of the firm. In R. Lamb, ed., *Competitive strategic management*, pp.556–70. Englewood Cliffs, MD: Prentice Hall.

Schleicher, D. J., Bull, R. A., and Green, S. G. 2009. Rater reactions to forced distribution rating systems. *Journal of Management*, 35(4), pp.899–927.

Scullen, S. E., Bergey, P. K., and Aiman-Smith, L. 2005. Forced distribution rating systems and the improvement of workforce potential: a baseline simulation. *Personnel Psychology*, 58, pp.1–32.

Sonnenberg, M., Van Zijderveld, V., and Brinks, M. 2014. The role of talent-perception incongruence in effective talent management. *Journal of World Business*, 49(2), pp.272–80.

Sonnenberg, M., and Van Zijderveld, V. 2011. *Talent: key ingredients*. Amsterdam: Accenture.

Sparrow, P. R. 2007. Globalization of HR at function level: four UK-based case studies of the international recruitment and selection process. *The International Journal of Human Resource Management*, 18(5), pp.845–67.

Swailes, S. 2013. The ethics of talent management. *Business Ethics: A European Review*, 22, pp.32–46.

Swailes, S., and Blackburn, M. 2016. Employee reactions to talent pool membership. *Employee Relations*, 38(1), pp.112–28.

Spence, M. 1973. Job market signaling. *The Quarterly Journal of Economics*, 87, pp.355–74.

Teece, D. J., Pisano, G., and Shuen, A. 1997. Dynamic capabilities and strategic management. *Strategic Management Journal*, 18, pp.509–33.

Vaiman, V., Scullion, H., and Collings, D. 2012. Talent management decision making. *Management Decision*, 50(5), pp.925–41.

Wayne, S. J. 2015. Attracting and retaining talent through differential treatment. In D. Ulrich, W. A. Schiemann, and L. Sartain, eds., *The rise of HR: wisdom from 73 thought leaders*, pp. 271–276. Alexandria, VA: HR Certification Institute.

Wright, P. M., and Boswell, W. R. 2002. Desegregating HRM: a review and synthesis of micro and macro human resource management research. *Journal of Management*, 28, pp.247–76.

Wright, P. M., and McMahan, G. C. 2011. Exploring human capital: putting "human" back into strategic human resource management. *Human Resource Management Journal*, 21(2), pp.93–104.

CHAPTER 17

SUCCESSION PLANNING

Talent Management's Forgotten, but Critical Tool

ANTHONY J. NYBERG, DONALD J. SCHEPKER,
ORMONDE R. CRAGUN, AND PATRICK M. WRIGHT

17.1 INTRODUCTION

SUCCESSION planning has long been a critical tool in the talent-management toolkit because it is the element of talent management concerned with planning for and putting in place the human capital to perform the required tasks necessary to advance the organization's strategy. Specifically, "Succession planning describes a process of anticipating and then planning for the replacement of important employees in an organization … It is an organizational practice or system of practices for addressing succession events" (Cappelli, 2011: 673). A fundamental assumption of succession planning is that internal development and work-based learning will prepare candidates to fill future openings (Cappelli, 2011). Therefore, succession planning combines workforce planning, replacement planning, and employee development.

Without well-considered succession planning, organizations can either run leanly staffed organizations or maintain surplus workforce capacity. If organizations run lean, then they must react to staffing events, scrambling after departures to identify, recruit, select, and train workers. Since each of these activities takes time (the more idiosyncratic or important the job, the longer the process), waiting until needs arise ensures that the organization will constantly be performing with suboptimal talent. These problems are exacerbated as turnover increases or firms grow, creating new staffing needs. Over time, this leads to employee burnout, lower employee satisfaction, increased turnover, and, ultimately, lower organizational performance (Reilly et al., 2014). Alternatively, an organization could maintain surplus talent, but this can result in excessive owing to unused or underutilized resources.

In addition to identifying the talent needed and replacing talent efficiently, succession planning can improve strategic performance. Both occur through identifying critical roles and the employees who are likely to achieve future success in those roles (Cappelli and Keller, 2017; Collings, 2017; Friedman and Singh, 1989). Thus, overall, succession planning is the key mechanism for identifying strategic talent needs and ensuring the necessary talent to accommodate these needs. Hence, succession planning, if done well, is a key feature for creating, maintaining, and sustaining economic value.

17.1.1 Succession-Planning Problems

While succession planning can help organize and prepare talent, the implementation of succession plans rarely achieves the desired smoothness of transition (Cappelli, 2000, 2008). Succession-plan implementation requires accurately forecasting talent demands (e.g., How will the business grow? What future skills will be required?) and understanding the organization's current talent supply. Naturally, it is often difficult to forecast future talent demand because it requires knowing how the organization will grow and strategically respond to such growth, neither of which are easily predictable (Cappelli and Keller, 2014, 2017).

Environmental factors also challenge succession-planning efficacy. As markets become more globally competitive, it becomes that much more difficult for organizations to plan for future, often unpredictable, events. It requires predicting the future marketplace and figuring out how competitors (including those that do not yet exist) will act. However, without a plan, it is not possible to forecast the jobs and knowledge, skills, abilities, and other characteristics required to meet future needs. Thus, strategic forecasting is a challenging but key succession-planning tool. Environmental uncertainty also affects succession planning. In volatile environments, firms may choose executives who have generic skills that maximize adaptation. In contrast, imparting firm-specific knowledge in situations where knowledge may quickly become outdated may be less relevant in firms that face unstable contexts than in those that face more stable contexts. Hence, succession planning is likely to be influenced by the competitive environment faced by the firm, and environmental changes may alter succession-planning strategies.

Understanding the organization's current talent supply is similarly challenging. Even if organizations are thorough in assessing new hires, employee skills and interests change over time, and few organizations continually update employee-skill inventories enough to understand current employee skills, let alone the skills necessary to advance. Forecasting supply and demand is even more challenging as organizations try to think about how to fill jobs that may be two or three higher levels within the organizational hierarchy, while addressing the uncertainties of turnover (e.g., jobs that are not likely to open soon, open unexpectedly, or change in volume).

17.2 REVIEW OF CURRENT RESEARCH

Succession planning can be viewed in six different employee segments, each with unique attributes and challenges: chief executive officer (CEO); top-management team (TMT); non-TMT executives; star performers (stars); high-potential employees; and other employees. (See Table 17.1 for definitions, attributes, and challenges.) The vast majority

Table 17.1 Levels of Succession

Segment	Definition	Attributes	Research Challenges
Chief executive officer (CEO)	The highest-ranking person in an organization, including non-CEO titles	• Selected by the board of directors • CEO can prepare successors • Responsible for succession across roles	• Lack of substantive data • Lack of visibility into the process • Relatively rare event
Top-management team (TMT)	Responsible for strategic decisions for the organization Typically, direct reports to the CEO—also C-Suite	• Selected by the CEO • Potential CEO successors • Responsible for functionality succession	• Lack of data beyond the five most highly paid employees • Frequently change with the CEO
Executives not on the TMT	Senior, non-TMT executives Often report to the TMT	• Selected by the TMT and CEO • Some groomed to be the CEO • In competition to fill TMT positions	• Few empirical studies • Lack of access to data • Each level adds complexity
Stars	Employees with disproportionately high and prolonged (1) performance, (2) visibility, and (3) relevant social capital	• Small set of individuals • Often in key strategic positions • Exist in non-managerial hierarchical roles	• Lack of data • Overlap with high potentials • Distinguishing between star status and position
High potentials	Employees who can rise multiple levels High potentials can exist throughout an organization	• Identified by the organization • High-potential pools are refreshed by monitoring, evaluating, and identifying new high potentials from lower-level employees	• Lack of access to data • Idiosyncratic to companies • Various levels of utilization of succession
Everyone else	Employees not in other categories Typically lower organizational levels	• Succession rarely part of a formal processes • Managers identify and train replacements	• Lack of formal system • Organizational importance unclear

of succession research concerns the CEO. Therefore, we begin by briefly commenting on succession planning of other areas in the organization, and then focus our review on CEO-succession planning.

17.2.1 Non-CEO Succession

Succession regarding the TMT has received more attention than other non-CEO areas, but not nearly as much attention as the CEO, despite also being viewed as a critical element in the organization (Hambrick, 2007; Bigley and Wiersema, 2002). Since the interaction and combination of the TMT and the CEO together determine the TMT's performance, and because TMT turnover often follows CEO succession (Barron et al., 2011), the majority of TMT-succession research has been conducted in conjunction with CEO research. That which we do know about TMT succession parallels much of what we know about CEO succession. For instance, organizational performance (Haveman, 1993) and size both influence TMT turnover rates (Grusky, 1961). The volatility of the environment and the organization, as well as the politics of the organization, can also affect TMT turnover (Virany et al., 1992). There are also substantive unanswered questions regarding how and who is groomed for TMT roles. More research is needed to understand the processes between TMT members being groomed or moving to the CEO role and what this means for subsequent succession planning for executives that are not currently on the TMT. That said, research has illustrated that TMT turnover has negative effects on firm performance, though these are attenuated when the TMT has spent more time working together (Messersmith et al., 2013).

The few studies that have investigated non-TMT executive succession look at succession among sports team managers (e.g., Grusky, 1963), hospital leaders (Pfeffer and Salancik, 1977), publisher leaders (Carroll, 1984), and deans (Welsh and Dehler, 1988). Succession appears to depend in part on the corporation's business life cycle (Navin, 1971). There are also implications for new managers who bring a previous subordinate along to the new position; over time, the previous subordinate becomes an additional layer of authority, potentially creating added communication challenges (Grusky, 1969). Succession at this level also appears to be tied to the organization's climate and the levels of satisfaction and commitment among managers (Huang, 2001). Although succession research in this area is sparse, this is a critical area for future research because non-TMT executives are the organizational level where succession events happen more frequently (a result of having more employees in these roles), where employees are groomed for C-Suite jobs, and where the execution of strategy often resides.

Some research has focused on employees noted as high potentials or star employees, as these employees influence firm performance at a disproportionate rate compared with peers. Research involving stars, high potentials, and high performers has shown that high performers are more likely to voluntarily leave the organization than are average performers (Maltarich et al., 2010; Hausknecht, 2017; Trevor et al., 1997), but it is not clear if stars, who are a subset of the high-performer group with greater social capital and visibility than high performers (Call et al., 2015b), behave similarly. Promotion rates, pay growth, perceived pay-for-performance (Nyberg, 2010), and actively being recruited from outside the organization (Lee et al., 2008) all influence the likelihood of departure. These may be even more prominent issues for high performers with high visibility, which means that they will have an easier ability to gain meaningful employment elsewhere than non-stars would (Aguinis and O'Boyle, 2014; Nyberg and Ployhart, 2013). One common conclusion appears to be that part of the manner of dealing with succession planning is to retain star employees and this may be facilitated by managing the star's social network, as well as the star's pay (Aguinis and O'Boyle, 2014). Cappelli (2008, 2011) suggests identifying high potentials early, and that development should include broad managerial competencies and business exposure. Early development of broad skills allows for customized development later, when exact needs are identified, thus reducing the risk of wasting time on developing the wrong skills and avoiding the problem of staffing positions with unprepared talent. However, this can also mean making employees simultaneously more marketable and less productive because they would then have more skills that are applicable to anyone, but, potentially, less competencies in their current tasks.

Although most researchers and many practitioners consider succession planning only for the most senior and strategically relevant members, succession planning can apply to all positions. However, as described, research on non-TMT members is paltry. This minimal research may be reasonable if the value of these other positions are minimal or the ability to replace and train an employee is high, in which case it may not be worth investing time and resources to invoke succession planning (Cappelli, 2008) or, consequently, research.

17.2.2 CEO Succession

As stated, much of what we think we know about succession comes from research involving the CEO. The focus on CEO succession derives from upper-echelons theory that argues the CEO disproportionately affects organizational performance. For instance, the strength of the CEO effect has grown over time; it is stronger than both the industry and year effect and is thought to account for between 16% and 26% of the firm's performance variance (Quigley and Hambrick, 2015). For these reasons, we focus the bulk of our review on CEO succession.

17.2.2.1 *Performance as an Antecedent to CEO Succession*

There are five primary causes of CEO succession: poor performance (Osborn et al., 1981); scapegoating (Boeker, 1992); strategic shift (Kesner and Dalton, 1985); planned succession such as retirement (Smith and White, 1987); and unexpected succession such as death (Worrell and Davidson, 1987). Dismissal usually occurs when poor performance, scapegoating, or strategic shift is the reason for CEO succession, and there is a great deal of research studying the relationship between poor performance and CEO dismissal (Finkelstein et al., 2009).

Not surprisingly, firms that perform poorly are more likely to replace their CEOs (Crossland and Chen, 2013), and this likelihood increases when there are a greater number of candidates and the process may be subject to politics (Mobbs and Raheja, 2012). Furthermore, when the board's performance expectations are not met, the likelihood of CEO succession increases (Puffer and Weintrop, 1991; Farrell and Whidbee, 2000). Analyst forecasts (Wiersema and Zhang, 2011) and strategic and operational actions (Bruton et al., 1997) have been used as proxies of the board's expectations. Another way boards develop expectation is by comparing firm performance to similar companies; this type of comparison has increasingly been recognized as central to establishing board expectations (Jenter and Kanaan, 2015).

When a CEO has power, this decreases the likelihood of CEO succession (Boeker, 1992; Zajac and Westphal, 1996). For example, embeddedness (Allgood and Farrel, 2000), ownership (Pi and Lowe, 2011), being a founder (Allgood and Farrel, 2000), and holding additional positions and titles beyond CEO (Davidson et al., 2008) all provide the CEO with more power. As expected, more and stronger relationships between the CEO and the board are associated with less CEO succession (Boeker, 1992). This includes board members appointed by the CEO and when the CEO has formal authority over them because they are thought to be indebted or beholden to the CEO (Ocasio and Kim, 1999).

Additionally, CEO similarity to the board diminishes CEO-succession likelihood. Similarities in regard to demographics, insider and outsider status, tenure, and experience all reduce CEO-succession likelihood (Zajac and Westphal, 1996). In contrast, CEO succession is more likely when boards are powerful, well networked (Zajac and Westphal, 1996), or have private-equity representation (Gong and Wu, 2011) or institutional block holders (Nguyen, 2011). Stakeholders not on the board can also influence CEO-succession planning. Non-board stakeholders such as lenders (Ozelge and Saunders, 2012), activist shareholders (Helwege et al., 2012), and state powers (Jiang et al., 2013) all influence CEO succession. Changing political and regulatory landscapes also increase succession (Haveman et al., 2001). However, while poor organizational performance increases the likelihood of CEO succession in the United States, the same is not true in Japan (Sakano and Lewin, 1999) or Thailand (Rachpradit et al., 2012), presumably because, on average, the external societal pressures for immediate, short-term performance are not as prevalent in these countries as they are in the United States.

17.2.2.2 *Strategy, Structure, Operations, and Lifecycle*

Frequent mergers and divestitures (Osborn et al., 1981), bad acquisitions (Lehn and Zhao, 2006), overinvestment (Hornstein, 2013), and being acquired (Buchholtz et al., 2003) are predictors of CEO succession. However, poor performance is less likely to lead to CEO succession when the firm is well diversified (Berry et al., 2006), when the chief operating officer (COO) or president is different from the CEO (Zhang, 2006), when firms are run by the state (Kato and Long, 2006), or when the CEO is a founder (Wasserman, 2003).

In close relation to strategy, the firm's structure matters, such that poor performance is less likely to lead to CEO succession when the firm is well diversified (Berry, Bizjak, Lemmon, and Naveen, 2006) or when the COO or president position is different than the CEO (Zhang, 2006). Firms that are run by the state are also less likely to have CEO succession (Kato and Long, 2006). Based on our review it appears as though the structure of the organization moderates direct relationships with CEO succession. For example, larger firms are more likely to be associated with CEO succession (Harrison et al., 1988). So too are firms where the CEO has more control of risk decisions (Bushman et al., 2010).

The firm's lifecycle is also associated with CEO succession. Initially, with a founding CEO there is less CEO change, even with poor firm performance (Wasserman, 2003). However, after its first product, new financing, or new investors, CEO-succession likelihood increases (Wasserman, 2003). Other than the circulation-of-power theory—which posits that CEOs follow a cycle of slowly gaining power, and then lose power at the end of their tenure (Ocasio, 1994; Ocasio and Kim, 1999)—very little research explains how or why firm lifecycle affects CEO succession.

17.2.2.3 *The Environmental Context*

The environmental context, including market, industry, candidate pools, shifts in regulation, and location, can affect CEO succession. For example, market and industry performance are likely to influence firm performance and increasingly are considered a basis of comparison (Jenter and Kaanan, 2015). Another market-driven component is the pool of available successor candidates. The availability of candidates appears to influence the CEO-succession process. When there appear to be a greater number of candidates, there is also a greater likelihood of CEO succession (Mobbs and Raheja, 2012). While poor performance increases the likelihood of CEO succession in US environments (Crossland and Chen, 2013); the same is not necessarily true in other countries. For example, Japanese CEO succession does not appear to be associated with strategic reorientation (Sakano and Lewin, 1999), and in Thailand, sensitivity to poor performance is higher with CEO duality and low board independence (Rachpradit et al., 2012). This is likely because of the increased pressure in many Western contexts, particularly in the United States, to continually deliver short-term economic return for shareholders.

Changing political and regulatory landscapes can also affect succession. Haveman and co-authors (2001), Powell and Lim (2009), and Wang and co-authors (2010) all found that legislative changes can lead to increased CEO succession because new legislation can require the firm to change and adapt to survive in a new environment. One critical shift in legislation was the Sarbanes-Oxley Act (SOX). The vast majority of empirical research (e.g., Arthaud-Day et al., 2006; Billger and Hallock, 2005; Daily and Dalton, 1995; Farrell and Whidbee, 2003; Fosberg, 2001) uses data on companies from before the implementation of key provisions of SOX. In response to high-profile corporate-accounting scandals in the early 2000s, SOX became law in July 2002, and many key aspects were implemented in 2004. SOX was designed to change financial disclosure and corporate governance rules (Wang, et al., 2010: 367). There is some anecdotal evidence that SOX affected board involvement in the governance process (Goel and Thakor, 2008; Wang et al., 2010). Some of these changes appear to include an increased professionalization of boards and an increased sense of responsibility toward protecting constituent interests.

17.2.2.4 *CEO-Succession Candidates*

The number, quality, and availability of candidates affect who will be selected, including the likelihood of whether the firm will select an insider or an outsider. It has been proposed that the greater the firm's reputation, network, and recruiting resources, the larger the external candidate pool and, hence, the greater the likelihood that the next CEO will be hired from outside the firm (Parino, 1997; Mobbs and Raheja, 2012; Pissaris et al., 2010). Additionally, although it is suggested that that larger, better candidate pools affect the CEO-succession process, how these pools are identified and the determination of fit remain understudied (Pissaris et al., 2010). There is not as much understanding regarding how the board determines which outside candidates have the personality and behavioral characteristics that will meet the firm's needs. Some knowledge, skills, abilities, and other attributes (KSAOs) that have been studied include firm-specific skills, often determined by whether the person was a firm insider or outsider (Zhang and Rajagopalan, 2004), functional experience (Chen and Hambrick, 2012), tenure (Bigley and Wiersema, 2002), and education level and quality (Martinson, 2012). Researchers have also examined CEO demographics including age (Martinson, 2012), gender (Lee and James, 2007), and hair color (Takeda et al., 2006). While the majority of KSAOs studied look at the candidates' functional and technical skills, as well as strategic perspective, very little has been done in regards to style or leadership capability.

Insider and outsider status has been used heavily as a measure of CEO characteristics, with mixed results, and has recently been challenged as an inaccurate measure (Karaevli, 2007; Shen and Cannella, 2002). Scholars now question the use of insider and outsider status as a measure because it is insufficient at capturing the degree to which a CEO or candidate has the characteristics typified by outsider or insider definitions (Karaevli, 2007; Pitcher et al., 2000; Shen and Cannella, 2002). As a result, there has been a proliferation of insider and outsider definitions to capture better who is truly an insider or an outsider. This confounds the issue because scholars are using the same language (i.e., insider vs. outsider) but are using substantially different measures. Alternative definitions such as that put forth by Barron and colleagues (2011) use the terms *contender, follower,* and *outsider* to better differentiate insiders who will challenge the status quo versus those that will not. Davidson and colleagues (2002) use the term *outsiderness,* based on how related the industry origin of the new CEO is to the new firm.

The degree of ownership is a measure of *power*, which is a key concept in CEO-succession research. There is evidence that candidates who have greater ownership positions are more likely to be selected as CEO (Boyer and Ortiz-Molina, 2008). The position of the CEO candidate also has bearing on if he or she will be selected. The next CEO is likely to come from the same functional background as the current CEO (Carpenter and Wade, 2002). Candidates designated as heirs apparent to the CEO or who have had positions on the board are also more likely to be selected as CEO (Boivie, Graffin, and Pollock, in press; Cannella and Shen, 2001), unless the firm is performing poorly before the succession event (Zhang and Rajagopalan, 2004). In addition, boards are more likely to select candidates that are like themselves (Davidson et al., 2006; Westphal and Fredrickson, 2001).

Researchers have compared candidate features with firm characteristics, such as size (Ang et al., 2003), industry (Datta and Rajagopalan, 1998), lifecycle stage (Martinson, 2012), structure (Wilson and Stranahan, 2000), and strategy (White, 1997) to predict the type of candidate to be selected. For example, a firm with acceptable performance, but an anticipated need for a strategic shift, is more likely to select an outsider (Lant et al., 1992). Another example is that firms that spend heavily in R&D are more likely to select a CEO with a technical background (Datta and Guthrie, 1994). In a similar vein, heavy advertising spending has been associated with selecting CEOs with low tenure (Guthrie and Datta, 1997).

17.2.2.5 *Consequences of CEO Succession*

The start of a new CEO's tenure can result in numerous changes. Having a new CEO has been linked to strategic reorientation (Lant et al., 1992), executive turnover (Barron et al., 2011), general turnover (Khaliq et al., 2006), director turnover (Marcel et al., 2013), climate changes (Friedman and Saul, 1991), accounting changes (Geiger and North, 2011), divestitures (Weisback, 1995), discontinued operations (Barron et al., 2011), internationalization (Liu et al., 2012), and investment allocation changes (Du and Ting-Ting, 2011). Outsiders are associated with more change than insiders are (Barron et al., 2011; Lant et al., 1992). Climate changes are also more likely to be positive when the new CEO replaces someone with a performance deficiency (Friedman and Saul, 1991). Accounting changes are more likely when both the CEO and the chief financial officer are replaced (Geiger and North, 2011). Divestitures are more likely when the previous CEO made poor investment decisions or there is a poor rate of return on one of the company's businesses (Weisback, 1995). Recently, more attention has focused on the speed of change after a new CEO takes office (Karaevli, 2007). Novel research by Crossland and co-authors (2014) shows how new CEO career variety (having a diverse set of experiences and background) affects a firm's strategy by changing the way the firm allocates resources to become distinct from competitors.

Performance outcomes linked to CEO succession include profitability (Fong et al., 2010), return on assets, return on equity (Ang et al., 2003), cost efficiency, revenue efficiency (He et al., 2011), the achievement of firm goals (Khaliq et al., 2006), growth (Jalal and Prezas, 2012), firm value (Adams and Mansi, 2009), and long-term performance (Denis and Denis, 1995). There is also evidence that stock prices are higher after a succession event or announcement. This tends to be a function of the quality of the new CEO (Ang et al., 2003), forced versus voluntary succession, outsider versus insider replacements (Adams and Mansi, 2009), the level of board social and human capital (Tian et al., 2011), issuance of stock grants to the new CEO (Blackwell et al., 2007), and the new CEO's prior experience (Hamori and Koyuncu, 2015).

Markets often react more strongly to unanticipated CEO-succession announcements (Rhim et al., 2006; Worrell and Davidson, 1987). Additionally, after a CEO dismissal, new CEOs are likely to increase investments in research and development and advertising (Du and Ting-Ting, 2011). The type of succession also matters: Zhang and Rajagoplan (2004) found that relay succession leads to better post-succession performance, although Intintoli (2013) did not find decreased performance during the period of a marathon succession.

The environmental context also provides key contingencies for post-CEO-succession outcomes. These include industry, industry dynamism, environmental uncertainty, competitive dynamics, and competitive uncertainty. Industry is a factor in determining post-succession outcomes (He et al., 2011); however, industry *dynamism* (Ballinger and Marcel, 2010; Marcel et al., 2013), uncertainty, and turbulence of the environment (Chen, 2008; Gordon et al., 2000; Karaevli, 2007; Westphal et al., 2006) have been examined with mixed results. In another example, Marcel and colleagues (2013) found evidence that the impact of an interim CEO on board turnover was weaker in dynamic industries. In addition, Chen (2008) found that in succession involving turnaround situations, where the incumbent CEO had a long tenure, subsequent performance was more positive. Overall, many correlational studies compare CEO-succession events with post-succession outcomes. In total, these studies show that the succession event is extremely disruptive, and the outcome depends on the organization, CEO, and environmental context.

17.2.2.6 *The CEO-Succession Process*

Unfortunately, there is very little information about the process by which CEO succession occurs. For instance, information regarding the steps taken to identify and develop potential successors is not well understood. Further, considerable research focuses on the succession of the CEO and the announcement of the successor as the event of interest, while succession decisions may be undertaken well in advance of an announcement in order to groom a CEO's replacement. One conclusion from this research is that differences between insider and outsider candidates matter. Insiders know the firm's dynamics, internal processes, TMT, and culture. One disadvantage of insiders is that they can be embedded and therefore hesitant to take action, particularly if performance has been positive. In contrast, outsiders bring fresh perspectives, new ideas, and other KSAOs. Additionally, outsiders are less beholden to social norms and restrictive practices that may inhibit making changes. However, outsiders can lack organizational understanding and therefore can make decisions that are not accepted within the firm. As such, outsiders are thought to be most beneficial when significant strategic changes are necessary to respond to poor organizational performance or a firm's lack of fit with its environmental context.

In results primarily based on pre-Sarbanes-Oxley Act (SOX) data, there seems to be a clear split in terms of who leads the succession activities. When the CEO is leading the succession process, it is typically in times of good performance and when the exit strategy and departure plans of the CEO are expected and known, such as in a retirement. When the board leads the succession process, it is usually in the involuntary removal of the CEO, or in an unexpected event such as illness, injury, or death (Friedman and Singh, 1989; Zajac, 1990; Zajac and Westphal, 1996). Third-party firms can help augment the generation of a candidate pool and interviewing but can also bias the selection process by encouraging and leading boards to select candidates who are the most charismatic but not necessarily the best fit with the strategic needs of the firm (Bonet and Hamori, 2017; Zhang and Rajagopalan, 2010). They may also lead firms to select outsiders for whom the search firm will receive more credit, and sometimes greater compensation.

Internal candidates are primarily identified and developed through setting up a *horse-race*, where candidates compete for the CEO position (Kesner and Sebora, 1994); a *relay* succession, where one candidate succeeds the CEO—this usually involves designating an heir apparent (Kesner and Sebora, 1994); or a marathon, which is a prolonged search for the CEO (Intintoli, 2013). When CEO succession is unplanned or arises because of a crisis, it can lead to using an interim CEO (Ballinger and Marcel, 2010). This is likely even after announcing an heir apparent or during the early years of a CEO's tenure (Mooney et al., 2014). While some research predicts when a particular method will be used (Zajac, 1990), and many studies look at relay succession (i.e., Zhang and Rajagopolan, 2004), with the exception of Mobbs and Raheja (2012), research rarely compares the effectiveness between types of CEO succession. There is research showing that the effectiveness of insider versus outsider succession seems to have changed over time. Specifically, in the 1980s and 1990s, insider successors resulted in higher organizational performance, while outside CEO successors resulted in poorer organizational performance. However, organizational performance following CEO succession shows the opposite results in the 2000s (Schepker et al., 2015). Regardless of whether the CEO successor is an insider or an outsider, the importance of succession planning is illustrated by research indicating that interim CEOs are likely to perform poorly (Ballinger and Marcel, 2010) and are more likely to manage earnings in order to increase their chances of promotion (Chen et al., 2015).

The implementation process includes considering how a CEO will be removed from office (Ertugrul and Krishnan, 2011), the timing of CEO departure (Tichy, 1996), informing the unsuccessful candidates of their status (Cannella and Shen, 2001), informing the stakeholders of who was selected as the new CEO (Chen, 2008), and onboarding the new CEO. One illustrative example regarding how boards try to manage this process comes from evidence gathered by Graffin and colleagues (2011), who suggest that boards routinely try to mask the differences between the exiting and incoming CEOs to avoid potential negative stock market reactions. This process is critical, as investors have been shown to respond negatively to both the hiring of an interim CEO and the removal of a CEO without a named replacement (Gangloff et al., 2015).

17.3 UNANSWERED SUCCESSION QUESTIONS

There is so much more that needs to be addressed regarding succession planning that it is easy to generate a long list of questions. However, generating interesting research questions without first developing the underlying theoretical mechanisms could result in continued lack of progress in our understanding of the phenomenon. We suggest that research should focus on understanding, developing, and testing succession-planning theory to help understand its underlying theoretical mechanisms. The theories most commonly applied include upper-echelons, power, and agency theories, and extending these theories to more thoroughly consider CEO-succession processes could help better explain some of the unanswered questions. Additionally, integrating these theories with individual-level theories, such as information-asymmetry or decision-making theory, can provide opportunities for better understanding how individual actions aggregate to affect the succession process. This approach would encourage research that is more theoretically connected and facilitate a more programmatic progression.

Additionally, as we noted, the specific processes involved in CEO-succession research is severely under-researched. Most of what we know about processes comes from single companies (e.g., Brooks, 2014; Durst and Wilhelm, 2012; Rochadel, 2015) or from studies with small sample sizes. These studies are best described as comparative case studies (e.g., Conger and Fulmer, 2003; Greer and Virick, 2008; Kim, 2010). To address this gap, the Center for Executive Succession (CES) at the University of South Carolina started the HR@Moore survey to research the specific processes of succession for the C-Suite, with emphasis on the CEO (Wright et al., 2013, 2014, 2015a). CES is a partnership designed to bring together academics and executives including directors, CEOs, and chief human resource officers (CHROs) to discuss senior-leader succession. Early experience is demonstrating that this environment provides a secure environment for sensitive knowledge to be discussed, disguised, and distributed.

Early CES surveys find a broad spectrum of how much responsibility resides with the board versus the CEO regarding the CEO-succession process, with the central tendency being a 40% to 60% split in favor of either the board or the CEO. This reveals that there are multiple sets of processes involved in C-Suite succession, including processes internal to the TMT and processes primarily associated with the board of directors. It is also increasingly becoming clear that there is usually a tension between the board and the incumbent CEO regarding CEO succession—this is even true when the company is doing well and the CEO is voluntarily planning retirement. This tension results from the board having fiduciary responsibilities to long-term shareholder interests, while the incumbent CEO may have a distinct agenda and is often able to control much of the information flow to the board. This leads the board to rely on *disinterested* brokers among the incumbent TMT to help understand and maneuver the succession process, and in many companies this is becoming the CHRO's responsibility.

The four most prevalent practices for developing talent include giving candidates exposure to the board, defining who has ownership of succession processes, conducting ongoing assessment of candidates, and scheduling conversations with the CEO; the least prevalent practice is exploring the external market for successors. At the C-Suite level, the four most prevalent practices for developing talent are: (1) providing high potentials access to senior leadership; (2) developing high potentials through job and role change or expansion to broaden through new challenges and to fill experience gaps; (3) providing experiences required for critical leadership positions and mapping high potentials; and (4) providing rotational assignment for high potentials across departments and or functions. High-level exposure and practical experience are critical for developing talent.

In an open-ended response format, respondents cited special projects, job rotations and stretch assignments, leadership development programs, extensive assessment, and interaction with the board as some of the innovative practices used to build the C-Suite pipeline. Our findings also indicate inconsistencies across organizations, and it seems likely that the same succession practice may produce different outcomes in different organizations. The surveys also reveal that onboarding is a critical component to making a CEO successful after the transition. Formal onboarding processes include the creation of a structured plan, new leader assimilation, listening and town hall tours, and transitioning internally.

17.4 IDEAS FOR APPROACHING
UNANSWERED SUCCESSION QUESTIONS

Succession research has primarily looked at the CEO and been performed by those focused on macro or strategic research topics. However, through integrating additional literature and research domains while recognizing succession may differ across employee populations, we can promote a greater understanding of the nuanced microfoundations underlying succession processes. Some of these areas include selection, development, turnover, teams, and matching.

17.4.1 Selection

We know plenty about individual selection (e.g., Highhouse and Brooks, 2017; Ployhart et al., 2006), but this knowledge is rarely incorporated in succession-planning research. Within the I/O psychology and strategic HR domains, there is a vast selection literature, but this research primarily focuses on lower levels in the firm (Ployhart, 2012), and this knowledge has not been overtly applied to succession planning. To the extent that we can apply some of the knowledge accumulated over the decades in selection research, it may facilitate our understanding of the processes involved in succession research across the organization. In other words, appropriately choosing employees with valuable KSAOs for the organization is an important first step in succession planning.

For instance, best practices dictate a formalized selection process to identify the necessary KSAOs to perform the necessary tasks. When organizations hire not only for the skills required, but also for how the KSAOs of the new hire will contribute to the overall interaction of the combination of KSAOs of the firm, they increase the ability to create a valuable, rare, inimitable, and non-substitutable resource, which can lead to competitive advantage (Barney, 1991; Ployhart et al., 2014). Therefore, how the KSAOs of a new hire or newly promoted member of the team combine with the KSAOs of existing members becomes an essential consideration. Recent research has also expanded theorizing about how individual selection can lead to emergence at collective level resources (Ployhart and Moliterno, 2011; Ployhart et al., 2014).

17.4.2 Development

Talent development has long been recognized as a critical cog in maintaining organizational performance (Huselid et al., 1997). Unfortunately, very little succession research includes a developmental role. For instance, there is evidence that developmental assignments, particularly those that provide growth opportunities, are associated with higher competencies (Day and O'Connor, 2017; Dragoni et al., 2009). However, much more research is needed to understand how such competencies translate to better performance as individuals move to higher-level jobs.

17.4.3 Turnover

Succession necessarily involves turnover. However, most succession research fails to incorporate the turnover literature. This is particularly surprising given that most of succession literature begins by focusing on a CEO turnover event, and individual turnover is one of the more researched human resources areas and one where we know a great deal (Holtomb et al., 2008).

Recent research has spent more time theorizing about how to explore the causes, consequences, and processes involved in human capital resource reductions (Ployhart et al., 2014), primarily through considering collective turnover (e.g., Hausknecht and Holwerda, 2013; Hausknecht and Trevor, 2011; Nyberg and Ployhart, 2013). When a new CEO takes office, it often results in multiple changes to the TMT (Boyer and Ortiz-Molina, 2008) and the board (Farrell and Whidbee, 2000; Marcel et al., 2013), resulting in collective turnover. Another collective effect of CEO succession occurs when a high-performing CEO is hired by another firm and takes key talent with her to build the KSAOs of the newly formed TMT (Groysberg and Lee, 2009). Succession events also have cascading effects. For instance, if a person is promoted from chief financial officer

(CFO) to CEO, then the CEO-succession event also creates a succession event at the CFO level, and if this is filled internally, that executive's role must then be filled, etc. This is a particularly meaningful concern as we are only beginning to learn more about the criticality of base levels of Human Capital Resources (Call et al., 2015a) and how replacements can mitigate such reductions (Reilly et al., 2014).

17.4.4 Teams

Teams are essential throughout the organization (Kehoe, Rosikiewicz, and Tzabbar, 2017; Mathieu et al., 2008). The firm's ability to develop and implement a strategy to create a sustained competitive advantage is dependent on the interaction between the CEO and the rest of the TMT, including their joint ability to make decisions and take strategic action. For example, a TMT that compliments the CEO's strengths and weaknesses may lead to stronger team (and consequently organizational) performance than a TMT that duplicates the CEO's strengths and weaknesses. Similarly, after a CEO changes, the fit between the new CEO and the TMT may dramatically change because of different characteristics of the new CEO, and a firm may do better to replace other TMT members to strengthen the overall team. Thus, understanding how the new CEO will combine and interact with the TMT will help scholars and directors understand what conditions increase the likelihood of success, and understanding this is fundamentally a team's research question. This is compounded because turnover among teams at all levels of the firm can exert substantive disruptions on the functioning of that team and the performance of those the team affects.

For example, workers could focus too much on personal outcomes while neglecting team or organizational performance (Deckop et al., 1999; Mitchell and Silver, 1990; Morrison, 1994; Shaw et al., 2002). Some also suggest an inherent social dilemma occurs when individual- and group-level incentives are mixed. It is claimed that this creates a conflict between individual interests and collective interests (Barnes et al., 2008; Sniezek et al., 1990; Wageman, 1995), but such pay mixtures are ubiquitous among most TMTs. Using what we know from teams-based research (e.g., Mathieu et al., 2008) could inform succession researchers about how best to plan for changing team dynamics. This could mitigate disruptions to teams throughout the organization, as well as optimizing team decision making.

17.4.5 Fit

The importance of fit (e.g., person-environment fit, person-job fit, etc.) is well known (Edwards, 1991; Kristof, 1996; Kristof-Brown et al., 2005), but this knowledge has not been applied to succession planning. This is disturbing because recent research has found that one of the most common reasons for succession failure is poor fit with the culture or the members of the TMT (Wright et al., 2015b). Fit is particularly important for creating firm-specific human capital because better fit in heterogeneous firms makes it more difficult for competitors to emulate (Lazear, 2009).

One way to think about creating optimal fit is through continual talent matching or optimizing human capital with necessary tasks (Weller et al., 2015). This is accomplished by optimizing internal labor-market flexibility to create better matches, value, and competitive advantage (Reilly et al., 2014). Given that many firms have multiple job requirements, stimulating internal labor markets may motivate individuals to invest in additional skill sets. Consequently, there is potential for value creation and performance advantages through internal markets or improved talent-matching flexibility (Way et al., 2015; Wright and Snell, 1998). Of course, optimizing matching through flexibility requires knowing the needs of the organization and employee skill sets.

For instance, at the beginning of the CEO-succession process, much could be gained from learning more about how desirable characteristics of the new CEO are determined. We did not find any research detailing the selection and onboarding processes, even though the announcement of the CEO during the onboarding process is an event that affects firm performance and stakeholder expectations (Jalal and Prezas, 2012). Additionally, apart from the announcement itself, we could not find any research that discusses how well the succession process was implemented. At the same time, little research exists that examines the impact, or how to minimize unwanted disruptions, when the new CEO takes office. Further, it would be valuable to understand how firms determine whether the best candidate was actually selected for the position, outside of simply evaluating the new CEO's performance.

17.5 Conclusion

Overall, our findings raise questions of the effectiveness of CEO succession and show that researchers know very little about what constitutes best practices. It is not even clear that researchers understand what constitutes a successful process (e.g., is it simply shareholder return, the person keeping the job for a specified period of time, etc.). What we do know is that organizations claim that the chief human resource officer can help develop C-Suite candidates by managing the succession process, through assessment of high potentials, by supporting the development of individual development plans, and through coaching. Additionally, organizations say that considering diversity implications when identifying high potentials, using metrics to measure the strength of the leadership pipeline, and informing high potentials of their status is more important than looking for high potentials outside of the organization or using current high potentials to help identify future high potentials (Wright et al., 2015a).

Not surprisingly, one of the biggest challenges in succession processes is the uncertainty of future talent requirements. For example, with regard to forecasting CEO departure, 80% of respondents state there is no agreed upon timeline for the CEO to retire. Of the few that did have a plan, responses on the timeline spanned timeframes between 6 months and 5 years, with more than 20% responding over 5 years. This variety makes the succession timeframe very idiosyncratic to each organization. With the added complexity of future strategy changes, this makes the future staffing requirement very uncertain. Cappelli (2008, 2011) suggests dealing with this uncertainty by running staff lean and hiring from the outside to address talent gaps while avoiding overproducing costly talent. We also suggest using knowledge garnered from other research areas (e.g., fit, teams, turnover, development, selection) to help determine succession-planning best practices that can be a key tool for optimizing managing talent.

References

Adams, J. C., and Mansi, S. A. 2009. CEO turnover and bondholder wealth. *Journal of Banking & Finance*, 33(3), pp.522–33.

Aguinis, H., and O'Boyle, E. H. 2014. Star performers in twenty-first-century organizations. *Personnel Psychology*, 67, pp.313–50.

Allgood, S., and Farrell, K. A. 2000. The effect of CEO tenure on the relation between firm performance and turnover. *Journal of Financial Research*, 23(3), pp.373–90.

Ang, J., Lauterbach, B., and Vu, J. 2003. Efficient labor and capital markets: evidence from CEO appointments. *Financial Management*, 32(2), pp.27–52.

Arthaud-Day, M., Certo, S. T., Dalton, C. M., and Dalton, D. R. 2006. A changing of the guard: executive and director turnover following corporate financial restatements. *Academy of Management Journal*, 49(6), pp.1119–36.

Ballinger, G. A., and Marcel, J. J. 2010. The use of an interim CEO during succession episodes and firm performance. *Strategic Management Journal*, 31(3), pp.262–83.

Barnes, C. M., Hollenbeck, J. R., Wagner, D. T., DeRue, D. S. et al. 2008. Harmful help: the costs of backing-up behavior in teams. *Journal of Applied Psychology*, 93(3), pp.529–39.

Barney, J. 1991. Firm resources and sustained competitive advantage. *Journal of Management*, 17(1), pp.99–120.

Barron, J. M., Chulkov, D. V., and Waddell, G. R. 2011. Top management team turnover, CEO succession type, and strategic change. *Journal of Business Research*, 64(8), pp.904–10.

Berry, T. K., Bizjak, J. M., Lemmon, M. L., and Naveen, L. 2006. Organizational complexity and CEO labor markets: evidence from diversified firms. *Journal of Corporate Finance*, 12(4), pp.797–817.

Bigley, G. A., and Wiersema, M. F. 2002. New CEOs and corporate strategic refocusing: how experience as heir apparent influences the use of power. *Administrative Science Quarterly*, 47(4), pp.707–27.

Billger, S. M., and Hallock, K. F. 2005. Mass layoffs and CEO turnover. *Industrial Relations*, 44(3), pp.463–89.

Blackwell, D. W., Dudney, D. M., and Farrell, K. A. 2007. Changes in CEO compensation structure and the impact on firm performance following CEO turnover. *Review of Quantitative Finance and Accounting*, 29(3), pp.315–38.

Boeker, W. 1992. Power and managerial dismissal: scapegoating at the top. *Administrative Science Quarterly*, 37(3), pp.400–21.

Boivie, S., Graffin, S. D., and Pollock, T. G. 2012. Time for me to fly: predicting director exit at large firms. *Academy of Management Journal*, 55(6), pp.1334–59.

Boivie, S., Graffin, S. D, and Pollock, T. G. In press. *Academy of Management Journal*.

Bonet, R., and Hamori, M. 2017. Talent Intermediaries. In D. G. Collings, K. Mellahi, and W. F. Cascio, eds., *Oxford handbook of talent management*, pp. 251–69. Oxford: Oxford University Press.

Boyer, M. M., and Ortiz-Molina, H. 2008. Career concerns of top executives, managerial ownership and CEO succession. *Corporate Governance: An International Review*, 16(3), pp.178–93.

Brooks, S. 2014. Strategic, future-proof succession planning connects Telefónica with success: how HR was able to move the process on. *Human Resource Management International Digest*, 22(2), pp.28–30.

Bruton, G., Fried, V., and Hisrich, R. D. 1997. Venture capitalist and CEO dismissal. *Entrepreneurship: Theory and Practice*, 21(3), pp.41–55.

Buchholtz, A. K., Ribbens, B. A., and Houle, I. T. 2003. The role of human capital in postacquisition CEO departure. *Academy of Management Journal*, 46(4), pp.506–14.

Bushman, R., Dai, Z., and Wang, X. 2010. Risk and CEO turnover. *Journal of Financial Economics*, 96(3), pp.381–98.

Call, M. L., Nyberg, A. J., Ployhart, R. E., and Weekley, J. 2015a. The dynamic nature of collective turnover and unit performance: the impact of time, quality, and replacements. *Academy of Management Journal*, 58(4), pp.1208–32.

Call, M. L., Nyberg, A. J., and Thatcher, S. M. B. 2015b. Stargazing: an integrative conceptual review, theoretical reconciliation, and extension for star employee research. *Journal of Applied Psychology*, 100(3), pp.623–640.

Cannella, A. A., and Shen, W. 2001. So close and yet so far: promotion versus exit for CEO heirs apparent. *Academy of Management Journal*, 44(2), pp.252–70.

Cappelli, P. 2000. A market-driven approach to retaining talent. *Harvard Business Review*, 78, pp.103–11.

Cappelli, P. 2011. Succession planning. In *APA handbook of industrial and organizational psychology*, pp.673–90. Washington, DC: American Psychological Association.

Cappelli, P. 2008. Talent management for the twenty-first century. *Harvard Business Review*, 86(3), pp.74–81.

Cappelli, P., and Keller, JR. 2014. Talent management: conceptual approaches and practical challenges. *Annual Review of Organizational Psychology and Organizational Behavior*, 1(1), pp.305–31.

Cappelli, P., and Keller, JR. 2017. The historical context of talent management. In D. G. Collings, K. Mellahi, and W. F. Cascio, eds., *Oxford handbook of talent management*, pp. 23–43. Oxford: Oxford University Press.

Carpenter, M. A., and Wade, J. B. 2002. Microlevel opportunity structures as determinants of non-CEO executive pay. *Academy of Management Journal*, 45(6), pp.1085–103.

Carroll, G. R. 1984. Dynamics of publisher succession in newspaper organizations. *Administrative Science Quarterly*, 29(1), pp.93–113.

Chen, G. 2008. Three essays on CEO replacement in turnaround situations. Unpublished doctoral dissertation, Smeal College of Business.

Chen, G., and Hambrick, D. C. 2012. CEO replacement in turnaround situations: executive (mis) fit and its performance implications. *Organization Science*, 23(1), pp.225–43.

Chen, G., Luo, S., Tang, Y., and Tong, J. Y. 2015. Passing probation: earnings management by interim CEOs and its effect on their promotion prospects. *Academy of Management Journal*, 58(5), pp.1389–418.

Collings, D. G. 2017. Workforce differentiation. In D. G. Collings, K. Mellahi, and W. F. Cascio, eds., *Oxford handbook of talent management*, pp. 301–17. Oxford, Oxford University Press.

Conger, J. A., and Fulmer, R. M. 2003. Developing your leadership pipeline. *Harvard Business Review*, 81(12), pp.76–85.

Crossland, C., and Chen, G. 2013. Executive accountability around the world: sources of cross-national variation in firm performance–CEO dismissal sensitivity. *Strategic Organization*, 11(1), pp.78–109.

Crossland, C., Zyung, J., Hiller, N. J., and Hambrick, D. C. 2014. CEO career variety: effects on firm-level strategic and social novelty. *Academy of Management Journal*, 57(3), pp.652–74.

Daily, C. M., an Dalton, D. R. 1995. CEO and director turnover in failing firms: an illusion of change? *Strategic Management Journal*, 16(5), pp.393–400.

Datta, D. K., and Guthrie, J. P. 1994. Executive succession: organizational antecedents of CEO characteristics. *Strategic Management Journal*, 15(7), pp.569–77.

Datta, D. K., and Rajagopalan, N. 1998. Industry structure and CEO characteristics: an empirical study of succession events. *Strategic Management Journal*, 19(9), pp.833–52.

Davidson III, W. N., Nemec, C., and Worrell, D. L. 2006. Determinants of CEO age at succession. *Journal of Management & Governance*, 10(1), pp.35–57.

Davidson III, W. N., Nemec, C., Worrell, D. L., and Lin, J. 2002. Industrial origin of CEOs in outside succession: board preference and stockholder reaction. *Journal of Management and Governance*, 6(4), pp.295–321.

Davidson III, W. N., Ning, Y., Rakowski, D., and Elsaid, E. 2008. The antecedents of simultaneous appointments to CEO and Chair. *Journal of Management and Governance*, 12(4), pp.381–401.

Day, D. V., and O'Connor, P. 2017. Talent development: building organizational capability. In D. G. Collings, K. Mellahi, and W. F. Cascio, eds., *Oxford handbook of talent management*, pp. 343–60. Oxford: Oxford University Press.

Deckop, J. R., Mangel, R., and Cirka, C. C. 1999. Research notes. Getting more than you pay for: organizational citizenship behavior and pay-for-performance plans. *Academy of Management Journal*, 42(4), pp.420–28.

Denis, D. J., and Denis, D. K. 1995. Performance changes following top management dismissals. *The Journal of Finance*, 50(4), pp.1029–57.

Dragoni, L., Tesluk, P. E., Russell, J. E., and Oh, I. S. 2009. Understanding managerial development: integrating developmental assignments, learning orientation, and access to developmental opportunities in predicting managerial competencies. *Academy of Management Journal*, 52(4), pp.731–43.

Du, C., and Lin, T. T. 2011. CEO turnover, equity-based compensation and firms investment decisions. *Journal of Business & Economics Research*, 9(8), pp.19–40.

Durst, S., and Wilhelm, S. 2012. Knowledge management and succession planning in SMEs. *Journal of Knowledge Management*, 16(4), pp.637–49.

Edwards, J. R. 1991. Person-job fit: a conceptual integration, literature review, and methodological critique. In C. L. Cooper and I. T. Robertson, eds., *International review of industrial and organizational psychology*, pp.283–357. Oxford: John Wiley & Sons.

Ertugrul, M., and Krishnan, K. 2011. Can CEO dismissals be proactive? *Journal of Corporate Finance*, 17(1), pp.134–51.

Farrell, K. A., and Whidbee, D. A. 2000. The consequences of forced CEO succession for outside directors (digest summary). *Journal of Business*, 73(4), pp.597–627.

Finkelstein, S., Hambrick, D. C., and Cannella, A. A., Jr. 2009. *Strategic leadership: theory and research on executives, top management teams, and boards*. New York: Oxford University Press.

Fong, E. A., Misangyi, V. F., and Tosi, H. L. 2010. The effect of CEO pay deviations on CEO withdrawal, firm size, and firm profits. *Strategic Management Journal*, 31(6), pp.629–51.

Fosberg, R., 2001. CEO replacement and compensation around dividend omissions. *Corporate Governance*, 9(1), pp.25–35.

Friedman, S. D., and Saul, K. 1991. A leader's wake: organization member reactions to CEO succession. *Journal of Management*, 17(3), pp.619–42.

Friedman, S. D., and Singh, H. 1989. CEO succession and stockholder reaction: the influence of organizational context and event content. *Academy of Management Journal*, 32(4), pp.718–44.

Gangloff, K. A., Connelly, B. L., and Shook, C. L. 2016. Of scapegoats and signals: investor reactions to CEO succession in the aftermath of wrongdoing. *Journal of Management*, 42(6), pp. 1664–34.

Geiger, M. A., and North, D. S. 2011. Do CEOs and principal financial officers take a "bath" separately or together? An investigation of discretionary accruals surrounding appointments of new CEOs and PFOs. *Academy of Accounting and Financial Studies Journal*, 15(1), pp.1–30.

Goel, A. M., and Thakor, A. V. 2008. Overconfidence, CEO selection, and corporate governance. *The Journal of Finance*, 63(6), pp.2737–84.

Gong, J. J., and Wu, S. Y. 2011. CEO turnover in private equity sponsored leveraged buyouts. *Corporate Governance: An International Review*, 19(3), pp.195–209.

Gordon, S. S., Stewart, W. H., Sweo, R., and Luker, W. A. 2000. Convergence versus strategic reorientation: the antecedents of fast-paced organizational change. *Journal of Management*, 26(5), pp.911–45.

Graffin, S. D., Carpenter, M. A., and Boivie, S. 2011. What's all that (strategic) noise? Anticipatory impression management in CEO succession. *Strategic Management Journal*, 32(7), pp.748–70.

Greer, C. R., and Virick, M. 2008. Diverse succession planning: lessons from the industry leaders. *Human Resource Management*, 47(2), pp.351–67.

Groysberg, B., and Lee, L. E. 2009. Hiring stars and their colleagues: exploration and exploitation in professional service firms. *Organization Science*, 20(4), pp.740–58.

Grusky, O. 1961. Corporate size, bureaucratization, and managerial succession. *American Journal of Sociology*, 67(3), pp.261–9.

Grusky, O. 1963. Managerial succession and organizational effectiveness. *American Journal of Sociology*, 69(1), pp.21–31.

Grusky, O. 1969. Succession with an ally. *Administrative Science Quarterly*, 14(2), pp.155–70.

Guthrie Datta, J. P., and Deepak, K. 1997. Contextual influences on executive selection: firm characteristics and CEO experience. *Journal of Management Studies*, 34(4), pp.537–60.

Hambrick, D. C. 2007. Upper echelons theory: an update. *Academy of Management Review*, 32(2), pp.334–43.

Hamori, M., and Koyuncu, B. 2015. Experience matters? The impact of prior CEO experience on firm performance. *Human Resource Management*, 54(1), pp.23–44.

Harrison, J. R., Torres, D. L., and Kukalis, S. 1988. The changing of the guard: turnover and structural change in the top-management positions. *Administrative Science Quarterly*, 33(2), pp.211–32.

Hausknecht, J. 2017. Talent turnover. In D. G. Collings, K. Mellahi, and W. F. Cascio, eds., *Oxford handbook of talent management*, pp. 261–74. Oxford: Oxford University Press.

Hausknecht, J. P., and Holwerda, J. A. 2013. When does employee turnover matter? Dynamic member configurations, productive capacity, and collective performance. *Organization Science*, 24(1), pp.210–25.

Hausknecht, J. P., and Trevor, C. O. 2011. Collective turnover at the group, unit, and organizational levels: evidence, issues, and implications. *Journal of Management*, 37(1), pp.352–88.

Haveman, H. A. 1993. Ghosts of managers past: managerial succession and organizational mortality. *Academy of Management Journal*, 36(4), pp.864–81.

Haveman, H. A., Russo, M. V., and Meyer, A. D. 2001. Organizational environments in flux: the impact of regulatory punctuations on organizational domains, CEO succession, and performance. *Organization Science*, 12(3), pp.253–73.

He, E., Sommer, D. W., and Xie, X. 2011. The impact of CEO turnover on property–liability insurer performance. *Journal of Risk and Insurance*, 78(3), pp.583–608.

Helwege, J., Intintoli, V. J., and Zhang, A. 2012. Voting with their feet or activism? Institutional investors' impact on CEO turnover. *Journal of Corporate Finance*, 18(1), pp.22–37.

Highhouse, S., and Brooks, M. 2017. Selecting for talent. In D. G. Collings, K. Mellahi, and W. F. Cascio, eds., *Oxford handbook of talent management*, pp. 251–69. Oxford: Oxford University Press.

Holtom, B. C., Mitchell, T. R., Lee, T. W., and Eberly, M. B. 2008. Turnover and retention research: a glance at the past, a closer review of the present, and a venture into the future. *The Academy of Management Annals*, 2(1), pp.231–74.

Hornstein, A. S. 2013. Corporate captial budgeting and CEO turnover. *Journal of Corporate Finance*, 20, pp.41–58.

Huang, T. C. 2001. Succession management systems and human resource outcomes. *International Journal of Manpower*, 22(8), pp.736–47.

Huselid, M. A., Jackson, S. E., and Schuler, R. S. 1997. Technical and strategic human resource management effectiveness as determinants of firm performance. *Academy of Management Journal*, 40(1), pp.171–88.

Intintoli, V. J. 2013. The effects of succession choice surrounding CEO turnover announcements: evidence from marathon successions. *Financial Management*, 38, pp.211–38.

Jalal, A. M., and Prezas, A. P. 2012. Outsider CEO succession and firm performance. *Journal of Economics and Business*, 64(6), pp.399–426.

Jenter, D., and Kanaan, F. 2015. CEO turnover and relative performance evaluation. *The Journal of Finance*, 70(5), pp.2155–84.

Jiang, F., Huang, J., and Kim, K. A. 2013. Appointments of outsiders as CEOs, state-owned enterprises, and firm performance: evidence from China. *Pacific-Basin Finance Journal*, 23, pp.49–64.

Karaevli, A. 2007. Performance consequences of new CEO "outsiderness": moderating effects of pre- and post-succession contexts. *Strategic Management Journal*, 28(7), pp.681–706.

Kato, T., and Long, C. 2006. CEO turnover, firm performance, and enterprise reform in China: Evidence from micro data. *Journal of Comparative Economics*, 34(4), pp.796–817.

Kehoe, R., Rosikiewicz, B. L., and Tzabbar, D. 2017. Talent and teams. In D. G. Collings, K. Mellahi, and W. F. Cascio, eds., *Oxford handbook of talent management*, pp. 153–68. Oxford: Oxford University Press.

Kesner, I. F., and Dalton, D. R. 1985. The effect of board composition on CEO succession and organizational performance. *Quarterly Journal of Business and Economics*, 24(2), pp.3–20.

Kesner, I. F., and Sebora, T. C. 1994. Executive succession: past, present and future. *Journal of Management*, 20(2), pp.327–72.

Khaliq, A. A., Thompson, D. M., and Walston, S. L. 2006. Perceptions of hospital CEOs about the effects of CEO turnover. *Hospital Topics*, 84(4), pp.21–7.

Kim, Y., 2010. Measuring the value of succession planning and management: a qualitative study of multinational companies. *Performance Improvement Quarterly*, 23(2), pp.5–31.

Kristof, A. L. 1996. Person-organization fit: an integrative review of its conceptualizations, measurement, and implications. *Personnel Psychology*, 49(1), pp.1–49.

Kristof-Brown, A. L., Zimmerman, R. D., and Johnson, E. C. 2005. Consequences of individuals' fit at work: a meta-analysis of person-job, person-organization, person-group, and person-supervisor fit. *Personnel Psychology*, 58(2), pp.281–342.

Lant, T. K., Milliken, F. J., and Batra, B. 1992. The role of managerial learning and interpretation in strategic persistence and reorientation: an empirical exploration. *Strategic Management Journal*, 13(8), pp.585–608.

Lazear, E. P. 2009. Firm-specific human capital: a skill-weights approach. *Journal of Political Economy*, 117(5), pp.914–40.

Lee, P. M., and James, E. H. 2007. She'-e-os: Gender effects and investor reactions to the announcements of top executive appointments. *Strategic Management Journal*, 28(3), pp.227–41.

Lee, T. H., Gerhart, B., Weller, I., and Trevor, C. O. 2008. Understanding voluntary turnover: path-specific job satisfaction effects and the importance of unsolicited job offers. *Academy of Management Journal*, 51(4), pp.651–71.

Lehn, K. M., and Zhao, M. 2006. CEO turnover after acquisitions: are bad bidders fired? *The Journal of Finance*, 61(4), pp.1759–811.

Liu, Y., Yu, H. Y., and Valenti, A. M. 2012. Presuccession performance, CEO succession, top management team, and change in a firm's internationalization: the moderating effect of CEO/chairperson dissimilarity. *Canadian Journal of Administrative Sciences*, 26, pp.67–78.

Maltarich, M. A., Nyberg, A. J., and Reilly, G. 2010. A conceptual and empirical analysis of the cognitive ability–voluntary turnover relationship. *Journal of Applied Psychology*, 95(6), pp.1058–70.

Marcel, J. J., Cowen, A. P., and Ballinger, G. A. 2013. Are disruptive CEO successions viewed as a governance lapse? Evidence from board turnover. *Journal of Management*. DOI: 10.1177/0149206313503011.

Martinson, B., 2012. And the winner is! Corporate life cycle stage as an antecedent to CEO selection characteristics. *American Journal of Business and Management*, 1(4), pp.248–58.

Mathieu, J., Maynard, M. T., Rapp, T., and Gilson, L. 2008. Team effectiveness 1997–2007: a review of recent advancements and a glimpse into the future. *Journal of Management*, 34(3), pp.410–76.

Messersmith, J. G., Lee, J. Y., Guthrie, J. P., and Ji, Y. Y. 2013. Turnover at the top: executive team departures and firm performance. *Organization Science*, 25, pp.776–93.

Mitchell, T. R., and Silver, W. S. 1990. Individual and group goals when workers are interdependent: effects on task strategies and performance. *Journal of Applied Psychology*, 75(2), pp.185–93.

Mobbs, S., and Raheja, C. G. 2012. Internal managerial promotions: insider incentives and CEO succession. *Journal of Corporate Finance*, 18(5), pp.1337–53.

Mooney, C. H., Semadeni, M., and Kesner, I. F. 2014. The selection of an interim CEO: boundary conditions and the pursuit of temporary leadership. *Journal of Management*. DOI: 10.1177/0149206314535433.

Morrison, E. W. 1994. Role definitions and organizational citizenship behavior: the importance of the employee's perspective. *Academy of Management Journal*, 37(6), pp.1543–67.

Navin, T. R. 1971. Passing on the mantle. *Business Horizons*, 14(5), pp.83–93.

Nguyen, B. D. 2011. Ownership structure and board characteristics as determinants of CEO turnover in French-listed companies. *Finance*, 32(2), pp.53–89.

Nyberg, A. J. 2010. Retaining your high performers: moderators of the performance–job satisfaction–voluntary turnover relationship. *Journal of Applied Psychology*, 95(3), pp.440–53.

Nyberg, A. J., and Ployhart, R. E. 2013. Context-emergent turnover (CET) theory: a theory of collective turnover. *Academy of Management Review*, 38(1), pp.109–31.

Ocasio, W. 1994. Political dynamics and the circulation of power: CEO succession in US industrial corporations, 1960–1990. *Administrative Science Quarterly*, 39(2), pp.285–312.

Ocasio, W., and Kim, H. 1999. The circulation of corporate control: selection of functional backgrounds of new CEOs in large US manufacturing firms, 1981–1992. *Administrative Science Quarterly*, 44, pp.532–62.

Osborn, R. N., Jauch, L. R., Martin, T. N., and Glueck, W. F. 1981. The event of CEO succession, performance, and environmental conditions. *Academy of Management Journal*, 24(1), pp.183–91.

Ozelge, S., and Saunders, A. 2012. The role of lending banks in forced CEO turnovers. *Journal of Money, Credit and Banking*, 44(4), pp.631–59.

Parrino, R. 1997. CEO turnover and outside succession: a cross-sectional analysis. *Journal of Financial Economics*, 46(2), pp.165–97.

Pi, L., and Lowe, J. 2011. Can a powerful CEO avoid involuntary replacement? An empirical study from China. *Asia Pacific Journal of Management*, 28(4), pp.775–805.

Pissaris, S., Weinstein, M., and Stephan, J. 2010. The influence of cognitive simplification processes on the CEO succession decision. *Journal of Management Research*, 10(2), pp.71–86.

Pitcher, P., Chreim, S., and Kisfalvi, V. 2000. CEO succession research: methodological bridges over troubled waters. *Strategic Management Journal*, 21(6), pp.625–48.

Powell, K. S., and Lim, E. 2009. Nonroutine CEO turnover in Korean Chaebols. *Journal of Asia-Pacific Business*, 10(2), pp.146–65.

Puffer, S. M., and Weintrop, J. B. 1991. Corporate performance and CEO turnover: the role of performance expectations. *Administrative Science Quarterly*, 36(1), pp.1–19.

Pfeffer, J., and Salancik, G. R. 1977. Organizational context and the characteristics and tenure of hospital administrators. *Academy of Management Journal*, 20(1), pp.74–88.

Ployhart, R. E. 2012. Personnel selection and the competitive advantage of firms. In *International review of industrial and organizational psychology*, pp.153–95. Indianapolis: Wiley.

Ployhart, R. E., and Moliterno, T. P. 2011. Emergence of the human capital resource: a multilevel model. *Academy of Management Review*, 36(1), pp.127–50.

Ployhart, R. E., Nyberg, A. J., Reilly, G., and Maltarich, M. A. 2014. Human capital is dead; long live human capital resources! *Journal of Management*, 40(2), pp.371–98.

Ployhart, R. E., Schneider, B., and Schmitt, N. 2006. *Staffing organizations: contemporary practice and theory*, 3rd edn. Mahwah, NJ: Lawrence Erlbaum Associates.

Quigley, T. J., and Hambrick, D. C. 2014. Has the "CEO effect" increased in recent decades? A new explanation for the great rise in America's attention to corporate leaders. *Strategic Management Journal*, 36(6), pp.821–30.

Rachpradit, P., Tang, J. C. S., and Khang, D. B. 2012. CEO turnover and firm performance: evidence from Thailand. *Corporate Governance*, 12(2), pp.164–78.

Reilly, G., Nyberg, A. J., Maltarich, M. A., and Weller, I. 2014. Human capital flows: using context-emergent turnover (CET) theory to explore the process by which turnover, hiring, and job demands affect patient satisfaction. *Academy of Management Journal*, 57(3), pp.766–90.

Rhim, J. C., Peluchette, J. V., and Song, I. 2006. Stock market reactions and firm performance surrounding CEO succession: antecedents of succession and successor origin. *American Journal of Business*, 21(1), pp.21–30.

Rochadel, W. 2015. Knowledge management and succession planning: case study in a food industry from the state of Paraná, Brazil. *International Journal of Knowledge Engineering and Management*, 4(8), pp.1–22.

Sakano, T., and Lewin, A. Y. 1999. Impact of CEO succession in Japanese companies: a coevolutionary perspective. *Organization Science*, 10(5), pp.654–71.

Schepker, D. J., Kim, Y., Patel, P., Campion, M. et al. 2015. The value of external hires: effects of external versus internal CEO successors on firm performance over time. Unpublished manuscript. University of South Carolina.

Shen, W., and Cannella, A. A., Jr. 2002. Revisiting the performance consequences of CEO succession: the impacts of successor type, postsuccession senior executive turnover, and departing CEO tenure. *Academy of Management Journal*, 45(4), pp.717–33.

Shaw, J. D., Gupta, N., and Delery, J. E. 2002. Pay dispersion and workforce performance: moderating effects of incentives and interdependence. *Strategic Management Journal*, 23(6), pp.491–512.

Smith, M., and White, M. C. 1987. Strategy, CEO specialization, and succession. *Administrative Science Quarterly*, 32(2), pp.263–80.

Sniezek, J. A., May, D. R., and Sawyer, J. E. 1990. Social uncertainty and interdependence: a study of resource allocation decisions in groups. *Organizational Behavior and Human Decision Processes*, 46(2), pp.155–80.

Takeda, M. B., Helms, M. M., and Romanova, N. 2006. Hair color stereotyping and CEO selection in the United Kingdom. *Journal of Human Behavior in the Social Environment*, 13(3), pp.85–99.

Tian, J. J., Haleblian, J. J., and Rajagopalan, N. 2010. The effects of board human and social capital on investor reactions to new CEO selection. *Strategic Management Journal*, 32(7), pp.731–47.

Tichy, N. 1996. Simultaneous transformation and CEO succession: key to global competitiveness. *Organizational Dynamics*, 25(1), pp.45–59.

Trevor, C. O., Gerhart, B., and Boudreau, J. W. 1997. Voluntary turnover and job performance: curvilinearity and the moderating influences of salary growth and promotions. *Journal of Applied Psychology*, 82(1), pp.44–61.

Virany, B., Tushman, M. L., and Romanelli, E. 1992. Executive succession and organization outcomes in turbulent environments: an organization learning approach. *Organization Science*, 3(1), pp.72–91.

Wageman, R. 1995. Interdependence and group effectiveness. *Administrative Science Quarterly*, 40(1), pp.145–80.

Wang, H., Davidson, W. N., III, and Wang, X. 2010. The Sarbanes-Oxley Act and CEO tenure, turnover, and risk aversion. *Quarterly Review of Economics and Finance*, 50(3), pp.367–76.

Wasserman, N. 2003. Founder-CEO succession and the paradox of entrepreneurial success. *Organization Science*, 14(2), pp.149–72.

Way, S. A., Tracey, J. B., Fay, C. H., Wright, P. M. et al. 2015. Validation of a multidimensional HR flexibility measure. *Journal of Management*, 41(4), pp.1098–131.

Welsh, M. A., and Dehler, G. E. 1988. Political legacy of administrative succession. *Academy of Management Journal*, 31(4), pp.948–61.

Weisbach, M. S. 1995. CEO turnover and the firm's investment decisions. *Journal of Financial Economics*, 37(2), pp.159–188.

Weller, I., Nyberg, A. J., and Abdulsalam, D. 2015. Talent matching as a dynamic capability: integrating economic and strategic human resource management perspectives. Paper presented at the Strategic Management Society conference, Denver.

Westphal, J. D., Boivie, S., and Ming Chng, D. H. 2006. The strategic impetus for social network ties: reconstituting broken CEO friendship ties. *Strategic Management Journal*, 27(5), pp.425–45.

Westphal, J. D., and Fredrickson, J. W. 2001. Who directs strategic change? Director experience, the selection of new CEOs, and change in corporate strategy. *Strategic Management Journal*, 22(12), pp.1113–37.

Wiersema, M. F., and Zhang, Y. 2011. CEO dismissal: the role of investment analysts. *Strategic Management Journal*, 32(11), pp.1161–82.

White, M. C. 1997. CEO succession: overcoming forces of inertia. *Human Relations*, 50(7), pp.805–28.

Wilson, C. N., and Stranahan, H. 2000. Organizational characteristics associated with hospital CEO turnover. *Journal of Healthcare Management*, 45(6), pp.395–404.

Worrell, D. L., and Davidson, W. N., III, 1987. The effect of CEO succession on stockholder wealth in large firms following the death of the predecessor. *Journal of Management*, 13(3), pp.509–15.

Wright, P. M., Call, M. L., Nyberg, A. J., Schepker, D. J. et al. 2015a. *Building the C-suite talent pipeline*. Darla Moore School of Business, University of South Carolina.

Wright, P. M., Nyberg, A. J., Schepker, D. J., and Ulrich, M. 2013. *The critical role of CHROs in CEO succession*. Darla Moore School of Business, University of South Carolina.

Wright, P. M., Nyberg, A. J., Schepker, D. J., and Ulrich, M. 2014. *CEO assessment and onboarding*. Darla Moore School of Business, University of South Carolina.

Wright, P. M., Schepker, D. J., Call, M. L., Nyberg, A. J. et al. 2015b. *C-suite succession failures: causes, effects, and prevention*. Darla Moore School of Business, University of South Carolina.

Wright, P. M., and Snell, S. A. 1998. Toward a unifying framework for exploring fit and flexibility in strategic human resource management. *Academy of Management Review*, 23(4), pp.756–72.

Zajac, E. J. 1990. CEO selection, succession, compensation and firm performance: a theoretical integration and empirical analysis. *Strategic Management Journal*, 11(3), pp.217–30.

Zajac, E. J., and Westphal, J. D. 1996. Who shall succeed? How CEO board preferences and power affect the choice of new CEOs. *Academy of Management Journal*, 39(1), pp.64–90.

Zhang, Y. 2006. The presence of a separate COO/president and its impact on strategic change and CEO dismissal. *Strategic Management Journal*, 27(3), pp.283–300.

Zhang, Y., and Rajagopalan, N. 2004. When the known devil is better than an unknown god: an empirical study of the antecedents and consequences of relay CEO successions. *Academy of Management Journal*, 47(4), pp.483–500.

Zhang, Y., and Rajagopalan, N. 2010. Once an outsider, always an outsider? CEO origin, strategic change, and firm performance. *Strategic Management Journal*, 31(3), pp.334–46.

CHAPTER 18

TALENT DEVELOPMENT

Building Organizational Capability

DAVID V. DAY AND PATRICIA M. G. O'CONNOR

AN important aspect of any organizationally driven talent-management system is attention to the investments—often considerable in terms of time and money—made in talent development. Developing individuals and their capabilities involves movement from one state or level to a more desired one over time. Thus, at the heart of any developmental initiative is individual and/or collective change. The focus of such developmental change for present purposes is talent, whether it is defined in terms of within-person capabilities or more holistically as between-person capacity, but it also involves time. In essence, talent development addresses how to change individuals and collectives in desired ways over time.

In terms of the plan of this chapter, an overview summary of the literature on talent development in young people is provided. Although often overlooked, this literature is rigorous and generally relevant to understanding talent processes in organizations. Talent development in young people elaborates on how nature, in the form of certain traits, and nurture, with regard to experiences, interact to shape development. This perspective is applied in understanding focal issues concerning building organizational capability through talent. Talent development among adult managers and leaders focuses on developing collective capability through the creation of systems, processes, practices, and cultures focused on achieving strategic objectives and doing so in a sustainable manner. Talented individuals are integral to designing and implementing collective phenomena, as well as responsible for executing, stewarding, and improving them. Taking a broad-focused approach to building organizational capability means going beyond a select group of especially talented (i.e., high-potential) employees to focusing on the development of broad-based organizational capacity for leadership. In general, this involves facilitating an inclusive approach to talent development in which nurturing the growth of every employee is essential (see Kegan and Lahey, 2016, on building an "everyone culture" in becoming a deliberately developmental organization).

To appreciate better these different perspectives and the implications for talent development in organizations, we first briefly review background theory on talent and its development independent of organizational contexts, to better understand the foundations of talent development in organizations and what is involved in developing broad-based leadership capacity.

18.1 THEORETICAL BACKGROUND ON TALENT DEVELOPMENT

Understanding the history of talent development requires a quick revisiting of the classic nature-versus-nurture distinction that has been the focus of much of the early psychological research on individual differences. In a nutshell, nature refers to those capabilities that are largely genetically inherited, such as personality and general intelligence (i.e., cognitive ability or *g*). At the other end of the continuum is nurture, which asserts that environmental factors such as education, training, and deliberate practice are the primary drivers of the development of exceptional capabilities or what has been called talent. The contemporary understanding of the nature–nurture issue is that talent develops as a function of both nature and nurture (Meyers, van Woerkom, and Dries, 2013). There is a certain innate capacity to excel in a given domain that is enhanced through environmental interventions such as coaching, training, and extensive practice.

Much of the attention on talent development historically has been on young people (i.e., children and adolescents) who become exceptional performers in specific domains such as sport, science, music, and sophisticated games such as chess (e.g., Bloom, 1985). A focal question of interest in this field is how young people develop into such exceptional performers and such early ages. An example might be a 16-year-old chess grand master or a 12-year-old concert violinist. Clearly, these young people are performing at levels that far exceed what typical individuals of their age can accomplish. Is it all a function of innate ability or is it mainly due to extensive, dedicated practice over time? If it is a combination of nature and nurture, then how do these two forces work in tandem to develop talent and talented individuals?

Perhaps the most extensive theoretical treatment of talent and its development stems from the work of Simonton, who defined *talent* as "any innate capacity that enables an individual to display exceptionally high performance in a domain that requires special skills and training" (1999: 436). He notes that it is conceivable for a given talent to be innate without being genetic; however, the non-genetic influences, such as in the intrauterine environment, are argued to occur very early in life.

Of particular relevance to the nature–nurture discussion, Simonton's (1999) model consists of two parts, with the first involving *emergenic* and domain-specific individual differences (e.g., social potency in the leadership domain, which might be termed charisma in contemporary leadership vernacular). An emergenic trait is "an emergent property of a configuration of genes or … more basic traits that are themselves genetic in origin" (Lykken, McGue, Tellegen, and Bouchard, 1992: 1569). As an aside, an inherited individual difference in the form of general intelligence would not be considered an emergenic trait because it is not domain-specific. Social potency or charisma would be considered emergenic traits because they are specific to the leadership domain.

The second part of Simonton's model focuses on how these innate individual differences develop across the formative years of a person's life in an *epigenetic* or nurture-based fashion. As noted by Bloom in his ambitious program of research on talent development in young people, there is "strong evidence that no matter what the initial characteristics (or gifts) of the individuals, unless there is a long and intensive process of encouragement, nurturance, education, and training, the individuals will not attain extreme levels of capability in these particular fields" (1985: 3). Whereas Bloom places stronger emphasis on the epigenetic forces in developing talent, Simonton (1999) takes a more balanced two-pronged approach.

But Simonton (1999) offers a relevant caution to his two-part model by stating that talent development may not operate in the same manner across all domains. This raises questions regarding the applicability of talent-development models devoted to predicting and explaining exceptional performance in general to the domain of talent and its development in organizations. How might organizational-based talent development differ from what Simonton and others have offered?

One such contextual difference is the focus on employed adults in organization-based talent development rather than youths pursuing their passion. As such, factors associated with adult development (e.g., adult learning, goal management, and self-regulation) would be considered to be highly relevant, more so than child or adolescent perspectives on development (Day, Harrison, and Halpin, 2009). This raises a key question as to whether emergenesis (Lykken, McGue, Tellegen, and Bouchard, 1992) is a relevant process in examining talent development in adulthood. If so, what are the most relevant epigenetic programs for developing these domain-specific individual differences in high-potential employees? This brings us back to the central concern of this chapter: the topic of talent development in organizations and why it is important, including identifying whom to invest in and how to change individuals and collectives in desired ways over time.

18.2 TALENT DEVELOPMENT IN ORGANIZATIONS

The topic of talent development in organizations requires a basic appreciation of the context in which development takes place. Specifically, both the meaning of talent and the developmental initiatives undertaken are contextually embedded. What constitutes talent in one organization might not be seen as such in a different organization, perhaps even in the same industry (an even broader context). Supporting the assertion that talent is a function of organization context, Groysberg (2010) reported that Wall Street investment analysts, as well as General Electric executives, demonstrated significant drops in performance when moving to different organizations, requiring different forms of human capital skills (see also Dokko and Jiang, 2017; Groysberg, Lee, and Nanda, 2008; Minbashian, 2017).

It is also the case that the assessments used to identify talent in a given organization would differ from those used in other organizations, as might the processes used for development (i.e., to bring about individual and collective change). Indeed, such assessments and developmental processes should differ across organizations if the goal is to develop a sustainable competitive advantage through talent (Barney, 1991; Collings and Melahi, 2009, 2013). Put differently, if every organization used identical assessments and developmental practices, what would be the source of value, rareness, non-imitability, and non-substitutability (i.e., sustainable competitive advantage) of talent development? By definition, there would be no such advantage.

Context in this arena differs from how context is typically used in the development of talent in young people, as discussed by Bloom (1985) and Simonton (1999). In the case of young people, talent is domain-specific, in that someone who is a world-class tennis player would probably not be a world-class sprinter or chess grandmaster. The context is the specific domain in which expertise is demonstrated (tennis, track, and chess, respectively). In the former case of organizational talent, individuals would be expected to be expert across a number of relevant functions or domains (e.g., finance, operations, marketing, and people development) but within the boundaries of the given organization. The boundary around talent development in organizations is the organization itself and not the function, whereas with talent development in youth outside of organizational contexts the boundary is the particular functional domain (e.g., tennis, track, chess, etc.).

18.2.1 Why Invest in Talent Development?

Given that talent development is a cost center in organizations—and potentially a very substantial one—a question arises as to *why* it is necessary at all. One approach might be to try and buy needed talent in the form of hiring stars away from competing organizations; however, Groysberg (2010) demonstrated that this is unlikely to be a winning strategy in the long term. The other option is to make or develop talent internally. In general, the dual drivers for investments in talent development are (a) an organization's need to leverage its human talent to deliver results, secure and hold a competitive advantage, and attain a strong reputation with a diverse array of stakeholders (e.g., board members, shareholders, customers, suppliers, current and potential employees); and (b) individual employee needs for competence, mastery, challenge, achievement, relatedness, and a meaningful career (Gagné and Deci, 2005; Ryan and Deci, 2000). Although factors beyond talent-development investments influence the fulfillment of these organization and individual needs, it could be argued that any organization is realizing a return on its talent investments if it is consistently delivering results, staying competitive, enjoying a positive reputation, and retaining motivated, high-performing, and committed talent.

Specific reasons for making investments in talent development include as in the case of one nonprofit healthcare system: (a) identifying high-potential executives with a capacity for greater responsibility in the organization, (b) building a pipeline of talented leaders committed to carrying on the organization's mission and values, and (c) developing a greater sense of shared commitment in executives across different geographic regions (see Day, 2007b: 28). The latter issue can be framed in terms of developing a sense of collective identity (e.g., defining oneself in terms of organizational membership), which has been argued to be an important component at more senior levels because of the enhanced need to adopt a holistic systems perspective on the organization in understanding "who we are" and "what we can do" (Day and Harrison, 2007). Although these specific reasons for investing in talent development were provided by a single nonprofit organization in the healthcare sector, they would not be at odds with reasons provided by many for-profit organizations in other industry sectors (see Ready and Peebles, 2015).

To best maximize returns, investments in talent development should be connected to a broader organizational strategy (Collings and Melahi, 2009, 2013; Silzer and Dowell, 2010). Strategic investments in talent development begin with a prioritization exercise to determine where to focus the investment to best enhance organizational capability. This should flow from an organization's overall strategy and then be further grounded in the specific business challenges related to delivering on that strategy. See the example provided in Table 18.1 as to how the strategic imperatives in a large conglomerate organization (200,000+ employees) give rise to specific leadership challenges and require targeted capability to be developed.

18.2.2   Whom to Develop

After successful identification of requisite collective organizational capabilities, a next step is to make decisions regarding *whom* to target for developmental investments. In the context of organizations, one recognized approach to defining talent refers to those individuals who have the current or future potential to differentially contribute to firm performance by being incumbent and delivering in strategic jobs (Cappelli and Keller, 2014). As such, it is not entirely a person or personal-capability approach to talent, as with developing talent in young people, nor does it limit the identification of talent to specific jobs. Rather, talent is conceptualized using a *person-in-job* perspective. It is not solely the innate capabilities of the person because an employee must be in a pivotal or so-called corporate critical position to be able to contribute to firm performance or influence achievement of strategic objectives (Collings and Mellahi, 2009). From this perspective, talent is the combination of individual potential enacted within a given organization role. But it is also the case that there must be sufficiently wide variability in

Table 18.1 Aligning Business Strategy and Talent Development

Strategic Imperative	Leadership Challenge	Targeted Capability
Win in a competitive talent market	Leading teams	Attract, identify, develop, and retain strong senior talent
International expansion	Managing stakeholders	Establish credibility and rapport with external stakeholders (e.g., governments, regulators, policy makers, media, analysts, and unions)
Turn around underperforming business	Driving financial performance	Manage the profitability over time, balancing short term and long term
Respond to an unexpected competitor	Prioritizing and executing	Appropriately balance monitoring and controls with empowered teams
Post-acquisition integration	Managing and simplifying internal complexity	Manage scale and high-volume decision making
Weather an economic downturn	Managing challenging external conditions	Identification of new growth opportunities while managing risks (e.g., strategic, operational, financial, and reputational)

Note. Each targeted capability has implications at both a collective and an individual level as the relative effectiveness of the culture, systems, teams, and leaders together determine the likelihood of attaining and deploying the capability, in service of the overall strategic imperative.

the quality of work displayed by incumbents in the corporate critical position for it to be considered an "A position" (Huselid, Beatty, and Becker, 2005).

According to a classic perspective, performance in any domain, including exceptional performance, is an interactive function of motivation, ability, and opportunity (see Collings and Mellahi, 2009). In terms of work performance, motivation might be conceptualized in terms of aspiration, as with certain perspectives on high-potential employees (e.g., Corporate Leadership Council, 2005) but it inherently involves a desire to contribute in strategically important ways. Ability refers to individual capabilities, whether they are emergenic, epigenetic, or some combination of those factors. Opportunity conveys the importance of occupying a strategically important organizational role. All three factors must be present to enhance work performance.

A related but somewhat different conceptualization of talent is reflected in the practice of identifying *talent pools* (Cappelli and Keller, 2017; Collings and Mellahi, 2009; Silzer and Church, 2010). This approach aggregates talent into categories that help decision-makers prioritize and customize the type of development investment to make in each pool. The categories can be based on any number of factors, including critical job families, role size, risk profile, compensation level, and/or depth of experience. Regardless of the factors taken into consideration, the identification and management of talent pools is driven by the recognition that shallow or weak pools can put the business at risk by limiting an organization's ability to deliver on its strategy. See the example in Table 18.2 as to how one large organization defines their top leadership talent pools, which span senior manager (Pool 5) through managing director and CEO levels (Pool 1).

Along with identifying organizational capabilities, the talent-development process involves identifying current talent by identifying key roles as well as potential incumbents to those roles. It is a matter of which talented people are in the best position (e.g., in terms of role, visibility, networks, supportive manager, or some combination) and condition (e.g., emergenic or innate talent, experience, mental toughness and resilience) to deliver at increasingly greater levels of effectiveness (Meyers, van Woerkom, and Dries, 2013). From this perspective talent development involves targeted investments in those individuals with the greatest potential to build and deploy capacity to influence significantly the achievement of strategic organizational objectives *and develop the capacity in others to do so.*

Taking a broader perspective to include developing others' capacity highlights an important point that contemporary state-of-the-art talent development goes beyond developing just the human capital capacity of a limited number of high-potential or star employees (Aguinis and O'Boyle, 2014; O'Boyle and Kroska, 2017). There must also be the demonstrated willingness and ability to develop those more removed from high-level positions to prepare them for the future possibility of occupying strategic positions. It also recognizes that performance is usually a function of groups of people engaged in shared work rather than outcomes associated solely with the efforts of one individual (Groysberg, 2010; Kehoe, Rosikiewicz, and Tzabbar, 2017). In this manner, state-of-the-art talent

Table 18.2 Example Talent Pools with Performance Expectations

Pool	Definition	Performance Expectation
Pool 1: talent-portfolio owners	Senior executives: divisional MDs and corporate functional heads	Achieve divisional and functional advantage
Pool 2: critical executives	Executives in roles strategically critical to the business	Drive organizational growth and model responsible long-term management
Pool 3: proven executives	Executives in roles ensuring business continuity	Strengthen businesses through operational excellence and customer satisfaction
Pool 4: new executives	Executives in roles less than 18 months	Make a material impact that lifts the bar on previous practice
Pool 5: potential executives	Managers with the potential to take on an executive role in the next 12–36 months	Deliver in current role while demonstrating motivation and capacity to broaden impact

development focuses on developing collective capability, which includes the creation of systems, processes, practices, and culture required to achieve strategic objectives in a sustainable manner. This sort of broad-focused approach to building organizational capability does not rely on any one or just a handful of extraordinarily talented people (Kegan and Lahey, 2016). Creating collective capability involves going beyond assessing performance and potential solely in financial terms to examining the track records of developing others, plus assessing the skills and motivation to do so in the future. Expectations regarding this responsibility need to be made explicit, with the reward system aligned to recognize the accomplishment of this talent-development objective.

As an example, research conducted in the context of Wall Street analysts employed in investment banks found that research directors (senior managers) who took talent-development responsibilities seriously encouraged their senior analysts to function as ongoing mentors for more junior analysts. This was done by highlighting the importance of institution building as a shared value and by making substantive mentoring of juniors a criterion in assessing performance and in determining compensation of senior analysts (Groysberg, 2010).

On a related note, it is common for incumbents in senior roles to have responsibility for developing at least one successor. This can be called a replacement plan if it is done mainly to ensure continuity and reduce disruption to the business when succession occurs, but it may not constitute talent development if the successor brings no more value than the current incumbent has. To drive continuous growth and competitive advantage, organizations typically seek successors with the capacity and motivation to "raise the bar" on past practice and performance. It should be noted that the development of others (usually subordinates) is a joint effort between the line manager and HR, but the line manager must adopt co-ownership of this process. This can get lost or overlooked if the organization prioritizes and rewards other deliverables—for example, revenue or return on capital—to the exclusion of development of future leaders and the broader leadership culture. For successful talent development to occur, it cannot be the sole responsibility of HR and must be an explicitly communicated and rewarded expectation of line managers.

18.3 How to Develop Talent in Organizations

This section briefly reviews a handful of state-of-the-art practices regarding *how* to develop talent in organizations. This is not an exhaustive treatment of this topic, but the focus is on those practices that are thought to add the most value in the talent-development process. It is important to note that the distinction between talent development and leadership development becomes fuzzy, especially as the focal position level moves into senior-management ranks (i.e., general manager and above). As such, most initiatives directed at enhancing leadership capabilities are indistinguishable from those designated as talent development. Both developmental foci (leadership and talent) are part of the broader talent-management and succession-management processes in organizations (Day, 2007a). A potential explanation for the overlap is that the more senior the position, the more leadership responsibility is likely to be required. At the more senior levels, exceptional performance is considered to be less reliant on developing technical sorts of skills, which are thought to be mastered at lower levels or earlier career stages, and more on the so-called soft skills of leadership.

In general, talent development is enriched when practices are appropriately designed and connected to measureable outcomes, are well timed in terms of the developmental readiness of those targeted for investment (ideally involving readiness assessment), and are introduced at appropriate junctures (e.g., at the beginning of a stretch assignment). The various kinds of developmental initiatives can be grouped into categories of practice types including *experiential learning* (e.g., action learning and cross-functional or global job rotations), *education* (e.g., formal programs, including executive MBA), *assessment* (e.g., 360-degree feedback), and *coaching* (e.g., mentoring and executive coaching) (Day, 2007a). It is generally the case that the more engaging, interactive, or "hands on" the initiative that also requires an individual to move out of his or her comfort zone, the greater the potential developmental impact (Tesluk and Jacobs, 1998). But it is also the case that any initiative can be made more developmentally powerful by incorporating all three aspects of assessment, challenge, and support (McCauley, Van Velsor, and Ruderman, 2010).

One way to enhance developmental "punch" is through systemically linking various initiatives. Using 360-degree or multisource feedback provides individuals with relevant assessment data regarding their impact across various perspectives (e.g., subordinates, peers, and superiors). This type of assessment has become ubiquitous in organizations (Waldman, Atwater, and Antonioni, 1998), but by itself it only provides data summaries to individuals, which can be bewildering in their inconsistency across sources. Thus, it is more developmentally potent to link 360-degree feedback (assessment) with a relevant stretch assignment (challenge) to address a developmental gap identified in the assessment that also includes access to high-quality personal coaching (support). Research has shown that challenging experiences reach a plateau in terms of learning and development unless there is also ready access to support (DeRue and Wellman, 2009). The message is that no single developmental initiative or practice is a panacea to enhancing organizational capability. State-of-the-art talent development is very much about creating systems of various practices that are linked together in systematic and holistic ways.

18.3.1 State-of-the-Art Practices in Talent Development

18.3.1.1 *General Principles*

Although talent-development practices differ across organizations, industries, and countries, there is a set of fundamental principles that guide all practice considered state-of-the art (see Table 18.3). As discussed, high return on investment in talent requires it to be grounded in strategy, addressing a compelling need and targeting a prioritized audience. Drilling down further into executing the practice, a few other principles merit discussion.

As development is essentially about change, it is important for organizations to develop and communicate a transparent and specific description of the aspired state. Some organizations refer to it as "what good looks like." This typically is addressed through both collective and individual level factors. Examples of collective factors include core organizational capabilities such as customer insight, cultural values, and global benchmarks of similar talent. At an individual level, this may include behavioral descriptors, such as those found in competency models and 360-degree assessments, as well as descriptors that are more dispositional, such as those measured through assessments of personality and cognitive functioning (e.g., general intelligence). It is through the latter types of assessments that the epigenetic factors discussed by Simonton (1999) are incorporated into organization-based talent development.

Flowing from a clarification of the aspired state is the application of that model or framework through the deployment of evidenced-based assessment. While it may occur at both an organizational and an individual level, the state of the art incorporates a multisource approach. It should be noted that this form of multisource assessment does not involve personalized feedback. Rather, it gathers information across a variety of assessment sources (e.g., senior executive judgment, individual assessments, and in-depth interview) to evaluate a high-potential candidate against the senior executive leadership model. Figure 18.1 provides an example of how one organization incorporates multiple sources into their assessment of senior executive pipeline candidates. This approach produces a more nuanced and complete picture of the specific factor under examination (e.g., leadership competency and personal attribute) and can help to somewhat reduce human bias associated with relying solely on executive judgment. Multisource assessment in this form serves to clarify the most essential developmental priorities and thus to focus investments.

Table 18.3 Key Principles Guiding Talent–Development Practice

- Grounded in organizational and talent-management strategy
- Addresses a compelling and well-defined organizational need
- Targets a prioritized audience
- Driven by a transparent and specific model of "what good looks like"
- Clarifies development priorities through evidence-based, multisource assessment
- Designs development experiences to be relevant to the target audience
- Incorporates a range of developmental methodology
- Employs multiple data sources when evaluating the impact of investment
- Adopts a continuous-improvement mindset, to ensure relevance and impact over time

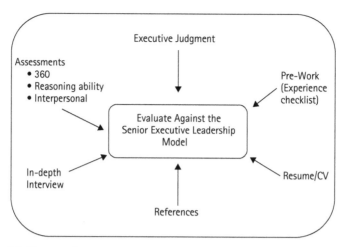

FIGURE 18.1 Multisource Assessment

This next principle may seem self-evident but it is a common oversight in the practice of talent development. State-of-the-art practice ensures that talent-development investment objectives are clearly relevant to the target individual or group in the immediate term. Given the performance pressure and competing priorities experienced by an organization's most talented employees, it is essential for the developmental objective to be perceived as not merely a "nice to have" but rather a "need to have" factor for delivering increasingly greater value to the organization. If the alignment is achieved, motivation to develop increases and the likelihood of applying the new capabilities in the day-to-day context is enhanced.

State-of-the-art practice also incorporates a variety of developmental methods. The three primary methods include *structured learning* (e.g., formal programs, study tours, and self-directed study; Conger, 2010), *developmental relationships* (e.g., coaching, mentoring, and shadowing; McCauley and Douglas, 2004), and *experiential learning* (e.g., stretch assignments, action-learning projects, cross-functional or global job rotation, and existing work; Yost and Mannion Plunket, 2010). The relative weighting of these three methods—popularly referred to as the 70-20-10 rule, or 70% experience, 20% relationships, 10% formal programs—prioritizes the use of experiential development (McCall, 2010). Wherever possible, talent development involves leveraging the developmental power of naturally occurring work that the business is already engaged in and committed to (O'Connor, 2014). Experiential approaches are powerful in that they deliver outcomes of tangible value to the organization and accelerate talent development through just-in-time implementation and feedback. But providing such experiences is insufficient for development to occur. There is also the corresponding epigenetic need to help employees learn from experience and engage in deliberate practice to realize the full potential of experiential approaches to talent development (Day, 2010).

As with all investments, there is the need to measure and increase the return on talent-development investments, or what some authors have referred to as return-on-development investments (RODI; Avolio, Avey, and Quisenberry, 2010). Just as state-of-the-art practice incorporates multiple data sources when assessing individuals and groups, it is equally important to employ multiple data sources when evaluating a given developmental practice or process. The classic four-level approach to evaluating training and development practices (reactions, learning, behavior, and results; Kirkpatrick, 1994) is the one most commonly adopted by organizations. A relevant and important aspect of Kirkpatrick's model is recognizing that training effectiveness is multifaceted, and relying only on relatively basic (and often biased) level-1 reaction data or so-called smile sheets provides a potentially contaminated but surely deficient evaluation of training effectiveness. Isolating and explaining the impact of a single investment on an individual's behavior, or a team's or organization's effectiveness, is challenging given the general acknowledgment that there are myriad possible causal factors influencing effectiveness.

For example, in assessing the impact of a leader-development program, factors such as the opportunity to practice and apply learning, the relative support of the manager, the motivation and readiness of the individual to step outside of their comfort zone, and the competing priorities encountered back in the business all exert an influence on the program's effectiveness. State-of-the-art practice takes into consideration a variety of data when evaluating developmental-investment impact (Hannum, Martineau, and Reinelt, 2007). These include direct measures, such as changes in individual or team capability, and indirect measures, such as role change, promotion, and retention rates. Best practice also adopts a long-term approach to evaluating impact, based on longitudinal research, which better captures the trajectory of development over time and across changing organizational contexts. Adopting a multifaceted approach to evaluating investments in talent development can provide valuable data on where the returns meet or exceed expectations and where further efforts are needed to improve the intervention.

The final general principle guiding state-of-the-art talent-development practice is the adoption of a continuous-improvement mindset. To reflect the dynamic nature of both organizations overall and talent development specifically, the core facets of why, who, and how need to be reviewed and revised on a continuous basis. This helps ensure that practices retain high relevance and deliver material impact over time.

18.3.1.2 *Development in Context*

It is also the case that state-of-the-art talent development does not take people away from their work in order to develop them. Instead, development is embedded in ongoing work and the work context. In his research on Wall Street analysts, Groysberg provides the compelling example of Schroder Wertheim, a "second-tier, underfunded bank" (2010: 234, Kindle Edition) that could not afford to buy its talent externally. It also did not have the resources to buy developmental experiences in the form of formal programs or external coaching. Instead, one of the developmental practices it adopted was *critique*, in which all members of a department regardless of seniority "mentored" each other by critiquing forthcoming publications to the Street. The firm's research director explained the process this way:

> On Friday afternoon we would give out copies [of manuscripts] to the entire research department. Everybody was expected to read it over the weekend, and we would assemble on Monday morning to critique the work. This accomplished three things. First, the Monday-morning meetings supplemented my work: it made the product better than it would have been if I were the only outside contributor. Second, the fact that we took several hours out of everyone's time to critique a report spoke volumes about our values. It was the single most important thing that reinforced with great regularity that we were focused on high-quality investment thought more than any of the other trappings of Wall Street research. Third, the discussions in those meetings provided me another window into each analyst's stage of development. It was a very useful management tool. (235, Kindle Edition)

This provides a tangible example of how talent-development practices can be embedded in the context of ongoing organizational work. As noted by the research director, the benefits of this Monday-morning practice were threefold: product improvement; values reinforcement; and providing assessment data on each analyst's developmental level. Although no evidence of this potentially additional benefit was provided, it might also be expected that the critique process developed the critical thinking skills of department members over time to make them more broad-based, sophisticated (i.e., talented) analysts. There are costs associated with this practice in terms of analysts' time; however, the benefits appear to far outweigh such costs. One of the most important factors needed to embed talent development in ongoing work is the discipline to implement it regularly.

18.3.1.3 *Creating Facilitative Norms and Systems*

This practice of embedding talent development in ongoing work is very much in line with what has been argued is an important job of strategic leaders: to act as social architects in helping to generate normative conditions that facilitate development (Day, 2007b). Inherent to human development and therefore talent development is learning. Indeed, it is reasonable to conclude that it is impossible for complex skills or more sophisticated thinking to develop without learning. For this reason, it is important to foster a learning orientation both individually and collectively, in which an accepted goal is to enhance mastery and further development rather than solely proving competence or avoiding failure (Dweck, 1986). Having analysts review and critique research that is not central to their own areas of expertise emphasizes the role of learning in building new forms of expertise in different industry or market segments. As noted by Groysberg (2010), analysts with different foundations of expertise often forge reciprocal, symbiotic relationships in which they promote each other's development.

Weekly report critiques can also serve to enhance psychological safety among department members, which refers to perceptions of security in taking interpersonal risks in a particular context (Edmondson and Lei, 2014). In the context of weekly report critiques, interpersonal risks might take the form of questioning certain taken-for-granted industry assumptions, admitting a lack of understanding regarding arguments or data, or other forms of expressing interpersonal vulnerability. In other words, enhancing psychological safety builds trust among group members, and as research has demonstrated, safety and trust can facilitate and accelerate team learning (Edmondson, 1999).

Thus, there is a tangible connection between certain kinds of norms that are fostered through practices such as weekly report critiques and talent development in organizations. In this way, senior leaders can act as social architects in fostering interpersonal conditions that enhance ongoing learning and development on the job. The types of dense developmental networks that evolve with these contextually embedded practices not only help to develop talent in individuals, they also contribute to the overall strength or capability of the firm (Groysberg, 2010; Kegan and Lahey, 2016).

18.3.1.4 *Personalizing Talent Development*

It is generally recognized that people develop in different ways and across different time scales. Talent differ in their respective abilities, interests, aspirations, and developmental gaps. In other words, individuals progress along different developmental trajectories (Smith, 2009). Despite this recognition, most talent-development approaches—with the possible exception of executive coaching—fail to recognize the individualized nature of development. The good news is that through the advent of sophisticated measurement and modeling procedures, as well as mobile technology that facilitates access 24/7 to developmental resources, it is becoming feasible to personalize talent development.

Day and Barney (2012) provide an overview of an approach adopted by a global software and professional services firm to enhance a personalized approach to talent development. Included in the approach are psychometrically rigorous assessments that are linked to flexible and efficient Computer Adaptive Testing, even for what are usually time-consuming 360-degree feedback processes. The data that are gathered over time are then used to chart individual trajectories of development to personalize further developmental needs and opportunities. The overarching goal is to help the organization individualize and focus developmental investments in areas that pay off more effectively.

It is also the case that we are living in the age of the algorithm, which has potentially profound implications for talent development (Buckingham, 2012). Organizations across a wide array of industries (e.g., social media, online merchants, and digital news providers) use mathematical algorithms to personalize content delivery to users. In a similar vein, technology has evolved in the space of leadership and talent development. One such approach (www.leaderamp.com) links personalized assessment, artificial intelligence, and expert coaching within a mobile application. This tailors development to the individual user and makes it available anytime, anywhere. This promises to contribute to an exciting future for the science and practice of talent development in organizations.

18.4 CONCLUSIONS AND FUTURE RESEARCH DIRECTIONS

Talent development is an investment in building organizational capability to deliver against strategy. For this reason, the process of talent development as part of a broader talent-management system in organizations requires it to be grounded in and driven by strategy for it to matter in terms of providing meaningful returns on investment (Silzer and Dowell, 2010). There are also lessons to be learned from the foundational literature devoted to understanding talent and its development in youths (e.g., Bloom, 1985; Simonton, 1999), especially regarding the respective influences of nature and nurture on talent development. Further integration of the literature would help to inform and potentially enhance them both, and provide greater insights into core questions pertaining to talent and its development.

In addressing the issues of why talent development should be invested in, whom to invest in, and how to facilitate it, perhaps the most provocative aspect of this review concerns the question of whom to develop. State-of-the-art practice goes beyond identifying those individuals with the greatest individual potential to build and deploy capacity to influence strategic organizational objectives, to require demonstrated motivation and ability to develop the capacity in others to do so as well. From this perspective, so-called star performers are only stars if they are willing to move beyond their own stellar orbits to recognize the broader galaxy in which they shine and commit to improving it.

In terms of future research needs, there are any number of topics and research streams requiring additional evidence. We need a much deeper understanding of human potential in organizations, and how to measure it accurately. It is also the case that potential is unlikely to be a static concept, so charting and understanding individual trajectories of development (e.g., Day and Sin, 2011) as part of talent-development and succession-management processes would potentially open new avenues of research and practice. There is also much to learn about developing an inclusive approach to talent development that is not shackled to the identification and development exclusively of high-potential employees. In this area, the work of Kegan and Lahey (2016) with what they term deliberately developmental organizations is notable and worthy of more research attention. There is little or no empirical understanding of the developmental impact that occurs among experts who play key roles in talent-development initiatives. Specifically, what, if any, development occurs among those internal (often senior) executives who are tapped to contribute to leader-led talent initiatives by contributing judgment to talent-pipeline assessments, conveying technical knowledge by facilitating classroom modules, or sharing lessons of experience as mentors? A more complete empirical understanding which emergenic versus epigenetic processes explain differences between those that demonstrate the ability to develop others and those that do not (or do so to a lesser degree) is also needed. Finally, a better understanding of the "differences that matter" to better inform criteria for composing diverse teams or cohorts who will share a development experience is greatly needed. These are just a few of the many pressing research needs in building a more complete and evidence-based understanding of talent development in organizations.

In conclusion, talent development is a vitally important area of study and practice because it is devoted to improving the welfare of individuals and organizations. Understanding how and why individuals and broader collectives such as organizations progress along different trajectories of development poses difficult and important challenges for those responsible for talent-management initiatives. These are the same kinds of challenges that organizational scholars should try to answer in their research. Advancing the science and practice of talent development depends on it.

References

Aguinis, H., and O'Boyle, E. 2014. Star performers in twenty-first century organizations. *Personnel Psychology*, 67, pp.313–50.

Avolio, B. J., Avey, J. B., and Quisenberry, D. 2010. Estimating return on leadership development investment. *The Leadership Quarterly*, 21, pp.633–44.

Barney, J. B. 1991. Firm resources and sustained competitive advantage. *Journal of Management*, 17, pp.99–120.

Bloom, B. S., ed. 1985. *Developing talent in young people*. New York: Ballantine.

Buckingham, M. 2012. Leadership development in the age of the algorithm. *Harvard Business Review*, 90(6), pp.86–94.

Cappelli, P., and Keller, JR. 2014. Talent management: conceptual approaches and practical challenges. *Annual Review of Organizational Psychology and Organizational Behavior*, 1, pp.305–31.

Cappelli, P., and Keller, JR. 2017. The historical context of talent management. In D. G. Collings, K. Mellahi, and W. Cascio, eds., *The Oxford handbook of talent management*, pp.23–42. Oxford: Oxford University Press.

Collings, D. G., and Mellahi, K. 2009. Strategic talent management: a review and research agenda. *Human Resource Management Review*, 19, pp.304–13.

Collings, D. G., and Mellahi, K. 2013. Commentary on: "Talent—innate or acquired? Theoretical considerations and their implications for talent management." *Human Resource Management Review*, 23, pp.322–5.

Conger, J. A. 2010. Developing leadership talent: delivering on the promise of structured programs. In R. Silzer and B. E. Dowell, eds., *Strategy-driven talent management: a leadership imperative*, pp.281–311. San Francisco: Jossey-Bass.

Corporate Leadership Council. 2005. *Realizing the full potential of rising talent (vol. I): a quantitative analysis of the identification and development of high-potential employees*. Washington, DC: Corporate Executive Board.

Day, D. V. 2007a. *Developing leadership talent: a guide to succession planning and leadership development* (SHRM Foundation's Effective Practice Guidelines Series). Alexandria, VA: Society for Human Resource Management Foundation.

Day, D. V. 2007b. Structuring the organization for leadership development. In R. Hooijberg, J. G. Hunt, J. Antonakis, K. B. Boal, and N. Lane, eds., *Being there even when you are not: leading through strategy, structures, and systems* (Monographs in Leadership and Management, Vol. 4.), pp.13–31. Amsterdam: Elsevier.

Day, D. V. 2010. The difficulties of learning from experience and the need for deliberate practice. *Industrial and Organizational Psychology: Perspectives on Science and Practice, 3,* pp.41–4.

Day, D. V., and Barney, M. F. 2012. Personalizing global leader development @ Infosys. In W. H. Mobley, Y. Wang, and L. Ming, eds., *Advances in global leadership,* Vol. 7, pp.173–95. London: Emerald.

Day, D. V., and Harrison, M. M. 2007. A multilevel, identity-based approach to leadership development. *Human Resource Management Review, 17,* pp.360–73.

Day, D. V., Harrison, M. M., and Halpin, S. M. 2009. *An integrative approach to leader development: connecting adult development, identity, and expertise.* New York: Routledge.

Day, D. V., and Sin, H.-P. 2011. Longitudinal tests of an integrative model of leader development: charting and understanding developmental trajectories. *The Leadership Quarterly, 22,* pp.545–60.

DeRue, D. S., and Wellman, N. 2009. Developing leaders via experience: the role of developmental challenges, learning orientation, and feedback availability. *Journal of Applied Psychology, 94,* pp.859–75.

Dokko, G. and Jiang, W. 2017. The portability of individual performance. In D. G. Collings, K. Mellahi, and W. Cascio, eds., *The Oxford handbook of talent management,* pp.115–33. Oxford: Oxford University Press.

Dweck, C. S. 1986. Motivational processes affecting learning. *American Psychologist, 41,* pp.1040–8.

Edmondson, A. 1999. Psychological safety and learning behavior in work teams. *Administrative Science Quarterly, 44,* pp.350–83.

Edmondson, A. C., and Lei, Z. 2014. Psychological safety: the history, renaissance, and future of an interpersonal construct. *Annual Review of Organizational Psychology and Organizational Behavior, 1,* pp.23–43.

Gagné, M., and Deci, E. L. 2005. Self-determination theory and work motivation. *Journal of Organizational Behavior, 36,* pp.331–62.

Groysberg, B. 2010. *Chasing stars: the myth of talent and the portability of performance.* Princeton, NJ: Princeton University Press.

Groysberg, B., Lee, L.-E., and Nanda, A. 2008. Can they take it with them? The portability of star knowledge workers' performance. *Management Science, 54,* pp.1213–30.

Hannum, K. M., Martineau, J. W., and Reinelt, C. eds. 2007. *The handbook of leadership development evaluation.* San Francisco: Jossey-Bass.

Huselid, M. A., Beatty, R. W., and Becker, B. E. 2005. A players or A positions? *Harvard Business Review, 83*(12), pp.110–17.

Kegan, R., and Lahey, L. L. 2016. *An everyone culture: becoming a deliberately developmental organization.* Boston: Harvard Business Review Press.

Kehoe, R. R., Rosikiewicz, B. L., and Tzabbar, D. 2017. Talent and teams. In D. G. Collings, K. Mellahi, and W. Cascio, eds., *The Oxford handbook of talent management,* pp.153–68. Oxford: Oxford University Press.

Kirkpatrick, D. L. 1994. *Evaulating training programs: the four levels.* San Francisco: Berrett-Koehler.

Lykken, D. T., McGue, M., Tellegen, A., and Bouchard, T. J. 1992. Emergenesis: genetic traits that may not run in families. *American Psychologist, 47,* pp.1565–77.

McCall, M. W., Jr. 2010. Recasting leadership development. *Industrial and Organizational Psychology: Perspectives on Science and Practice, 3*, pp.3–19.

McCauley, C. D., and Douglas, C. A. 2004. Developmental relationships. In C. D. McCauley and E. Van Velsor, eds., *The Center for Creative Leadership handbook of leadership development*, 2nd edn., pp.85–115. San Francisco: Jossey-Bass.

McCauley, C. D., Van Velsor, E., and Ruderman, M. N. 2010. Introduction: our view of leadership development. In E. Van Velsor, C. D. McCauley, and M. N. Ruderman, eds., *The Center for Creative Leadership handbook of leadership development*, 3rd edn., pp.1–26. San Francisco: Jossey-Bass.

Meyers, M. C., Van Woerkom, M., and Dries, N. 2013. Talent—innate or acquired? Theoretical considerations and their implications for talent management. *Human Resource Management Review, 23*, pp.305–21.

Minbashian, A. 2017. Within-person variability in performance. In D. G. Collings, K. Mellahi, and W. Cascio, eds., *The Oxford handbook of talent management*, pp.66–86. Oxford: Oxford University Press.

O'Boyle, E., and Kroska, S. 2017. Star performers. In D. G. Collings, K. Mellahi, and W. Cascio, eds., *The Oxford handbook of talent management*, pp.43–65. Oxford: Oxford University Press.

O'Connor, P. M. G. 2014. Leveraging the developmental power of core organizational work. In C. D. McCauley, D. S. DeRue, P. R. Yost, and S. Taylor, eds. *Experience-driven leader development: models, tools, best practices and advice for on-the-job development*, pp.57–63. San Francisco: Wiley.

Ready, D. A., and Peebles, M. E. 2015. Developing the next generation of enterprise leaders. *MIT Sloan Management Review, 57*(1), pp.43–51.

Ryan, R. M., and Deci, E. L. 2000. Self-determination theory and the facilitation of intrinsic motivation, social development, and well-being. *American Psychologist, 55*, pp.68–78.

Silzer, R., and Church, A. H. 2010. Identifying and assessing high-potential talent: current organizational practices. In R. Silzer and B. E. Dowell, eds., *Strategy-driven talent management: a leadership imperative*, pp.213–79. San Francisco: Jossey-Bass.

Silzer, R., and Dowell, B. E. 2010. Strategic talent management matters. In R. Silzer and B. E. Dowell, eds., *Strategy-driven talent management: a leadership imperative*, pp.3–72. San Francisco: Jossey-Bass.

Simonton, D. K. 1999. Talent and its development: an emergenic and epigenetic model. *Psychological Review, 106*, pp.435–57.

Smith, G. T. 2009. Why do different individuals progress along different life trajectories? *Perspectives on Psychological Science, 4*, pp.415–21.

Tesluk, P. E., and Jacobs, R. R. 1998. Toward an integrated model of work experience. *Personnel Psychology, 51*, pp.321–55.

Waldman, D. A., Atwater, L. E., and Antonioni, D. 1998. Has 360-degree feedback gone amok? *Academy of Management Executive, 12*(2), pp.86–94.

Yost, P. R., and Mannion Plunket, M. 2010. Developing leadership talent through experiences. In R. Silzer and B. E. Dowell, eds., *Strategy-driven talent management: a leadership imperative*, pp.313–48. San Francisco: Jossey-Bass.

CHAPTER 19

TALENT AND TURNOVER

JOHN P. HAUSKNECHT

19.1 INTRODUCTION: WHY CARE ABOUT TOP-TALENT TURNOVER?

ALTHOUGH researchers and practitioners have long been in interested in understanding and managing turnover across all employees, additional focus on the mobility of specific employee groups—notably high performers and "stars"—has intensified in recent years. Such interest reflects beliefs that certain employees contribute a disproportionate amount to organizational goals, have greater potential to occupy key leadership positions in the future, are more difficult and more costly to replace, and diminish an organization's status when they leave (Aguinis and O'Boyle, 2014; O'Boyle and Kroska, 2017; Call, Nyberg, and Thatcher, 2015; Groysberg, Lee, and Nanda, 2008; Kehoe, Lepak, and Bentley, 2016). For these reasons, scholars and practitioners have begun to focus on *talent retention* rather than (or in addition to) employee retention, broadly defined.

The focus on retaining top talent is not new, but its importance is increasing. Lawler characterizes *talent* as "the fundamental building block when it comes to creating an organization capable of innovating and changing and using this as a source of competitive advantage" (2008: 5). Cappelli (2008) cites numerous practitioner surveys that place talent concerns front and center among CEOs. He cites a 2004 Conference Board study where 65% of companies reported talent-management concerns as "dramatically or considerably more important" than in 2001. Finally, globalization heightens the need to locate and retain top talent. Given that employers now compete for talent regionally and globally, they demand a workforce with specialized skills who are adept at entering new markets (Farndale, Scullion, and Sparrow, 2010).

Given these developments, it is an opportune time to review scholarly literature that focuses specifically on talent retention. The goals of this chapter are to review *talent* definitions, examine current findings, identify emerging issues, and outline future research needs. The review is organized around several key questions that have garnered the most attention to date. These include:

1. How is *talent* defined and measured?
2. Are talented employees more likely to quit?
3. What frameworks help us understand star performers?
4. What are the drawbacks of attempting to retain top talent?
5. What future research is needed?

19.2 How Is *Talent* Defined and Measured?

As a starting point, it is informative to consider how authors have defined *talent* and related concepts such as *high performers, high potentials, stars, critical roles,* and *core employees.* Table 19.1 lists these terms along with a definition, sample measurement approaches, and citations to selected papers. Looking across terms, *talent* serves as an umbrella concept for all other terms. That is, depending on the context (and organizational goals), *talent* may be defined in terms of high performance, high potential, star status, or critical roles, and/or in reference to a core-employee group. Operationally, organizations often identify key talent through formal talent-review systems that involve managers and other relevant stakeholders. Ratings of performance, potential, and related concepts often feed into these types of evaluations.

High performers are those who excel at executing core job/role responsibilities and they are often identified operationally via supervisory performance ratings (and/or objective measures when available and job-appropriate). *High potentials* are those who managers believe have the ability to move into higher-level positions over time. Large organizations often have formalized systems for identifying and grooming high-potential employees (Derr, Jones, and Toomey, 1988), though systematic studies examining turnover of high potentials have yet to appear in the scholarly literature.

Stars have been defined in numerous ways, but most definitions emphasize disproportionately high performance (relative to others) that is externally visible and sustained over time (Aguinis and O'Boyle, 2014; Call, Nyberg, and Thatcher, 2015; Groysberg, Lee, and Nanda, 2008; O'Boyle and Kroska, 2017). Given that much of the recent literature addresses star employees, I elaborate on these and other definitional nuances in a subsequent section.

Finally, numerous authors have pointed out that organizations often rely on a smaller set of *critical roles* and/or *core employees* in their pursuit of sustained competitive advantage (Boudreau and Ramstad, 2005; Humphrey, Morgeson, and Mannor, 2009). These roles (and those who are selected to occupy them) become the focus, as opposed to identifying a set of high performers that cut across pivotal and non-pivotal roles (Collings,

Table 19.1 Definitions of *Talent* and Related Concepts

Concept	Definition	Notes	Sample Measurement Approaches	Selected Papers
Talent	Incumbents in an organization's talent pool who occupy (or will occupy) pivotal strategic positions (Collings and Mellahi, 2009: 306)	• Most general definition (often incorporates some or all of the concepts shown below)	Manager identification (e.g., via formal talent-review systems)	Björkman et al. (2013); Collings and Mellahi (2009)
High performers	An individual who is highly effective in completing core job/role responsibilities (Conway, 1999)	• Performance can reflect actual levels and/or be relative to others	Supervisors' annual performance-review ratings (e.g., top end of a 5-point scale); objective indicators of output (e.g., top 10%)	Beck, Beatty, and Sackett (2014); Nyberg (2010); O'Boyle and Aguinis (2012); Salamin and Hom (2005); Trevor Gerhart, and Boudreau (1997)
High potentials	"The ability to move up into specific managerial positions to which the corporation attaches value" (Derr, Jones, and Toomey, 1988: 275)	• Companies may differentiate potential based on number of levels above the current position	Executive/manager identification	Derr, Jones, and Toomey (1988)
Stars	Those who "consistently generate exorbitant output levels that influence the success or failure of their organizations and even society as a whole" (Aguinis and O'Boyle, 2014: 314)	• Some definitions account for star visibility, status, and/or social capital (e.g., Call, Nyberg, and Thatcher, 2015; Kehoe, Lepak, and Bentley, 2016) • Performance often defined relative to others	Institutional investor rankings; publication counts; percentiles	Aguinis and O'Boyle (2014); Call, Nyberg, Ployhart, and Weekley, (2015); Groysberg, Lee, and Nanda, (2008); Oldroyd and Morris (2012); Tzabbar and Kehoe (2014)
Critical roles	Positions that most directly affect strategic success (Boudreau and Ramstad, 2005: 129)		Judgment	Boudreau and Ramstad, (2005); Collings and Mellahi (2009)

(continued)

Table 19.1 Continued

Concept	Definition	Notes	Sample Measurement Approaches	Selected Papers
Core employees	"The role or roles on a team that (a) encounter more of the problems that need to be overcome in the team, (b) have a greater exposure to the tasks that the team is performing, and (c) are more central to the workflow of the team" (Humphrey, Morgeson, and Mannor, 2009: 50)		Judgment	Humphrey, Morgeson, and Mannor (2009); Siebert and Zubanov (2009)

2017; Collings and Mellahi, 2009). Despite the obvious strategic importance of focusing on critical roles and/or core employees, very little empirical work in the turnover domain has adopted this lens on "talent" (see Siebert and Zubanov, 2009, for an exception).

19.3 ARE TALENTED EMPLOYEES MORE LIKELY TO QUIT?

Existing research that addresses whether talented employees are more or less likely to quit largely adopts the "high performer" definition of *talent* and relies upon annual performance appraisal ratings to identify such workers. In the following sections, I consider theory and evidence that explains why high performers are generally more likely to leave organizations (compared with average performers), unless they are adequately rewarded for their contributions.

19.3.1 Theoretical Foundations

March and Simon's (1958) classic theory of organizational equilibrium explains why employees quit, in general, and it has been refined to explain high-performer quit patterns, in particular. March and Simon's model includes two dimensions as key turn-over antecedents: (i) perceived ease of movement, and (ii) perceived desirability of movement. Turnover risk increases as ease of movement (often measured in terms of job alternatives) and desirability of movement (often indexed in terms of job satisfaction) increase. Applying the model to high performers affords straightforward predictions regarding ease of movement. Given their superior accomplishments and abilities, they should be highly sought after by competing firms, increasing their external opportunities, and therefore their likelihood of leaving. Concerning desirability of movement, however, high performers are likely sensitive to the level of rewards (e.g., pay and promotions) received in exchange for their superior inputs (Trevor, Gerhart, and Boudreau, 1997). When rewards are closely tied to performance (and consistent with equity theory), desirability of movement is lessened, which would offset the relatively greater access to alternatives expected among high performers. In short, turnover risk is theorized to increase for high performers, especially so when their performance goes unrewarded.

19.3.2 Meta-Analytic Results

Meta-analytic evidence summarizing average correlations between performance and turnover provides support for a negative relationship, indicating that turnover risk decreases as performance increases (Griffeth, Hom, and Gaertner, 2000). Summarizing across seventy-two effect sizes drawn from over 25,000 employees, Griffeth and colleagues found an average corrected correlation of −.17 between performance and turn-over. Although this finding suggests that it is generally low performers who leave (for a variety of reasons, such as having low intrinsic motivation, feeling "pushed out," and so forth), later research challenged the view that this relationship holds as one looks across successive levels of performance.

19.3.3 Curvilinearity and Context

Scholars have contested the assumption of a linear performance-turnover association and, consistent with the rationale outlined above, argued that contextual factors (e.g., pay growth, promotions, and the like) would moderate this relationship. Two studies supported an "inverted-U" relationship wherein high and low performers were more likely than average performers were to quit (Salamin and Hom, 2005; Trevor, Gerhart, and Boudreau, 1997). The increased turnover risk among higher performers, however, was lessened to the extent that workers received sizable pay growth, higher rate of promotions, and larger merit bonuses. Nyberg (2010) replicated the pay-growth moderation patterns found in previous studies using a measure of total pay growth and also showed that high performers found alternatives more readily (i.e., had lower survival probabilities) when unemployment rates were high, thus supporting the notion that high performers have greater ease of movement, even during difficult economic times.

In sum, research evidence shows that turnover likelihood is greatest among poor performers, diminishes for average performers, and rises again for high performers; the increased turnover risk among high performers, however, is lessened to the extent that rewards are closely linked with performance. Stated simply, high performers are more likely to leave than average performers are, unless they have good reason to stay.

19.4 What Frameworks Help Us Understand Star Performers?

Complementing the extant research on turnover among high performers, scholars have recently proposed definitional and theoretical refinements that further specify characteristics of exceptional contributors or "stars" (Aguinis and O'Boyle, 2014; Call, Nyberg, and Thatcher, 2015; Groysberg , Lee, and Nanda, 2008; Kehoe, Lepak, and Bentley, 2016; O'Boyle, 2017; Oldroyd and Morris, 2012). To various degrees, these papers seek to: (a) explain what differentiates stars from other employees, (b) examine consequences of star employee movement into, through, and out of work groups and organizations, (c) theorize how turnover operates for star performers, and (d) document the shape of performance distributions. I discuss each of these broad aims in the following sections.

19.4.1 How Are Stars Different?

Several studies aim to differentiate star employees from other types of employees, both conceptually and operationally. Two such papers provide typologies of star employees that help explain how and why stars differ from high performers and other types of talent. First, Call, Nyberg, and Thatcher, (2015) provide an integrative review of stars research and construct a multidimensional typology that explains the core dimensions of star employees relative to other, conceptually distinct types of employee groups. In their analysis, star employees are those with "disproportionately high and prolonged (a) performance, (b) visibility, and (c) relevant social capital" (Call, Nyberg, and Thatcher, 2015: 624). By "disproportionately high and prolonged," the authors suggest that stars must exhibit superior performance, visibility, and social capital *relative to their peers* (rather than in any absolute sense) and for a long enough duration that high performance is attributable to the person rather than the circumstances. Unlike traditional high-performer conceptualizations, their analysis suggests that to be labeled as a star, someone's performance must be visible, whether internally or externally. Finally, the authors include the concept of relevant social capital (i.e., the value generated from internal and external relationships) in their *stars* definition, arguing, "stars capitalize on valuable relationships" (627). The Call typology differs from other talent definitions in its argument that high performance is a necessary but insufficient condition for star performance; such output must also be highly visible and include a strong social capital dimension, and all three elements must be sustained over time.

A second paper by Kehoe and colleagues (2016) aims to differentiate different types of star employees and explains the conditions under which stars create organizational value. It begins with a *stars* definition that includes both exceptional productivity and high external visibility (consistent with parts of Call, Nyberg, and Thatcher [2015] and with previous work by Groysberg, Lee, and Nanda [2008] and Oldroyd and Morris [2012]), but raise two limitations of this view. Kehoe and colleagues note that stars vary in their performance and visibility over their careers (suggesting that other definitions may be overly restrictive in reserving star status for situations where both performance and visibility are high) and question the assumption that stars must have both high performance *and* high visibility to create organizational value. Instead, they argue for a focus on the broader concept of *external status* rather than visibility, to capture "the amount of respect, influence, and admiration an individual enjoys in the eyes of others" (2015: 3). They propose that these two dimensions—performance and status—can be crossed to identify three types of stars, which they label "universal stars" (high performance and high status), "performance stars" (high performance only), and "status stars" (high status only). They further divide status stars into three types, based on whether they derived their status from affiliation with other prestigious individuals or institutions, previous exceptional task performance, or a deep and extensive external network.

Comparing across recent papers, there is emerging consensus that stars are defined not only by high performance, but also by the visibility and/or status that they maintain externally. Less certain is whether a person must excel on multiple dimensions for a sustained period (e.g., performance, visibility, and social capital) to achieve star status (which is more in line with Call, Nyberg, and Thatcher, 2015), or whether star status can emerge from high standing on a single dimension, which may persist into the future, despite drops in performance, status, or both (which is more in line with Kehoe et al., 2016). In any case, both perspectives are consistent in specifying that high performance alone is only one ingredient in determining whether one qualifies as a star employee. As Groysberg and colleagues noted:

> Any industry will have many high-performing individuals, but the handful of super-stars at the top will receive disproportionate attention from competitors and clients (and in some industries, the media), making their performance public and observable. (2008: 1215)

19.4.2 What Does the Addition, Presence, and Departure of Stars Mean for Work Groups and Organizations?

Several scholars have examined the repercussions associated with star movement from one firm to another. For instance, Groysberg and colleagues (2008) tracked star security analysts' performance following a move to a new firm and found that their performance declined immediately and remained depressed for at least five years. Further, they showed that declines were strongest when analysts' moves were solo and when they moved to firms with lesser capabilities. Their findings reveal that star performance is at least partly firm-specific and depends on the level of support provided by the star's firm and his or her colleagues.

Tzabbar and Kehoe (2014) examined how star-scientist turnover affected biotechnology firms' subsequent exploitation and exploration activities. Exploitation characterizes situations where firms pursue novel ideas within the bounds of existing expertise (e.g., building on ideas from past patents), whereas exploration involves seeking new knowledge beyond existing capabilities (e.g., patenting novel ideas that are unrelated to existing patents). They hypothesized that star-scientist turnover would decrease exploitation because of the loss of organizational memory, the disruption caused by human capital loss, and the erosion of social capital once associated with the star scientist. Conversely, they hypothesized that star-scientist turnover would *increase* exploration because remaining members would have: (a) freedom to pursue new initiatives; (b) increased opportunities to develop new routines; and (c) greater exposure to new ideas from colleagues. Results from 197 firms confirmed both predictions: Exploitation was 14% lower in firms that experienced a star-scientist departure, while exploration was 22% higher following a star departure. (Results were also sensitive to several moderating characteristics related to the star's collaborative involvement with colleagues and overall innovative involvement within the firm.) Related work by Groysberg and Lee (2009) revealed that star performers experience a short-term performance drop when moving for exploitation purposes, but suffer short- and long-term performance drops when moving to a new firm for exploration purposes. They theorized that exploitation settings allowed star analysts to leverage existing resources, routines, and capabilities (and thus maintain high performance), whereas those hired for exploration operated "essentially solo in all aspects of the job, from producing research reports to selling those reports to clients" (Groysberg and Lee, 2010: 752), which then led to persistent overall performance deficiencies.

19.4.3 What Are the Likely Drivers of Star Turnover?

Aside from the handful of studies described above, little else has been published that documents the causes and consequences of star turnover. However, recent theory is suggestive of potential patterns. Call, Nyberg, and Thatcher (2015) suggest that if stars behaved like high performers, they would be more likely than average performers to leave, because of greater ease of movement and heightened sensitivity to pay growth, promotions, and the like. Moreover, they argue that, given their high external visibility, stars will be much more susceptible to poaching from rival organizations. Finally, these authors contend that stars with a deep internal social network would be less likely to leave because of their embeddedness and the associated sacrifices that would be made if they left.

Aguinis and O'Boyle (2014) note that traditional turnover theories may not apply well to star performers. For example, they point out that most individual-level turnover theories posit job search as a proximal cause of turnover intentions and decisions to leave. However, job search "may not be relevant to stars because they do not need to contact employers … employers contact them" (Aguinis and O'Boyle, 2014: 330). They further argue that the likely agent in the job search will be the competing organization rather than the star, which "circumnavigates the plethora of predictors, mediators, and moderators that play such central roles in current conceptualizations of turnover theory" (330). Ultimately, Aguinis and O'Boyle propose that the job search-turnover relationship will be weaker when considering star performers versus non-stars. They also suggest that stars would be more sensitive to psychological contract breaches and injustice, which further reinforces the notion that rewards and other enticements should be especially important when considering star retention.

19.4.4 How Rare Is Exceptional Performance?

A related stream of work has emerged that challenges conventional views about the distribution of job performance. The longstanding view is that employee performance is normally distributed—or "clusters around a mean and then fans out into symmetrical tails" (O'Boyle and Aguinis, 2012: 79). However, these authors provide sizable evidence showing that performance resembles power-law distributions, or those "typified by unstable means, infinite variance, and a greater proportion of extreme events" (80). Beck, Beatty, and Sackett described such distributions as being "characterized by the highest number of performers falling at the low end rather than in the center, and by a consistently decreasing number of performers at each subsequent higher level of performance" (2014: 532). O'Boyle and Aguinis presented data from five studies that span industries, occupations, and performance metrics and showed that data better fit a power-law distribution versus a conventional normal distribution. Consequently, a large proportion of performers actually fell below the mean (66% to 83% across the samples analyzed). At the high end of the distribution were extreme performers whose output far exceeded what would be expected under normal distribution assumptions.

From a talent-turnover standpoint, one implication is that organizations may be better served by focusing their efforts on retaining a select few star performers rather than the upper end of an artificially imposed normal distribution. From a utility standpoint, their work suggests that these "elites" are actually much more valuable than previously believed. In the conventional, normal distribution view, organizations would attempt to make fine gradations between a large number of better-than-average and top performers; however, when considered from a power-law distribution standpoint, they would target a much smaller set of stars who contribute substantially to overall performance.

Despite the ample evidence put forth to substantiate power-law performance distributions, Beck, Beatty, and Sackett (2014) cautioned that these extreme departures from normality may be attributable to measurement artifacts. They identified seven measurement criteria that, when met, should lead researchers to find that performance distributions resemble better a normal rather than a power-law distribution. Based on their logic, these measures would: (a) address behavior; (b) aggregate multiple behaviors; (c) be collected for all performers; (d) include the full performance range; (e) give performers an equal opportunity to perform; (f) apply to comparable jobs; and (g) be free from motivations to distort ratings. They presented a series of data sets that met many or most of the criteria identified and showed better fit to a normal versus a power-law distribution. In contrast to the implications identified by O'Boyle and Aguinis, Beck, Beatty, and Sackett (2014) argued that failing to account for measurement artifacts could result in mislabeling employees as "superstars" when, in reality, such outliers could be easily explained by other factors (e.g., greater opportunity to perform). Taking them together, a conservative conclusion that can be drawn from these two contrasting papers is that if: (a) measurement criteria identified by Beck and colleagues are satisfied, and (b) performance distributions continue to conform to a power law rather than normal distribution per O'Boyle and Aguinis, then organizations would be wise to focus retention efforts on the small number of star performers who far exceed the output of others.

19.5   What Are the Drawbacks of Trying to Retain Top Talent?

Despite the logic that stars disproportionately improve firm performance, and are therefore prime targets for retention efforts, losing stars may not be so problematic under some conditions. As discussed above, firms pursuing innovation strategies (i.e., exploration vs. exploitation) may be served better by occasional talent renewal and may not suffer the usual performance losses when stars leave (Tzabber and Kehoe, 2014). In other cases, firms could benefit when losing (or gaining) talent from "cooperator" firms (i.e., those that a focal firm might do business with following employee movement) because of deepened social networks associated with departing (joining) employees (Somaya, Williamson, and Norikova, 2008). Beyond this, star departures can also create career opportunities for remaining members, lessen entrenched conflict, and reduce costs (Call, Nyberg, and Thatcher, 2015). Further, along with exceptional performance, stars can also bring disproportionate levels of arrogance and narcissism; thus, losing stars could promote teamwork and cohesiveness (Lucey, Sedmak, Notestine, and Souba, 2010). Consistent with these ideas, Pfeffer (2001) argued against engaging in the "war for talent" because doing so promotes an individualistic culture, impedes learning and knowledge sharing, glorifies outsider talent, and reinforces a simplistic view that there are only two types of employees: stars and non-stars. Despite the logical appeal of these arguments, little evidence is available to substantiate the benefits of top-talent turnover, particularly regarding the conditions under which firms would be well served to encourage star performer exits.

19.6 What Future Research Is Needed?

Interestingly, at present, theory and propositions dominate the talent/turnover landscape, and empirical studies have been slow to emerge. Thus, there are numerous opportunities to contribute to our understanding of the causes and consequences of top-talent turnover. One finding that seems clear from extant work is that top performers are highly sensitive to input-reward ratios, which is consistent with equity-theory propositions from decades ago. That is, given their visibility and ease of movement, turnover risk among top performers is higher than that for average performers. Beyond this consistent finding, many directions are possible for future research.

19.6.1 Research Direction #1: Further Investigate Drivers of Top Talent and Star Turnover

Despite valuable findings from performance-turnover studies (e.g., Nyberg, 2010; Trevor, Gerhart, and Boudreau, 1997), these studies do not identify "stars" as recently defined. Additional work that helps uncover whether turnover theories, processes, and outcomes differ for the highly visible, socially connected, exceptionally productive stars has yet to emerge. New measurement approaches that better match *emerging star* definitions are needed to contrast findings against those that use the more typical design involving extant performance-review data.

19.6.2 Research Direction #2: Study Stars in Context

Much of the writing on star performers leaves aside the massive group of "non-stars" who appear quite capable of augmenting or depressing stars' performance (e.g., Groysberg, Lee, and Nanda, 2008). Further, potential negative characteristics of some stars (e.g., high narcissism and low cooperation) would surely offset their superior individual productivity and hinder group performance (Pfeffer, 2001). Additional studies of star–non-star relationships would be worthwhile, including how the presence of a star affects the attitudes and behaviors (e.g., turnover) of surrounding members (e.g., Groysberg and Lee, 2010).

19.6.3 Research Direction #3: Track Star Mobility across Time

Call et al. nicely outline the importance of addressing timing in stars research. They suggest drawing on the career-development literature to understand better the "lifespan" of stars, including how they "develop, behave, perform, and grow over time" (2015: 634). Such a focus on within-person development seems extremely valuable and can incorporate multiple definitions of *talent* as presented here (e.g., moving from high potential to high performer, gaining visibility and eventually status; see Kehoe, Lepak, and Bentley, 2016). Addressing the role of turnover in enhancing or constraining a star's career trajectory would be valuable.

19.6.4 Research Direction #4: Address the Conditions under which Star-Performer Turnover Is Desirable

There is at least some evidence that losing stars promotes innovation (Tzabbar and Kehoe, 2014), but the notion of identifying when the addition, presence, and/or departure of star performers is actually detrimental (to team function, performance, and so forth) also seems worthwhile. Further studies (akin to Somaya, Williamson, and Norikova, 2008) that track how star mobility affects the spread of social capital across firms, for instance, could add to our understanding of star turnover benefits. Other work that tracks the group dynamics associated with star performers would also be interesting and worthwhile.

19.6.5 Research Direction #5: Address Turnover for Critical Roles, Core Employees, and High Potentials

As noted at the outset, little work has adopted the critical-role or core-employee lens when studying talent and turnover. The same can be said for high potentials. These omissions are surprising given the strategic importance of focusing retention efforts on those positions most likely to drive current and future organizational performance (Collings and Mellahi, 2009). Focusing on these groups differs from research that adopts other talent definitions because critical roles and/or core members may or may not consist of high performers or stars. Different turnover theories and/or processes may be needed to explain behaviors of these employee types. Finally, additional research on high potentials would also be of value. Organizations sometimes decide to tell employees they are high potential, which likely increases their perceived ease of movement, status, and other dimensions that could increase turnover risk. Thus, future work should address the dynamics surrounding high potentials and their turnover behavior.

19.7 Summary

Although the corporate mantra to "retain top talent" remains widespread, scholarly research that investigates talent and turnover is only beginning to emerge. Talent definitions range from the more traditional high-performer lens to the more recent, nuanced views of stars that incorporate visibility, status, and social capital. Evidence is clear that high performers are more likely than average performers to leave, but much less is known about the factors that drive stars to leave organizations. Further, there is reason to suspect that star-performer retention is not always desirable. Future research that addresses these and other questions would help organizations make informed decisions about when, why, and how to retain top talent.

References

Aguinis, H., and O'Boyle Jr., E. 2014. Star performers in twenty-first century organizations. *Personnel Psychology*, 67, pp.313–50.

Beck, J. W., Beatty, A. S., and Sackett, P. R. 2014. On the distribution of job performance: the role of measurement characteristics in observed departures from normality. *Personnel Psychology*, 67, pp.531–66.

Björkman, I., Ehrnrooth, M., Makela, K., Smale, A. et al. 2013. Talent or not? Employee reactions to talent identification. *Human Resource Management*, 52, pp.195–214.

Boudreau, J. W., and Ramstad, P. M. 2005. Talentship, talent segmentation, and sustainability: a new HR decision science paradigm for a new strategy definition. *Human Resource Management*, 44(2), pp.29–36.

Call, M. L., Nyberg, A. J., Ployhart, R. E., and Weekley, J. 2015. The dynamic nature of collective turnover and unit performance: the impact of time, quality, and replacements. *Academy of Management Journal*, 58(4), pp.1208–32.

Call, M. L., Nyberg, A. J., and Thatcher, S. M. B. 2015. Stargazing: an integrative conceptual review, theoretical reconciliation, and extension for star employee research. *Journal of Applied Psychology*, 100, pp.623–40.

Cappelli, P. 2008. *Talent on demand: managing talent in an age of uncertainty.* Boston: Harvard Business Press.

Collings, D. G. 2017. Workforce differentiation. In D. G. Collings, K. Mellahi, and W. F. Cascio, eds., *Oxford handbook of talent management*, pp.301–17. Oxford: Oxford University Press.

Collings, D. G., and Mellahi, K. 2009. Strategic talent management: a review and research agenda. *Human Resource Management Review*, 19, pp. 304–13.

Conway, J. 1999. Distinguishing contextual performance from task performance for managerial jobs. *Journal of Applied Psychology*, 84(1), pp.3–13.

Derr, C. B., Jones, C., and Toomey, E. L. 1988. Managing high-potential employees: current practices in thirty-three U.S. corporations. *Human Resource Management*, 27, pp.273–90.

Farndale, E., Scullion, H., and Sparrow, P. 2010. The role of the corporate HR function in global talent management. *Journal of World Business*, 45, pp.161–8.

Griffeth, R. W., Hom, P. W., and Gaertner, S. 2000. A meta-analysis of antecedents and corre-lates of employee turnover: update, moderator tests, and research implications for the next millennium. *Journal of Management*, 26, pp.463–88.

Groysberg, B., and Lee, L. 2009. Hiring stars and their colleagues: exploration and exploitation in professional service firms. *Organization Science*, 20, pp.740–58.

Groysberg, B., and Lee, L. 2010. Star power: colleague quality and turnover. *Industrial and Corporate Change*, 19, pp.741–65.

Groysberg, B., Lee, L., and Nanda, A. 2008. Can they take it with them? The portability of star knowledge workers' performance. *Management Science*, 54, pp.1213–30.

Humphrey, S. E., Morgeson, F. P., and Mannor, M. J. 2009. Developing a theory of the strategic core of teams: a role composition model of team performance. *Journal of Applied Psychology*, 94, pp.48–61.

Kehoe, R. R., Lepak, D. P., and Bentley, F. S. 2016. Let's call a star a star: task performance, external status, and exceptional contributors in organizations. *Journal of Management*, DOI: 10.1177/0149206316628644.

Lawler, E. E., III. 2008. *Talent: making people your competitive advantage*. San Francisco: Jossey-Bass.

Lucey, C. R., Sedmak, D., Notestine, M., and Souba, W. 2010. Rock stars in academic medicine. *Academic Medicine*, 85, pp.1269–75.

March, J. G., and Simon, H. A. 1958. *Organizations*. New York: Wiley.

Nyberg, A. 2010. Retaining your high performers: moderators of the performance-job satisfaction-voluntary turnover relationship. *Journal of Applied Psychology*, 95, pp.440–53.

O'Boyle, E., and Kroska, S. 2017. Star performers. In D. G. Collings, K. Mellahi, and W. F. Cascio, eds., *Oxford handbook of talent management*, pp.43–65. Oxford: Oxford University Press.

O'Boyle Jr., E., and Aguinis, H. 2012. The best and the rest: revisiting the norm of normality of individual performance. *Personnel Psychology*, 65, pp.79–119.

Oldroyd, J. B., and Morris, S. S. 2012. Catching falling stars: a human resource response to social capital's detrimental effect of information overload on star employees. *Academy of Management Review*, 37, pp.396–418.

Pfeffer, J. 2001. Fighting the war for talent is hazardous to your organization's health. *Organizational Dynamics*, 29, pp.248–59.

Salamin, A., and Hom, P. W. 2005. In search of the elusive u-shaped performance-turnover relationship: are high performing Swiss bankers more liable to quit? *Journal of Applied Psychology*, 90, pp.1204–16.

Siebert, W. S., and Zubanov, N. 2009. Searching for the optimal level of employee turnover: a study of a large U.K. retail organization. *Academy of Management Journal*, 52, pp.294–313.

Somaya, D., Williamson, I. O., and Lorinkova, N. 2008. Gone but not lost: the different perfor-mance impacts of employee mobility between cooperators versus competitors. *Academy of Management Journal*, 51, pp.936–53.

Trevor, C. O., Gerhart, B., and Boudreau, J. W. 1997. Voluntary turnover and job performance: curvilinearity and the moderating influences of salary growth and promotions. *Journal of Applied Psychology*, 82, pp.44–61.

Tzabbar, D., and Kehoe, R. R. 2014. Can opportunity emerge from disarray? An examination of exploration and exploitation following star scientist turnover. *Journal of Management*, 40, pp.449–82.

CHAPTER 20

HR METRICS AND TALENT ANALYTICS

ALEXIS A. FINK AND MICHAEL C. STURMAN

20.1 INTRODUCTION

ONCE again, there is buzz about organizations working to apply numbers to managing their talent. The opportunities created by "big data" in human resources (HR), along with the continuous pressure for greater effectiveness and productivity, have renewed calls for more analytical HR management as the way of the future. But we have heard this call in HR many times. We heard it associated with HR accounting in the 1970s (e.g., Flamholtz, 1999), utility analysis in the 1980s (e.g., Boudreau, 1991; Cascio, 1981), HR scorecards in the 1990s (e.g., Becker, Huselid, and Ulrich, 2001), and HR metrics in the 2000s (e.g., Boudreau and Ramstad, 2007). Is there really anything new today or is this just the same old analytical angst wrapped up in fresh and different colorful wrappings? A cynical view of HR's analytical history may suggest recurring rounds of clarion calls for quantifiable approaches to HR, each one leading to a new dead end where the promises of greater sophistication are not fulfilled because of the limitations in the data and decision makers at whom the advances are targeted. In this chapter, however, we argue that this history is indicative of an evolving decision science (Boudreau and Ramstad, 2007). We see the combination of current technologies, past experiences, and varied analytical approaches to HR leading to a new set of emerging methods and tactics. This chapter shows that, while the field of HR is still far from a definitive resolution to its analytical challenges, we can learn from the various efforts to quantify HR, combining and coordinating these efforts to yield a better understanding of the various ways analytical HR processes build upon each other. We argue that the union of past analytical approaches to HR with a recognition of the opportunities presented today, owing to technology and data availability, culminates in what is now known as talent analytics.

Many may be challenged to define *talent analytics*, let alone differentiate it from HR metrics and other jargon of the near and far past. For the purposes of this chapter, we are treating HR metrics as an operational measurement. HR metrics addresses how efficient, effective, and impactful an organization's HR practices are. That is, HR metrics quantify waste in programs and investments (efficiency), whether programs deliver the outcomes planned (effectiveness), and whether those outcomes have a material effect on the firm (impact) (Boudreau and Ramstad, 2007; Dulebohn and Johnson, 2013). In contrast, talent analytics focus on decision points, guiding investment decisions (Boudreau and Ramstad, 2007; Fitz-Enz, 2010). Whereas HR metrics tell you about "what" is going on, talent analytics gets at the decision-making about HR, driven by both good data and good science (Boudreau and Ramstad, 2007). Thus, metrics are about getting the numbers right, and analytics are about finding answers in the data (Cascio and Boudreau, 2011; Levenson, 2015).

Unfortunately, practitioners wishing to deliver excellent HR metrics, let alone a talent analytics system, don't have much to go on in the way of guidance. Despite repeated calls for HR research to help drive evidence-based management (Briner and Rousseau, 2011; Rousseau, 2006), the gap between research and practice with regard to talent analytics remains quite extensive (Dulebohn and Johnson, 2013). Quite arguably, even state-of-the-art research often lacks clear practical applicability. For example, issues of scale create an additional layer of complexity between primary research, often done with controlled samples of modest size, and complex organizations that may vary in size from hundreds of thousands to fewer than twenty (Cascio and Boudreau, 2014). Conversely, practices developed at leading organizations and covered in the business press may be difficult to translate into different organizational contexts. Thus, while there may be clear consensus for the need for talent analytics, implementation remains a major problem.

The purpose of this chapter is to provide an overview of the historic roots and current practices around HR metrics and talent analytics in organizations. Over the course of this discussion, we will review the distinctions between HR metrics and talent analytics, as well as the distinctions among different types of HR metrics, such as efficiency, effectiveness, and impact. We'll also explore the role, benefits, and risks of benchmarking and utility analyses as two common approaches to setting HR metrics in organizations. We will close with a discussion on fostering talent analytics within organizations, as a natural outgrowth and companion to a robust HR metrics portfolio.

20.2 Current Practical and Theoretical Approaches

Basic HR data points, such as overall headcount or payroll expenditures, should not be confused with HR metrics. While these are nearly ubiquitous, and clearly are reporting HR-related information, these sorts of measures don't capture HR effectiveness. Cascio and Boudreau (2011) refer to this most fundamental level of sophistication as "counting." Reports that simply reflect numbers like these quantify the workforce, but don't add much value in terms of informing judgments about how well HR is doing as a function. Thus, we make a distinction between basic HR reporting, which captures basic facts about an organization or team and has value in helping managers and leaders track and manage their own teams and workforces, and HR metrics, which help HR and the organization evaluate the efficiency, effectiveness, and impact of their HR systems, programs, and processes. Cascio and Boudreau (2011) refer to this greater level of HR sophistication as both "clever counting" (which extrapolates from descriptive data to yield new insights) and "insight" (which helps reveal the drivers of trends discovered through "clever counting"). HR reporting quantifies the current state, and HR metrics add an evaluative component that tells us how well HR is performing for a particular function.

20.2.1 Benchmarking

In seeking to build measurement systems for HR and to improve HR functioning through measurement, practitioners often turn first to benchmarking. Benchmark information is readily available through consultants, nonprofit organizations, and specialized reporting groups, and benchmarks are available for a vast array of HR items (Becker, Huselid, and Ulrich, 2001; Dulebohn and Johnson, 2013). Benchmarks provide a ready-made bundle of evaluation methods and target values that can be appealing. For example, the Society for Human Resources Management offers a library of benchmarking reports, toolkits, and calculators as one of its services (e.g., Dooney, 2013). The Saratoga Institute, an innovator in HR benchmarking nearly a half-century ago and now a part of PWC, offers a dizzying array of metrics and custom benchmarking solutions (cf. PWC, 2015). Social comparison is a strong human urge and, at least intuitively, comparing one's processes or own performance to those of peers seems like a useful first step. Benchmarking studies can help organizations identify areas in their HR systems that are atypical, although benchmarking alone may not be able to help organizations determine whether that is an atypical result of failure that should be mitigated or a strategic investment that should be preserved (Levenson, 2015).

Additionally, benchmarking studies, whether from consulting firms or organizations like the Conference Board, are often accompanied by best-practice sharing. These are often presented as small case studies. Many benchmarking studies will highlight practices from multiple organizations to highlight different approaches, or different nuances to the same general approach. This can serve as a source of inspiration.

Benchmarking, while dominant, is an imperfect approach to HR metrics. Benchmarking studies often do not include rigorous evaluation of the practices being highlighted. Further, many benchmarking studies are produced by consulting firms with a clear commercial interest in the practices being touted. Benchmarking is further complicated in that organizational context and strategy are typically lost in the process. Benchmarking can run the risk of contributing to a mindless "me too" mentality that wastes resources. By its very nature, benchmarking facilitates the process of one organization copying the processes and results of another organization, which contrasts directly with the concept of developing a sustained competitive advantage (Bromiley and Rau, 2015; Hitt, Carnes, and Xu, 2015). Indeed, the best a firm could ever hope to be, if it relies only on benchmarking, is a composite of elements from other firms; yet, competitive advantage comes from doing something different from everyone else.

While excessive attention to benchmarking can be a net negative for organizations, the specific calculations used in many studies can provide clarity and inspiration for developing HR metrics and ultimately developing a talent analytics system. That is, while the specific benchmark practices or target scores on metrics may not be suited to a particular organization's strategy or situation, borrowing or gaining inspiration from benchmarked methods of calculation can speed the process of developing and finalizing the optimal suite of metrics for a given organization. For example, a medium-sized, stable organization with low turnover and limited internal movement, operating in a single line of business, is likely to need different levels of successor bench strength, as measured by ready-now candidates, and likely to need a different efficiency profile in investing in those select few candidates than a fast-growing, global business with 30% turnover and multiple, diverse business lines. However, the two organizations could learn from one another in the methods they use to evaluate their succession-planning system, such as perhaps judging efficiency of succession-planning investments in terms of dollars spent per successor placed, rather than dollars spent per potential successor. While the target dollars per placement would likely differ for the two organizations, the focus on efficiency of investment per outcome (successors placed) may help both organizations avoid imbalanced investments that leave them with too many potential successors in one part of an organization and too few in another.

20.2.2 Balanced Scorecards

Some organizations have applied Balanced-scorecard (Kaplan and Norton, 1992) thinking to their talent systems. Balanced scorecards have helped the cause of HR metrics in that they pushed organizations to measure and manage non-financial items. Some organizations have even applied balanced scorecards to their talent systems (e.g., Becker, Huselid, and Ulrich, 2001), and many scorecards specifically take into account HR measures (e.g., Denton and White, 2000). Given that HR topics are often included in a balanced scorecard, organizations using them typically have at least perfunctory HR metrics systems.

Many HR organizations build and publish slates of key metrics, such as cost per hire, span-of-control ratios, success rate of employee referrals versus other hire sources, percentage of high potentials promoted in a given year, employee engagement, training spend per employee, or attrition among top versus low performers. Depending on the priorities of the organization and the maturity of the measurement system, balanced scorecards may include basic reporting, performance against external benchmarks, or performance against internal standards of efficiency, effectiveness, and impact. HR scorecards will be composed, at least in part, by HR metrics, ideally chosen in such a way that helps explain and drive valued organizational outcomes.

A simpler HR scorecard, based on reporting efficiency metrics, might include such things as attendance, cost per hire, number of hires, number of exits, or number of training days (Huselid, Becker, and Beatty, 2005). These reporting approaches often include a backward-looking component, such as percentage change from a prior period, for example, the prior month, quarter, or year. However, while those backward-looking comparisons are provided, the reporting system itself does not generally add a value judgment to the metrics reported in these schemes, and, under different business conditions, the same number could have a very different meaning.

Scorecards that are more sophisticated may include measures of effectiveness or even outcomes. Such scorecards could contain metrics such as percentage turnover by performance level, percent of workforce that is promotable, retention of core competency workforce, proportion of workforce possessing requisite skill levels, increase in sales attributable to a training program, reduction in turnover attributable to a new orientation system, and others (cf., Huselid, Becker, and Beatty, 2005). Regardless of the level of sophistication, the scorecards are most typically divided by HR functional area—staffing, employee relations, and so forth—and rarely sum to an overall measure. Indeed, where systems are composed largely of reporting, such a sum would be nonsensical.

Often, HR scorecards include a target value and a scoring schema to indicate trouble areas (Huselid, Becker, and Beatty, 2005). For example, the target number of days to fill an open requisition might be thirty-eight, and that line on a scorecard may be coded as green if it is thirty-eight or fewer, yellow if it is thirty-nine to forty-five days (15% over target), and red if it is forty-five days or longer. HR organizations that use this approach will often regularly assess performance against those target values or goals, most often with a simple color-coding scheme as noted in this example. Simple color codes allow quick attention to focus on problematic items. However, even setting those simple color codes can become fraught as practitioners determine, for example, if yellow means "in danger of being worse than target" or "slightly worse than target, but still recoverable," and as the size of the ranges around a target are set.

Organizations can set their goals based on external comparisons, such as performance against an external benchmark or industry standard, or based on internal strategies. It is unfair to oversimplify and suggest that sophisticated organizations use their own standards and unsophisticated ones "chase the taillights" of the industry leaders. A thoughtful approach to HR metrics will generally incorporate target values or goals from a variety of sources, both internal and external, depending on the strategic importance and uniqueness of the items in question (Huselid, Becker, and Beatty, 2005). Thus, a well-built HR scorecard is likely to include some external benchmark information as well as some internal references, and that same scorecard is likely to reflect a mix of efficiency, effectiveness, and impact measures. The more that an HR scorecard is tailored to the specific characteristics and HR strategy of a given organization, though, the more likely it is that internal comparisons will be needed over external benchmarks. It is easier to benchmark "time to fill," for example, than it is to benchmark the ROI from a sales training program.

20.2.3 Research-Based Approaches

There is actually quite a long history to HR metrics from the academic literature (e.g., Brogden, 1949; Cronbach and Gleser, 1957; Taylor and Russell, 1939). Repeated efforts have been made to create a mechanism that links individual behaviors and organizational value. Perhaps the most historically prominent among these approaches are Kirkpatrick's (1959) framework of learning evaluation—which provides an approach for conceptualizing different ways in which an HR intervention has effects at different levels of impact—and utility analysis, which applies mathematical conventions to assign a monetary value to an intervention's effect on organizational outcomes (Cascio and Boudreau, 2014; Sturman, 2012).

20.2.3.1 *Kirkpatrick's Model of Learning Evaluation*

Theoretical taxonomies have been put forth for nearly every corner of HR practice. These often reflect the maturity of a particular process, and are very useful in providing a language for debate internally as strategic decisions are made. It is logical to apply the same models that influenced the design of a system or program to measurement of that system or program.

Kirkpatrick (1959) created a now classic model that outlined four levels of learning evaluation (reactions, learning, behaviors, and outcomes or results). Each higher level is purported to be progressively more useful, but also increasingly difficult to implement. Despite long-standing evidence questioning the assumptions behind this model (cf. Alliger and Janak, 1989; Holton, 1996; Snyder, Raben, and Farr, 1980), it continues to be regularly employed in the evaluation of training (e.g., Grohmann and Kauffeld, 2013; Salas, Wildman, and Piccolo, 2009; Taras et al., 2013; Yorks, Beechler, and Ciporen, 2007). The first two levels—reactions and learning—account for the vast majority of learning-measurement projects (Grohmann and Kauffeld, 2013; Kirkpatrick and Kirkpatrick, 2005; Noe, 2013; Salas, Wildman, and Piccolo, 2009). This is not because organizations don't believe that changing behavior and ultimately getting results are not important outcomes; rather, such measurement is more challenging logistically and from a design standpoint. Despite Kirkpatrick's more than 10,000 citations for this model (according to Google Scholar), the high-level evaluation of HR training programs remains an elusive goal.

Outcome data are often not easily available, and by definition, they require time to collect and analyze. As is often the case, organizations focus on what is easy to measure, which, at times, can be counterproductive (Kerr, 1975). Managers may also want to include metrics they know they can do well on, or focus their efforts on achieving better scores on the metrics at the expense of other parts of their jobs that are not well measured. Indeed, there is a large body of literature describing how individuals use various impression-management tactics in order to increase performance ratings (cf. Bolino, Kacmar, Turnley, and Gilstrap, 2008). Measuring and rewarding specific metrics will likely encourage managers to behave in ways that increase scores on those metrics. A well-designed system can be quite productive. But if the set of metrics is not complete, or if the incentives are such that they encourage unethical behaviors in order to manipulate the metrics, then such measurement systems may actually cause more harm than good in the long run.

Continuing the Kirkpatrick example, some organizations surely focus on reactions (did participants like the training?) and learning (did participants gain knowledge from the training?) because they do well on those measures, and can more directly influence them. Changes in behavior and the resulting ultimate change in performance are influenced by many factors, and they are much less certain as results of learning interventions. Thus, organizations may intend to invest in the higher-level outcomes, but as long as measurement systems focus on the lower-level outcomes, they are less likely to achieve their stated objectives. Ironically, there may even be an inverse relationship between achieving the stated objectives and driving measurement, so long as that measurement is focused on a different part of the system. For example, imagine a company is sending high-level managers to an off-site location for a training program designed to enhance their financial analytical skills. For this, the company would likely want an intensive program that effectively teaches high-level financial concepts and gives the trainees practice with difficult problems so they can apply the skills when they return to their positions. But if the training program is evaluated purely based on reactions (as opposed to learning, behaviors, or outcomes), it is highly plausible that an entertaining course with a light workload (and plenty of time for the trainees to enjoy the site's amenities) would be rated more positively than would an intensive and challenging course that makes the trainees work long hours, devote considerable mental energy to the course, and miss out on all those nice amenities at the training location.

The opportunity to finally, truly capture the full robustness of data required to deliver compelling HR metrics may be found in the emergence of new data sources and analytic methods brought about by increases in computing power and innovations in data capture. With so much of modern work being digital, data-mining technologies can be used to evaluate data on engagement, sales activities, personality variables, and other work efforts to create metrics of individual performance (Chamorro-Premuzic, Winsborough, Sherman, and Hogan, 2016). At the same time, we are seeing technology advances that allow personality to be predicted from mobile phone records (de Montjoye, Quoidbach, Robic, and Pentland, 2013) or with social media information (Lambiotte and Kosinski, 2014). Phone records can also be used to predict employees' stress (Bogomolov et al., 2014). Increasingly, HR information systems are integrating with other workplace computer systems and building not only HR reporting but also HR metrics into their out-of-the-box offerings. All of this suggests that automated methods for assessing individuals can be used to evaluate the behavioral changes and results attributable to training (or other HR) interventions.

20.2.3.2 *Human Resource Accounting*

According to the American Accounting Association's Committee on Human Resource Accounting (1973), HR accounting is "the process of identifying and measuring data related to HR and communicating this information to interested parties." Given the importance of an organization's employees for its own success, it would be valuable to have the means to understand the cost of developing human capital and the return on investment from training and development (Cherian and Farouq, 2013). Over the years, a body of research, techniques, and tools has emerged to help make the ideas of HR accounting feasible to implement (Flamholtz, 1999).

Research on HR accounting has sought to create a means to measure the value of employee talent, ultimately with the intent of helping drive better investment decisions in human capital and deepening our understanding of the implications of HR decisions (Flamholtz, 1999). Unfortunately, despite research on the topic and many advances over the years, companies (and HR professionals) are not willing to engage in HR accounting (Cherian and Farouq, 2013). The fundamental need of HR accounting was an objective measure representing employee value, but it never fully materialized (Cascio and Boudreau, 2011; Mirvis and Lawler, 1983; Roselender and Dyson, 1992; Scarpello and Theeke, 1989). So, as Scarpello and Theeke noted more than twenty-five years ago, while "at the theoretical level, HR accounting is an interesting concept" (1989: 275), its use as a decision aid remains negligible. The few studies we occasionally see today continue to indicate a lack of awareness of HR accounting, as well as other major obstacles to its implementation (cf. Paki and Azar, 2015), and others cite many continuing impediments despite the appeal of fulfilling HR accounting's goals (Cherian and Farouq, 2013).

20.2.3.3 *Utility Analysis*

Another longstanding effort to quantify the impact of HR is utility analysis. With utility analysis, HR works to speak the language of business, calculating the value of specific investments in the HR system. By quantifying the value of employee performance and estimating the effect of HR interventions on the bottom line through their influence on employee performance, utility analysis provides an estimate of the result (e.g., the fourth level of Kirkpatrick's framework) of HR interventions (Sturman, 2012).

One of the great strengths of utility analysis is that it explicitly addresses HR expenditures and resource commitments, not as costs, but as investments in outcomes. Most typically, utility analyses are calculated in financial terms, and over the years the model has been expanded to consider a host of financial and contextual factors (Boudreau, 1983; Sturman, 2000). Yet despite its sophistication, or perhaps because of it (Sturman, 2000), utility analyses may be viewed skeptically by the very audiences they are intended to influence (Latham and Whyte, 1994; Whyte and Latham, 1997), and thus the adoption of utility analysis has been minimal at best.

The extensive literature on utility analysis also held out the hope for a research-driven, practically applicable means of combining HR metrics with improved decision making. This literature provided multiple and sophisticated methodological approaches to its implementation (e.g., Boudreau, 1983, 1991; Boudreau and Berger, 1985; Cascio and Boudreau, 2011; De Corte, 1994; Murphy, 1986; Sturman, 2000, 2001). Moreover, studies have even shown how the method can be used to demonstrate the practical implications of research findings and how they may be leveraged to improve HR decision making (e.g., Sturman, Trevor, Boudreau, and Gerhart, 2003). Unfortunately, like HR accounting, utility analysis relied upon a means of quantifying the economic value of employee performance, which is considered by many to be a major reason for the failure of the methodology to become practically widespread (Boudreau, 1991; Boudreau, Sturman, and Judge, 1994; Cascio, 1992; Macan and Highhouse, 1994; Schmidt, Hunter, McKenzie, and Muldrow, 1979). Thus, despite early indications of promise (e.g., Brogden, 1949; Brogden and Taylor, 1950; Cronbach and Gleser, 1957), and even some continued hope for its value as a theoretical tool (Sturman, 2012), utility analysis has not become the bridge between HR metrics and talent analytics.

Research on strategic HR management (SHRM) makes claims on a causal link between HR practices and organizational performance (Becker and Gerhart, 1996; Becker and Huselid, 1998; Guest, 1997; Huselid and Becker, 2011; Way, 2002). There is great value from this research, as the metrics used in these studies, such as surveys of high-performance work practices (Becker and Huselid, 1998; Huselid, 1995; Guthrie, 2001; Way, 2002), may be a starting point for HR metrics that have an established link with operational or financial outcomes. Yet this work remains arguably too macro (e.g., items include a simple assessment of whether a company uses pay-for-performance), making its influence on day-to-day HR metrics limited at best.

20.3 Types of Metrics

Previous sections have established the difference between HR reporting, HR metrics, and talent analytics. In many ways, these differences parallel the levels of sophistication in talent analytics described by Cascio and Boudreau (2011), which progress from counting (HR reporting), to clever counting and insight (HR metrics), to influence (talent analytics). As with this categorization, one can see that there are different potential categories of HR metrics. Although the Cascio and Boudreau (2011) categorization focuses on sophistication, we turn to a categorization by Boudreau and Ramstad (2007), which categorizes metrics based on the nature of what is being measured. Specifically, Boudreau and Ramstad (2007) categorize HR metrics as (a) metrics of efficiency, (b) metrics of effectiveness, and (c) metrics of impact. Each type of metric can play a role in helping to describe the results of a HR system, but each type also comes with its share of pitfalls. The benefits to talent analytics, though, will have to be built upon, and therefore dependent upon, the foundation of appropriate HR metrics (Cascio and Boudreau, 2011).

20.3.1 Efficiency

Often the first type of HR metric adopted is a measure of efficiency. Efficiency metrics focus on things like speed and ratios of resources to outcomes. Efficiency as a HR metrics concept has roots in and shares priorities with multiple other disciplines, such as the economic concepts of efficiency (Farrell, 1957).

Typical efficiency metrics include measures like cost per hire, time to fill, training investment per high-potential employee promoted, and HR expenses as a proportion of all company expenses. Measures such as these help reveal the ability of these various HR functions to avoid waste—be it of time, money, or effort. While avoiding waste can clearly be beneficial, the danger of efficiency metrics is the potential interpretation that the focal processes are best off when the measures are either maximized or minimized. Yet, this is not always the case. For example, time to fill is not necessarily better as it approaches zero. Rather, it should be targeted at the optimal point where candidate quality and supply balance for the needs of the role and the organization.

HR operations, such as managing payroll or managing employee service centers, can also apply concepts of efficiency in the sense of minimizing waste. Here again, however, there is a natural tension in the concept of efficiency. For example, wait times for employees calling or chatting with a service center are necessarily a function of call volume, call complexity, center staffing, and center resources. A metric of wait times needs to balance the waste that a wait time represents for an employee against the waste that idle agents represent for the service center. Managing the request queue such that a "hotline" for higher-value customers is always answered first is a way of prioritizing waste differently for different segments.

The risk associated with efficiency as a focus of measurement is that efficiency can become a goal in and of itself, thus potentially creating inappropriate and strategically misaligned priorities. For example, time to fill a position may be used as a way of measuring how efficiently managers perform the staffing function. As companies want managers to pay attention to the ever-important staffing need and to keep a group's productivity at desired levels, it makes sense to be concerned regarding this process, as overly long staffing times may be detrimental. Yet if the use of the metric leads to a goal of minimizing the metric, it may motivate undesirable behaviors. In this example, it would be possible to greatly reduce time to fill if no consideration were given to the qualifications of potential new hires. Effective construction of an HR metric must carefully balance the competing interests or tensions inherent in the process being monitored. So, while "time to fill" is essentially unidimensional as initially presented, the overall goal of the hiring process includes both quality and speed. Thus, to be useful, efficiency metrics should generally be designed to capture and balance multiple criteria, and be represented in such a way that reveals the critical tensions that exist between the various desired outcomes. Monitoring a single criterion or a unidimensional metric is likely to lead to unintended and undesired consequences.

20.3.2 Effectiveness

Having established the efficiency with which HR processes and services are delivered, many organizations move on to measuring the effectiveness of those products and services. Here, we evaluate the extent to which HR programs and services deliver the outcomes they were designed to deliver.

Effectiveness metrics commonly include measures like quality of hire, availability of ready-now successors for key leadership roles, differentiation in rewards, changes in attrition because of specific retention/attrition programs, and so forth. Whereas efficiency metrics generally examine a single resource to be minimized (e.g., expense, time), effectiveness metrics tend to balance aspects of resource expenditure with performance improvements. So whereas an efficiency metric may capture time to fill a position (implying a desire to minimize time), an effectiveness measure may capture the number of new hires that pass the probationary period (i.e., did the company hire individuals of sufficiently high quality that constituted acceptable employees?). Effectiveness metrics can be tuned to represent the quality of HR efforts in broad systems, such as recruitment, staffing, training, compensation, performance appraisal, labor relations, etc. The creation of effectiveness measure forces the HR decision maker to think beyond the resources needed to engage in a HR task, and particularly think about the benefits that should be exhibited by the system or intervention.

Effectiveness measures are not without pitfalls. Measuring effectiveness typically requires measurement at multiple process points, and it may require additional measurement beyond what naturally accumulates in the HR data systems or additional manipulation and cleaning in order to analyze the data effectively. These are not trivial challenges. Identifying the appropriate outcome measures requires a sophisticated understanding of the strategic purpose behind the processes undertaken, and generating measurements may require significant stakeholder engagement. It also requires the collection of appropriate HR data, not just easily measured HR data (Boudreau and Ramstad, 2007). These barriers may be sufficiently cumbersome to warrant using a sampling approach to measurement, rather than the population-level measurement that is more common among HR metrics. In addition, such metrics may not be perfectly accurate, as they will be approximated with error. Yet such error is acceptable as long as the measure is getting at the type of information needed to inform a particular decision. A relevant measure approximated with error is more valuable than a different, perfectly estimated, but irrelevant measure.

20.3.3 Impact

Finally, the ultimate goal of many HR programs and services is, or should be, material impact on the business. Thus, a practice has emerged around metrics that attempts to gauge the impact of HR investments. These impact measures are driven by the same underlying philosophy that drove the classic utility analysis approach discussed above; however, where utility analyses attempted to create direct financial connections, impact analyses may measure HR programs against a variety of different business outcomes. Such outcomes may be customer-focused, process or HR-outcome-related, or financial in nature.

Impact measures differ from measures of efficiency and effectiveness in that they are more tightly aligned to unique company strategy and specific programs and services, and thus have fewer commonly shared measures across organizations. Thus, while measures of effectiveness are likely bounded to outcomes within the HR system, measures of impact typically expand beyond the HR system into business outcomes. Some outcomes may be widely visible across an industry, such as online ratings of satisfaction from third-party sources (e.g., Yelp! and TripAdvisor). Others may be very company-specific (e.g., a quality rating for a specific product or service or a measure of turnover for a particular group).

Although impact measures offer advantages over measures of efficiency and effectiveness, they have their own downsides. Impact measures generally seek to tie HR programs and processes to business outcomes, which creates multiple technical challenges. First, the data are rarely housed in compatible systems. Many organizations have separate HR hierarchies, which reflect the reporting lines in an organization, and business or finance hierarchies, which reflect how customer accounts, P&Ls, or other business processes are reported. Second, while HR data are most often stored and measured at the individual level of analysis, business metrics are often tracked taken together, across teams, organizations, regions, product lines, or other segments. This creates levels-of-analysis problems. Third, the actual percentage of variance that any HR process or procedure has on actual business outcomes is likely to be relatively small, given all the other sources of variance in those outcomes, such as competitor actions, economic conditions, market position, inventory levels, and a host of other factors. Finally, many HR interventions are conducted at the enterprise level, and thus they lack sufficient variability to isolate truly the unique variance contributed by a specific process. This, in essence, is a restriction-of-range problem. These challenges do not mean that it is impossible or even inadvisable to conduct impact analyses. Rather, they serve as a caution to be thoughtful in isolating specific processes and specific outcomes, and to consider project-management strategies, like rolling implementation, that would allow for more variability and thus better signal detection. Companies can implement policies and collect data in a way consistent with quasi-experimental designs (Shadish, Cook, and Cambell, 2002). This allows HR data to be collected in such a way as to lend insights into the causes and effects of specific HR interventions. A key aspect to using HR metrics to inform decision making is not simply what is collected, but also how data are collected to allow for the most insight into the effects of HR actions.

20.4 TALENT ANALYTICS

Talent analytics is distinct from HR metrics in that the goal underlying talent analytics is to identify patterns that can inform strategic decisions (e.g., Boudreau and Ramstad,

2007). In this way, talent analytics functions as a decision science. The recent attention on talent analytics is exciting, as it is bringing opportunities to create better workplaces and better organizational outcomes.

20.4.1 HR Metrics and Talent Analytics Work Together

The purpose of talent analytics is to yield better decisions. As such, metrics are needed both to identify problems and to evaluate solutions. For example, talent analytics may reveal that a particular university produces the most successful new hires in a particular area, thus causing the HR department to change its recruitment tactics. To reach this decision, HR metrics would have had to gauge the company's ability to hire, evaluate, and retain the graduates from that program, as well as from alternative programs. Similarly, talent analytics may reveal that a top risk factor for attrition is commute time. An organization may choose to address this through changing its recruiting practices, supporting employee relocation, or providing commuting options like buses, work-from-home, a satellite office, or hoteling options. Metrics would come into play both to help reveal the issue (i.e., metrics on turnover and commute time) and to monitor the success—efficiency, effectiveness, and impact—of the solutions used to address the commute-related attrition. It is talent analytics, though, that uses the HR metrics to drive HR decision making to understand the problem and yield a solution to it.

As seen in these examples, a key distinction between HR metrics and talent analytics is that metrics tend to be ongoing, whereas talent analytics is oriented toward decision making. Measures of HR data, employee turnover and performance, other potential predictors, key outcomes, and comparisons among groups or across points in time are essential. Talent analytics, though, tends to occur in the context of discrete projects, with clear beginning and ends, used with the intent of moving from an identified problem to evaluating a solution.

As is most commonly applied, talent analytics is a challenging manual task. HR decision makers must act as researchers, looking for evidence of problems, either with a priori hypotheses (e.g., "I suspect that commute time increases turnover"), or as exploratory questions (e.g., "Does where we recruit affect the quality of our hires?"). Advances in HR data systems and big data methods that capitalize on large volumes of employee data, however, may yield more talent analytics indicators that function in a continually adaptive and even automated way. Advances in visual display of patterns in data, generally referred to as data visualization, are facilitating the process of talent analytics, allowing decision makers to search for patterns in data based on ad hoc or evolving hypotheses. To continue our attrition example from above, a dynamic data visualization of employee-movement data can enable a user to examine turnover data, expand those exits by key segment, and then drill into the top reasons why people leave that segment, all in a matter of moments. Simultaneously, big data systems can continuously scan quantitative and qualitative data, looking for patterns and predictors of organizational-critical outcomes. Such efforts are often aided by the use of extensive data dictionaries.

Data dictionaries are centralized repositories of information about data, providing information about the meaning of specific words, the relationships of those words to other words in the database, the usage of the words, format, and origin (McDaniel, 1994). Data dictionaries help in the evaluation of large qualitative sources of data, allowing patterns of meaning to be deduced from the vast content of unstructured qualitative data. Qualitative data dictionaries can be built and used to scan large volumes of employee surveys for indicators of managerial trouble or antecedents of turnover. In short, because of the combination of business needs, refinement in the HR field and in HR information, and the availability of technology applicable to HR issues and decision making, HR is now reaching new levels of sophistication.

20.5 Fostering Talent Analytics

20.5.1 Evolving Decision Science

Decision science applies statistical analysis as part of strategic analysis to inform organizational investments and choices (Boudreau and Ramstad, 2007). This is a categorically different approach from the use of numbers in an HR system. Where HR reporting reflects what has happened, and HR metrics evaluate what is happening, the decision science around talent analytics provides recommendations about what should happen. Interest in and efforts at more sophisticated HR require a progression in sophistication (Cascio and Boudreau, 2011), as well as the tools and human capital within the HR group to engage in the decision science.

While industrial/organizational (I/O) psychology has a century-long history, broad interest outside of HR in using statistical approaches in talent management to drive broad business success is a fairly recent phenomenon (Davenport, Harris, and Shapiro, 2010). One of the key differentiators between the historical practice of I/O psychology and the emerging decision science around talent analytics is the tight and compelling connection to business strategy (Levenson, 2015). In this way, the current practice of talent analytics shares roots with HR accounting, utility analysis, and the impact metrics we discussed earlier. Talent analytics, however, tends to be focused explicitly on informing organizational decision making. A fair amount of the traditional practice of I/O psychology focused on optimizing processes that had already been identified as important. Thus, the analytic projects began after the key decisions as to where to invest had been made. Talent analytics often begins at a different point—identifying which problems to address in the first place, based on data describing the effects associated with prior decisions and circumstances. Furthermore, talent analytics often expands beyond the traditional areas of I/O psychology, such as selection, performance appraisal, leadership, and employee performance, and it considers questions around items such as strategic workforce planning or team social structures. Additionally, where historically I/O psychology has relied heavily on experimental designs and parametric statistics, talent analytics tends to incorporate a wider range of analytic methods of both greater (i.e., machine learning and big data analytics) and lesser (i.e., data visualization) analytic complexity. The emergence of talent analytics has implications for data systems, measurement systems, the HR data teams that work with the data, and, perhaps most importantly, the opportunity for HR to influence organizational decisions.

While talent analytics holds tremendous promise for improving organizations, and the lives of the people in and around them, the field is not without challenges and risks. Perhaps the first obstacle is the actual human capital in HR itself. The implementation of talent analytics places a great burden on future HR managers, who need to possess sophistication in both the practices of HR and the analytical processes needed to employ talent analytics.

Once there are people in the field with the ability to implement talent analytics, the raw resources to create the opportunity for it are necessary. Many talent analytics projects require huge amounts of data; however, these data are often highly unstructured (Gandomi and Haider, 2015). Other data often include personally identifiable information, which requires special consideration (Guzzo et al., 2015). The risk of data breaches for such large volumes of information is non-trivial (Zafar, 2013). The rapid surge in interest in talent analytics means that many teams working on these problems lack useful training in employment law and ethical treatment of human subjects. Care must be taken to ensure the security and privacy of employees' information (Kovach, Hughes, Fagan, and Maggitti, 2002; Zafar, 2013).

Talent analytics also runs the risk of inadvertently using processes that are inappropriate or even illegal. Data-mining processes may find patterns in the data that are correlated with protected-class characteristics. For example, a system may find patterns in hiring successes that are associated with particular zip codes, but policies based on such patterns may lead to disparate impacts in hiring decisions. Care must be taken to ensure that the decision-making facilitated by talent analytics addresses all the goals of the HR department, including ethical standards, and it does not focus exclusively on maximizing a single goal (King, Tonidandel Cortina, and Fink, 2016).

20.5.2 Fostering Metrics

Many organizations are struggling to transition their HR data from a system designed to support transactions to a system designed to support measurement and analytics. Many HR data systems, particularly at established companies, were not built to be analyzable systems. Rather, many of them were optimized for handling transactions. This means many data are not stored or data are stored in ways that are difficult to disaggregate to analyzable component parts or impossible to link together across datasets or all of the above at once.

Companies with such systems may find that, for example, fields are overwritten to contain only the most recent information. In other cases, data are not stored at all. This is efficient from a storage standpoint, and it ensures that only the most recent information is used; however, it creates obstacles for conducting analyses of HR effectiveness. For example, if only the most current information is stored in a way that can be analyzed, it becomes difficult (and sometimes impossible) to examine individual performance over time. This may prevent analyses such as looking at which managers are most effective at developing and promoting women, or if certain interviewers are better at identifying future top performers, or what career paths are most efficient at producing effective leaders. A system designed only to be able to display and analyze the most current data loses the potential to consider what occurs over time. As so much about HR systems is the development of people over time in their jobs and careers, such deficiencies in HRISs preclude the ability to study many of the sort of questions that may most need to be addressed to assess the effectiveness of HR investments.

Data limitations are genuine constraints on organizations' ability to use HR metrics, which ultimately constrains the use of talent analytics. Although increasing availability and usability of commercially available HR data systems and tools with standard reporting packages is helping, many organizations still manage key processes, like succession plans, special retention-bonus programs, or expensive expatriate or executive-education processes, manually, on spreadsheets stored on an individual's hard drive. Notes from exit interviews may be handwritten and not transcribed, much less categorized or rated. Organizations built by acquisition may have entirely separate data systems, with different fields and values within those fields. Reorganizations may limit the ability to understand the impact of an intervention or process over time.

The implementation of talent analytics is challenged by more mundane data-system barriers as well. Cloud providers' contracts may not include sharing of raw data. Data-retention policies designed to protect privacy and mitigate risk may make things like impact measures, which necessarily require the passage of time and the ability to link across systems, impossible. Limitations like these can severely hobble the potentially very promising future of talent-analytic programs.

20.6 CONCLUSION

HR metrics has a decades-long history of theoretical contributions that advance thinking but haven't definitively advanced the field. The emergence of talent analytics, in a milieu of increased global competition, increased data availability, increased general analytic sophistication, and increased availability of data storage and computing power, has finally cracked that challenge.

As we've seen above, effective talent analytics sits at the confluence of business imperatives and competitiveness, internal talent systems, and data infrastructure. Thus, to address this space effectively, a talent analytics team needs to encompass strong business acumen, deep HR content expertise, robust statistical and methodological depth, and well-informed data systems capabilities. The interdisciplinary nature of these requirements means that individuals on the team must also be effective at collaborative problem solving, and good at respecting expertise beyond their own. Further, talent analytics teams should cultivate solid relationships with their legal counsel to ensure that issues such as privacy are thoughtfully considered, and requirements for Equal Employment Opportunity and Uniform Guidelines for Selection Procedures are unfailingly met.

Opportunities for sophistication in the HR function thus now exist in ways that have never existed before, and organizations are increasingly being motivated, and hiring those in HR with the right abilities, to take advantage of these opportunities. Together, HR metrics and talent analytics form a powerful approach to optimizing the utilization and experience of the chief resource of most organizations—the people.

REFERENCES

Alliger, G. M., and Janak, E. A. 1989. Kirkpatrick's levels of training criteria: thirty years later. *Personnel Psychology*, 42(2), pp.331–42.

American Accounting Association Committee of Accounting for Human Resources. 1973. Report of the Committee on Human Resource Accounting. *The Accounting Review Supplement*, 48, pp.169–85.

Becker, B. E., and Gerhart, B. 1996. The impact of human resource management on organizational performance: progress and prospects. *Academy of Management Journal*, 39, pp.779–801.

Becker, B. E., and Gerhart, B. 1998. High performance work systems and firm performance. A synthesis of research and managerial implications. In G. R. Ferris, ed., *Research in personnel and human resource management*, Vol. 16, pp.53–101. Stamford, CT: JAI Press.

Becker, B. E., Huselid, M. A., and Ulrich, D. 2001. *The HR scorecard: linking people, strategy, and performance*. Boston: Harvard Business Press.

Bogomolov, A., Lepri, B., Ferron, M., Pianesi, F. et al. 2014. Pervasive stress recognition for sustainable living. In *Pervasive Computing and Communications Workshops (PERCOM Workshops), 2014 IEEE International Conference on*. pp.345–50. New York, NY: IEEE.

Bolino, M. C., Kacmar, K. M., Turnley, W. H., and Gilstrap, J. B. 2008. A multi-level review of impression management motives and behaviors. *Journal of Management*, 34, pp.1080–109.

Boudreau, J. W. 1983. Economic considerations in estimating the utility of human resource productivity improvements. *Personnel Psychology*, 36, pp.551–7.

Boudreau, J. W. 1991. Utility analysis for decisions in human resource management. In M. D. Dunnette and L. M. Hough, eds., *Handbook of industrial and organizational psychology*, Vol. 1, pp.621–745. Palo Alto, CA: Consulting Psychologist Press.

Boudreau, J. W., and Berger, C. J. 1985. Decision-theoretic utility analysis applied to external employee movement. *Journal of Applied Psychology*, 70, pp.581–612.

Boudreau, J. W., and Ramstad, P. M. 2007. *Beyond HR: the new science of human capital*. Boston: Harvard Business School Press.

Boudreau, J. W., Sturman, M. C., and Judge, T. A. 1994. Utility analysis: what are the black boxes and do they affect decisions? In N. Anderson and P. Herriot, eds., *Assessment and selection in organizations*, pp.77–96. John Wiley & Sons: New York.

Briner, R. B., and Rousseau, D. M. 2011. Evidence-based I-O psychology: not there yet. *Industrial and Organizational Psychology*, 4, pp.3–22

Brogden, H. E. 1949. When testing pays off. *Personnel Psychology*, 2, pp.171–83.

Brogden, H. E., and Taylor, E. K. 1950. The dollar criterion: applying the cost accounting concept to criterion construction. *Personnel Psychology*, 3, pp.133–54.

Bromiley, P., and Rau, D. 2015. Operations management and the resource based view: another view. *Journal of Operations Management*, 41, pp.95–106.

Cascio, W. F. 1981. *Costing human resources: the financial impact of behavior in organizations*. Cincinnati: Southwestern.

Cascio, W. F. 1992. Assessing the utility of selection decisions: Theoretical and practical considerations. In N. Schmidt, W. C. Borman, and Associates, eds., *Personnel selection in organizations*, pp.310–40. San Francisco: Josset-Bass.

Cascio, W., and Boudreau, J. 2011. *Investing in people: financial impact of human resource initiatives*, 2nd edn. Upper Saddle River, NJ: Pearson Education Inc.

Cascio, W., and Boudreau, J. 2014. Evidence-based management at the bottom of the pyramid: why human resources standards and research must connect more closely. *Oxford handbooks online*, Nov. 2014. http://www.oxfordhandbooks.com/view/10.1093/oxfordhb/9780199935406.001.0001/oxfordhb-9780199935406-e-12.

Chamorro-Premuzic, T., Winsborough, D., Sherman, R. A., and Hogan, R. 2016. New talent signals: shiny new objects or brave new world? *Industrial and Organizational Psychology: Perspectives on Science and Practice*, 9(3), pp.621–40.

Cherian, J., and Farouq, S. 2013. A review of human resource accounting and organizational performance. *International Journal of Economics and Finance*, 5, pp.74–83.

Cronbach, L. J., and Gleser, G. C. 1957. *Psychological tests and personnel decisions*. Urbana: University of Illinois Press.

Davenport, T. H., Harris, J., and Shapiro, J. 2010. Competing on talent analytics. *Harvard Business Review* (Oct.), pp.2–6.

De Corte, W. 1994. Utility analysis for the one-cohort selection-retention decision with a probationary period. *Journal of Applied Psychology*, 79, pp.402–11.

de Montjoye, Y. A., Quoidbach, J., Robic, F., and Pentland, A. S. 2013. Predicting personality using novel mobile phone-based metrics. In SPB, *Social computing, behavioral-cultural modeling and prediction*, pp.48–55. Berlin: Springer.

Denton, G. A., and White, B. 2000. Implementing a balanced-scorecard approach to managing hotel operations: the case of White Lodging Services. *Cornell Hotel and Restaurant Administration Quarterly*, 41(1), pp.94–107.

Dooney, J. 2013. Benchmarking human capital metrics. *SHRM Online* (Mar. 26). http://www.shrm.org/templatestools/toolkits/pages/benchmarkinghumancapitalmetrics.aspx. Accessed 1/26/2016.

Dulebohn, J. H., and Johnson, R. D. 2013. Human resource metrics and decision support: a classification framework. *Human Resource Management Review*, 23, pp.71–83.

Farrell, M. J. 1957. The measure of productive efficiency. *Journal of the Royal Statistical Society Series A*, 125, pp.252–67.

Fitz-Enz, J. 2010. *The new HR analytics: predicting the economic value of your company's human capital investment*. New York: American Management Association.

Flamholtz, E. G. 1999. *Human resource accounting: advances in methods and applications*, 3rd edn. New York: Spring Science+Business Media.

Gandomi, A., and Haider, M. 2015. Beyond the hype: big data concepts, methods, and analytics. *International Journal of Information Management, 35*(2), pp.137–44.

Grohmann, A., and Kauffeld, S. 2013. Evaluating training programs: development and correlates of the questionnaire for professional training evaluation. *International Journal of Training and Development, 17*(2), pp.135–55.

Guest, D. E. 1997. Human resource management and performance: a review and research agenda. *International Human Resource Management, 8*, pp.263–76.

Guthrie, J. 2001. High involvement work practices, turnover, and productivity: evidence from New Zealand, *Academy of Management Journal, 44*, pp.180–90.

Guzzo, R. A., Fink, A. A., King, E., Tonidandel et al. 2015. Big data recommendations for industrial-organizational psychology. *Industrial and Organizational Psychology: Perspectives on Science and Practice, 8*, pp.491–508.

Hitt, M. A., Carnes, C. M., and Xu, K. 2015. A current view of resource based theory in operations management: a response to Bromiley and Rau. *Journal of Operations Management, 41*(10), pp.107–9.

Holton, E. F. 1996. The flawed four-level evaluation model. *Human Resource Development Quarterly, 7*(1), pp.5–21.

Huselid, M. A. 1995. The impact of human resource management practices on turnover, productivity, and corporate financial performance. *Academy of Management Journal, 38*, pp.635–70.

Huselid, M. A., and Becker, B. E. 2011. Bridging micro and macro domains: workforce differentiation and strategic human resource management. *Journal of Management, 37*, pp.421–28.

Huselid, M. A., Becker, B. E., and Beatty, R. W. 2005. *The workforce scorecard: managing human capital to execute strategy*. Boston: Harvard Business School Press.

Kaplan, R. S., and Norton, D 1992. The balanced scorecard: measures that drive performance. *Harvard Business Review, 70*(1), pp.71–9.

Kerr, S. 1975. On the follow of rewarding A while hoping for B. *Academy of Management Journal, 18*, pp.769–83.

King, E., Tonidandel, S., Cortina, J., and Fink, A. A. 2016. Building understanding of the data science revolution and IO psychology. In S. Tonidandel, E. King, and J. Cortina, eds., *Big data at work, pp. 1–15*. New York: Taylor & Francis/ Routledge.

Kirkpatrick, D. L. 1959. Techniques for evaluating training programs. *Journal of American Society for Training and Development, 13*, pp.11–12.

Kirkpatrick, D. L., and Kirkpatrick, J. D. 2005. *Transferring learning to behavior*. San Francisco: Berrett-Koehler Publishers.

Kovach, K., Hughes, A., Fagan, P., and Maggitti, P. 2002. Administrative and strategic advantages of HRIS. *Employment Relations Today, 29*, pp.43–8.

Lambiotte, R., and Kosinski, M. 2014. Tracking the digital footprints of personality. *Proceedings of the IEEE, 102*(12), pp.1934–9.

Latham, G. P., and Whyte, G. 1994. The futility of utility analysis. *Personnel Psychology, 47*, pp.31–46.

Levenson, A. 2015. *Strategic analytics: advancing strategy execution and organizational effectiveness*. San Francisco: Berrett-Koehler Publishers.

Macan, T. H., and Highhouse, S. 1994. Communication the utility of human resource activities: a survey of I/O and HR professionals. *Journal of Business Psychology, 8*, pp.425–36.

McDaniel, G., ed. 1994. *IBM dictionary of computing*. New York: McGraw-Hill.

Mirvis, P. H., and Lawler, E. E. 1983. Systems are not solutions: issues in creating information systems that account for the human organization. *Accounting, Organizations and Society*, 8(2-3), pp.175–90.

Murphy, K. R. 1986. When your top choice turns you down: effect of rejected offers on the utility of selection tests. *Psychological Bulletin*, 99, pp.133–8.

Noe, R. A. 2013. *Employee training and development*, 6th edn. New York: McGraw-Hill.

Paki, H., and Azar, S. F. 2015. Identification and prioritization of obstacles of implementation of human resource accounting system by TOPSIS. *Journal of Management Sciences*, 1(3), pp.23–31.

PWC. 2015. *Trends in people analytics.* http://www.pwc.com/us/en/hr-management/publications/assets/pwc-trends-in-the-workforce-2015.pdf. Accessed Jan. 26, 2016.

Roselender, R., and Dyson, J. R. 1992. Accounting for the worth of employees: a new look at an old problem. *British Accounting Review*, 24, pp.311–29.

Rousseau, D. M. 2006. Is there such a thing as evidence-based management? *Academy of Management Review*, 31, pp.256–69.

Shadish, W. R., Cook, T. D., and Campbell, D. T. 2002. *Experimental and quasi-experimental designs for generalized causal inference.* Houghton, Mifflin and Company.

Salas, E., Wildman, J. L., and Piccolo, R. F. 2009. Using simulation-based training to enhance management education. *Academy of Management Learning & Education*, 8(4), pp.559–73.

Scarpello, V., and Theeke, H. A. 1989. Human resource accounting: a measured critique. *Journal of Accounting Literature*, 8, pp.265–80.

Schmidt, F. L., Hunter, J. E., McKenzie, R. C., and Muldrow, T. W. 1979. Impact of valid selection procedures on work-force productivity. *Journal of Applied Psychology*, 64, pp.609–26.

Snyder, R. A., Raben, C. S., and Farr, J. L. 1980. A model for the systematic evaluation of human resource development programs. *Academy of Management Review*, 5, pp.431–44.

Sturman, M. C. 2012. Employee value: combining utility analysis with strategic human resource management research to yield strong theory. In N. Schmitt, ed., *Oxford handbook of personnel assessment and selection*, pp.768–92. Oxford: Oxford University Press.

Sturman, M. C. 2000. Implications of utility analysis adjustments for estimates of human resource intervention value. *Journal of Management*, 26, pp.281–99.

Sturman, M. C. 2001. Utility analysis for multiple selection devices and multiple outcomes. *Journal of Human Resources Costing and Accounting*, 6, pp.9–28.

Sturman, M. C., Trevor, C. O., Boudreau, J. W., and Gerhart, B. 2003. Is it worth it to win the talent war? Evaluating the utility of performance-based pay. *Personnel Psychology*, 56, pp.997–1035.

Taras, V., Caprar, D. V., Rottig, D., Sarala, R. M. et al. 2013. A global classroom? Evaluating the effectiveness of global virtual collaboration as a teaching tool in management education. *Academy of Management Learning & Education*, 12(3), pp.414–35.

Taylor, H. C., and Russell, J. T. 1939. The relationship of validity coefficients to the practical effectiveness of tests in selection: discussion and tables. *Journal of Applied Psychology*, 23, pp.565–78.

Way, S. A. 2002. High performance work systems and intermediate indicators of firm performance within the US small business sector. *Journal of Management*, 28, pp.765–85.

Whyte, G., and Latham, G. P. 1997. The futility of utility analysis revisited: when even an expert fails. *Personnel Psychology*, 50, pp.601–10.

Yorks, L., Beechler, S., and Ciporen, R. 2007. Enhancing the impact of an open-enrollment executive program through assessment. *Academy of Management Learning & Education*, 6(3), pp.310–20.

Zafar, H. 2013. Human resource information systems: information security concerns for organizations. *Human Resource Management Review*, 23, pp.105–13.

SECTION 5

TALENT MANAGEMENT IN CONTEXT

CHAPTER 21

TALENT MANAGEMENT IN THE GLOBAL CONTEXT

SHAISTA E. KHILJI AND RANDALL S. SCHULER

21.1 TALENT MANAGEMENT IN THE GLOBAL CONTEXT

INTEREST in talent management in the business context and the global context increased significantly in the 1990s, when a group of McKinsey consultants coined the phrase *war for talent* in late 1990s to emphasize the critical importance of employees to the success of top-performing companies (Michaels, Hanfield-Jones, and Axelford, 2001). Much of this work is detailed in the other chapters in this book (e.g., Cappelli and Keller, 2017). However, to recap, scholars (e.g., Collings and Mellahi, 2009; Lewis and Hackman, 2006) have identified three distinct strands within the talent-management literature, focusing upon functional HR practices (to include recruitment, selection, and training), succession planning, and management of talented people. While certainly important, this approach to talent management tends to focus mainly on the individual and organizational levels, and minimizes several macro or country aspects of the global environment that are proving to be invaluable for talent management at the individual and organizational levels (Khilji, Tarique, and Schuler, 2015; Oxford Economics, 2014; Strack et al., 2014). This is despite the longstanding interest in talent management in the global context, or at the macro (country) level. In particular, non-governmental organizations such as the World Economic Forum, the World Competitiveness Center, and the Organization for Economic Cooperation and Development began publishing reports about the importance of talent, education, and quality of a country's workforce in the 1980s. Since then several studies have highlighted the macro-national aspect of talent management (Cooke, Saini, and Wang, 2014; Economist, 2011; Heidrick and Struggles, 2012; Khilji, Tarique, and Schuler, 2015; Oxford Economics, 2014). These studies and reports showed that many governments (e.g.,

Australia, Canada, Germany, the United Kingdom, and the United States) have joined the hunt for global talent by developing immigrant-friendly policies. Some governments (e.g., China, Indonesia, and India) have also been luring back skilled members of diasporas, and many others have been making serious investments in the education and human development of their own citizens with the purpose of spurring economic growth by upgrading local capabilities and building innovative capacities for the firms in their countries (Khilji, Tarique, and Schuler, 2015; Lanvin and Evans, 2014; Ragazzi, 2014; Oettl and Agarawal, 2008; Tung and Lazarova, 2006; Zweig, 2006; Saxenian, 2005).

Active involvement of various governmental and non-governmental organizations in attracting and developing talent makes talent management truly a global issue, which reaches beyond a single organization and its talent-management activities. It draws attention to the complexity of the macro environment within which organizations develop their talent-management systems and individuals make career choices (Khilji, Tarique, and Schuler, 2015; Khilji and Keilson, 2014). It incorporates cross-border flow of talent, diaspora mobility, and government policies to attract, grow, develop, and retain the talent nationally in support of innovation, productivity, and competitiveness, which facilitates talent-management activities within organizations.

It is therefore important that the scope of talent management extends beyond an individual and organizational analysis to incorporate the macro level in order to fully comprehend the complexities of managing talent in today's globalized world, where organizations are not only competing with each other, but governments and their societies have also joined the race (Lanvin and Evans, 2014; Ragazzi, 2014; The Economist, 2011). As such, we propose a definition of macro talent management (MTM) as:

> Factors such as the demographics, the economic, educational, social and political conditions of countries and the policies, programs and activities that are systematically developed by governmental and non-governmental organizations expressly for the purpose of enhancing the quality and quantity of talent within and across countries and regions to facilitate productivity, innovation and competitiveness of their domestic and multinational enterprises for the benefit of their citizens, organizations, and societies for long term advantage.

By promoting the macro perspective, we want to broaden the scope of talent management beyond its current focus (on the individual and organizational levels). To reiterate for clarity, what we are describing is not "global talent management" (which is focused on the individual and organizational levels), but talent management in the global context, which is focused on the macro level, or country level. (It is both within a single country and/or across countries.) At this macro level, *talent* is defined to include a large majority of a country's population, similar to companies that pursue an inclusive approach in their talent-management activities. However, research has also shown that many countries also pursue an exclusive approach to target a small portion of the portion (e.g., youth programs and assistance for high-performing citizens in Bangladesh and Pakistan; Khilji and Keilson, 2014).

To help facilitate this view in the chapter, we propose a conceptual framework of MTM that encapsulates environmental factors, processes, and outcomes related to MTM. We hope that this conceptual framework can serve to show MTM as an interdisciplinary phenomenon, and provide building blocks for future research.

21.2 CONCEPTUAL FRAMEWORK

Talent management has become an increasingly complex phenomenon in today's marketplace, with enhanced talent mobility and national-level competition for talent globally. Hence, it requires theoretical explanations (and developments) that are multilevel and deeply embedded contextually. As we start to extend our understanding of talent management to complex aspects that relate to an economic development agenda or competitiveness of countries (and increasingly cities and states), we begin viewing talent management from a macro perspective.

In order to highlight the significance of MTM, disparate research has referred to several factors that have contributed to its advancement, including competitive global environment (Farndale, Scullion, and Sparrow, 2010; McDonnell, Gunnigle, Lamare, and Lavelle, 2010), shifting demographics (Heid and Murphy, 2007; Khilji and Keilson, 2014), the rise of emerging economies and international mobility (Cooke, 2017; Collings, 2014; Khilji and Keilson, 2014; Li and Scullion, 2010), and demand–supply gaps or talent shortages (McDonnell, 2011; Oxford Economics, 2014; Stahl et al., 2007). Overall, scholars have concluded that MTM is a timely topic, and that organizations must build new capabilities in order to revitalize their competitive standing. In discussing the importance of global talent management (GTM), Tarique and Schuler (2010) gave some attention to factors external to the organization. For example, they referred to the talent flow related to migration of individuals across countries, differences in the population dynamics of developed and developing countries, and talent shortages globally to develop an integrative framework of GTM in multinational corporations (MNCs), but their primary focus for talent management was at the individual and organizational level. Khilij and co-authors (2015) expanded the Tarique and Schuler (2010) framework and developed the macro context of talent management to present GTM as an interdisciplinary field. This chapter offers a further expansion and development of the Khilij and colleagues (2015) model (refer to Figure 21.1), to include environmental factors, MTM functions, and processes, functions, and outcomes.

21.2.1 The MTM Macro Environment

We begin with a description of the macro-environmental factors, which are captured in Figure 21.1. These factors highlight the importance of MTM. In what follows, we discuss how environment serves as a push factor behind many MTM policies around the world.

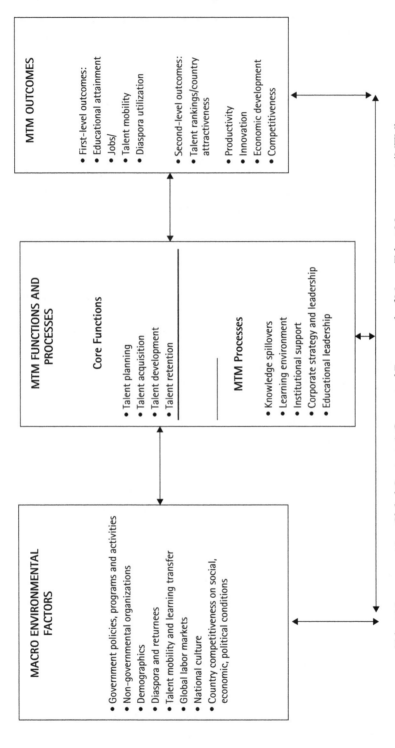

FIGURE 21.1 Talent Management in a Global Context: A Conceptual Framework of Macro Talent Management (MTM)

21.2.1.1 *Governmental Policies, Programs, and Activities*

We have mentioned previously that many national governments have been pursuing policies that focus upon upgrading local capabilities and developing innovative capacities through their human talent. A review of a wide range of these country initiatives indicates these are predominantly human development- and immigration-focused. Below we explain each focus, highlighting many country examples.

21.2.1.1.1 *Education Focused*

In the past few decades, many countries, such as South Korea, Taiwan, Malaysia, Pakistan, and Singapore, have made serious investments in the education and human development of their own citizens (Khilji, Tarique, and Schuler, 2015; Oxford Economics, 2014). Singapore, a small country with no natural resources, is a particularly good example. It is consistently ranked as one of the world's most competitive countries (World Economic Forum [WEF], 2014, 2015) with the best business climate (Lanvin and Evans, 2014; Evans and Lanvin, 2015) and a highly skilled and cosmopolitan workforce (Evans and Lanvin, 2015; Global Talent Competitiveness Index (GTCI) (see Heidrick and Struggles, 2015)). Scholars have argued this success is primarily due to its strong emphasis on people-development programs (Osman-Ghani, 2004) and the ready availability of scientists and engineers (WEF, 2014, 2015). WEF reports that a country's competitiveness is reinforced by a strong focus on education, providing individuals with the skills needed for a rapidly changing global economy (WEF, 2014, 2015). Over the past several decades, the Singaporean government has spent millions of dollars on developing an excellent educational system that develops talented and driven individuals. It has also developed a skill-upgrading system to help individuals continually develop their core competencies within the changing global environment. The chair of the EDB of Singapore, which develops and implements talent-development initiatives, states: "EDB's home strategy is to have companies use Singapore as their strategic location to grow, to expand their business, their innovation, their talent activities to help them grow [not just] in Asia but globally" (Business Climate, 2011).

While Singapore is a unique case because it has (probably) the clearest national strategy to grow and attract the best talent (Lanvin and Evans, 2014; Evans and Lanvin, 2015), a recent GTCI Report (Lanvin and Evans, 2014) indicates that other countries (e.g., Switzerland and Denmark) are also leading the global war for talent. In addition, the United Kingdom and Sweden are pursuing a strategy to become "talent competitive" via quality education (Lanvin and Evans, 2014). All of these countries also have a longstanding commitment to providing quality education and continuous training. Further details of how these and other countries improve the talent of their citizens can be found in the reports and rankings published in the GTCI, as well as the Global Competitiveness Index (GCI) of the WEF and the World Talent Report of the IMD to be described below in the section on NGOs.

21.2.1.1.2 *Educational Institutions*

Within this environment of accelerating and emphasizing human development, educational institutions have also emerged as important players in MTM. In developed countries, they are forging global partnerships with other universities and exchange programs worldwide to train talent and get greater access to global talent pool (Wildavsky, 2010). Currently, they are also recipients of large numbers of students from emerging economies. For example, in the United States, approximately 1 million foreign students enrolled in a variety of higher educational institutions in 2013–14 (Institute of International Education, 2015). This was a 10% increase, the highest since 1978–9. These international students gain valuable global experience and often fill important positions upon returning to their home countries (Gareis, 2012). They also provide cheap and easy access to global knowledge that exists elsewhere.

21.2.1.1.3 *Immigration Policies*

It is clear from the above examples that talent development has been adopted as a national agenda by many countries (Guo and Al Ariss, 2015; Khilji, Tarique, and Schuler, 2015). Several countries have also been competing for the world's most skilled and qualified workers in an increasingly global labor market via their immigration policies. Kapur and McHale state: "official pronouncement on immigration policy has been couched in the language of 'national competitiveness,' especially in knowledge-intensive sectors" (2005: 37). This is clearly apparent in the immigration strategies adopted by countries such as Germany and Canada. Germany's immigration policy is embedded in its ongoing need to bolster its economic development and maintain a dynamic workforce (Oezcan, 2004), especially in view of its aging population and continuing low fertility rates. The number of foreigners living in Germany is growing at the fastest rate in twenty years (Ferdman and Yanofsky, 2013); between 2007 and 2012, it increased by 72% (Faiola, 2014). Similarly, Britain has pursued a Highly Skilled Migrant Program and Tier 1 (General) Plan in its efforts to keep its economy globally competitive (UK Border Agency, 2012). Canada is one of the world's friendliest nations to immigrants and has the highest per capita admission rate. It has offered residency to approximately 200,000 immigrants (and refugees) per year for the past decade and has earned a reputation for an "open arms" attitude toward highly skilled talent (Council for Foreign Relations, 2006).

21.2.1.2 *NGOs*

Many of the programs and activities being pursued by governments are encouraged and driven in part by the activities of non-governmental organizations (NGOs). One of the most prominent is the Organizational for Economic Cooperation and Development (OECD). The OECD ranks countries on their levels of educational attainment for many age categories of their citizens. One of its most famous rankings is the Program for International Student Assessment, which ranks 15-year-old students on the basis of the achievement in math, sciences, and reading. The International Labor Organization also provides information on a country's skills, knowledge, and employability. The World Bank's *Doing Business Index* ranks countries on several aspects of doing business, from ease of starting a company and tax rates to employability of the workforce, including its skill levels (World Bank, 2017). Another group of NGOs that have been active in evaluating countries on their talent-management factors includes the WEF and its GCI; the IMD and its World Talent Rankings; and INSEAD/Human Capital

Leadership Institute of Singapore/Adecco and its Global Talent Competitiveness Index (GTCI). Because these NGOs highlight the qualities of countries as related to their talent management, the results are oftentimes used by countries to compare themselves to other countries, providing guidance (e.g., for educational initiatives) on how they can improve their supply of talented employees and how they can become more attractive for employers, both domestic and international. As a consequence, they can also serve as outcome measures in the evaluation of governmental programs and activities to improve country-level talent management. Hence, it might be useful to highlight briefly the content of some of the rankings.

In the GCI, the pillars that are most reflective of how a country is managing their talent are mainly the Fourth Pillar (Health and Primary Education), the Fifth Pillar (High Education and Training), the Seventh Pillar (Labor Market Efficiency), and the Twelfth Pillar (R&D Innovation). Similarly, the IMD *World Talent Report* is specifically focused on how well a country is managing its talent, using three major factors: (i) investment and development; (ii) appeal; and (iii) readiness. Under each of these are multiple indicators that can be used by countries to measure how well they are doing in managing talent at the country level and how attractive the country is to local and international businesses. The *GTCI* measures a country on six talent-management-relevant pillars: (i) enabling; (ii) attracting; (iii) growing; (iv) retaining; (v) vocational knowledge; and (vi) global knowledge. The Economist Intelligence Unit and the consulting firm of Heidrick and Struggles (2012) compile an index they call the *Global Talent Index*. As the title suggests, all seven of its dimensions capture some aspect of talent and talent management, to include: (i) demographics; (ii) compulsory education; (iii) university education; (iv) quality of the labor force; (v) talent environment; (vi) openness; and (vii) proclivity to attracting talent (Heidrick and Struggles, 2012).

21.2.1.3 *Demographics and Mobility*

In addition to the quality of the talent pool of countries provided by the NGO rankings, sheer quantity of the talent/population pool is also important for talent management in the global context (Chand and Tung, 2014; Khilji, 2012).

A majority of the future growth in the world population is expected to occur in developing or emerging economies (Population Reference Bureau, 2017). As a matter of fact, nearly half of the increment to the world population is estimated to come from only six countries: India (22%); China (11%); and Pakistan, Nigeria, Bangladesh, and the United States (17%, at approx. 4% each). This presents an interesting paradox because, on one hand, some countries in Asia Pacific and Europe (including France, Spain, Japan, and Germany) are aging fast and the proportion of the working-age people in the population is shrinking (McDonnell, Collings, and Burgess, 2012). On other hand, in countries such as India, Bangladesh, and Pakistan, 31%–36% of the workforce is fourteen years of age or below (Khilji, 2012; Khilji and Keilson, 2014). These countries are faced with the crisis of making them employable for an increasingly complex and global environment. By 2050, developed countries will not have enough workers to support the higher cost of their aging populations. Developing countries with younger populations will not have enough jobs. Khilji and Keilson (2014) argue that a global generational divide is likely to emerge as a workforce issue, where a majority of the young will be based in or come from developing countries, and the aging from the developed countries. Japan is already providing lessons for other countries and companies in talent management with a hyper-aging society (Adachi, Ishida, and Oka, 2015), as are several other countries mentioned previously. Khilji and Keilson (2014) offer a detailed review of government-led policies of several South Asian countries (including Pakistan, India, and Bangladesh) to highlight the importance of MTM in a demographically shifting world.

21.2.1.4 *Diaspora and Returnees*

Two other important factors in the global context of talent management are brain circulation and efforts to maximize the diaspora effect (Saxenian, 2005; Tung and Lazarova, 2006). Both of these phenomena can have a big impact on governmental programs. For example, those countries with large populations that emigrated elsewhere (mostly to the West) for better opportunities decades earlier are luring back talented members of the diaspora in order to benefit from their expertise and connections and develop younger talent effectively (e.g., China, Pakistan, and India, with their policies to bring back their diasporic persons for shorter to longer durations (Ragazzi, 2014; Khilji and Keilson, 2014). Thus while this discussion could be placed under "governmental activities," it is instead placed here because of its singular importance.

There are 232 million first-generation migrants around the world (United Nations, 2014). As 3.25% of the world's population, immigrants could make up a nation as big as Brazil. "There are more Chinese people living outside China than there are French people in France. Some 22 million Indians are scattered all over the globe" (The Economist, 2011: 13). Diasporic networks have always been a potent economic force (Chand, 2013; Tung and Lazarova, 2006). However, particularly in recent years, the ability to connect the home economy to international business networks by leveraging the reputation, education, and experiences of this population has been instrumental in successful development efforts, as in the case of Bangalore, the Indian IT hub and global destination of off-shoring, and the rapid economic development of China (Chand, 2012; Chen, 2008; Kapur and McHale, 2005; Saxenian, 2005). Diasporas have shaped global business, politics, and social development. More than half a million Chinese who have studied abroad and returned to dominate think-tanks and advise the government are moving up the ranks of the Communist Party, establishing new businesses, and thus having a positive impact on technology transfer and economic development (Chen, 2008; Liu et al., 2011; The Economist, 2011).

China, following in Korean and Taiwanese footsteps, provides a good example of a country that has successfully embarked on a comprehensive policy of luring back diasporic persons. Zweig (2006) traces Chinese interest in diasporas to the 1990s, when the central government realized that in order to improve science and technology in China, it had to let people go abroad freely, and then compete for them in the international market by creating a domestic environment that would attract them. Subsequently, the Chinese government improved the environment for immigrants and returnees by developing job introduction centers, offering preferential policies (of giving them more living space and higher professional titles), establishing a national association of returned students, and increasing support for scientific research. Local governments also started competing for talent by instituting their own policies. At the same time, universities and government-funded research organizations also actively started recruiting immigrants and returnees. Many other countries in Asia and Eastern Europe have adopted similar practices to lure back highly skilled persons to support their respective economic development (Ragazzi, 2014; Tung and Lazarova, 2006).

These programs and incentives have resulted in a reverse brain drain globally, or what Saxenian refers to as "brain circulation" (2005: 36)—that is, the ability of the diasporic and returnees to establish business relationships or to start new businesses while maintaining their social and professional ties elsewhere (countries they graduated from and gained experience in). These returnees have proven critical to the overall development of talent nationally, by transferring their knowledge and experience to the people they work with (DeVoretz and Zweig, 2008; Kapur and McHale, 2005; Tung and Lazarova, 2006) and establishing a new form of economic growth model through entrepreneurship and experimentation (Saxenian, 2005).

21.2.1.5 *Global Labor Markets*

A central factor in the global context of talent management is the development of global labor markets over the past thirty years. Global labor markets have been created in part due to government-led initiatives that prioritize talent acquisition, retention, and development. These have been facilitated by technological advancements and ease of global communication. In turn, greater workforce mobility, extensive diasporas, and international migration (along with brain circulation and knowledge flows) have exposed the macro implications and country effects of MTM. It is to be expected that both of these macro aspects of MTM will continue to evolve and transform over the next decade, based on the characteristics and desires of the large generation of millennials who are now in the position of having and wanting international assignments (PWC, 2015). As we continue to adopt a macro perspective in GTM, it is important to review how global markets are evolving particularly in view of a likely "global generational divide" (Khilji and Keilson, 2014).

21.2.1.6 *National Culture*

While these data indicate where talent pools are likely to be found, additional information about the national culture of a country can be important in establishing a country's reputation as a good place for doing business. For example, cultural characteristics such as work orientation, work ethics, comfort with uncertainty, and the need for structure at work have been shown to be important characteristics of a country's labor force, that is, its talent (Hofstede, 1980). In addition, a plethora of evidence suggests that national culture can help determine the appropriateness of the many possible talent-management policies a company can use in a particular country. For example, Cooke, Saini, and Wang (2014) describe the Chinese cultural characteristics and discuss how these impact the talent-management programs of companies in China. One of their findings is that the Chinese respondents are likely to value life-long learning and growth advancement as key criteria for joining and staying in the firm. These reflect Confucian values of life-long learning and advancement. Another example of how national culture can influence comapnies' talent management within a country is a study by Latukha (2015). Primarily focused on the specific talent-management practices within companies in Russia, Latuka found that these practices reflect the Russian culture especially for Russian companies, and less so for multinational companies within Russia.

While the degree to which a strong relationship between country culture and a company's talent-management practices is linked to the effectiveness of specific talent-management practices remains to be explored, companies may still to choose to tailor their programs for managing talent with sensitivity to the local country's cultural conditions. For example, because of the need to manage their talent within a global framework, companies such as Huawei, YUM, IKEA, and LG encase their talent-management program within a global/local context (Schuler, 2015).

21.2.1.7 *Country Competitiveness on Social, Economic, and Political Conditions*

Country competitiveness is the set of institutions, policies, and factors that determine the level of productivity of a country (WEF, 2015). The level of productivity in turn sets the level of prosperity that can be reached by the society. As described above, the WEF ranks these institutions (i.e., pillars) in more than 150 countries. Four of the fourteen pillars directly measure indicators of talent management, while the remaining ten measure broader aspects of a country's institutional environment including social, economic, and political ones. Hence, the premise is that the country that scores the best on all fourteen pillars is the most competitive and thus the most likely to be productive and provide prosperity for its citizens. So efforts to boost the talent-management pillars are in vain if not also accompanied by similar efforts to boost all the other pillars. Thus companies depending on developing the quality of the labor force in a country may hesitate to enter the country if it does not score well on the ten pillars of the WEF that describe the country's social, political, and economic conditions.

In summary, we are aware that the macro, global environment of talent management is dynamic and uncertain; thus, none of the identified factors is likely to remain stable or the same. For example, by 2030, population dynamics may have already changed, depending upon the development and demographic priorities of many developing and developed countries globally (Kunzig, 2011). Hence, an understanding of MTM needs to be continuously updated in order to refine existing knowledge to keep pace with the evolving world and remain relevant (Cheng, Guo, and Skousen, 2011; Khilji, 2012).

21.2.2 MTM Functions and Processes

Here we include the essential functions of MTM at the country level—talent planning, talent acquisition, talent development, and talent retention—as part of the MTM processes.

21.2.2.1 *Core Functions*

A plethora of research indicates that these core functions transfer/mediate/shape/ modify the impact of the macro-environmental factors on the MTM outcomes/consequences (Tarique and Schuler, 2010; Scullion, Collings, and Caligiuri, 2010; Khilij, Tarique, and Schuler, 2015). For example, the diaspora effect (mentioned previously) at the country level is associated with a country's ability to plan, attract, and retain talent, and education-led initiatives are focused upon developing human talent.

21.2.2.2 *Core MTM Processes*

These are the forces that influence how, when, why, and if the environmental factors transfer/mediate/shape/modify the impact of the macro-environmental factors on the MTM outcomes/consequences. These events might include:

- Talent mobility
- Knowledge spillovers
- Learning and knowledge sharing
- Institutional support
- Educational leadership
- Corporate strategy and leadership

Scholars have argued that talent produces knowledge flows, causes spillovers, and can be used for knowledge sharing and (organizational and national) learning. As discussed previously, it is clear that macro-institutional support, educational leadership, and corporate strategy and leadership can facilitate and/or hinder MTM in an environment. We present these aspects as MTM processes because they describe how talent relates to organizational and country-level changes over time, identify patterns of activities, and explain observed relationships between talent and the desired outcomes of (e.g.,) national competitiveness, innovation, and economic development (Liu et al., 2011; Oettl and Agrawal, 2008).

It is worth repeating that both governmental/NGO programs and organizational-level activities influence MTM processes. For example, greater global talent mobility stimulates international transmission of ideas (Agarwal, McHale, Kapur, and Oettl, 2011; Kapur, and McHale, 2005; Liu et al., 2011), produces knowledge flows (Di Maria and Lazarova, 2009; Carr, Inkson, and Thorn, 2005), enhances learning (Furuya, Stevens, Bird, Oddou, and Mendenhall, 2009) and improves efficiency of the innovation process (Oettl and Agrawal, 2008). As people move and interact across organizations and societies, they provide greater access to knowledge and reduce the need to recreate knowledge that already exists elsewhere. They also gain diverse experiences and hence serve as a prime source of learning for organizations and societies (Di Maria and Lazarova, 2009).

Emerging evidence in international business literature indicates the importance of the impact of talent mobility on country-level innovation performance, well beyond the much-understood firm-level innovative capacities. For example, Oettl and Agrawal's

(2008) study of cross-border movement of inventors (diasporas) presents an analysis of knowledge-flow patterns as people move from one country (and firm) to another. Their analysis indicates that knowledge flows don't necessarily follow organizational boundaries as diasporas continue to develop and tap social relationships. They conclude that the receiving country (that members of diaspora return to) learns and gains above and beyond the knowledge-flow benefits enjoyed by the receiving firm. Based upon the findings, they emphasize the need for and the extensive role of national learning (from the diaspora) outside the traditional market mechanisms. Liu and colleagues' (2011) study of panel data, constituting technological characteristics of Chinese firms and innovative performance, also indicates that talent mobility is an important source of knowledge spillovers. They argue that returning diaspora's presence facilitates technology transfer to other firms in the receiving country, thereby leading to enhanced learning and economic growth. Both of these studies are pioneers in examining the value of talent mobility to the global economy. These provide evidence of the complexity of MTM as a phenomenon in the global marketplace and the role of corporate strategy and leadership, and offer good insights for broadening the scope of talent management to include discussions relating to knowledge flows, innovation, learning, and competitiveness, topics that have not been sufficiently addressed in core talent-management literature.

21.2.3 MTM Outcomes

The outcomes/consequences of MTM are many. Sparrow, Scullion, and Tarique (2014) suggest that it is possible to think of them of occurring over time or in sequence. For example, the outcomes of educational attainment, jobs, and global mobility/immigration flows/diasporas can be considered first-level outcomes that result from the macro-environmental factors and the MTM processes. These outcomes are directly related to talent within the country (in terms of its development, retention, and utilization). In addition, there are several second-level outcomes, including talent rankings, country attractiveness, productivity, innovation, economic development, and competitiveness. These second-level outcomes are cumulative in nature. They relate to the strengthened economies and are the direct result of effective first-level outcomes. In other words, if a country has managed to enhance the educational attainment of its people, create jobs, and capitalize on human capital global mobility, it can have a positive impact on enhancing its national innovative capacities, productivity, and competitiveness.

21.3 FUTURE RESEARCH SUGGESTIONS FOR MTM

We hope that researchers recognize the broader scope of MTM as explored in this chapter, and use the conceptual framework proposed in Figure 21.1 to engage further in interdisciplinary research, practice, and policy related to MTM at not only the country and cross-country but also the individual and organizational levels. Our intention is not to bifurcate talent management into camps of micro and macro experts but to engage scholars in integrative analyses, thereby improving understanding of its theory, policy, and practice. But certainly the thrust of this chapter is expounding on talent management at the macro level, in the global context first.

We would like to offer a word of caution here. The conceptual framework presented in Figure 21.1 should not be viewed as a matter of linear or simple relationships. Scholars argue that societies and organizations are complex social systems (Anderson, 1999). The rapid pace of globalization has also added new elements of complexity to the human dynamics (Lane, Mazenvski, Mendenhall, and McNett, 2004). Accordingly, the MTM model should be viewed as being made up of large numbers of parts that interact in a complex manner (Phene and Tallman, 2012; Simon, 1962). Applying this understanding to macro MTM presents it as a system that requires interactions between different partners on a number of issues and levels, representing varying levels of complexity. We would also like to mention that the proposed framework doesn't capture an exhaustive list of trends, outcomes, and processes. As scholars continue to explore the multiple aspects of macro MTM as a phenomenon, they are likely to unravel and add other issues to this framework. Hence, we admit we have merely scratched the surface, based upon our current understanding of the global environment. We hope other researchers continue to critique and build upon it. Here are just a few research questions that one could begin with:

1. Do government policies targeting effective utilization, development, and retention of talent relate directly and positively to stronger economies?
2. Do NGOs have a significantly positive impact on how effectively countries manage their talent?
3. Does more successful management of diaspora members and returnees guarantee a higher talent-management ranking? What other cultural, economic, and organizational factors could contribute to it?
4. How does a country's higher talent-management ranking impact growth of multinational activity?
5. How does educational leadership, as well as corporate leadership/strategy, relate to higher levels of MTM outcomes?
6. How does talent mobility expand international knowledge and learning mechanisms and lead to enhanced levels of global competitiveness?
7. What type of environment facilitates learning? What types of socioeconomic and organizational mechanisms enhance the learning of individuals and the transfer of knowledge?

MTM calls for governments around the world to rethink their role in the society (Khilji, Tarique, and Schuler, 2015). They will have to become more active in the talent-management activities necessary for companies and individuals to thrive and be productive. They will need to enhance the attractiveness of their countries, although the processes for doing so will require real long-term thinking (Woetzel, 2015).

21.4 Data Sources and Theories to Utilize for Research

The topics for future research listed above are just a sample of what could be done (see Al Ariss, Cascio, and Paauwe, 2014; Khilji, Tarique, and Schuler, 2015 for more specific questions that could be examined). Fortunately, these questions and many others can be explored, at least in part, by existing databases. Virtually all the reports that establish rankings of countries have extensive data sets that could be utilized as secondary databases. Some of them are also based on existing databases. For example, the ranking reports of the GTCI and the *Global Talent Index* reveal many of their secondary data sources, as well as any primary databases that they use. In addition, the GCI has impressive data useful for direct indicators of talent management and indicators of the social, political, and economic environments of many countries.

The limited list of research suggestions is relevant in a dynamic and constantly evolving global context for talent management. Researchers could explore them in a variety of ways, using interdisciplinary approaches and multilevel analyses. Examining these questions is likely to establish MTM as an important field that is able to provide valuable insights to overall economic and human development within and beyond multinational organizations (Cheng, Guo, and Skousen, 2011; Cheng, Henisz, Roth, and Swaminath, 2009; Hitt, Beamish, Jackson, and Mathieu, 2007; Khilji and Keilson, 2014; Kuhn, 1962). For a discussion of talent management within multinationals, see Björkman and colleagues (2017).

Scholars have argued that a majority of the existing research on MTM is based upon anecdotal or limited information (Tarique and Schuler, 2010) and thus suffers from a number of theoretical deficiencies (Al Ariss, Cascio, and Paauwe, 2014; Khilji, Tarique, and Schuler, 2015; Farndale, Scullion, and Sparrow, 2010; Tarique and Schuler, 2010). Conceptualizing rigorous research questions that cut across several theoretical boundaries is likely to engage scholars in empirically based research and lead to lively discussions of an expansive scope and interdisciplinary understanding of MTM. Fortunately, there are several theoretical perspectives that might be used, including the institutional theory, resource-based view (RBV), knowledge-based theories (e.g., knowledge-spillover effects, and knowledge sharing), and transformative learning and human capital theory (HCT). Khilji and Keilson's (2014) study of ongoing MTM initiatives in South Asia is just one example of a study that employs RBV and HCT, concurrently, to highlight the importance of MTM in talent management. They argue that both RBV and HCT underscore the importance of people to national and organizational competitive advantage by emphasizing them as rare and socially complex resources (Hitt, Biermant,

Shimizu, and Kochhar, 2001). However, HCT goes a step further to link human capital to economic growth (Lepak and Snell, 1999). It suggests that individuals and societies derive economic benefits from investments in people (Becker, 1992; Sweetland, 1996). According to Becker (1992), investments in education and training are the most relevant types of investment in human capital. Hence, HCT is particularly relevant for studies adopting a macro view in GTM, in that it directly relates talent development to economic development (Lepak and Snell, 2002; Khilji, 2012). Such a view is important for informing many research questions, including questions 1 and 3 posed previously. Similarly, knowledge sharing, as the fundamental means through which people can contribute to innovation and competitive advantage (Wang and Noe, 2010), can aid studies focused upon exploring innovation capabilities, as well as building knowledge capabilities (such as in questions 6 and 7). Institutional theory, with its emphasis on the environment, imitative or mimetic processes, and normative transmission of social facts, can provide useful MTM analyses related to the role of NGOs (question 2), multinational activity (question 4), and other social structures in implementing and delineating MTM policy impacts. A transformative learning theory can be used to focus upon fundamental shifts in perspectives and frames of reference that MTM policies and practices may bring about at the individual, organizational, and even societal levels. The multiphased transformation of perspective process outlined by Mezirow (1991) could also be helpful in examining acquisition of new knowledge, building new competence, and planning new roles and actions; all of these are critical to the study of MTM.

The aforementioned serve as a few examples of interdisciplinary work employing a few theories that we can relate to. As MTM offers an encompassing view, it is likely to open up new possibilities to researchers in terms of employing diverse perspectives and theories. We hope that, given the interdisciplinary nature and wide scope of MTM, future studies are able to expand the scope of theoretical relevance and contributions and thus offer new insights into MTM activities, processes, and outcomes.

21.5 IMPLICATIONS FOR MANAGERS AND POLICY MAKERS

There is much evidence to suggest that talent shortages will continue in the near future (despite the effects of the financial crisis). Hence, organizations cannot become complacent (Lanvin and Evans, 2014; Evans and Lanvin, 2015; McDonnell, Gunnigle, Lamare, and Lavelle, 2010). Managers need to recognize fully the broad scope of MTM and develop new organizational capabilities that enable them to acquire, grow, and retain talent globally, with the purpose of improving their innovation and competitiveness (Khilji, Tarique, and Schuler, 2015). As talent mobility increases, a new cadre of global workers will develop multiple identities and start taking control of their own careers. Managers will have to consider how to interact with them, what strategies to use in order to benefit from their expertise, what reward mechanisms to use to retain them, and how to plan their careers if they are not willing to slot their careers into strategic corporate plans (Carr, Inkson, and Thorn, 2005). Managers will also need to develop organizational mechanisms and policies that promote environments conducive for individual and organizational learning, as this is critical to developing effective MTM outcomes. Working in cooperation with city, state, and national governmental bodies and NGOs might facilitate an appropriate supply of talent to meet the demand of organizations, in both the short and the long run.

Recognizing demographic global changes, in particular a *global generational divide* (Khilji and Keilson, 2014), and interdependencies of talent shortages is critical for national policy makers (Woetzel, 2015). They need to develop more integrated and collaborative MTM policies in order to better compete for talent (Lanvin and Evans, 2014; Manning, Massini, and Lewin, 2008). Governments also need to become more concerned not only with attracting migrants and members of diasporas but also with capturing and institutionalizing their skills for national learning and technological developments (Adachi, Ishida, and Oka, 2015). They may have to create national diaspora networks composed of virtual networks of nationals based overseas who are willing to provide expertise to their countries of birth (Carr, Inkson, and Thorn, 2005). Finally, much like managers and practitioners, they also need to create socioeconomic environments that facilitate and enhance social and national learning. Creating opportunities for research, innovation, and entrepreneurship can stimulate the flow of talent and provide access to international innovation networks (Woetzel, 2015). All of these changes will help attract new companies and create more opportunities for productivity, growth, and gains in standards of living for their citizens.

Based on country conditions/attractiveness/educational levels, companies will continue to make major decisions on where to locate operations, determined by which countries have favorable conditions for acquiring local firms or entering into joint ventures.

21.6 Conclusions

The chapter contributes in a number of ways to the literature on talent management. First, it proposes several theoretical arguments for examining the processes through which aspects of the external environment such as economic development and competitiveness influence and have the potential to advance the research on MTM outcomes. Second, it offers several arguments for examining the role of "MTM process" in explaining the relationship between the external environment and talent-management outcomes. Third, by integrating several streams of research this study attempts to contribute to new theory-building in talent management by offering a theoretical framework that provides a foundation for others to build from and improve upon. Fourth, it suggests that further research might extend its focus to include more non-American contexts (Collings, Scullion, and Vaiman, 2011). Finally, we argue that talent management, especially in the macro, global context, is a complex phenomenon and we propose an interdisciplinary research agenda. The proposed MTM framework (Figure 21.1) makes a value-added contribution to the literature because it combines ideas from multiple disciplines that enhance its scope and provide a more comprehensive view of talent management. This could not have been obtained by relying on a single discipline and/or field. We hope that it is able to stimulate interest in MTM from a wider variety of disciplines, thus enriching our understanding of core MTM issues.

As with any research proposing a new and broad conceptual framework, there are limitations to this study. First, the operationalization of some constructs can be a major concern. Although most of the constructs are adapted from prior research on GTM, future work should include measures of the constructs in this study that are more refined. Second, "model specification" is an important concern: It is important to determine whether all relevant variables have been included in our model (Schuler, 2015). Third, the ability to generalize our framework across countries may not be reasonable. More research is needed to explore these issues further.

Overall, we believe that MTM offers a rich new avenue for research. Given its complexity and overarching influence, the field offers an opportunity for scholars to incorporate interdisciplinary perspectives and engage in research that is able to cut across and synthesize individual, organizational, and societal levels.

References

Adachi, M., Ishida, R., and Oka, G. 2015. Japan: lessons from a hyperaging society. *McKinsey Quarterly*, March. www.mckinsey.com/global-themes/asia-pacific/japan lessons-from-a-hyperaging-society.

Agarwal, A., Kapur, D., McHale, J., and Oettl, A. 2011. Brain drain or brain bank? The impact of skilled emigration on poor country innovation. *Journal of Urban Economics*, 69, pp.43–55.

Anderson, P. 1999. Complexity theory and organization science. *Organization Science*, 10, pp.216–32.

Al Ariss, A. A., Cascio, W. F., and Paauwe, J. 2014. Talent management: current theories and future research directions. *Journal of World Business*, 49, pp.173–9.

Becker, T. E. 1992. Foci and bases of commitment: are they distinctions worth making? *Academy of Management Journal*, 35(1), pp.232–44.

Blass, E. 2007. *Talent management: maximizing talent for business performance*. London: Chartered Management Accounting and Ashridge Consulting.

Björkman, I., Ehrnrooth, M., Makela, K., Smale, A. et al. 2017. Talent management in multinational corporations. In D. G. Collings, K. Mellahi, and W. C. Cascio, eds., *Oxford handbook of talent management*. Oxford: Oxford University Press.

Business Climate. 2011. Singapore's investment climate best in the world. http://www.singaporesetup.com/singapore's-investment-climate-best-in-the-world-survey/.

Cappelli, P., and Keller, JR. 2017. Introduction: talent management. In D. G. Collings, K. Mellahi, and W. C. Cascio, eds., *Oxford handbook of talent management*. Oxford: Oxford University Press.

Carr, S. C., Inkson, K., and Thorn, K. 2005. From global careers to talent flow: reinterpreting "brain drain." *Journal of World Business*, 40, pp.386–98.

Chand, M. 2013. A catalyst for globalization and knowledge flows: the South Asian diaspora. In S. E. Khilji and C. Rowley, eds., *Globalization, change and learning in South Asia*, pp.39–61. Oxford: Elsevier.

Chand, M. S. 2012. Diasporas, migration and trade: the Indian diaspora in North America. *Journal of Enterprising Communities*, 6(4), pp.383–96.

Chand, M. S., and Tung, R. L. 2014. The aging of the world's population and its effects on global business. *Academy of Management Perspectives*, 26(4), pp.409–29.

Chen, Y .O. C. 2008. The limits of brain circulation: Chinese returnees and technological development in Beijing. *Pacific Affairs*, 81(2), pp.195–215.

Cheng, J. L.C., Guo, W., and Skousen, B. 2011. Advancing new theory development in the field of international management. *Management International Review*, 51, pp.787–802.

Cheng, J. L. C., Henisz, W., Roth, K. and Swaminath, A. 2009. From the editors: advancing interdisciplinary research in the field of international business: prospects, issues and challenges. *Journal of International Business Studies*, 40, pp.1070–4.

Collings, D. G. 2014. Integrating global mobility and global talent management: exploring the challenges and strategic opportunities. *Journal of World Business*, 49(2), pp.253–61.

Collings, D. G., and Mellahi, K., 2009. Strategic talent management: a review and research agenda. *Human Resource Management Review*, 19(4), pp.304–13.

Collings, D. G., Scullion, H., and Vaiman, V. 2011. European perspectives on talent management. *European Journal of International Management*, 5(5), pp.453–62.

Cooke, F. L. 2017. Talent management in emerging economies. In D. G. Collings, K. Mellahi, and W. C. Cascio, eds., *Oxford handbook of talent management*. Oxford: Oxford University Press.

Cooke, F. L., Saini, D. S., and Wang, J. 2014. Talent management in China and India: a comparison of management perceptions and human resource practices. *Journal of World Business*, 49, pp.225–35.

Council for Foreign Relations. 2006. Canada's immigration policy. http://www.cfr.org/canada/canadas-immigration-policy/p11047.

DeVoretz, D., and Zweig, D. 2008. An overview of the 21st century Chinese "brain circulation." *Pacific Affairs*, 81(2), pp.171–4.

Di Maria, C., and Lazarova, E. A. 2011. Migration, human capital formation and growth: an empirical investigation. *World Development*, 40(5), pp. 938–55.

Doing Business Report. 2017. Equal opportunities for all. In *The World Bank*, 14th edn. Available at http://www.doingbusiness.org/~/media/WBG/DoingBusiness/Documents/Annual-Reports/English/DB17-Report.pdf. Accessed June 3, 2017.

Economist. 2011. The magic of diasporas. Economist (Nov. 19), http://ssrn.com/abstract=1517647.

Evans, P., and Lanvin, B. 2015. The world's most talent ready countries. www.knowledge.insead.edu/talent-management.

Faiola, A. 2014. The new land of opportunity for immigrants is Germany. *The Washington Post*, July 27.

Farndale, E., Scullion, H., and Sparrow, P. 2010. The role of corporate HR function in global talent management. *Journal of World Business*, 45, pp.161–8.

Farndale, E., Pai, A., Sparrow, P., and Scullion, H. 2014. Balancing individual and organizational goals in global talent management: a mutual-benefits perspective. *Journal of World Business*, 49(2), pp.204–14.

Ferdman, R. A., and Yanofsky, D. 2013. Germany opened its immigration and the rest of Europe came pouring in. *Quartz.* http://qz.com/138807/germany-opened-its-immigration-gates-and-the-rest-of-europe-came-pouring-in/.

Furuya, N., Stevens, M. J., Bird, A., Oddou, G., and Mendenhall, M. 2009. Managing the learning and transfer of global management competence: antecedents and outcomes of Japanese repatriation effectiveness. *Journal of International Business Studies, 40*, pp.200–15.

Gareis, E. 2012. Intercultural friendship: effects of home and host region. *Journal of International and Intercultural Communication, 5*(4), pp.309–28.

Guo, C., and Al Ariss, A. 2015. Human resource management of international migrants: current theories and future research. *International Journal of Human Resource Management, 26*(9–10), pp.1287–97.

Heidrick and Struggles. 2012. *The Global Talent Index Report: the outlook to 2015*. New York: Heidrick and Struggles.

Heidrick and Struggles. 2015. Global talent index. Available at http://www.globaltalentindex.com/Resources/gti-map.aspx#. Accessed June 3, 2017.

Heid, M. C., and Murphy, W. 2007. It is 2012. Do you know where your talent is? *Financial Executive, 23*(10), pp.28–31.

Hitt, M. A., Beamish, P. W., Jackson, S. E., and Mathieu, J. 2007. Building theoretical and empirical bridges across levels: multilevel research in management. *Academy of Management Journal, 50*, pp.1385–99.

Hitt, M. A., Biermant, L. Shimizu, K., and Kochhar, R. 2001. Direct and moderating effects of human capital on strategy and performance in professional service firms: a resource-based perspective. *Academy of Management Journal, 44*(1), pp.13–28.

Hofstede, G. 1980. *Culture's consequences*. London: Sage Publications.

Institute of International Education (IIE). 2015. http://www.iie.org/.

Kapur, D., and McHale, J. 2005. *Give us your best and brightest: the global hunt for talent and its impact on the developing world*. Washington, DC: Center for Global Development.

Khilji, S .E. 2012. Does South Asia matter? Rethinking South Asia as relevant in international business research. *South Asian Journal of Global Business Research, 1*(1), pp.8–21.

Khilji, S. E., and Keilson, B. 2014. In search of global talent: Is South Asia ready? *South Asian Journal of Global Business Research, 3*(2), pp.114–34.

Khilji, S. E., Tarique, I., and Schuler, R. S. 2015. Incorporating the macro view in global talent management. *Human Resource Management Review, 25*(3), pp.236–48.

Kuhn, T. S. 1962. *The structure of scientific revolutions*. Chicago: University of Chicago Press.

Kunzig, R. 2011. Population 7 billion. *National Geographic*. fhttp://ngm.nationalgeographic.com/2011/01/seven-billion/kunzig-text.

Lane, H. W., Mazenvski, M. L., Mendehall, M E., and McNett, J. 2004. *Blackwell handbook of global management: a guide to managing complexity*. Oxford: Blackwell.

Lanvin, B., and Evans, P. 2014. *The global talent competitiveness index 2014*. Human Capital Leadership Institute (INSEAD and Adecco Group).

Latukha, M. 2015. Talent management in Russian companies: domestic challenges and international experience. *International Journal of Human Resource Management, 26*(8), pp.1051–75.

Lepak, D. P., and Snell, S. A. 2002. The human resource architecture: towards a theory of human capital allocation and development. *Academy of Management Review, 24*(1), pp.31–48.

Lewis, R. E., and Heckman, R. J. 2006. Talent management: a critical review. *Human Resource Management Review, 16*(2), pp.139–54.

Li, S., and Scullion, H. 2010. Developing local competence of expatriate managers for emerging markets: a knowledge based approach. *Journal of World Business*, 45, pp.190–6.

Liu, X., Lu, J., Filatotchev, I., Buck, T. et al. 2011. Returnee entrepreneurs, knowledge spillovers and innovation in high-tech firms in emerging economies. *Journal of International Business Studies*, 41, pp.183–97.

Manning, S., Massini, S. and Lewin, A. Y. 2008. A dynamic perspective on next-generation offshoring: the global sourcing of science and engineering talent. *Academy of Management Perspectives*, 22, pp.35–54.

McDonnell, A. 2011. Still fighting the "war for talent"? Bridging the science versus practice gap. *Journal of Business and Psychology*, 26(2), pp.169–73.

McDonnell A., Collings, D., and Burgess, J. 2012. Guest editors' note: talent management in the Asia Pacific. *Asia Pacific Journal of Human Resources*, 50, pp.391–8.

McDonnell, A., Lamare, R., Gunnigle, P., and Lavelle, J. 2010. Developing tomorrow's leaders: evidence of global talent management in multinational enterprises. *Journal of World Business*, 45, pp.150–60.

Mezirow, J. 1991. *Transformative dimensions of adult learning*. San Francisco: Jossey Bass.

Michaels, E., Hanfield-Jones, H., and Axelford, B. 2001. *War for talent*. Boston: Harvard Business School Press.

Oettl, A., and Agrawal, A. 2008. International labor mobility and knowledge flow externalities. *Journal of International Business Studies*, 39, pp.1242–60.

Oezcan, V. 2004. Germany: immigration in transition. *Social Science Immigration Center*. http://www.migrationinformation.org/Profiles/display.cfm?ID=235.

Osman-Ghani, A. 2004. Human capital development in Singapore: an analysis of national policy perspectives. *Advances in Developing Human Resources*, 6, pp.276–87.

Oxford Economics. 2014. Global talent 2021: how the new geography of talent will transform human resource strategies. https://www.oxfordeconomics.com/Media/Default/Thought%20Leadership/global-talent-2021.pdf.

Phene, A., and Tallman, S. 2012. Complexity, context, and governance in biotechnology alliances. *Journal of International Business Studies*, 43, pp.61–83.

PWC Millenials Survey. 2015. Millennials at work: reshaping the workplace. http://www.pwc.com/gx/en/managing-tomorrows-people/future-of-work/millennials-survey.html.

Population Reference Bureau. 2017. 2016 World Population Data. Available at http://www.prb.org/Publications/Datasheets/2016/2016-world-population-data-sheet.aspx. Accessed June 3, 2017.

Puri, R. D. 2017. Is talent in Singapore digital-ready? Future Ready Singapore. Available at https://www.futurereadysingapore.com/2017/is-talent-in-singapore-digital-ready.html. Accessed June 3, 2017.

Ragazzi, F. 2014. A comparative analysis of diaspora policies. *Political Geography*, 41, pp.74–89.

Saxenian, A. L. (2005). From brain drain to brain circulation: transnational communities and upgrading in China and India. *Studies in Comparative International Development*, 40, pp.35–61.

Schuler, R. S. 2015. The five-C framework for managing talent. *Organizational Dynamics*, 44, pp.15–29.

Simon, R. 1962. The architecture of complexity. *Proceedings of the American Philosophical Society*, 106(6), pp.467–82.

Scullion, H., Collings, D., and Caligiuri, P. 2010. Global talent management: introduction. *Journal of World Business*, 45, pp.105–8.

Sparrow, P. R., Scullion, H., and Tarique, I. 2014. Strategic talent management: future directions. In P. R. Sparrow, H. Scullion, and I. Tarique, eds., *Strategic talent management: contemporary issues in international context*, pp.278–302. Cambridge: Cambridge University Press.

Sparrow, P. R., and Markam, H. 2015. What is the value of talent management: building value-driven processes within a talent management architecture. *Human Resource Management Review*, 25(3), pp.249–63.

Stahl, G. K., Björkman, I., Farndale, E., Morris, S. et al. 2007. *Global talent management: how leading multinationals build and sustain their talent pipeline*. Faculty & Research Working Paper. Fontainebleau, France: INSEAD.

Strack, R., Von Der Linden, C., Booker, M., and Strohmayr, A. 2011. *Decoding global talent*. Boston: Boston Consulting Group.

Sweetland, S. R. 1996. Human capital theory: foundations of a field of inquiry. *Review of Educational Research*, 66(3), pp.341–59.

Tarique, I., and Schuler, R. 2010. Global talent management: literature review, integrative framework, and suggestions for future research. *Journal of World Business*, 45, pp.122–33.

Tung, R. L., and Lazarova, M. B. 2006. Brain drain versus brain gain: an exploratory study of ex-host country nationals in Central and East Europe. *International Journal of Human Resource Management*, 17(11), pp.1853–72.

UK Border Agency. 2012. Home page. http://www.ukba.homeoffice.gov.uk/.

United Nations. 2014. 232 million international migrants living abroad worldwide (UN press Release), Department of Economic and Social Affairs. http://esa.un.org/unmigration/wall-chart2013.htm.

Wang, S., and Noe, R. A. 2010. Knowledge sharing: a review and directions for future research. *Human Resource Management Review*, 20, pp.115–31.

WEF. 2014. *Global Competitiveness Report 2013–2014: country profile highlights*. http://www3.weforum.org/docs/GCR2013-14/GCR_CountryHighlights_2013-2014.pdf.

WEF. 2015. *Global Competitiveness Report 2014–2015: country profile highlights*. http://www.weforum.org/reports/global-competitiveness-report-2014-2015.

Wildavsky, B. 2010. *The great brain race: how global universities are shaping the world*. Hartford, CT: Princeton Press.

Woetzel, J. 2015. How Asia can boost productivity and economic growth. McKinsey and Company, March. www.mckinsey.com/global-themes/employment-andgrowth/how-asia-can-boost-productivity-and-economic-growth.

World Bank. 2014. *Doing business*. http://www.doingbusiness.org/rankings.

Zucker, L. G. 1987. Institutional theories of organizations. *Annual Review of Sociology*, 13, pp.443–64.

Zweig. D. 2006. Competing for talent: China's strategies to reverse brain drain. *International Labor Review*, 145(1), pp.65–89.

....

CHAPTER 22

TALENT MANAGEMENT IN THE PUBLIC SECTOR

Managing Tensions and Dualities

....

PAUL BOSELIE AND MARIAN THUNNISSEN

22.1 INTRODUCTION

....

TALENT management, performance management, and leadership development are popular themes in private sector companies and organizations (Stahl et al., 2012). Performance management and leadership have found their way to public sector organizations and research (see, e.g., Van Dooren, Boukaert, and Halligan [2015] on performance management, and Tummers and Knies [2013] on public sector leadership). Talent management in the public sector, however, is an underexplored field of research (Thunnissen, Boselie, and Fruytier, 2013; Gallardo-Gallardo and Thunnissen, 2016), but it is most likely to be one of the key areas of attention in the near future in both theory and practice. This chapter on talent management in the public sector is very much focused on the relevance of context. In general, the attention to the impact of the institutional context, the organizational configuration, and the characteristics of the workforce on talent management is very weak in talent-management research and the literature (Collings, 2014; Gallardo-Gallardo and Thunnissen, 2016). The aim of this chapter is to define *talent management* in the public sector context by putting talent management in a public sector Human Resource Management (HRM) framework and linking talent management to public sector developments and tendencies in order to present some key issues, tensions, and dualities regarding talent management in the public sector. Moreover, we address future research avenues and some practical applications. To achieve these aims, we apply a multidisciplinary approach to talent management, using insights from HRM, public administration, and public management.

22.2 HRM in the Public Sector: A Theoretical Framework

The public sector context is complex because of the significant impact of institutional mechanisms (often stronger than in private companies; see, e.g., Christensen, Laegrid, Roness, and Rovik, 2007). The public sector context is characterized by issues of ownership, the presence and influence of multiple stakeholders inside and outside public sector organizations, the role of the government (including the authorizing environment), the relevance of politics, the impact of public values linked to institutions and culture, and the employment of professionals in public service jobs such as judges in courts, medical specialists in hospitals, and teachers in education (Leisink, Boselie, Hosking, and Van Bottenburg, 2013). Because of these factors, the public sector is diverse. There is no singular public sector context, although different public sectors (e.g., education, health care, and local governments) can have significant similarities. Moreover, as a result of privatization and new public management (NPM), some public sector organizations (e.g., airports and railways) are more closely related to private sector companies than other public sector organizations. And there are differences between countries as a result of differences in institutions, politics, culture, and legislation. In summary, public sector organizations are often very different from private sector organizations. Finally, there are significant differences between public sector organizations owing to sectoral differences.

Institutional factors affect relevant organizational concepts such as (a) the concept of organizational and individual performance, (b) the concept of employee motivation (e.g., translated into public service motivation), and (c) the way public sector organizations and its staff can be managed. Vandenabeele, Leisink, and Knies (2013) have integrated public administration and public management insights and theory in HRM, in particular, into the HR value chain of Wright and Nishii (2013) (see Figure 22.1). Their model differs from the Wright and Nishii (2013) model because it contextualizes the HR value chain and includes a range of factors that can help understand the shaping of HRM (and therefore also talent management) in different public sector contexts.

The upper half of the model illustrates the direct and continuous impact of contextual factors on the development and implementation of HR practices in public sector organizations. In this specific public sector context, Vandenabeele and colleagues (2013) make a distinction between the authorizing environment and public values. The authorizing environment consists of politician and stakeholder influences. The stakeholders can be situated outside and inside the organization: for example, governmental policy makers, political parties, unions, audit offices, and governmental advisory bodies, as well as managers and public service workers within the organization (internal stakeholders). Public values refer to the public sector's contribution to society (e.g., service to society as a whole, social cohesion, and sustainability), and how public sector organizations and their employees should behave in relation to their environment such as politicians

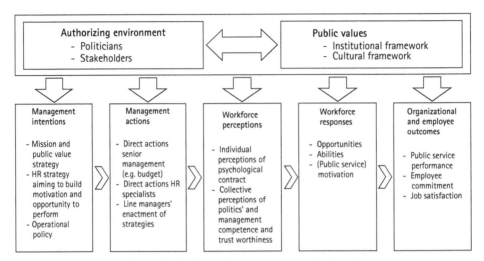

FIGURE 22.1 Integrated Model of Public Administration and Public Management Insights and HRM Theory

and citizens (referring to values such as loyalty, responsiveness, accountability, honesty, and integrity) (Jørgensen and Bozeman, 2007). The public values are determined by the existing institutional and cultural framework.

The lower half of the model focuses on the HRM process. Regarding the workforce responses to the implemented HR practices, the model is adapted to some specific characteristics of the public service workers. It includes insights from the AMO model (employee abilities, motivation, and opportunity to participate), in particular the employee motivation, which is adapted to the concept of public service motivation (PSM) widely studied in public administration (Perry and Vandenabeele, 2015). PSM is a specific type of employee motivation associated with public sector work.

In this chapter we apply the basic principles of Vandenabeele and co-authors' model to talent management in the public sector context, given that talent management is a sort of micro-HRM in itself (Boselie, 2014: Chapter 10). First, we describe the relevant public sector characteristics and developments. Next, we define talent management in the public sector context based on what we already know from previous research and the literature. Third, we discuss key issues, dualities, and tensions regarding talent management in the public sector. Finally, we focus on a future research agenda for talent management in public sector contexts, and present some implications for practitioners.

22.3 PUBLIC SECTOR CHARACTERISTICS AND DEVELOPMENTS

We want to highlight three significant characteristics of public sector organizations that are important for understanding fully a talent-management debate in these contexts.

22.3.1 Characteristics of Public Sector Organizations

First, in many countries, there is a strong historical tradition of the government as "the good employer," putting the well-being of the individual employee central in terms of employment security, payment, and development. This has resulted in life-long careers within one organization, as depicted in the (classic) internal labor market (ILM) model (see, e.g., Baron and Kreps, 1999). This "good employer" intention is not an organizational strategy as such, but it has often become a way of organizational life within public sector organizations. It is questionable whether this starting point can be maintained, given the necessary organizational flexibility and employability notions for individual employees.

Second, the principle of equality implying that all workers are equal and should be treated as far as is possible also has a strong tradition in many public sector organizations (Boselie, Leisink, and Vandenabeele, 2011). Adapting this principle to the workplace implies that all employees should get the same chances to develop and grow, including equal promotion opportunities. This leaves little room for differentiation and often leads to additional mechanisms, such as various possibilities for internal and external grievance procedures. Employees who do not get a promotion, for example, can file a formal complaint against a public sector organization.

Third, most public sectors have specific legislation for civil servants and employees (Leisink, Boselie, Van Bottenburg, and Hosking, 2013), ranging from maximum employment security to a sector-specific court for employees in the case of military services. This means that the dismissal of employees is often more difficult for public sector organizations than for private sector organizations. In addition, there are often professional bodies and networks linked to the professionals who work in the public sector organization—such as for doctors and other medical professionals, judges, and academics—that monitor professional quality standards, provide professional development, and even have their own regulations. Many professions are protected by law and are therefore highly institutionalized. In a way the socialization and development of these public sector workers cannot be completely controlled by the organization, but is also in the hands of external organizations or networks.

These three characteristics of the public employer are under pressure and, therefore, changing. First, most countries are facing governmental cuts, often directly related to the global financial crisis that started in 2008 (Boselie, Brewster, and Vos, 2013). These governmental cuts can be sector- and country-specific. The health care sector, for example, is under pressure, given increasing health care costs and the problem of an aging population. In some countries, the military budget is reduced as a direct result of politics and the public opinion, whereas in other countries this budget is increased because of terrorist threats or war. Second, besides the financial cutbacks, many Western countries show the tendency of decreasing the size of governmental and public sector organizations: less government and more privatization. This has resulted in a decline in the total number of public service workers in many countries. In addition, we also see an increase in employees with flexible contracts and a decrease in permanent contracts, with the ultimate aim to increase organizational flexibility. The ILM model (e.g., Baron and Kreps, 1999) is now challenged by high-performance work systems models (Boselie, 2014: Chapter 6). Third, in line with the latter point is what is nowadays called NPM, which is focused on increasing the organizational effectiveness and accountability of public sector organizations. The managerial and efficiency logics are dominant in NPM (Noordegraaf, 2015). As a result of NPM, many private company concepts, such as performance management and lean management, have found their way to public sector organizations (Van den Brink, Fruytier, and Thunnissen, 2013). Fourth, there is increased social pressure for accountability and legitimacy of the public sector organizations: for example, related to top-management pay, bonuses, and public money spending in a broad sense (value-for-money discussions) (Boselie, Brewster, and Vos, 2013). Public organizations are placed under increased pressure to provide efficient and effective services to citizens and users, along with demonstrating value for money.

22.3.2 Motives to Work in the Public Sector

Although some scholars claim that the public sector is not regarded as an attractive one (e.g., Swailes and Orr, 2008), most public sector workers—once working in it—show little intention to leave. For example, less than one third of the employees in the Dutch public sector claim to be looking for another job, and those who are show a strong preference for a new job within their own organization or in another public sector organization. Additionally, the tendency to switch jobs decreases significantly from the age of thirty-five (Ministry of Interior and Kingdom Relations, 2015). The following questions arise: why do people choose a job in the public sector, and what makes them stay? A cross-country study of Van der Walle, Steijn, and Jilke (2015) showed that individual characteristics are a more important determinant of public sector employment than country-level labor market conditions. At the country level only, the dominant career system in the public sector has a significant influence: the public sector is a more preferred sector of employment when it has a career-based system of employment instead of a position-based system, probably because a career-based system provides greater security. Income, weak economic conditions, and the level of unemployment in a country show little or no impact, according to the study of Van der Walle and colleagues (2015).

On the individual level, both service motivation (PSM) and extrinsic motivation are important drivers for the preference for a job in the public sector (Van de Walle et al., 2015). The extrinsic motivation is related to job security, security of income, and possibilities for advancement. PSM implies that people are attracted to a public sector job because they want to contribute to society or to the public good. People who attach value to intrinsic work values (e.g., an interesting job, work independently, pleasure, and enjoyment) show more preference for a job in a private sector organization. Therefore, Delfgaauw and Dur (2008) conclude that two types of workers are especially attracted to the public sector: the "lazy" and the "dedicated."

Since this chapter is about talent management, we want to focus on the "dedicated" public service workers and pay more attention to the concept of PSM. PSM can be described as "the belief, the values and attitudes that go beyond self-interest and organizational interest, that concern the interests of a larger political entity and that motivate individuals to act accordingly whenever appropriate" (Vandenabeele, 2007: 549). Van Loon (2015) illustrates that the values associated with PSM vary across subsectors. She makes a distinction between people-changing and people-processing service providers. People-changing service providers often focus on realizing change and improvement in users. They include professionals working in public schools, health care, and prisons. These employees need to identify with the users (patients, students, and inmates) to know how to change them, and therefore tend to emphasize affective motives (i.e., out of compassion and identification with others). On the other hand, people-processing service providers deal with all kinds of "users" and only change the status or location of a user. They include city hall administrators of a local government and police officers. Employees in people-processing services often attach more value to normative motives (i.e., a commitment to the public interest and a feeling of duty); they feel the need to fight injustice (police) or to take care of democracy (local government).

If the job provides opportunities to satisfy PSM, it leads to higher job satisfaction, organizational commitment, and individual performance, and lower turnover intensions (Perry, Hondeghem, and Wise, 2010). This relationship between PSM and performance is particularly confirmed for jobs with a high perceived societal impact: when employees have a high PSM but do not perceive opportunities to contribute to society through their job, high levels of PSM are not related to higher performance, and may even decrease performance slightly or result in burn out (Van Loon, 2015).

PSM is not a stable trait; it can change over time (Van Loon, 2015). This implies that public sector organizations can influence the motivation of their staff. For public sector workers, financial incentives are less attractive and effective than intrinsic rewards are (Perry, Mesch, and Paalberg, 2006; Perry, Hondeghem, and Wise, 2010). Also, other extrinsic incentives such as control or output steering—both crucial steering mechanisms in NPM—are regarded as less effective to enhance performance of public service workers. According to Perry and co-authors (2006, 2010), public sector organizations need to have a broader range of inducements, such as job redesign, supporting the social significance of work tasks, and employee participation in decision making.

To conclude, public sector organizations have adjusted their HR policies and practices to fit the demands from the external context. As a result, the soft "developmental" approach to HRM that was so common in public sector organizations has shifted toward "performance." The rational and managerial logics underpinning NPM, which caused this shift, stand in sharp contrast with the professional logics of the public service workers, whose behavior is based on public service motives. The abovementioned traditional "good employer" orientation to HRM (putting the well-being of the individual employee central) seems to be more appropriate to satisfy employees' affective, normative, and instrumental motives. We expect that these characteristics of the public service worker and the public sector organizations as an employer affect talent management in public sector organizations. In the next section, we discuss this in more detail.

22.4 Defining Talent Management in the Public Sector: What Do We Know by Now?

Contemporary talent-management literature highlights the talent-management issues of a select category of organizations. The majority of the talent-management publications focuses on talent management in private sector organizations, multinationals, and organizations in the US context (Powell et al., 2012; Vaiman and Collings, 2013; Gallardo-Gallardo and Thunnissen, 2016). In some empirical talent-management studies, data are collected in both the public and private sectors, but the relevance of the organizational context is not taken into consideration since the researchers do not make a distinction between these sectors in their discussion of the findings. There are also some papers on talent management in public administration journals, but these conceptual papers discuss talent management in general, without linking it to the public sector (e.g., Garrow and Hirsch, 2008; Calo, 2008). All in all, just a handful of publications pay explicit attention to talent-management issues in nonprofit or public organizations, such as health care institutes (e.g., Groves, 2011; Powell et al., 2012), (higher) education institutes (e.g., Davies and Davies, 2010; Van den Brink, Boselie, and Paauwe, 2017, 2013; Thunnissen, 2015), or local or central government organizations (e.g., Glenn, 2012; Harrisr and Foster, 2010). In our search for relevant literature, we found twenty publications (articles, books, and book chapters) that focused specifically on talent management in the public sector. Below we discuss the most relevant topics in the field of talent management and the specific issues raised in the limited amount of papers on talent management in the public sector that we found.

22.4.1 Definition of Talent

Talent management is often described as the systematic attraction, identification, development, engagement/retention, and deployment of talents (e.g., Scullion, Collings, and Caligiuri, 2010; CIPD, 2006). Within the talent-management definitions, authors adopt different terms for *talent*, such as *excellent abilities*, but also terms like *key employees, high potentials*, or *those individuals with high potential who are of particular value to an organization*. The variety of terms used to define talent reflects one of the most central debates in talent management: whether talent management is an inclusive approach that focuses on (the talents or abilities of) all employees, or an exclusive approach aimed at attracting and retaining a select group of employees (Gallardo-Gallardo, Dries, and Gonzalez-Cruz, 2013). In the exclusive approach, the select group could refer to specific persons (e.g., high potentials or A-players) or to some scarce and valuable positions in the organizations (e.g., management positions). Although in the academic talent-management debate the definition of talent seems to shift toward an exclusive approach (Gallardo-Gallardo and Thunnissen, forthcoming), Stahl and co-authors (2012) argue that in practice the inclusive interpretation is also present, as are combinations of the inclusive and exclusive talent-management approaches. In response to these developments, talent-management scholars recently started to explore the possibilities of differentiated talent-management architectures and approaches—a principle adopted from the field of marketing, in which the specific needs and preferences of various groups of employees are addressed simultaneously.

The literature shows that both inclusive and exclusive approaches occur in public sector organizations, yet few articles point to the rationales behind the talent-management approaches. According to Glenn (2012), the inclusive approach is more likely to occur in collective bargaining environments:

> formalized talent-management programming has been largely limited to executives and non-bargaining executive feeder groups. This is not to say that talent management cannot occur in collective bargaining environments, but it is obviously much easier to manage talent in a systematic, formalized way without the discipline imposed by collective bargaining. (2012: 43)

Also, developments in the internal and external labor markets affect the talent-management approach. In the case of increased retirement or shortages in the labor market, public sector organizations show a tendency to develop an exclusive approach to fill the pipeline for scarce and valuable positions (e.g., Kock and Burke, 2008; Glenn, 2012; Delfgaauw and Dur, 2010; MacFarnlane et al., 2012).

But to what extent is this focus on an exclusive or specific category of employees completely new for public sector organizations? The field of foreign affairs has a long tradition of recruiting, selecting, and developing the best students to become future diplomats. Very few candidates are selected, and often these newcomers receive an exclusive HRM approach. Another example of widely applied talent-management principles in public sector contexts is the people management of expatriates working in international governmental organizations such as the North Atlantic Treaty Organization, International Monetary Fund, the World Bank, and the United Nations (Boselie, Brewster, and Vos, 2013). These employees are sent to other countries, regularly accompanied by their families. These expats often get special treatment and benefit from exclusive HR policies, including an attractive employee benefit package. A third example of talent-management principle application is directly related to the HRM of professionals such as judges, prosecutors, professors, technicians, and medical specialists. These professionals and/or specialists receive specific training, development, rewards, and benefits in combination with relatively high degrees of autonomy, given their professional work. Although these professionals are under increasing pressure (Noordegraaf, Schneider, Boselie, and Van Rensen, 2016), it could still be argued that a lot of professionals receive special treatment or have a special position within public sector organizations. They are often considered to be among the most valuable workers of the public sector organization. Except from some articles on scholars working in higher education (e.g., Van den Brink, Fruytier, and Thunnissen, 2013; Bradley, 2016), the literature pays little attention to talent-management issues related to these specialists. Most of the articles on talent management in the public sector focus on the attraction and retention of managers. The public sector is in need of "the best and brightest managers in the public sector" (Delfgaauw and Dur, 2008; Day et al., 2014), and to win the battle for talent, specific talent-management programs are developed to attract and retain talented (line) managers. However, leaders of public sector organizations have always been considered special and valuable (Tummers and Knies, 2013).

22.4.2 Talent-Management Outcomes

Next to the definition of talent, the operationalization of the intended outcomes of talent management is a crucial topic in the talent-management literature. For what purpose does talent have to be managed? With regard to this issue, talent-management scholars are unanimous: The achievement of organizational goals prevails (Thunnissen, Boselie, and Fruytier, 2013). However, influential talent-management scholars such as Collings (2014) stress the importance of a broader scope taking in performance and discuss the value of talent management at the employee, organizational, and societal levels. In particular, discussion of the value of talent management at the macro level is new, but some economists have started to explore this avenue and have considered the Global Talent Competitiveness Index or research on the skills gap or oversupply in a region or country (e.g., Rodriguez, 2015; for a discussion of global talent management see Khilji and Schuler, in this volume). Thunnissen and co-authors (2013) argue that this broad orientation toward outcomes is particularly relevant for public sector organizations, because of the multiplicity of stakeholders and organizational objectives. Yet, the papers on talent management in the public sector barely pay proper attention to the outcomes of talent management or to the meaning of performance in the context of public sector organizations as presented in the model by Vandenabeele and co-authors (2013).

22.4.3 Talent-Management Practices

Now the question arises as to what practices and instruments are implemented by organizations to achieve the intended talent-management objectives. Up until now, the majority of publications on talent management have lacked a clear description of relevant practices involved in talent management (Dries, 2013). A broad variety of instruments regarding recruitment, staffing, development, and retention has been presented and prescribed, with no further classification or structuring. Current talent-management literature seems to promote the "hard" production-focused approach to talent management, with its preference for high performance (in the exclusive approach) and organizational objectives (Thunnissen, 2016). In talent management, the "soft" approach can be connected to the inclusive talent-management approach that is adopted by some talent-management scholars, in which the strengthening and developing of the talents of all employees is underlined.

The literature on talent management indicates that in public sector organizations the talent-management practices are poorly applied, and talent management can be characterized as ad hoc, scattered, and reactive (e.g., Barkhuizen, 2014; Lynn, 2001). Some studies point at a "hard" approach to talent management in the organizations under investigation. The study of MacFarlane and co-authors (2012) showed that in the UK National Health Service, talent management is increasingly rationalistic, bureaucratic, centralized, standardized, and performance-managed. The authors state that the UK National Health Service has adopted an approach that is even harder than in many private sector organizations: "Successful private sector companies, even when they espouse hard talent management, take a more nuanced approach which recognizes the limitations of over-standardized procedures and reductive metrics of progress" (MacFarlane et al., 2012: 451). Thunnissen (2015) also makes record of a "hard" approach to talent management in her study on talent management in Dutch public universities. Buttiens (2016) shows that the Flemish government intends to adopt an inclusive talent-management approach yet at times it takes an exclusive approach in practice: "an exclusive approach in disguise."

22.5 DISCUSSION

In this second part of the chapter, we address the tension between the rational and managerial logics incorporated in NPM and in public sector HRM on the one hand, and the professional logics of the public service workers (whose behavior is based on the intrinsic drive to help people and to deliver good public services) on the other. We assume that this tension would have an impact on talent-management approaches in the public sector. Although some critical issues are addressed in the current talent-management literature, current research on talent management in the public sector does not address these tensions thoroughly. In particular with regard to defining *talent* and the extent of employee differentiation and in the link between talent management and performance and commitment, we notice issues of duality, paradox, ambiguity, and balance, which we will discuss below (see also Table 22.1).

Table 22.1 Overview of Discussion Points and Questions for Talent Management in Public Sector Contexts

"The good employer"	Past: ILM model
	Present/future: High Commitment model, HPWS and/or HIWS
	What is the impact of a possible transition from ILM to innovative models, and how does this transition affect talent management?
Equality	What is the degree of possible and acceptable employee differentiation given equality principles within public sector contexts?
Public sector specific legislation, regulations, and procedures (including professional norms)	Bureaucracy, administrative barriers (red tape), and possible grievance procedures:
	- Within the organization
	- Within the sector
	- Through professional bodies
	How does bureaucracy affect talent management in practice?
Governmental cuts	What is the leeway for talent-management initiatives and investments?
NPM and (new) managerial programs such as lean, six sigma, performance management, and talent management	How is talent management perceived, and what meaning is given to *talent management* by those involved?
	How does this affect employee attitudes and behaviors?
Organizational performance, individual goals, and implications for talent management	What drives public service workers? How does PSM affect their performance, and can it be influenced by talent management?
	If defining and measuring performance is complex in public sector organizations, what does this mean for individual employee goals and the shaping of talent management?
Combining exclusive and inclusive talent-management approaches: is it the best of both worlds?	To what extent can talent-management approaches that are more exclusive for specialists (professionals) and management be combined with inclusive talent-management approaches for all employees?

22.5.1 Defining Talent: Equality versus Differentiation

Based on the review above, we conclude that one of the crucial issues in talent management in the public sector is the definition of talent. The discussion about the conceptualization of talent is highly influenced by the tension between equality and differentiation. Employee differentiation (Lepak and Snell, 1999), as suggested in the exclusive approach, is most likely causing tension with the principle of equality (all workers are equal and should be treated as equal as possible), which is closely related to the inclusive approach of talent management. In the exclusive talent-management approach, a strict distinction is made between talent and non-talent, implying that the talent are the "happy few," and the non-talent are the "have nots." But on what basis is this distinction made? Employee differentiation toward specialists (e.g., different medical specialists in hospitals) is probably generally accepted, given the specific knowledge, skills, and abilities of these professionals in combination with the institutionalization of these professions. However, applying HRM differentiation and talent-management principles to other functions that are less specialized, such as management trainees, managers, and leaders, might cause equality issues in public sector contexts. This group of employees is placed centrally in literature on talent management in the public sector. MacFarlane and colleagues (2012), in their article on talent management in UK health care, question whether talent management should focus on the "dedicated" public service workers instead of future leaders, since front-line patient care is not provided by managers but by medical staff.

Several authors discuss the tension between the traditional public sector values of equality, equity, and fairness on the one hand, and the exclusive orientation which implies that not all workers are equal nor treated equally on the other hand (e.g., Swailes and Orr, 2008; Harrisr and Foster, 2010; Lynn, 2001; Poocharoen and Lee, 2013; Swailes and Blackburn, 2016). Because of this tension, Harrisr and Foster (2010) found that line managers in UK public sector organizations prefer an inclusive approach. The authors therefore stress the importance of procedural and distributive justice, expressed in a transparent and fair selection process (see also Poocharoen and Lee, 2013).

22.5.2 The Outcomes of Talent Management: Delivering Public Value versus Organizational Excellence

Ulrich and Ulrich (2010) use the AMO model to argue that one only speaks of talent when high motivation (to serve the client and society) in combination with excellent abilities leads to an outstanding performance. Yet, in the public sector, performance is a diffuse construct. First of all, current talent-management literature particularly draws attention to boosting and controlling individual performance, but public service and public value are often not offered alone but are rather the result of a team effort.

Second, many HRM scholars have difficulty defining performance in the context of public sector organizations, given that public sector organizations have multiple goals and priorities that often conflict with each other owing to the demands of different stakeholder groups (central government, citizens, service users, and local politicians). The demands for efficiency, effectivity, and value for money which are the basis of NPM can stand in sharp contrast with the creation of public value as discussed in section two of this chapter. This ambiguity about performance affects the debate on talent-management outcomes in the public sector as well.

22.5.3 Talent-Management Practices: Influencing Commitment and Motivation versus Performance

The government as the "good employer" offering lifetime employment, employment security, vertical growth and development, and pay increases strongly linked to tenure—elements of the ILM model (e.g., Baron and Kreps, 1999) that is still dominant in most public sector organizations—does not fit the challenges public organizations are confronted with. These challenges include governmental cuts, privatization and deregulation (less government, more free market), NPM, and greater emphasis on accountability and legitimacy. One of the risks regarding talent management in the public sector is the governmental cuts in public sector contexts, which put serious constraints on HRM investments, including recruitment, selection, training, development, and pay. This can also negatively affect talent-management initiatives and investments, simply because there are no budgets for these policies. NPM is reflected in the increased attention to performance-improving management practices such as lean management and six sigma programs. These programs have become popular given the recent performance and efficiency focus as a result of governmental cuts and public accountability. The connotations of the specific programs, however, are often perceived as highly managerial (read "in the interest of the organization"), potentially negatively affecting employee attitudes and behaviors toward these programs (Van Den Broek, Boselie, and Paauwe, 2014; Buttiens, 2016). Van Den Broek and co-authors (2014), for example, found that a specific autonomous team program for nurses in hospitals called "The Productive Ward— Releasing Time to Care" was perceived as a managerial tool for increasing efficiency with little or no effect on patient care. Talent management can easily be subject to similar perceptions by those involved.

Instead of a hard performance orientation, the characteristics of the public sector and in particular of the public service worker stress the importance of enhancing individual and societal well-being (Boselie, 2014: Chapter 6). Instead of an ILM-dominated system, several authors suggest some kind of high-commitment approach or high-involvement work system (Boxall and Macky, 2009; Paauwe, 2009). Applying this approach to talent management in the public sector would imply that the focus is not on directly increasing

and controlling performance (the "hard" approach to talent management), but emphasizes the indirect motivational path to stimulate performance. This also fits the aforementioned importance of PSM. Highlighting motivation is in line with Collings and
Mellahi's argument that "the emphasis for HR practices should be on building the motivation, commitment and development of those in the talent pool, and a shift from a
short-term 'transactional' psychological contract toward a more long-term 'relational'
psychological contract" (2009: 309). From these high-commitment systems approaches,
the "good employer" model in public sector organization could include training and
development aimed at employability, horizontal growth through task enrichment and
autonomy, competency development in combination with knowledge and skill development, job redesign supporting the social significance of work tasks and knowledge sharing in a team, increasing employee participation in decision making, and team or group
rewards for excellent performance. Yet, the different motives grounded in PSM need to
be taken into account to select the right set of practices.

We are aware that the consequences of applying these innovative systems implies, as
discussed above, a further differentiation of HRM policies and practices toward individual employees and employee groups. A possible transition from an ILM model toward
innovative HRM system approaches in the public sector context is a challenge in itself
for both theory and practice. Yet, we believe that differentiation in talent management—
when it is approached as a combination of inclusive and exclusive approach—is an
interesting option for public sector organizations to balance the needs of multiple stakeholders (i.e., the organization and the employees).

22.5.4 Agenda for Talent-Management Research in
Public Sectors

Public sector contexts incorporate transitions (e.g., from more ILM models toward
high-performance work systems models), conflicting interests and outcomes (e.g.,
between different stakeholders), and competing logics (e.g., professional logics versus
efficiency/business/managerial logics), which often result in "wicked problems" that are
not easily solved. These logics, interests, and outcomes co-exist in today's public sector organizations and create tensions that affect talent-management policy and practice (Thunnissen, 2016). They create tensions, dualities, ambiguities, and paradoxes with
which public sector organizations have to deal. Future talent-management research in
the public sector could benefit from the paradox theory model presented by Smith and
Lewis (2011), who define a paradox as "Contradictory yet interrelated elements (dualities) that exist simultaneously and persist over time; such elements seem logical when
considered in isolation, but irrational, inconsistent, and absurd when juxtaposed"
(Smith and Lewis, 2011: 387). In our interpretation of the paradox theory model, context matters, and the contextual factors (e.g., presented in the model by Vandenabeele
and co-authors [2013] in our chapter) are interrelated with the policies, interventions,

perceptions, and outcomes within organizations. The paradox theory model could be a good starting point for further talent-management research in public sector contexts through both theoretical insights and alternative methodologies. The paradox theory can help in investigating the dilemmas, tensions, and paradoxes regarding talent management in the public sector in more detail and it gives insight into how public sector organizations deal with them. It would also be interesting to compare this with research on paradoxes and dilemmas in talent management in private sector organizations to find out if these tensions are exclusive to the public sector or occur in the private sector as well.

Institutional theory is generally applied in public administration, public management, and to some degree HRM as well (see, e.g., Paauwe and Boselie, 2003). Institutional theory provides a strong fundament for future talent-management research in different public sectors, in particular, given the possible differences between professionals working in these contexts (judges, professors, teachers, medical specialists, etc.). Although talent-management scholars refer to the institutional theory in their papers—according to Gallardo-Gallardo, Nijs, Dries, and Gallo (2015), it is found in 10% of the talent-management articles—they often fail to use it as a comprehensive framework for the data gathering and discussion of the findings. We therefore recommend talent-management scholars take a more rigorous research design. We echo Gallardo-Gallardo and co-authors (2015) in saying that instead of agreeing on which theoretical frameworks to use, it is more important that scholars make deliberate choices in terms of theoretical framing and apply these consistently within one and the same project, which can help the field to surpass descriptive research designs and identify and clarify correlations and causality between variables.

PSM is widely studied within public administration and public management (Perry and Vandenabeele, 2015) and further research can be focused on, for example:

- The integration of the AMO theory in HRM and the lessons from previous PSM studies when studying talent management.
- The link between talent management and PSM in public sector contexts.
- The link between talent management, PSM, and performance.

The link between talent management, PSM, and performance can be extended by a recent publication of Beer, Boselie, and Brewster (2015) on a revised version of the Harvard model, thirty years after its emergence in 1984. This model emphasizes the relevance of a multidimensional performance construct, taking into account organizational effectiveness, individual well-being, and societal well-being. In addition, the authors state that employee influence (through participation, involvement, and agency) is the most important HRM domain and that HRM, in an ideal situation, is a social system. These claims fit nicely into the public sector context, with its multiple stakeholders, regulations, and institutions (including rules and procedures on participation and involvement) and its multifaceted performance, including organizational effectiveness, individual well-being ("the good employer"), and public values that reflect the link to societal well-being.

The model by Vandenabeele and colleagues (2013) appears to be a good conceptual one and includes several of the theoretical building blocks mentioned above. This conceptual model is a good framework for HRM research in public sector organizations and for future talent-management research as well. However, regarding talent management, we have to add an element to the model. The model only focuses on institutional mechanisms, and it excludes market mechanisms. Yet, several studies on talent management in the public sector indicated that developments in the internal and external labor markets had affected the talent-management approach in the organization. We call for more research on talent-management issues and approaches in nonprofit and/or public organizations in general. Further, a comparison between different kinds of public sector organizations could be particularly valuable in identifying the impact of organizational factors on talent management. This comparison will help to clarify what public sector organizations aim to achieve with talent management (and why), how, and how effective they are in doing so. A multilevel approach in which both representatives of the organization (HRM and managers) and employees are included is valuable to the effectiveness of talent management. In addition, we recommend more cross-country comparisons.

22.6 Implications for Practitioners

Talent management is most likely to gain popularity in the daily practices of public sector organizations as a result of societal developments and NPM, in particular, focused on performance, efficiency, and the competition for talent. Table 22.1 in this chapter shows an overview of key issues for future talent-management research in public sector contexts and highlights a number of relevant questions that can have direct implications and relevance for public sector practitioners interested in applying talent management, including concrete questions such as: How is talent management perceived and what meaning is given to talent management by those involved? How does this affect employee attitudes and behaviors? There are no simple solutions for talent management in public sector organizations and "best practices" are not likely to exist on a large scale. It is therefore important to avoid imitation of "simplistic" talent-management practices from other public sector or private organizations without a critical analysis of the organization's own internal and external context. Context sensitivity is relevant for HRM, in general, and talent management, in particular, to avoid ineffective HRM and talent-management investments that could lead to employee frustration, dissatisfaction, and demotivation; decreased service quality and labor productivity; and reputational damage (societal well-being) of the public sector organization.

22.7 CONCLUDING REMARKS

Talent management in public sector organizations is a form of micro-HRM in a specific context. Many of the ongoing debates on contextuality in HRM are relevant and comparable with new debates on talent management in public sector organizations. Overall, we conclude that context matters and there are no easy solutions for talent management in these specific contexts. Therefore, we need the rigor of possible theories, conceptual models, and methods (including paradox theory, AMO theory, PSM theory, and the model by Vandenabeele and co-authors [2013]), in combination with the context-specific approach, to explore, understand, and unwrap the talent-management relevance in public sector contexts.

REFERENCES

Barkhuizen, N. 2014. How relevant is talent management in South African local government institutions? *Mediterranean Journal of Social Sciences*, 5(20), p.2223.

Baron, J., and Kreps, D. 1999. *Strategic human resources: frameworks for general managers.* New York: John Wiley & Sons, Inc.

Beer, M., Boselie, P., and Brewster, C. 2015. Back to the future: implications for the field of HRM of the multi-stakeholder perspective proposed 30 years ago. *Human Resource Management*, 54(3), pp.427–38.

Boselie, J., Leisink, P., and Vandenabeele, W. 2011. Human resource management. In M. Noordegraaf, K. Geuijen, and A. Meijer, eds., *Handboek publiek management*, pp.315–38. Den Haag: Boom Lemma.

Boselie, P. 2014. *Strategic human resource management: a balanced approach*, 2nd edn. London: McGraw-Hill Higher Education.

Boselie, P., Brewster, C., and Vos, E. 2013. *The impact of the global crisis on the HRM of international organizations.* Geneva: Association of HRM in International Organizations.

Boxall, P., and Macky, K. 2009. Research and theory on high-performance work systems: progressing the high involvement stream. *Human Resource Management Journal*, 19(1), pp.2–23.

Bradley, A. P. 2016. Talent management for universities. *Australian Universities' Review*, 58(1), p.13.

Buttiens, D. 2016. *Talent management in de Vlaamse overheid*, doctoral thesis. Leuven, Belgium: KU Leuven.

Calo, T. J. 2008. Talent management in the era of the aging workforce: the critical role of knowledge transfer. *Public Personnel Management*, 37(4), pp.403–16.

Christensen, T., Laegrid, P., Roness, P. G., and Rovik, K. A. 2007. *Organization theory for the public sector. Instrument, culture and myth.* Florence: Routledge.

CIPD. 2006. *Talent management: understanding the dimensions.* London: CIPD.

Collings, D. 2014. Toward mature talent management: beyond shareholder value. *Human Resource Development Quarterly*, 25(3), pp.301–19.

Collings, D., and Mellahi, K. 2009. Strategic talent management: a review and research agenda. *Human Resource Management Review*, 19(4), pp.304–13.

Davies, B., and Davies, B. J. 2010. Talent management in academies. *International Journal of Educational Management*, 24(5), pp.418–26.

Day, M., Shickle, D., Smith, K., Zakariasen, K. et al. 2014. Training public health superheroes: five talents for public health leadership. *Journal of Public Health*, 36(4), pp.552–61.

Delfgaauw, J., and Dur, R. 2008. Incentives and workers' motivation in the public sector. *The Economic Journal*, 118(525), pp.171–91.

Dries, N. 2013. The psychology of talent management: a review and research agenda. *Human Resource Management Review*, 23(4), pp.272–85.

Gallardo-Gallardo, E., Dries, N., and González-Cruz, T. 2013. What is the meaning of talent in the world of work? *Human Resource Management Review*, 23(4), pp.290–300.

Gallardo-Gallardo, E., Nijs, S., Dries, N., and Gallo, P. 2015. Towards an understanding of talent management as a phenomenon-driven field using bibliometric and content analysis. *Human Resource Management Review*, 25, pp.264–79.

Gallardo-Gallardo, E., and Thunnissen, M. 2016. Standing on the shoulders of giants? A review of empirical talent management research, *Employee Relations*, 38(1), pp.31–56.

Garrow, V., and Hirsh, W. 2008. Talent management: issues of focus and fit. *Public Personnel Management*, 37(4), pp.389–402.

Glenn, T. 2012. The state of talent management in Canada's public sector. *Canadian Public Administration*, 55(1), pp.25–51.

Groves, K. S. 2011. Talent management best practices: how exemplary health care organizations create value in a down economy. *Health Care Management Review*, 36(3), pp.227–40.

Harrisr, L., and Foster, C. 2010. Aligning talent management with approaches to equality and diversity. *Equality, Diversity and Inclusion: An International Journal*, 29(5), pp.422–35.

Jørgensen, T. B., and Bozeman, B. 2007. Public values: an inventory. *Administration & Society*, 39(3), pp.354–81.

Khilji, S. E., and Schuler, S. R. 2017. Talent management in a global context. In D. G. Collings, K. Mellahi, and W. F. Cascio, eds., *Oxford handbook of talent management*. Oxford: Oxford University Press.

Kock, R., and Burke, M. 2008. Managing talent in the South African public service. *Public Personnel Management*, 37(4), pp.457–70.

Leisink, P., Boselie, P., Van Bottenburg, M. and Hosking, D. M. 2013. *Managing social issues: a public values perspective*. Cheltenham: Edward Elgar.

Lepak, D., and Snell, S. 1999. The human resource architecture: toward a theory of human capital allocation and development. *Academy of Management Review*, 24, pp.31–48.

Lynn, D. 2001. Succession management strategies in public sector organizations building leadership capital. *Review of Public Personnel Administration*, 21(2), pp.114–32.

Noordegraaf, M. 2015. *Public management: performance, professionalism and politics*. Basingstoke: Palgrave.

Noordegraaf, M., Schneider, M., Boselie, P., and Van Rensen, E. 2016. Cultural complementarity—reshaping professional and organizational logics in developing frontline medical leadership. *Public Management Review*.

Macfarlane, F., Duberley, J., Fewtrell, C., and Powell, M. 2012. Talent management for NHS managers: human resources or resourceful humans? *Public Money & Management*, 32(6), pp.445–52.

Ministry of Interior and Kingdom Relations. 2015. *Werken in de publieke sector 2015. Cijfers en Trends*.

Paauwe, J. 2009. HRM and performance: achievements, methodological issues and prospects. *Journal of Management Studies*, 46(1), pp.129–42.

Paauwe, J., and Boselie, P. 2003. Challenging "strategic HRM" and the relevance of the institutional setting. *Human Resource Management Journal*, 13(3), pp.56–70.

Perry, J., Hondeghem, A., and Wise, L. 2010. Revisiting the motivational bases of public service: twenty years of research and an agenda for the future. *Public Administration Review*, 70(5), pp.681–90.

Perry, J., Mesch, D., and Paarlberg, L. 2006. Motivating employees in a new governance era: the performance paradigm revisited. *Public Administration Review*, 66, pp.505–14.

Perry, J., and Vandenabeele, W. 2015. Public service motivation research: achievements, challenges, and future directions. *Public Administration Review*, 75(5), pp.692–99.

Poocharoen, O., and Lee, C. 2013. Talent management in the public sector: a comparative study of Singapore, Malaysia, and Thailand. *Public Management Review*, 15(8), pp.1185–1207.

Powell, M., Durose, J., Duberley, J., Exworthy et al. 2012. *Talent management in the NHS managerial workforce.* Final report, National Institute for Health Research.

Rodriguez, M. 2015. *The economic meaning of talent: finding the right match of skills and work environment for productivity to thrive.* Paper presented at the 4th EIASM Workshop on Talent Management, Valencia-Spain.

Scullion, H., Collings, D. G., and Caligiuri, P. 2010. Global talent management. *Journal of World Business*, 45(2), pp.105–8.

Smith, W., and Lewis, M. 2011. Toward a theory of paradox: a dynamic equilibrium model of organizing. *Academy of Management Review*, 36(2), pp.381–403.

Stahl, G., Björkman, I., Farndale, E., Morris, S. et al. 2012. Six principles of effective global talent management. *MIT Sloan Management Review*, 53, pp.24–32.

Swailes, S., and Blackburn, M. 2016. Employee reactions to talent pool membership. *Employee Relations*, 38(1), pp.112–28.

Swailes, S., and Orr, K. 2008. Talent management in the UK: public/private sector differences and implications for reward. In *Reward management—facts and trends in Europe*, pp.275–93. Berlin: PABST.

Truss, C., Gratton, L., Hope-Hailey, V., McGovern, P., and Stiles, B. 1997. Soft and hard models of human resource management: a reappraisal. *Journal of Management Studies*, 34(1), pp.53–73.

Thunnissen, M. 2016. Talent management: for what, how and how well? An empirical exploration of talent management in practice. *Employee Relations*, 38(1), pp.57–72.

Thunnissen, M., Boselie, P., and Fruytier, B. 2013. A review of talent management: "infancy or adolescence?" *The International Journal of Human Resource Management*, 24(9), pp.1744–61.

Tummers, L., and Knies, E. 2013. Leadership and meaningful work in the public sector. *Public Administration Review*, 73(6), pp.859–68.

Ulrich, D., and Ulrich, M. 2010. Marshalling talent. Paper accepted at the *2010 Academy of Management Annual Meeting*, Montreal.

Vaiman, V., and Collings, D. G. 2013. Talent management: advancing the field. *International Journal of Human Resource Management*, 24(9), pp.1737–43.

Vandenabeele, W. 2007. Toward a public administration theory of public service motivation. *Public Management Review*, 9(4), pp.545–56.

Vandenabeele, W., Leisink, P., and Knies, E. 2013. Public value creation and strategic human resource management: public service motivation as a linking mechanism. In P. Leisink,

P. Boselie, M. Van Bottenburg, and D. Hosking, eds., *Managing social issues: a public values perspectives*, pp.37–54. Cheltenham, UK, and Northampton, MA: Edward Elgar.

Van den Brink, M., Fruytier, B., and Thunnissen, M. 2013. Talent management in academia: performance systems and HRM policies. *Human Resource Management Journal*, 23(2), pp.180–95.

Van den Broek, J., Boselie, P., and Paauwe, J. 2014. Multiple Institutional logics in health care—"Productive Ward: Releasing Time to Care." *Public Management Review*, 16(1), pp.1–20.

Van den Broek, J., Boselie, P., and Paauwe, J. 2017. Cooperative innovation through a talent management pool: a qualitative study on competition in healthcare. *European Management Journal*, doi.org/10.1016/j.emj.2017.03.012.

Van de Walle, S., Steijn, B., and Jilke, S. 2015. Extrinsic motivation, PSM and labour market characteristics: a multilevel model of public sector employment preference in 26 countries. *International Review of Administrative Sciences*, 81(4), pp.833–55.

Van Dooren, W., Bouckaert, G., and Halligan, J. 2015. *Performance management in the public sector*, 2nd edn. London: Routledge.

Van Loon, N. 2015. *The role of public service motivation in performance: examining the potentials and pitfalls through an institutional approach*. Doctoral thesis, Utrecht University, Utrecht, Netherlands.

Wright, P., and Nishii, L. 2013. Strategic HRM and organizational behavior: integrating multiple levels of analysis. In J. Paauwe, D. Guest, and P. Wright, eds., *HRM and performance: achievements and challenges*, pp. 97-108. Chichester: John Wiley & Sons.

....

CHAPTER 23

TALENT MANAGEMENT IN EMERGING ECONOMIES

....

FANG LEE COOKE

23.1 INTRODUCTION

....

A distinct feature of economic globalization in the past two decades, especially following the global financial crisis in 2008, has been the growing significance of emerging economies (also referred to as emerging markets). A crucial factor that contributes to, but also constrains, the rapid economic growth of emerging economies is the availability of talent. As such, talent-management research and practices in emerging economies form an integral and significant part of our knowledge on talent management in the global context. For the purpose of this chapter, we adopt Collings and Mellahi's definition of *strategic talent management* as:

> activities and processes that involve the systematic identification of key positions which differentially contribute to the organisation's sustainable competitive advantage, the development of a talent pool of high potential and high performing incumbents to fill these roles, and the development of a differentiated human resource architecture to facilitate filling these positions with competent incumbents and to ensure their continued commitment to the organisation. (2009: 304)

The task of this chapter is to present to readers debates and practices related to (2009: 304) talent management in various emerging economies, drawing on existing research on the topic. It also highlights a number of research gaps that may be fruitful avenues for future studies in the field.

The definition of *emerging economies* is rather loose, and there is no consensus as to which countries should be included in this evolving category. For the purpose of this chapter, we adopt an inclusive approach, to include in our discussion Brazil, China, India, Indonesia, Malaysia, the Philippines, Russia, South Africa, Thailand, Turkey, and Vietnam. We do so not least because they are the main emerging-economy countries recognized, but also because they are the countries on which literature on talent management published in the English language is available for review. Where appropriate, we also include Arab Gulf States (e.g., Sidani and Al Ariss, 2014) and Central and Eastern European countries (e.g., Skuza, Scullion, and McDonnell, 2013) for discussion because of their relatively high economic growth. It is important to note that emerging economies are a nonhomogeneous group with different institutional and cultural characteristics, educational and skill levels, and varied stages of economic development (Tymon, Stumpf, and Doh, 2010).

Few studies of talent management in emerging economies have provided a working definition of *talent* for the purpose of their study. But from reading the articles, one can infer that most studies see talent as high-performing employees or managerial and professional employees who can make a significant difference to the firm's performance. In other words, most studies tend to adopt an exclusive approach when referring to talent and talent management (e.g., Chuai, Preece, and Iles, 2008). This is with a few exceptions that take an inclusive approach, notably in the equal-opportunity-oriented studies (e.g., Kulkarni and Scullion, 2015). In line with this volume, we focus on, as talent, those holding critical positions in the employing organizations, specifically managers (e.g., Zhang and Bright, 2012; Cooke, Saini, and Wang, 2014) and professional employees (e.g., Tymon, Stumpf, and Doh, 2010; Doh, Smith, Stumpf, and Tymon, 2011; Cooke, Saini, and Wang, 2014) who are highly sought after in the labor market.

Talent management is a relatively new concept in many emerging economies. It is believed that talent-management challenges are more acute and complex in these countries (Sparrow, Scullion, and Tarique, 2014). Despite the lead of Western MNCs in promoting talent-management practices (Iles, Chuai, and Preece, 2010; Vaiman and Holden, 2011), recent research suggests that talent-management practices in emerging economies are far from converging with Western models (Skuza, Scullion, and McDonnell, 2013; Skuza, McDonnell, and Scullion, 2015). For example, Liu and Pearson's study of talent management in the Chinese context revealed the lack of consensus in talent-management terminology and cautioned against the pursuit of a "universalistic form of talent management in Chinese organizations, given the semantical and jargon language barriers" (2014: 165). Other researchers (e.g., Elegbe, 2010; Zhang and Bright, 2012) also argued that talent is situation-specific and its definition needs to take into account the individual context.

In the rest of the chapter, we address the following key questions by reviewing the talent-management literature in the emerging-economies context:

1. What are the key issues and debates in talent management?
2. What do talent and their employers want, respectively?
3. What are the main challenges to talent management?
4. What is the role of the state in talent management?
5. What talent-management practices have been researched and how effective are they?
6. What may be the implications of talent-management research and practices?

23.2 EXISTING RESEARCH ON TALENT MANAGEMENT: KEY ISSUES AND DEBATES

Existing research on talent management in emerging economies has been limited, particularly in high-quality research outlets. The bulk of the studies have been rather descriptive and "normative" (Golik and Blanco, 2014), and mainly focusing on the following aspects (see the following sections for more discussion):

- The status quo of talent management in the country/countries of study (e.g., Harvey, 2014);
- Whether talent management is different from HRM in the emerging-economies context (e.g., Chuai, Preece, and Iles, 2008);
- Reasons for talent shortages (often focusing on the macro level in terms of skill/ human capital development, and how the national education system is lagging behind the needs of rapid economic growth) (e.g., Ready, Hill, and Conger, 2008; Horwitz, 2013; Khilji and Keilson, 2014);
- Key challenges to talent management, highlighting talent attraction and retention as the main issues (e.g., Horwitz, 2013);
- Initiatives at the macro level for talent attraction and development (e.g., human resources development and the role of the state/government); and
- Suggestions of HRM practices for talent management to improve talent performance and organizational commitment, thus retention (e.g., Ready, Hill, and Conger, 2008; Sovanjeet, 2014).

While not all studies make a distinction between talent management and HRM, those that do suggest a difference between the two exists. For example, Chuai and colleagues' study of whether or not there are any differences between HRM and talent management in China concluded that talent management is not old wine in new bottles. Rather, it is "a new management ideology that may make a difference to the success and competitive advantage" (2008: 908) of at least the organizations in their study.

In reviewing the limited studies of talent management in the Russian context, Holden and Vaiman (2013) singled out three key contributions in this emerging body of literature. The first contribution focuses on the individual level, that is, the importance of wisdom in managing *talent*, which is defined as the capability of managers to "use past experience to solve new problems" (Konstantinov, 2011; cited in Holden and Vaiman, 2013: 135). Here, the emphasis is the manager's ability to incentivize and motivate talented employees to solve problems and deliver results (Holden and Vaiman, 2013). A second contribution takes on a very different view from a societal perspective (Fryer, 2011; cited in Holden and Vaiman, 2013). Taking a broader view, the author points out the unpopularity of top managers in Russia, who are seen as "overpaid" and "scandal ridden," and calls for an ethical approach to talent management to establish societal trust (cited in Holden and Vaiman, 2013). The third contribution is by Ridderstrale (2011; cited in Holden and Vaiman, 2013), in which the author draws our attention to Russia's problem of brain drain in the context of globalization.

23.2.1 What Talent Desire

To understand the challenges to talent management, important issues to establish are what talent value from their employers, as well as what their aspirations are, in order for employers to meet their demands or select those whose aspirations can be met and aligned with the organizational goals. This requires a differentiated approach to talent management instead of a universalist perspective, which appears to be common in the bulk of (Western-oriented) talent-management literature. Such a differentiated approach should take into account not only individual variations but also societal distinctiveness that underpins individual variations. For example, Ernst and Young's (2014) study of global talent-management highlights the fact that different aspects of employers' brands vary across countries and that companies need to vary their recruitment messages to improve their employer brand in order to attract the best talent. For example, Brazil and India place emphasis on corporate social responsibility, which is an important element of a firm's global employer brand, whereas in China the prestige of the company is highly valued by job seekers. In addition, in Brazil, Russia, and India, job seekers tend to focus on the financial strength of their prospective employer and particularly value clear career paths and future earning potentials (Ernst and Young, 2014).

Research on talent management in South Africa (Horwitz, 2012; Bluen, 2014) also showed that professionals in knowledge-intensive firms rate autonomy at work, challenging and stimulating work, good workplace relations, work-life balance, development opportunities, and competitive pay as important talent-management practices for motivation and retention. In addition, Nzukuma and Bussin's study of 208 African black senior managers regarding retention issues in South Africa revealed that "African Black senior managers do not trust organizations with their career development" and that they "would rather take control of their own career development by moving from organization to organization to build their repertoire of skills and competence" (2011: 258).

23.2.2 Talent Sought by Employers and Talent Shortages

Extant research suggests that the quality of talent sought by employers differs across societal contexts among emerging economies as a result of diverse political, economic, and social traditions. For instance, a survey of 1,109 professionals between the ages of twenty-five and forty in the BRIC (Brazil, Russia, India, and China) countries conducted by Ernst and Young (2014) reveals that in China, the complex nature of working with the government and the growing competitiveness of state-owned enterprises mean that a premium is placed on management skills gained in the country, at all levels, rather than abroad. In Brazil, the dominant mining and oil industries absorb a large amount of engineering talent. Less developed mathematics and science education means that people who can fill non-management engineering roles are at a premium. In India, the hugely successful indigenous IT sector, made up of companies seen locally as Indian champions, has made working for a foreign company's IT function seem far less attractive. This means that foreign companies with great recruitment brands at home may struggle to fill vacancies in India.

Cooke and co-authors' (2014) comparative study of 178 non-HR managers' views of talent management in China and India reveals that Indian employers tend to focus on the technical and managerial skills of their talent, whereas Chinese employers pay attention to not only the technical competence but also the behavior of their talent, and emphasize their overall "quality," known as *suzhi* (素质). *Suzhi* includes one's knowledge, skills, morality, and manners in general. According to Li (2013: 14), "it is the development of one's '*suzhi*' that gives one positional advantage in all aspects of social and economic life." As such, the discourse of *suzhi* has stronger explanatory power in terms of understanding the concept as a broader social phenomenon than as a narrow instrument to employability (Li, 2013). In addition, the dominant role of *guanxi* in getting business done in China means that Chinese employers may put more emphasis on the networking ability and social networks that the candidate possesses than on their technical competences (e.g., Zhang and Bright, 2012; Liu and Pearson, 2014; Wang, Cooke, and Huang, 2014).

Talent shortage has been a common finding of academic studies and a collective *cri de coeur* from employers (e.g., Tymon, Stumpf, and Doh, 2010; Chatterjee, Nankervis, and Connell, 2014; Cooke, Saini, and Wang, 2014). However, insufficient supply is not the only cause of the problem. Instead, underutilization may be a strong contributing factor to the talent shortage. For instance, Furusawa and Brewster's (2015) study of Japanese immigrants and their descendants (known as *Nikkeijin*) in Japanese MNCs in Brazil reveals that the bilingual and bicultural skills of *Nikkeijin* are largely untapped as a boundary-spanning international competence. Using two different surveys, Furusawa and Brewster find that while this group is recognized as a source of talent by Japanese MNCs, the HRM practices of these firms "are not appropriate to attract and use them in their global talent management programmes" (2015: 133). Similarly, Kulkarni and Scullion (2015) adopted a broad notion of talent to refer to productive individuals with diverse background who may be highly valuable to employers. With this broad concept in mind, they examined talent-management activities of disability training and placement agencies in India and found that persons with a disability in India have been largely underutilized and that external stakeholders such as training placement agencies have an important role to play in identifying, developing, and placing this talent for organizations.

23.3 CHALLENGES TO TALENT MANAGEMENT IN EMERGING ECONOMIES

Extant studies of talent management in emerging economies have highlighted various challenges confronting organizations across different industrial sectors and professional groups, reflecting current societal conditions. For example, recruiting ready-trained talent instead of growing talent internally, or even poaching, seems to be common in China, India, and Malaysia (e.g., Zheng, Soosay, and Hyland, 2007; Cooke, Saini, and Wang, 2014; Liu and Pearson, 2014). This reduces the incentives for firms to invest in talent development. In Russia, the lack of an empowerment tradition, a just-in-time approach to HR needs, and "entrenched bossdom" "(a unique brand of management that somehow combines authoritarian sternness with paternalism)" (Holden and Vaiman, 2013: 136) are the main challenges. In addition, brain drain has been a particular problem for talent acquisition and retention, not least owing to the emigration of talented young people (Holden and Vaiman, 2013). South Africa also faces a similar problem of brain drain (e.g., Amankwah-Amoah and Debrah, 2011; Cooke, Wood, and Horwitz, 2015).

Perhaps the most critical challenge to talent management is the deficiency in corporate strategic capabilities in global talent management. For instance, a survey conducted by Deloitte Consulting LLP of 376 senior business leaders and HR executives showed that only 30% of respondents believed they have sufficient capabilities for managing global talent, and only 28% reported to be investing actively to improve those capabilities (Deloitte, 2013). Similarly, Hartmann, Feisel, and Schober's case study of seven European and US-owned MNCs operating in China found that these firms tend to transfer their talent-management practices to China without much change, "focusing specifically on the development of talented employees (i.e., succession planning) and the creation of an organizational culture" (2010: 169). Findings of the same study also suggest that "integrated and strategic talent management strategies have not yet been fully implemented" (Hartmann, Feisel, and Schober, 2010: 169).

The deficiency of corporate strategic capability in global talent management also tends to exhibit itself in various aspects of talent management. For example, Preece and co-authors' (2013) study of an automotive manufacturing MNC with a regional headquarters in the Asia Pacific region reveals that, among other HR challenges, recruiting mid-ranking managers was a main problem because the junior members of staff were not ready for promotion. According to Preece and colleagues (2013), two factors contributed to the talent-shortage problem. One was the focus on senior managers in the early days of setting up the regional headquarters; the other was that local staff tended to follow instructions and rules with little mentoring from their superiors on strategic matters.

Another key challenge to talent management is the mismatch of demand and supply expectations. Shi and Handfield's study of talent management in global logistic firms in China found that the talent shortage in this industry problem is manifold: there is a lack of qualified graduates from universities, lack of attraction of multinational logistics enterprise roles, and a mismatch between the expectations of Chinese employees and the "perceived reality of foreign managers relative to what constitutes competitive salary, benefits, and job satisfaction conditions" (2012: 163). As a study by Deloitte (2013) reported, talented people in emerging economies are increasingly aware of their value and are adopting a free-agent mentality and changing jobs readily in order to pursue their career goals, be they promotion, financial incentives, improved working conditions, or all of them.

Knowledge transfer in the MNC context presents a further challenge to talent management. Vance, Chow, Paik, and Shin's study of knowledge transfer from Korean expatriates to Chinese employees in the Chinese subsidiaries revealed several gaps between Korean expatriates and Chinese employees "in areas of perceived importance for training Chinese employees," which may become "obstacles to optimal knowledge transfer in ongoing efforts to improve global talent management" (2013: 999). The study also found that national culture is a much stronger factor than organizational culture in influencing Chinese employees' learning. These findings have strong implications for Korean MNCs as an increasing number of them are developing core employees, such as engineers and professionals, from the host countries for senior management positions (Vance, Chow, Paik, and Shin, 2013).

In short, talent-management challenges in emerging economies are interlocked, from strategic to operational. As Wang-Cowham (2011: 393–4) summarizes, organizations face four key challenges in developing talent in China. These include the scarcity of managerial talent, which means that companies may need to mobilize internal and external labor markets; strategic alignment with talent criteria and critical organizational capability; designing training and development programs to align organizational and individual needs with greater flexibility for job rotation and emphasis on strategic development rather than functional skills development; and difficulties in implementing training and development programs owing to the lack of career-advancement support mechanisms, such as succession planning and transparency and communication of talent-development plans.

23.4 Talent Attraction and Development at the Macro Level

Strong state intervention is characteristic of emerging economies, in which the developmental state plays an important role in human resource development at the macro level through not only its formal education system but also its talent-attraction programs (e.g., Khilji and Shuler, 2017; Cooke, 2011; Zweig and Wang, 2013). In particular, after some years of "brain drain," in which talent has been lost through immigration, emerging economies have been implementing initiatives to reverse the situation (also known as reverse brain drain) (e.g., Dickson, 2006; Chacko, 2007). For instance, the Chinese government has launched a number of talent-management programs aimed at attracting highly educated overseas Chinese professionals and academics to return to China since the late 1990s, including the "1000 Talents" plan implemented since 2008 (see Zweig and Wang, 2013 for a detailed review). However, the extent to which these programs have been successful has not been assessed fully, and existing evidence suggests that these programs have been more successful in attracting certain types of talent (e.g., entrepreneurs) than others have (e.g., scientists and academics) (Zweig and Wang, 2013).

Sidani and Al Ariss's (2014) study that examines how organizations in the Gulf Cooperation Council (GCC) states adopt and implement talent-management practices suggests that enforcing the localization rule in the GCC poses major challenges to an efficient talent-management process as it forces companies to employ a minimum percentage of local people who may not be best qualified. The existence of "symbolic talent management" in the GCC means that some locals may be "automatically attached to talent management programs, yet without a serious commitment from them or their organizations to talent management issues" (Sidani and Al Ariss, 2014: 221). Nevertheless, having an equal-opportunity law in place will help companies to consider local talent more naturally and provide locals with more opportunities in the long term.

23.5 WHAT IS BENEFICIAL TO TALENT MANAGEMENT: ROLES, PRACTICES, AND TECHNIQUES

The bulk of the studies of talent management at the organizational level in emerging economies have taken a strategic-management perspective, explicitly or implicitly. They are empirical studies, often aiming to provide "best-practice" advice for firms to enhance their talent-management capacity and organizational performance (e.g., Sharma and Bhatnagar, 2009). These studies have identified a number of conditions beneficial to talent management, ranging from the role of talent-management stakeholders to talent-management practices and techniques for talent attraction, development to retention, and their likely impacts.

23.5.1 Role of Talent-Management Stakeholders

Current studies of talent management in the emerging-economy context have primarily focused on the role of the corporate HR function in effective talent management (e.g., Farndale, Scullion, and Sparrow, 2010). Only a few studies (e.g., Chahal and Kumari, 2013; Kulkarni and Scullion, 2015) have examined the role of other stakeholders in talent management. For example, Chahal and Kumari's study of the key role of the board of directors in corporate governance (CG) practices found that CG plays an "indirect but key role in the way top talent is selected, and the way in which a process that applies to succession management is developed" (2013: 199). Further, they argued, "the talent developed within the framework of CG can be seen as a key requirement of any approach relating to" talent management and that "the CEO can improve organisational performance through effective CG practices, which subsequently will nurture and develop talent at all levels" (Chahal and Kumari, 2013: 199).

Taking a broad approach to talent management, Kulkarni and Scullion's (2015) study revealed how placement agencies for workers with a disability may play an important role in sourcing and placing talent required by employers. This research has particularly important implications for emerging economies and other less developed countries, where equal opportunity of employment may not be a top priority of business despite suffering from acute skill shortages (see below for further discussion).

23.5.2 Talent-Management Practices, Techniques, and Environments and Their Effects

Several studies have examined the effectiveness of talent-management practices in relation to talent-management outcomes and organizational outcomes. For instance, using the marketing concept of brand equity, Jiang and Iles's (2011: 97) qualitative study identified the process that leads employees and prospective applicants to be attracted and remain in the company in the private sector in Zhejiang province, China. The study found that "prospective applicants and employees evaluate job offers or organizational positions based both on organizational attractiveness (OA) and on employee-based brand equity (EBBE) perceptions" (Jiang and Iles, 2011: 97).

Golik and Blanco's survey study of 112 Argentina-based companies on their talent-identification and development practices found that companies utilizing more talent-identification processes (performance management and potential identification) tend to make use of a greater number of development tools, and that "the presence of a Development Department encourages the implementation of identification and development tools" (2014: 23).

Compared with recruitment in HRM, firms seem to make more use of Internet and social networking sites (SNS) for talent attraction. For instance, Rao's study of the role of SNS in talent recruitment in India and Mexico found that both countries "have welcome various forms of SNS as strategic organizational tools for talent management" (2014: 259) and that SNS is highly effective in creating brand awareness, augmenting recruiting, enhancing learning, broadening communication, reducing traditional costs, and also simulating work environments.

Tymon and co-authors' study aimed at developing and testing a talent-management model across twenty-eight Indian firms, involving 4,811 professional-level employees, found that the "intrinsic rewards experienced are a critical element in employee reten-tion, satisfaction with the organization, and career success" (2010: 109). The four ante-cedents of intrinsic rewards used for this study include "the social responsibility of the employer, pride in the organization, manager support, and performance management" (Tymon, Stumpf, and Doh, 2010: 109). Tymon and colleagues' (2010) study highlights the universal values of non-pecuniary practices to talent management in the Indian context. By contrast, Bhatnagar's (2007) study of the role of engagement and talent man-agement in the Indian business process outsourcing (BPO)/ITES sector revealed that a good level of engagement may lead to high retention for only a limited period. The study suggests that engagement practices proven effective in the Western context may have limited utility in the Indian BPO/ITES sector because of the severe skill shortage and abundant labor market opportunities for talented young engineers. Further, more homegrown and rigorous employee-engagement design may be needed.

In a similar vein, Srivastava and Bhatnagar's (2008) case study of talent acquisition in Motorola India MDB found that aligning recruitment needs with cultural fits seems to create a workplace environment in which employees feel more passionate about their work and exhibit the behaviors that are required by the organizations to achieve better results. The authors conclude that during "talent acquisition, due diligence is required in assessing the person-organization fit and providing an enabling work environment to keep the talent anchored to the organization" and that "organizations should make efforts to build effective, practical and holistic talent strategies that are not only able to attract talent but also address employee engagement and the retention of key skills thus boosting the productivity and business performance" (Srivastava and Bhatnagar, 2008: 253).

Corporate mindset appears to be a crucial factor in talent management. For exam-ple, a study by Bhatnagar and Sharma (2009) of an Indian pharmaceutical company also found that having a "talent mindset" has helped the company recruit the best talent from the best pharmaceutical companies on the one hand, and retain the top and valued talent on the other, in part through succession planning. The findings of the study point to the importance of using a competency-profiling approach to develop a talent-man-agement strategy as part of strategic HRM. At the international level, Raman, Chadee, Roxas, and Michailova's (2013: 342) quantitative study of talent management in the Indian offshore IT services context shows that global mindset, talent management, and part-nership quality significantly contribute to the performance of offshore service-providing firms. The significant positive impact of global mindset and talent management accentu-ates the significance of talent in the IT outsourcing industry (Raman, Chadee, Roxas, and Michailova, 2013). And this has strong implications for emerging economies that are favorite offshore destination countries for IT outsourcing, such as China and India.

Talent management and knowledge sharing/transfer also appear to be favorite top-ics for talent-management research (e.g., Wang-Cowham, 2011; Vance, Chow, Paik, and Shin, 2013). Wang-Cowham's (2011: 391) qualitative study of twenty Chinese HR practi-tioners explored the connection between talent development and knowledge-sharing mechanisms from a social-exchange perspective. Findings of the study suggest that "incorporating a knowledge-sharing socialization mechanism with talent development programs has a nurturing and supporting effect on learning and development" and that the "mechanism can be used to facilitate organization-wide knowledge sharing and support both organization-led and self-managed talent development programs" (Wang-Cowham, 2011: 391).

Having a shared external environment, for example in the setting of industrial clusters, may be symbiotic in talent development. Weng's (2008) study examining why there are favorable growing environments in industrial clusters in China revealed a number of insights. For example, an industrial clusters economy has a positive direct impact on talent growth; an industrial clusters HR policy has a positive direct impact on talent growth; an industrial clusters living setting has a positive direct impact on talent growth; and the HRM of companies in the industrial clusters has a positive direct impact on talent growth. The findings of this study suggest that industrial clusters may be conducive to talent management, particularly if a high level of coordination and practice sharing across organizational boundaries exists. Industrial clusters in the Chinese context may be unique, in part owing to the on-site working and living arrangements in a collectivist cultural setting. In such a context, it is relatively easy to make collective investments, often with the support of local government in order, to develop infrastructure (e.g., transportation, satellite communications, water and power supplies, and laboratories) to create favorable working environments to facilitate talent growth (Weng, 2008).

A small number of studies have attempted to assess the impact of talent management and business performance. Using profit per employee, revenue per employee, and market capitalization per employee as part of the measurements, Soewignyo and Soewignyo's (2015) study examined talent factors that may influence business performance of the Indonesian finance industry. The study showed that "the greater the number of audit committee members, the higher the profit per employee" and that "higher remuneration for directors and commissioners induced better business performance, as measured by [the] three indicators" (Soewignyo and Soewignyo, 2015: 76). However, the same study found that number of employees is negatively associated with profit per employee, revenue per employee, and market capitalization per employee.

Ulrich and Allen's study examined talent trends and how investment in talent is linked to business results in top Asian companies. Based on data from more than 570 separate businesses in Singapore, China, and India, with thirteen talent-management processes, the study found that "investments in managing current talent have more impact on business performance than hiring new talent or retaining existing talent [with job quit intent]" (Ulrich and Allen, 2014: 1).

In a similar vein, Zheng's survey study of talent retention in 281 service MNCs in six Asian countries and regions (Indonesia, Malaysia, Philippines, Singapore, Taiwan, and Thailand) found "statistically significant linkages between HR practices, talent retention and firm performance," as perceived by managers surveyed. The same study also found that not all formalized HRM practices lead to talent retention. Instead, informal recruitment methods "that are used more by Asian-bred firms have contributed to better retention rates" (Zheng, 2009: 482). Findings of this study suggest that talent management "is influenced by country-specific variables," and firms need to "focus on strategic selection of both formal and informal HR practices in order to deliver high quality service and to drive service firm growth" (Zheng, 2009: 482).

Indeed, a number of studies in the emerging-economy context have highlighted the significance of societal culture in influencing talent management. For example, Cooke and colleagues' (2014) comparative study of China and India reveals the centrality of materialistic values in the employment relationships in the two countries. The findings shed light on the different needs of capacity-building for the HR institutions in each of the two countries, as well as the need to adopt a more particularistic (vs. a universalist) approach to conceptualizing and operationalizing talent management in the international context. Similarly, Li and Scullion's study that explored the processes and mechanisms through which expatriate managers' local competence can be developed in the emerging-economy context found that "knowledge in emerging markets differs significantly from corporate knowledge transferred to those markets, and that its very nature determines its critical importance to expatriate managers' business performance" (2010: 190). Based on this finding, Li and Scullion conclude, "conventional local competence development strategies may not be effective methods for developing global managers for emerging markets" (2010: 190).

23.6 PROSPECTS OF TALENT MANAGEMENT IN EMERGING ECONOMIES: RESEARCH AND PRACTICAL IMPLICATIONS

Existing studies of talent management in emerging economies have made a highly valuable contribution in extending our knowledge in this field, both intellectually and empirically. However, a number of related research gaps remain, as is often the case with any emerging field of study. On this occasion, the advancement of the field may be hampered by two challenges. One is that foreign researchers may face added challenges to gaining good-quality access for data collection and language/culture barriers. The other is that the majority of indigenous researchers may not yet have acquired a sufficient level of research capacity and language competence to enable them to publish papers in good-quality academic journals in the English language. A strategic and fruitful way forward in addressing these deficiencies would be for Western and indigenous researchers to team up and use complementary resources in their research as has been the case in other business and management fields. In the rest of this section, we will highlight a number of related implications for future research.

23.6.1 Research Agendas

The bulk of the literature on talent management in emerging economies has come from a strategic-management perspective (focusing mainly on the firm level) or a human capital development perspective (focusing on the macro level). While the persistent influence of national culture in talent management has been highlighted in several studies, this factor was only revealed as part of the findings, rather than as a research angle in its own right.

23.6.1.1 *Theoretical Perspectives and Interdisciplinary Approach*

Given the fact that societal culture has been an important research angle and key to findings in international HRM literature, and given the rich and diverse cultures derived from religious and other societal norms and traditions in emerging economies, which are mostly high-context research settings, it may be fruitful to study the role of societal culture in greater depth to examine the extent to which talent management may be influenced by societal culture, compared with HRM. This includes, for example, whether talent management can adopt a more universalist approach than HRM. Such studies can also be conducted in a cross-group and cross-nation comparative setting. Similarly, while a handful of studies have adopted an organizational psychology perspective (e.g., employee engagement) in examining what motivates and helps to retain talent, more studies are needed that focus on the psychological state and outcome of individuals from a talent-management angle. In short, talent-management research in the emerging-economy context may benefit from the mobilization of a wider range of perspectives and greater depth than those of existing research.

23.6.1.2 *Research Design and Methods*

Most of the existing studies of talent management in emerging economies are either review papers (e.g., Li and Scullion, 2010) or empirical studies that are relatively small in scale, with interviews and case studies as the main methods (e.g., Anand, 2011; Chahal and Kumari, 2013). A small number are quantitative studies (e.g., Tymon, Stumpf, and Doh, 2010; Raman, Chadee, Roxas, and Michailova, 2013), and only a few studies contain a large sample size and deploy both quantitative and qualitative methods that are carefully designed (e.g., Ulrich and Allen, 2014). Building on the existing body of research, more in-depth and well-designed empirical studies may be conducted to test the frameworks and models advanced by authors in their review or conceptual papers (e.g., Li and Scullion, 2010) and to address research avenues identified below (see also Preece, Iles, and Jones, 2013, for another set of research avenues).

23.6.1.3 *More Studies on Less Examined Countries*

The majority of studies of talent management in emerging economies published in the English-language journals use China and India as the research locales. This is to some extent understandable, as they are the largest emerging economies and both are facing acute talent shortage, recruitment, and retention problems. However, as other emerging economies are stepping up in the global economy ladder and more and more Western MNCs are relocating or offshoring to new emerging markets beyond China and India (or what some would call "further south"), more research attention to talent management in these countries will help inform business decisions and enhance intellectual understanding of what goes on and why in these settings, and how it may impact the rest of the world.

23.6.1.4 *Corporate Capacity in Talent Management*

In general, firms in emerging economies possess a relatively low level of HRM competences, and the talent mindset may not yet have developed. As an increasing number of domestic firms are entering the global market, how do they develop their talent-management strategy in relation to their global talent strategy as part of their overall business strategy (e.g., Sparrow, Scullion, and Tarique, 2014)? Given the fact that talent management mobilizes marketing (e.g., employer branding) and supply-chain management concepts and techniques, what may be the implications for the competence development of HR professionals as an aspect of corporate HRM capacity-building (e.g., Bluen, 2014)?

23.6.1.5 *Ownership Variations in Talent Management*

Existing talent-management studies in emerging economies (notably China and India) have focused primarily on Western MNCs operating in these host countries (e.g., Chuai, Preece, and Iles, 2008; Hartmann, Feisel, and Schober, 2010; Preece, Iles, and Jones, 2013; Schmidt, Mansson, and Dolles, 2013), using HR and non-HR executives as the main research targets. Future studies may investigate how domestic firms attract and manage their talent, including talented individuals as the main research targets. Future studies may also extend the work by Cooke and co-authors (2014) to study talent-management issues across ownership forms across countries.

23.6.1.6 *Diverse Social Groups of Talent*

Extant research on talent management in emerging economies has treated talent implicitly as a homogenous group of (able and young) managerial and professional employees. Future research should broaden the scope to examine talent management with regard to diversity management that goes beyond the study of women's empowerment (e.g., Sovanjeet [2014] in the Indian context) to include, for example, older, ethnic minority, and physically challenged employees as underutilized talent pools (e.g., Kulkarni and Scullion, 2015). Future studies should also examine the career needs and expectations of different categories of talent—for example, managerial and professional talent—and the crossover of the two groups as individual career needs change (e.g., from professional to managerial for progression for younger people, and from managerial back to professional role as a result of lifestyle change for older people). Similarly, expatriates, as MNCs' talent from emerging economies in host countries, may be a fruitful avenue of research, given the rising number of emerging MNCs.

23.6.1.7 *A Wider Set of Talent-Management Stakeholders*

The majority of the empirical studies of talent management have focused on talent management within organizations and stakeholders within them (Kulkarni and Scullion, 2015). There is plenty of scope to adopt a broader approach to studying the role of institutional actors (not just employers and employees) in talent management. Research could include, for example, employment agencies. In China and India the use of agency employment is widespread, even for knowledge workers, such as in the finance and IT sector. Research could also include the role of recruitment consultants/businesses as labor market agencies in recruiting and poaching talent who might not have thought of leaving a company initially, and in disseminating information and reducing information asymmetry.

23.6.1.8 *Role of Technology in Talent Management*

The important role of social media in promoting employer branding and recruiting talent has been highlighted. For example, Rao's (2014) study of the use of social networking sites (SNS) in talent recruitment as mentioned earlier in this chapter reveals that local recruiters in Brazil and India are using Orkut, Facebook, and LinkedIn to recruit talent in different categories, with Facebook being used to target overseas Indians, Orkut and Facebook primarily for entry level, and LinkedIn for upper-level talent. Twitter is also being used creatively by recruiters to source applicants. However, the adoption of SNS for talent recruitment in emerging economies may be hampered by the inadequate telecommunications infrastructures in the less well-developed areas in these countries, with those who are underprivileged being disadvantaged. Without a wider and more detailed research scope, we cannot adequately assess the likely effect of SNS on talent recruitment and management, as well as how it may affect different groups of talent in varied ways. Future studies could examine the role of SNS, and more broadly the role of ICT, in a range of talent-management issues in emerging economies.

23.6.1.9 *Effects of State-Led Talent Programs*

As shown above, macro-level talent-management studies have drawn our attention to the role of the developing state in developing human capital in general and in reversing the brain-drain trend specifically to support their countries' accelerated economic development. As a result, talent from emerging economies who were trained and had work experience overseas have been returning to their home country—also known as "brain gain" (e.g., Harvey, 2014). However, the effect of these state-led talent-management initiatives/programs on talent development and utilization at the organizational level has not been systematically assessed. Nor do we have much knowledge as to how, if at all, the career aspirations and expectations of the returning talent may differ from those of their domestic counterparts. It is important to note that state-led programs may not always yield positive outcomes for individuals and organizations. As Sidani and Al Ariss's (2014) study argued, an inequitable HR system may have a negative impact on the talent-management process when favorable conditions are granted to local employees, which foster an inflated sense of entitlement in some and undermine the enthusiasm of (disadvantaged) foreign workers for talent-management initiatives. Coordinated research efforts at a high level, especially if conducted in cross-country comparative modes, are likely to generate valuable insights to inform policy and management decisions.

23.6.1.10 *Linking Talent Management with Employee and Business Outcomes*

Not all talent-management practices will work or have the same effect on all groups of talent across emerging economies. Existing research on talent-management practices have focused largely on Western practices, with limited insights offered into practices that are home-grown in emerging economies (Sparrow, Scullion, and Tarique, 2014). For example, the Western talent-management approach assumes implicitly that talent-management practices may help retain talent. However, in the Chinese and Indian context, young employees prefer to change jobs regularly in order to gain experience and career advancement (e.g., Nankervis, Cooke, Chatterjee, and Warner, 2013). As Ulrich and Allen's (2014) study found, investing in talent retention has a limited effect on business performance. Here, a key question to contemplate is: Should companies make efforts to retain talent vis-à-vis the talent's desire for job mobility for personal growth? More in-depth studies of talent-management practices in domestic firms may identify indigenous practices that may be better aligned with employees' needs and thus yield preferable outcomes. Equally, future studies may be conducted to measure the qualitative and quantitative outcomes of talent-management practices and their benefits to employees and businesses.

In short, emerging economies present fertile ground for research on talent management, owing to differences in their institutional and cultural backgrounds, stages, and patterns of economic development. In researching talent-management practices at the organizational level, we need to examine in greater depth the consistency between the practices (Golik and Blanco, 2014) in order to understand what and how talent-management practices and processes may contribute to the business strategically. Researchers can design their studies to examine various talent-management issues as indicated in Table 23.1.

In researching the avenues identified above, researchers may mobilize different theories and perspectives. For example, in examining various aspects of the process of talent management, a multilevel approach may be adopted to assess the strength of the talent-management practices adopted by the organization as perceived by those (talented employees) who are targeted for talent management. Here, Ostroff and Bowen's (2016) conceptualization and argument about strengths in the constructs of HR systems related to the HRM-performance linkages may be mobilized to inform the research design. In researching the strategic aspects of talent management, Collings and Mellahi's argument that "the key focus for organizations should be on maximizing value creation through calibrating the level of talent required by the organization and ensuring that talent are deployed in those strategic jobs with the greatest potential for value creation" (2013: 322) will be valuable in informing the research design. In addition, research design, both quantitative and qualitative, may take into account the importance of the organizational context within which "the translation of talent into performance" is to take place (Collings and Mellahi, 2013: 322). Johns defines context as "situational opportunities and constraints that affect the occurrence and meaning of organizational behavior as well as

Table 23.1 Talent Management: Some Related Questions for Research and Practice

	Talent-management functions (internal and external focus)	Talent-management context and outcomes (internal and external focus)
What should we focus on in the **process**?	• Determining what talent-management tools are effective and in what professional, organizational, industrial, and societal context • Evaluating the effectiveness of talent-management practices	• Determining the business strategy • Identifying the talent pool and the stakeholders • Discovering how talent management is linked to business results • Measuring talent management and organizational performance
What should we focus on in the **strategic** domain?	• Learning to align talent needs and business needs • Identifying and making use of better talent-management techniques and practices	• Making sense of new markets and market trends • Determining what corporate capabilities are needed for long-term development

functional relationships between variables" (2006: 386). Yet, (quantitative) research has tended to design out contextual factors rather than treating them as an important component of the study in itself (Johns, 2006). Given the differentiated nature of talent and key positions, and given the diversity of business contexts in the global economy, more attention should be given to context in talent-management research.

23.7 CONCLUSIONS

This chapter has reviewed the status quo of research on talent management in nations with emerging economies, highlighting a number of major challenges confronting these nations, as well as some of these states' initiatives to combat the bottleneck caused by talent shortage in their economic development. In short, this review shows that research on talent management in emerging economies has largely focused on a small number of countries (mainly China and India) and MNCs, which in general take a strategic approach to talent management and thus are better at attracting talent than domestic firms are. While there is a growing level of understanding of the effectiveness and types of talent-management activities in different national contexts and organizational settings (Kulkarni and Scullion, 2015), future research in this field would benefit from drawing on a broader set of disciplinary perspectives, achieving more robust research design, and conducting systematic analysis of practices, processes, and outcomes.

So far, talent management in emerging economies has focused on relatively small, elite groups of employees. Given the persisting social and economic inequalities exhibited at various degrees across these countries, a approach to talent management that includes nontraditional stakeholders external to the organization and groups of underutilized candidates may help alleviate talent-shortage problems and create opportunities for talented individuals to fulfill their career aspirations. It will also contribute to the corporate social-responsibility agenda much needed for development in these countries.

Finally, it is important for researchers and practitioners to bear in mind that there are differences not just between developed and emerging economies, but also among emerging economies. At the same time, there are similarities in talent management for particular industries (e.g., IT) across developed and emerging economies. For firms to adopt a more sophisticated approach to talent attraction and retention beyond simply spending more money, we need nuanced insights into what talent value from their employers, by country and by profession (Ernst and Young, 2014), in order to create a better alignment between individual aspirations and corporate goals.

References

Amankwah-Amoah, J, and Debrah, Y. A. 2011. Competing for scarce talent in a liberalised environment: evidence from the aviation industry in Africa. *The International Journal of Human Resource Management*, 22, pp.3565–81.

Anand, P. 2011. Talent development and strategy at telecom major Bharti Airtel. *Strategic HR Review*, 10(6), pp.25–30.

Bhatnagar, J. 2007. Talent management strategy of employee engagement in Indian ITES employees: key to retention. *Employee Relations*, 29(6), pp.640–63.

Bluen, S. 2014. Talent management challenges in emerging markets. In D. van Eeden, ed., *The role of the chief human resources officer*, pp.107–51. Randburg: KnowRes Publishing.

Chacko, E. 2007. From brain drain to brain gain: reverse migration to Bangalore and Hyderabad, India's globalizing high tech cities. *GeoJournal*, 68(2-3), pp.131–40.

Chahal, H., and Kumari, A. 2013. Examining talent management using CG as proxy measure: a case study of State Bank of India. *Corporate Governance: The International Journal of Business in Society*, 13(2), pp.198–207.

Chatterjee, S., Nankervis, A., and Connell, J. 2014. Framing the emerging talent crisis in India and China: a human capital perspective. *South Asian Journal of Human Resources Management*, 1(1), pp.25–43.

Chuai, X., Preece, D., and Iles, P. 2008. Is talent management just "old wine in new bottles"? The case of multinational companies in Beijing. *Management Research News*, 31(12), pp.901–11.

Collings, D., and Mellahi, K. 2013. Commentary on: "talent—innate or acquired? Theoretical considerations and their implications for talent management. *Human Resource Management Review*, 23(3), pp.322–5.

Collings, D. G., and Mellahi, K., 2009. Strategic talent management: a review and research agenda. *Human Resource Management Review*, *19*(4), pp.304–13.

Cooke, F. L. 2011. The role of the state and human resource management in China. *International Journal of Human Resource Management*, *22*(18), pp.3830–48.

Cooke, F. L., Saini, D., and Wang, J. 2014. Talent management in China and India: a comparison of management perceptions and human resource practices. *Journal of World Business*, *49*(2), pp.225–35.

Cooke, F. L., Wood, G., and Horwitz, F. 2015. Multinational firms from emerging economies in Africa: implications for research and practice in human resource management. *The International Journal of Human Resource Management*, *26*(21), pp.2653–75.

Deloitte. 2013. Emerging market talent: managing risks and strategies. http://deloitte.wsj.com/riskandcompliance/2013/12/18/emerging-market-talent-managing-risks-and-strategies/. Accessed July 7, 2015.

Dickson, D. 2006. Competing for talent: China's strategies to reverse the brain drain. *International Labour Review*, *145*, pp.1–2.

Doh, J. P., Smith, R. R., Stumpf, S. A., and Tymon, Jr., W. G. 2011. Pride and professionals: retaining talent in emerging economies. *Journal of Business Strategy*, *32*(5), pp.35–42.

Elegbe, J. A. 2010. *Talent management in the developing world adopting a global perspective.* Burlington, VT: Gower.

Ernst & Young. 2014. Differentiating for success: securing top talent in the BRICs. http://www.ey.com/Publication/vwLUAssets/EY-Securing-top-talent-in-the-BRICs/$FILE/EY-Securing-top-talent-in-the-BRICs.pdf. Accessed December 6, 2015.

Farndale, E., Scullion, H., and Sparrow, P. 2010. The role of the corporate HR function in global talent management. *Journal of World Business*, *45*, pp.161–8.

Furusawa, M., and Brewster, C. 2015. The bi-cultural option for global talent management: the Japanese/Brazilian Nikkeijin example. *Journal of World Business*, *50*, pp.133–43.

Golik, M. N., and Blanco, M. R. 2014. Talent identification and development tools. *Management Research: The Journal of the Iberoamerican Academy of Management*, *12*(1), pp.23–39.

Hartmann, E., Feisel, E., and Schober, H. 2010. Talent management of Western MNCs in China: balancing global integration and local responsiveness. *Journal of World Business*, *45*, pp.169–78.

Harvey, W. S., 2014. Winning the global talent war. *Journal of Chinese Human Resource Management*, *5*(1), pp.62–74.

Holden, N., and Vaiman, V. 2013. Talent management in Russia: not so much war for talent as wariness of talent. *Critical Perspectives on International Business*, *9*(1/2), pp.129–46.

Horwitz, F. M. 2012. Evolving human resource management in Southern African multinational firms: towards an Afro-Asian nexus. *The International Journal of Human Resource Management*, *23*, pp.2938–58.

Horwitz, F. M. 2013. An analysis of skills development in a transitional economy: the case of the South African labour market. *The International Journal of Human Resource Management*, *24*, pp.2435–51.

Iles, P., Chuai, X., and Preece, D. 2010. Talent management and HRM in multinational companies in Beijing: definitions, differences and drivers. *Journal of World Business*, *45*, pp.179–89.

Jiang, T, and Iles, P. 2011. Employer-brand equity, organizational attractiveness and talent management in the Zhejiang private sector, China. *Journal of Technology Management in China*, *6*(1), pp.97–110.

Johns, G. 2006. The essential impact of context on organizational behaviour. *Academy of Management Review*, 31(2), pp.386–408.

Khilji, S. E., and Keilson, B. 2014. In search of global talent: Is South Asia ready? *South Asian Journal of Global Business Research*, 3(2), pp.114–34.

Khilji, S. E., and Schuler, R. S. 2017. Talent management in global context. In D. G. Collings, K. Mellahi, and W. C. Cascio, eds., *Oxford handbook of talent management*. Oxford: Oxford University Press.

Kulkarni, M., and Scullion, H. 2015. Talent management activities of disability training and placement agencies in India. *The International Journal of Human Resource Management*, 26(9), pp.1169–81.

Li, S., and Scullion, H. 2010. Developing the local competence of expatriate managers for emerging markets: a knowledge-based approach. *Journal of World Business*, 45, pp.190–6.

Li, Z. 2013. A critical account of employability construction through the eyes of Chinese post-graduate students in the UK. *Journal of Education and Work*, 26(5), pp.473–93.

Liu, Y., and Pearson, C. A. L. 2014. The importance of talent management: a study of Chinese organisations. *Journal of Chinese Economic and Foreign Trade Studies*, 7(3), pp.153–72.

Nankervis, A., Cooke, F. L., Chatterjee, S., and Warner, M. 2013. *New models of human resource management in China and India*. London: Routledge.

Nzukuma, K. C. C., and Bussin, M. 2011. Job-hopping amongst African Black senior management in South Africa. *South African Journal of Human Resource Management*, 9, pp.258–69.

Ostroff, C. L., and Bowen, D. E. 2016. Reflections on the 2014 decade award: is there strength in the construct of HR system strength? *Academy of Management Review*, 41(2), pp.196–214.

Preece, D., Iles, P., and Jones, R. 2013. MNE regional head offices and their affiliates: talent management practices and challenges in the Asia Pacific. *The International Journal of Human Resource Management*, 24(18), pp.3457–77.

Raman, R., Chadee, D., Roxas, B., and Michailova, S. 2013. Effects of partnership quality, talent management, and global mindset on performance of offshore IT service providers in India. *Journal of International Management*, 19, pp.333–46.

Rao, P. 2014. Social networking sites (SNS): talent management in emerging markets—India and Mexico. *Social Media in Strategic Management*, pp.259–76. Published online September 11, 2014.

Ready, D. A., Hill, L. A., and Conger, J. A. 2008. Winning the race for talent in emerging markets. *Harvard Business Review*, 86(11), pp.62–70.

Schmidt, C., Mansson, S., and Dolles, H. 2013. Managing talents for global leadership positions in MNCs: responding to the challenges in China. *Asian Business & Management*, 12, pp.477–96.

Sharma, R., and Bhatnagar, J. 2009. Talent management—competency development: key to global leadership. *Industrial and Commercial Training*, 41(3), pp.118–32.

Shi, Y., and Handfield, R. 2012. Talent management issues for multinational logistics companies in China: observations from the field. *International Journal of Logistics Research and Applications: A Leading Journal of Supply Chain Management*, 15(3), pp.163–79.

Sidani, Y., and Ariss, A. A. 2014. Institutional and corporate drivers of global talent management: evidence from the Arab Gulf region. *Journal of World Business*, 49, pp.215–24.

Skuza, A., Scullion, H., and McDonnell, A. 2013. An analysis of the talent management challenges in a post-communist country: the case of Poland. *The International Journal of Human Resource Management*, 24, pp.453–70.

Skuza, A., McDonnell, A., and Scullion, H. 2015. Talent management in the emerging markets. In F. Horwitz and P. Budhwar, eds., *Handbook of human resource management in emerging markets*, pp.225–43. Cheltenham: Edward Elgar.

Soewignyo, F., and Soewignyo, T. I. 2015. The influence of talent factors on business performance. *Issues in Social and Environmental Accounting*, 9(1), pp.76–99.

Sovanjeet, M. 2014. HR issues and challenges in pharmaceuticals with special reference to India. *Review of International Comparative Management*, 15(4), pp.423–30.

Sparrow, P., Scullion, H., and Tarique, I. 2014. Strategic talent management: future directions. In P. Sparrow, H. Scullion, and I. Tarique, eds., *Strategic talent management contemporary issues in international context*, pp.278–302. Cambridge: Cambridge University Press.

Srivastava, P., and Bhatnagar, J. 2008. Talent acquisition due diligence leading to high employee engagement: case of Motorola India MDB. *Industrial and Commercial Training*, 40(5), pp.253–60.

Tymon, W. G., Stumpf, Jr., S. A., and Doh, J. P. 2010. Exploring talent management in India: the neglected role of intrinsic rewards. *Journal of World Business*, 45, pp.109–21.

Ulrich, D., and Allen, J. 2014. Talent accelerator: understanding how talent delivers performance for Asian Firms. *South Asian Journal of Human Resources Management*, 1(1), pp.1–23.

Vaiman, V., and Holden, N. 2011. Talent management in Central and Eastern Europe: challenges and trends. In D. Collings and H. Scullion, eds., *Global talent management*, pp.178–93. London: Routledge.

Vance, C. M., Chow, I. H. S., Paik, Y., and Shin, K. Y. 2013. Analysis of Korean expatriate congruence with Chinese labor perceptions on training method importance: implications for global talent management. *International Journal of Human Resource Management*, 24(5), pp.985–1005.

Wang, J., Cooke, F. L., and Huang, W. H. 2014. How resilient is the (future) workforce in China? A study of the banking sector and implications for human resource development. *Asia Pacific Journal of Human Resources*, 52(2), pp.132–54.

Wang-Cowham, C. 2011. Developing talent with an integrated knowledge-sharing mechanism: an exploratory investigation from the Chinese human resource managers' perspective. *Human Resource Development International*, 14(4), pp.391–407.

Weng, Q. 2008. Role of the HR environment on talent growth: an empirical study of industrial clusters in China. *Chinese Management Studies*, 2(1), pp.14–31.

Zhang, S., and Bright, D. 2012. Talent definition and talent management recognition in Chinese private owned enterprises. *Journal of Chinese Entrepreneurship*, 4(2), pp.143–63.

Zheng, C. 2009. Keeping talents for advancing service firms in Asia. *Journal of Service Management*, 20(5), pp.482–502.

Zheng, C., Soosay, C., and Hyland, P. 2007. Manufacturing to Asia: who will win the emerging battle for talent between dragons and tigers? *Journal of Manufacturing Technology Management*, 19(1), pp.52–72.

Zweig, D., and Wang, H. 2013. Can China bring back the best? The Communist Party organizes China's search for talent. *The China Quarterly*, 215, pp.590–615.

....

CHAPTER 24

TALENT MANAGEMENT IN MULTINATIONAL CORPORATIONS

....

INGMAR BJÖRKMAN, MATS EHRNROOTH,
KRISTIINA MÄKELÄ, ADAM SMALE,
AND JENNIE SUMELIUS

24.1 INTRODUCTION

INTEREST in talent management has proliferated over the last decade, with the global shortage of leadership talent being touted as one of the highest HR concerns for multinational corporations (MNCs) today (Cappelli, 2008; Guthridge, Komm, and Lawson, 2008). Consequently, MNCs have directed increasing attention to global talent management (Farndale, Scullion, and Sparrow, 2010; McDonnell, Lamare, Gunnigle, and Lavelle, 2010; Stahl et al., 2012), which can be defined as "all organizational activities for the purpose of attracting, selecting, developing, and retaining the best employees in the most strategic roles (those roles necessary to achieve organizational strategic priorities) on a global scale" (Scullion, Collings, and Caligiuri, 2010: 106; see also Chapter 2 of this book).[1] Although approaches vary, talent management usually focuses on a pool of employees who rank at the top in terms of performance and competencies, and are therefore considered either present or future leaders or key professionals (Collings and Mellahi, 2009; Lewis and Heckman, 2006).[2] In MNCs, talent-management decisions are increasingly global in that employees may be identified as "talent" or "high potentials" regardless of whether they are parent-country nationals, expatriates, or local employees working in foreign subsidiaries (Collings, Scullion, and Morley, 2007).

In this chapter, we will review current research on talent management in MNCs. The focus is on the practices used by MNCs to manage employees defined as "talent." We will examine the content of corporate practices, the actors involved in carrying out these practices, and the roles they are playing, and the effects of these practices on outcomes at different levels of analysis. Efforts are then made to identify promising ways to enhance our knowledge of talent management in the context of MNCs. By way of an illustration of the kinds of issues covered, we present the talent-management practices of one MNC in particular, the Finland-based elevator and escalator company KONE. A comparative review and discussion of talent management across countries falls outside the scope of the chapter (see Chapter 23 for talent management in a global context).

24.2 TALENT MANAGEMENT IN MNCs: OVERVIEW

Talent management consists of a system of organizational practices used to attract, identify, develop, and retain individuals considered key to the performance of the MNC. KONE illustrates some of the key central talent-management practices that MNCs engage in. With some USD 10 billion in sales and close to 50,000 employees, KONE is one of the leading players in the elevator and escalator industry. At the heart of global talent management in KONE is an annual leadership and talent review (LTR), which focuses on the occupants of 500 leadership roles worldwide. During this review of key people and positions, all businesses and geographic areas must identify high potentials, nominate successors to key positions, and decide on development actions for people in key positions. Areas and businesses are expected to nominate 1%–5% of their staff for review, and there are about 300 high potentials (HiPos) worldwide who do not currently occupy key positions. Identifying high potential at an early career stage (six months from the commencement of employment) is seen as desirable so that individuals can benefit from special development through, for example, KONE leadership training programs, cross-functional and geographical moves, and mentoring, as well as coaching.

To steer this review process, top management sets annual targets, including diversity (gender and nationality), development (proportion undergoing job rotation), and recruitment (external versus internal sourcing). "High potential" is defined as the ability, commitment, and motivation to succeed in senior leadership positions. A "walk and write" approach is used at LTR meetings to stimulate input and discussion about the candidates. Reviewing the succession plan for the top positions is also part of the meeting, giving a measure of the "bench strength" of areas and businesses, as well as an indication of the need for external recruitment and the urgency of renewal in management teams. As is common practice in the Nordic countries, HiPos and succession candidates are not usually informed of their status. KONE believes that 70% of development happens through job, project, and rotational challenges; 20% by learning through others (HiPos have mentors and many receive special coaching); and 10% through formal education and training.[3]

In the next sections we will examine different issues related to talent management in MNCs, using KONE as an illustration of the issues at hand. In particular, we will focus on the delicate balancing act between global integration and local responsiveness in tal-ent-management policies and practices, as well as the integration and user internaliza-tion of talent-management practices across the MNC. Further, we will discuss the role that the HR function plays in managing talent globally and locally.

24.3 GLOBAL INTEGRATION VERSUS LOCAL RESPONSIVENESS

It is common within international HRM research to use the global standardization/integration versus local adaptation/responsiveness framework, originally introduced by Doz and Prahalad (1991), to examine people-management practices in MNCs across countries (Rosenzweig and Nohria, 1994). *Global standardization* refers to the extent to which the MNC uses the same talent-management practices throughout the organ-ization, and local adaptation has to do with the need to apply different practices in dif-ferent countries owing to local cultural, institutional, and economic factors (Doz and Prahalad, 1991). The tensions inherent in the integration/responsiveness framework are also very relevant to talent management (Hartmann, Feisel, and Schober, 2010; Tarique and Schuler, 2010), several of which have been key issues in KONE, as the example of their Chinese operations illustrates.

China posed particular challenges for the global talent-management process in KONE. The company entered the Chinese market after its main international competi-tors but set out in 2005 to catch up, and managed to secure a leading position by 2013. Recruiting 1,000 new staff each year, a recruitment slogan was "Come to work for the fastest growing company," which helped overcome KONE's lack of visibility. KONE staff, teaching at fifty technical schools, also assisted in recruitment. But there was a shortage of high potentials: few of the Chinese managers satisfied the global Basic Requirements, notably fluent English. The size and growth of China, virtually a continent unto itself, led KONE to relax the global criteria, allowing also local HiPos to be nominated who did not speak English. The relaxation of language requirements also prompted more exclu-sive use of Chinese as the language of communication, which motivated local managers to speak up and become more proactive. However, cultural diversity within and mobil-ity into and out of the China organization—KONE's fastest growing market and largest country by employment—have remained a challenge. Partly in response to expectations of rapid career progression among Chinese employees, the high-potential identification process in China was pushed down to the branch level.

Global standardization of talent-management practices has many advantages. First, the firm can employ best practices throughout the organizations, and by doing so improve their effectiveness. It also makes it easier for the firm to identify and compare talent in different units, reducing potential biases of location or visibility (Mäkelä, Björkman, and Ehrnrooth, 2010). While many MNCs have thus put global talent-management practices in place, many more are still described as having an ad-hoc approach (McDonnell, Lamare, Gunnigle, and Lavelle, 2010).

At the same time, and as seen in the KONE case, there are also benefits associated with at least some degree of local responsiveness in talent management. Cultural differences are often cited, but they are by no means the only ones. Institutional factors are equally if not even more important, and characteristics of the local labor market play a significant role (Pudelko and Harzing, 2007; see also Chapter 23 on talent management in the global context). Such local characteristics may be particularly important in high-velocity labor markets such as China, in which high turnover of qualified local employees is an acute concern (Hartmann, Feisel, and Schober, 2010; Ready, Hill, and Conger, 2008). Considerable research attention has been paid to general HRM practices across countries within MNCs, and there are some suggestions of convergence across MNCs from different countries in terms of talent management (Stahl et al., 2012). However, there is relatively little work specifically focusing on global standardization and/or local adaptation of talent management (Vaiman and Collings, 2015), in particular work that examines how macro, country-level effects are influencing global–local tensions within talent management (Khilji, Tarique, and Schuler, 2015). In line with research on HRM in MNCs in general, cultural and institutional perspectives, investigations of social capital (Kostova and Roth, 2002) could also be used to shed further light on similarities and differences in the patterns of talent-management practices found within MNCs that span a variety of settings.

A key issue in global talent management is that of *implementation*, particularly in terms of the implementation of globally standardized policies. Wright and Nishii (2013) suggest that actual implemented practices in local subsidiaries often vary significantly from those that are intended by the headquarters. Previous research provides plenty of evidence that planned transfers of management practices to foreign subsidiaries are often far from successful (Björkman and Lervik, 2007), and the question of MNC headquarters intentions versus actual practices is therefore an important one for both scholars and practicing managers.

In part to explain differences in implementation, Kostova (1999) introduced the notion of *internalization* of organizational practices to the international management literature. Internalization has to do with how committed managers and employees are to a certain organizational practice, and how much value they attribute to it (Kostova, 1999). Unless managers really believe in a certain organizational practice, they are unlikely to put much effort into its use; as a result the practice may only be ceremonially or superficially implemented and is likely to have disappointing results (Cascio, 2006). The consideration of key-stakeholder internalization of talent-management practices is also supported by the HRM-process perspective developed by Bowen and Ostroff (2004, 2016), which emphasizes the role of management in shaping the signals sent by the people-management system concerning the kind of behavior that is expected and rewarded in the organization. If the talent-management system is to send the kind of signals intended by the corporation, it is vital that key actors have internalized the practices in question (Ahlvik and Björkman, 2015).

A related issue is that of *integration*, which in this context refers to the extent to which the talent-management practices that are implemented in a subsidiary, geographical region, or at a global scale, are linked to other relevant HRM practices, such as performance management, training and development, and compensation. The importance of this internal fit, or linkage across practices, is widely acknowledged in the HRM literature both more generally (MacDuffie, 1995; Lepak et al., 2006) and within research on talent management in particular (Pucik, Evans, Björkman, and Morris, 2017). In talent management, the integration of talent identification and leadership-development practices is a crucial one (McCall, Lombardo, and Morrison, 1988). In the KONE case, for example, much effort was placed on ascertaining that those individuals identified as talent had opportunities to participate in leadership educational programs. They were also expected to go through cross-functional and/or geographical moves as part of their development program within three years of being identified. However, evidence suggests that this kind of systematic integration across different elements of the talent-management system does not always materialize (McDonnell, 2010). Both top-down and bottom-up approaches to managing global mobility have been reported in the literature (see Vaiman and Collings, 2015). However, further empirical research on this issue is clearly warranted.

Table 24.1 summarizes key issues related to the implementation, internalization, and implementation of talent management in MNCs.

Table 24.1 A Summary of Implementation, Internalization, and Integration Issues in the Context of Talent Management in MNCs

Dimensions of practice transfer (Ahlvik and Björkman, 2015)	Key issues
Implementation	*To what extent is talent management taking place in the subsidiary?* Refers to the extent of use of talent-management practices in the subsidiary (Kostova and Roth, 2002) Practices implemented in the subsidiary may vary from those intended by headquarters (Wright and Nishii, 2013)
Internalization	*To what extent are key stakeholders committed to the company's talent-management practices?* Refers to the attitudes of key actors in the MNC/subsidiary and how they influence the attitudes and actions of others: if they do not actually believe in the talent-management practices, they may not put much effort into using them, which in turn may result in only ceremonial or superficial implementation (Kostova, 1999; cf. Bowen and Ostroff, 2004)
Integration	*To what extent are talent-management practices connected to other HRM practices in the MNC?* Refers to internal fit and alignment among the company's talent-management practices and other HRM practices (Delery and Doty, 1996): for instance, the integration of talent-management practices and leadership-development practices is important (McCall, Lombardo, and Morrison, 1988)

To date there appears to be little explicitly comparative work on the talent-management practices in MNCs from different countries (cf. McDonnell, Lavelle, and Gunnigle, 2014; Pudelko and Harzing, 2007). Further, we are not aware of research that, in line with the traditions of the comparative HRM field (Brewster and Mayrhofer, 2012; Mayrhofer, Brewster, Morley, and Ledolter, 2011), has investigated possible processes of international convergence and crossvergence in talent-management practices in MNCs.

24.4 The Role of the HR Function

Another key issue for talent management in MNCs has to do with the role the HR function plays in the design and implementation of talent-management practices. The HR function typically has the primary responsibility of handling functional processes, tools, procedures, and policies related to talent management, including the attraction (into the company) and identification (within the company) of talent, the performance-management processes that link into talent reviews, and the development and training of the identified talent (Mäkelä, Björkman, and Ehrnrooth, 2010). Often talent management has a global process owner at the headquarters, who works with local business partners or unit HR managers.

Returning to the KONE example, the head of talent management is responsible for the global talent-management policy, process, and tools and for driving the process together with the business leaders and unit HR directors. She also leads the global talent-management process and does this by communicating guidelines each year, kicking off the LTR process, providing definitions and tools, and traveling to all area- and unit-level LTR workshops to ensure they are run effectively. KONE has come a long way in creating a talent culture in which managers openly talk about individuals from the perspective of personal growth and thinking about developmental opportunities. One significant factor that is attributed to the evolution of this talent mindset is the support and commitment that comes from the highest levels of management, including the CEO. Another factor has been the development of global tools and processes. However, KONE's HR team acknowledges that the real success of KONE's global talent management should not simply be measured in terms of implementation, but in terms of impact—impact on the moves, career paths, and development actions of key people, and the business impact of these on KONE's competitiveness. In response to challenges in ensuring sufficient numbers of competent, ready, and available successor candidates and meeting job rotation and diversity targets, KONE HR has made improvements in recruitment quality through global recruitment training for all line managers, initiated a number of employer-branding projects, become more active in helping managers to identify rotation opportunities, and ramped up efforts to identify HiPos earlier, by going down levels in the organization and introducing country-level LTR workshops.

The HR function typically also plays a key role in influencing the attitudes that line managers and employees have toward (their internalization of) talent management. While we seem to have only limited research-based knowledge on this issue (cf. Farndale, Scullion, and Sparrow, 2010; Sparrow, Farndale, and Scullion, 2013), the talent-management-related roles played by actors in the HR functions are likely to differ across MNCs and also across the different units within the firm, and this will influence the way in which top executives and line managers (a) view or internalize talent issues and (b) respond to them.

Further empirical work is needed on the roles played by the HR function in talent management in MNCs. The HR function often has little formal authority, so the question is to what extent, through which tools, and with which tactics do they influence line and top managers? In the general HRM research area, a stream of research has shed light on the various roles played by the HR function. This body of work has focused on the HR function as an organizational actor, contributing with several typologies of the HR function's work domain (e.g., Caldwell, 2003; Ulrich, 1997; Welch and Welch, 2012). Research has also advanced in terms of how HR roles are enacted (Welch and Welch, 2012), the ways in which contextual factors influence and are influenced by HR (Caldwell, 2008), and how the HR function deals with increasing ambiguities, pressures, and conflicts driven by different role and stakeholder demands (Hope-Hailey, Farndale, and Truss, 2005; Mäkelä et al., 2013). In one of very few papers focusing more specifically on talent management, Farndale, Scullion, and Sparrow (2010) outline four different roles that HR can play in management talent in MNCs.

Building on research done within the strategy-as-practice literature (see, e.g., Vaara and Whittington, 2012), we propose that talent-management research would also gain from incorporating the practices, practitioners, and praxis of talent management (i.e., a shift from only studying "talent-management practices" to doing research on the "practice of talent management" more generally). This would imply going beyond studying talent-management tools, processes, and procedures to a focus on talent-management praxis (the situated, social activities of those individuals and groups involved in talent-management work) and the practitioners involved in doing talent management (the agency and actions of key actors from the HR function, as well as line and top managers) (see Jarzabkowski, Balogun, and Seidl, 2007; see also Björkman et al. [2014] for an effort at developing such a research agenda for work on HRM in general). We believe that a "talent management-as-practice" approach would contribute novel insights into how talent-related decisions are made, implemented, and enacted in organizations, as well as how different stakeholders interpret and engage with talent management, how HR actors in MNCs become more effective and influential organizational agents (Ferris et al., 2002; Mäkelä et al., 2013), and what the short-term and more long-term effects of these actions and activities are.

Similar to our suggestion concerning MNC talent-management practices, we suggest that scholars engage in comparative work concerning the praxis of talent management and the practitioners involved in this work. Such work could build on the research that has already been done on the devolution of responsibility for HRM issues to line managers (e.g., Brewster, Brookes, and Gollan, 2015).

24.5 Outcomes of Talent Management in MNCS

Following on from Section 2 of this book regarding talent-management and performance, of considerable scholarly and practical interest is the influence of MNC talent-management practices and praxis on a range of key outcomes. Building on traditions in international business research, we suggest that three different levels of analysis are relevant: *the MNC as a whole*; *MNC units* such as country subsidiaries; and *individuals* (both persons identified as talent and those not identified). In terms of outcomes, one can make a distinction between *proximal outcomes* of talent management (i.e., outcomes that are likely to be directly impacted by the practices) and more *distant outcomes* of talent management—the latter likely to be mediated by the proximal outcomes (cf. Björkman and Welch, 2015).

First, corporate-wide human and social capital enhancement (Taylor, 2007; Morris, Snell, and Björkman, 2016), for example via talent mobility (Bozkurt and Mohr, 2011; Reiche, Harzing, and Kraimer, 2009), can be considered one of the intended outcomes of talent management at the MNC level of analysis, although some research suggests that corporations do not always succeed in this endeavor (Espedal, Gooderham, and Stensaker, 2013). Second, international and cross-functional mobility assignments, interunit skills training, and the like are likely to have an impact on knowledge sharing and transfer across units in the MNC (see, e.g., Minbaeva et al., 2003; Reiche, 2012). Third, the extent to which there are shared values, beliefs, and norms across units in the MNC as a whole can also be viewed and studied as an important outcome of HRM in general (Chatman and Cha, 2003; Levy, Taylor, and Boyacigiller, 2010; Smale et al., 2015), but also talent management more specifically (Stahl et al., 2012). A fourth and somewhat related outcome is organizational climate: the degree to which managers and employees have shared perceptions of what is important and what behaviors are expected and rewarded (Schneider, 1990), the strength of which is likely to be influenced by features of the practices (Bowen and Ostroff, 2004; Sumelius et al., 2014), as well as differences in societal values about talent (Cooke, Saini, and Wang, 2014).

Fifth, employee turnover might be influenced by how talent are managed—for instance, MNCs that do not invest in or live up to employee expectations concerning training and development may experience higher turnover rates among individuals for whom there is high demand in the labor market. In this respect, studies reveal the importance of careful and honest communication and regularly reviewing judgments on potential (Fernández-Aráoz, Groysberg, and Nohria, 2011), as well as organizational-justice perceptions (Gelens, Hofmans, Dries, and Pepermans, 2014). Lastly, employer branding in MNCs (Martin, Gollan, and Grigg, 2011; Stahl et al., 2012) may be viewed as an additional relatively proximate outcome of how talent are managed in the corporation, epitomized by MNCs such as GE, which has become known as a "talent machine" (Bartlett and McClean, 2003). KONE has recently been given the prestigious titles of "Most Attractive Employer" with the "Best CEO" and "Best HR" in its native Finland. In many countries, the average length of employment of a KONE employee is over a decade. Much of this is attributed to the investments KONE has made in global talent management.

There are potentially more distant organization-level outcomes of MNC talent management, including worldwide innovativeness, flexibility, market share, and both financial and stock market performance (see, e.g., Joyce and Slocum, 2012; Schuler and Tarique, 2007). Talent management should also influence the composition of top-management teams in MNCs, at least over time. When it comes to the background of those at the senior levels—and despite decades of attention to diversity in talent management—top-leadership positions in most MNCs still remain dominated by parent-country nationals (van Veen and Marsman, 2008). For example, fewer than 15% of global Fortune 500 firms have a CEO or top-management executive who was born outside of the country in which the corporation has its headquarters (Ghemawat and Vantrappen, 2015). The question remains, therefore, whether a truly global approach to talent-change management possesses the potential to change this (cf. Mäkelä, Björkman, and Ehrnrooth, 2010).

Several of the issues mentioned above are also relevant at the MNC unit level of analysis. For instance, returning to the KONE example, investments in talent management were seen by the corporation as an important reason why the corporation managed to reduce the turnover rate among its high potentials (HiPos) and managers in China. The perceptions held about the talent-management practices can also be surmised to impact the employer brand of the MNC in a certain country. Echoing the kinds of findings that have appeared in the general international HRM literature, Burbach and Royle (2010) found that the transfer and subsequent effectiveness of headquarters' talent-management practices in foreign subsidiaries are influenced by stakeholder involvement and top-level support, micropolitical exchanges, and the integration of talent management with a supporting global HRM information system. What remains less clear is the degree to which transferred talent-management practices can be regarded as distinctly different from other HRM practices (Iles, Chuai, and Preece, 2010), and if so, whether they face similar dualistic pressures from headquarters and the host-country context to certain other individual HRM practices (e.g., Smale, Björkman, and Sumelius, 2013). Indeed, there may be good grounds to assume that transfers of talent-management practices will encounter some unique barriers, given talent management's often controversial nature and alleged management fad status (Iles, Preece, and Chuai, 2010).

At the *individual* level of analysis, talent-management practices have been found to be significantly related with a range of attitudinal outcomes. Social exchange theory suggests that when individuals know or perceive that corporations invest in them, employees are likely to reciprocate these corporate investments in positive ways

(Cropanzano and Mitchell, 2005), providing a useful lens through which to understand the mechanisms involved in how employees interpret and react to organizational talent-management practices (Höglund, 2012). In line with this theoretical reasoning, Björkman and Mäkelä (2013) found that employees who perceived that they have been identified as talent (as compared with other managers and professionals) showed a higher level of commitment to increasing performance demands, to building competencies that are valuable for their employers, and to supporting actively its strategic priorities. They also showed greater identification with the focal MNC unit and lower turnover intent. Similarly, Gelens and colleagues (2014) found that employees identified as talent were more satisfied in their jobs and displayed more work effort compared with those not identified as talent. Sonnenberg, van Zijderveld, and Brinks (2014) found that the greater use of talent-management practices was positively related to psychological-contract fulfillment, as perceived by employees. Further, Dries and De Gieter (2014) suggest that identifying talent, and communicating their special status to them, may cause changes in the employment relationship, in terms of raising the talent's expectations about special treatment and development opportunities in the organization. Together these studies suggest that the communication of talent status in the organization tends to correspond with positive attitudes in particular among the identified talent, and that organizations need to pay due attention to perceptions of incongruence and injustice concerning the process of talent identification (cf. Mäkelä, Björkman, and Ehrnrooth, 2010).

Within MNCs, there are likely to be contextual differences in both actual talent-management practices and in how these impact employee attitudes (Farndale, Scullion, and Sparrow, 2010). For instance, there is likely to be significant variation—regardless of MNC policies—in terms of how and if individual supervisors communicate about their subordinates' talent status, ranging from explicit formal assertions to informal and indirect clues (see, e.g., Sonnenberg, van Zijderveld, and Brinks, 2014). More comparative research is called for to shed light on the effects of the communication practices of superiors and the HR function across countries, as well as how individuals make sense of and react to the signals they are sent, formally and informally, about their talent status.

Similar to the MNC and MNC unit level of analysis, we consider individual human and social capital development, as well as interpersonal knowledge transfer, to be both desirable and likely outcomes of talent-management practices. We further argue that not only work-life balance but also workload and stress deserve to be included as individual-level outcomes in research on talent management in MNCs, thus pointing to the potential negative effects of talent-management practices on individual employees and their families (cf. Ehrnrooth and Björkman, 2012).

Finally, individual long-term career progression (Cappellen and Janssens, 2010) is an important, yet more distant outcome of talent management. A study by Claussen, Grohsjean, Luger, and Probst (2014) finds that human capital and experience are important for promotions at middle- and senior-management levels, but that the size of a person's network is only useful for midlevel promotions. This finding would seem to support global talent-management practices that provide or encourage personal development, but it is at odds with other descriptive research reporting that around 40% of internal job moves involving high potentials end in failure (Martin and Schmidt, 2010). Although being identified as talent is associated with a greater willingness to take on challenging global leadership-development activities (Björkman and Mäkelä, 2013), research that sheds light on whether these investments pay off for the MNC and the individual is sorely needed.

We summarize the discussion about possible outcomes of talent management in MNCs in Table 24.2.

Table 24.2 Illustrative Example of Potential Outcomes of Talent Management at Different Levels

Level of analysis	Proximal outcomes of TM	Distant outcomes of TM
Corporate level	- Increased knowledge sharing and transfer as a result of various international and cross-unit talent trainings and assignments (Minbaeva et al., 2003; Reiche, 2012) - Corporate-wide human and social capital enhancement through talent mobility (Reiche, Harzing, and Kraimer, 2009) - Shared values (Stahl et al., 2012) - Reduced employee turnover (Gelens Hofmans, Dries, and Pepermans, 2014) - Employer branding (Bartlett and McClean, 2003) and organizational reputation (Rindova et al., 2005)	- Worldwide innovativeness, flexibility, market share, and financial and stock market performance (Joyce and Slocum, 2012; Schuler and Tarique, 2007) - Composition of top-management team (cf. Mäkelä et al., 2010)
Individual Level	- Increased work motivation and commitment (Collings and Mellahi 2009) and efforts to fulfill the psychological contract (Sonnenberg, van Zijderveld, and Brinks, 2014) - Additional attitudinal outcomes such as willingness to take on demanding work, to build valuable competencies, to support company strategic priorities, and MNC identification (Björkman and Mäkelä, 2013) - Job satisfaction (Gelens, Hofmans, Dries, and Pepermans, 2014) - Human and social capital development and interpersonal knowledge transfer (Reiche, Harzing, and Kraimer, 2009) - Work-life balance and workload, stress (Ehrnrooth and Björkman, 2012)	- Long-term career progression/success (Briscoe et al., 2012; Cappellen and Janssens, 2010) - Global mindset (Levy, Beechler, Taylor, and Boyacigiller, 2007) - Global leadership effectiveness (Caligiuri and Tarique, 2012)

24.6 Conclusions

Talent management continues to be a key concern for MNCs. In this chapter, we focused on practices used by MNCs for managing talent, as well as the role of the HR function and other actors in managing talent and the outcomes of it. We started by arguing for the usefulness of an integration/responsiveness lens for examining talent-management issues in MNCs, since managing talent across borders results in several global–local tensions. The case of KONE in China also illustrates this well, showing how the company had to adapt its talent-pool criteria considerably in order for it to be meaningful in the Chinese context.

Next, we discussed the implementation of talent-management practices, focusing in particular on the importance of management internalization of talent-management practices and the integration of these practices with other relevant HRM practices. In particular, we highlighted the need for a linkage between talent management and leadership development, which means that MNCs should make sure that those identified as talent actually get the opportunity to participate in relevant leadership programs and take on different roles in various functional and geographical areas within the company as a part of their development. This is also linked to outcomes of talent management at the individual level, where one key question that MNCs struggle with is whether to communicate talent status to employees. Issues that require more research in the future include whether companies communicate talent status and with what consequences, and in particular how the communication of both talent status and the whole talent-management system is carried out and with what consequences in different contexts.

As for outcomes of talent management more generally, we posit that we still only have scant knowledge of the outcomes of talent-management practices in MNCs. We suggested three different levels of analysis: MNC level; unit/subsidiary level; and individual level, discussing proximal and more distant outcomes at each of these levels. Moreover, we discussed the role of the HR function and other actors, such as top executives and line managers, in talent management. We suggested that in addition to examining talent-management *practices*, research in this field would benefit from a shift toward the practice of talent management, which is in line with a strategy-as-practice (Vaara and Whittington, 2012) and, more specifically, an HR-as-practice perspective (Björkman et al., 2014) implies extending the focus also to the practitioners (actors) and praxis of talent management.

To conclude, we hope this overview serves to highlight some of the key challenges with managing talent in MNCs, and that it provides some useful suggestions for areas for future research efforts.

Notes

1. For a detailed discussion of different perspectives on talent management, see also Vaiman and Collings (2015).

2. For a detailed discussion of the different ways to define, operationalize, and measure talent, see Nijs, Gallardo-Gallardo, Dries, and Sels (2014).
3. The description of global talent management in KONE is based on Smale, Björkman, and Saarinen (2015).

References

Ahlvik, C., and Björkman, I. 2015. Towards explaining subsidiary implementation, integration, and internalization of MNC headquarters HRM practices. *International Business Review, 24,* pp.497–505.

Bartlett, C. A., and McLean, A. N. 2003. *GE's talent machine: the making of a CEO.* Case study no. 12128659. Harvard Business School, Boston.

Björkman, I., Ehrnrooth, M., Mäkelä. K., Smale, A. et al. 2013. Talent or not? Employee reactions to talent identification. *Human Resource Management, 52,* pp.195–214.

Björkman, I., Ehrnrooth, M., Mäkelä. K., Smale, A. et al. 2014. From HRM practices to the practice of HRM: setting a research agenda. *Journal of Organizational Effectiveness: People and Performance, 1,* pp.122–40.

Björkman, I., and Lervik, J. E., 2007. Transferring HR practices in multinational corporations. *Human Resource Management Journal, 17,* pp.320–35.

Björkman, I., and Mäkelä, K. 2013. Are you willing to do what it takes to become a senior global leader? Explaining the willingness to undertake challenging leadership development activities. *European Journal of International Management, 7,* pp.570–86.

Björkman, I., and Welch, D. 2015. Framing the field of international human resource management research. *International Journal of Human Resource Management, 26,* pp.136–50.

Bowen, D. E., and Ostroff, C. 2004. Understanding HRM-firm performance linkages: the role of the "strength" of the HRM system. *Academy of Management Review, 29,* pp.203–21.

Bowen, D. E., and Ostroff, C. 2016. Reflections on the 2014 Decade Award: is there strength in the construct of HR system strength? *Academy of Management Review, 41,* pp.194–214.

Bozkurt, Ö., and Mohr, A. T. 2011. Forms of cross-border mobility and social capital in multinational enterprises. *Human Resource Management Journal, 21,* pp.138–55.

Brewster, C., Brookes, M., and Gollan, P. J. 2015. The institutional antecedents of the assignment of HRM responsibility to line managers. *Human Resource Management, 54,* pp.577–97.

Brewster, C., and Mayrhofer, W. 2012. *Handbook of research on comparative human resource management.* Cheltenham: Edward Elgar Publishing.

Briscoe, J. P., Hall, D. T., and Mayrhofer, W. 2012. *Careers around the world: individual and contextual perspectives.* New York: Routledge.

Burbach, R., and Royle, T. 2010. Talent on demand? Talent management in the German and Irish subsidiaries of a US multinational corporation. *Personnel Review, 39,* pp.414–31.

Caldwell, R. 2003. The changing roles of personnel managers: old ambiguities, new uncertainties. *Journal of Management Studies, 40,* pp.983–1004.

Caldwell, R. 2008. HR business partner competency models: re-contextualizing effectiveness. *Human Resource Management Journal, 18,* pp.275–94.

Caligiuri, P., and Tarique, I. 2012. Dynamic cross-cultural competencies and global leadership effectiveness. *Journal of World Business, 47,* pp.612–22.

Cappellen, T., and Janssens, M. 2010. The career reality of global managers: an examination of career triggers. *International Journal of Human Resource Management*, 21, pp.1834–1910.

Cappelli, P. 2008. *Talent on demand: managing talent in an age of uncertainty*. Boston: Harvard Business Press.

Cascio, W. F. 2006. Global performance management system. In G. K. Stahl, and I. Björkman, eds., *Handbook of research in international human resource management*, pp.176–96. Cheltenham: Edward Elgar.

Chatman, J., and Chan, S. E. 2003. Leading by leveraging culture. *California Management Review*, 45, pp.20–34.

Claussen, J., Grohsjean, T., Luger, J., and Probst, G. 2014. Talent management and career development: what it takes to get promoted. *Journal of World Business*, 49, pp.236–44.

Collings, D. G., and Mellahi, K. 2009. Strategic talent management: a review and research agenda. *Human Resource Management Review*, 19, pp.304–13.

Collings, D. G., Scullion, H., and Morley, M. J. 2007. Changing patterns of global staffing in the multinational enterprise: challenges to the conventional expatriate assignment and emerging alternatives. *Journal of World Business*, 42, pp.198–213.

Cooke, F. L., Saini, D. S., and Wang, J. 2014. Talent management in China and India: a comparison of management perceptions and human resource practices. *Journal of World Business*, 49, pp.225–35.

Cropanzano, R., and Mitchell, M. S. 2005. Social exchange theory: an interdisciplinary review. *Journal of Management*, 31, pp.874–900.

Delery, J. E., and Doty, D. H. 1996. Modes of theorizing in strategic human resource management: tests of universalistic, contingency, and configurational performance predictions. *Academy of Management Journal*, 39, pp.802–35.

Doz, Y., and Prahalad, C. K. 1991. Managing DMNCs: a search for a new paradigm. *Strategic Management Journal*, 12, pp.145–64.

Dries, N., and De Gieter, S. 2014. Information asymmetry in high potential programs: a potential risk for psychological contract breach. *Personnel Review*, 43, pp.136–62.

Ehrnrooth, M. and Björkman, I. 2012. The HRM process, employee performance and workload: a study of the mechanisms of HRM's influence. *Journal of Management Studies*, 49, pp.1109–35.

Espedal, B., Gooderham, P. N., and Stensaker, I. G. 2013. Developing organizational social capital or prima donnas in MNEs? The role of global leadership development programs. *Human Resource Management*, 52, pp.607–25.

Farndale, E., Pauuwe, J., Morris, S. S., Stahl, G. K. et al. 2010. Context-bound configurations of corporate HR functions in multinational corporations. *Human Resource Management*, 49, pp.45–66.

Farndale, E., Scullion, H., and Sparrow, P. 2010. The role of the corporate HR function in global talent management. *Journal of World Business*, 45, pp.161–8.

Fernández-Aráoz, C., Groysberg, B., and Nohria, N. 2011. How to hang on to your high potentials. *Harvard Business Review*, 89(10), pp.76–83.

Ferris, G., Hochwarter, W., Douglas, C., Blass, F. et al. 2002. Social influence processes in organizations and human resources systems, *Research in Personnel and Human Resources Management*, 21, pp.65–127.

Gelens, J., Hofmans, J., Dries, N., and Pepermans, R. 2014. Talent management and organisational justice: employee reactions to high potential identification. *Human Resource Management Journal*, 24, pp.159–75.

Ghemawat, P., and Vantrappen, H. 2015. How global is your C-suite? *MIT Sloan Management Review*, 56(4), pp.78–82.

Guthridge, M., Komm, A. B., and Lawson, E. 2008. Making talent a strategic priority. *McKinsey Quarterly*, 1, pp.49–59.

Hartmann, E., Feisel, E., and Schober, H. 2010. Talent management of Western MNEs in China: balancing global integration and local responsiveness. *Journal of World Business*, 45, pp.169–78.

Höglund, M. 2012. Quid pro quo? Examining talent management through the lens of psychological contracts. *Personnel Review*, 41, pp.126–42.

Hope-Hailey, V., Farndale, E., and Truss, C. 2005. The HR department's role in organisational performance. *Human Resource Management Journal*, 15, pp.49–66.

Iles, P., Chuai, X., and Preece, D. 2010. Talent management and HRM in multinational companies in Beijing: definitions, differences and drivers. *Journal of World Business*, 45, pp.179–89.

Iles, P., Preece, D., and Chuai, X. 2010. Talent management as a management fashion in HRD: towards a research agenda. *Human Resource Development International*, 13, pp.125–45.

Jarzabkowski, P., Balogun, J., and Seidl, D. 2007. Strategizing: the challenges of a practice perspective. *Human Relations*, 60, pp.5–27.

Joyce, W. F., and Slocum, J. W. 2012. Top management talent, strategic capabilities, and firm performance. *Organizational Dynamics*, 41, pp.183–93.

Khilji, S. E., Tarique, I., and Schuler, R. S. 2015. Incorporating the macro view in global talent management. *Human Resource Management Review*, 25, pp.236–48.

Kostova, T. 1999. Transnational transfer of strategic organizational practices: a contextual perspective. *Academy of Management Review*, 24, pp.308–24.

Kostova, T., and Roth, K. 2002. Adoption of organizational practice by subsidiaries of multinational corporations: institutional and relational effects. *Academy of Management Journal*, 45, pp.215–33.

Lepak, D. P., Lio, H., Chung, Y., Harden, E. E. et al. 2006. A conceptual review of human resource management systems in strategic human resource management research. *Research in Personnel and Human Resource Management*, 25, pp.217–71.

Levy, O., Taylor, S., and Boyacigiller, N. A. 2010. On the rocky road to strong global culture. *MIT Sloan Management Review*, 51(4), pp.20–2.

Lewis, R. E., and Heckman, R. J. 2006. Talent management: a critical review. *Human Resource Management Review*, 16, pp.139–54.

MacDuffie, J. P. 1995. Human resource bundles and manufacturing performance: organizational logic and flexible production systems in the world auto industry. *Industrial and Labor Relations Review*, 48, pp.197–221.

Mäkelä, K., Björkman, I., and Ehrnrooth, M. 2010. How do MNCs establish their talent pools? Influences on individuals' likelihood of being labeled as talent. *Journal of World Business*, 45, pp.134–42.

Mäkelä, K., Björkman, I., Ehrnrooth, M., Smale, A. et al. 2013. Serving many masters: the evaluation of HRM capabilities within the MNC. *Journal of International Business Studies*, 44, pp.813–32.

Martin, G., Gollan, P. J., and Grigg, K. 2011. Is there a bigger and better future for employer branding? Facing up to innovation, corporate reputations and wicked problems in SHRM. *The International Journal of Human Resource Management*, 22, pp.3618–37.

Martin, J., and Schmidt, C. 2010. How to keep your top talent. *Harvard Business Review*, 88(5), pp.54–61.

Mayrhofer, W., Brewster, C., Morley, M., and Ledolter, J. 2011. Hearing a different drummer? Evidence of convergence in European HRM. *Human Resource Management Review*, 21, pp.50–67.

McCall, M. W., Lombardo, M. M., and Morrison, A. M. 1988. *The Lessons of Experience: how successful executives develop on the job*. New York: Free Press.

McDonnell, A., Lamare, R., Gunnigle, P., and Lavelle, J. 2010. Developing tomorrow's leaders— evidence of global talent management in multinational enterprises. *Journal of World Business*, 45, pp.150–60.

McDonnell, A., Lavelle, J., and Gunnigle, P. 2014. Human resource management in multinational enterprises: evidence from a late industrializing economy. *Management International Review*, 54, pp.361–80.

Minbaeva, D., Pedersen, T., Björkman, I., Fey, C. A. et al. 2003. MNC knowledge transfer, subsidiary absorptive capacity, and HRM. *Journal of International Business Studies*, 35, pp.586–99.

Morris, S., Snell, S., and Björkman, I. 2016. An architectural framework for global talent management. *Journal of International Business Studies*, 47, pp.723–47.

Nijs, S., Gallardo-Gallardo, E., Dries, N., and Sels, L. 2014. A multidisciplinary review into the definition, operationalization, and measurement of talent. *Journal of World Business*, 49, pp.180–91.

Pucik, V., Evans, P., Björkman, I., and Morris, S. 2017. *The global challenge: international human resource management*, 3rd edn, Chicago: Chicago Business Press.

Pudelko, M., and Harzing, A-W. K. 2007. Country-of-origin, localization, or dominance effect? An empirical investigation of HRM practices in foreign subsidiaries. *Human Resource Management*, 46, pp.535–59.

Ready, D., Hill, L., and Conger, J. 2008. Winning the race for talent in emerging markets. *Harvard Business Review*, 86(11), pp.63–70.

Reiche, B. S. 2012. Knowledge benefits of social capital upon repatriation: a longitudinal study of international assignees. *Journal of Management Studies*, 49, pp.1052–77.

Reiche, B. S., Harzing, A. W., and Kraimer, M. L. 2009. The role of international assignees' social capital in creating inter-unit intellectual capital: A cross-level model. *Journal of International Business Studies*, 40, pp.509–26.

Rindova, V. P., Williamson, I. O. and Petkova, A. P. 2005. Being good or being known: an empirical examination of the dimensions, antecedents, and consequences of organizational reputation. *Academy of Management Journal*, 48, pp.1033–49.

Rosenzweig, P., and Nohria, N. 1994. Influences on human resource management practices in multinational corporations. *Journal of International Business Studies*, 25, pp.229–51.

Schneider, B. 1990. Organizational climate and culture. San Francisco: Jossey-Bass.

Schuler, R. S., and Tarique, I. 2007. International human resource management: a North American perspective, a thematic update and suggestions for future research. *The International Journal of Human Resource Management*, 18, pp.717–44.

Scullion, H., Collings, D. G., and Caligiuri, P. 2010. Global talent management. *Journal of World Business*, 45, pp.105–8.

Smale, A., Björkman, I., Ehrnrooth, M., and John, S. et al. 2015. Dual values- based organizational identification in MNC subsidiaries: a multilevel study. *Journal of International Business Studies*, 46, pp.761–83.

Smale, A., Björkman, I., and Saarinen, J. 2015. *Pushing the right buttons: global talent management at KONE corporation*. The Case Centre, case no. 415-111-1.

Smale, A., Björkman, I., and Sumelius, J. 2013. HRM integration mechanisms in MNCs: European subsidiaries in China. *Journal of World Business*, 48, pp.232–40.

Sonnenberg, M., van Zijderveld, V., and Brinks, M. 2014. The role of talent-perception incongruence in effective talent management. *Journal of World Business*, 49, pp.272–80.

Sparrow, P., Farndale, E., and Scullion, H. 2013. An empirical study of the role of the corporate HR function in global talent management in professional and financial service firms in the global financial crisis. *The International Journal of Human Resource Management*, 24, pp.1777–98.

Stahl, G., Björkman, I., Farndale, E., Morris, S. et al. 2012. Six principles of global talent management. *MIT Sloan Management Review*, 53(2), pp.25–32.

Sumelius, J., Björkman, I., Ehrnrooth, M., Mäkelä, K. et al. 2014. What determines employee perceptions of HRM process features? The case of performance appraisal in MNC subsidiaries. *Human Resource Management*, 53, pp.569–92.

Tarique, I., and Schuler, R. S. 2010. Global talent management: literature review, integrative framework, and suggestions for further research. *Journal of World Business*, 45, pp.122–33.

Taylor, S. 2007. Creating social capital in MNCs: the international human resource management challenge. *Human Resource Management Journal*, 17, pp.336–54.

Ulrich, D. 1997. *Human resource champions*. Boston: Harvard Business School Press.

Vaara, E., and Whittington, R. 2012. Strategy as practice: taking social practices seriously. *Academy of Management Annals*, 6, pp.285–336.

Vaiman, V., and Collings, D. 2015. Global talent management. In D. G. Collings, G. T. Wood, and P. M. Caligiuri, eds., *The Routledge companion to international human resource management*, pp.210–25. London: Routledge.

van Veen, K., and Marsman, I. 2008. How international are executive boards of European MNCs: nationality diversity in 15 European countries. *European Management Journal*, 26, pp.188–98.

Welch, C. L., and Welch, D. E. 2012. What do HR managers really do? HR roles on international projects. *Management International Review*, 52, pp.597–617.

Wright, P., and Nishii, L. 2013. Strategic HRM and organizational behavior: integrating multiple levels of analysis. In D. Guest, J. Paauwe, and P. Wright, eds., *HRM and Performance: Building the Evidence Base*, pp.97–110. San Francisco, CA: Wiley.

CHAPTER 25

··

TALENT MANAGEMENT IN SMALL- AND MEDIUM-SIZED ENTERPRISES

··

MARION FESTING, KATHARINA HARSCH,
LYNN SCHÄFER, AND HUGH SCULLION

25.1 INTRODUCTION

TODAY, talent management is one of the most important issues for every company—and it is likely to remain so in the years to come (Strack, 2014). Regardless of their size, industry, or business location, organizations have to overcome the challenge of attracting and retaining key employees from the declining pool of highly qualified talent, if they wish to be competitive (Beechler and Woodward, 2009; CIPD, 2007; ILO, 2009). To design and implement an appropriate talent-management approach, the organizational context should be taken into account (Iles, Chuai, and Preece, 2010; Sparrow and Makram, 2015).

When looking at the corporate landscape, it becomes obvious that the majority of companies are small- and medium-sized enterprises (SMEs). SMEs play a crucial role in the global economy. For instance, more than 99% of all companies in OECD and G20 countries fall under this category, and in most OECD countries, SMEs generate between 55% and 75% of the value added[1] (OECD, 2015). As a result of their special characteristics, SMEs may be confronted with particular challenges regarding talent management. For example, it is said that they have fewer resources, are less professional, and are characterized by a centralized management style (Hudson, Smart, and Bourne, 2001). Because of such factors, SMEs find it much more difficult to attract and retain talent (see also Festing, 2007).

Despite the economic importance of SMEs, academic publications on talent management in the context of SMEs are scarce. While there are academic articles on talent management in multinational enterprises (MNEs) (see e.g., Collings, 2014; McDonnell and Collings, 2011; Stahl et al., 2007), only a few authors have addressed the topic of talent management in an SME context (for exceptions, see Festing, Schäfer, and Scullion, 2013; or Valverde, Scullion, and Ryan, 2013). However, research on HRM in SMEs highlights significant differences between SMEs and large firms in relation to their approach to HRM (Rabi and Gilman, 2012). In this chapter, we address this topic by answering the questions: What particularities affect the management of human resources and therefore the management of talent in SMEs with regard to the attraction and retention of employees, and how do they affect it? In order to answer these questions, we draw on the latest findings in academic research on corporate talent-management practices in SMEs.

The remainder of this chapter is organized as follows. After describing the main particularities of SMEs discussed in academia and demonstrating their impact on the management of human resources, we provide a brief overview of the comparatively young research field of talent management and its importance for SMEs. We then review the scant literature on talent management in SMEs, and as one example, we outline how they can join forces in order to compete as networks and with cooperation agreements in industry clusters in the war for talent. We conclude with a short summary and implications for future research in this area.

25.2 SMEs: Relevance and Particularities

In most countries, SMEs play a crucial role for the economy. A recent OECD study demonstrates that more than 99% of the companies in OECD and G20 countries are SMEs[2] (OECD, 2015). Moreover, they employ more than 50% of the workforce,[3] generate between 30% and 84% of the value added, and make a decisive contribution to national and global economic growth (OECD, 2015).

SMEs can be defined by quantitative criteria (European Commission, 2005) or by qualitative criteria regarding the particularities that make them special (IfM Bonn, 2016). The most commonly used definition of SMEs in Europe is the one provided by the European Commission, referring to quantitative criteria: SMEs employ fewer than 250 persons, generate less than 50 million euro turnover per year, and their annual balance sheet does not exceed 43 million euro (European Commission, 2005). Taking qualitative criteria into account, the IfM Bonn defines SMEs in a German context, which is referred to as the German "Mittelstand,"[4] by the unity of ownership and management, whereby the owner, for instance, has significant personal influence on the business, bears the entrepreneurial risk, and generates his/her income through the business (IfM Bonn, 2016). Therefore, larger companies can also be found in the group of SMEs.

Although SMEs differ from each other in size, legal form, or ownership, they still share common characteristics that differentiate them from the majority of larger companies (Hudson, Smart, and Bourne, 2001; OECD, 2015). As argued by Storey (1994), SMEs are not scaled-down versions of large companies; therefore, we cannot understand their particularities, challenges, and needs simply by making small what was large (Ates, Garengo, Cocca, and Bititci, 2013). Hudson and co-authors (2001) summarize the key characteristics of SMEs as follows. In SMEs, often a personalized management style aligned with centralized authority prevails. They are characterized through flat and flexible structures, a reactive, fire-fighting mentality, and informal, dynamic strategies. In addition, SMEs exhibit high innovatory potential. However, resources in terms of management, finance, and workers are scarce. Moreover, they often rely only on a small number of customers, are specialized, and operate in limited markets.

These characteristics influence the management of human resources and, as a result, the management of talent. We will address both fields later. The management of employees has long been recognized as an important challenge facing SMEs (Dundon and Wilkinson, 2009), and HR practices overall are recognized as important contributors to the success of small firms (Heneman, Tansky, and Camp, 2000; Wilkinson, 1999). However, there is limited conceptual or empirical research on HRM and talent management in SMEs, and often HR concepts are not adapted to suit the SME context (Festing et al., 2013; Heneman, Tansky, and Camp, 2000). In the next section, before we examine talent-management issues in SMEs, we briefly highlight some important differences between SMEs and large firms in relation to their overall approach to HRM.

25.3 Human Resource Management in SMEs

Research has highlighted that SMEs and large firms differ in their overall approach to HRM and in adopted HR practices (e.g. Rabi and Gilman, 2012). The limited research suggests that small firms adopt a distinctive approach to their HR practices. Furthermore, the research highlights that large organizations adopt more sophisticated HR practices owing to pressures to gain legitimacy combined with more important resource endowments compared with SMEs (Festing, 2007; Valverde, Scullion, and Ryan, 2013). Therefore, compared with small organizations, they are more likely to adopt sophisticated staffing and training approaches (Cappelli, 2010; Conaty and Charan, 2010), while SMEs tend to be more focused on how to utilize existing resources more efficiently and effectively (Festing et al., 2013). Human resource issues in these firms are rarely a top priority because the strategic emphasis is placed on ensuring and expanding market power while closely observing and reacting to changing market and customer demands (Edwards and Ram, 2009). On the contrary, there is evidence that SMEs spend fewer resources on the employment of HR professionals (Kinnie et al., 1999; Klaas, McClendon, and Gainey, 2000) and on the implementation of formalized, professional HRM systems and policies (Cardon and Stevens, 2004; de

Kok, Uhlaner, and Thurik, 2006); consequently, HRM in SMEs is often highly informal and mainly concentrated on administrative tasks. This is confirmed by a study by Kabst, Wehner, Meifert, and Kötter (2009), who indicated that small companies are less likely to have an HR strategy than large companies are.

Generally, SMEs invest less in making themselves visible in the labor market and tend to recruit from labor markets separate from large firms (Cappelli, 2010; Storey et al., 2010). In addition, compensation levels that can be afforded by SMEs are limited by the abovementioned resource constraints, which also limit their ability to invest in the sophisticated HR practices adopted by some large firms (Edwards and Ram, 2009). Finally, it is significant that we have not seen the emergence of best practice leaders in HR systems in the SME sector, in contrast with the considerable literature on large enterprises which highlights best practices in global MNEs (Cappelli, 2008, 2010). However, it is important to note that strategic HRM and operational HR issues in SMEs are often decided by the founder/owner of the organization (Kühlmann, 2000), who may not be an expert in HRM but clearly has the HR–business link in mind.

Valverde and co-authors (2013) summarize three characteristics of HRM in SMEs. First, there has been work suggesting how *similar* SMEs are in relation to their approaches to HRM. Edwards and Ram (2009) have suggested that homogeneity may be found among SMEs, depending on external factors (e.g., industry sector and technology base), as well as internal factors (e.g., the ownership of the company or the characteristics of employees). Second, a high degree of *informality*, both in the general approach to HRM and in relation to specific HR practices, is recognized as a key characteristic of HRM in SMEs (Dundon and Wilkinson, 2009). This informality has been identified as a source of competitive advantage for SMEs (Bacon, Ackers, Storey, and Coates, 1996; Edwards and Ram, 2009; Storey et al., 2010), and its importance to the organizational culture in SMEs may affect approaches to talent management and talent identification. Third, HRM in SMEs is also characterized by the *presence of powerful owner managers* who determine both the strategic approach to the organization and operational approaches to HRM (Rabi and Gilman, 2012; Wilkinson, 1999). Additionally, specialized HR functions may not be present in many SMEs (Edwards and Ram, 2009; Valverde, Scullion, and Ryan, 2013). Overall, research on HRM in SMEs highlights that these companies face distinctive HRM challenges and need HR policies to suit their particular context; applying HR policies from the large firm context will be unlikely to work (Heneman, Tansky, and Camp, 2000; Rabi and Gilman, 2012).

Taking the employee perspective, recent research suggests that employees may choose to work in an SME for a variety of reasons, including better job quality, less bureaucracy (Storey et al., 2010), greater job satisfaction, higher flexibility, and more informality in the workplace (Dundon and Wilkinson, 2009). Given the distinct HRM practices and approaches, as well as the seeming attractiveness of small firms to potential employees, we will consider below the issue of how attracting and retaining talent works in the SME context. However, we will first outline the relevance of talent management in general—and in SMEs in particular.

25.4 RELEVANCE OF TALENT MANAGEMENT

Societal developments in many countries make talent management one of the most important challenges for organizations, both currently and, most likely, in the years to come (Strack, 2014), and one of the most rapidly emerging topics for research (Sparrow, Scullion, and Tarique, 2014). The rapid growth of knowledge-based economies increases the demand for highly qualified employees, and demographic changes, characterized by an aging workforce and declining birth rates in many industrialized societies, reduce the supply of skilled labor (Beechler and Woodward, 2009; CIPD, 2007; ILO, 2009).

After McKinsey consultants designated the increasing competition for companies to attract and retain highly qualified employees as "the war for talent" in the late 1990s, talent management gained the attention of HR practitioners and consultancy firms (Chambers et al., 1998). Only nearly a decade later did it emerge as a growing field in academia (Chambers et al., 1998; Collings and Mellahi, 2009; Gallardo-Gallardo, Nijs, Dries, and Gallo, 2015; Thunnissen, Boselie, and Fruytier, 2013). Although several researchers in this area emphasize the growing maturity of this comparatively young research field (see, e.g., Gallardo-Gallardo, Nijs, Dries, and Gallo, 2015; Sparrow and Makram, 2015; Thunnissen, Boselie, and Fruytier, 2013), there is still no commonly accepted definition of *talent* or *talent management* (Al Ariss, Cascio, and Paauwe, 2014; Cappelli and Keller, 2014; Dries, 2013; Meyers and van Woerkom, 2014). The primary controversial issue in this academic discussion is whether talent management should be more inclusive, addressing all employees, or exclusive, focusing on key employees (Collings and Mellahi, 2009; Lewis and Heckman, 2006; Schuler, Jackson, and Tarique, 2011).

Most of the attempts to define *talent* are based on the resource-based view, which entails an exclusive talent-management approach (Cappelli and Keller, 2014). Taking this perspective, talent is seen as a key strategic resource, creating a competitive advantage, and is supposed to have an important influence on organizational performance (Collings and Mellahi, 2009). In this case, talent are "high performers," having special, often firm-specific knowledge, experience, and behaviors and/or high potentials, with the ability to develop and grow within the organizational context (Festing and Schäfer, 2014; Sparrow and Makram, 2015). They can be seen as a "small elite of employees whose skills (in the broadest sense) are assumed to be rare, hard to find, difficult to replace, and to add a disproportionate amount of value to the organization compared to other employees" (Sparrow and Makram, 2015: 251). Therefore, resources should be allocated to attracting and retaining such employees. On the other hand, the inclusive approach of talent management sees the potential of every employee to add value to the organization. This view also argues that resources for developing employees should be allocated more or less evenly across the organization (Al Ariss, Cascio, and Paauwe, 2014; Dries, 2013; Festing et al., 2013). In this sense, organizational talent management focuses on providing a good working environment and employee wellbeing for all employees, to prevent the inequality and injustice that can be fostered by an exclusive talent-management approach, with its classification of employees and the uneven distribution of resources (Thunnissen, Boselie, and Fruytier, 2013). In accordance with Dries (2013), these extreme interpretations of the notions of talent can be seen as the ends of a continuum in which an appropriate talent-management approach can be positioned.

For the purpose of this chapter, we have chosen a broad definition suggested by Stahl and colleagues (2007), where individual talent-management practices are emphasized. Thus, organizational talent management includes internally consistent, complementary, and reinforced practices utilized to attract, select, develop, evaluate, and retain talented employees. These practices should be aligned with the organizational culture of the company and be related to an organization's strategy and overall goals (Stahl et al., 2007). Furthermore, there is a growing consensus that talent-management practices vary by contextual factors such as the type of organization, country, etc. (Festing et al., 2013; Vaiman, Scullion, and Collings, 2012). Therefore, when defining and conducting talent-management practices, the specific context matters.

25.5 TALENT MANAGEMENT IN SMES

In this section, we first outline the importance of talent management in the specific context of SMEs, following which we address the challenges in more detail and present some opportunities for talent management in SMEs identified by recent research.

25.5.1 Importance of Talent Management in SMEs

The increasing demand for talented employees in times of progressively scarce supply caused by demographic changes challenges organizations (CIPD, 2007; ILO, 2009). Therefore, talent management is gaining more and more importance for companies, including SMEs (Beechler and Woodward, 2009; Strack, 2014). In fact, researchers propose that this topic will become even more significant in the future, owing to the growing number of SMEs worldwide and the increase in "micro-multinationals" (Festing, 2007; Scullion and Brewster, 2002). Consequently, the competition for talent has become more intense, and attracting and retaining qualified managers is now the key challenge for many SMEs (Scullion and Brewster, 2002). SMEs embedded in a global competitive environment are confronted with challenges that are more acute when it comes to attracting scarce talent, as the resources and support for international assignments which are available in MNEs are much scarcer for applicants in SMEs (Festing, 2007). Furthermore, if HR practices are important contributors to the success of small firms (Carlson, Upton, and Seaman, 2006), the lack of resources and formal approaches to HRM in SMEs adds additional difficulties and challenges regarding the management of HR, and talent in particular (Cardon and Stevens, 2004; Cassell, Nadin, Gray, and Clegg, 2002; Festing et al., 2013).

25.5.2 Challenges for Talent Management in SMEs

As introduced above, owing to the lack of resources, the dominance of the owner, the tendency toward reactive management practices, or the lack of formalized processes, SMEs seem to be confronted with different challenges compared with their larger counterparts. Therefore, challenges in talent management (i.e., in attracting and retaining talents) may occur (Cardon and Stevens, 2004; Festing, 2007). We explain these in detail in the following sections.

25.5.2.1 *Talent Attraction*

Attracting suitable employees is highly relevant for the competitiveness, economic success, and growth of SMEs (Festing et al., 2013; Williamson, 2000). However, recruitment and selection can be problematic. A global study by ADP (2010), a leading service company for HRM in Europe, shows that the greatest HR challenge faced within SMEs is the recruitment of qualified employees to fill key positions. One reason may lie in the abovementioned fact that SMEs often do not have an appropriate strategy (Heneman and Berkley, 1999) and lack professional HR resources for recruiting. In addition, they are viewed as lacking visibility in the labor market in comparison with large firms (Cardon and Stevens, 2004). Furthermore, as resources in SMEs are often scarce, only convenient and cheap instruments are used to attract, select, and recruit employees (Heneman and Berkley, 1999). Also, it is argued by Williamson (2000) that they may lack employer legitimacy, meaning that the company is not seen as an attractive employer by potential applicants. Moreover, through their actions, they may not comply with the norms, values, beliefs, and definitions of the respective industry and may therefore appear to be unattractive. Another issue that makes it more difficult for SMEs to find adequate employees is that the requirements for working in such a firm are high. First, because of the smallness of the company, employees often have multiple tasks to fulfill in their day-to-day work (Cardon and Stevens, 2004), which is why SMEs look for employees with more generalist than specialist knowledge (Festing, 2007). Second, for SMEs, norms, values, and beliefs play a crucial role in recruitment, and so the person–organization fit is essential (Cardon and Stevens, 2004; Williamson, 2000). These factors make attracting and recruiting talent in the SME context even more complex and difficult.

25.5.2.2 *Talent Retention*

Retention of employees is an important topic for all organizations, as turnover entails various negative consequences, such as interrupted workflows, the rise of accident rates, and a reduction in customer service, quality, and overall financial resources required to recruit and train a replacement, which often exceed 100% of the annual pay of the position (Allen, Bryant, and Vardaman, 2010; Hausknecht, 2017; Hom, Mitchell, Lee, and Griffeth, 2012). In the academic discussion on why employees might leave their company, factors such as job satisfaction, organizational commitment, work environment, development opportunities, or compensation are identified as being important. While there is little research on retention in SMEs, a study by Kühlmann (2000) in the German context shows how their positive and negative aspects as employers are perceived by the external labor market. On the positive side, SMEs are said to provide a good working atmosphere, are less anonymous, offer a high degree of information, and require less mobility. On the negative side, he states that they provide less career opportunities, offer fewer benefits, and are less progressive regarding organization, training and development, compensation, and international working opportunities. In order to retain employees, SMEs should foster positive aspects in this regard and improve the negative ones (Festing, 2007).

Regarding the compensation of employees as a means of retention, the particularities characterizing SMEs play a dominant role. As outlined in the context of HRM in SMEs, usually it is more difficult for them to provide attractive compensation packages for their employees than it is for the majority of large companies (Cardon and Stevens, 2004). In addition, compensation in SMEs often differs with respect to the applied reference values. For instance, innovative creative behavior, the willingness to take risks, and cooperative relationships between employees are valued more in small and entrepreneurial firms (Cardon and Stevens, 2004). Moreover, the hierarchies are generally rather flat, and in terms of compensation, "rewards are not indicative of status differences among employees" (Cardon and Stevens, 2004: 307).

Another important issue when retaining employees includes training and development opportunities. Owing to scarcer financial and material resources, SMEs might not be able to afford expensive, formalized training programs with external providers and consultancies, and so instead they focus on informal, on-the-job training to prepare their employees for the multiple tasks common in SMEs (Cardon and Stevens, 2004; Cassell, Nadin, Gray, and Clegg, 2002). This could be perceived as a disadvantage, as employees cannot "upgrade" their CV with training programs at well-known business schools, etc. This is one reason why SMEs recruit in labor markets different from those frequented by large firms (Storey et al., 2010).

Despite the importance of and the challenges in this topic, there is very limited conceptual or empirical research on talent management in SMEs. The following section therefore outlines some of the opportunities that recent research has identified.

25.5.3 Opportunities for Talent Management in SMEs

Besides a few studies in the context of developing countries (see, e.g., for the Nigerian context, Epie, 2014; for the Indian context, Kaur, Sharma, Kaur, and Sharma, 2015), there are, to our knowledge, only two studies on talent management in SMEs examining the definition and management of talent and explicitly considering the particularities of the SME context.[5] Both were published in the *International Journal of Human Resource Management* in 2013, but each has a different contextual focus. We describe both studies in particular detail in this chapter.

The study by Valverde and co-authors (2013) investigated the concepts and practices of talent management in Spanish medium-sized companies. It used multiple case studies based on semi-structured interviews with different stakeholders (director or owner,

HR manager, and employees) in six companies that had between 48 and 350 employees. The key finding of the study was that most of the companies were not aware of formal talent-management policies and practices and preferred approaches that are more informal; nevertheless, in practice they were able to define talent and identify talent in their company. The focus was on employees' attitudes and performance. For instance, loyalty, commitment, trustworthiness, and consistency were identified as important characteristics defining talent in an SME context. Furthermore, this study suggested that there is no common practice defining talent in SMEs as inclusive or exclusive, since both approaches were applied in the companies within the sample. In companies where an exclusive approach was adopted, talent received more training, as well as preferential treatment due to being part of an inner circle and having greater autonomy regarding their job, which resulted in perceived injustice on the part of non-talent. Contrary to previous research, the SMEs in this study had no problems attracting and retaining talent, although they did not have formal policies in place. Overall, the study highlighted the differences in talent management in SMEs and large MNEs and provided some insights into and an overview of how talent is managed in the context of the SME sector.

The study by Festing et al. (2013) examined talent management in medium-sized German companies by using a quantitative approach, including a survey of 700 companies. Furthermore, they focused on larger medium-sized companies (along the definition of the German "Mittelstand"), with up to 2,000 employees. The authors assumed that in this group of companies there is a certain degree of HRM—and, therefore, talent-management professionalization—in place, but they argued at the same time that these medium-sized companies still differ from large enterprises with more than 2,000 employees in their HRM and talent management. The authors identified three distinct clusters of talent-management intensity in SMEs, which are described briefly below:

- *Highly engaged talent management*: these SMEs are very active and engaged regarding talent-management practices. This can be seen, for instance, in high investments in training and measures to retain employees. However, a strong focus also lies on the attraction and recruitment of talent. This cluster rather comprises larger medium-sized companies.
- *Reactive talent management*: companies in this cluster are not engaged and are more reactive in terms of talent management. Their investment in training and other measures to retain key employees is low and they only focus on HR planning.
- *Retention-based talent management*: talent management in companies of this cluster focuses on training and development, as well as succession and career planning to retain employees. Practices attracting and recruiting employees are not that important in this cluster.

A key finding of the study was that most of the SMEs in this sample followed an inclusive approach to talent management. This is a different picture compared with the data gathered by Valverde and colleagues (2013), who identified a mixed approach in the Spanish sample, and it is also contrary to previous research in the context of MNEs, where the exclusive approach prevails (Collings and Mellahi, 2009; Lewis and Heckman, 2006; Schuler, Jackson, and Tarique, 2011).

Another particularity of talent management in SMEs found by this study is that cooperation and networks with other companies and institutions were used to enhance talent-management practices (Festing and Schäfer, 2013). Clusters, such as Silicon Valley, represent an important economic factor and include many companies and institutions, although it is not always clear how single actors and firms in a regional cluster benefit from cooperation with their competitors within a cluster. Following the conceptualization of clusters as value-adding webs (VAWs), according to Brown and co-authors (2010, 2007, 2008), clusters can be defined as "a series of linkages between single firms in a certain surrounding. Understanding clusters as VAWs takes the connectivity of individual firms on different levels in a cluster into account. Value is added by horizontal, vertical, and lateral actors" (Brown et al., 2008: 159). As such, between these different actors, relationships and interdependencies of different strengths and quality exist—not only in industry and production terms but also with respect to knowledge, the exchange of HR, cooperation, and talent management. However, research on HRM and talent-management practices, or networks in clusters, is scarce. Festing and Schäfer (2013) investigated how active participation in a regional cluster environment, exemplified by a German IT cluster with 173 different actors (OstWestfalenLippe Marketing GmbH, 2016), might contribute to a firm's and a cluster's value creation in the area of HRM and talent management, by focusing on SMEs. In this example of an IT industry cluster, SMEs who were faced with limited resources to set up complex, professional HRM functions on their own (Festing, 2007) started to create networks to promote and benefit from cooperation in various areas of HRM and talent management with other horizontal, vertical, and lateral cluster actors (Festing, Schäfer, Massmann, and Englisch, 2012). Companies that usually competed in the war for talent for the same type of talent (e.g., electrical engineer) exchanged ideas and experiences; initiatives and networks in the areas of talent attraction, recruiting, and retention were created with the purpose of joining forces in order to improve the overall employer attractiveness of that region. As outcomes, for example, the number of hires in this region increased, and companies which formerly could not afford an HR specialist for employee development joined forces and used the support of lateral actors and service companies in that cluster to hire a HR specialist together with other cluster actors. As such, while they were competitors, they shared resources, exchanged ideas, teamed up for a common, higher goal, and, through these networks and cooperation, created various interdependencies (Picot, Dietl, and Franck, 2008; Thompson, 1967), thus generating a competitive advantage for the whole cluster region, also through HRM and talent management. This example of a German IT cluster focusing on SMEs is clearly not representative. However, it again highlights the more inclusive approach to talent management that is typical of Germany (Festing et al., 2013).

As can be seen from these two examples, knowledge on talent management in SMEs is still limited, so we need additional insights to shed light on the subject. The research agenda below identifies some key areas for future research in this highly relevant and important economic context of SMEs.

25.6 FUTURE RESEARCH AGENDA

In this section, we will highlight some issues for future research. The first issue is what does *talent* mean in an SME context? Who is categorized as *talent*—everyone or some? As indicated above, recent research suggests that an inclusive approach to talent management may be more appropriate in SMEs, but further research is required on whether an inclusive approach to talent management applies to the majority of SMEs in a wider range of countries (Valverde, Scullion, and Ryan, 2013).

Another important issue for future research concerns the particular challenges faced by SMEs in the labor market. To what extent are SMEs disadvantaged in the labor market because of a lack of visibility and a lack of organizational legitimacy (Edwards and Ram, 2009)? What are the implications for approaches to recruitment and selection and the overall approach to talent management? Related to this point, further research is required on the reasons why workers choose to work in SMEs and their experience of doing so.

Research is also needed to address the question of whether talent in SMEs is innate or acquired and how this is influenced by the need for many employees to perform multiple roles with unclear boundaries and job responsibilities. In addition, the extent to which talent categorization in SMEs is influenced by organizational life stages, and to what extent identifying key jobs is an important consideration in talent management in SMEs, would be a challenging topic for research (Storey et al., 2010).

As SMEs are not a homogenous group and include firms of various sizes with varying degrees of complexity in management organization and practices (Edwards and Ram, 2009), further research is required to understand the meaning of talent in this particular cohort. In addition, further research is needed on the question of whether SMEs primarily "make or buy talent." There is very little research on this question in the SME context.

Additionally, more research is required on country-specific differences in talent management systems in SMEs—new contributions from different national cultures could enhance our understanding of talent, and would yield insights into the contextualized meaning of talent management in different contexts (Festing et al., 2013). For example, will the inclusive approach be stronger in comparably collectivistic countries such as those found in the CEE region? Finally, research is urgently needed on talent management in SMEs in emerging markets, since they account for the largest proportion of employment (consider, e.g., India), but there is a dearth of research in the area (Skuza, McDonnell, and Scullion, 2015).

Overall, we can only underline that there is a need for theoretical perspectives and conceptual developments to increase understanding in this area, and more generally to explain why talent management in SMEs differs from that in large organizations.

25.7 CONCLUSION

As this chapter has shown, research on talent management in SMEs is very important and highly necessary in today's challenging economic environment. First, as the majority of all companies are SMEs, they represent the backbone of the global economy and are therefore of high economic relevance (OECD, 2015). Second, talent management in SMEs is different from that in MNEs because of the special characteristics of the former, such as the liability of smallness or scarcer resources (Cardon and Stevens, 2004; Cassell, Nadin, Gray, and Clegg, 2002; Festing et al., 2013). Consequently, SMEs are different, not just small versions of MNEs, and existing research on talent management in MNEs cannot easily be transferred to SMEs (Ates, Garengo, Cocca, and Bititci, 2013). This is why we need to know more about challenges and talent-management practices in the specific context of SMEs. It is surprising that this has not yet happened and that the field of talent management in SMEs is still under-researched (Festing et al., 2013; Valverde, Scullion, and Ryan, 2013). However, insights taken from the few existing studies summarized above, and the theoretical discussion about HRM and talent-management networks and cooperation in industry clusters, already indicate unique, context-specific, and interesting findings that may be helpful for practitioners.

NOTES

1. *Value added*: the difference between production and intermediate consumption.
2. In this study, SMEs are defined according to the definition of the European Commission. In terms of employees, this means, for example, a maximum of 250 employees.
3. With the exception of India.
4. IfM Bonn is a research institute addressing topics concerning the German "Mittelstand."
5. The Epie (2014) study only investigated the single case of a Nigerian sports radio station and was therefore excluded from our literature review. Kaur and co-authors (2015) conducted a quantitative study with a sample of 147 employees from twenty small and medium IT firms in India regarding the influence of social media use on employer branding. However, there is only a small reference to SMEs, and this is done without considering their particularities. Therefore, we decided not to include the study.

REFERENCES

ADP. 2010. *HR challenges and solutions for SMEs.* www.international.adp.com/assets/vfs/Family-31/pdf/hrchallengesandsolutions-e.pdf.

Al Ariss, A., Cascio, W. F., and Paauwe, J. 2014. Talent management: current theories and future research directions. *Journal of World Business* 49(2), pp.173–9.

Allen, D. G., Bryant, P. C., and Vardaman, J. M. 2010. Retaining talent: replacing misconceptions with evidence-based strategies. *Academy of Management Perspectives*, 24(2), pp.48–64.

Ates, A., Garengo, P., Cocca, P., and Bititci, U. 2013. The development of SME managerial practice for effective performance management. *Journal of Small Business and Enterprise Development*, 20(1), pp.28–54.

Bacon, N., Ackers, P., Storey, J., and Coates, D. 1996. It's a small world: managing human resources in small businesses. *The International Journal of Human Resource Management*, 7(1), pp.82–100.

Beechler, S., and Woodward, I. C. 2009. The global war for talent. *Journal of International Management*, 15(3), pp.273–85.

Brown, K., Burgess, J., Festing, M., and Royer, S., eds. 2010. *Value adding webs and clusters—concepts and cases*. München and Mering: Rainer Hampp Verlag.

Brown, K., Burgess, J., Festing, M., and Royer et al. 2007. The value adding web—a conceptual framework of competitive advantage realisation in clusters. *Working Paper No. 27*. Berlin: ESCP-EAP Europäische Wirtschaftshochschule Berlin.

Brown, K., Burgess, J., Festing, M., and Royer, S. et al. 2008. Single firms and competitive advantage in clusters—context analysis identifying the embeddedness of a winery in the Hunter Valley. In M. Festing and S. Royer, eds., *Current issues in international human resource management and strategy research*, pp.157–78. München and Mering: Rainer Hampp Verlag.

Cappelli, P. 2008. Talent management for the twenty-first century. *Harvard Business Review*, 86(3), pp.74–83.

Cappelli, P. 2010. The rise and decline of managerial development. *Industrial and Corporate Change*, 19(2), pp.509–48.

Cappelli, P., and Keller, JR. 2014. Talent management: conceptual approaches and practical challenges. *Annual Review of Organizational Psychology and Organizational Behavior*, 1(1), pp.305–31.

Cardon, M. S., and Stevens, C. E. 2004. Managing human resources in small organizations: what do we know? *Human Ressource Management Review*, 14(3), pp.295–323.

Carlson, D. S., Upton, N., and Seaman, S. 2006. The impact of human resource practices and compensation design on performance: an analysis of family-owned SMEs. *Journal of Small Business Management*, 44(4), pp.531–43.

Cassell, C., Nadin, S., Gray, M., and Clegg, C. 2002. Exploring human resource management practices in small and medium sized enterprises. *Personnel Review*, 31(6), pp.671–92.

Chambers, E. G., Foulon, M., Handfield-Jones, H., Hankin, S. M. et al. 1998. The war for talent. *McKinsey Quarterly*, 1(3), pp.44–57.

CIPD. 2007. Annual survey report 2007: recruitment, retention and turnover. CIPD, London.

Collings, D. G. 2014. Integrating global mobility and global talent management: exploring the challenges and strategic opportunities. *Journal of World Business*, 49(2), pp.253–61.

Collings, D. G., and Mellahi, K. 2009. Strategic talent management: a review and research agenda. *Human Resource Management Review*, 19(4), pp.304–13.

Conaty, B., and Charan, R. 2010. *The talent masters: why smart leaders put people before numbers*. London: Random House Business.

De Kok, J. M., Uhlaner, L. M., and Thurik, A. R. 2006. Professional HRM practices in family owned-managed enterprises. *Journal of Small Business Management*, 44(3), pp.441–60.

Dries, N. 2013. The psychology of talent management: a review and research agenda. *Human Resource Management Review*, 23(4), pp.272–85.

Dundon, T., and Wilkinson, A. 2009. HRM in small and medium-sized enterprises (SMEs). In D. G. Collings and G. Wood, eds., *Human resource management: a critical approach*, pp.130–47. London: Routledge.

Edwards, P., and Ram, M. 2009. HRM in small firms: respecting and regulating informality. In *The Sage handbook of human resource management*, pp.524–40. London: Sage.

Epie, C. 2014. Improving talent retention in an SME in the Nigerian environment. *International Journal of Employment Studies*, 22(1), pp.60–76.

European Commission. 2005. *The new SME definition: user guide and model declaration*. Office for Official Publications of the European Communities. http://ec.europa.eu/growth/smes/business-friendly-environment/sme-definition_en.

Festing, M. 2007. Globalisation of SMEs and implications for international human resource management research and practice. *International Journal of Globalisation and Small Business*, 2(1), pp.5–18.

Festing, M., and Schäfer, L. 2013. Value creation through human resource management and talent management. In K. Brown, J. Burgess, M. Festing, and S. Royer, eds., *Resources and competitive advantage in clusters*, pp.170–89. Munich and Mering: Rainer Hampp Verlag.

Festing, M., and Schäfer, L. 2014. Generational challenges to talent management: a framework for talent retention based on the psychological-contract perspective. *Talent Management*, 49(2), pp.262–71.

Festing, M., Schäfer, L., Massmann, J., and Englisch, P. 2012. Mit vereinten Kräften. *Personalwirtschaft*, 2, pp.52–4.

Festing, M., Schäfer, L., and Scullion, H. 2013. Talent management in medium-sized german companies: an explorative study and agenda for future research. *The International Journal of Human Resource Management*, 24(9), pp.1872–93.

Gallardo-Gallardo, E., Nijs, S., Dries, N., and Gallo, P. 2015. Towards an understanding of talent management as a phenomenon-driven field using bibliometric and content analysis. *Human Resource Management Review*, 25(3), pp.264–79.

Hausknecht, J. 2017. Talent turnover. In D. G. Collings, K. Mellahi, and W. F. Cascio, eds., *Oxford handbook of talent mangement*. Oxford: Oxford University Press.

Heneman, H. G., and Berkley, R. A. 1999. Applicant attraction practices and outcomes among small businesses. *Journal of Small Business Management*, 37(1), pp.53–74.

Heneman, R. L., Tansky, J. W., and Camp, S. M. 2000. Human resource management practices in small and medium-sized enterprises: unanswered questions and future research perspectives. *Entrepreneurship: Theory and Practice*, 25(1), pp.11–26.

Hom, P. W., Mitchell, T. R., Lee, T. W., and Griffeth, R. W. 2012. Reviewing employee turnover: focusing on proximal withdrawal states and an expanded criterion. *Psychological Bulletin*, 138(5), pp.831–58.

Hudson, M., Smart, A., and Bourne, M. 2001. Theory and practice in SME performance measurement systems. *International Journal of Operations and Production Management*, 21(8), pp.1096–115.

IfM Bonn. 2016. *Mittelstandsdefinition des IfM Bonn*. www.ifm-bonn.org/definitionen/mittelstandsdefinition-des-ifm-bonn/.

Iles, P., Chuai, X., and Preece, D. 2010. Talent management and HRM in multinational companies in Beijing: definitions, differences and drivers. *Journal of World Business*, 45(2), pp.179–89.

ILO. 2009. Global employment trends, January 2009. Geneva, Switzerland: International Labour Office.

Kabst, R., Wehner, M. C., Meifert, M., and Kötter, P. M. 2009. *Personalmanagement im internationalen Vergleich. Ergebnisbericht der siebten Erhebung des Cranfield Project on International Human Resource Management (Cranet)*. Giessen: Justus-Liebig-Universität Giessen.

Kaur, P., Sharma, S., Kaur, J., and Sharma, S. K. 2015. Using social media for employer branding and talent management: an experiential study. *IUP Journal of Brand Management*, 12(2), pp.7–20.

Kinnie, N., Purcell, J., Hutchinson, S., Terry, M. et al. 1999. Employment relations in SMEs: market-driven or customer-shaped? *Employee Relations*, 21(3), pp.218–36.

Klaas, B. S., McClendon, J., and Gainey, T. W. 2000. Managing HR in the small and medium enterprise: the impact of professional employer organizations. *Entrepreneurship: Theory and Practice*, 25(1), pp.107–24.

Kühlmann, T. M. 2000. Internationalisierung des Mittelstands als Herausforderung für die Personalauswahl und-entwicklung. In J. Gutmann and R. Kabst, eds., *Internationalisierung im Mittelstand. Chancen, Risiken, Erfolgsfaktoren*, pp.357–71. Wiesbaden: Springer.

Lewis, R. E., and Heckman, R. J. 2006. Talent management: a critical review. *The New World of Work and Organizations*, 16(2), pp.139–54.

McDonnell, A., and Collings, D. G. 2011. The Identification and evaluation of talent in MNEs. In H. Scullion and D. G. Collings, eds., *Global talent management*, pp.56–73. London: Routledge.

Meyers, M. C., and Van Woerkom, M. 2014. The influence of underlying philosophies on talent management: theory, implications for practice, and research agenda. *Talent Management*, 49(2), pp.192–203.

OECD. 2015. Taxation of SMEs in OECD and G20 countries. *OECD Tax Policy Studies No. 23.* Paris: OECD Publishing. DOI: 10.1787/9789264243507-en.

OstWestfalenLippe Marketing GmbH. 2016. *Intelligente Technische Systeme OstWestfalenLippe.* http://www.its-owl.de/home/.

Picot, A., Dietl, H., and Franck, E. 2008. *Organisation: Eine ökonomische Perspektive*, 5th edn. Stuttgart: Schäffer-Poeschel Verlag.

Raby, S. O., and Gilman, M. W. 2012. Human resource management in small to medium-sized enterprises. In R. Kramar and J. Syed, eds., *Human resource management in a global context. a critical approach*. pp.424–55. Basingstoke: Palgrave MacMillan.

Schuler, R. S., Jackson, S. E., and Tarique, I. 2011. Global talent management and global talent challenges: strategic opportunities for IHRM. *Journal of World Business*, 46(4), pp.506–16.

Scullion, H., and Brewster, C. 2002. The management of expatriates: messages from Europe? *Journal of World Business*, 36(4), pp.346–65.

Skuza, A., McDonnell, A., and Scullion, H. 2015. Talent management in the emerging markets. In F. Horwitz and P. Budhwar, eds., *Handbook of human resource management in emerging markets*, pp.225–43. Cheltenham: Edward Elgar.

Sparrow, P., and Makram, H. 2015. What is the value of talent management? Building value-driven processes within a talent management architecture. *Human Resource Management Review*, 25(3), pp.249–63.

Sparrow, P., Scullion, H., and Tarique, I. 2014. *Strategic talent management: contemporary issues in international context*. Cambridge: Cambridge University Press.

Stahl, G., Björkman, I., Farndale, E., Morris, S. et al. 2007. *Global talent management: how leading multinationals build and sustain their talent pipeline*. INSEAD faculty and research Working Papers 24, Fontainebleau.

Storey, D. J. 1994. *Understanding the small business sector*. London: Routledge.

Storey, D. J., Saridakis, G., Sen-Gupta, S., Edwards, P. K. et al. 2010. Linking HR formality with employee job quality: the role of firm and workplace size. *Human Resource Management*, 49(2), pp.305–29.

Strack, R. 2014. *Creating people advantage: how to set up great HR functions: connect, prioritize, impact.* Boston: The Boston Consulting Group, Inc.

Thompson, J. D. 1967. *Organizations in action.* New York: Mc Graw-Hill.

Thunnissen, M., Boselie, P., and Fruytier, B. 2013. Talent management and the relevance of context: towards a pluralistic approach. *Human Resource Management Review,* 23(4), pp.326–36.

Vaiman, V., Scullion, H., and Collings, D. G. 2012. Talent management decision making. *Management Decision,* 50(5), pp.925–41.

Valverde, M., Scullion, H., and Ryan, G. 2013. Talent management in Spanish medium-sized organisations. *International Journal of Human Resource Management,* 24(9), pp.1832–52.

Wilkinson, A. 1999. Employment relations in SMEs. *Employee Relations,* 21(3), pp.206–17.

Williamson, I. O. 2000. Employer legitimacy and recruitment success in small businesses. *Entrepreneurship Theory and Practice,* 25(1), pp.27–42.

CHAPTER 26

TALENT MANAGEMENT OF NONSTANDARD EMPLOYEES

WAYNE F. CASCIO AND JOHN W. BOUDREAU

MORE and more workers are operating outside the traditional confines of regular, full-time employment. They may be "free agents" or "e-lancers" (i.e., freelancers in the digital world) who work for themselves, or they may be employees of an organization a firm is allied with, employees of an outsourcing or temporary-help firm, or even volunteers. Last year, almost 18 million people toiled as nonstandard workers for 15 hours or more a week (Bensinger, 2015). Software maker Intuit estimates that 40% of the American workforce will be nonstandard workers by 2020 (Sveen, 2015). It is already happening now in a number of industries. For example, 90% of the hands-on crew in an offshore oil-exploration project work for contractors (Barrett and Elgin, 2015). On any given day, experts estimate, as much as 24% of the American workforce may be nonstandard workers (Pofeldt, 2015), and this number excludes the 16.2% whom the US Government Accountability Office categorizes as "standard part-time workers."

Nonstandard workers are appearing in an increasingly broad range of work—not just low-level clerical tasks, but also managerial and professional work. You can find LinkedIn freelance profiles for directors of marketing communications and freelance CEO, CFO, and COO jobs on Indeed.com. Nonstandard workers may be less costly than their regular full-time counterparts, especially since they typically are not eligible for benefits. Nonstandard work allows the workforce to expand or contract faster when demand is volatile (Davis-Blake and Uzzi, 1993). Nonstandard work allows organizations to tailor the skill sets they need without hiring and firing full-time employees.

Two factors combine to make nonstandard work more feasible for organizations and workers. The first is technology. Internet-based communication tools, including collaborative workspaces and the opportunity for remote monitoring by companies, make nonstandard work attractive to individuals, as well as organizations (Cascio and Montealegre, 2016). Second, creativity and problem-solving skills play critically important roles in production and value creation in today's knowledge-based economy, and those can originate either inside or outside organizational boundaries. For certain specialized skills, the best way to obtain and keep them current is a freelance or nonstandard work ecosystem (Boudreau, Jesuthasan, and Creelman, 2015; Meyer, Somaya, and Williamson, 2012).

These factors have combined to create a virtuous circle. That is, the more nonstandard work exists as a model of how to do work and to conduct a career over a lifetime, the more legitimate it becomes as a work form and life pattern. The more legitimate it becomes, the more firms and employees will choose to engage in it (Ashford, George, and Blatt, 2007; Boudreau, Jesuthasan, and Creelman, 2015).

At the same time, there are risks associated with nonstandard workers. Will they be as committed as full-timers? Will their rapid turnover require extensive orientation and training of new workers? Will they stick around long enough to develop the kind of depth of understanding of people and operations that will enable them to contribute meaningfully? Can work arrangements appropriately protect workers and balance worker and organizational rights and needs?

Ashford, George, and Blatt (2007) correctly noted that nonstandard work is a topic worthy of studying on its own, and it is an ideal context for testing and developing theory about organizations, work, and workers. What is the pattern of research on nonstandard work and what are its implications? This chapter offers a review of research on nonstandard work through the lens of the talent-management lifecycle. We set out to map existing research, to discover where research has been plentiful and sparse, whether research frameworks applied to nonstandard work are similar to those applied to traditional, regular full-time employment, and the implications for future research.

We begin by defining nonstandard workers and explaining the various categories that make up this segment of the workforce. Section 26.2 addresses why and when organizations choose to use nonstandard workers, as illustrated by several well-known companies' decisions to use them. Section 26.3 describes the stages and the objectives of the talent lifecycle. Section 26.4 maps the talent-lifecycle stages and objectives against several categories of nonstandard work, and the distribution of research attention across that map. Analyzing that distribution reveals large areas of very sparse research, as well as two significant clusters of research. One focuses on more traditional arrangements (contractors, temporary, and outsourced work), and the other on less traditional arrangements (freelance platforms and crowdsourcing). Section 26.5 delves more deeply into these two clusters, revealing striking differences in their respective research questions, theoretical frameworks, and disciplinary foundations. Our final section, 26.6, offers questions and opportunities for future research, to deepen our understanding of this growing phenomenon.

26.1 DEFINITION AND TYPES OF NONSTANDARD WORKERS

Ashford, George, and Blatt (2007) defined *nonstandard workers* as "something other" than standard workers—those who work on a fixed schedule, at the employer's place of business, under the employer's control, and with mutual expectations of continued employment. Ashford, George, and Blatt (2007) excluded part-time workers because some expect employment continuity, while others do not. In this chapter, we include part-timers, and we note when research identified those with expectations of continuous employment.

Pfeffer and Baron (1988) described three dimensions of attachment between workers and organizations: The degree of physical proximity between employer and employee; the extent of administrative control that the employer exerts; and the expected duration of employment. Table 26.1 shows these three types of attachment, and various categories of nonstandard work that describe each one.

In Table 26.1, PEOs are professional employer associations. A PEO enables an organization to outsource the management of HR, employee benefits, payroll, and workers' compensation. That is, both the PEO and client company have an employment relationship with the worker. They share and allocate responsibilities and liabilities for compliance with employment laws (National Association of Professional Employer Associations, 2015).

Table 26.1 Three Types of Attachment and Types of Nonstandard Work that Describe Each One

Dimension	Temporal attachment	Administrative attachment	Physical attachment
Definition	Extent to which workers expect employment to last over the long term	Extent to which workers are under the organization's administrative control	Extent to which workers are physically proximate to the organization
Examples	Temporary workers PEOs Volunteers Borrow Loan	Contract workers Outsourcers Virtual workers Talent platform Crowdsource	Teleworkers Part-time* Flexitime

* Assumes part-time workers are part of a secondary labor market, work limited hours, and have no expectations of long-term employment.

26.2 Why Organizations Choose Nonstandard Workers

Should you "build" or "buy" the capabilities your organization needs to get work done? What about borrowing employees from another organization or soliciting volunteers? When should you use each alternative? Leaders who choose to "build" hire full-time employees, often for strategically important jobs. Then they offer them many opportunities for development, formal as well as informal, on the job, to develop the kinds of knowledge, skills, abilities, and other characteristics that their organizations need to get work done. Their time horizon is long and assumes that these employees will remain with the organization, typically for three to five years. Leaders do this for two key reasons: to ensure that high-value talent is readily available and to protect that talent from competitors. Other ways to get work done, especially when it needs to be done in a shorter period, include borrowing workers, seeking volunteers, or hiring contract workers who already have the kinds of capabilities the organization needs.

Theory can help guide these decisions. Traditionally, work was performed inside the boundaries of an organization. Those boundaries may be horizontal (defined by the scope of products and markets) or vertical (defined by the scope of activities undertaken in the industry value chain) (Santos and Eisenhardt, 2005). The same authors identified four distinct conceptions of boundaries: efficiency, power, competence, and identity. Each deals with a fundamental organizational issue—cost (efficiency), autonomy (power), growth (competence), and coherence (identity). As work flows across boundaries that are more permeable, it has implications for each of these issues.

The most dominant conception of organizational boundaries is cost (efficiency), whether a transaction (e.g., a task or project) should be conducted inside the organization or outside through a market exchange. Transaction-cost economics (Coase, 1993) argues that boundaries should be set at the point that minimizes the cost of governing activities. However, in the contexts of bounded rationality and exchange uncertainty, the precise terms of transactions are costly to define, monitor, and enforce, leading to incomplete contracts.

Alternatively, the competence conception of boundaries views the organization as a unique bundle of resources, and asks what resources the organization should possess. In less dynamic environments, organizations tend to become configurations of deeply entwined resources, such as in "lean manufacturing" (Prahalad and Hamel, 1990). In moderately dynamic environments, resources are often more loosely coupled. For example, a study of US medical firms (Karim and Mitchell, 2000) revealed that managers use acquisitions to alter horizontal boundaries. Finally, in high-velocity environments, characterized by ambiguity, nonlinear turbulence, and fast pace, the underlying strategic logic shifts further from leveraging existing resources to seizing opportunities using novel combinations of new and existing resources. As noted by the CEO of Philips, "We used to start by identifying our core competencies and then looking for market opportunities. Now we ask what is required to capture an opportunity, and then either try to get those skills via alliances or develop them internally to fit" (Struggling with a supertanker, 2002).

As the environment becomes increasingly volatile and uncertain (high-velocity), alternatives beyond alliances have emerged, such as outsourcing, crowdsourcing, using independent contractors or talent platforms, professional employer organizations, and even borrowing employees from another firm (Boudreau, Jesuthasan, and Creelman, 2015). These go well beyond simple "build or buy" decisions that have typically been the focus of theory and research. Consider the business model that Apple (and, more recently, Google) has forged with application developers. Hundreds of thousands of applications exist for the iPhone, iPad, and Android operating systems. The developers of those "apps" do not work for Apple, nor Google, nor a phone manufacturer. In another example, Apple collaborated with Visa to develop the Apple Pay payment system (Boudreau, Jesuthasan, and Creelman, 2015). The partnership required that Visa and Apple combine their respective engineers into a project team and that they share detailed proprietary elements of each other's products and systems, because that was necessary for the team to have the necessary insights to create the combined Apple Pay system. Apple developed a similar partnership with IBM, combining Apple's capability in product design with IBM's expertise and relationships for building enterprise systems. Boudreau and co-authors (2015) also described how Siemens invented a pediatric hearing aid and forged a partnership with the Walt Disney Corporation, through which Disney marketing employees developed the storybooks, character-themed packaging, and displays for physicians' offices, to help market the hearing aid.

This implies that the discourse must evolve from the optimal way to minimize the costs of transactions to creating and maintaining the optimal resource portfolio for superior profitability and growth.

Decisions to acquire talent outside the traditional boundaries of an organization are typically based on considerations such as cost (efficiency) and opportunities for growth (by increasing competence) to pursue new market opportunities. If an organization does decide to move outside its traditional boundaries to acquire talent, there are numerous alternative channels for doing that, such as outsourcing, crowdsourcing, independent contractors, talent platforms, borrowing employees from other organizations, or even seeking volunteers. Such decisions have potentially significant implications for every element of talent management, such as sourcing, rewarding, developing, and engaging workers. So, we next define the *talent lifecycle* and its objectives, as one foundation for mapping and interpreting research.

26.3 THE TALENT LIFECYCLE

The effects of nonstandard work on the HR discipline and HR functions are complex, so it's helpful to use a familiar frame: the *talent lifecycle*. The talent lifecycle describes HR processes as a series of employment life stages, beginning when a person enters an organization, capturing his or her experiences as he or she encounters its rewards and development opportunities, and finally ending when the person separates from the organization. Figure 26.1 depicts the talent lifecycle graphically.

Typical names of the stages of the talent lifecycle are shown in the outer circle. The cycle starts with "planning," through which an organization estimates the current and future supply of workers and demands for work. It develops strategies and tactics to match projected demand to projected supply. "Attracting and sourcing" identifies the sources from which workers are drawn, as well as the activities to attract workers to engage with the work. "Selecting" involves choices and decisions regarding which of the willing workers will be matched with specific work to be done. "Deploying" moves a worker through different work experiences, locations, and assignments over time. "Developing" builds the capacity of workers through experiences, such as training, experiential learning, and challenges. "Rewarding" conveys an array of benefits to workers through explicit exchange or through implicit experiences via the work itself. Finally, "separating" ends a relationship between a worker and a particular work assignment or experience.

FIGURE 26.1. Talent Lifecycle and Objectives

Adapted from Boudreau, J. W., Jesuthasan, R., and Creelman, D. 2015. *Lead the work*. Hoboken, NJ: Wiley.

Traditionally, the lifecycle is expressed in terms of entry, movement within, and movement out of a particular organization, and it is shown in terms of a series of jobs contained within that organization. It is often called the "employment lifecycle," and it begins when a person joins and ends when a person leaves a particular organization. We have been careful here to avoid referring to a single organization and its jobs. As we shall see, if we use the words *work* and *worker* instead of *organization, job*, or *employee*, this familiar model can become a powerful organizing metaphor for a world beyond employment. The idea is that all of these lifecycle stages still occur, but not necessarily within the boundary of a single employer and not necessarily through work experiences organized as jobs.

The middle of the circle includes a set of broad outcomes or objectives of the employment lifecycle. Here, we have included engagement, leadership, diversity, performance, and culture. *Engagement* refers to employee commitment, loyalty, identity, passion, and satisfaction with their relationship with the organization. *Leadership* refers to setting a vision and values, inspiring followers, and communicating a strategy and mission. *Diversity* refers to an environment that is inclusive of differences, encourages disparate perspectives, and allows interactions among those with different demographic, lifestyle, professional, and cultural backgrounds. *Performance* refers to the results produced by individuals and groups, as well as the systems that evaluate, communicate, and track those results. *Culture* refers to the often unstated beliefs, norms, values, and customs of the work. Again, these are traditionally framed to focus on a particular organization, with terms such as *employee engagement, job performance, company culture*, or *top [name of the company] leadership*. Once more, we have been careful to frame these ideas in terms of the work and the worker, so that they can encompass not only traditional employment but also a world beyond traditional employment.

26.4 HOW DOES RESEARCH ON NONSTANDARD WORK MAP AGAINST THE TALENT-MANAGEMENT LIFECYCLE ACTIVITIES AND OBJECTIVES?

Now that we have established the definitions of nonstandard work categories and the talent-lifecycle stages and objectives, it is possible to combine the two frameworks to map the research literature on nonstandard work. Our objective is to identify how comprehensively the intersections have been addressed, and to describe where research attention has been plentiful versus sparse.

26.4.1 Methodology

We undertook a literature search for studies addressing nonstandard work. We included in our search the following nonstandard work arrangements:

- Independent contractor
- Outsourcing and temporary-help agency
- Part-time employment
- Professional employment organizations (PEOs)
- Freelance platforms
- Crowdsourcing
- Volunteers
- Borrowing employees from another organization
- Loaning employees to another organization

The ordering of these arrangements is not random. We have attempted to place them in order starting with nonstandard arrangements that have been used for a longer time, and thus are likely better known to organizations and workers, progressing toward arrangements that are newer and perhaps less known to organizations and workers. In addition, the work arrangements of freelance platforms, crowdsourcing, and volunteers (e.g., gamers) are often enabled by cloud-based social technology, a relatively newer development compared with the more traditional approaches at the top of the list.

We coded each article by the type of nonstandard work it addressed and by the following elements of the talent lifecycle, beginning with the elements in Figure 26.1 and then expanding them to reflect other significant HR activities found in the literature. This produced the following talent-lifecycle elements:

- Plan
- Attract
- Source
- Select
- Onboard
- Train
- Deploy
- Appraise
- Goal Set
- Develop
- Reward
- Separate
- Rehire

We also coded the articles according to the HR outcomes they addressed, beginning with those in Figure 26.1 and then expanding them as we discovered the most frequent topics in the literature, to include these outcomes:

- Engagement
- Leadership
- Diversity
- Performance
- Culture
- Compliance
- Cost
- Risk

We completed the literature search during the period September 1–16, 2015, using the database ABI/INFORM Complete. We included only articles containing certain keywords in the abstract and that were from peer-reviewed, scholarly journals. The keywords included *free-agent, contract work, borrowed employees, freelance work, non-traditional employment, non-employee worker, trades and tours of duty, deconstructed work, talent trades, piecework rewards, labor market intermediaries, PEOs, temporary work, temporary work agency, temporary-help service, outplacement services, creative collaboration, crowdsourcing, open innovation, knowledge sharing, recognition awards, dual-incentive structure, contingent work or labor,* and *idiosyncratic deals.* We refined the resulting literature further to include only those articles that addressed the relationships between non-traditional work arrangements and HR management practices and outcomes. Our search uncovered 291 articles.

We assigned a number to each article, and we entered its number in the cells of a matrix with HR lifecycle stages and objectives as rows and work types as columns. We assigned each article to one or more cells if it addressed any of the lifecycle and objective categories.

26.4.2 Results

Table 26.2 shows the frequency with which we coded articles into each of the cells representing the intersection of a talent-lifecycle element or objective in the rows, and a type of nonstandard work in the columns. Note that we counted articles multiple times if the same article addressed multiple lifecycle elements or multiple nonstandard work arrangements.

Looking at the totals at the bottom of the table, by far the greatest attention to the HR implications of nonstandard work has been devoted to the more traditional nonstandard work arrangements of outsourcing, temporary-help agencies, and part-time workers. This is followed by moderate levels of attention to PEOs, freelance platforms, and

Table 26.2 Frequency of Articles Addressing Combinations of Nonstandard Work and Talent–Lifecycle Elements

	Independent Contractor	Outsourcer/ Temporary Agency	Part-Time	PEO	Freelance Platform	Crowdsource	Volunteer	Borrow	Loan	Total
Talent-Management Lifecycle										
Plan	29	53	17	5	4	3	0	0	0	117
Attract	2	5	2	0	3	4	0	0	0	18
Source	6	15	2	2	8	9	0	0	0	45
Select	9	16	5	0	4	4	0	0	0	44
Onboard	1	2	1	0	1	1	0	0	0	6
Train	11	27	8	0	0	0	0	0	0	51
Deploy	3	7	1	0	1	1	0	0	0	16
Appraise	4	3	1	1	2	1	0	0	0	14
Goal Set	2	2	1	0	1	2	0	0	0	10
Develop	20	26	8	2	0	0	0	0	0	65
Reward	20	30	15	3	3	3	0	1	2	84
Separate	8	17	9	0	0	0	0	0	0	35
Rehire	1	1	1	0	0	0	0	0	0	3

(continued)

Table 26.2 Continued

Talent-Management Objectives	Independent Contractor	Outsourcer/ Temporary Agency	Part-Time	PEO	Freelance Platform	Crowdsource	Volunteer	Borrow	Loan	Total
Engagement	53	101	33	7	5	7	0	1	2	209
Leadership	6	11	4	3	2	3	0	1	1	31
Diversity	3	7	4	0	2	0	0	0	0	16
Performance	11	30	9	2	4	6	0	1	1	64
Culture	3	9	1	1	1	1	0	0	0	16
Compliance	12	21	4	4	1	1	0	1	1	45
Cost	19	38	7	4	0	0	0	1	1	70
Risk	11	20	2	1	0	0	0	0	0	34
Totals	234	441	135	35	42	46	0	7	10	

crowdsourced work. Very few studies attend to volunteers or borrowing and loaning employees between organizations.

Looking at the totals on the right, the most studied element is the engagement objective. Other objectives that appeared frequently were performance and cost. Least addressed talent outcomes were diversity and culture. Among the lifecycle activities, planning is by far the most frequently studied, whereas rewarding, developing, and training were addressed moderately frequently. Least addressed HR activities were onboarding, rehiring, and goal setting.

One conclusion from the pattern of results is that there is ample opportunity to extend research attention to work arrangements outside of contractor and outsource/temporary, and to talent-management elements beyond engagement. Why might there be such a preponderance of research in the first two columns? It may be that research reflects the temporal emergence of nonstandard work arrangements, with the more traditional arrangements on the left being far more frequently addressed. We may see additional research devoted to the work arrangements on the right of the table, as they are used over a longer time, and experience with them reveals data sources and interesting research questions.

Why the preponderance of attention to engagement? As we shall see, much of the engagement-focused research reflects an interest in determining whether nonstandard workers have similar attitudes on topics such as work satisfaction, commitment, and motivation. This research often proceeded from a hypothesis that nonstandard work may be exploitative, and thus produce less positive worker attitudes and responses. This reflects significant social and legal attention to the dangers of worker exploitation, particularly during the mid- to late-twentieth century, when many of these arrangements became more widespread. A similar logic may explain the large number of studies that addressed the outcomes of compliance and cost, again largely concentrated in the nonstandard arrangements of independent contractor and outsourced/temporary work. Research in these areas also reflected social interest and concern about whether such new arrangements actually reduced labor costs and how they might create a danger of noncompliance with existing labor legislation, perhaps because they were the first nonstandard arrangements to emerge as alternatives to standard work. For decades, fulltime, in-house employment was the presumed way that work was done, and that was reflected in existing legislation, cost estimates, and planning models. Thus, research tended to apply frameworks developed for standard work, and examined the earliest forms of nonstandard work through the lenses typically used to describe and regulate standard work.

Yet, these same issues of engagement, cost, and compliance are equally applicable to nonstandard work arrangements that have emerged more recently, including freelance platforms and crowdsourcing. Have they received the same emphasis? Table 26.2 shows that among the talent-management objectives studied, when it comes to these two nonstandard work arrangements, engagement revealed the highest cell counts. Yet, the performance row reveals the same amount of research attention as engagement for these two work arrangements. This is in sharp contrast to the work arrangements of independent contractor, outsourced/temporary, and part-time, where attention to performance appears far less often than engagement. Moreover, in the columns for freelance platforms and crowdsourcing, the number of references that dealt with compliance and cost are very few or none.

It thus appears from Table 26.2 that there may be a fundamental difference in the research on the nonstandard work arrangements on the left, which emerged earlier, and those on the right, which emerged more recently. This may also be due, in part, to the disciplinary foundations of the scholars in each area. Scholars studying contractors and outsourced work bring backgrounds in human resources, labor relations, labor economics, and industrial psychology, and the citations reflect this. Scholars studying freelance platforms and crowdsourcing bring backgrounds in organizational design, group processes, and operations management. Thus, the unit of analysis, important conceptual connections, and independent and dependent variables, differ significantly.

Because a comprehensive treatment of all the cells in Table 26.2 is beyond the scope of this chapter, we decided to conduct an illustrative examination of the cells were most populated, at the same time providing clues to the differences in how researchers have addressed the nonstandard work arrangements. Specifically, we decided to focus on studies that were coded as relevant to the engagement and performance rows of Table 26.2. One group represents early emerging, nonstandard work arrangements: independent contractor and outsourced/temporary. The contrasting group represents more recent nonstandard work arrangements: freelance platform and crowdsource. Focusing on these cells allowed us to capture the area of the greatest attention (engagement of independent contractors and outsourced/temporary workers), and to contrast it with the newer work arrangements, in the areas that have received the most attention. Our next section describes studies that reveal some important gaps in each type of research, and important lessons that each category of research can learn from the other.

26.5 Comparing Research on Traditional (Contractors and Temporary/Outsourced) versus less Traditional (Freelance Platforms and Crowdsourced) Nonstandard Work

Our review unearthed fundamental and consistent differences between research that addressed contractors and temporary/outsourced work versus freelance platforms and crowdsourced work. We can see this quite vividly when we look at how research on each category of nonstandard work addressed the outcomes of engagement and performance.

Overall, the two categories of research emanate from very different conceptual bases. Research on more traditional forms of nonstandard work (contractors and temporary/ outsourced work) focus on cognitive and attitudinal reactions of the workers, often compared with regular full-time workers. In contrast, research on the less traditional forms of nonstandard work (freelance platforms and crowdsourcing) is more often framed in terms of the process steps or the particular outcomes of the process, rather than the cognitive or behavioral experiences, attitudes, or actions of individuals. For example, when incentives for performance are examined with regard to outsourced and contract workers, the theory base often draws on psychological and behavioral theories of rewards. When incentives are examined with regard to freelance and crowdsourced work, the focus is on the differential effect of incentives on the sorts of ideas, comments, and insights produced by the group as a whole. The individual cognitive and behavioral responses to incentives are implicit in research on crowdsourcing and freelance platforms, while such responses are often the focus in research on outsourced or contractor arrangements. In contrast, research on contractors and outsourced work frequently leaves implicit the question of the work processes and outcomes. Indeed, researchers studying contractors and outsourced work often control for the work processes by ensuring that all the subjects are doing the same tasks, even to the point of having standard workers working in close physical proximity with nonstandard workers. We have illustrated this in Tables 26.3 and 26.4, which contrast the two types of nonstandard work, focusing on those that used employee engagement and/or performance as a dependent variable. Table 26.3 reveals a variety of theories or research frameworks that have been used to investigate more traditional nonstandard work arrangements, such as independent contractors, outsourcers, and temporary-help agencies, as related to the objectives of engagement or performance. We refer to these types of work arrangements as Category 1. Table 26.4 shows research frameworks applied to two newer types of nonstandard work arrangements—freelance platforms and crowdsourcing—as related to the objectives of engagement or performance. We refer to these types of work arrangements as Category 2.

The difference in theories and research frameworks applied to Categories 1 and 2 is quite striking. For example, research on Category 1 nonstandard work arrangements typically focuses on enhancing individual behaviors. For Category 2 nonstandard work arrangements, in contrast, research typically focuses on enhancing collective outcomes.

The terms *engagement* and *performance* are common to both Tables 26.3 and 26.4, but they seem to be defined and studied quite differently for each category of nonstandard work arrangements. For example, in Category 1, the focus of the studies was primarily on cognition and attitudes, with performance often mentioned only as a potential outcome. When the focus in Category 1 was "engagement," researchers typically studied cognition, health, and attitudes in depth. In contrast, in Category 2, even when the objective was engagement, researchers did not measure it per se, but rather discussed it as a potential explanation for their main focus—outcomes or process. Conversely, when the objective was "performance" for Category 2 workers, performance was a major focus, with very detailed and tangible measurement that often included nuances such

Table 26.3 Representative Theories or Research Frameworks Applied to Independent Contractors, Outsourcers, and Temporary–Help Agencies

Framework	Objective*	Representative citations
Social-Exchange	E/P	Ang, Van Dyne, and Begley (2003); Chambel and Sobral (2011)
Career Theories	E/P	De Cuyper, De Witte, and Van Emmerik (2011); Mallon (1998); Mirvis and Hall (1994); Peel and Inkson (2004); Zeitz, Blau, and Fertig (2009)
Organizational Justice (procedural, distributive, interpersonal, and informational)	E/P	Ang, Van Dyne, and Begley (2003); Collinson (1999); Feldman, Doerpinghaus, and Turnley (1994); McAllister (1998); Rogers and Henson (1997)
Psychological Contract	E/P	Chambel and Castanheira (2006); George (2003); Guest (2004); Ho, Ang, and Strau (2003); Lapalme, Simard, and Tremblay (2011); McDonald and Makin (2000); Millward and Brewerton (1999)
Organizational Citizenship	E	Broschak and Davis-Blake (2006); Chiu, Lin, and Han (2015); Moorman and Harland (2002); Uzzi and Barsness (1998); Van Dyne and Ang (1998); Wheeler and Buckley (2001)
Role Theory	E	Broschak and Davis-Blake (2006); Ho, Ang, and Strau (2003); Krausz, Brandwein, and Fox (1995); Parker, Griffin, Sprigg, and Wall (2002); Sverke, Gallagher, and Hellgren (2000)
Commitment	E/P	Beard and Edwards (1995); Boswell et al. (2012); Van Breugel, Van Olffen, and Olie (2005); Chambel and Castanheira (2012); Chambel and Sobral (2011); Clinton, Bernhard-Oetell, Rigotti, and de Jong (2011); Ellingson, Gruys, and Sackett (1998); Feldman (2006); Felfe, Schmook, Schyns, and Six (2008); Gallagher and Sverke (2005); Krausz, Brandwein, and Fox (1995); Pearce (1993)

Framework	Objective*	Representative citations
Work-Family Conflict	E/P	Ang and Slaughter (2001); Gallagher and Parks (2001)
Well-Being	E	Bardasi and Francesconi (2004); Bernhard-Oettel, Sverke, and De Witte (2005); Virtanen et al. (2003)
Employee Voice	E	Davis-Blake and Uzzi (2003)
Volition	E/P	De Jong and Schalk (2010); DiNatale (2001); Ellingson, Gruys, and Sackett (1998); Hardy and Walker (2003); Isaksson and Bellagh (2002); Polivka and Nardone (1989)
Perceived Organizational Support	E/P	Buch, Kuvaas, and Dysvik (2010); Liden, Wayne, Kraimer, and Sparrowe (2003); Chambel and Sobral (2011)
Job Design	E/P	Allan and Sienko (1997); Ang and Slaughter (2001); Pearce (1993)
Training	E/P	Chambel and Sobral (2011); Hanratty (2000); Lowry, Simon, and Kimberley (2002)
Job Satisfaction	E/P	Aletraris (2010); Bardasi and Francesconi (2004); Clinton, Bernhard-Oetell, Rigotti, and de Jong (2011); De Cuyper and De Witte (2006); Ellingson, Gruys, and Sackett (1998); Torka and Schyns (2007); Wilkin (2013)
Social Identity Theory	E	Chattopadhyay and George (2001)
Theory of Majority-Minority Group Relations	E	Broschak and Davis-Blake (2006)
Integration/Trust	E/P	Broschak, Davis-Blake, and Block (2008); Chattopadhyay and George (2001); Davis-Blake, Broschak, and George (2003); de Gilder (2003); Lautsch (2003); Pearce (1993); Yang (2012)
Knowledge Sharing	E/P	Galup, Saunders, Nelson, and Cerveny (1997); Matusik and Hill (1998)

*E = Engagement; P = Performance.

Table 26.4 Research Frameworks Applied to Freelance Platforms and Crowdsourcing

Framework	Objective*	Representative citations
Use of Social Networks to Facilitate Virtual Collaboration	E/P	Garrigos-Simon, Alcami, and Ribera, (2012)
Effects of Technology	E/P	Kane (2014)
Contests to Create Incentives	E/P	Morgan and Wang (2010)
Appropriate Configuration of HR Practices	E/P	Lepak and Snell (2002)
Maximizing Payoffs from Crowdsourcing	E	Prpic, Shukla, Kietzmann, and McCarthy (2015)
Managing Crowds to Enhance Innovation Outcomes	E	Malhotra and Majchrzak (2014)
Generating Innovative Ideas from Innovation Contests	E	Armisen and Majchrzak (2015)
Expectancy Theory to Motivate Effort	E	Sun, Wang, Yin, and Zhang (2015)
Psychological Contracts and Nonstandard Workers	E/P	Parks, Kidder, and Gallagher (1998)
Health Consequences of Contingent Work	E	Quinlan, Mayhew, and Bohle (2001)
Training of Teleworkers	E/P	Solomon and Templer (1993)
Effects of Internet-Based Technologies on Labor	P	Freeman (2002)
Effects of IT-Based Supplier Relationships	P	McDonald and Kotha (2014)
Organizational Learning with Freelance, Crowdsourced Workers	P	Schlagwein and Bjorn-Andersen (2014)

* E = Engagement; P = Performance.

as whether ideas were creative or integrative. What might account for the stark differences in the research shown in Tables 26.3 and 26.4?

Our reading of the literature suggests that this may be because the research on contract and outsourced work emphasizes the issue of whether workers are exploited by such arrangements, relative to more standard employment (regular full-time jobs). For example, Broschak and Davis-Blake used "data collected from workers at two US locations of a large, multinational financial services firm. We selected these two locations because both were responsible for similar activities (payment processing, account reconciliation, and inquiry/complaint handling), and local managers regularly utilized nonstandard workers to supplement the standard workforce" (2006: 380). The concern with comparing standard workers to nonstandard workers is not prominent among researchers studying crowdsourcing and freelance platforms.

The difference may also reflect the distinct disciplinary foundations of the scholars in each area. The unit of analysis, the important conceptual connections, and independent and dependent variables differ significantly. We can illustrate this by comparing a sample of articles that addressed engagement as an outcome, from each category of research. (Space constraints do not allow us to include a similar sampling of the outcome performance.)

26.5.1 Research on Engagement in Freelance Platform and Crowdsourced Work

Malhotra and Majchrzak (2014) provide suggestions for getting innovation contests to generate ideas with greater competitive potential. These include fostering different crowd roles to ensure a diversity of contributions, offering knowledge-integration instructions and incentives, and offering explicit instructions for sharing different knowledge. They focus mainly on the process of generating ideas, invoking few behavioral theories. Morgan and Wang (2010) cite empirical studies about incentives and the construction of idea tournaments, and provide decision trees to help leaders decide how to create them. They mention the "theory of network effects" (phones are not valuable until they exist in a network), returns to non-pecuniary incentives such as reputation, and the concepts of social interactions, secrecy, and arbitrage. Prpic, Shukla, Kietzmann, and McCarthy (2015) focus mainly on the practical issues of creating crowdsource-based contests, and offer some useful frameworks for constructing rewards, participant interactions, sourcing participants, etc. They refer to resource-based theory in discussing how to make crowdsourced information non-replicable, but the frameworks are mostly about the structure of innovation, not behavioral or attitudinal experiences of the workers.

Armisen and Majchrzak (2015) also focus on elements that make innovation contests more effective when an innovative post is made: (a) variety of participant familiarity with the topic; (b) amount of collaboration versus argumentation in the discussion; and (c) whether the poster had previous posts in that discussion before his or her innovative one. Sun, Wang, Yin, and Zhang's is the only article in this cell that actually invokes a behavioral theory. The article uses expectancy theory to examine the effects of reward valence, trust, and self-efficacy, including a nonlinear relationship between self-efficacy and effort and the moderating role of task complexity. The results show that: "(1) reward valence and trust positively influence effort; and (2) when task complexity is high (low), there will be a convex (concave) relationship between self-efficacy and effort" (2015: 267).

26.5.2 Research on Engagement in Contractor and Temporary/Outsourced Work

Now consider a sampling of the articles in the cells of Table 26.2 that intersect the engagement objective with the nonstandard work types of independent contractors and outsourcer/temporary agency. They show that the themes are far more focused on test-ing behavioral theories and on examining the attitudinal and behavioral characteristics of such workers. They often compare those workers to regular, full-time workers who are doing the same job or even working physically with the nonstandard workers.

The review by Connelly and Gallagher (2004) is an excellent illustration of the research on contingent workers and its emphasis on various behavioral, attitudinal, and cognitive responses by those workers. Connelly and Gallagher organize the conclusions of their review according to several key attitudinal and behavioral outcomes. They con-clude that findings about organizational commitment are mixed, and studies of "dual commitment" to the client and to temporary placement firms often find them to be pos-itively correlated. Regarding job satisfaction,

> Within the context of contingent work arrangements, research on satisfaction as well as other attitudinal and behavioral measures has also been closely linked to the issue of volition. Simply stated, positive worker responses to their jobs are closely tied to the extent to which they feel that their choice to work as a contingent was voluntary rather than from the lack of an alternative (e.g., Krausz, Brandwein, and Fox, 1995; Ellingson, Gruys and Sackett, 1998). (2004: 964)

Regarding role ambiguity and conflict, they conclude that "most empirical research shows virtually no evidence of a strong or systematic relationship with status as a contin-gent worker" (e.g., Krausz et al., 1995; Sverke, Gallagher, and Hellgren, 2000). "However, some research on direct-hire temporary workers in the manufacturing sector suggests that contingent workers actually have lower levels of role overload and role conflict in comparison to the permanent employees" (Parker, Griffin, Sprigg, and Wall, 2002: 964). They note that a key moderator between contingent or part-time work and posi-tive work experiences is volition. Individuals who voluntarily choose or prefer such arrangements have more positive experiences and reactions than those who are doing such work because they cannot find permanent employment. They note, "There is evi-dence to suggest that a sizeable majority of contingents working through temporary-staff firms or direct-hire arrangements would prefer permanent employment" (Hardy and Walker, 2003; Isaksson and Bellagh, 2002; Polivka and Nardone, 1989). "In con-trast, it is estimated that only a small minority of all independent contractors are inter-ested in securing more permanent contractual arrangements" (DiNatale, 2001: 965). This is a consistent theme: nonstandard workers are not invariably less satisfied or dis-advantaged compared to permanent workers, and the underlying relationship is more nuanced. A meta-analysis by Wilkin (2013) reached a similar conclusion, finding that results from seventy-two studies (N = 237,856) suggest that contingent workers experi-ence slightly, but statistically significantly, lower job satisfaction compared with perma-nent employees (d = 0.06). However, contingent workers are not homogeneous. Some (e.g., agency workers) experience lower job satisfaction than permanent employees do, but others (e.g., contractors) experience similar job satisfaction compared with perma-nent employees.

Clinton, Bernhard-Oetell, Rigotti, and de Jong (2011) surveyed 1,169 temporary workers in Europe. They found that prior experience as a temporary worker associated positively with individual performance, but it was not associated with job insecurity, job satisfaction, or organizational commitment. Guest's (2004) review reached a similar conclusion, noting that workers on flexible contracts are not invariably disadvantaged, and that knowledge workers pursuing boundaryless careers are especially likely to report positive outcomes. Allan and Sienko (1997) administered the Job Diagnostic Survey of Hackman and Oldham (1980) to 149 permanent and 48 contingent workers doing the same types of jobs in six locations of a large unit of a telecommunications company in various US locations. Results showed contingent workers to have higher motivating potential scores, owing to higher task identity and feedback scores. Contingents also scored higher on knowledge of results and growth-need strength, while permanent employees were higher in satisfaction with job security. Bardasi and Francesconi (2004) examined subjective indicators of mental health, general health status, life satisfaction, and job satisfaction. To do that they compared workers with temporary contracts, part-time workers, and full-time workers, using a panel of 7,000 workers from the first ten waves of the British Household Panel Survey, 1991–2000. They found that, "Controlling for background characteristics, atypical employment does not appear to be associated with adverse health consequences for either men or women" (Bardasi and Francesconi, 2004: 1671).

26.6 CONCLUSIONS AND FUTURE DIRECTIONS

Our review of theories and research frameworks that focus on the domain of nonstandard workers revealed stark differences between the kinds of questions studied with respect to more traditional and more recent nonstandard work arrangements. Research concerned with the former—outsourcing, temporary-help agencies, and part-time workers—tended to address cognition and attitudes. The latter include commitment, job satisfaction, volition, role conflict or role ambiguity, integration, trust, knowledge sharing, perceived organizational support, justice/unfair treatment, psychological contract, well-being, and organizational citizenship behaviors. Research with more recent forms of nonstandard work—freelance platforms and crowdsourcing—tends to emphasize processes or outcomes (use of social networks to enhance virtual collaboration, use of contests to create incentives, maximizing payoffs from crowdsourcing, and generating useful ideas from innovation contests).

Collings (2014) has defined talent management as the management and development of high-performing and high-potential incumbents in critical organizational roles. The term *incumbents* is typically oriented toward traditional, standard employment arrangements, but if we substitute *workers* for *incumbents*, then the definition seems to apply equally well to nonstandard workers. If the focus is on managing and developing high-performing and high-potential workers—whether inside or outside organizational boundaries—then talent management of nonstandard workers is a research topic that is fully appropriate in its own right. The relevant domain is large, and it constitutes a "big tent."

Our review provides several observations that may direct future research. First, Table 26.2 suggests that only a few regions of the map of work arrangements and talent-lifecycle elements are well populated. The cells with small numbers or zeros offer opportunities to extend research in more populated arenas to those with very little attention. In particular, despite the fact that it is clear that nonstandard work arrangements can fundamentally change virtually all talent-management practices and outcomes (Boudreau, Jesuthasan, and Creelman, 2015), only a small amount of research has examined any of the practices through the lens of particular nonstandard work arrangements.

Second, the research on newer forms of nonstandard work (Category 2) may fruitfully draw upon existing research on older forms of such work (Category 1). There is much to learn about the cognitions and attitudes of nonstandard workers in Category 2, yet these questions have gone largely unstudied. Processes and outcomes are undoubtedly important, but scientific disciplines are distinguished not so much by the subject matter they study as by the questions they ask. Social scientists focus on behavior, individual or collective, and the demand for deeper understanding of the behavioral effects of nonstandard employment is strong and continuing.

Third, one can make a symmetrical observation about what research on older forms of nonstandard work (Category 1) might learn from research on newer forms (Category 2). Studies of Category 2 work arrangements demonstrate ways to measure and compare work outcomes and processes under different talent practices, such as rewards and talent sourcing. Research on Category 1 work arrangements (and others) might benefit from incorporating process and outcome variables. For example, Connelly and Gallagher (2004) suggested that supervisors may narrow the scope of the tasks assigned to contingent workers. Doing so limits their jobs, but positively affects their job attitudes. We know very little about whether the work processes and assignments of nonstandard workers vary from those of standard workers, and how that may explain differences in attitudes as well as performance.

Among social scientists, numerous questions remain unanswered in the domain of talent management of nonstandard workers. We hope that this article may help point the way toward fruitful discoveries.[1]

Note

1. Special thanks to Nora O. Hilton, of the Center for Effective Organizations, for her assistance and support in preparing the literature review and analysis.

REFERENCES

Aletraris, L. 2010. How satisfied are they and why? A study of job satisfaction, job rewards, gender and temporary agency workers in Australia. *Human Relations*, 63(8), pp.1129–55.

Allan, P., and Sienko, S. 1997. A comparison of contingent and core workers' perceptions of their jobs' characteristics and motivational properties. *SAM Advanced Management Journal*, 62(3), pp.4–9.

Ang, S., and Slaughter, S. A. 2001. Work outcomes and job design for contract versus permanent information systems professionals on software development teams. *MIS Quarterly*, 25(3), pp.321–50.

Ang, S., Van Dyne, L., and Begley, T. M. 2003. The employment relationships of foreign workers versus local employees: a field study of organizational justice, job satisfaction, performance, and OCB. *Journal of Organizational Behavior*, 24, pp.561–83.

Armisen, A., and Majchrzak, A. 2015. Tapping the innovative business potential of innovation contests. *Business Horizons*, 58(4), pp.389–99.

Ashford, S. J., George, E., and Blatt, R. 2007. Old assumptions, new work: the opportunities and challenges of research on nonstandard employment. *Academy of Management Annals*, 1(1), pp.65–117.

Bardasi, E., and Francesconi, M. 2004. The impact of atypical employment on individual wellbeing: evidence from a panel of British workers. *Social Science and Medicine*, 58, pp.1671–88.

Barrett, P. M., and Elgin, B. 2015. The Arctic or bust. *Bloomberg Businessweek*, August 10, pp.58–63.

Beard, K. M., and Edwards, J. R. 1995. Employees at risk: contingent work and the psychological experience of contingent workers. In C. L. Cooper and D. M. Rousseau, eds., *Trends in organizational behavior*, Vol. 2, pp.109–26. Chichester: Wiley.

Bensinger, G. 2015. Startups scramble to define "employee." *The Wall Street Journal*, July 30, B1, B5.

Bernhard-Oettel, C., Sverke, M., and De Witte, H. 2005. Comparing three alternative types of employment with permanent full-time work: how do employment contract and perceived job conditions relate to health complaints? *Work and Stress: An International Journal of Work, Health and Organisations*, 19(4), pp.301–18.

Boswell, W. R., Watkins, M. B., Triana, M. D. C., Zardkoohi, A. et al. 2012. Second-class citizen? Contract workers' perceived status, dual commitment, and intent to quit. *Journal of Vocational Behavior*, 80, pp.454–63.

Boudreau, J. W., Jesuthasan, R., and Creelman, D. 2015. *Lead the work*. Hoboken, NJ: Wiley.

Broschak, J. P., and Davis-Blake, A. 2006. Mixing standard work and nonstandard deals: the consequences of heterogeneity in employment arrangements. *Academy of Management Journal*, 49(2), pp.371–93.

Broschak, J. P., Davis-Blake, A., and Block, E. S. 2008. Nonstandard, not substandard: the relationship among work arrangements, work attitudes, and job performance. *Work and Occupations*, 35(1), pp.3–43.

Buch, R., Kuvaas, B., and Dysvik, A. 2010. Dual support in contract workers' triangular employment relationships. *Journal of Vocational Behavior*, 77, pp.93–103.

Cascio, W. F., and Montealegre, R. 2016. How technology is changing work and organizations. *Annual Review of Organizational Psychology and Organizational Behavior*, 3, pp.349–75.

Chambel, M. J., and Castanheira, F. 2006. Different temporary work status, different behaviors in organization. *Journal of Business and Psychology*, 20(3), pp.351–67.

Chambel, M. J., and Castanheira, F. 2012. Training of temporary workers and the social exchange process. *Journal of Managerial Psychology*, 27(2), pp.191–209.

Chambel, M. J., and Sobral, F. 2011. Training is an investment with return in temporary workers. *Career Development International*, 16(2), pp.161–77.

Chattopadhyay, P., and George, E. 2001. Examining the effects of work externalization through the lens of social identity theory. *Journal of Applied Psychology*, 86(4), pp.781–88.

Chiu, S. F., Lin, S. T., and Han, T. S. 2015. Employment status and employee service-oriented organizational citizenship behaviour. *Career Development International*, 20(2), pp.133–46.

Clinton, M., Bernhard-Oetell, C., Rigotti, T., and de Jong, J. 2011. Expanding the temporal context of research on non-permanent work. *Career Development International*, 16(2), pp.114–39.

Coase, R. H. 1993. The nature of the firm: influence. In O. E. Williamson and S. G. Winter, eds., *The nature of the firm*, pp.61–74. New York: Oxford University Press.

Collinson, D. L. 1999. "Surviving the rigs": safety and surveillance on North Sea oil installations. *Organization Studies*, 20(4), pp.579–600.

Connelly, C. E., and Gallagher, D. G. 2004. Emerging trends in contingent work research. *Journal of Management*, 30(6), pp.959–83.

Davis-Blake, A., Broschak, J. P., and George, E. 2003. Happy together? How using nonstandard workers affects exit, voice, and loyalty among standard employees. *Academy of Management Journal*, 46(4), pp.475–85.

Davis-Blake, A., and Uzzi, B. 1993. Determinants of employment externalization: a study of temporary workers and independent contractors. *Administrative Science Quarterly*, 38(2), pp.195–223.

De Cuyper, N., and De Witte, H. 2006. Autonomy and workload among temporary workers: their effects on job satisfaction, organizational commitment, life satisfaction, and self-rated performance. *International Journal of Stress Management*, 13(4), pp.441–59.

De Cuyper, N., De Witte, H., and Van Emmerik, H. 2011. Temporary employment: costs and benefits for (the careers of) employees and organizations. *Career Development International*, 16(2), pp.104–13.

de Gilder, D. 2003. Commitment, trust and work behaviour. *Personnel Review*, 32(5), pp.588–604.

de Jong, J., and Schalk, R. 2010. Extrinsic motives as moderators in the relationship between fairness and work-related outcomes among temporary workers. *Journal of Business and Psychology*, 25(1), pp.175–89.

DiNatale, M. 2001. Characteristics of and preference for alternative work arrangements, 1999. *Monthly Labor Review*, 124, pp.28–49.

Ellingson, J. E., Gruys, M. L., and Sackett, P. R. 1998. Factors related to the satisfaction and performance of temporary employees. *Journal of Applied Psychology*, 83, pp.913–21.

Feldman, D. C. 2006. Toward a new taxonomy for understanding the nature and consequences of contingent employment. *Career Development International*, 11(1), pp.28–47.

Feldman, D. C., Doerpinghaus, H. I., and Turnley, W. H. 1994. Managing temporary workers: a permanent HRM challenge. *Organizational Dynamics*, 23(2), pp.49–63.

Felfe, J., Schmook, R., Schyns, B., and Six, B. 2008. Does the form of employment make a difference?—Commitment of traditional, temporary, and self-employed workers. *Journal of Vocational Behavior*, 72, pp.81–94.

Freeman, R. B. 2002. The labour market in the new information economy. *Oxford Review of Economic Policy*, 18(3), pp.288–305.

Gallagher, D. G., and Parks, J. M. 2001. I pledge thee my troth … contingently: commitment and the contingent work relationship. *Human Resource Management Review*, 11, pp.181–208.

Gallagher, D. G., and Sverke, M. 2005. Contingent employment contracts: are existing employment theories still relevant? *Economic and Industrial Democracy*, 26(2), pp.181–203.

Galup, S., Saunders, C., Nelson, R. E., and Cerveny, R. 1997. The use of temporary staff and managers in a local government environment. *Communication Research*, 24(6), pp.698–730.

Garrigos-Simon, F. J., Alcami, R. L., and Ribera, T. B. 2012. Social networks and Web 3.0: their impact on the management and marketing of organizations. *Management Decision*, 50(10), pp.1880–90.

George, E. 2003. External solutions and internal problems: the effects of employment externalization on internal workers' attitudes. *Organization Science*, 14(4), pp.386–402.

Guest, D. 2004. Flexible employment contracts, the psychological contract and employee outcomes: an analysis and review of the evidence. *International Journal of Management Reviews*, 5/6(1), pp.1–19.

Hackman, J. R., and Oldham, G. R. 1980. *Work redesign*. Reading, MA: Addison-Wesley Publishing Co.

Hanratty, T. 2000. The impact of numerical flexibility on training for quality in the Irish manufacturing sector. *Journal of European Industrial Training*, 24(9), pp.505–12.

Hardy, D. J., and Walker, R. J. 2003. Temporary but seeking permanence: a study of New Zealand temps. *Leadership and Organization Development Journal*, 24(3), pp.141–52.

Ho, V. T., Ang, S., and Straub, D. 2003. When subordinates become IT contractors: persistent managerial expectations in IT outsourcing. *Information Systems Research*, 14, pp.66–86.

Isaksson, K. S., and Bellagh, K. 2002. Health problems and quitting among female "temps." *European Journal of Work and Organizational Psychology*, 11(1), pp.27–38.

Kane, G. C. (2014). Leveraging the extended enterprise: MITRE's Handshake Tool builds virtual collaboration. *MIT Sloan Management Review*, Reprint #56111. http://mitsmr.com/1v6KaFO.

Karim, S., and Mitchell, W. 2000. Path-dependent and path-breaking change: reconfiguring business resources following acquisitions in the US medical sector, 1978–1995. *Strategic Management Journal*, 21(10/11) pp.1061–81.

Krausz, M., Brandwein, T., and Fox, S. 1995. Work attitudes and emotional responses of permanent, voluntary, and involuntary temporary-help employees: an exploratory study. *Applied Psychology: An International Review*, 44(3), pp.217–32.

Lapalme, M. E., Simard, G., and Tremblay, M. 2011. The influence of psychological contract breach on temporary workers' commitment and behaviors: a multiple agency perspective. *Journal of Business Psychology*, 26, pp.311–24.

Lautsch, B. A. 2003. The influence of regular work systems on compensation for contingent workers. *Industrial Relations*, 42(4), pp.565–88.

Lepak, D. P., and Snell, S. A. 2002. Examining the human resource architecture: the relationships among human capital, employment, and human resource configurations. *Journal of Management*, 28(4), pp.517–43.

Liden, R. C., Wayne, S. J., Kraimer, M. L., and Sparrowe, R. T. 2003. The dual commitments of contingent workers: an examination of contingents' commitment to the agency and the organization. *Journal of Organizational Behavior*, 24, pp.609–25.

Lowry, D. S., Simon, A., and Kimberley, N. 2002. Toward improved employment relations practices of casual employees in the New South Wales registered clubs industry. *Human Resource Development Quarterly*, 13(1), pp.53–70.

Malhotra, A., and Majchrzak, A. 2014. Managing crowds in innovation challenges. *California Management Review*, 56(4), pp.103–23.

Mallon, M. 1998. The portfolio career: pushed or pulled to it? *Personnel Review*, 27(5), pp.361–77.

Matusik, S. F., and Hill, C. W. L. 1998. The utilization of contingent work, knowledge creation, and competitive advantage. *Academy of Management Review*, 23(4), pp.680–97.

McAllister, J. 1998. Sisyphus at work in the warehouse: temporary employment in Greenville, South Carolina. In K. Barker and K. Christensen, eds., *Contingent work: American employment relations in transition*, pp.221–42. Ithaca, NY: ILR Press.

McDonald, D. J., and Makin, P. J. 2000. The psychological contract, organizational commitment and job satisfaction of temporary staff. *Leadership and Organizational Development Journal*, 21(1/2), pp.84–91.

McDonald, R., and Kotha, S. 2014. *Boeing 787: the Dreamliner*. Boston: Harvard Business School, Case No. N456–789.

Meyer, K. J., Somaya, D., and Williamson, I. O. 2012. Firm-specific, industry-specific, and occupational human capital and the sourcing of knowledge work. *Organization Science*, 23(5), pp.1311–29.

Millward, L. J., and Brewerton, P. M. 1999. Contractors and their psychological contracts. *British Journal of Management*, 10, pp.253–74.

Mirvis, P. H., and Hall, D. T. 1994. Psychological success and the boundaryless career. *Journal of Organizational Behavior*, 15(4), pp.365–80.

Moorman, R. H., and Harland, L. K. 2002. Temporary employees as good citizens: factors influencing their OCB performance. *Journal of Business and Psychology*, 17(2), pp.171–87.

Morgan, J., and Wang, R. 2010. Tournaments for ideas. *California Management Review*, 52(2), pp.77–97.

National Association of Professional Employer Associations. 2015. *What is a PEO?* www.napeo.org/peoindustry/faq.cfm.

Parker, S. K., Griffin, M. A., Sprigg, C. A., and Wall, T. D. 2002. Effect of temporary contracts on perceived work characteristics and job strain: a longitudinal study. *Personnel Psychology*, 55, pp.689–719.

Parks, J. M., Kidder, D. L., and Gallagher, D. G. 1998. Fitting square pegs into round holes: mapping the domain of contingent work arrangements onto the psychological contract. *Journal of Organizational Behavior*, 19, pp.697–730.

Pearce, J. L. 1993. Toward an organizational behavior of contract laborers: their psychological involvement and effects on employee co-workers. *Academy of Management Journal*, 36(5), pp.1082–96.

Peel, S., and Inkson, K. 2004. Contracting and careers: choosing between self and organizational employment. *Career Development International*, 9(6/7), pp.542–58.

Pfeffer, J., and Baron, J. N. 1988. Taking the workers back out: recent trends in the structuring of employment. In L. L. Cummings, and B. M. Staw, eds., *Research in organizational behavior*, Vol. 10, pp.257–303. Greenwich, CT: JAI Press Inc.

Pofeldt, E. 2015. Shocker: 40% of workers now have "contingent" jobs, says US Government. *Forbes*. http://www.forbes.com/sites/elainepofeldt/2015/05/25/shocker-40-of-workers-now-have-contingent-jobs-says-u-s-government/.

Polivka, A. E., and Nardone, T. 1989. On the definition of "contingent work." *Monthly Labor Review*, 112, pp.9–16.

Prahalad, C. K., and Hamel, G. 1990. The core competence of the corporation. *Harvard Business Review*, 68(3), 79–91.

Prpic, J., Shukla, P. P., Kietzmann, J. H., and McCarthy, I. P. 2015. How to work a crowd: developing crowd capital through crowdsourcing. *Business Horizons*, 58(1), pp.77–85.

Quinlan, M., Mayhew, C., and Bohle, P. 2001. The global expansion of precarious employment, work disorganization, and consequences for occupational health: placing the debate in a comparative historical context. *International Journal of Health Services*, 31(3), pp.507–36.

Rogers, J. K., and Henson, K. D. 1997. Hey, why don't you wear a shorter skirt? Structural vulnerability and the organization of sexual harassment in temporary clerical employment. *Gender and Society*, 11, pp.215–37.

Santos, F. M., and Eisenhardt, K. M. 2005. Organizational boundaries and theories of organization. *Organization Science*, 16(5), pp.491–508.

Schlagwein, D., and Bjorn-Andersen, N. 2014. Organizational learning with crowdsourcing: the revelatory case of LEGO. *Journal of the Association for Information Systems*, 15, pp.754–78.

Solomon, N. A., and Templer, A. J. 1993. Development of non-traditional work sites: the challenge of telecommuting. *The Journal of Management Development*, 12(5), pp.21–32.

Struggling with a supertanker. 2002. *The Economist*, February 7, 362, pp.52–3.

Sun, Y., Wang, N., Yin, C., and Zhang, J. X. 2015. Understanding the relationships between motivators and effort in crowdsourcing marketplaces: a nonlinear analysis. *International Journal of Information Management*, 35, pp.267–76.

Sveen, L. 2015. Changing social norms also changing the norms of work. *The Denver Post*, April 5, p.2K.

Sverke, M., Gallagher, D. G., and Hellgren, J. 2000. Alternative work arrangements: job stress, well-being and work attitudes among employees with different employment contracts. In K. Eriksson, C. Hogstedt, C. Eriksson, and T. Theorell, eds., *Health hazards in the new labour market*. pp.145–67. London: Kluwer Academic/Plenum Press.

Torka, N., and Schyns, B. 2007. On the transferability of "traditional" satisfaction theory to non-traditional employment relationships: temp agency work satisfaction. *Employee Relations*, 29(5), pp.440–57.

Uzzi, B., and Barsness, Z. I. 1998. Contingent employment in British establishments: organizational determinants of the use of fixed-term hires and part-time workers. *Social Forces*, 76(3), pp.967–1007.

Van Breugel, G., Van Olffen, W., and Olie, R. 2005. Temporary liaisons: the commitment of "temps" towards their agencies. *Journal of Management Studies*, 42(3), pp.539–66.

Van Dyne, L., and Ang, S. 1998. Organizational citizenship behavior of contingent workers in Singapore. *Academy of Management Journal*, 41(6), pp.692–703.

Virtanen, M., Kivimaki, M., Virtanen, P., Elovainio, M. et al. 2003. Disparity in occupational training and career planning between contingent and permanent employees. *European Journal of Work and Organizational Psychology*, 12(1), pp.19–36.

Wheeler, A. R., and Buckley, M. R. 2001. Examining the motivation process of temporary employees. *Journal of Managerial Psychology*, 16(5), pp.339–54.

Wilkin, C. L. 2013. I can't get no job satisfaction: meta-analysis comparing permanent and contingent workers. *Journal of Organizational Behavior*, 34, pp.47–64.

Yang, X. 2012. Contingent worker, permanent loser?—How perceived trust shapes communication between contingent workers and standard workers in knowledge-based organizations. *International Journal of Business and Social Science*, 3(8), pp.172–80.
Zeitz, G., Blau, G., and Fertig, J. 2009. Boundaryless careers and institutional resources.
The International Journal of Human Resource Management, 20(2), pp.372–98.

CHAPTER 27

....

INTEGRATING TALENT AND DIVERSITY MANAGEMENT

....

DARREN T. BAKER AND ELISABETH K. KELAN

27.1 INTRODUCTION

WHEREAS talent management is a relatively new, specialist, and strategic subarea of HR management, largely emerging from debates in the 1990s on the "war for talent" (Chambers et al., 1998), diversity management has a longer history, emerging from the civil rights movements of the 1960s, and in some organizations it now represents a broad range of practices affecting the full business value chain. Talent and diversity management are often presumed to be complementary and interdependent practices because, broadly speaking, both seek to develop and nurture strategic human capital assets for organizations, which have to operate in an increasingly complex globalized marketplace. However, this chapter challenges this perspective by analyzing how talent management has been dominated by an exclusionary paradigm, which has focused on treating a small number of employees more favorably than others. We argue in particular that talent management espouses neoliberal, meritocratic ideologies, which are problematic for the efficacy of equality, especially in their assumption that everyone is endowed with equal opportunity. We also explore how microinequalities emerge in specific talent-management practices including recruitment and selection, performance management, and leadership.

The chapter is organized as follows. In this first section, we explain how talent-management practices in many organizations have been dominated by an exclusionary paradigm. This has sought to nurture and develop the talents of an elite few in organizations. We then similarly trace the different paradigms and approaches to diversity management in Section 27.2. In Section 27.3, we explore some of the tensions that have emerged between the founding principles of collectivism and social justice and the more recent economic and business case-fused approaches to equality. In particular, we focus on how talent-management practices and meritocratic ideologies have undermined equality efforts in organizations. In the penultimate section, we go on to identify a number of ways in which microinequalities emerge and play out in talent recruitment and selection, performance management, and leadership practices. In the final section, we propose a number of recommendations as to how talent management could catalyze equality progress in organizations, and we raise some key indicative questions regarding the intersection between equality and talent management, which future researchers could explore.

27.2 THE EXCLUSIONARY PARADIGM TO TALENT MANAGEMENT

There remains considerable terminological confusion over the meaning of *talent management*, and a detailed exploration of the multifaceted nature of the term can found elsewhere in this dictionary (see Cappelli and Keller, 2017). For the purposes of this chapter, however, talent management at a very broad level concerns the attraction, development, retention, mobilization, and succession planning of employees and leaders (CIPD, 2009; Tansley et al., 2013). Organizational concerns regarding the management of talent emerged in part as a result of changes to workforce demographics (Lacey and Groves, 2014). For instance, in the United States, organizations have had to respond to the risk that a third of the entire workforce will soon reach the retirement age, which means that half of those in management positions will exit from organizations over the next five years (Lacey and Groves, 2014: 400).

This represents a medium- to long-term challenge for organizations to meet current and future workforce requirements. In response, organizations have begun to invest considerable financial resources into the development of future leaders. This response gained traction and eminence with the publication of the McKinsey and Company practitioner literature, which coined the term *war on talent* (Michaels, Handfield-Jones, and Axelrod, 2001). This recommended that organizations respond to the talent deficit by developing and supporting those perceived as high-performing or high potential in their organization (Björkman et al., 2007; Cappelli and Keller, 2017; Ready and Conger, 2007; Collings and Mellahi, 2009; Chambers et al., 1998; Tansley et al., 2007; Schuler and Tarique, 2012; Gallardo-Gallardo, Dries, and Gonzales-Cruz, 2013). This is based in part on Pareto's "law of the vital few," which asserts that 80% of the value of the organization derives from only 20% of the employees (Lacey and Groves, 2014; O'Boyle, 2017). High performers are, thus, acclaimed for taking more initiative and delivering higher quality work (Stahl et al., 2007), and overall perceived as generating more organizational value than the majority of their peers.

One of the main ways organizations have sought to develop their high performers is through the design and implementation of HiPo ("high potential") development programs. Typically, admission onto such a program involves senior-level leaders nominating individual employees whom they perceive as leaders of the future (Lacey and Groves, 2014). Those admitted undertake specialized training, which is intended to fine-tune, nurture, and prepare individuals to ascend the organizational hierarchy and assume influential roles in the organization (Lacey and Groves, 2014). Additional opportunities are also opened up, including invitations to attend events with senior leaders in the organization, which helps them build professional and personal relationships with senior leaders, and increase their visibility within the organization (see also Day and O'Connor, 2017).

27.3 DIVERSITY MANAGEMENT PARADIGMS AND APPROACHES OVER TIME

Similar to talent management, the term *diversity management* has been subject to significant criticism by scholars who view the term as broad and inconsistent (Wrench, 2002). While some scholars and practitioners define it in terms of demographics such as race, gender, or sexuality (McGrath et al., 1995), the term is contemporaneously understood as referring to unobservable attributes including the skills, beliefs, and personality of an individual (Wrench, 2002). However, in comparison to talent management, which has been dominated by an exclusionary approach, diversity management has a much longer history, during which a number of different organizational paradigms and approaches have emerged largely in response to cultural shifts and legislative demands at the national and supranational level.

First, the "discrimination-and-fairness" paradigm in organizations emerged as a result of affirmative action legislation in the United States (Thomas and Ely, 1996; Vermeulen and Coetzee, 2011). The civil rights movements of the 1960s and the subsequent Civil Rights Act made it unlawful for organizations to discriminate based on race, color, religion, sex, or origin. Affirmative action was the main approach to emerge from this paradigm and its purpose was to ensure equal opportunities for those minority groups (Thomas, 1992). This was founded on moral and ethical principles of compensatory justice for groups that had historically been discriminated against (Kellough, 2006). The impact of this paradigm was that organizations began to seek demographic variation in their workforce through increasing opportunities for minority groups, particularly through recruitment and retention, but also through value-added initiatives such as providing mentoring and development opportunities.

However, during the late 1970s and 1980s, there was a paradigmatic shift from legal compliance to a focus on "difference" at an individual level. This was spurred on by the release of the *Workforce 2000* report, which forecasted how the US workforce would become increasingly diverse and segmented (Johnston and Packer, 1987). This was driven by economic shifts during the 1960s and 1970s (cf. Kooistra, 2006), which saw the decline of manufacturing and mass production for a homogenous market, and the rise and dominance of the service sector and flexible, precarious forms of employment (Jackson and Alvarez, 1992). Women, in particular, were positioned as the new employee par excellence under the new economic regime, as flexible working patterns were perceived as enabling women to enter the workforce while maintaining domestic duties. The second paradigm, "access-and-legitimacy," emerged advocating the business benefits of diversity, and aligning the strategic imperatives of the organization with the talents, attributes, and "requirements" of its diverse workforce (Wentling and Palma-Rivas, 1997; Cox, 1991). However, despite organizations integrating diversity into their strategies, organizational structures, such as performance and reward processes, remained largely untouched (Kulik and Roberson, 2008).

The third and most recent paradigm, "learning-and-effectiveness," was proposed by Thomas (1990) and sought to understand how diverse workers could to be managed. In this paradigm there is a focus on inclusion, in which individuals are integrated and valued as a way to increase productivity and effectiveness and affect the bottom line (Thomas, 1990; Roberson, 2006). The first step is to reduce the inhibitors to progress and good performance between different groups (Miller and Katz, 2002). The second is for organizations to leverage all the unique talents and attributes of their entire workforce, which Miller and Katz (2002) infamously termed "lifting the playing field." Additional aspects of driving an inclusive organizational culture include resolving and learning from conflicts emerging from difference and monitoring the impact of diversity management, particularly using metrics such as retention, promotion, and team effectiveness.

27.4 THE MYTH OF MERITOCRACY AND STICKING POINTS TO EQUALITY

In this section, we explore the tensions in equality progress between collective and social justice-inspired approaches on the one hand, and individualistic and business case inspired approaches on the other. We also explore how talent management has added to this tension by espousing neoliberal meritocratic ideologies, which also challenge the efficacy of diversity and equality.

The social justice approach, which aligns with the aforementioned "discrimination-and-fairness" paradigm, focuses on increasing the representation of minority groups across all levels of an organization. It is achieved through, for instance, the implementation of targets and quotas. In the United States, this is done through affirmative action policies, which proactively seek to increase the representation of minority groups within organizations while satisfying the skill and talent requirements of the role. Interventionist approaches are often argued to be the most effective way to guarantee equality outcomes in organizations. Wang and Kelan (2013), for instance, in studying the effects of the imposed 40% gender quotas on executive boards in Norway, found that redressing gender parity on executive boards had a positive "trickle-down" impact on the succession pipeline of an organization. However, such interventionist approaches are often criticized for neglecting to challenge the cultural drivers of inequality. The implication of not doing this is that diverse individuals are expected to assimilate into a homogenous organizational culture (Gottfredson, 1992; Thomas and Ely, 1996), which can result in increased conflict between minority and dominant groups (Mckay and Avery, 2005).

However, during the 1980s and 1990s, there was an "economic turn" from the moral, emotive, and legislatively driven social justice approach toward a more individual-istic and business case approach (Jack and Lorbiecki, 2000). This reflects broader economic changes in the global economy toward liberalization and deregulation (cf. Harvey, 2005). In diversity management, this shift is associated with the "learning-and-effectiveness" paradigm, which represented genuine attempts, according to Greene and Kirton (2009), to revitalize organizational equality efforts. European Union laws buttressed this paradigm by encouraging organizations to create a meritocratic culture, in which the unique attributes of each individual were respected and leveraged.

It was during the same period that formalized talent-management practices emerged. They focused on developing and nurturing the talents of a small, elite segment of the workforce (Swailes, 2013). This exclusionary paradigm is underpinned by meritocratic ideologies that are used as the main rationale for making key decisions regarding selec-tion, reward, and promotion in organizations (Scully, 2003). However, this is problem-atic for equality for four reasons.

First, segmenting the workforce as such runs the risk of violating fundamental under-standings of equity and equality, as it neglects the majority of the employee-stakeholder group. This may cause feelings of neglect, unworthiness, and emotional distress when employees see others being favored in their workplace. Further, it may have implications on the commitment, engagement, and productivity of certain parts of the workforce (see Collings, 2017; Meyers, De Boeck, and Dries, 2017).

Second, meritocratic ideologies fail to recognize the exclusionary and unfair pro-cesses that structure organizations. For instance, in the case of talent management, the idea that privileges should be given to those perceived as more talented incorrectly assumes that everyone has been endowed with the same opportunities and rights, and that success is therefore the direct result of hard work and/or ability (cf. Young, 1990). This assumption neglects the unequal systems of distribution that structure society and the barriers and obstacles to access and progression within organizations (Bradley and van Hoof, 2005; Acker, 2006; McDowell, 2003; Noon, 2010). In turn, inequality influ-ences different groups disproportionately more than other groups. In the workplace, discursive constructions of the "ideal" employee or leader are deeply inflected in gen-dered, classist, and racialized ways. Thus, the ideal worker is indirectly perceived of as masculine, Western, white, and middle or upper class (Acker, 2006; Bebbington and Özbilgin, 2013; Kang, Cheng, and Gray, 2007; Tatli, Vassilopoulou, and Özbilgin, 2013).

Third, even when minority individuals assume positions of power in organizations, their perceived embodiment can still put them at a significant disadvantage. In her book *Space Invaders* (2004), Puwar explains how in elite institutions, women and ethnic minorities are measured against a "universal somatic norm," which is defined as the white, heterosexual male. When bodies that lie outside this definition enter such spaces, they are rendered visible and marked as "alien." In particular, when these individuals assume positions of authority they are perceived as intruders and a threat to established orders. Diverse individuals in positions of power are thus subjected to what Puwar terms "infantilization," in which they are perceived as less competent. The implication of this is that diverse individuals have to negotiate their identities with the dominant culture in complex ways, while simultaneously being more likely to be subjected to increased scrutiny.

However, fourth, one of the core features of neoliberal meritocratic organizational cultures is that discrimination and unfairness have become individualized. In the neoliberal economy, individuals are constructed as self-reliant, autonomous, and continuously self-assessing and self-marketing (Bauman, 2001; Beck and Beck-Gernsheim, 1995; Giddens, 1991; McRobbie, 2009). When discrimination occurs, individuals do not place themselves within broader social or organizational structures, as using this rationale negates the opportunity for the individual to construct themselves in a morally appropriate way within the context of the neoliberal individualistic and independent "ethic" (Scharff, 2012). Neoliberal subjects, therefore, espouse the idea of an individual who, through hard work and talent, can navigate inequalities and seize opportunities, without the support of a collective. The wider implication of this is that individuals who do not have success only have themselves to blame. Bauman (2001) explains that these "individualizing" processes emerged as a result of contemporary economic uncertainty. Risk and failure are becoming personalized (Beck, 1992). Whereas during the industrial and manufacturing era, employees could collectively act on and negotiate with managers, capital today has cut itself loose from its dependency on labor, resulting in more precarious forms of employment, added to by severe attacks on the powers of unions (Castells, 1996, 1989).

Kelan (2014) explains that despite the increase in precarious and insecure work, "inequalities have become unspeakable" in organizations (cf. Gill, 2014). This does not mean that inequalities have disappeared but rather that, under the cloak of neoliberalism, they are not spoken of. For example, Kelan (2008) explored how men and women make sense of insecurity. Despite the fact that the neoliberal subject is constructed as gender-neutral, a masculine subtext remains which, for instance, constructs women as less at risk of redundancy in comparison to their male colleagues; instead, gendered issues regarding balancing work and family life are constructed as related to age rather than gender. In other words, gendered inequalities are discursively redefined as age-related and, therefore, something that both men and women are exposed to and at risk of. In her more recent study, Kelan (2014) explored the intersection of age and gender among young professionals and discovered how gender was discursively rendered invisible through ways in which professionals link sexist behavior to the past and previous generations, despite the fact that the men and women were aware of or had experienced it in the workplace. In sum, while inequalities continue to exist, they are often not articulated as such, but a failure to succeed is seen as an individual failure.

The net sum of much of this is that equality discourses have become buried in neoliberal meritocratic ideologies that reinforce discrimination rather than break it down. As Noon (2010) explains, neoliberal rationales delegitimize but at the same time repackage historical social justice arguments on equality so that they are more palatable for managers responsible for the day-to-day practice of equality with subordinates. This "diminishes the significance of identify by trivializing it and overlooking the negative impact of social group characteristics" (Noon, 2007: 774) by instead focusing on inclusion, which dilutes group-level identities (Baker and Kelan,2015). This is done in order to negate more collectivist action with regard to inequality (Jonsen, Tatli, Özbilgin, and Bell, 2013). As Özbilgin and Tatli (2011) explain, by focusing on individual employees and defining difference as a matter of individual uniqueness, individualism serves to obscure the collective dimension of inequality and discrimination.

27.5 MICROPRACTICES OF INEQUALITY IN TALENT MANAGEMENT

In the previous section we explored the challenges to equality progress with a specific focus on the role of talent management, which we argued has espoused neoliberal, meritocratic ideologies. In this section, we consider some of the micropractices of inequality that can emerge in talent-management practices.

27.5.1 Talent Recruitment and Selection

Talent recruitment and selection is an important area where diversity and inclusion matter. *Recruitment* refers to the process of generating a pool of candidates based on an analysis of the job requirements, job specification, and advertisement of the role. *Selection* is the process of choosing the most suitable candidate from the pool by identifying and deciding on the required skills and talents for the role, and by using techniques including structured and semistructured interviews and psychometric testing, including ability tests, which measure knowledge, and personality tests, which measure attitudes and values.

Senior leaders are, however, at risk of taking biased decisions on talent recruitment and selection. For instance, there is evidence that decision makers may fall into the trap of the "halo effect" and "horn effect," which is when interviewers, managers, and leaders over-emphasize a positive attribute, in the former, and a negative attribute, in the latter, when judging another person (Sorcher and Brant, 2002; Heery and Noon, 2001). A number of studies reflect how individuals are perceived positively or negatively because of their group membership. King and co-authors (2006), for example, gave 155 white male participants fictitious CVs of either an

Asian-American, a Mexican-American, an African-American, or a Caucasian man that was of either high or low quality. Participants were asked to evaluate the CVs based on intelligence, motivation, and likelihood of being hired and give a rating on suitability for various occupations based on high- or low-status jobs. Overall, African-Americans were rated the least positively, while Asian-Americans were rated the most positively. Asian-Americans were rated as most suitable for high-status jobs. Mexican-Americans were rated as the most suitable for low-status jobs. Caucasians were rated the least suitable for low-status jobs. Similarly, Biernat and Manis (1994) examined the stereotype that women are more verbally able than men, and that Caucasian individuals are more verbally able than ethnic minorities. A total of 143 participants viewed photographs of individuals from the different groups, specified alongside definitions of two words. The participants rated the verbal ability of the individuals represented in the photographs and the ethnic minority individuals were perceived as having lower verbal ability than Caucasian individuals, which implies that the participants perceived ethnic minorities as less verbally able.

Based on sixty-one in-depth interviews with female, classically trained musicians, Scharff (2015) explored the complex negotiations they had to make with regards to their sexuality, particularly when performing in concerts. Female musicians had to ensure that they maintained respect and their "reputation" as serious classical artists by not "overdoing" femininity. Owing to the risks of sexualization and gender stereotypes, Scharff (2015b) recommends the introduction of "blind" auditions, where those auditioning are not visible, particularly in conservatoires and orchestras. In her examination of the reasons why women were underrepresented in radio DJing, Gill (1993) found that the reasons given by DJs and producers for not hiring were often contradictory. For example, many of the accounts assume that the reasons for the lack of women are "lying in women themselves" or presumed perceptions of what "the audience wants."

There is also evidence of microinequalities in performance-management processes, which often perceive the archetypal employee as white and male (Acker, 1990, 2006). Festing, Knappert, and Kornau (2015) examined global performance management (GPM) systems to identify gender-specific preferences and whether masculine preferences matched the processes in place. They found that GPM systems correspond better to the preferences of male managers, whereas female managers preferred different approaches, for instance including more supervisor involvement and more directness and involvement in the feedback process. This indicates not only that women were less satisfied with the GPM systems but also that these structures are themselves biased in favor of men. Bauer and Baltes (2002) examined individual performance-evaluation practices for gender-biased stereotypes. Drawing on the performance ratings that 247 college students gave to two vignettes depicting the performance of a male and a female academic, it was found that raters who held more stereotypical views of women rated them less accurately than how they performed.

27.5.2 Leadership

Leadership development also poses a range of diversity and inclusion challenges. As with the "ideal employee," organizational conceptions of the "ideal leader" are inflected with embodied expectations rooted in historical associations of leaders as masculine, Western, white, and middle and upper class. One reason why, for instance, corporate boards remain largely white and male (cf. Davies, 2015) is that they draw on their existing networks when profiling for a potential new board member (Holgersson, 2012). Such networks are sociodemographically homogenous, as the contact between similar people occurs at a higher rate than among dissimilar people, which reproduces the established networks and power (Nickerson, 1998; McPherson, Smith-Lovin, and Cook, 2001). Those who do not embody the attributes expected within these groups are disadvantaged. In her ethnographic study of gender-inclusive managers, for instance, Kelan (2015) explored a number of moments when gender discrimination emerged in day-to-day interactions, including an example when a male leader wanted to hire a man for a new position "as they reminded them of themselves at their age." Brown, Kelan, and Humbert (2015), drawing on their longitudinal qualitative study, explained that 70% of board appointments continue to go to men, as men are more likely to be sponsored than are women, who proactively support men to make headway towards the boardroom.

27.6 CONCLUSION

In this chapter, we have attempted to pull apart the presumption that talent and diversity management are interrelated and complementary practices. We have done this by highlighting the deep tensions and contradictions between equality and the individualistic meritocratic ideologies espoused in talent management. This includes how conceptions of the ideal worker and leader are inflected in gendered, classist, and racialized ways. In the penultimate section, we also attempted to show how microinequalities emerge in specific talent-management practices, such as performance management, recruitment, and retention.

This then raises the question: how can organizations seeking to create equality in the workplace begin to unpick and redress these complex contradictions? We now outline a number of ways in which talent management can attempt to catalyze equality progress in organizations.

27.6.1 Inclusive Career-Enhancing Development Practices

Whereas exclusionary talent-management practices prepare an elite segment of the workforce to be future leaders, inclusive talent-management practices develop the entire stakeholder group. Thus, inclusive talent-management practices consider "talent" as everyone in the organization and everyone having a role in the enablement of an organizational strategy (Gallardo-Gallardo, Dries, and González-Cruz, 2013; Tansley et al., 2007). There are a number of ethical arguments for inclusive talent-management practices. First, when an employee enters into a contract with an employer, it leaves the employee vulnerable to risks. For example, over the short term, they can experience career stagnation, unfair treatment by colleagues, and lack of opportunities to develop, and, over the long term, a potential loss of future income and fewer opportunities after exiting an organization (cf. Lacey and Groves, 2014). Second, as organizations often reap benefits of such risks, there is thus an ethical responsibility for employers to prepare employees for an increasingly competitive labor market, including equipping them with the skills and competencies needed to ensure their success both within and outside the organization (Lacey and Groves, 2014). In other words, organizations have a duty to prepare employees with the skills to meet existing and future organizational imperatives, while developing them for career progression within the wider market.

These actions can also have indirect organizational returns such as greater collaboration, improved commitment, and morale among staff (Groysberg, Nanda, and Nohria, 2004). One example where inclusive talent-management practices could be implemented is in the identification of employees for a HiPo development program. It would obviously be very costly and impractical to put all employees through the program. Instead, to ensure that the program was inclusive, participation could be based on self-nomination. This would, first, allow those individuals who are willing to invest the time and effort to access the opportunity and acquire new skills, and, second, avoid any biases that emerge from nominations of individuals by managers and leaders. As minority groups, particularly women, are less likely to self-promote, organizations must proactively encourage and engage with all workforce demographics—for instance, in terms of gender, class background, and sexuality—through tailored communications, events, and direct support without nomination from sponsors and mentors.

27.6.2 Inclusive-Leadership Training

Developing leaders who demonstrate inclusive behaviors is pivotal to ensuring that diverse employees feel attached to the organization. This means identifying the behaviors required, along with when and where they should be performed. Concerning driving gender parity, for instance, Kelan (2014) identified six pivotal inclusive-leadership behaviors based on the responses of CEOs. First, leaders need to drive accountability down the command chain, for instance through performance outcomes of subordinates and team managers. They must also develop ownership of gender parity through, for instance, critically questioning the performance evaluation of women and other diverse individuals. Further, both internal and external communication is a vital process in winning the hearts and minds of individuals, particularly middle managers. Next is leading by example, in which leaders will openly talk about their personal commitments, such as picking up their children after school, which opens up the opportunity for others to do the same. From the study, CEOs tended to throw their weight behind a number of initiatives such as questioning, challenging, or calling for action on a small number of specific issues. Finally, CEOs must drive culture change over the long term and many were conscious of their organizational legacy.

In a later study on inclusive male middle managers, Kelan (2015) recommended four gender-inclusive leadership practices for male middle managers. First, managers "celebrating and encouraging women," for example, focus on how women are less likely to put themselves forward to take on new opportunities and responsibilities, and how managers can explain the career benefits of doing so in order to encourage a woman or diverse individual; then, "calling out biases" involves managers making visible the moments when biases emerge in a sensitive and constructive way; next, "championing and defending gender initiatives" involves male managers defending or sponsoring gender-parity initiatives and promoting these activities with others; finally, "challenging working practices" includes problematizing gendered metaphors used in everyday organizational discourse.

27.6.3 Implicit Bias Awareness Training

Many employees are unaware of their own implicit biases, and how these affect their workplace interactions. Implicit biases can result in the application of derogatory, offensive, and discriminatory behaviors, which can affect key talent-management practices such as performance management, selection, and recruitment, as discussed in the previous section. Training can help managers and leaders first to identify their own biases, and second to manage them. One-off training sessions may have an impact on behaviors in the short term but are unlikely to break habits over the long term. However, Devine, Forscher, Austin, and Cox (2012) explain that addressing implicit bias effectively involves, first, individuals being aware of their biases, and, second, educating employees to be concerned with the effects of biases on others. This requires regular implicit bias training and the full integration of biases in all organizational systems, processes, and practices—for instance, prompts during the performance-evaluation process to indicate moments or key decisions when common biases may emerge.

27.6.4 Checking Your Privilege Training Courses

Privilege is commonly understood as having an advantage over someone else in the workplace. However, many privileged employees forget the unequal systems that structure the workplace, and employ meritocratic ideologies to justify their positions and advantages. Although many privileged groups may recognize the disadvantage of another group, for instance the underrepresentation of individuals from working-class backgrounds in elite occupations such as law and banking, they may not recognize or accept their own "over-privilege." The objective of such training would be to get advantaged employees to check their power and privilege, and reflect on this alongside other components of socioeconomic inequality, such as race, gender, faith, and sexuality. The course would aim to put individuals within the wider context of structures and recognize patterns, while respecting the history of each individual. Rather than blaming an individual for their privilege, such a program would help employees to start unpacking the myth of meritocracy in organizations, and open up constructive dialogues for redress.

However, these recommendations must be considered within a broader and drastically changing talent-management landscape. Talent-management practices are likely to continue to become global in the search for elite talent, and therefore more demographically diverse, and demands for talent will become more temporally and geographically specific (Ariss, Cascio, and Paauwe, 2014). As a result, there is likely to be an increasing individualization of techniques which aim to empower the individual to assume responsibility for their own careers (Ariss, Cascio, and Paauwe, 2014). However, in parallel, the increasing role of corporate social responsibility activities, in addition to equality and diversity, means that talent-management practices increasingly have to consider their ethical and moral obligations to both the individual and wider society, and not just organizational shareholders. Possible future areas of research must therefore explore the following unexhausted list of questions:

- What is the ethical imperative for talent-management practices? What are the positive and negative repercussions of talent-management practices both internally and externally for organizations?
- How can ethics be incorporated into leadership training and development? What are the impacts of these programs on both the organization and society?
- How, within workplaces dominated by individualistic and independent cultures, can talent management help build more interdependent and ethical relations between workers and leaders?
- What are the impacts of talent-management provisions such as "inclusive-leadership training" and "checking your privilege" on an organization? To what extent are these programs successful?
- How can organizations collaborate with not-for-profit, public, and philanthropic organizations to create a vibrant economy and shared value?
- What are the linkages between global diversity and talent management? How can these be fostered and improved?
- How can talent-management practices be used to create stronger links between schools and workplaces and address issues around social mobility for those from lower socioeconomic backgrounds?
- In a contemporary service sector economy dominated by precarious, low-skilled, and poorly paid work, how can organizations better support, train, and improve the chances of those from lower socioeconomic backgrounds, and, thus, improve intragenerational mobility? How can this be looked at from an intersectional perspective?

References

Acker, J. 1990. Hierarchies, jobs, bodies: a theory of gendered organizations. *Gender and Society*, 4(2), pp.139–58.

Acker, J. 2006. Inequality regimes—gender, class, and race in organizations. *Gender and Society*, 20(4), pp.441–64.

Al Ariss, A., Cascio, W. F., and Paauwe, J. 2014. Talent management: current theories and future research directions. *Journal of World Business*, 49(2), pp.173–9.

Baker, D. T, and Kelan, E. K. 2015. Policy and practice of diversity management in the workplace. In J. Syed and M. Ozbilgin, eds., *Managing diversity and inclusion: an international perspective*, pp.78–106. SAGE Publications Ltd.

Bauer, C., and Baltes, B. 2002. Reducing the effects of gender stereotypes on performance evaluations. *Sex Roles*, 47(9/10), pp.465–76.

Bauman, Z. 2001. *The individualized society*. Cambridge: Blackwell Publishers Ltd.

Bebbington, D., and Özbilgin, M. 2013. The paradox of diversity in leadership and leadership for diversity. *Management International/International Management*, 17, pp.14–24.

Beck, U. 1992. *Risk society: towards a new modernity*. London: SAGE Publication.

Beck, U., and Beck-Gernsheim, E. 1995. *The normal chaos of love*. Cambridge: Polity Press.

Biernat, M., and Manis, M. 1994. Shifting standards and stereotype-based judgments. *Journal of Personality and Social Psychology*, 66(1), pp.5–20.

Bjorkman, I., Fey, C., and Park, H. 2007. Institutional theory and MNC subsidiary HRM practices: evidence from a three country study. *Journal of International Business Studies*, 38(3), pp.430–46.

Bradley, H., and Van Hoof, J. 2005. *Young people in Europe: labour markets and citizenship*. Bristol: Policy Press.

Brown, S., Kelan, E., and Humbert, A. 2015. *Black box of board appointments: women's and men's routes to the boardroom*. London. Economic and Social Research Council (ESRC) and Sapphire Partners.

Cappelli, P., and Keller, JR. 2017. Talent management in historical content. In D. G. Collings, K. Mellahi, and W. C. Cascio, eds. *Oxford handbook of talent management*, pp.23–42. Oxford: Oxford University Press.

Castells, M. 1989. *The informational city: information technology, economic restructuring and the urban-regional process*. Oxford: Blackwell.

Castells, M. 1996. *The rise of the network society*. Oxford: Blackwell.

Chambers, E. G., Foulon, M., Handfield-Jones, H., Hankin, S. M. et al. 1998. The war for talent. *McKinsey Quarterly*, 1(3), pp.44–57.

CIPD. 2009. *The war on talent? Talent management under threat in uncertain times*. New York, United States: McKinsey and Company.

Collings, D. G. 2017. Workforce differentiation and talent management. In D. G. Collings, K. Mellahi, and W. C. Cascio, eds., *Oxford handbook of talent management*, pp. 301–17. Oxford: Oxford University Press.

Collings, D. G., and Mellahi, K. 2009. Strategic talent management: a review and research agenda. *Human Resource Management Review*, 19(4), pp.304–13.

Cox, T. 1991. The multi-cultural organization. *The Executive*, 5(2), pp.34–47.

Davies, E. M. 2015. *Improving gender balance on British boards: Women on Boards Davies Review Five Year Summary Review*. Cranfield School of Management Female FTSE reports 2010-2015.

Day, D. V., and O'Connor, P. G. 2017. Talent development: building organizational capability. In D. G. Collings, K. Mellahi, and W. C. Cascio, eds., *Oxford handbook of talent management*, pp.343–60. Oxford: Oxford University Press.

Devine, P. G., Forscher, P. S., Austin, A. J., and Cox, W. T. 2012. Long-term reduction in implicit race bias: a prejudice habit-breaking intervention. *Journal of Experimental Social Psychology*, 48(6), pp.1267–78.

Festing, M., Knappert, L., and Kornau, A. 2015. Gender-specific preferences in global performance management: an empirical study of male and female managers in a multinational context. *Human Resource Management*, 54(1), pp.55–79.

Gallardo-Gallardo, E., Dries, N., and González-Cruz, T. F. 2013. What is the meaning of "talent" in the world of work? *Human Resource Management Review*, 23(4), pp.290–300.

Giddens, A. 1991. *Modernity and self-identity*. Cambridge: Polity Press.

Gill, R. 1993. Justifying injustice: broadcasters' accounts of inequality in radio. In E. Burman and I. Parker, eds., *Discourse analytic research: repertoires and readings of texts in action*, pp. 137–151. London: Routledge.

Gill, R. 2014. Unspeakable inequalities: post feminism, entrepreneurial subjectivity, and the repudiation of sexism among cultural workers. *Social Politics: International Studies in Gender, State and Society*, 21(4), pp.509–28.

Gottfredson, L. S. 1992. Dilemmas in Developing Diversity Programs. In S. E. Jackson, ed., *Diversity in the workplace: human resources initiatives*, pp.279–305. New York: Guilford.

Greene, A. M., and Kirton, G. 2009. *Diversity management in the UK: organizational and stakeholder experiences*. London: Routledge.

Groysberg, B., Nanda, A., and Nohria, N. 2004. The risky business of hiring stars. *Harvard Business Review*, 82(5), pp.92–100.

Harvey, D. 2005. *A brief history of neoliberalism*. Oxford and New York: Oxford University Press.

Heery, E., and Noon, M. 2001. *A dictionary of human resource management*. Oxford: Oxford University Press.

Holgersson, C. 2012. Recruiting managing directors: doing homosociality. *Gender, Work and Organization*, 20(4), pp.454–66.

Jack, G., and Lorbiecki, A. 2000. Critical turns in the evolution of diversity management. *British Journal of Management*, 11(Special Issue), pp.S17–S31.

Jackson, S. E., and Alvarez, E. B. 1992. Working through diversity as a strategic imperative. In S. E. Jackson, ed., *Diversity in the workplace*, pp.13–29. New York: Guilford Press.

Johnston, W., and Packer, A. 1987. *Workforce 2000: work and workers for the 21st century*. Indianapolis: Hudson Institute.

Jonsen, K., Tatli, A., Özbilgin, M. F., and Bell, M. P. 2013. The tragedy of the uncommons: reframing workforce diversity. *Human Relations*, 66(2), pp.271–94.

Kang, H., Cheng, M., and Gray, S. J. 2007. Corporate governance and board composition: diversity and independence of Australian boards. *Corporate Governance*, 15(2), pp.194–207.

Kelan, E. 2008. *Gender, risk and employment insecurity: the masculine breadwinner subtext*, *Human Relations*, 61(9), pp. 1171–1202.

Kelan, E. 2015. *Linchpin—men, middle managers and gender inclusive leadership*, Cranfeld University School of Management. *http://www.som.cranfield.ac.uk/som/dinamiccontent/research/Linchpin. pdf.*

Kelan, E. K. 2014. From biological clocks to unspeakable inequalities: the intersectional positioning of young professionals. *British Journal of Management*, 25, pp.790–804.

Kelan, E. K. 2014. *Winning hearts and minds: how CEOs talk about gender parity*. KPMG International and King's College London.

Kellough, J. E. 2006. *Understanding affirmative action: politics, discrimination, and the search for justice*. Washington, DC: Georgetown University Press.

King, E. B., Mendoza, S. A., Madera, J. M., Hebl, M. R. et al. 2006. What's in a name? A multi-racial investigation of the role of occupational stereotypes in selection decisions. *Journal of Applied Social Psychology*, 36(5), pp.1145–59.

Kooistra, A. 2006. Putting identity to work post-Fordist modes of production and protest. *NEXUS*, 19, pp.58–184.

Kulik, C. T., and Roberson, L. 2008. Diversity initiative effectiveness: what organizations can (and cannot) expect from diversity recruitment, diversity training, and formal mentoring programs. In A. P. Brief, ed., *Diversity at work*, pp. 265–317. Cambridge: Cambridge University Press.

Lacey, M., and Groves, K. 2014. Talent management collides with corporate social responsibility: creation of inadvertent hypocrisy. *Journal of Management Development*, 33(4), pp.399–409.

McDowell, L. 2003. Masculine identities and low paid work: young men in urban labour markets. *International Journal of Urban and Regional Research*, 27(December), pp.828–48.

McGrath, J. E., Berdahl, J. L., and Arrow, H. 1995. Traits, expectations, culture and clout: the dynamics of diversity in work groups. In S. E. Jackson and M. N. Ruderman, eds., *Diversity in work teams*, pp.17–45. Washington, DC: American Psychological Association.

Mckay, P. F., and Avery, D. R. 2005. Warning! Diversity recruitment could backfire. *Journal of Management Inquiry*, 14(4), pp.330–6.

McPherson, M., Smith-Lovin, L., and Cook, J. M. 2001. Birds of a feather: homophily in social networks. *Annual Review of Sociology*, 27, pp.415–44.

McRobbie, A. 2009. *The aftermath of feminism: gender, culture and social change*. London: SAGE Publications Ltd.

Meyers, M. C., De Boeck, G., and Dries, N. 2017. Talent or not: reactions to talent designations. In D. G. Collings, K. Mellahi, and W. C. Cascio, eds., *Oxford handbook of talent management*, pp.169–92. Oxford: Oxford University Press.

Michaels, E., Handfield-Jones, H., and Axelrod, B. 2001. *The war for talent*. Boston: Harvard Business School Press.

Miller, F. A., and Katz, J. H. 2002. *The inclusion breakthrough: unleashing the real power of diversity*. San Francisco: Berrett-Koehler Publishers.

Nickerson, R. S. 1998. Confirmation bias: a ubiquitous phenomenon in many guises. *Review of General Psychology*, 2(2), pp.175–220.

Noon, M. 2007. The fatal flaws of diversity and the business case for ethnic minorities. *Work Employment and Society*, 21(4), pp.773–84.

Noon, M. 2010. The shackled runner: time to rethink positive discrimination? *Work, Employment and Society*, 24(4), pp.728–39.

O'Boyle, E., and Kroska, S. 2017. Star performers. In D. G. Collings, K. Mellahi, and W. C. Cascio, eds., *Oxford handbook of talent management*, pp.43–65. Oxford: Oxford University Press.

Özbilgin, M., and Tatli, A. 2011. Mapping out the field of equality and diversity: rise of individualism and voluntarism. *Human Relations*, 64(9), pp.1229–53.

Puwar, N. 2004. *Space invaders: race, gender and bodies out of place*. Oxford: Berg Publishers.

Ready, D. A., and Conger, J. A. 2007. Make your company a talent factory. *Harvard Business Review*, 85(6), pp.68–70.

Roberson, Q. M. 2006. Disentangling the meanings of diversity and inclusion in Organizations. *Group and Organization Management*, 31(2), pp.212–36.

Scharff, C. 2012. *Repudiating feminism: young women in a neoliberal world*. Surrey, UK and Burlington, VT: Ashgate Publishing Limited.

Scharff, C. 2015a. Blowing your own trumpet: exploring the gendered dynamics of self-promotion in the classical music profession. *The Sociological Review*, 63(2015), pp.97–112.

Scharff, C. 2015b. *Equality and diversity in the classical music profession*, London: King's College.

Schuler, R. S., and Tarique, I. 2012. Global talent management: Theoretical perspectives, systems, and challenges. In G. K. Stahl, I. Bjo¨rkman, and S. Morris, eds., *Handbook of research in international human resource management*, pp.205–19. Cheltenham, UK and Northampton, MA: Edward Elgar.

Scully, M. 2003. Meritocracy. In R. J. Ely, E. G. Foldy, and M. A. Scully, eds., *Reader in gender, work, and organization*, pp.284–6. Malden, MA: Blackwell Publishing Ltd.

Sorcher, M., and Brant, J. 2002. Are you picking the right leaders? *Harvard Business Review*, 80(2), pp.78–85.

Stahl, G. K., Björkman, I., Farndale, E., Morris, S. S., Paauwe, J. et al. 2007. Global talent management: how leading multinationals build and sustain their talent pipeline. *INSEAD Faculty and Research Working Papers*, 24.

Swailes, S. 2013. The ethics of talent management. *Business Ethics: A European Review*, 22(1), pp.32–46.

Tansley, C., Turner, P., Foster, C., Harris, L. et al. 2007. *Talent: strategy, management, measurement*. London: Chartered Institute of Personnel & Development (CIPD).

Tatli, A., Vassilopoulou, J., and Özbilgin, M. 2013. An unrequited affinity between talent shortages and untapped female potential: the relevance of gender quotas for talent management in high growth potential economies of the Asia Pacific region. *International Business Review*, 22(3), pp.539–53.

Thomas, D. A., and Ely, R. J. 1996. Making differences matter: a new paradigm for managing diversity. *Harvard Business Review*, 74(5), pp.79–90.

Thomas, R. 1990. From affirmative action to affirming diversity. *Harvard Business Review*, 68, pp.107–17.

Thomas, R. R. 1992. Managing diversity: a conceptual framework. In S. E. Jackson, ed., *Diversity in the workplace*, pp.306–17. New York: Guilford Press.

Vermeulen, L. P., and Coetzee, M. 2011. Perceptions of the dimensions of the fairness of affirmative action: a pilot study. *South African Journal of Business Management*, 37(2), pp.53–64.

Wang, M., and Kelan, E. K. 2013. The gender quota and female leadership: effects of Norwegian gender quota on board chairs and CEOs. *Journal of Business Ethics*, 117, pp.449–66.

Wentling, R. M., and Palma-Rivas, N. 1997. Diversity in the workforce: a literature review. *Diversity in the Workforce Series Report No. 1*. University of California at Berkeley: National Centre for Research in Vocational Education.

Wrench, J. 2002. Diversity management, discrimination and ethnic minorities in Europe: Clarifications, critiques and research agenda. *Occasional Papers and Reprints on Ethnic Studies*, 19, CEUS, Sweden.

Young, I. 1990. *Justice and the politics of difference*. Princeton: Princeton University Press.

CHAPTER 28

HOW IS TECHNOLOGY CHANGING TALENT MANAGEMENT?

PATRICK GAVAN O'SHEA AND KERRIN E. PUENTE

EVER since humans began bending the natural world to their will—transforming the earth's resources into tools, using those tools to cultivate food and create homes, and taming the power of fire to heat and light our world—technological advances have continuously changed humanity in myriad ways. While it is natural to view the impact of these advances through the lens of personal experience, today's global citizens (particularly those living in developed countries) could be forgiven for asserting that these advances have increased dramatically in recent years. Innovations such as smartphones and cloud computing continue to revolutionize the ways we communicate, travel, consume, recreate, and work, with each new year bringing the promise of breakthrough transformations.

Within the broad domain of work, we focus on mapping the ways that technology has changed both how organizations manage talent, and how individuals identify and develop their own skills. Our work is guided by the definition of *talent management* offered by Cappelli and Keller: *the process through which organizations anticipate and meet their needs for talent in strategic jobs* (Chapter 2, this volume). The chapter is organized around the contours of the talent-management lifecycle, which we have labeled *Identifying Talent, Acquiring Talent, Developing Talent*, and *Evaluating Talent*. It is important to note that entire books have been written to address the question posed by our chapter's title (e.g., Schweyer, Newman, and DeVries, 2009). Accordingly, our strategy is to highlight the key technological innovations within these four domains, and then direct the reader to resources offering a more detailed treatment of specific topics. Each section of the chapter closes with a set of five questions that we hope will guide future research.

In considering technology's impact, we focus on the sorts of outcomes familiar to any HR practitioner or industrial-organizational (I-O) psychologist, such as efficiency, effectiveness, reliability, and validity. In most cases, improving such metrics is the goal when technology is used to enhance a talent-management process. At the same time, we also seek to highlight cases where technology may introduce unintended consequences, such as when automating various aspects of a recruiting system leads to fewer face-to-face interactions among managers and potential hires. For quite some time, many of our leading minds have warned us to guard against the potential for technology to impoverish the human experience, with even Albert Einstein purportedly stating that "the human spirit must prevail over technology." Accordingly, we highlight examples of the thoughtful use of technology that promote effective collaboration and interactions whenever possible.

28.1 IDENTIFYING TALENT

Organizations have relied on web-based recruiting tools to attract and identify job candidates since the dawn of the Internet. As Dineen and Allen (2013) proclaim, such advances have fundamentally altered the recruitment paradigm. Where the historical emphasis was on the accurate and legal screening of candidate qualifications, technology-enhanced recruitment adds a focus on proactively generating qualified and diverse talent pools and improving the efficiency of the recruitment process (Chapman and Webster, 2003). The e-Recruitment landscape continues to develop swiftly, with a bounty of new, innovative methods on the rise. We begin by examining traditional e-Recruitment methods, including their limitations, and then turn to a discussion of more recent technology-enhanced recruitment innovations.

The trend toward e-Recruitment began with the advent of static technologies such as Internet-based job boards (e.g., Indeed.com, Monster.com) and career websites designed to communicate openings and occupational information to a wider audience, as well as applicant tracking systems (ATS) designed to improve the efficiency of the recruitment lifecycle. The preponderance of research in the e-Recruitment realm has focused on understanding how the design features of these technologies (e.g., media richness, customization, and usability) influences applicant attraction: for thorough reviews, see Dineen and Allen (2013) and Dineen and Soltis (2011). However, the impact of e-Recruitment on actual candidate engagement and placement has not received sustained attention. These tools arguably generate larger pools of job candidates (Breaugh and Starke, 2000; Cappelli, 2001), but their effectiveness in generating a high-quality, diverse applicant pool is less clear (Stone, Deadrick, Lukaszewski, and Johnson, 2015; Stone, Lukaszewski, Stone-Romero, and Johnson, 2013).

Stone and her colleagues (2015) note that these early manifestations of e-Recruitment were often impersonal, generating an artificial distance between candidates and the organization that undermined their effectiveness—though enhancements such as cookie-based recruitment-message customization (e.g., targeting individuals whose

Internet-browsing patterns reflect interest in a given career) and mobile compatibility have addressed this to some degree. Several emerging interactive technologies have significantly enhanced the personalization and effectiveness of e-Recruitment, supporting organizations' proactive efforts to engage and motivate previously inaccessible or "passive" candidates (Dineen and Allen, 2013; Stone et al., 2015). This is a critical facet of effective talent management. In the remained of this section, we discuss two of the most promising examples of these interactive technologies: social recruiting and rich-media simulations.

28.1.1 Social Recruitment

Recent surveys suggest that more than 90% of recruiters currently use social media platforms to source job candidates (most prominently LinkedIn, followed by Facebook and Twitter), making social recruiting one the most prevalent e-Recruitment trends today (JobVite, 2015; Society for Human Resource Management, 2011). Anecdotal evidence suggests that social media is a powerful way to identify, segment, and screen candidates at minimal cost, but there is a significant lack of research exploring the detailed methods used and the overall effectiveness of organizational recruitment via social media (Ollington, Gibb, and Harcourt, 2013). Likewise, little is known about the regulatory context or legal ramifications associated with subjective evaluations of social media content.

In an effort to standardize the use of data gleaned from social media sites, e-Recruitment leaders such as JobVite have begun automating the evaluation of social media profiles as an integrated component of their ATS. Research investigating the validity of these techniques has followed suit, including validating a method to assess applicants' Big Five personality traits through open-vocabulary (or rich text) analysis of the language used on Facebook sites (Park et al., 2014) and the successful application of data-mining algorithms that automatically rank-order applicants based on LinkedIn content with levels of consistency that rival those of human recruiters (Faliagka, Tsakalidis, and Tzimas, 2012).

The image or "brand" that an employer promotes via social networks is also a key component in attracting new candidates, providing an opportunity to connect with the larger community and locate talent in niche or underrepresented groups (Cascio and Graham, 2016; Ollington, Gibb, and Harcourt, 2013). For example, the global logistics company UPS hosts videos highlighting women in leadership roles on its Facebook page and shares application information with potential candidates via Twitter—strategies that it has linked to hiring successes (Raphael, 2011). Social media content can also help organizations convey their value propositions to potential candidates. In a recent campaign to shift its image to that of a digital company, GE has shared engaging and amusing YouTube videos, where new hires explain to family and friends that they will not simply be working in manufacturing, but as programmers striving to "transform the way the world works."

28.1.2 Rich-Media Simulations

Organizations are increasingly incorporating interactive rich-media simulations within their e-Recruitment efforts to communicate desired images and share job-related information. For example, the US Department of Justice's Community-Oriented Policing Services office has developed a Virtual Ride Along that allows candidates to experience a "day in the life" of a police officer (http://discoverpolicing.org). By providing clear and accurate information about the duties involved in community policing, the tool seeks to counteract widespread, yet at least partially inaccurate, occupational stereotypes promulgated by the entertainment industry. A corresponding self-assessment provides real-time feedback to help users gauge their interest in and suitability for the roles and responsibilities of a police officer.

Online gaming applications are also emerging as another type of engaging self-assessment tool that allow candidates to make informed application decisions. Knack, a mobile pioneer in this arena, uses data-driven algorithms to create games that help organizations quickly and consistently screen candidates. In one example known as "Wasabi Waiter," candidates assume the role of a waiter in a sushi restaurant who has to balance multiple responsibilities while maintaining customer service (Peck, 2013). Because they present job-related challenges in an entertaining way, these games can potentially serve as both job previews and screening tools—after completing the assessment, applicants can accurately assess their organizational fit and decide whether to apply for a job (Laumer, Eckhardt, and Weitzel, 2012).

Although the research evidence generally indicates that rich-media recruitment tools positively influence candidates' organizational perceptions and intent to pursue a job (e.g., Allen, Van Scotter, and Otondo, 2004; Cable and Yu, 2006), a caveat is in order. One of the few direct comparisons between digital and non-digital media found that the use of digital media (in this case virtual worlds) may actually detract from the acquisition

Table 28.1 Research Questions—Identifying Talent

1. How do the methods of recruitment—traditional recruitment processes, passive e-Recruitment methods (e.g., Internet job boards, career websites), or interactive e-Recruitment technologies (e.g., social media recruiting, rich-media simulations)—affect the quality of applicant pools, the frequency of successful job placements, and applicant retention?
2. How do e-Recruitment methods affect the diversity of applicant pools? For example, does the digital divide systematically limit minorities' access to e-Recruitment-based opportunities, or does technology allow organizations to access and attract these populations more effectively?
3. How does job-irrelevant information presented on social media affect the validity and potential bias of inferences made during applicant identification and screening?
4. What techniques or best practices maximize the decision consistency and validity of social media-based applicant screening?
5. What design features maximize applicant perceptions of face validity and perceived utility of online gaming applications in evaluating person-job fit?

of factual information (Badger, Kaminsky, and Behrend, 2014), most likely because the interactive elements of the simulation are relatively more cognitively demanding.

In addition to the recruitment arena, technology has also significantly changed the way organizations acquire new talent. Following our sharing several questions in Table 28.1 that we hope will guide future researchers interested in exploring technology's impact on talent identification, we explore talent acquisition in the next section.

28.2 ACQUIRING TALENT

Technology's impact has colored all aspects of the talent-acquisition process, from expanding the reach of assessment programs through web-based administration to altering even the fundamental nature of the assessments themselves. We begin by covering administration-related issues, and then discuss an assessment method that arguably has harnessed technology's full potential more than any other—interactive, rich-media online simulations.

28.2.1 Assessment Administration

Organizations continue to accelerate the trend away from paper-and-pencil administration of hiring assessments, with the vast majority (at least in the United States) currently administered electronically (Stone et al., 2013). As a result, it is not surprising that research in the e-Selection arena has largely focused on evaluating the measurement equivalence of paper-and-pencil versus computer-administered assessments. Stone and her colleagues (2013) provide a comprehensive overview of this literature organized by assessment type (e.g., ability tests, situational judgment tests [SJTs], and personality tests). Although the results of this literature resist unequivocal conclusions, Scott and Mead (2011) note that rigorously developed computerized assessments in both cognitive and non-cognitive domains can measure the same constructs as their paper-and-pencil analogs, with the consistent exceptions being (a) those with considerable reading requirements and (b) cognitive tests that involve speeded administration. Consistent with these conclusions, Reynolds and Rupp (2010) highlight the lack of equivalence often observed for speeded tests. Some studies have also found slightly lower scores for computer-administered cognitive-ability tests relative to paper-and-pencil versions (Mead and Dragow, 1993; Potosky and Bobko, 2004). Stone and co-authors (2013) suggest that such differences may be driven by test takers' lack of familiarity with computers, as well as needing to attend to two tasks in the web-based context (taking the test and interacting with the computer system). Along with computer illiteracy in general, investigating the impact of test takers' lack of familiarity with online testing, specifically smartphone-based assessment, could be a fruitful avenue for future research.

At least for some assessment types, there appear to be psychometric benefits associated with electronic administration. A study comparing paper-and-pencil with computer-administered SJTs found that the computerized version had increased variance, a distribution that more closely approximated a normal curve, higher reliability estimates, and stronger relations with other measures (Ployhart, Weekley, Holtz, and Kemp, 2003). As we alluded to above, though, it is often difficult to draw clear, unambiguous conclusions from measurement-equivalence research—and not simply because of the somewhat mixed results across studies. Reynolds and Dickter (2010) raise a very important point by noting that many measurement-equivalence studies do not randomly assign participants to groups, so any differences across administration modes cannot be unambiguously attributed to the administration medium. In light of this issue, coupled with the fact that certain assessment methods have received more equivalence-focused research attention than others, we recommend consulting reviews of this literature (e.g., Stone et al., 2013; Scott and Mead, 2011) before making decisions about how best to implement a web-enabled assessment administration program.

Technological advances have expanded the reach of many large-scale selection programs beyond the walls of proctored test centers, allowing applicants to complete assessments at any time or location via a secure Internet connection. Two chief concerns in such situations are that applicants neither cheat nor copy test content. Remote proctoring, where applicants complete the assessment under the watchful eye of a proctor via a live-streaming webcam, is one potential way to mitigate these concerns. This service is offered by most major assessment-delivery companies, as well as through cloud-based solutions such as Remote Proctor NOW (RPNow). Rooted in evidence that individuals have unique typing patterns, keystroke analytics offer one way to verify the test-taker's identity in unproctored settings by having applicants complete a baseline typing measure that is then compared with the patterns generated during the assessment administration (Arthur and Glaze, 2011); other methods include making the test available only to known test takers through individually assigned login IDs and passwords that allow a single login (Bartram, 2011). In situations where a selection battery is administered in an unproctored setting, we suggest that follow-up proctored verification testing be conducted for individuals whom the organization is seriously considering hiring. Though organizations vary as to whether they accept the unproctored or proctored results as the official score, Arthur and Glaze (2011) recommend having the results generated in the proctored setting serve as the score of record.

Several "under the hood" technological innovations, most notably computer-adaptive testing (CAT) and linear on-the-fly testing (LOFT), have shattered the century-long reign of the static test form. Using item-response theory-based (IRT) scoring, CAT programs update test-taker ability estimates following each item administration, and then adaptively present items tailored to that estimate. Because individuals are only presented with items that have difficulty levels falling close to their estimated ability, and because each test taker completes a unique form, CAT results in shorter testing times and enhanced test security (McCloy and Gibby, 2011). LOFT also promotes security by automatically generating a test form "on the fly" (i.e., immediately before a test taker begins an assessment) according to a predefined test blueprint. Despite the clear benefits of LOFT and CAT, one drawback is that they require relatively large item pools. The IRT-based scoring rubrics that underlie CAT (and many LOFT) programs also often need considerable data to reach stable item-parameter estimates, although research has shown that using a large pool of items (i.e., fifty) in the calibration set to generate such estimates can mitigate the need for large samples (Hoffman, 2012).

28.2.2 Assessment Content

One of the most widespread technology-driven changes within the assessment-content arena is the transition from written to video- and picture-based content. Beyond applicants generally preferring video formats (Chan and Schmitt, 1997), this trend has had important practical benefits. For example, Chan and Schmitt (1997) found less adverse impact associated with a video-based SJT relative to a paper-and-pencil version. Furthermore, Lievens and Sackett (2006) found that a video-based, interpersonally oriented SJT had higher predictive validity than its written analog, as well as higher incremental validity and lower correlations with cognitively oriented predictors.

The use of videos and pictures can reap particularly large benefits when employers expect the targeted applicant pool to have limited reading ability. Marriott International uses an innovative assessment to select housekeepers that first shows applicants an image of a model hotel room and a brief description of the actions that have made it so (i.e., place three small pillows in front of three large pillows on the bed) (Malamut, Van Rooy, and Davis, 2011). In a subsequent image of a hotel room, applicants must count the number of deficiencies present. The limited amount of text included within the assessment, which applicants can access in audio form, remains at an eighth-grade or lower reading level.

At an even deeper level, technological advances have led recently to the emergence of assessments that did not even exist a decade ago. Perhaps the best example of this phenomenon is the advent of online simulations, which we see as the latest and most technologically sophisticated incarnation of the successful use of content-valid, "day in the life" scenario-based assessments. In our view, an effective way to highlight the evolution of online simulations is to frame them against the backdrop of traditional assessment centers. In a traditional assessment center, individuals assume a specific identity (e.g., a first-line supervisor just starting a new job), review background materials that evoke a specific context, and then complete a series of exercises (e.g., role play, in-basket, analysis exercise, leaderless group discussion) over the course of several hours or even a full day. Trained assessors typically watch individuals complete each exercise, take detailed notes and generate ratings across several competencies, and then meet at the end of the day to generate consensus ratings for each individual.

Assessment centers clearly offer an unparalleled opportunity to observe behavior directly in a rich, detailed, content-valid context, but they are also very expensive and administratively time-consuming. The recent global recession and the reduced spending it triggered within both private and public sectors has led to a search for more efficient and lower-cost alternatives (McNelly, Ruggeberg, and Hall, 2011; Tsacoumis, 2016), and technology has offered several options. As described by Grubb (2011), the US Federal Bureau of Investigation (FBI) uses a phone-based system where all assessors operate out of a centralized call center, and can interact with candidates and enter their notes and ratings via computer. Darden Restaurants Inc. has also integrated phone-based interactions into its assessment program, as well as a simulated office environment that includes the ability to send e-mails and schedule meetings (McNelly et al., 2011). Given the near-universal application of technology in today's organizations, these technological enhancements increase content validity and assessment realism (Reynolds and Rupp, 2010). Digital recordings also allow the Darden assessments to be scored at any time by trained assessors. Because it was important for Darden to retain some "high touch" program elements, McNelley and colleagues note that applicants complete the assessments at a centralized location where they are greeted by an onsite facilitator.

While the examples noted above involve human judges scoring candidate behaviors and responses, a new class of simulations has emerged that automate even that element of the process. Tsacoumis (2016) offers a detailed set of lessons learned across a series of assessment efforts that employ these simulations. One such simulation is known as a Virtual Role Play (VRP). Similar to a traditional role play, candidates assume a given role, review information, and interact with others in the service of solving a set of problems and challenges that arise—but in the case of the VRP, this all occurs in an online environment, using rich-media animation. Fetzer (2013) has noted that many simulations are still linear, in that the choices users make early in the simulation do not affect the way the scenario unfolds at later stages. In contrast, VRPs use intelligent branching to create unique "paths" that reflect the decisions made by users (e.g., what information they chose to review and who they decide to meet with). At critical junctures, users provide ratings in response to questions or prompts that assess their judgments about the effectiveness of various actions, the extent to which they see certain issues as problems, and the actions they would prioritize taking. The scores for each response option, which are linked to the competencies targeted by the assessment, are generated automatically by comparing the user's ratings with SME-generated expert ratings.

Along with the cutting-edge work summarized by Tsacoumis (2016) and Fetzer (2013), technology is continuing to drive the assessment process down exciting new avenues. One example is provided by Adler (2011), who describes assessments developed by Prinsloo and her colleagues in South Africa that assess various facets of cognitive ability by first teaching applicants a novel symbolic language and then measuring their learning speed, the errors generated in the learning process, and the fluency and creativity associated with use of the new language. Aguinis, Henle, and Beaty (2001) also highlight how virtual reality technologies (e.g., haptic devices simulating force and tactile feedback; environments shifting in response to user gaze) can provide a safe means of testing applicants' ability to deal with conditions that could never be tested in the "real world," such as handling dangerous chemicals. As we highlight in the following section, simulations also can be very effective development tools. Before engaging with that topic, we close this section with a set of research questions in Table 28.2.

Table 28.2 Research Questions—Acquiring Talent

1. With respect to simulations, what types of rating scales (e.g., rate the effectiveness of certain behaviors, prioritize specific actions, rate the extent to which issues are critical problems) exhibit the strongest psychometric properties and validity results, and why?
2. How does varying the degree of fidelity/job realism (i.e., an assessment that closely mirrors a target job versus a "serious game" that bears little resemblance to any specific job) affect applicant reactions to simulations used for selection and promotion purposes?
3. To what extent do users' experience with and attitudes about smartphone-based assessment impact their performance on such assessments?
4. What specific elements of the assessment design, implementation, and administration process impact the degree of measurement equivalence observed for technology-enhanced and traditional versions of a given assessment?
5. How can technology help further reduce barriers to accurate assessment of certain groups (e.g., individuals with disabilities, individuals with very low reading levels)?

28.3 DEVELOPING TALENT

From the early days of immersive scenario-based military training simulations, to the more recent emergence of leadership-development vodcasts (i.e., podcasts with video content) available 24/7 via a user's smartphone apps, technology has had a profound impact on training and development. This impact appears to be growing exponentially, with organizations' use of e-Learning more than doubling since the turn of the century (Brown and Charlier, 2013). Beyond simply increasing a program's reach, technology is dramatically changing the fundamental ways that people experience the learning process. The age-old stereotype of training consisting of an instructor transmitting information to a classroom full of passive learners is becoming less and less relevant with each passing day. As the title of a recent paper aptly recognized, technology is bringing "power to the people" (Orvis, Fisher, and Wasserman, 2009), by placing decisions about when, how, and where training and development occurs firmly in the hands of users.

This power brings with it a number of challenges. In a traditional in-person training environment, the instructor has direct access to participants' reactions and level of engagement—questions, quizzical looks, and both verbal and non-verbal feedback can all help a trainer adapt his or her strategy on the fly and adjust the pacing, use of examples, and level of detail presented (Orvis, Fisher, and Wasserman, 2009). When training is delivered via a vodcast or other technology-mediated mechanism, and this type of instructor-led adaptation is not possible, there is potentially a greater risk of a participant disengaging if he or she experiences content that is confusing or irrelevant. Simply put, it is much easier to shut down a computer program or close an app than it is to walk out of an in-person training session. Training professionals clearly recognize this when they argue that participant motivation and satisfaction are particularly critical in e-Learning contexts (Brown and Charlier, 2013).

Of course, e-Learning approaches will never totally replace in-person training and development, nor should they. Initiatives such as those focused on developing collaborative leadership among a small team of corporate officers would undoubtedly lose much of their impact and power without face-to-face interactions. For financial and other reasons, though, many organizations are deciding that e-Learning is the optimal choice in many situations—and in keeping with the "power to the people" theme, resources such as podcasts, vodcasts, and MOOCs (massively open online courses) have dramatically expanded access to a wide range of content either for free or at a very low cost. Bersin (2015a) notes that MOOC providers claim to have trained more than two million people during the past two years. This enthusiastic assertion should be considered in light of a study conducted by the University of Pennsylvania's School of Education, which found that approximately half of those individuals who registered for an online course never viewed a lecture, and less than 5% completed the course (Lewin, 2013). Despite these sobering results, it does appear that e-Learning is here to stay. Thankfully, the research literature offers some very practical suggestions that developers would be wise to heed as they create high-quality e-Learning offerings (Brown and Charlier, 2013; Orvis, Fisher, and Wasserman, 2009).

In the context of generating a model of e-Learning usage, Brown and Charlier (2013) note that one of the primary benefits that it offers is user control. However, research indicates that simply providing control does not always lead to positive outcomes because users do not consistently make choices that enhance the learning process—they may end the training too soon, skip valuable information, fail to use online resources, or not fully engage with the process (e.g., they may multitask, or lose interest over time). Although the results are equivocal, research indicates that learner control over the amount of instruction and the context provided with examples may have more consistent positive outcomes than allowing users to control the timing and sequencing of training content (Brown and Charlier, 2013). That said, Orvis and co-authors (2009) found that letting users control the order, pacing, and the communication medium of an e-Learning process did lead to enhanced learning, but the results were mediated by user reactions. Once again, this indicates that for the full benefits of e-Learning to be realized, ensuring that users are fully engaged is absolutely critical. In the remainder of this section, we first provide several examples where learner control is deployed very effectively to promote an engaging learning process. Next, we share examples of how technology has helped create "virtual communities" in situations where distance would normally preclude such interactions.

28.3.1 Learner Control

For the past several years, Bersin by Deloitte has presented WhatWorks® Awards to recognize programs reflecting innovation and excellence across the talent-management spectrum. The set of 2015 finalists included several cases where technology played a central role in providing an engaging employee learning and development experience

(Mallon, 2015). For example, Autotrader (an online marketplace for new and used car buyers and sellers) developed an online training program that includes components such as a virtual scavenger hunt (participants must locate pricing guides, business rules, etc.) that tests employees' ability to address client questions quickly and accurately in a fun, engaging way. Participants also have direct control and input over the learning process by using iPads to produce training videos that address specific sales scenarios, with the best videos chosen to train new hires. The many impressive outcomes associated with this program include reductions in training time from several days to 5–7 hours and in product-launch times by 70%–80%, savings of more than $1 million, and a return in revenue of more than $500,000 (Mallon, 2015).

In Section 28.2, we discussed how rich-media online simulations that allow participants to control their path through the assessment via intelligent branching (e.g., the participant decides which of several possible actions to take next) are being successfully used in the hiring and promotion arena (Tsacoumis, 2016). Because such assessments evoke the targeted competencies in a realistic and engaging job-relevant context, they can also serve as valuable developmental tools. For example, the Society for Human Resource Management (SHRM) has developed a VRP rich-media assessment that allows HR practitioners to obtain valuable developmental feedback rooted in SHRM's Competency Model (O'Shea, 2014).

28.3.2 Virtual Communities

The ultimate winner of Bersin's 2015 WhatWorks® Award focused on employee learning and development during the onboarding process, a particularly critical phase where new talent must be successfully integrated into the organization. Marriott's new global leadership-development program (Voyage) not only immerses participants in a virtual learning environment and provides mentoring and on-the-job development, but also includes a virtual portal where they can communicate with other "Voyagers," view program content, and interact with senior organizational leaders. Ladkin and her colleagues note that such virtual collaborations can be an extremely effective component of online leadership-development programs (Ladkin, Case, Wicks, and Kinsella, 2009). In the context of the program Ladkin and colleagues describe, the virtual online community allows participants to pose and respond to questions, react to readings and videos, and communicate with their coaches. The authors note the paradox inherent in the clear potential for distance learning to actually bring participants closer in time and place to where real learning occurs—because they can immediately engage with the virtual community as they struggle to apply what they are learning within their workplace, reflect on what they learn through the program content, and pose questions and reactions as soon as they emerge.

Along with fostering the development of virtual communities, technology has also drastically expanded coaching's reach. In addition to face-to-face settings, technology allows coaching to occur via Skype or over the phone, which has facilitated

---

Table 28.3 Research Questions—Developing Talent

---

1. How do individual differences (e.g., personality, interests, age, experiences) interact to influence reactions to technology-enhanced training and development opportunities?
2. What features of technology-enhanced training and development tools (e.g., type and extent of animation, manual versus auditory response modality) enhance user engagement and learning?
3. How can technology enhance the coaching process and behavioral change in general (e.g., through goal tracking, reminders that prompt certain behaviors, and apps that track behaviors and/or emotions and display the results for clients)?
4. How can technology be employed to optimize the delivery of developmental feedback?
5. How can technology be integrated into traditional face-to-face training programs in ways that enhance their effectiveness (e.g., apps that track trainee reactions and feed them back to the trainer in real time)?

---

the integration of coaching into virtual leadership-development programs. Indeed, some of the most innovative learning and development programs combine engaging online simulations with developmental coaching. For example, the Interpublic Group of Companies, Inc. has implemented a development program targeting high-potential mid- to senior-level leaders that includes both online role plays and in-basket exercises, as well as coaching (Hartog, 2011). Across the program's seven weeks, participants alternate between assessments and coaching, with the coaches helping participants integrate assessment feedback and use it to plan development efforts.

Ideally, talent-development processes are coordinated with and closely informed by clear and accurate talent appraisals. After sharing this section's research questions in Table 28.3, we address technology's impact on the talent evaluation process.

28.4 Evaluating Talent

Supervisors and their direct reports often dread the performance-management process. Aside from the fact that it can evoke bruised egos and difficult conversations, much of this dread is generated by the administrative burden the process places on all involved parties. In recent years, however, a variety of technology vendors (e.g., Cornerstone, Halogen, HRsmart/Deltek, Kenexa/IBM, Oracle, Saba, SilkRoad, SuccessFactors, and Workday) have launched performance-management solutions that have lessened this burden considerably. These systems, which are typically one facet of an integrated talent-management solution, include components that allow managers to select target competencies for each subordinate, identify relevant goals and objectives, solicit rater input, display performance notes collected throughout the review cycle, generate reports, send reminders and acknowledgment notes, and obtain approvals (Schweyer, Newman, and DeVries, 2009). In turn, employees are able to enter input such as targeted developmental goals and self-assessments, as well as commendations received during the review cycle (Krauss and Snyder, 2009). Beyond simply alleviating administrative burdens, these systems can significantly improve the quality of the appraisal process. Some monitor ratings for potential errors such as leniency, and then send raters tailored messages emphasizing the need for accuracy and sharing tips for how to differentiate among employees effectively. Employees can also update the system to reflect the completion of a project, which automatically triggers the solicitation of feedback from relevant stakeholders. This feature allows feedback to be collected at the ideal moment—when it is most likely to be timely, accurate, and detailed—rather than solely during an artificial annual performance appraisal cycle.

Despite these technological advances, performance management remains a significant challenge for many organizations. Recent survey research indicates that only 12% of organizations feel that the time they put into their performance-management processes is worth it (Deloitte Development LLC, 2015). This dissatisfaction is reflected in (and perhaps stimulated by) a recent avalanche of practitioner and academic writing on the topic, including books encouraging companies to *Get Rid of the Performance Review!* (Culbert and Rout, 2010) and journal articles questioning Why is performance management broken?" (Pulakos and O'Leary, 2011). While the root of performance management's ills and the suggested remedies vary somewhat across these writings, the zeitgeist is clearly moving away from programs grounded in formal, ratings-based, administratively burdensome appraisals toward those that do away with ratings in favor of informal feedback, coaching, and a clear developmental focus. Many well-known global companies have embraced this trend and decided to forgo performance ratings, including Accenture, Adobe, The Gap, and GE.

A number of software applications have emerged recently that allow employees to share and receive immediate and unvarnished informal feedback, typically referred to as instant feedback (Wright, 2015) or microfeedback. As an example, Reflektive enables users to provide feedback to their colleagues directly in Outlook while sending e-mails, and Waggl provides a forum for meeting attendees to send feedback immediately after the meeting ends (Bersin, 2015b). GE uses an application called PD@GE, where employees can post messages of encouragement, advice or suggestions, and criticism within categories such as "insight," "consider," and "continue." A pilot of PD@GE produced encouraging results, and GE is now planning to expand the program to include the entire white-collar workforce of 175,000 by the end of 2016 (Streitfeld, 2015). Amazon has also implemented a program called "Anytime Feedback" that allows users to submit anonymous praise or criticism to managers, and the financial firm Capco has an application that allows colleagues to review each other's goals and send "nudges" and "cheers" in response (Streitfeld, 2015).

All of these tools aim to increase the quantity and quality of the feedback shared within organizations, which raises two critical issues. First, organizations must decide whether the feedback is captured and shared anonymously or whether providers are identified. Bersin (2015b) argues for anonymity, seeing it as a critical way to guard against retaliation and foster honest, critical feedback. If trust is not a strong feature of an organization's culture and/or the culture emphasizes peer competition, though, such systems can become powerful weapons used to intimidate and sabotage rivals. Kurtzberg, Naquin, and Belkin highlight the critical role of organizational culture when they note that "to truly understand a tool, you must understand not only its physical properties, but also *the way people think about it, treat it, and its symbolic representation in an organization*" (2005: 224, emphasis added). For organizations that do choose to allow anonymity, we recommend outlining clear guidelines around the nature of what can be shared, such as Netflix's rule: "don't say anything online that you would not say in person" (Bersin, 2015b). Establishing such rules is critical in light of research findings indicating that technology-mediated feedback does tend to be relatively more negative because the communication context engenders less social obligation to be respectful and polite (Kurtzberg, Naquin, and Belkin, 2005).

The second issue is really a caution, in that organizations must be prepared to address the impact of unleashing tools that essentially act as feedback multipliers. As any leader who has received a 360-degree feedback report knows, the ratings and comments are rarely straightforward and unambiguous, and people need help interpreting and acting upon them. Rather than replacing the need for face-to-face meetings with managers, these tools actually increase it. When Sears Holding Corporation (SHC) introduced a new 360-degree feedback system among its salaried staff, called Soundboard, employees were able to provide non-anonymous feedback to their supervisors, peers, and subordinates at any point throughout the year. At the same time, SHC replaced annual performance-review meetings with quarterly objective-setting and check-in meetings. As a result, the amount of time employees spent having performance-related conversations with their managers more than tripled (Moretti, 2015). Finally, as Krauss and Snyder (2009) wisely argue, using technology to communicate about emotionally charged topics like job performance is fraught with the potential for confusion and frustration. Establishing clear guidelines around the acceptable use of such tools can help mitigate these risks.

Table 28.4 Research Questions—Evaluating Talent

1. How and to what extent does technologically mediated rater feedback (e.g., systems that automatically monitor ratings for potential biases and then send raters immediate feedback) influence outcomes such as rating quality and rater satisfaction with the appraisal process?
2. What dimensions of an organization's culture (e.g., tolerance for conflict, innovation, people orientation) differentiate among positive versus negative employee reactions to technology-mediated anonymous instant feedback?
3. What individual differences (e.g., personality, age, work experience) influence employees' receptivity to technology-mediated anonymous instant feedback?
4. What behaviors can supervisors, mentors, and coaches engage in to help employees interpret and act upon instant feedback that is inconsistent (e.g., team members who anonymously provide very different reactions to a colleague's presentation to the group)?
5. What is the long-term impact of introducing organization-wide, technology-enhanced instant feedback systems on employee engagement and firm performance?

As we noted above, some technology vendors include a performance-management component within a larger talent-management solution. Following our sharing this section's research questions in Table 28.4, we briefly touch on the relatively recent emergence of these integrated solutions. We then close the chapter with a look toward the future and some concluding thoughts.

28.5 INTEGRATED TALENT-MANAGEMENT SOLUTIONS

Schweyer and co-authors (2009) note that when talent-management technologies began appearing in the 1990s, they focused almost exclusively on a single phase of the process (e.g., recruitment or hiring). As a result, organizations typically purchased separate applications for each function, and the result was often "four or five different loosely integrated niche products and large amounts of redundant data" (Schweyer, Newman, and DeVries, 2009: 41). In the ensuing years, vendors began to see the value in creating talent-management systems that combined ATS, learning-management systems, performance-management systems, and other functions into a seamless, integrated solution. While one can argue whether a truly "end-to-end" system has emerged to date, these more comprehensive solutions clearly help promote a unified, holistic view of talent management within organizations and reduce the potential incompatibilities and redundancies inherent in the use of separate solutions for each talent management function. Integrated talent-management solutions also facilitate explorations of the links among data from the various system elements (e.g., recruiting, hiring, and performance management), helping organizations to capitalize on the potential for "big data" to effectively drive organizational decision making and strategy. Ideally, such systems generate a continual stream of talent-management data, which has the potential to improve significantly the way organizations manage their talent. This rich source of data can be used to build statistical workforce-planning models and even recast traditionally episodic activities like assessment validation into dynamic processes that can be evaluated over time (Putka and Oswald, 2015).

While the benefits of integrated systems are very clear, they may not be the best (or at least not the only) solution in every case. In a thoughtful analysis of the talent-management technology landscape, Schweyer and co-authors (2009) note that there is a tension within this market between the breadth provided by an integrated solution and the deep functionality offered by niche providers. Echoing this view, Bersin (2015b) notes that the niche-oriented startups are moving the fastest to introduce innovative feedback apps, although the legacy software providers are also investing in such tools. For organizations planning to acquire an off-the-shelf talent-management solution, Schweyer and co-authors' (2009) book includes a very helpful (and, at nearly 400 pages, a very detailed) "buyer's guide." The guide highlights company information, product specifications, and a functionality matrix that lists the key components (e.g., recruiting/job posting functionality, candidate experience, sourcing, assessment/interview capabilities, offer management/onboarding, and system security) for most of the major vendors.

28.6 Looking Toward the Future: Self-Initiated Talent Management

We defined *talent management* in the chapter's opening pages as including employee-initiated activities that may transcend the boundaries of traditional employment relationships. As we look to the future, we see evidence that such activities will become increasingly prevalent. One example of this type of trend is e-Lancing, which is currently practiced by millions of individuals across the globe and promises to fundamentally transform the employer-employee bond (Aguinis and Lawal, 2013; see also Chapter 26 of this volume by Cascio and Boudreau). In e-Lancing arrangements, employees find work by bidding on the chance to complete relatively short-term tasks posted by potential customers to a wide variety of online marketplaces, including eLance.com, freeLancer.com, guru.com, oDesk.com, microworkers.com, and Amazon's Mechanical Turk (mturk.com). These online marketplaces, which typically collect a 5% to 15% commission directly from participants' profit margins, have become increasingly sophisticated in recent years; most integrate procedures to match employers and employees, provide online training, verify employee skills, record time spent on specific tasks, manage quality control, and evaluate employee performance. Indeed, maintaining stellar customer reviews and quality metrics is the primary way employees differentiate themselves within e-Lancing marketplaces, ideally providing them with the autonomy to design jobs that consist of a constellation of tasks performed for a variety of employers that are an excellent match for their skills and interests.

Another even more recent example of how technology is allowing individuals to manage proactively their own talent is YouScience's (www.youscience.com) *Latitude* career planning and assessment system. Students as young as fifteen years old can complete Latitude's online cognitive-ability assessments, which include numerical reasoning, spatial visualization, and associative memory, and receive a detailed set of educational, job, and career options mapped to their identified strengths. The Latitude platform also integrates information on approximately 500 different jobs, including the educational path needed to attain the job, the salary range, the projected number of openings over the next decade, and whether the job is a good fit given the user's ability profile (McGee, 2013). Latitude and e-Lancing are just two examples of the many different tools and systems that are helping individuals develop and deploy their talents in increasingly proactive ways.

28.7 A CONCLUDING RESEARCH CALL

In preparing this chapter, we were struck by the fact that nearly all of the published commentary covering similar topics notes that practice is far outpacing research (e.g., Reynolds and Rupp, 2010; Tsacoumis, 2016). Given that technological advances have come at lightning speed in recent decades and considering the tendency for HR research to follow rather than drive workplace trends (Cascio and Aguinis, 2008), this is not surprising. Nevertheless, the gap seems relatively large, particularly in light of the many interesting and important research questions that remain unanswered— ranging from exploring the measurement benefits of technology-enhanced assessments (Reynolds and Rupp, 2010) to the impact of removing performance appraisal ratings while simultaneously providing more feedback. Without sound research to guide decision making, however, organizations run the risk of becoming dazzled by captivating technologies that add no demonstrable value. In our view, it is hard to imagine a research domain within talent management where the potential theoretical and practical benefits are greater, and we hope that the research questions we have included in each section of this chapter will help stimulate future work. For researchers and practitioners fascinated by the intersection of talent management and technology, these are exciting times indeed.[1]

NOTE

1. The authors wish to thank Wayne Cascio, Molly O'Shea, Cheryl Paullin, Nick Puente, and Suzanne Tsacoumis for very helpful feedback, encouragement, and support throughout the process of developing this chapter. Please direct any chapter-related correspondence to Gavan O'Shea at gavanoshea@gmail.com.

REFERENCES

Adler, S. 2011. Concluding comments: open questions. In N. T. Tippins and S. Adler, eds., *Technology-enhanced assessment of talent*, pp.418–36. San Francisco: Jossey-Bass.

Aguinis, H., and Lawal, S. O. 2013. eLancing: a review and research agenda for bridging the science-practice gap. *Human Resource Management Review*, 23, pp.6–17.

Aguinis, H., Henle, C. A., and Beaty, Jr., J. C. 2001. Virtual reality technology: a new tool for personnel selection. *International Journal of Selection and Assessment*, 9, pp.70–83.

Allen, D. G., Van Scotter, J. R., and Otondo, R. F. 2004. Recruitment communication media: impact on prehire outcomes. *Personnel Psychology*, 57, pp.143–71.

Arthur, W., and Glaze, R. M. 2011. Cheating and response distortion on remotely delivered assessments. In N. T. Tippins and S. Adler, eds., *Technology-enhanced assessment of talent*, pp.99–152. San Francisco: Jossey-Bass.

Badger, J., Kaminsky, S., and Behrend, T. 2014. Media richness and information acquisition in internet recruitment. *Journal of Managerial Psychology*, 29, pp.866–83.

Bartram, D. 2011. International issues, standards, and guidelines. In N. T. Tippins and S. Adler, eds., *Technology-enhanced assessment of talent*, pp.224–50. San Francisco: Jossey-Bass.

Bersin, J. 2015a. *HR technology for 2016: 10 big disruptions on the horizon*. Deloitte Development, LLC. http://marketing.bersin.com/hr-technology-for-2016.html.

Bersin, J. 2015b. Feedback is the killer app: a new market and management model emerges. *Forbes*. August 26. www.forbes.com.

Breaugh, J. A., and Starke, M. 2000. Research on employee recruitment: so many studies, so many remaining questions. *Journal of Management*, 26, pp.405–34.

Brown, K. G., and Charlier, S. D. 2013. An integrative model of e-learning use: leveraging theory to understand and increase usage. *Human Resource Management Review*, 23, pp.37–49.

Cable, D. M., and Yu, K.Y.T. 2006. Managing job seekers' organizational image beliefs: the role of media richness and media credibility. *Journal of Applied Psychology*, 91, pp.828–40.

Cappelli, P. 2001. On-line recruiting. *Harvard Business Review*, 79, pp.139–46.

Cappelli, P., and Keller, JR. 2017. The historical context of talent management. In D. G. Collings, K. Mellahi, and W. F. Cascio, eds., *The Oxford handbook of talent management*. Oxford: Oxford University Press.

Cascio, W. F., and Aguinis, H. 2008. Research in industrial and organizational psychology from 1963 to 2007: changes, choices, and trends. *Journal of Applied Psychology*, 93, pp.1062–81.

Cascio, W. F., and Boudreau, J. W. 2017. Talent management of nonstandard employees. In D. G. Collings, K. Mellahi, and W. F. Cascio, eds., *The Oxford handbook of talent management*. Oxford: Oxford University Press.

Cascio, W. F., and Graham, B. Z. 2016. New strategic role for HR: leading the employer-branding process. *Organization Management Journal*, 13, pp.182–92.

Chan, D., and Schmitt, N. 1997. Video-based versus paper-and-pencil methods of assessment in situational judgment tests: subgroup differences in test performance and face validity perceptions. *Journal of Applied Psychology*, 82, pp.143–59.

Chapman, D. S., and Webster, J. 2003. The use of technologies in the recruiting, screening, and selection processes for job candidates. *International Journal of Selection and Assessment*, 11, pp.113–20.

Culbert, S. A., and Rout, L. 2010. *Get rid of the performance review! How companies can stop intimidating, start managing—and focus on what really matters*. New York: Business Plus.

Deloitte Development LLC. 2015. *Global human capital trends 2015: leading in the new world of work*. http://www2.deloitte.com/us/en/pages/human-capital/articles/introduction-human-capital-trends.html.

Dineen, B. R., and Allen, D. G. 2013. Internet recruiting 2.0: shifting paradigms. *The Oxford handbook of recruitment*, pp.382–401. New York: Oxford University Press.

Dineen, B. R., and Soltis, S. M. 2011. Recruitment: a review of research and emerging directions. In Sheldon, S., ed., *APA handbook of industrial and organizational psychology*, pp.43–66. Washington, DC: American Psychological Association.

Fetzer, M. 2013. Future directions. In M. Fetzer and K. Tuzinski, eds., *Simulations for personnel selection*, pp.259–64. New York: Springer.

Faliagka, E., Tsakalidis, A., and Tzimas, G. 2012. An integrated e-recruitment system for automated personality mining and applicant ranking. *Internet Research*, 22, pp.551–68.

Grubb, A. D. 2011. Promotional assessment at the FBI: how the search for a high-tech solution led to a high-fidelity low-tech simulation. In N. T. Tippins and S. Adler, eds., *Technology-enhanced assessment of talent*, pp.293–306. San Francisco: Jossey-Bass.

Hartog, S. B. 2011. Innovation in senior-level assessment and development: grab 'em when and where you can. In N. T. Tippins and S. Adler, eds., *Technology-enhanced assessment of talent*, pp.307–23. San Francisco: Jossey-Bass.

Hoffman, R. G. 2012. IRT 3PL parameter estimation for future tests: exploration of data collection requirements using archival data. In C. Paullin (Chair), *Practical IRT: Applications in real-world situations*. Symposium held at the 27th Annual Conference of the Society for Industrial and Organizational Psychology, San Diego, CA.

Jobvite. 2015. The Jobvite recruiter nation survey. *Jobvite*. http://www.jobvite.com/wp-content/uploads/2015/09/jobvite_recruiter_nation_2015.pdf.

Krauss, A. D., and Snyder, L. A. 2009. Technology and performance management. In J. W. Smither and M. London, eds., *Performance management: putting research into practice*, pp.445–91. San Francisco: Jossey Bass.

Kurtzberg, T. R., Naquin, C. E., and Belkin, L. Y. 2005. Electronic performance appraisals: the effects of e-mail communication on peer ratings in actual and simulated environments. *Organizational Behavior and Human Decision Processes*, 98, pp.216–26.

Ladkin, D., Case, P., Wicks, P. G., and Kinsella, K. 2009. Developing leaders in cyber-space: the paradoxical possibilities of on-line learning. *Leadership*, 5, pp.193–212.

Laumer, S., Eckhardt, A., and Weitzel, T. 2012. Online gaming to find a new job—examining job seekers' intention to use serious games as a self-assessment tool. *German Journal of Research in Human Resource Management*, 26, pp.218–40.

Lewin, T. 2013. After setbacks, online courses are rethought. *The New York Times*. December 10.

Lievens, F., and Sackett, P. R. 2006. Video-based versus written situational judgment tests: a comparison in terms of predictive validity. *Journal of Applied Psychology*, 91, pp.1181–8.

Malamut, A., Van Rooy, D. L., and Davis, V. A. 2011. Bridging the digital divide across a global business: development of a technology-enabled selection system for low-literacy applicants. In N. T. Tippins and S. Adler, eds., *Technology-enhanced assessment of talent*, pp.267–92. San Francisco: Jossey-Bass.

Mallon, D. 2015. *The WhatWorks® Awards 2015*. Bersin by Deloitte: Deloitte Consulting LLP.

Mead, A. D., and Drasgow, F. 1993. Equivalence of computerized and paper-and-pencil cognitive ability tests: a meta-analysis. *Psychological Bulletin*, 114, pp.449–58.

McCloy, R. A., and Gibby, R. E. 2011. Computerized adaptive testing. In N. T. Tippins and S. Adler, eds., *Technology-enhanced assessment of talent*, pp.153–89. San Francisco: Jossey-Bass.

McGee, J. 2013. YouScience helps students find best career for them before investing in college. *The Tennessean*. December 9. www.tennessean.com.

McNelly, T., Ruggeberg, B. J., and Hall, Jr., C. R. 2011. Web-based management simulations: technology-enhanced assessment for executive-level selection and development. In N. T. Tippins and S. Adler, eds., *Technology-enhanced assessment of talent*, pp.253–66. San Francisco: Jossey-Bass.

Moretti, D. 2015. *Performance enablement at Sears Holdings Corporation*. Presentation at the Society for Industrial-Organizational Psychology's Leading Edge Consortium, Boston, MA.

O'Shea, G. 2014. *Assessing the SHRM competency model through engaging online simulations*. Presentation at the 30th Annual Kentucky Society for Human Resource Management (SHRM) Conference, Louisville, KY.

Ollington, N., Gibb, J., and Harcourt, M. 2013. Online social networks: an emergent recruiter tool for attracting and screening. *Personnel Review*, 42, pp.248–65.

Orvis, K. A., Fisher, S. L., and Wasserman, M. E. 2009. Power to the people: Using learner control to improve trainee reactions and learning in web-based instructional environments. *Journal of Applied Psychology*, 94, pp.960–71.

Park, G., Schwartz, H. A., Eichstaedt, J. C., Kern, M. L. et al. 2014. Automatic personality assessment through social media language. *Journal of Personality and Social Psychology*, 108, pp.934–52.

Peck, D. 2013. They're watching you at work. *The Atlantic*. http://www.theatlantic.com/magazine/archive/2013/12/theyre-watching-you-at-work/354681/.

Ployhart, R. E., Weekley, J. A., Holtz, B. C., and Kemp, C. 2003. Web-based and paper-and-pencil testing of applicants in a proctored setting: are personality, biodata, and situational judgment tests comparable? *Personnel Psychology*, 56, pp.733–52.

Potosky, D., and Bobko, P. 2004. Selection testing via the Internet: practical considerations and exploratory empirical findings. *Personnel Psychology*, 57, pp.1003–34.

Pulakos, E. D., and O'Leary, R. S. 2011. Why is performance management broken? *Industrial and Organizational Psychology: Perspectives on Science and Practice*, 4, pp.146–64.

Putka, D. J., and Oswald, F. L. 2015. Implications of the big data movement for the advancement of I-O science and practice. In S. Tonidandel, E. B. King, and J. M. Cortina, eds., *Big data at work: the data science revolution and organizational psychology*, pp.181–212. New York: Routledge.

Raphael, T. 2011. UPS says it's now delivering hires not just fans and followers. *EREmedia*. http://www.eremedia.com/ere/ups-says-its-now-delivering-hires-not-just-fans-and-followers/.

Reynolds, D. H., and Dickter, D. N. 2010. Technology and employee selection. In J. L. Farr and N. T. Tippins, eds., *Handbook of employee selection*, pp.171–94. New York: Taylor and Francis.

Reynolds, D. H., and Rupp, D. E. 2010. Advances in technology-facilitated assessment. In J. C. Scott and D. H. Reynolds, eds., *Handbook of workplace assessment: evidence-based practices for selecting and developing organizational talent*, pp.609–41. San Francisco: Jossey-Bass.

Schweyer, A., Newman, E., and DeVries, P. 2009. *Talent management technologies: a buyer's guide to new, integrated solutions*. Bloomington, IN: AuthorHouse.

Scott, J. C., and Mead, A. D. 2011. Foundations for measurement. In N. T. Tippins and S. Adler, eds., *Technology-enhanced assessment of talent*, pp.21–65. San Francisco: Jossey-Bass.

Society for Human Resource Management. 2011. *SHRM research spotlight: social networking websites and staffing*. https://www.shrm.org/Research/SurveyFindings/Documents/Social%20Networking %20Flyer_Staffing%20Conference_FINAL1.pdf.

Stone, D. L., Deadrick, D. L., Lukaszewski, K. M., and Johnson, R. 2015. The influence of technology on the future of human resource management. *Human Resource Management Review*, 25, pp.216–31.

Stone, D. L., Lukaszewski, K. M., Stone-Romero, E. F., and Johnson, T. L. 2013. Factors affecting the effectiveness and acceptance of electronic selection systems. *Human Resource Management Review*, 23, pp.50–70.

Streitfield, D. 2015. Data crunching is coming to help your boss manage your time. *The New York Times*. August 17. http://nyti.ms/1Mt6Ne6.

Tsacoumis, S. 2016. Rich-media interactive simulations: lessons learned. In Y. Rosen, S. Ferrara, and M. Mosharraf, eds., *Handbook of research on technology tools for real-world skill development*, pp.261–83. Hershey, PA: IGI Global.

Wright, G. 2015. *Employee feedback apps on the rise: using technology for real-time employee performance reviews*. Alexandria, VA: Society for Human Resource Management. https://www.shrm.org/hrdisciplines/technology/articles/pages/employee-feedback-apps.aspx.

INDEX

Note: "(fig.)" relates to Figures and "(t)" relates to Tables.

Lightning Source UK Ltd.
Milton Keynes UK
UKHW030741161019
351696UK00003B/5/P